Expert MySQL

Second Edition

Charles Bell

Apress·

Expert MySQL: Second Edition

ISBN-13 (pbk): 978-1-4302-4659-6

ISBN-13 (electronic): 978-1-4302-4660-2

President and Publisher: Paul Manning
Lead Editor: Jonathan Gennick
Technical Reviewers: Alfranio Correia, Sven Sandberg, Luis Soares, Marco Tusa, Geert Vanderkelen
Editorial Board: Steve Anglin, Ewan Buckingham, Gary Cornell, Louise Corrigan, Morgan Ertel, Jonathan Gennick, Jonathan Hassell, Robert Hutchinson, Michelle Lowman, James Markham, Matthew Moodie, Jeff Olson, Jeffrey Pepper, Douglas Pundick, Ben Renow-Clarke, Dominic Shakeshaft, Gwenan Spearing, Matt Wade, Tom Welsh
Coordinating Editor: Kevin Shea
Copy Editor: Pat Morris
Compositor: SPi Global
Indexer: SPi Global
Artist: SPi Global
Cover Designer: Anna Ishchenko

Distributed to the book trade worldwide by Springer Science+Business Media New York, 233 Spring Street, 6th Floor, New York, NY 10013. Phone 1-800-SPRINGER, fax (201) 348-4505, e-mail orders-ny@springer-sbm.com, or visit www.springeronline.com.

For information on translations, please e-mail rights@apress.com, or visit www.apress.com.

Apress and friends of ED books may be purchased in bulk for academic, corporate, or promotional use. eBook versions and licenses are also available for most titles. For more information, reference our Special Bulk Sales–eBook Licensing web page at www.apress.com/bulk-sales.

Any source code or other supplementary material referenced by the author in this text is available to readers at www.apress.com. For detailed information about how to locate your book's source code, go to www.apress.com/source-code.

I dedicate this book to my biggest fan—my big sister.
You were the catalyst for my academic and writing success.

—Charles Bell

Contents at a Glance

Contents

About the Author

Dr. Charles A. Bell conducts research in emerging technologies. He is a member of the Oracle MySQL Development team as team lead for the MySQL Utilities team. He lives in a small town in rural Virginia with his loving wife. He received his Doctor of Philosophy in Engineering degree from Virginia Commonwealth University in 2005. His research interests include database systems, software engineering, and sensor networks. He spends his limited free time as a practicing Maker focusing on microcontroller projects.

Dr. Bell's research projects and development of an advanced database-versioning system make him uniquely qualified to write this book. An expert in the database field, he has extensive knowledge and experience in modifying the MySQL source code. With more than 30 years experience in enterprise development and systems architecture, his experience enables him to create a book that gives excellent insight into developing and modifying open-source systems.

About the Technical Reviewers

Sven Sandberg leads the MySQL Replication Core subteam at Oracle. He has worked as a developer at MySQL for the last five years and has a PhD in computer science from Uppsala University in Sweden.

Luís Soares is a Senior Software Engineer and the MySQL Replication team lead at Oracle. His research interests include replication technologies, dependable systems, and high availability.

Before joining the MySQL team, he was both a postgraduate student and a researcher at the University of Minho, Portugal, where he designed and implemented group-based replication protocols. Before that, he worked for a Portuguese multinational company as a system analyst.

Geert J.M. Vanderkelen is a member of the MySQL Developer Team at Oracle. He is based in Germany and has worked for MySQL AB since April 2005. Before joining MySQL, he worked as a developer, DBA, and SysAdmin for various companies in Belgium and Germany. After working more than six years for the MySQL Support team, Geert is now part of the MySQL Utilities team and is the lead developer of MySQL Connector/Python.

Marco Tusa has run his own international practice for the past twenty-five years. His experience and expertise are in a wide variety of information technology and information management fields of application. He has been involved in research, development, analysis, database management, quality control, and project management. Learn more at his website: www.tusacentral.net.

Acknowledgments

I would like to thank all of the many talented and energetic professionals at Apress. I appreciate the understanding and patience of my editor, Jonathan Gennick, and managing editor, Kevin Shea. They were instrumental in the success of this project. I would also like to thank the army of publishing professionals at Apress for making me look so good in print. Thank you all very much!

I'd like to especially thank the technical reviewers, my colleagues at Oracle for their constructive criticism, and my academic colleagues for encouraging me to write this edition. Most important, I want to thank my wife, Annette, for her unending patience and understanding.

Introduction

MySQL has been identified as the world's most popular open-source database and the fastest-growing database system in the industry. This book presents some of the topics of advanced database systems, examines the architecture of MySQL, and provides an expert's workbook for examining, integrating, and modifying the MySQL source code for use in enterprise environments. The book provides insight into how to modify the MySQL system to meet the unique needs of system integrators and educators alike.

Whom This Book Is For

I have written this book with a wide variety of readers in mind. Whether you have been working in database systems for years, or maybe have taken an introductory database-theory class, or have even just read a good Apress book on MySQL, you will get a lot out of this book. Best of all, you can even get your hands into the source code. If you ever wanted to know what makes a database system like MySQL tick, this is your book!

How This Book Is Structured

The material presented is divided into three parts followed by an appendix. Each part is designed to present a set of topics ranging from introductory material on MySQL and the open-source revolution to extending and customizing the MySQL system. There is even coverage on how to build an experimental query optimizer and execution engine as an alternative to the MySQL query engine.

Part One

The first part of the book introduces concepts in developing and modifying open-source systems. Part One provides the tools and resources necessary to begin exploring the more advanced database concepts presented in the rest of the book. Chapters include:

1. MySQL and the Open Source Revolution—This chapter is less technical and contains more narration than the rest of the book. It guides you through the benefits and responsibilities of an open-source system integrator. It highlights the rapid growth of MySQL and its importance in the open-source- and database-system markets. Additionally, it provides a clear perspective on the open-source revolution.

2. The Anatomy of a Database System—This chapter covers the basics of what a database system is and how it is constructed. The anatomy of the MySQL system is used to illustrate the key components of modern relational-database systems.

3. A Tour of the MySQL Source Code—A complete introduction to the MySQL source is presented in this chapter, along with how to obtain and build the system. You are introduced to the mechanics of the source code along with coding guidelines and best practices for how the code is maintained.

4. Test-driven MySQL Development—This chapter introduces a key element in generating high-quality extensions to the MySQL system. Software testing is presented along with the common practices of how to test large systems. Specific examples are used to illustrate the accepted practices of testing the MySQL system.

Part Two

This part of the book provides tools, using a hands-on approach to investigating the MySQL system. It introduces you to how the MySQL code can be modified and how the system can be used as an embedded-database system. Examples and projects illustrate how to debug the source code, how to modify the SQL commands to extend the language, and how to build a custom storage engine.

5. Debugging—This chapter provides you with debugging skills and techniques to help make development easier and less prone to failure. Several debugging techniques are presented, along with the pros and cons of each.

6. Embedded MySQL—This chapter presents you with a tutorial on how to embed the MySQL system in enterprise applications. Example projects assist you in applying the skills presented to your own integration needs.

7. Adding Functions and Command to MySQL—This chapter presents the most popular modification to the MySQL code. You are shown how to modify the SQL commands and how to build custom SQL commands. It presents examples of how to modify SQL commands to add new parameters, functions, and new commands.

8. Extending MySQL High Availability—This chapter provides an overview of the high-availability features of MySQL, including a tour of the replication source code and examples of how to extend the feature to meet your high-availability needs.

9. Developing MySQL Plugins—This chapter presents an introduction to the pluggable architecture in MySQL. You will discover how to build plugins and see a detailed example of an authentication plugin.

10. Building Your Own Storage Engine—This chapter demonstrates the pluggable-storage-engine feature. The architecture is explored using examples and projects that permit you to build a sample storage engine.

Part Three

This part of the book takes a deeper look into the MySQL system and provides you with an insider's look at what makes the system work. The section begins with an introduction into the more advanced database technologies. Theory and practices are presented in a no-nonsense manner to enable you to apply the knowledge gained to tackle the more complex topics of database systems. This section also presents examples of how to implement an internal-query representation, an alternative query optimizer, and an alternative query-execution mechanism. Examples and projects are discussed in detail. Chapters 12 through 14 provide the skills and techniques needed to alter the internal structure of the MySQL system to execute using alternative mechanisms. These chapters provide you with a unique insight into how large systems can be built and modified.

11. Database-systems Internals—This chapter is designed to present the more advanced database techniques by examining the MySQL architecture. Topics include query execution, multiuser concerns, and programmatic considerations.

12. Internal-query Representation—This chapter presents the MySQL internal-query representation. You are provided with an example alternative query representation. A discussion is included of how to alter the MySQL source code to implement an alternative query representation.

13. Query Optimization—This chapter presents the MySQL internal-query optimizer. You are provided with an example alternative query optimizer that uses the alternative query representation from the previous chapter. It discusses how to alter the MySQL source code to implement the alternative query optimizer.

14. Query Execution—This chapter combines the techniques from the previous chapters to provide you with instructions on how to modify the MySQL system to implement alternative query-processing-engine techniques.

Appendix

This section of the book provides a list of resources on MySQL, database systems, and open-source software.

Using the Book for Teaching Database-Systems Internals

Many excellent database texts offer coverage of relational theory and practice. Few, however, offer material suitable for a classroom or lab environment. There are even fewer resources available for students to explore the inner workings of database systems. This book offers an opportunity for instructors to augment their database classes with hands-on laboratories. This text can be used in a classroom setting in three ways:

1. The text can be used to add depth to an introductory undergraduate or graduate database course. Parts 1 and 2 can be used to provide in-depth coverage of special topics in database systems. Suggested topics for lectures include those presented in Chapters 2, 3, 4, and 6. These can be used in addition to more traditional database-theory or systems texts. Hands-on exercises or class projects can be drawn from Chapters 6 and 7.

2. An advanced database course for undergraduate or graduate students can be based on Parts 1 and 2; each chapter can be presented over the course of 8 to 12 weeks. The remainder of the lectures can discuss the implementation of physical storage layers and the notion of storage engines. Semester projects can be based on Chapter 10, with students building their own storage engines.

3. A special-topics course on database-systems internals for the senior undergraduate or graduate students can be based on the entire text, with lectures based on the first eleven chapters. Semester projects can be derived from Part 3 of the text, with students implementing the remaining features of the database experimental platform. These features include applications of language theory, query optimizers, and query-execution algorithms.

Conventions

Throughout the book, I've kept a consistent style for presenting SQL and results. Where a piece of code, a SQL reserved word, or a fragment of SQL is presented in the text, it is presented in fixed-width Courier font, such as:

```
select * from dual;
```

Where I discuss the syntax and options of SQL commands, I use a conversational style so you can quickly reach an understanding of the command or technique. This means that I haven't duplicated large syntax diagrams that better suit a reference manual.

Downloading the Code

The code for the examples shown in this book is available on the Apress web site, www.apress.com. A link can be found on the book's information page under the Source Code/Downloads tab. This tab is located underneath the Related Titles section of the page.

Contacting the Author

Should you have any questions or comments—or even spot a mistake you think I should know about—you can contact me at drcharlesbell@gmail.com.

## PART 1

Getting Started with MySQL Development

This section introduces you to concepts in developing and modifying open source systems. Chapter 1 guides you through the benefits and responsibilities of an open source system integrator. It highlights the rapid growth of MySQL and its importance in the open-source- and database-system markets. Chapter 2 covers the basics of what a database system is and how it is constructed. Chapter 3 provides a complete introduction to the MySQL source presented in this chapter along with how to obtain and build the system. Chapter 4 introduces a key element in generating high-quality extensions to the MySQL system. You'll learn about software testing as well as common practices for testing large systems.

CHAPTER 1

■ ■ ■

MySQL and The Open Source Revolution

Open source systems are rapidly changing the software landscape. Information technology professionals everywhere are taking note of the high quality, and in many cases world-class, development and support offered by open-source-software vendors. Corporations are paying attention, because for the first time they have an alternative to commercial proprietary software vendors. Small businesses are paying attention because open source software can significantly lower the cost of their information systems. Individuals are paying attention because they have more choices with more options than ever before. The majority of the underpinnings that make the Internet what it is today are based on open source software systems, such as Linux, Apache HTTP server, BIND, Sendmail, OpenSSL, MySQL, and many others.

The most common reason businesses use open source software is cost. Open source software, by its very nature, reduces the total cost of ownership (TCO) and provides a viable business model on which businesses can build or improve their markets. This is especially true of open-source database systems, as the cost of commercial proprietary systems can easily go into tens or hundreds of thousands of dollars.

For small businesses just starting, this outlay of funds could impact its growth. For example, if a startup has to spend a significant potion of its reserves, it may be unable to get its products to market and therefore may not be able to gain a foothold in a highly competitive market. Open source provides startups with the opportunity to defer their software purchases until they can afford the investment. That doesn't mean, however, that they are building an infrastructure out of inferior components.

Open source software once was considered by many to be limited to the hobbyist or hacker bent on subverting the market of large commercial software companies. Although some developers may feel that they are playing the role of David to Microsoft's Goliath, the open source community is not about that at all. It does not profess to be a replacement for commercial proprietary software, but rather, it proposes the open source philosophy as an alternative. As you will see in this chapter, not only is open source a viable alternative to commercial software, but it is also fueling a worldwide revolution in how software is developed, evolved, and marketed.

■ **Note**   In this book, the term "hacker" refers to Richard Stallman's definition: "someone who loves to program and enjoys being clever about,"[1] and not the common perception of a nefarious villain bent on stealing credit cards and damaging computer systems.

---

[1]http://www.gnu.org/gnu/thegnuproject.html

The following section is provided for those who may not be familiar with open source software or the philosophy of MySQL. If you are already familiar with open source software philosophy, you can skip to the section "Developing with MySQL."

What Is Open Source Software?

Open source software grew from a conscious resistance to the corporate-property mindset. While working for the Artificial Intelligence Lab at Massachusetts Institute of Technology (MIT) in the 1970s, Richard Stallman began a code-sharing movement. Fueled by the desire to make commonly used code available to all programmers, Stallman saw the need for a cooperating community of developers. This philosophy worked well for Stallman and his small community—until the industry collectively decided that software was property and not something that should be shared with potential competitors. This resulted in many of the MIT researchers being lured away to work for these corporations. Eventually, the cooperative community faded away.

Fortunately, Stallman resisted the trend and left MIT to start the GNU (GNU Not Unix) project and the Free Software Foundation (FSF). The goal of the GNU project was to produce a free Unix-like operating system. This system would be free (including access to the source code) and available to anyone. The concept of "free" was to not prohibit anyone from using and modifying the system.

Stallman's goal was to re-establish the cooperating community of developers that worked so well at MIT. He had the foresight, however, to realize the system needed a copyright license that guaranteed certain freedoms. (Some have called Stallman's take on copyright "copyleft," because it guarantees freedom rather than restricts it.) Stallman created the GNU Public License (GPL). The GPL, a clever work of legal permissions that permits the code to be copied and modified without restriction, states that derivative works (the modified copies) must be distributed under the same license as the original version without any additional restrictions. Essentially, this uses the copyright laws against copyrights by removing the proprietary element altogether.

Unfortunately, Stallman's GNU project never fully materialized, but several parts of it have become essential elements of many open source systems. The most successful of these include the GNU compilers for the C programming language (GCC) and the GNU text editor (Emacs). Although the GNU operating system failed to be completed, the pioneering efforts of Stallman and his followers permitted Linus Torvalds to fill the gap with his Linux operating system, then in its infancy, in 1991. Linux has become the free Unix-like operating system that Stallman envisioned (see "Why Is Linux So Popular?"). Today, Linux is the world's most popular and successful open source operating system.

WHY IS LINUX SO POPULAR?

Linux is a Unix-like operating system built on the open source model. It is, therefore, free for anyone to use, distribute, and modify. Linux uses a conservative kernel design that has proven to be easy to evolve and improve. Since its release in 1991, Linux has gained a worldwide following of developers who seek to improve its performance and reliability. Some even claim that Linux is the most well-developed of all operating systems. Since its release, Linux has gained a significant market share of the world's server and workstation installations. Linux is often cited as the most successful open source endeavor to date.

We can see the success of Linux in the many variants brought forth by smaller groups within the community. Many of these variants, such as Ubuntu, are owned by a corporation (Canonical) that controls the evolution of the product. While still Linux in practice, Ubuntu is a great example of how ownership can drive innovation and differentiation through value-added alterations of the core product.

There was one problem with the free software movement. "Free" was intended to guarantee freedom to use, modify, and distribute, not to be free as in no cost or free-to-a-good home (often explained as "free" as free speech, not free beer). To counter this misconception, the Open Source Initiative (OSI) formed and later adopted and promoted the phrase "open source" to describe the freedoms guaranteed by the GPL; visit the website at www.opensource.org.

The OSI's efforts changed the free software movement. Software developers were given the opportunity to distinguish between free software that is truly no cost and open software that was part of the cooperative community. With the explosion of the Internet, the cooperative community has become a global community of developers that ensures the continuation of Stallman's vision.

Open source software, therefore, is software that is licensed to guarantee the rights of developers to use, copy, modify, and distribute their software while participating in a cooperative community whose natural goals are the growth and fostering of higher-quality software. Open source does not mean zero cost. It does mean anyone can participate in the development of the software and can, in turn, use the software without incurring a fee. On the other hand, many open source systems are hosted and distributed by organizations that sell support services for the software. This permits organizations that use the software to lower their information technology costs by eliminating startup costs and in many cases saving a great deal on maintenance.

All open source systems today draw their lineage from the foundations of the work that Stallman and others produced in an effort to create a software utopia in which Stallman believed organizations should generate revenue from selling services, not proprietary property rights. There are several examples of Stallman's vision becoming reality. The GNU/Linux (henceforth referred to as Linux) movement has spawned numerous successful (and profitable) companies, such as Red Hat and Slackware, that sell customized distributions and support for Linux. Another example is MySQL, which has become the most successful open-source-database system.

Although the concept of a software utopia is arguably not a reality today, it is possible to download an entire suite of systems and tools to power a personal or business computer without spending any money on the software itself. No-cost versions of software ranging from operating systems and server systems such as database and web servers to productivity software are available for anyone to download and use.

Why Use Open Source Software?

Sooner or later, someone is going to ask why using open source software is a good idea. To successfully fend off the ensuing challenges from proponents of commercial proprietary software, you should have a solid answer. The most important reasons for adopting open source software are:

- Open source software costs little or nothing to use. This is especially important for nonprofits, universities, and community organizations, whose budgets are constantly shrinking and that must do more with less every year.

- You can modify it to meet your specific needs.

- The licensing mechanisms available are more flexible than commercial licenses.

- Open source software is more robust (tested) than commercial proprietary software.

- Open source software is more reliable and secure than commercial proprietary software.

Although you likely won't be challenged or asked to demonstrate any of these reasons for adopting open source software, you might be challenged by contradiction—that is, proponents of commercial proprietary software (opponents of open source) will attempt to discredit these claims by making statements about why you shouldn't use open source software for development. Let's examine some of the more popular reasons not to use open source software from a commercial proprietary software viewpoint and refute them with the open source view.

Myth 1: Commercial Proprietary Software Fosters Greater Creativity

The argument goes: Most enterprise-level commercial proprietary software provides application programming interfaces (API) that permit developers to extend their functionality, thus making the software more flexible and ensuring greater creativity for developers.

Some of this is true. APIs do permit developers to extend the software, but they often do so in a way that strictly prohibits developers from adding functionality to the base software. These APIs often force the developer into a sandbox, further restricting her creativity.

For example, the Microsoft .Net language C# has been critically acclaimed as being a very good language. APIs, however, are not easily modified. Indeed, one receives the binary form of the library only when installing the host product, Visual Studio. You can augment the APIs with class derivatives, but strictly speaking, you cannot edit the source code for the APIs in and of themselves.

■ **Note** Sandboxes are often created to limit the developer's ability to affect the core system, largely for security. The more open the API is, the more likely it is for villainous developers to create malicious code to damage the system or its data.

Open source software may also support and provide APIs, but it provides developers with the ability to see the actual source code of the core system. Not only can they see the source code, they are free (and encouraged) to modify it! (For example, you may want to modify the core system when a critical feature isn't available or you need the system to read or write a specific format.) Therefore, open source software fosters greater creativity than commercial proprietary software.

Myth 2: Commercial Proprietary Software Is More Secure Than Open Source Software

The argument goes: Organizations require their information systems in today's Internet-connected society to be more secure than ever before. Commercial proprietary software is inherently more secure because the company that sells the software has a greater stake in ensuring their products can stand against the onslaught of today's digital predators.

Although the goals of this statement are quite likely to appear on a boardroom wall as a mantra for any commercial software vendor, the realization of this goal, or in some cases marketing claim, is often misleading or unobtainable.

Studies have shown that the very nature of open source software development can help make the software more secure because open source software, by definition, is developed by a group and a community interested in seeking the very best for the product. Indeed, the rigorous review and openness of the source code ensures there is nothing that can be hidden from view, whether a defect or an omission. Because the source code is available to all, it is in every open source developer's best interest to harden his code—malicious or benign.

Myth 3: Commercial Proprietary Software Is Tested More Than Open Source Software

The argument goes: Software vendors sell software. The products they sell must maintain a standard of high quality or customers won't buy them. Open source software is not under any such pressure and therefore is not tested as stringently as commercial proprietary software.

This argument is very compelling. In fact, it sings to the hearts of all information-technology acquisition agents. They are convinced that something you pay for is more reliable and freer of defects than software that can be acquired without a fee. Unfortunately, these individuals are overlooking one important concept of open source software: It is developed by a global community of developers, many of whom consider themselves defect detectives (testers) and pride themselves on finding and reporting defects. In some cases, open source software companies have offered rewards for developers who find repeatable bugs.

It is true that software vendors employ software testers (and no doubt they are the best in their field), but more often than not, commercial software projects are pushed toward a specific deadline and are focused on the good of the product from the point of view of the company's goals – often driven by marketing opportunities. These deadlines are put in place to ensure a strategic release date or competitive advantage. Many times these deadlines force software vendors to compromise on portions of their software development process—which is usually the later part: testing. As you can imagine, reducing a tester's access to the software (testing time) means they will find fewer defects.

Open source software companies, by enlisting the help and support of the global community of developers, ensure that their software is tested more often by more people who have only the good of the product itself in mind and are not usually driven by goals that may influence their ability to scrutinize the software. Indeed, some open source community members can be at times merciless in their evaluation of a new feature or release. Believe me when I tell you that if it isn't up to their expectations, they will let you know.

Myth 4: Commercial Proprietary Systems Have More Complex Capabilities and More Complete Feature Sets Than Open Source Systems

The argument goes: Commercial proprietary database systems are sophisticated and complex server systems. Open source systems are neither large nor complex enough to handle mission-critical enterprise data.

Although some open source systems are good imitations of the commercial systems they mimic, the same cannot be said for a database system such as MySQL. Earlier versions of MySQL did not have all the features found in commercial proprietary database systems, but since version 5.0, and more so with the latest releases, MySQL includes major features and is considered the world's most popular open-source database system.

Furthermore, MySQL has been shown to provide the reliability, performance, and scalability that large enterprises require for mission-critical data, and many well-known organizations use it. MySQL is one open source system that offers all the features and capabilities of the best competing commercial proprietary database systems.

Myth 5: Commercial Proprietary Software Vendors Are More Responsive Because They Have a Dedicated Staff

The argument goes: When a software system is purchased, the software comes with the assurances that the company that produced it will provide assistance or help to solve problems. Because no one "owns" open source systems, it is far more difficult get assistance.

Most open source software is built by the global community of developers. The growing trend, however, is to base a business model on the open source philosophy and build a company around it, selling support and services for the software that the company oversees. Most major open source products are supported in this manner. For instance, Oracle Corporation, hence Oracle, owns the source code for its MySQL product. (For a complete description of Oracle's MySQL open source license, see www.mysql.com/company/legal/licensing/opensource-license.htm.)

Developers of open source software respond much more quickly to issues and problems than commercial developers do. Indeed, many take great pride in being open about their products and pay close attention to what the world thinks about them. On the other hand, it can be nearly impossible to talk to a commercial software developer directly. For example, Microsoft has a comprehensive support mechanism in place and can meet the needs of just about any organization. If you want to talk to a developer of a Microsoft product, however, you must go through proper channels. This requires talking to every stage of the support hierarchy—and even then are you not guaranteed contact with the developer.

Open source developers, on the other hand, use the Internet as their primary form of communication. Since they are already on the Internet, they are much more likely to see your question in a forum or news group. Additionally, open source companies such as Oracle actively monitor their community and can respond quickly to their customers.

Therefore, purchasing commercial proprietary software does not guarantee you quicker response times than that of open source software. In many cases, open source software developers are more responsive (reachable) than commercial software developers.

What If They Want Proof?

These are just a few of the arguments that are likely to cause you grief as you attempt to adopt open source software in your organization. Several researchers have attempted to prove open source is better than commercial software. One, James W. Paulson, conducted an empirical study of open source and commercial proprietary software (he calls it "closed") that examines the preceding arguments and proves that open source software development can demonstrate measurable improvements over commercial proprietary software development. See Paulson's article, "An Empirical Study of Open-Source and Closed-Source Software Products," in the April 2004 issue of IEEE Transactions on Software Engineering.

Is Open Source Really a Threat to Commercial Software?

Until recently, open source software was not considered a threat to the commercial proprietary software giants, but one of Oracle's competitors is beginning to exhibit the classic signs of responding to a competitive threat. While, despite its recent openness endeavor[2], Microsoft continues to speak out against open source software, denouncing MySQL as a world-class database server while passively ignoring the threat, Oracle is taking a considerably different tack.

Since acquiring MySQL with the Sun Microsystems acquisition, Oracle has continued to devote considerable resources in enhancing MySQL. Oracle has and continues to invest in development in the ongoing quest to make MySQL the world's best database system for the web.

The pressure of competition isn't limited to MySQL versus proprietary database systems. At least one open-source database system, Apache Derby, touts itself as an alternative to MySQL and recently tossed its hat into the ring as a replacement for the "M" in the LAMP stack (see "What Is the LAMP Stack?"). Proponents for Apache Derby cite licensing issues with MySQL and feature limitations. Neither has deterred the MySQL install base, nor have these "issues" limited MySQL's increasing popularity.

WHAT IS THE LAMP STACK?

LAMP stands for Linux, Apache, MySQL, and PHP/Perl/Python. The LAMP stack is a set of open source servers, services, and programming languages that permit rapid development and deployment of high-quality web applications. The key components are

Linux: A Unix-like operating system. Linux is known for its high degree of reliability and speed as well as its vast diversity of supported hardware platforms.

Apache: A web application server known for its high reliability and ease of configuration. Apache runs on most Unix operating systems.

---

[2]http://www.microsoft.com/en-us/openness/default.aspx#home

MySQL: The database system of choice for many web application developers. MySQL is known for its speed and small execution footprint.

PHP/Perl/Python: These are scripting languages that can be embedded in HTML web pages for programmatic execution of events. These scripting languages represent the active programming element of the LAMP stack. They are used to interface with system resources and back-end database systems to provide active content to the user. While most LAMP developers prefer PHP over the other scripting languages, each can be used to successfully develop web applications.

There are many advantages to using the LAMP stack for development. The greatest is cost. All LAMP components are available as no-cost open-source licenses. Organizations can download, install, and develop web applications in a matter of hours with little or no initial cost for the software.

An interesting indicator of the benefits of offering an open-source database system is the recent offering of "free" versions from some of the proprietary database vendors. Microsoft, which has been a vocal opponent of open source software, now offers a no-cost version of its SQL Server database system called SQL Server Express. Although there is no cost for downloading the software and you are permitted to distribute the software with your application, you may not see the source code or modify it in any way. This version has a limited feature set and is not scalable to a full enterprise-level database server without purchasing additional software and services.

Clearly, the path that Oracle is blazing with its MySQL server products demonstrates a threat to the proprietary database market—a threat that the commercial proprietary software industry is taking seriously. Although Microsoft continues to try to detract the open-source-software market, it, too, is starting to see the wisdom of no-cost software.

Legal Issues and the GNU Manifesto

Commercial proprietary software licenses are designed to limit your freedoms and to restrict your use. Most commercial licenses state clearly that you, the purchaser of the software, do not own the software but may use it under very specific conditions. In almost all cases, this means you cannot copy, distribute, or modify the system in any way. These licenses also make it clear that the source code is owned exclusively by the licenser, and that you, the licensee, are not permitted to see or re-engineer it.

■ **Caution** This section is a general discussion of the General Public License. Software providers often have their own forms of this license and may interpret the legalities in subtle but different ways. Always contact the software provider for clarification of any portion of the license that you wish to exercise. This is especially true if you wish to modify or include any portion of the software in your own products or services.

Open source systems are generally licensed using a GNU-based license agreement (GNU stands for GNU, not Unix) called General Public License (GPL). See http://www.gnu.org/licenses/ for more details. Most GPL licenses permit free use of the original source code with a restriction that all modifications be made public or returned to the originator as legal ownership. Furthermore, most open source systems use the GPL agreement, which states that it is intended to guarantee your rights to copy, distribute, and modify the software. Note that the GPL does not limit your rights in regard to how you use the software; in fact, it specifically grants you the right to use the software however you want. The GPL also guarantees your right to have access to the source code. All of these rights are specified in the GNU Manifesto and the GPL agreement (`www.gnu.org/licenses/gpl.html`).

Most interesting, the GPL specifically permits you to charge a distribution fee (or media fee) for distribution of the original source and provides you the right to use the system in whole or modified in order to create a derivative product, which is also protected under the same GPL. The only catch is that you are required to make your modified source code available to anyone who wants it.

These limitations do not prohibit you from generating revenue from your hard work. On the contrary, as long as you turn over your source code by publishing it via the original owner, you can charge your customers for your derivative work. Some may argue that this means you can never gain a true competitive advantage, because your source code is available to everyone, but the opposite is true in practice. Vendors such as Canonical, Red Hat, and Oracle have profited from business models based on the GPL.

The only limitations of the GPL that may cause you pause are the limitation on warranties and the requirement to place a banner in your software stating the derivation (original and license) of the work.

A limitation on expressed warranties isn't that surprising if you consider that most commercial licenses include similar clauses. The part that makes the GPL unique is the concept of nonliable loss. The GPL specifically frees the originator and you, the modifier (or distributor), from loss or damage as a result of the installation or use of the software. Stallman did not want the legal industry to cash in should there ever be a question of liability of open source software. The logic is simple. You obtained the software for free and you did not get any assurances about its performance or protection from damages as a result of its use. In this case, there is no quid pro quo and thus no warranty of any kind.

Opponents of the open source movement will cite this as a reason to avoid open source software, stating that it is "use at your own risk" and therefore introduces too much risk. While that's true enough, the argument is weakened or invalidated when you purchase support from open source vendors. Support options from open source vendors often include certain liability rights and further protections. This is perhaps the most compelling reason to purchase support for open source software. In this case, there is quid pro quo and in many cases a reliable warranty.

The requirement to place a banner in a visible place in your software is not that onerous. The GPL simply requires a clear statement of the software's derivation and origination as well as marking the software as protected under the GPL. This informs anyone who uses this software of their rights (freedoms) to use, copy, distribute, and modify the software.

Perhaps the most important declaration contained in the GNU manifesto is the statements under "How GNU Will Be Available." In this section, the manifesto states that although everyone may modify and redistribute GNU, no one may restrict its further redistribution. This means no one can take an open source system based on the GNU manifesto and turn it into a proprietary system or make proprietary modifications.

Property

A discussion of open-source-software licensing would be incomplete if the subject of property were not included. Property is simply something that is owned. While often think of property as something tangible, in the case of software, the concept becomes problematic. What exactly do we mean when we say software is property? Does the concept of property apply to the source code, the binaries (executables), the documentation, or all of them?

The concept of property is often a sticky subject when it comes to open source software. Who is the owner if the software is produced by the global community of developers? In most cases, open source software begins as a project someone or some organization has developed. The project becomes open source when the software is mature enough to be useful to someone else. Whether this is at an early stage, when the software is unrefined, or later, when the software reaches a certain level of reliability, is not important. What is important is that the person or organization that started the project is considered the owner. In the case of MySQL, the company, Oracle, originated the project and therefore it owns the MySQL system.

According to the GPL that MySQL adheres to, Oracle owns all the source code and any modifications made under the GPL. The GPL gives you the right to modify MySQL, but it does not give you the right to claim the source code as your property.

DOES ORACLE REALLY OWN MYSQL?

A detailed history of the evolution of MySQL as an organization is beyond the scope of this book. The MySQL brand, product, and its development organization is solely owned by Oracle Corporation. Oracle acquired MySQL as part of the Sun Microsystems merger executed in January 2010.

Despite some controversy over antitrust in Europe, the merger was successful, and Oracle pledged continued development and evolution of MySQL. To date, Oracle has lived up to those promises and continues to foster MySQL as the world's leading open-source database system. Oracle continues to position MySQL in the same light as it was in the past: the database for the web (the M in LAMP).

Since the acquisition, Oracle has released several versions of MySQL that include advancements in better performance, integration of InnoDB as the default database, Windows platform improvements, and numerous improvements and innovations to replication thereby enabling high availability capabilities. Oracle is indeed the owner of MySQL and has proved to be its greatest custodian to date.

The Ethical Side

Ethical dilemmas abound when you first start working with open source software. For example, open source software is free to download, but you have to turn over any improvements you make to the original owner. How can you make money from something you have to give away?

To understand this, you must consider the goal that Stallman had in mind when he developed the GNU license model: to make a community of cooperation and solidarity among developers throughout the world. He wanted source code to be publicly available and the software generated to be free for anyone to use. Your rights to earn (to be paid) for your work are not restricted. You can sell your derivative work. You just can't claim ownership of the source code. You are ethically (and legally!) bound to give back to the global community of developers.

Another ethical dilemma arises when you modify open source software for your own use. For example, you download the latest version of MySQL and add a feature that permits you to use your own abbreviated shortcuts for the SQL commands because you're tired of typing out long SQL statements (I am sure someone somewhere has already done this). In this case, you are modifying the system in a way that benefits only yourself. So why should you turn over your modifications? Although this dilemma is probably not an issue for most of us, it could be an issue for you if you continue using the software with your personal modifications and eventually create a derivative work. Basically, any productive and meaningful modification you make must be considered property of the originator regardless of its use or limits of its use.

If you modify the source code as an academic exercise (as I will show you how to do later in this book, however, you should discard the modifications after completing your exercises or experiments. Some open source software makes provisions for these types of uses. Most consider exploring and experimenting with the source code a "use" of the software and not a modification and so allow use of the source code in academic pursuits.

Let the Revolution Continue!

The idea of freedom drove Richard Stallman to begin his quest to reform software development. Although freedom was the catalyst for the open source movement, it has become a revolution, because organizations now can avoid obsolescence at the hands of their competitors by investing in lower-cost software systems while maintaining the revenue to compete in their markets.

Organizations that have adopted open source software as part of their product lines are perhaps the most revolutionary of all. Most have adopted a business model based on the GPL that permits them to gain all of the experience and robustness that come with open source systems while still generating revenue for their own ideas and additions.

Open source software is both scorned and lauded by the software industry. Some despise open source because they see it as an attack on the commercial proprietary software industry. They also claim open source is a fad and will not last. They see organizations that produce, contribute to, or use open source software as being on borrowed time and believe that sooner rather than later, the world will come to its senses and forget about open source software. Some don't despise open source as much as they see no possibility for profit and therefore dismiss the idea as fruitless.

Others see open source software as the savior that rescues us all from the tyrants of commercial proprietary software, and they believe that that sooner rather than later, the giant software companies will be forced to change their property models to open source or some variant thereof. The truth is probably in the middle. I see the open source industry as a vibrant and growing industry of similar-minded individuals whose goals are to create safe, reliable, and robust software. They make money by providing services based on and supporting open source software. Sometimes this is via licensing or support sales and sometimes this is via customization and consultation.

Whatever the method, it is clear that good open source software can become a business on its own. Similarly, whatever your perspective, you must conclude that the open source movement has caused a revolution among software developers everywhere.

Now that you have had a sound introduction to the open source revolution, you can decide whether you agree with its philosophy. If you do (and I sincerely hope I have convinced you to), then welcome to the global community of developers. *Viva le revolution!*

Developing with MySQL

You've taken a look at what open source software is and the legal ramifications of using and developing with open source software. Now you'll learn how to develop products using MySQL. As you'll see, MySQL presents a unique opportunity for developers to exploit a major-server software technology without the burden of conforming or limiting their development to a fixed set of rules or limited API suite.

MySQL is a relational database-management system designed for use in client/server architectures. MySQL can also be used as an embedded database library. Of course, if you have used MySQL before, you are familiar with its capabilities and no doubt have decided to choose MySQL for some or all of your database needs.

At the lowest level of the system, the server is built using a multithreaded model written in a combination of C and C++. Much of this core functionality was built in the early 1980s and later modified with a Structured Query Language (SQL) layer in 1995. MySQL was built using the GNU C compiler (GCC), which provides a great deal of flexibility for target environments. This means MySQL can be compiled for use on just about any Linux operating systems. Oracle has also had considerable success in building variants for the Microsoft Windows and Macintosh operating systems. The client tools for MySQL are largely written in C for greater portability and speed. Client libraries and access mechanism are available for .NET, Java, ODBC, and several others.

WHAT DOES THE ++ MEAN?

Once, while I was an undergraduate. I audited a C++ course primarily as a motivation to learn the language. I find learning a new programming language is futile if there is no incentive to master it—such as a passing grade. During the first day of class, a student (not me) asked the instructor what the ++ represented. His reply was, "the extra stuff." Based on that whimsical and not altogether historically correct answer, and the fact that the MySQL source code has portions that are truly C and portions that are truly C++, it is more like C+/− than C or C++. C++ was originally named "C with classes" by its creator but later changed to C++ in 1983, using a bad pun for the increment operator. In other words, C++ is C with evolutionary additions[3].

---

[3]http://www2.research.att.com/~bs/bs_faq.html#name

MySQL is built using parallel development paths to ensure product lines continue to evolve while new versions of the software are planned and developed. Software development follows a staged development process in which multiple releases are produced in each stage. The stages of a MySQL development process are:

1. *Development*—New product or feature sets are planned and implemented as a new path of the development tree.

2. *Alpha*—Feature refinement and defect correction (bug fixes) are implemented.

3. *Beta*—The features are "frozen" (no new features can be added) and additional intensive testing and defect correction is implemented.

4. *Release Candidate*—A stable beta state with no major defects, the code is frozen (only defects may be fixed) and final rounds of testing are conducted.

5. *Generally Available (GA)*—If no major defects are found, the code is declared stable and ready for production release.

You'll often see various versions of the MySQL software offered in any of these stages. Typically, only the beta, release candidate, and GA releases are offered for download, but depending on the significance of a feature or the status of a feature request made by a support subscription, alpha releases may be made available.

When a particular feature represents a major change in existing functionality or improves a particular feature significantly, a lab release may be offered on dev.mysql.com. A labs release is considered a preview of the feature and as such, it is meant for evaluation purposes. Typically, minimal or no documentation is available for labs releases. Indeed, Oracle states on the labs site, "not fit for production [use]." You can download lab releases from `http://labs.mysql.com/`.

When a set of features represents a major advancement in functionality or performance, there may be a development milestone release (DMR) offered. A DMR may have several features that may be at various stages of development. It is possible a DMR may have most features in a beta state, but a few may be at alpha or even near-release-candidate state. A DMR therefore is a key method of tracking and preparing for adopting major advances in MySQL development. You can find DMRs at `http://dev.mysql.com/downloads/mysql/#downloads`.

You can read more about general MySQL development, labs releases, and DMRs at `http://dev.mysql.com/doc/mysql-development-cycle/en/index.html`.

The parallel development strategy permits Oracle to maintain its current releases while working on new features. It is common to read about the new features in 5.6 while development and defect repair is continuing in 5.5. This may seem confusing, because we are used to commercial proprietary software vendors keeping their development strategies to themselves. MySQL version numbers are used to track the releases; they contain a two-part number for the product series and a single number for the release. For example, version 5.6.12 is the twelfth release of the 5.6 product line.

■ **Tip** Always include the complete version number when corresponding with Oracle. Simply stating the "alpha release" or "latest version" is not clear enough to properly address your needs.

This multiple-release philosophy has some interesting side effects. It is not uncommon to encounter organizations that are using older versions of MySQL. In fact, I have encountered several agencies that I work with who are still using the version 4.x product lines. This philosophy has virtually eliminated the upgrade shell game that commercial proprietary software undergoes. That is, every time the vendor releases a new version it ceases development, and in many cases support, of the old version. With major architectural changes, customers are forced to alter their environments and development efforts accordingly. This adds a great deal of cost to maintaining product lines based on commercial proprietary software. The multiple-release philosophy frees organizations from this burden by permitting them to keep their own products in circulation much longer and with the assurance of continued support. Even when new architecture changes occur, as in the case of MySQL version 5.6, organizations have a much greater lead time and can therefore expend their resources in the most efficient manner allowed to them without rushing or altering their long-term plans.

While you may download any version of MySQL, first consider your use of the software. If you plan to use it as an enterprise server in your own production environment, you may want to limit your download to the stable releases of the product line. On the other hand, if you are building a new system using the LAMP stack or another development environment, any of the other release stages would work for a development effort. Most users will download the stable release of the latest version that they intend to use in their environment.

WHICH VERSION SHOULD I USE WITH THIS BOOK?

For the purposes of the exercises and experiments in this book, any version (stage) of MySQL 5.6 will work well. MySQL 5.6 is a significant milestone in MySQL's evolution not only for its advanced features and performance improvements, but also for major changes in the architecture and significant changes to the source code. While some portions of this book may be fine for use in version 5.1 or 5.5 (for example, adding new functions), most examples are specific to version 5.6.

Oracle recommends using the latest stable release for any new development. What it means is if you plan to add features to MySQL and you are participating in the global community of developers, you should add new features to the server when it is most stable. This permits the greatest opportunity (exposure) for your code to be successful.

Also consider that, while the stage of the version may indicate its state with respect to new features, you should not automatically associate instability with the early stages or stability with the later ones. Depending on your use of the software, the stability may be different. For example, if you are using MySQL in a development effort to build a new ecommerce site in the LAMP stack, and you are not using any of the new features introduced during the alpha stage, the stability for your use is virtually the same as that of any other stage. The best rule of thumb is to select the version with the features that you need at the latest stage of development available.

CLONE WARS?

If you have spent time researching MySQL, you most likely have encountered at least one database system that claims to be a derivative of MySQL. While several vendors offer a variant (sometimes called a fork or port) of MySQL—some being backed by small startup companies and one by the original developers of MySQL—none of these will match the level of expertise and development prowess of Oracle's fostering of MySQL.

You may encounter variants that you may be able to use with this book. Given the major advances of MySQL in recent releases, however, you would do well to use the official MySQL source for your exploration of the source code. Some variants may eventually include the newest features, but at this time, it is unlikely they will be up to date with Oracle's releases. Vendors offering variants include MariaDB, SkySQL, and Percona.

Why Modify MySQL?

Modifying MySQL is not a trivial task. If you are an experienced C/C++ programmer and understand the construction of relational database systems, you can probably jump right in. The rest of us need to consider why we want to modify a database server system and carefully plan our modifications.

There are many reasons why you would want to modify MySQL. Perhaps you require a database server or client feature that isn't available. Or maybe you have a custom-application suite that requires a specific type of database behavior, and rather than having to adapt to a commercial proprietary system, it is easier and cheaper for you to modify

MySQL to meet your needs. It is most likely the case that your organization cannot afford to duplicate the sophistication and refinement of the MySQL database system, but you need something to base your solution on. What better way to make your application world-class than by basing it on a world-class database system?

▓ **Note**   If a feature is really useful and someone considers it beneficial, the beauty of open source is that the feature will work its way into the product. Someone, somewhere will contribute and build the feature.

Like all effective software developers, you must first plan what you are going to do. Start with the planning devices and materials that you are most comfortable with, and make a list of all of the things you feel you need the database server (or client) to do. Spend some time evaluating MySQL to see if any of the features you want already exist, and make notes concerning their behavior. After you've completed this research, you will have a better idea of where the gaps are. This "gap analysis" will provide you with a concentrated list of features and modifications needed. Once you have determined the features you need to add, you can begin to examine the MySQL source code and experiment with adding new features.

▓ **Warning**   Always investigate the current MySQL features thoroughly when planning your modifications. You will want to examine and experiment with all SQL commands that are similar to your needs. Although you may not be able to use the current features, examining the existing capabilities will enable you to form a baseline of known behavior and performance that you can use to compare your new feature. You can be sure that members of the global community of developers will scrutinize new features and remove those they feel are best achieved using a current feature.

This book will introduce you to the MySQL source code and teach you how to add new features, as well as the best practices for what to change (and what not to change).

Later chapters will also detail your options for getting the source code and how to merge your changes into the appropriate code path (branch). You will also learn the details of Oracle's coding guidelines that specify how your code should look and what code constructs you should avoid.

What Can You Modify in MySQL? Are There Limits?

The beauty of open source software is that you have access to its source code for the software (as guaranteed by its respective open source license). This means you have access to all of the inner workings of the entire software. Have you ever wondered how a particular open-source-software product works? You can find out simply by downloading the source code and working your way through it.

With MySQL, it isn't so simple. The source code in MySQL is very complex, and in some cases, it is difficult to read and understand. One could say the code has very low comprehensibility. Often regarded by the original developers as having a "genius factor," the source code can be a challenge for even the best C/C++ programmer.

While the challenges of complexities of the C/C++ code may be a concern, it in no way limits your ability to modify the software. Most developers modify the source code to add new SQL commands or alter existing SQL commands to get a better fit to their database needs. The opportunities are much broader than simply changing MySQL's SQL behavior, however. You can change the optimizer, the internal query representation, or even the query-cache mechanism.

One challenge you are likely to encounter will not be from any of your developers; it may come from your senior technical stakeholders. For example, I once made significant modifications to the MySQL source code to solve a challenging problem. Senior technical stakeholders in the organization challenged the validity of my project not because of the solution or its design, but because I was modifying foundations of the server code itself. One stakeholder was adamant that my changes "flew in the face of thirty years of database theory and tried and true implementation." I certainly hope you never encounter this type of behavior, but if you do and you've done your research as to what features are available and how they do not meet (or partially meet) your needs, your answer should consist of indisputable facts. If you do get this question or one like it, remind your senior technical stakeholder that the virtues of open source software is that it can be modified and that it frequently is modified. You may also want to consider explaining what your new feature does and how it will improve the system as a whole for everyone. If you can do that, you can weather the storm.

Another challenge you are likely to face with modifying MySQL is the question, "Why MySQL?" Experts will be quick to point out that there are several open-source-database systems to choose from. The most popular are MySQL, Firebird, PostgreSQL, and Berkeley DB. Reasons to choose MySQL for your development projects over some of the other database systems include:

- MySQL is a relational database-management system that supports a full set of SQL commands. Some open-source database systems, such as PostgreSQL, are object-relational database systems that use an API or library for access rather than accepting SQL commands. Some open source systems are built using architectures that may not be suited for your environment. For example, Apache Derby is based in Java and may not offer the best performance for your embedded application.

- MySQL is built using C/C++, which can be built for nearly all Linux platforms as well as Microsoft Windows and Macintosh OS. Some open source systems may not be available for your choice of development language. This can be an issue if you must port the system to the version of Linux that you are running.

- MySQL is designed as client/server architecture. Some open source systems are not scalable beyond a client-based embedded system. For example, Berkeley DB is a set of client libraries and is not a stand-alone database system.

- MySQL is a mature database server with a proven track record of stability owned by the world leader in database systems. Some open-source database systems may not have the install base of MySQL or may not offer the features you need in an enterprise database server.

Clearly, the challenges are going to be unique to the development needs and the environment in which the modifications take place. Whatever your needs are, you can be sure that you have complete access to all of the source code and that your modifications are limited only by your imagination.

MySQL's Dual License

MySQL is licensed as open source software under the GPL. The server and client software as well as the tools and libraries are all covered by the GPL. Oracle has made the GPL a major focal point in its business model. It is firmly committed to the GNU open source community.

■ **Tip** The complete GPLv2 license text for MySQL can be found at http://dev.mysql.com/doc/refman/5.6/en/ license-gnu-gpl-2-0.html. Read this carefully if you intend to modify MySQL or if you have never seen a GPL license before. Contact Oracle if you have questions about how to interpret the license for your use.

Oracle has gained many benefits by exposing its source code to the global community of developers. The source code is routinely evaluated by public scrutiny, third-party organizations regularly audit the source code, the development process fosters a forum of open communication and feedback, and the source code is compiled and tested in many different environments. No other database vendor can make these claims while maintaining world-class stability, reliability, and features.

MySQL is also licensed as a commercial product. A commercial license permits Oracle to own the source code (as described earlier) as well the copyright on the name, logo, and documentation (such as books). This is unique, because most open source companies do not ascribe to owning anything—rather, their intellectual property is their experience and expertise. Oracle has retained rights to the intellectual property of the software while leveraging the support of the global community of developers to expand and evolve it. Oracle has its own MySQL development team with more than 100 engineers worldwide. Although developers from around the world participate in the development of MySQL, Oracle employs many of them.

FREE AND OPEN SOURCE ("FOSS") EXCEPTION

Oracle's FOSS exception permits the use of the GPL-licensed client libraries in applications without requiring the derivative work to be subject to the GPL. If you are developing an application that uses MySQL client libraries, check out the MySQL FOSS exception for complete details.

http://www.mysql.com/about/legal/licensing/foss-exception/

Oracle offers several major MySQL editions, or versions, of the server. Most are commercial offerings that may not have a corresponding GPL release. For example, while you may download a GPL release of MySQL Cluster, you cannot download a commercial release of MySQL Cluster Carrier Grade Edition. Table 1-1 summarizes the various server editions currently available (when this chapter was written) from Oracle and their base licensing cost.

Table 1-1. *MySQL Server Products and Pricing*

Product	Description	License	Cost
MySQL Cluster Carrier Grade Edition	high-performance, in-memory clustered database solution that enables users to meet the challenges of high-demand web, cloud, and communications services.	Commercial	$10,000.00**
MySQL Enterprise Edition	advanced enterprise features including management tools and technical support to achieve the highest levels of MySQL scalability, security, reliability, and uptime. It is targeted for developing, deploying, and managing business-critical MySQL applications.	Commercial	$5,000.00**
MySQL Standard Edition	includes the InnoDB storage engine as the default engine making it a fully integrated transaction-safe, ACID compliant database. In addition, MySQL Replication allows you to deliver high-performance and scalable applications. It is targeted for scalable Online Transaction Processing (OLTP) applications.	Commercial	$2,000.00**
MySQL Classic	embedded database for ISVs, OEMs and VARs developing read-intensive applications using the MyISAM storage engine.	Commercial	Call MySQL sales for pricing
MySQL Embedded (OEM/ISV)	any of the above editions specifically licensed for OEM/ISV embedded application.	Commercial	Call MySQL sales for pricing
MySQL Community Edition	freely downloadable version of MySQL.	GPL	Free

**Costs shown are representative as of the publication of this work. Contact Oracle for accurate and up-to-date pricing.*

■ **Tip** Learn more about Oracle's pricing and purchasing options at `http://mysql.com/buy-mysql/`.

So, Can You Modify MySQL or Not?

You may be wondering, after a discussion of the limitations of using open source software under the GNU public license, if you can actually modify it after all. The answer is: it depends.

You can modify MySQL under the GPL, provided, of course, that if you intend to distribute your changes you surrender those changes to the owner of the project and thereby fulfill your obligation to participate in the global community of developers. If you are experimenting or using the modifications for personal or educational purposes, you are not obligated to turn over your changes.

The heart of the matter comes down to the benefits of the modifications. If you add capabilities of interest to someone other than yourself, you should share them. Regardless of the situation, always consult Oracle before making any modification that you intend to share.

Guidelines for Modifying MySQL

Take care when approaching a task such as modifying a system such as MySQL. A relational database system is a complex set of services layered in such a way as to provide fast, reliable access to data. You would not want to open the source code and start plugging in your own code to see what happens (but you're welcome to try). Instead, plan your changes and take careful aim at the portions of the source code that pertain to your needs.

Having modified large systems such as MySQL, I want to impart a few simple guidelines that will make your experience with modifying MySQL a positive one.

First, decide which license you are going to use. If you are using MySQL under an open source license already and can implement the modifications yourself, continue to use the GPL. In this case, you must perpetuate the open source mantra and give back to the community in exchange for what was freely offered. Under the terms of the GPL, the developer is bound to make these changes available. If you are using MySQL under the commercial license or need support for the modifications, purchase the appropriate MySQL Edition to match your server (number of CPU cores) and consult with Oracle on your modifications. If you are not going to distribute the modifications, however, and you can support them for future versions of MySQL, you do not need to change to the commercial license or change your commercial license to the GPL.

Another suggestion is to create a developer's journal and keep notes of each change you make or each interesting discovery you find. Not only will you be able to record your work step by step, but you can also use the journal to document what you are doing. You will be amazed at what you can discover about your research by going back and reading your past journal entries. I have found many golden nuggets of information scrawled within my engineering notebooks.

While experimenting with the source code, also make notes in the source code itself. Annotate the source code with a comment line or comment block before and after your changes. This makes it easy to locate all of your changes using your favorite text parser or search program. The following demonstrates one method for commenting your changes:

```
/* BEGIN MY MODIFICATION */
/* Purpose of modification: experimentation. */
/* Modified by: Chuck */
/* Date modified: 30 May 2012 */
if (something_interesting_happens_here)
{
do_something_really_cool;
}
/* END MY MODIFICATION */
```

Last, do not be afraid to explore the free knowledge base and forums on the MySQL website or seek the assistance of the global community of developers. These are your greatest assets. Be sure you have done your homework before you post to one of the forums. The fastest way to become discouraged is to post a message on a forum only to have someone reply with a curt (but polite) reference to the documentation. Make your posts succinct and to the point. You don't need to elaborate on the many reasons why you're doing what you're doing—just post your question and provide all pertinent information about the issue you're having. Make sure you post to the correct forum. Most are moderated, and if you are ever in doubt, consult the moderator to ensure you are posting your topic in the correct forum.

■ **Tip**   A great site to read about what is going on in the MySQL community is `http://planet.mysql.com/`, an aggregate of many blog postings from all over the world about MySQL.

A Real-World Example: TiVo

Have you ever wondered what makes your TiVo tick? Would you be surprised to know that it runs on a version of embedded Linux?

Jim Barton and Mike Ramsay designed the original TiVo product in 1997. It was pitched as a home network–based multimedia server serving streaming content to thin clients. Naturally, a device like this must be easy to learn and even easier to use, but most important, it must operate error free and handle power interruptions (and user error) gracefully.

Barton was experimenting with several forms of Linux, and while working at Silicon Graphics (SGI), he sponsored a port of Linux to the SGI Indy platform. Due mainly to the stable file system, network, memory handling, and developer tool support, Barton believed that it would be possible to port a version of Linux to the TiVo platform and that Linux could handle the real-time performance goals of the TiVo product.

Barton and Ramsay faced a challenge from their peers, however. At that time, many viewed open source with suspicion and scorn. Commercial software experts asserted that open source software would never be reliable in a real-time environment. Furthermore, they believed that basing a commercial proprietary product on the GPL would not permit modification and that if they proceeded, the project would become a nightmare of copyright suits and endless legal haranguing. Fortunately, Barton and Ramsay were not deterred and studied the GPL carefully. They concluded that not only was the GPL viable, it would permit them to protect their intellectual property.

Although the original TiVo product was intended to be a server, Barton and Ramsay decided that the bandwidth wasn't available to support such lofty goals. Instead, they redesigned their product to a client device, called the TiVo Client Device (TCD), which would act like a sophisticated video recorder. They wanted to provide a for-fee service to serve up the television guide and interface with the TCD. This would allow home users to select the shows they wanted in advance and program the TCD to record them. In effect, they created what is now known as a digital video recorder (DVR).

The TCD hardware included a small, embedded computer with a hard drive and memory. Hardware interfaces were created to read and write video (video in and video out) using a MPEG 2 encoder and decoder. Additional input/output (I/O) devices included audio and telecommunications (for accessing the TiVo service). The TCD also had to permit multiprocessing capabilities in order to permit the recording of one signal (channel) while playing back another (channel). These features required a good memory- and disk-management subsystem. Barton and Ramsay realized these goals would be a challenge for any control system. Furthermore, the video interface must never be interrupted or compromised in any way.

What Barton and Ramsay needed most was a system with a well-developed disk subsystem, supported multitasking, and the ability to optimize hardware (CPU, memory) usage. Linux, therefore, was the logical choice of operating system for the TCD. Production goals and budget constraints limited the choice of CPU. The IBM PowerPC

403GCX processor was chosen for the TCD. Unfortunately, there were no ports of Linux that ran on the chosen processor. This meant that Barton and Ramsay would have to port Linux to the processor platform.

While the port was successful, Barton and Ramsay discovered they needed some specialized customizations of the Linux kernel to meet the needs and limits of the hardware. For example, they bypassed the file-system buffer cache in order to permit faster movement, or processing, of the video signals to and from user space. They also added extensive performance enhancements, logging, and recovery features to ensure that the TCD could recover quickly from power loss or user error.

The application that runs the TCD was built on Linux-based personal computers and ported to the modified Linux operating system with little drama—a testament to the stability and interoperability of the Linux operating system. When Barton and Ramsay completed their porting and application work, they conducted extensive testing and delivered the world's first DVR in March 1999.

The TCD is one of the most widely used consumer products running a customized embedded Linux operating system. Clearly, the TCD story is a shining example of what you can accomplish by modifying open source software. The story doesn't end here, though. Barton and Ramsay published their Linux kernel port complete with the source code. Their enhancements have found their way into the latest versions of the Linux kernel.

CONVINCING YOUR BOSS TO MODIFY OPEN SOURCE SOFTWARE

If you have an idea and a business model to base it on, going the open source route can result in a huge time saving in getting your product to market. In fact, your project may become one that can save a great deal of development revenue and permit you to get the product to market faster than your competition. This is especially true if you need to modify open source software—you have already done your homework and can show the cost benefits of using the open source software.

Unfortunately, many managers have been conditioned by the commercial proprietary software world to reject the notion of basing a product on open source software to generate a revenue case. So how do you change their minds? Use the TiVo story as ammunition. Present to your boss the knowledge you gained from the TiVo story and the rest of this chapter to dispel the myths concerning GPL and reliability of open source software. Be careful, though. If you are like most open source mavens, your enthusiasm can often be interpreted as a threat to the senior technical staff.

Make a list of the technical stakeholders who adhere to the commercial proprietary viewpoint. Engage these individuals in conversation about open source software and answer their questions. Most of all, be patient. These folks aren't as thick as you may think, and eventually they will come to share your enthusiasm.

Once you have the senior technical staff educated and in the open source mindset, re-engage your management with a revised proposal. Be sure to take along a member of the senior technical staff as a shield (and a voice of reason). Winning, in this case, is turning the tide of commercial proprietary domination.

Summary

In this chapter, you explored the origins of open source software and the rise of MySQL to a world-class database-management system. You learned what open source systems are and how they compare to commercial proprietary systems. You saw the underbelly of open source licensing and discovered the responsibilities of being a member of the global community of developers.

You also received an introduction to developing with MySQL and learned characteristics of the source code and guidelines for making modifications. You read about Oracle's dual-license practices and the implications of modifying MySQL to your needs. Finally, you saw an example of a successful integration of an open source system in a commercial product.

In the chapters following, you will learn more about the anatomy of a relational database system and how to get started customizing MySQL to your needs. Later, in Parts 2 and 3 of this book, you will be introduced to the inner workings of MySQL and the exploration of the most intimate portions of the code.

CHAPTER 2

■ ■ ■

The Anatomy of a Database System

While you may know the basics of a relational database management system (RDBMS) and be an expert at administering the system, you may have never explored the inner workings of a database system. Most of us have been trained on and have experience with managing database systems, but neither academic nor professional training includes much about the way database systems are constructed. A database professional may never need this knowledge, but it is good to know how the system works so that you can understand how best to optimize your server and even how best to utilize its features.

Although understanding the inner workings of an RDBMS isn't necessary for hosting databases or even maintaining the server or developing applications that use the system, knowing how the system is organized is essential to being able to modify and extend its features. It is also important to grasp the basic principles of the most popular database systems to understand how these systems compare to an RDBMS.

This chapter covers the basics of the subsystems that RDBMSs contain and how they are constructed. I use the anatomy of the MySQL system to illustrate the key components of modern RDBMSs. Those of you who have studied the inner workings of such systems and want to jump ahead to a look at the architecture of MySQL can skip to "The MySQL Database System."

Types of Database Systems

Most database professionals work with RDBMSs, but several other types of database systems are becoming popular. The following sections present a brief overview of the three most popular types of database systems: object-oriented, object-relational, and relational. It is important to understand the architectures and general features of these systems to fully appreciate the opportunity that Oracle has provided by developing MySQL as open source software and exposing the source code for the system to everyone. This permits me to show you what's going on inside the box.

Object-Oriented Database Systems

Object-oriented database systems (OODBSs) are storage-and-retrieval mechanisms that support the object-oriented programming (OOP) paradigm through direct manipulation of the data as objects. They contain true object-oriented (OO)-type systems that permit objects to persist among applications and usage. Most, however, lack a standard query language[1] (access to the data is typically via a programming interface) and therefore are not true database-management systems.

OODBSs are an attractive alternative to RDBMSs, especially in application areas in which the modeling power or performance of RDBMSs to store data as objects in tables is insufficient. These applications maintain large amounts of data that is never deleted, thereby managing the history of individual objects. The most unusual feature of OODBSs is

---

[1]There are some notable exceptions, but this is generally true.

that it provides support for complex objects by specifying both the structure and the operations that can be applied to these objects via an OOP interface.

OODBSs are particularly suitable for modeling the real world as closely as possible without forcing unnatural relationships among and within entities. The philosophy of object orientation offers a holistic as well as a modeling-oriented view of the real world. These views are necessary for dealing with an elusive subject such as modeling temporal change, particularly in adding OO features to structured data. Despite the general availability of numerous open source OODBSs, most are based in part on relational systems that support query-language interfaces and therefore are not truly OODBSs; rather, they operate more like relational databases with OO interfaces. A true OODBS requires access via a programming interface.

Application areas of OO database systems include geographical information systems (GISs), scientific and statistical databases, multimedia systems, picture archiving and communications systems, semantic web solutions, and XML warehouses.

The greatest adaptability of the OODBS is the tailoring of the data (or objects) and its behavior (or methods). Most OODBS system integrators rely on OO methods for describing data and build their solutions with that expressiveness in the design. Thus, object-oriented database systems are built with specific implementations and are not intended to be general purpose or generalized to have statement–response-type interfaces like RDBMSs.

Object-Relational Database Systems

Object-relational database-management systems (ORDBMSs) are an application of OO theory to RDBMSs. ORDBMSs provide a mechanism that permits database designers to implement a structured storage-and-retrieval mechanism for OO data. ORDBMSs provide the basis of the relational model—meaning, integrity, relationships, and so forth—while extending the model to store and retrieve data in an object-centric manner. Implementation is purely conceptual in many cases, because the mapping of OO concepts to relational concepts is tentative at best. The modifications, or extensions, to the relational technologies include modifications to SQL that allow the representation of object types, identity, encapsulation of operations, and inheritance. These are often loosely mapped to relational theory as complex types. Although expressive, the SQL extensions do not permit the true object manipulation and level of control of OODBSs. A popular ORDBMS is ESRI's ArcGIS Geodatabase environment. Other examples include Illustra, PostgreSQL, and Informix.

The technology used in ORDBMSs is often based on the relational model. Most ORDBMSs are implemented using existing commercial relational database-management systems (RDBMSs) such as Microsoft SQL Server. Since these systems are based on the relational model, they suffer from a conversion problem of translating OO concepts to relational mechanisms. Some of the many problems with using relational databases for object-oriented applications are:

- The OO conceptual model does not map easily to data tables.

- Complex mapping implies complex programs and queries.

- Complex programs imply maintenance problems.

- Complex programs imply reliability problems.

- Complex queries may not be optimized and may result in slow performance.

- The mapping of object concepts to complex types[2] is more vulnerable to schema changes than are relational systems.

- OO performance for SELECT ALL...WHERE queries is slower because it involves multiple joins and lookups.

---

[2] This is especially true when the object types are modified in a populated data store. Depending on the changes, the behavior of the objects may have been altered and thus may not have the same meaning. Despite the fact that this may be a deliberate change, the effects of the change are potentially more severe than in typical relational systems.

Although these problems seem significant, they are easily mitigated by the application of an OO application layer that communicates between the underlying relational database and the OO application. These application layers permit the translation of objects into structured (or persistent) data stores. Interestingly, this practice violates the concept of an ORDBMS in that you are now using an OO access mechanism to access the data, which is not why ORDBMSs are created. They are created to permit the storage and retrieval of objects in an RDBMS by providing extensions to the query language.

Although ORDBMSs are similar to OODBSs, OODBSs are very different in philosophy. OODBSs try to add database functionality to OO programming languages via a programming interface and platforms. By contrast, ORDBMSs try to add rich data types to RDBMSs using traditional query languages and extensions. OODBSs attempt to achieve a seamless integration with OOP languages. ORDBMSs do not attempt this level of integration and often require an intermediate application layer to translate information from the OO application to the ORDBMS or even the host RDBMS. Similarly, OODBSs are aimed at applications that have as their central engineering perspective an OO viewpoint. ORDBMSs are optimized for large data stores and object-based systems that support large volumes of data (e.g., GIS applications). Last, the query mechanisms of OODBSs are centered on object manipulation using specialized OO query languages. ORDBMS query mechanisms are geared toward fast retrieval of volumes of data using extensions to the SQL standard. Unlike true OODBSs that have optimized query mechanisms, such as Object Description Language (ODL) and Object Query Language (OQL), ORDBMSs use query mechanisms that are extensions of the SQL query language.

The ESRI product suite of GIS applications contains a product called the Geodatabase (shorthand for geographic database), which supports the storage and management of geographic data elements. The Geodatabase is an object-relational database that supports spatial data. It is an example of a spatial database that is implemented as an ORDBMS.

■ **Note** Spatial database systems need not be implemented in ORDBMSs or even OODBSs. ESRI has chosen to implement the Geodatabase as an ORDBMS. More important, GIS data can be stored in an RDBMS that has been extended to support spatial data. Behold! That is exactly what has happened with MySQL. Oracle has added a spatial data engine to the MySQL RDBMS.

Although ORDBMSs are based on relational-database platforms, they also provide some layer of data encapsulation and behavior. Most ORDBMSs are specialized forms of RDBMSs. Those database vendors who provide ORDBMSs often build extensions to the statement-response interfaces by modifying the SQL to contain object descriptors and spatial query mechanisms. These systems are generally built for a particular application and are, like OODBSs, limited in their general use.

Relational Database Systems

An RDBMS is a data storage-and-retrieval service based on the Relational Model of Data as proposed by E. F. Codd in 1970. These systems are the standard storage mechanism for structured data. A great deal of research is devoted to refining the essential model proposed by Codd, as discussed by C. J. Date in *The Database Relational Model: A Retrospective Review and Analysis*.[3] This evolution of theory and practice is best documented in *The Third Manifesto*.[4]

---

[3]C. J. Date, The Database Relational Model: A Retrospective Review and Analysis (Reading, MA: Addison-Wesley, 2001).
[4]C. J. Date and H. Darwen, Foundation for Future Database Systems: The Third Manifesto (Reading, MA: Addison-Wesley, 2000).

The relational model is an intuitive concept of a storage repository (database) that can be easily queried by using a mechanism called a query language to retrieve, update, and insert data. The relational model has been implemented by many vendors because it has a sound systematic theory, a firm mathematical foundation, and a simple structure. The most commonly used query mechanism is Structured Query Language (SQL), which resembles natural language. Although SQL is not included in the relational model, SQL provides an integral part of the practical application of the relational model in RDBMSs.

The data are represented as related pieces of information (attributes) about a certain entity. The set of values for the attributes is formed as a *tuple* (sometimes called a *record*). Tuples are then stored in tables containing tuples that have the same set of attributes. Tables can then be related to other tables through constraints on domains, keys, attributes, and tuples.

RECORD OR TUPLE: IS THERE A DIFFERENCE?

Many mistakenly consider record to be a colloquialism for tuple. One important distinction is that a tuple is a set of ordered elements, whereas a record is a collection of related items without a sense of order. The order of the columns is important in the concept of a record, however. Interestingly, in SQL, a result from a query can be a record, whereas in relational theory, each result is a tuple. Many texts use these terms interchangeably, creating a source of confusion for many.

When exploring the MySQL architecture and source code, we will encounter the term record exclusively to describe a row in a result set or a row for a data update. While the record data structure in MySQL is ordered, the resemblance to a tuple ends there.

The query language of choice for most implementations is Structured Query Language (SQL). SQL, proposed as a standard in the 1980s,is currently an industry standard. Unfortunately, many seem to believe SQL is based on relational theory and therefore is a sound theoretical concept. This misconception is perhaps fueled by a phenomenon brought on by industry. Almost all RDBMSs implement some form of SQL. This popularity has mistakenly overlooked the many sins of SQL, including:

- SQL does not support domains as described by the relational model.

- In SQL, tables can have duplicate rows.

- Results (tables) can contain unnamed columns and duplicate columns.

- The implementation of nulls (missing values) by host database systems has been shown to be inconsistent and incomplete. Thus, many incorrectly associate the mishandling of nulls with SQL when in fact, SQL merely returns the results as presented by the database system.[5]

The technologies used in RDBMSs are many and varied. Some systems are designed to optimize some portion of the relational model or some application of the model to data. Applications of RDBMSs range from simple data storage and retrieval to complex application suites with complex data, processes, and workflows. This could be as simple as a database that stores your compact disc or DVD collection, or a database designed to manage a hotel-reservation system, or even a complex distributed system designed to manage information on the web. As I mentioned in Chapter 1, many web and social-media applications implement the LAMP stack whereby MySQL becomes the database for storage of the data hosted.

Relational database systems provide the most robust data independence and data abstraction. By using the concept of relations, RDBMS provide a truly generalized data storage-and-retrieval mechanism. The downside is, of course, that these systems are highly complex and require considerable expertise to build and modify.

---

[5] Some of the ways database systems handle nulls range from the absurd to the unintuitive.

In the next section, I'll present a typical RDBMS architecture and examine each component of the architecture. Later, I'll examine a particular implementation of an RDBMS (MySQL).

IS MYSQL A RELATIONAL DATABASE SYSTEM?

Many database theorists will tell you that there are very few true RDBMSs in the world. They would also point out that what relational is and is not is largely driven by your definition of the features supported in the database system and not how well the system conforms to Codd's relational model.

From a pure marketing viewpoint, MySQL provides a great many features considered essential for RDBMSs. These include, but are not limited to, the ability to relate tables to one another using foreign keys, the implementation of a relational algebra query mechanism, and the use of indexing and buffering mechanisms. Clearly, MySQL offers all of these features and more.

So is MySQL an RDBMS? That depends on your definition of relational. If you consider the features and evolution of MySQL, you should conclude that it is indeed an RDBMS. If you adhere to the strict definition of Codd's relational model, however, you will conclude that MySQL lacks some features represented in the model. But then again, so do many other RDBMSs.

Relational Database System Architecture

An RDBMS is a complex system comprising specialized mechanisms designed to handle all the functions necessary to store and retrieve information. The architecture of an RDBMS has often been compared to that of an operating system. If you consider the use of an RDBMS, specifically as a server to a host of clients, you see that they have a lot in common with operating systems. For example, having multiple clients means the system must support many requests that may or may not read or write the same data or data from the same location (such as a table). Thus, RDBMSs must handle concurrency efficiently. Similarly, RDBMSs must provide fast access to data for each client. This is usually accomplished using file-buffering techniques that keep the most recently or frequently used data in memory for faster access. Concurrency requires memory-management techniques that resemble virtual memory systems in operating systems. Other similarities with operating systems include network communication support and optimization algorithms designed to maximize performance of the execution of queries.

I'll begin our exploration of the architecture from the point of view of the user from the issuing of queries to the retrieval of data. The following sections are written so that you can skip the ones you are familiar with and read the ones that interest you. I encourage you to read all of the sections, however, as they present a detailed look at how a typical RDBMS is constructed.

Client Applications

Most RDBMS client applications are developed as separate executable programs that connect to the database via a communications pathway (e.g., a network protocol such as sockets or pipes). Some connect directly to the database system via programmatic interfaces, where the database system becomes part of the client application. In this case, we call the database an *embedded* system. For more information about embedded database systems, see Chapter 6.

Most systems that connect to the database via a communication pathway do so via a set of protocols called *database connectors*. Database connectors are most often based on the Open Database Connectivity (ODBC)[6] model.

---

[6] Sometimes defined as Object Database Connectivity or Online Database Connectivity, but the accepted definition is Open Database Connectivity.

MySQL also supports connectors for Java (JDBC), PhP, Python, and Microsoft .NET (see "MySQL Connectors."). Most implementations of ODBC connectors also support communication over network protocols.

ODBC is a specification for an application-programming interface (API). ODBC is designed to transfer SQL commands to the database server, retrieve the information, and present it to the calling application. An ODBC implementation includes an application designed to use the API that acts as an intermediary with the ODBC library, a core ODBC library that supports the API, and a database driver designed for a specific database system. We typically refer to the set of client access, API, and driver as a *connector*. Thus, the ODBC connector acts as an "interpreter" between the client application and the database server. ODBC has become the standard for nearly every relational (and most object-relational) database system. Hundreds of connectors and drivers are available for use in a wide variety of clients and database systems.

When we consider client applications, we normally take into account the programs that send and retrieve information to and from the database server. Even the applications we use to configure and maintain the database server are client applications. Most of these utilities connect to the server via the same network pathways as database applications. Some use the ODBC connectors or a variant such as Java Database Connectivity (JDBC). A few use specialized protocols for managing the server for specific administrative purposes. Others, such as phpMyAdmin, use a port or socket.

Regardless of their implementation, client applications issue commands to the database system and retrieve the results of those commands, interpret and process the results, and present them to the user. The standard command language is SQL. Clients issue SQL commands to the server via the ODBC connector, which transmits the command to the database server using the defined network protocols as specified by the driver. A graphical description of this process is shown in Figure 2-1.

Figure 2-1. *Client Application/database Server Communication*

MYSQL CONNECTORS

Oracle provides several database connectors for developers to enable applications to interact with MySQL. These connectors can be used with applications and tools that are compatible with industry standards, including ODBC and JDBC. This means that any application that works with ODBC or JDBC can use the MySQL connector. The MySQL connectors available for Oracle are:

- Connector/ODBC – standard ODBC connector for Windows, Linux, Mac OS X, and Unix platforms.

- Connector/J[ava] – for Java platforms and development.

- Connector/Net – Windows .Net applications development.

- Connector/MXJ – MBean for embedding the MySQL server in Java applications.

- Connector/C++ – C++ development.

- Connector/C (libmysql) – C applications development.

- Connector/Python – Python applications development.

You can view and download the connectors from at `http://www.mysql.com/downloads/connector/`

Query Interface

A query language such as SQL is a language (it has a syntax and semantics) that can represent a question posed to a database system. In fact, the use of SQL in database systems is considered one of the major reasons for their success. SQL provides several language groups that form a comprehensive foundation for using database systems. The *data definition language* (DDL) is used by database professionals to create and manage databases. Tasks include creating and altering tables, defining indexes, and managing constraints. The *data manipulation language* (DML) is used by database professionals to query and update the data in databases. Tasks include adding and updating data as well as querying the data. These two language groups form the majority of commands that database systems support.

SQL commands are formed using a specialized syntax. The following presents the syntax of a SELECT command in SQL. The notation depicts user-defined variables in italics and optional parameters in square brackets ([]).

```
SELECT [DISTINCT] listofcolumns
FROM listoftables
[WHERE expression (predicates in CNF)]
[GROUP BY listofcolumns]
[HAVING expression]
[ORDER BY listof columns];
```

The semantics of this command are:[7]

1. Form the Cartesian product of the tables in the FROM clause, thus forming a projection of only those references that appear in other clauses.

2. If a WHERE clause exists, apply all expressions for the given tables referenced.

3. If a GROUP BY clause exists, form groups in the results on the attributes specified.

4. If a HAVING clause exists, apply a filter for the groups.

5. If an ORDER BY clause exists, sort the results in the manner specified.

6. If a DISTINCT keyword exists, remove the duplicate rows from the results.

The previous code example is representative of most SQL commands; all such commands have required portions, and most also have optional sections as well as keyword-based modifiers.

---

[7] M. Stonebraker and J. L. Hellerstein, *Readings in Database Systems,* 3rd ed., edited by Michael Stonebraker (Morgan Kaufmann Publishers, 1998).

Once the query statements are transferred to the client via the network protocols (called *shipping*), the database server must then interpret and execute the command. A query statement from this point on is referred to simply as a query, because it represents the question for which the database system must provide an answer. Furthermore, in the sections that follow, I assume the query is of the SELECT variety, in which the user has issued a request for data. All queries, regardless whether they are data manipulation or data definition, follow the same path through the system, however. It is also at this point that we consider the actions being performed within the database server itself. The first step in that process is to decipher what the client is asking for—that is, the query must be parsed and broken down into elements that can be executed upon.

Query Processing

In the context of a database system operating in a client/server model, the database server is responsible for processing the queries presented by the client and returning the results accordingly. This has been termed *query shipping*, in which the query is shipped to the server and a payload (data) is returned. The benefits of query shipping are a reduction of communication time for queries and the ability to exploit server resources rather than using the more limited resources of the client to conduct the query. This model also permits a separation of how the data is stored and retrieved on the server from the way the data is used on the client. In other words, the client/server model supports data independence.

Data independence is one of the principal advantages of the relational model introduced by Codd in 1970: the separation of the *physical implementation* from the *logical model*. According to Codd,[8]

> *Users of large data banks must be protected from having to know how the data is organized in the machine ... Activities of users at terminals and most application programs should remain unaffected when the internal representation of data is changed.*

This separation allows a powerful set of logical semantics to be developed, independent of a particular physical implementation. The goal of data independence (called physical data independence by Elmasri and Navathe[9]) is that each of the logical elements is independent of all of the physical elements (see Table 2-1). For example, the logical layout of the data into relations (tables) with attributes (fields) arranged by tuples (rows) is completely independent of how the data is stored on the storage medium.

Table 2-1. *The Logical and Physical Models of Database Design*

Logical Model	Physical Model
Query language	Sorting algorithms
Relational Algebra	Storage mechanisms
Relational Calculus	Indexing mechanisms
Relvars	Data representation

One challenge of data independence is that database programming becomes a two-part process. First, there is the writing of the logical query—describing *what* the query is supposed to do. Second, there is the writing of the physical plan, which shows *how* to implement the logical query.

The logical query can be written, in general, in many different forms, such as a high-level language such as SQL or as an algebraic query tree.[10] For example, in the traditional relational model, a logical query can be described in

---

[8]C. J. Date, The Database Relational Model: A Retrospective Review and Analysis (Reading, MA: Addison-Wesley, 2001).

[9]R. Elmasri and S. B. Navathe, *Fundamentals of Database Systems*, 4th ed. (Boston: Addison-Wesley, 2003).

[10]A. B. Tucker, *Computer Science Handbook*, 2nd ed. (Boca Raton, FL: CRC Press, 2004).

relational calculus or relational algebra. The relational calculus is better in terms of focusing on *what* needs to be computed. The relational algebra is closer to providing an algorithm that lets you find what you are querying for, but still leaves out many details involved in the evaluation of a query.

The *physical plan* is a query tree implemented in a way that it can be understood and processed by the database system's query execution engine. A *query tree* is a tree structure in which each node contains a query operator and has a number of children that correspond to the number of tables involved in the operation. The query tree can be transformed via the optimizer into a plan for execution. This plan can be thought of as a program that the query execution engine can execute.

A query statement goes through several phases before it is executed; parsing, validation, optimization, plan generation/compilation, and execution. Figure 2-2 depicts the query processing steps that a typical database system would employ. Each query statement is parsed for validity and checked for correct syntax and for identification of the query operations. The parser then outputs the query in an intermediate form to allow the optimizer to form an efficient query execution plan. The execution engine then executes the query and the results are returned to the client. This progression is shown in Figure 2-2, where once parsing is completed the query is validated for errors, then optimized; a plan is chosen and compiled; and finally the query is executed.

Figure 2-2. *Query processing steps*

The first step in this process is to translate the logical query from SQL into a query tree in relational algebra. This step, done by the parser, usually involves breaking the SQL statement into parts and then building the query tree from there. The next step is to translate the query tree in logical algebra into a physical plan. Generally, many plans could implement the query tree. The process of finding the best execution plan is called *query optimization*. That is, for some query-execution-performance measure (e.g., execution time), we want to find the plan with the best execution performance. The plan should be optimal or near optimal within the search space of the optimizer. The optimizer starts by copying the relational-algebra query tree into its search space. The optimizer then expands the search space by forming alternative execution plans (to a finite iteration) and then searching for the best plan (the one that executes fastest).

At this level of generality, the optimizer can be viewed as the code-generation part of a query compiler for the SQL language. In fact, in some database systems, the compilation step translates the query into an executable program. Most database systems, however, translate the query into a form that can be executed using the internal library of execution steps. The code compilation in this case produces code to be interpreted by the query-execution engine, except that the optimizer's emphasis is on producing "very efficient" code. For example, the optimizer uses the database system's catalog to get information (e.g., the number of tuples) about the stored relations referenced by the query, something traditional programming language compilers normally do not do. Finally, the optimizer copies the optimal physical plan out of its memory structure and sends it to the query-execution engine, which executes the plan using the relations in the stored database as input and produces the table of rows that match the query criteria.

All this activity requires additional processing time and places a greater burden on the process by forcing database implementers to consider the performance of the query optimizer and execution engine as a factor in their overall efficiency. This optimization is costly, because of the number of alternative execution plans that use different access methods (ways of reading the data) and different execution orders. Thus, it is possible to generate an infinite number of plans for a single query. Database systems typically bound the problem to a few known best practices, however.

A primary reason for the large number of query plans is that optimization will be required for many different values of important runtime parameters whose actual values are unknown at optimization time. Database systems make certain assumptions about the database contents (e.g., value distribution in relation attributes), the physical schema (e.g., index types), the values of the system parameters (e.g., the number of available buffers), and the values of the query constants.

Query Optimizer

Some mistakenly believe that the query optimizer performs all the steps outlined in the query-execution phases. As you will see, query optimization is just one step that the query takes on the way to be executed. The following paragraphs describe the query optimizer in detail and illustrate the role of the optimizer in the course of the query execution.

Query optimization is the part of the query-compilation process that translates a data-manipulation statement in a high-level, nonprocedural language, such as SQL, into a more detailed, procedural sequence of operators, called a *query plan*. Query optimizers usually select a plan by estimating the cost of many alternative plans and then choosing the least expensive among them (the one that executes fastest).

Database systems that use a plan-based approach to query optimization assume that many plans can be used to produce any given query. Although this is true, not all plans are equivalent in the number of resources (or cost) needed to execute the query, nor are all plans executed in the same amount of time. The goal, then, is to discover the plan that has the least cost and/or runs in the least amount of time. The distinction of either resource usage or cost usage is a trade-off often encountered when designing systems for embedded integration or running on a small platform (with low resource availability) versus the need for higher throughput (or time).

Figure 2-3 depicts a plan-based query-processing strategy in which the query follows the path of the arrows. The SQL command is passed to the query parser, where it is parsed and validated, and then translated into an internal representation, usually based on a relational-algebra expression or a query tree, as described earlier. The query is then passed to the query optimizer, which examines all of the algebraic expressions that are equivalent, generating a different plan for each combination. The optimizer then chooses the plan with the least cost and passes the query to the code generator, which translates the query into an executable form, either as directly executable or as interpretative code. The query processor then executes the query and returns a single row in the result set at a time.

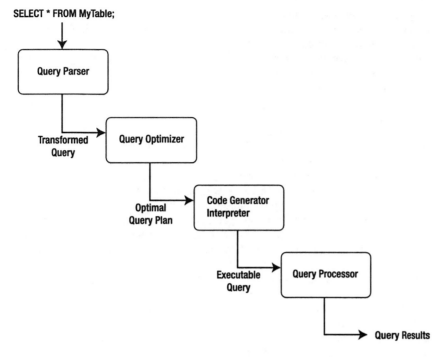

Figure 2-3. *Plan-based query processing*

This common implementation scheme is typical of most database systems. The machines that the database system runs on have improved over time, however. It is no longer the case that query plans have diverse execution costs. In fact, most query plans execute with approximately the same cost. This realization has led some database-system implementers to adopt a query optimizer that focuses on optimizing the query using some well-known best practices or rules (called *heuristics*), for query optimization. Some database systems use hybrids of optimization techniques that are based on one form while maintaining aspects of other techniques during execution.

The four primary means of performing query optimization are

- Cost-based optimization

- Heuristic optimization

- Semantic optimization

- Parametric optimization

Although no optimization technique can guarantee the best execution plan, the goal of all these methods is to generate an efficient execution for the query that guarantees correct results.

A cost-based optimizer generates a range of query-evaluation plans from the given query by using the equivalence rules, and it chooses the one with the least cost based on the metrics (or statistics) gathered about the relations and operations needed to execute the query. For a complex query, many equivalent plans are possible. The goal of cost-based optimization is to arrange the query execution and table access utilizing indexes and statistics gathered from past queries. Systems such as Microsoft SQL Server and Oracle use cost-based optimizers.

Heuristic optimizers use rules concerning how to shape the query into the most optimal form prior to choosing alternative implementations. The application of heuristics, or rules, can eliminate queries that are likely to be inefficient. Using heuristics to form the query plan ensures that the query plan is most likely (but not always) optimized prior to evaluation. The goal of heuristic optimization is to apply rules that ensure "good" practices for query execution. Systems that use heuristic optimizers include Ingres and various academic variants. These systems typically use heuristic optimization to avoid the really bad plans rather than as a primary means of optimization.

The goal of semantic optimization is to form query-execution plans that use the semantics, or topography, of the database and the relationships and indexes within to form queries that ensure the best practice available for executing a query in the given database. Though not yet implemented in commercial database systems as the primary optimization technique, semantic optimization is currently the focus of considerable research. Semantic optimization operates on the premise that the optimizer has a basic understanding of the actual database schema. When a query is submitted, the optimizer uses its knowledge of system constraints to simplify or to ignore a particular query if it is guaranteed to return an empty result set. This technique holds great promise for providing even more improvements to query processing efficiency in future RDBMSs.

Parametric query optimization combines the application of heuristic methods with cost-based optimization. The resulting query optimizer provides a means of producing a smaller set of effective query plans from which cost can be estimated, and thus, the lowest-cost plan of the set can be executed.

An example of a database system that uses a hybrid optimizer is MySQL. The query optimizer in MySQL is designed around a select-project-join strategy, which combines a cost-based and heuristic optimizer that uses known optimal mechanisms, thus resulting in fewer alternatives from which cost-based optimization can choose the minimal execution path. This strategy ensures an overall "good" execution plan, but it does not necessarily generate the best plan. This strategy has proven to work well for a vast variety of queries running in different environments. The internal representation of MySQL has been shown to perform well enough to rival the execution speeds of the largest of the production database systems.

An example of a database system that uses a cost-based optimizer is Microsoft's SQL Server. The query optimizer in SQL Server is designed around a classic cost-based optimizer that translates the query statement into a procedure that can execute efficiently and return the desired results. The optimizer uses information, or statistics,[11] collected from values recorded in past queries and the characteristics of the data in the database to create alternative procedures that represent the same query. The statistics are applied to each procedure to predict which one can be executed more efficiently. Once the most efficient procedure is identified, execution begins and results are returned to the client.

Optimization of queries can be complicated by using unbound parameters, such as a user predicate. For example, an unbound parameter is created when a query within a stored procedure accepts a parameter from the user when the stored procedure is executed. In this case, query optimization may not be possible, or it may not generate the lowest cost unless some knowledge of the predicate is obtained prior to execution. If very few records satisfy the predicate, even a basic index is far superior to the file scan. The opposite is true if many records qualify. If the selectivity is not known when optimization is performed because the predicate is unbound, the choice among these alternative plans should be delayed until execution.

The problem of selectivity can be overcome by building optimizers that can adopt the predicate as an open variable and perform query-plan planning by generating all possible query plans that are likely to occur based on historical query execution, and by utilizing the statistics from the cost-based optimizer, which include the frequency distribution for the predicate's attribute.

Internal Representation of Queries

A query can be represented within a database system using several alternate forms of the original SQL command. These alternate forms exist due to redundancies in SQL, the equivalence of subqueries and joins under certain constraints, and logical inferences that can be drawn from predicates in the WHERE clause. Having alternate forms of a query poses a problem for database implementers, because the query optimizer must choose the optimal access plan for the query regardless of how it was originally formed by the user.

Once the query optimizer has either formed an efficient execution plan (heuristic and hybrid optimizers) or has chosen the most efficient plan (cost-based optimizers), the query is then passed to the next phase of the process: execution.

---

[11] The use of statistics in databases stems from the first cost-based optimizers. In fact, many utilities in commercial databases permit the examination and generation of these statistics by database professionals to tune their databases for more efficient optimization of queries.

Query Execution

Database systems can use several methods to execute queries. Most use either an *iterative* or an *interpretative* execution strategy.

Iterative methods provide ways of producing a sequence of calls available for processing discrete operations (join, project, etc.), but they are not designed to incorporate the features of the internal representation. Translation of queries into iterative methods uses techniques of functional programming and program transformation. Several available algorithms generate iterative programs from algebra-based query specifications. For example, some algorithms translate query specifications into recursive programs, which are simplified by sets of transformation rules before the algorithm generates an execution plan. Another algorithm uses a two-level translation. The first level uses a smaller set of transformation rules to simplify the internal representation, and the second level applies functional transformations prior to generating the execution plan.

The implementation of this mechanism creates a set of defined compiled functional primitives, formed using a high-level language, that are then linked together via a call stack, or procedural call sequence. When a query-execution plan is created and selected for execution, a compiler (usually the same one used to create the database system) is used to compile the procedural calls into a binary executable. Due to the high cost of the iterative method, compiled execution plans are typically stored for reuse for similar or identical queries.

Interpretative methods, on the other hand, form query execution using existing compiled abstractions of basic operations. The query-execution plan chosen is reconstructed as a queue of method calls, which are each taken off the queue and processed. The results are then placed in memory for use with the next or subsequent calls. Implementation of this strategy is often called *lazy evaluation* because the set of available compiled methods is not optimized for best performance; rather, the methods are optimized for generality. Most database systems use the interpretative method of query execution.

One often-confusing area is the concept of *compiled*. Some database experts consider a compiled query to be an actual compilation of an iterative query-execution plan, but in Date's work, a compiled query is simply one that has been optimized and stored for future execution. I won't use the word *compiled,* because the MySQL query optimizer and execution engine do not store the query-execution plan for later reuse (an exception is the MySQL query cache). I don't think we can compare or mention query cache here. The evaluation of the executed query is not even related to a plan, but instead is related to a literary comparison between SQL received and SQL stored directly related to a Set of already retrieved information, nor does the query execution require any compilation or assembly to work. Interestingly, the concept of a stored procedure fits this second category; it is compiled (or optimized) for execution at a later date and can be run many times on data that meet its input parameters.

Query execution evaluates each part of the query tree (or query as represented by the internal structures) and executes methods for each part. The methods supported mirror those operations defined in relational algebra, project, restrict, union, intersect, and so on. For each of these operations, the query-execution engine performs a method that evaluates the incoming data and passes the processed data along to the next step. For example, only some of the attributes (or columns) of data are returned in a project operation. In this case, the query-execution engine would strip the data for the attributes that do not meet the specification of the restriction and pass the remaining data to the next operation in the tree (or structure). Table 2-2 lists the most common operations supported and briefly describes each.

Table 2-2. *Query Operations*

Operation	Description
Restrict	Returns tuples that match the conditions (predicate) of the WHERE clause (some systems treat the HAVING clause in the same or a similar manner). This operation is often defined as SELECT.
Project	Returns the attributes specified in the column list of the tuple evaluated.
Join	Returns tuples that match a special condition called the *join condition* (or *join predicate*). There are many forms of joins. See "Joins" for a description of each.

JOINS

The join operation can take many forms. These are often confused by database professionals and in some cases avoided at all costs. The expressiveness of SQL permits many joins to be written as simple expressions in the WHERE clause. While most database systems correctly transform these queries into joins, it is considered a lazy form. The following lists the types of joins you are likely to encounter in an RDBMS and describes each. Join operations can have join conditions (theta joins), a matching of the attribute values being compared (equijoins), or no conditions (Cartesian products). The join operation is subdivided into:

- *Inner:* The join of two relations returning tuples where there is a match.

- *Outer (left, right, full):* Returns all rows from at least one of the tables or views mentioned in the FROM clause, as long as those rows meet any WHERE search conditions. All rows are retrieved from the left table referenced with a left outer join; all rows from the right table are referenced in a right outer join. All rows from both tables are returned in a full outer join. Values for attributes of nonmatching rows are returned as null values.

- *Right outer:* The join of two relations returning tuples where there is a match, plus all tuples from the relation specified to the right, leaving nonmatching attributes specified from the other relation empty (null).

- *Full outer:* The join of two relations returning all tuples from both relations, leaving nonmatching attributes specified from the other relation empty (null).

- *Cross product:* The join of two relations mapping each tuple from the first relation to all tuples from the other relation.

- *Union:* The set operation in which only matches from two relations with the same schema are returned.

- *Intersect:* The set operation in which only the nonmatches from two relations with the same schema are returned.

Deciding how to execute the query (or the chosen query plan) is only half of the story. The other thing to consider is how to access the data. There are many ways to read and write data to and from disk (files), but choosing the optimal one depends on what the query is trying to do. File-access mechanisms are created to minimize the cost of accessing the data from disk and maximize the performance of query execution.

File Access

The file-access mechanism, also called the physical database design, has been important since the early days of database-system development. The significance of file access has lessened due to the effectiveness and simplicity of common file systems supported by operating systems, however. Today, file access is merely the application of file storage and indexing best practices, such as separating the index file from the data file and placing each on a separate disk input/output (I/O) system to increase performance. Some database systems use different file-organization techniques to enable the database to be tailored to specific application needs. MySQL is perhaps the most unique in this regard due to the numerous file-access mechanisms (called storage engines) it supports.

Clear goals must be satisfied to minimize the I/O costs in a database system. These include utilizing disk data structures that permit efficient retrieval of only the relevant data through effective access paths, and organizing data on disk so that the I/O cost for retrieving relevant data is minimized. The overriding performance objective is thus to minimize the number of disk accesses (or disk I/Os).

Many techniques for approaching database design are available. Fewer are available for file-access mechanisms (the actual physical implementation of the data files). Furthermore, many researchers agree that the optimal database design (from the physical point of view) is not achievable in general and, furthermore, should not be pursued. Optimization is not achievable, mainly because of the much-improved efficiency of modern disk subsystems. Rather, it is the knowledge of these techniques and research that permits the database implementer to implement the database system in the best manner possible to satisfy the needs of those who will use the system.

To create a structure that performs well, you must consider many factors. Early researchers considered segmenting the data into subsets based on the content or the context of the data. For example, all data containing the same department number would be grouped together and stored with references to the related data. This process can be perpetuated in that sets can be grouped together to form supersets, thus forming a hierarchical file organization.

Accessing data in this configuration involves scanning the sets at the highest level to access and scan only those sets that are necessary to obtain the desired information. This process significantly reduces the number of elements to be scanned. Keeping the data items to be scanned close together minimizes search time. The arrangement of data on disk into structured files is called *file organization*. The goal is to design an access method that provides a way of immediately processing transactions one by one, thereby allowing us to keep an up-to-the-second stored picture of the real-world situation.

File-organization techniques were revised as operating systems evolved in order to ensure greater efficiency of storage and retrieval. Modern database systems create new challenges for which currently accepted methods may be inadequate. This is especially true for systems that execute on hardware with increased disk speeds with high data throughput. Additionally, understanding database design approaches, not only as they are described in textbooks but also in practice, will increase the requirements levied against database systems and thus increase the drive for further research. For example, the recent adoption of redundant and distributed systems by industry has given rise to additional research in these areas to make use of new hardware and/or the need to increase data availability, security, and recovery.

Since accessing data from disk is expensive, the use of a cache mechanism, sometimes called a *buffer*, can significantly improve read performance from disk, thus reducing the cost of storage and retrieval of data. The concept involves copying parts of the data either in anticipation of the next disk read or based on an algorithm designed to keep the most frequently used data in memory. The handling of the differences between disk and main memory effectively is at the heart of a good-quality database system. The trade-off between the database system using disk or using main memory should be understood. See Table 2-3 for a summary of the performance trade-offs between physical storage (disk) and secondary storage (memory).

Table 2-3. *Performance Trade-offs*

Issue	Main Memory vs. Disk
Speed	Main memory is at least 1,000 times faster than disk.
Storage space	Disk can hold hundreds of times more information than memory for the same cost.
Persistence	When the power is switched off, disk keeps the data, and main memory forgets everything.
Access time	Main memory starts sending data in nanoseconds, while disk takes milliseconds.
Block size	Main memory can be accessed one word at a time, and disk one block at a time.

Advances in database physical storage have seen many of the same improvements with regard to storage strategies and buffering mechanisms, but little in the way of exploratory examination of the fundamental elements of physical storage has occurred. Some have explored the topic from a hardware level and others from a more pragmatic level of what exactly it is we need to store. The subject of persistent storage is largely forgotten, because of the capable and efficient mechanisms available in the host operating system.

File-access mechanisms are used to store and retrieve the data that are encompassed by the database system. Most file-access mechanisms have additional layers of functionality that permit locating data within the file more quickly. These layers are called *index mechanisms*. Index mechanisms provide access paths (the way data will be searched for and retrieved) designed to locate specific data based on a subpart of the data called a *key*. Index mechanisms range in complexity from simple lists of keys to complex data structures designed to maximize key searches.

The goal is to find the data we want quickly and efficiently, without having to request and read more disk blocks than absolutely necessary. This can be accomplished by saving values that identify the data (or keys) and the location on disk of the record to form an index of the data. Furthermore, reading the index data is faster than reading all of the data. The primary benefit of using an index is that it allows us to search through large amounts of data efficiently without having to examine, or in many cases read, every item until we find the one we are searching for. Indexing, therefore, is concerned with methods of searching large files containing data that is stored on disk. These methods are designed for fast random access of data as well as sequential access of the data.

Most, but not all, index mechanisms involve a tree structure that stores the keys and the disk block addresses. Examples include B-trees, B + trees, and hash trees. The structures are normally traversed by one or more algorithms designed to minimize the time spent searching the structure for a key. Most database systems use one form or another of the B-tree in their indexing mechanisms. These tree algorithms provide very fast search speeds without requiring a large memory space.

During the execution of the query, interpretative query execution methods access the assigned index mechanism and request the data via the access method specified. The execution methods then read the data, typically a record at a time; analyze the query for a match to the predicate by evaluating the expressions; and then pass the data through any transformations and finally on to the transmission portion of the server to send the data back to the client.

Query Results

Once all the tuples in the tables referenced in the query have been processed, the tuples are returned to the client, following the same, or sometimes alternative, communication pathways. The tuples are then passed on to the ODBC connector for encapsulation and presentation to the client application.

Relational Database Architecture Summary

In this section, I've detailed the steps taken by a query for data through a typical relational-database system architecture. As you'll see, the query begins with an SQL command issued by the client; then it is passed via the ODBC connector to the database system using a communications pathway (network). The query is parsed, transformed into an internal structure, optimized, and executed, and the results are returned to the client.

Now that I've given you a glimpse of all the steps involved in processing a query, and you've seen the complexity of the database system subcomponents, it is time to take a look at a real-world example. In the following section, I present an in-depth look at the MySQL database-system architecture.

The MySQL Database System

The MySQL source code is a highly organized and built using many structured classes (some are complex data structures and some are objects, but most are structures). While efforts toward making the system more modular through the addition of plugins are underway, the source code is not yet a truly modular architecture but is much closer now with the new plugin mechanism. It is important to understand this as you explore the architecture and more important later, when you explore the source code. This means that you will sometimes find instances in which no clear division of architecture elements exists in the source code. For more information about the MySQL source code, including how to obtain it, see Chapter 3.

Although some may present the MySQL architecture as a component-based system built from a set of modular subcomponents, the reality is that, while highly organized, it is neither component based nor modular. The source code is built using a mixture of C and C++, and a number of objects are utilized in many of the functions of the system. The system is not object oriented in the true sense of object-oriented programming. Rather, the system is built on the basis of function libraries and data structures designed to optimize the organization of the source code around that of the architecture, with some portions written using objects.

MySQL architecture is, however, an intelligent design of highly organized subsystems working in harmony to form an effective and highly reliable database system. All of the technologies I described previously in this chapter are present in the system. The subsystems that implement these technologies are well designed and implemented with the same precision source code found throughout the system. It is interesting to note that many accomplished C and C++ programmers remark upon the elegance and leanness of the source code. I've often found myself marveling at the serene complexity and yet elegance of the code. Indeed, even the code authors themselves admit that their code has a sort of genius intuition that is often not fully understood or appreciated until it is thoroughly analyzed. You, too, will find yourself amazed at how well some of the source code works and how simple it is once you figure it out.

■ **Note**   The MySQL system has proved to be difficult for some to learn and troublesome to diagnose when things go awry. It is clear, however, that once one has mastered the intricacies of the MySQL architecture and source code, the system is very accommodating and has the promise of being perhaps the first and best platform for experimental database work.

What this means is that the MySQL architecture and source code is often challenging for novice C++ programmers. If you find yourself starting to reconsider taking on the source code, please keep reading; I will be your guide in navigating the source code. But let's first begin with a look at how the system is structured.

MySQL System Architecture

The MySQL architecture is best described as a layered system of subsystems. While the source code isn't compiled as individual components or modules, the source code for the subsystems is organized in a hierarchical manner that allows subsystems to be segregated (encapsulated) in the source code. Most subsystems rely on base libraries for lower-level functions (e.g., thread control, memory allocation, networking, logging and event handling, and access control). Together, the base libraries, subsystems built on those libraries, and even subsystems built from other subsystems form the abstracted API that is known as the C client API. This powerful API permits the MySQL system to be used as either a stand-alone server or an embedded database system in a larger application.

The architecture provides encapsulation for a SQL interface, query parsing, query optimization and execution, caching and buffering, and a pluggable storage engine. Figure 2-4 depicts the MySQL architecture and its subsystems. At the top of the drawing are the database connectors that provide access to client applications. As you can see, a connector for just about any programming environment you could want exists. To the left of the drawing, the ancillary tools are listed grouped by administration and enterprise services. For a complete discussion of the administration and enterprise service tools, see Michael Kruckenberg and Jay Pipes's *Pro MySQL*,[12] an excellent reference for all things administrative for MySQL.

---

[12] M. Kruckenberg and J. Pipes. *Pro MySQL*. (Berkeley, CA: Apress, 2005).

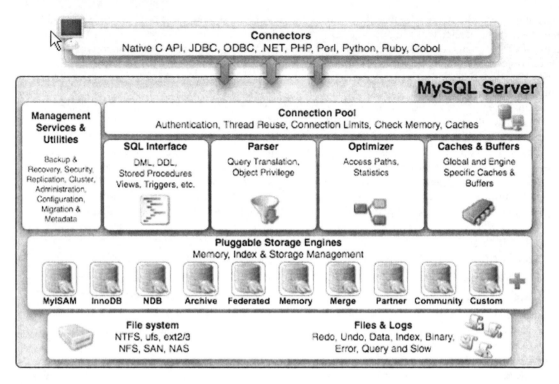

Figure 2-4. *MySQL server architecture (Copyright Oracle. Reprinted with kind permission.)*

The next layer down in the architecture from the connectors is the connection pool layer. This layer handles all of the user-access, thread processing, memory, and process cache needs of the client connection. Below that layer is the heart of the database system. Here is where the query is parsed and optimized, and file access is managed. The next layer down from there is the pluggable storage-engine layer. At this layer, part of the brilliance of the MySQL architecture shines. The pluggable storage-engine layer permits the system to be built to handle a wide range of diverse data or file storage and retrieval mechanisms. This flexibility is unique to MySQL. No other database system available today provides the ability to tune databases by providing several data storage mechanisms.

■ **Note** The pluggable storage-engine feature is available beginning in version 5.1.

Below the pluggable storage engine is the lowest layer of the system, the file-access layer. At this layer, the storage mechanisms read and write data, and the system reads and writes log and event information. This layer is the closest to the operating system, along with thread, process, and memory control.

Let's begin our discussion of the MySQL architecture with the flow through the system from the client application to the data and back. The first layer encountered once the client connector (ODBC, .NET, JDBC, C API, etc.) has transmitted the SQL statements to the server is the SQL interface.

SQL Interface

The SQL interface provides the mechanisms to receive commands and transmit results to the user. The MySQL SQL interface was built to the ANSI SQL standard and accepts the same basic SQL statements as most ANSI-compliant database servers. Although many of the SQL commands supported in MySQL have options that are not ANSI standard, the MySQL developers have stayed very close to the ANSI SQL standard.

Connections to the database server are received from the network communication pathways, and a thread is created for each. The threaded process is the heart of the executable pathway in the MySQL server. MySQL is built as a true multithreaded application whereby each thread executes independently of the other threads (except for certain helper threads). The incoming SQL command is stored in a class structure and the results are transmitted to the client by writing the results out to the network communication protocols. Once a thread has been created, the MySQL server attempts to parse the SQL command and store the parts in the internal data structure.

Parser

When a client issues a query, a new thread is created and the SQL statement is forwarded to the parser for syntactic validation (or rejection due to errors). The MySQL parser is implemented using a large Lex-YACC script that is compiled with Bison. The parser constructs a query structure used to represent the query statement (SQL) in memory as a *tree structure* (also called an abstract syntax tree) that can be used to execute the query.

■ **Tip** The sql_yacc.yy, sql_lex.h, and lex.h files are where you would begin to construct your own SQL commands or data types in MySQL. These files will be discussed in more detail in Chapter 7.

Considered by many to be the most complex part of the MySQL source code and the most elegant, the parser is implemented using Lex and YACC, which were originally built for compiler construction. These tools are used to build a lexical analyzer that reads a SQL statement and breaks the statement into parts, assigning the command portions, options, and parameters to a structure of variables and lists. This structure (named imaginatively Lex) is the internal representation of the SQL query. As a result, this structure is used by every other step in the query process. The Lex structure contains lists of tables being used, field names referenced, join conditions, expressions, and all the parts of the query stored in a separate space.

The parser works by reading the SQL statement and comparing the expressions (consisting of tokens and symbols) with rules defined in the source code. These rules are built into the code using Lex and YACC and later compiled with Bison to form the lexical analyzer. If you examine the parser in its C form (a file named /sql/sql_yacc. cc), you may become overwhelmed with the terseness and sheer enormity of the switch statement.[13]

A better way to examine the parser is to look at the Lex and YACC form prior to compilation (a file named /sql/sql_yacc.yy). This file contains the rules as written for YACC and is much easier to decipher. The construction of the parser illustrates Oracle's open source philosophy at work: why create your own language handler when special compiler construction tools such as Lex, YACC, and Bison are designed to do just that?

Once the parser identifies a regular expression and breaks the query statement into parts, it assigns the appropriate command type to the thread structure and returns control to the command processor (which is sometimes considered part of the parser, but more correctly is part of the main code). The command processor is implemented as a large switch statement with cases for every command supported. The query parser checks only the correctness of the SQL statement. It does not verify the existence of tables or attributes (fields) referenced, nor does it check for semantic errors, such as an aggregate function used without a GROUP BY clause. Instead, the verification is left to the optimizer. Thus, the query structure from the parser is passed to the query processor. From there, control switches to the query optimizer.

---

[13] Kruckenberg and Pipes compare the experience to a mind melt. Levity aside, it can be a challenge for anyone who is unfamiliar with YACC.

LEX AND YACC

Lex stands for "lexical analyzer generator" and is used as a parser to identify tokens and literals as well as the syntax of a language. YACC stands for "yet another compiler compiler" and is used to identify and act on the semantic definitions of the language. The use of these tools together with Bison (a YACC compiler) provides a rich mechanism for creating subsystems that can parse and process language commands. Indeed, that is exactly how MySQL uses these technologies.

Query Optimizer

The MySQL query-optimizer subsystem is considered by some to be misnamed. The optimizer used is a SELECT-PROJECT-JOIN strategy that attempts to restructure the query by first doing any restrictions (SELECT) to narrow the number of tuples to work with, then performs the projections to reduce the number of attributes (fields) in the resulting tuples, and finally evaluates any join conditions. While not considered a member of the extremely complicated query-optimizer category, the SELECT-PROJECT-JOIN strategy falls into the category of heuristic optimizers. In this case, the heuristics (rules) are simply:

- Eliminate extra data by evaluating the expressions in the WHERE (HAVING) clause.

- Eliminate extra data by limiting the data to the attributes specified in the attribute list. The exception is the storage of the attributes used in the join clause that may not be kept in the final query.

- Evaluate join expressions.

This results in a strategy that ensures a known-good access method to retrieve data in an efficient manner. Despite critical reviews, the SELECT-PROJECT-JOIN strategy has proven effective at executing the typical queries found in transaction processing. Figure 2-5 depicts a block diagram that describes the MySQL query processing methodology.

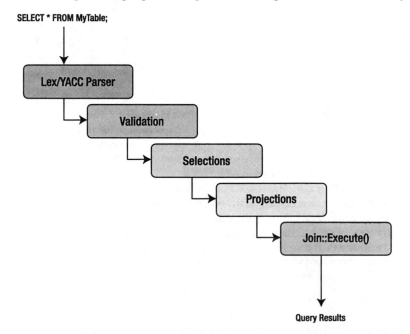

Figure 2-5. *MySQL query processing methodology*

The first step in the optimizer is to check for the existence of tables and access control by the user. If there are errors, the appropriate error message is returned and control returns to the thread manager, or listener. Once the correct tables have been identified, they are opened, and the appropriate locks are applied for concurrency control.

Once all the maintenance and setup tasks are complete, the optimizer uses the internal-query structure (Lex) and evaluates the WHERE conditions (a restrict operation) of the query. Results are returned as temporary tables to prepare for the next step. If UNION operators are present, the optimizer executes the SELECT portions of all statements in a loop before continuing.

The next step in the optimizer is to execute the projections. These are executed in a similar manner as the restrict portions, again storing the intermediate results as temporary tables and saving only those attributes specified in the column specification in the SELECT statement. Last, the structure is analyzed for any JOIN conditions that are built using the join class, and then the join::optimize() method is called. At this stage, the query is optimized by evaluating the expressions and eliminating any conditions that result in dead branches or always-true or always-false conditions (as well as many other similar optimizations). The optimizer is attempting to eliminate any known-bad conditions in the query before executing the join. This is done because joins are the most expensive and time consuming of all relational operators. Note that the join-optimization step is performed for all queries that have a WHERE or HAVING clause regardless of whether there are any join conditions. This enables developers to concentrate all of the expression-evaluation code in one place. Once the join optimization is complete, the optimizer uses a series of conditional statements to route the query to the appropriate library method for execution.

The query optimizer and execution engine is perhaps the second most difficult area to understand, because of its SELECT-PROJECT-JOIN optimizer approach. Complicating matters is that this portion of the server is a mixture of C and C++ code, where the typical select execution is written as C methods while the join operation is written as a C++ object. In Chapter 13, I show you how to write your own query optimizer and use it instead of the MySQL optimizer.

Query Execution

Execution of the query is handled by a set of library methods designed to implement a particular query. For example, the mysql_insert() method is designed to insert data. Likewise, there is a mysql_select() method designed to find and return data matching the WHERE clause. This library of execution methods is located in a variety of source-code files under a file of a similar name (e.g., sql_insert.cc or sql_select.cc). All these methods have as a parameter a thread object that permits the method to access the internal query structure and eases execution. Results from each of the execution methods are returned using the network-communication-pathways library. The query-execution library methods are clearly implemented using the interpretative model of query execution.

Query Cache

While not its own subsystem, the query cache should be considered a vital part of the query optimization and execution subsystem. The query cache is a marvelous invention that caches not only the query structure but also the query results themselves. This enables the system to check for frequently used queries and shortcut the entire query-optimization and -execution stages altogether. This is another technology unique to MySQL. Other database-systems cache queries, but no others cache the actual results. As you can appreciate, the query cache must also allow for situations in which the results are "dirty" in the sense that something has changed since the last time the query was run (e.g., an INSERT, UPDATE, or DELETE was run against the base table) and that the cached queries may need to be occasionally purged.

■ **Tip** The query cache is turned on by default. If you want to turn off the query cache for the specific SQL statment, use the SQL_NO_CACHE SELECT option: SELECT SQL_NO_CACHE id, lname FROM myCustomer;. Otherwise, it can be GLOBALY disable using the server variables (query_cache_type, query_cache_size to also deallocate the buffer).

If you are not familiar with this technology, try it out. Find a table that has a sufficient number of tuples and execute a query that has some complexity, such as a JOIN or complex WHERE clause. Record the time it took to execute, then execute the same query again. Note the time difference. This is the query cache in action.

Listing 2-1 illustrates this exercise using the SHOW command to display the system variables associated with the query cache. Notice how running the query multiple times adds it to the cache, and subsequent calls read it from the cache. Notice also that the SQL_NO_CACHE option does not affect the query cache variables (because it doesn't use the query cache).

Listing 2-1. The MySQL Query Cache in Action

```
mysql> CREATE DATABASE test_cache;
Query OK, 1 row affected (0.00 sec)

mysql> CREATE TABLE test_cache.tbl1 (a int);
Query OK, 0 rows affected (0.01 sec)

mysql> INSERT INTO test_cache.tbl1 VALUES (100), (200), (300);
Query OK, 3 rows affected (0.00 sec)
Records: 3  Duplicates: 0  Warnings: 0

mysql> USE test_cache;
Database changed

mysql> SELECT * FROM tbl1;
+------+
| a    |
+------+
|  100 |
|  200 |
|  300 |
+------+
3 rows in set (0.00 sec)

mysql> show status like "Qcache_hits";
+---------------+-------+
| Variable_name | Value |
+---------------+-------+
| Qcache_hits   | 0     |
+---------------+-------+
1 row in set (0.00 sec)
```

```
mysql> select length(now()) from tbl1;
+---------------+
| length(now()) |
+---------------+
|            19 |
|            19 |
|            19 |
+---------------+
3 rows in set (0.00 sec)

mysql> show status like "Qcache_hits";
+---------------+-------+
| Variable_name | Value |
+---------------+-------+
| Qcache_hits   | 0     |
+---------------+-------+
1 row in set (0.01 sec)

mysql> show status like "Qcache_inserts";
+----------------+-------+
| Variable_name  | Value |
+----------------+-------+
| Qcache_inserts | 1     |
+----------------+-------+
1 row in set (0.00 sec)

mysql> show status like "Qcache_queries_in_cache";
+-------------------------+-------+
| Variable_name           | Value |
+-------------------------+-------+
| Qcache_queries_in_cache | 1     |
+-------------------------+-------+
1 row in set (0.00 sec)

mysql> SELECT * FROM tbl1;
+------+
| a    |
+------+
|  100 |
|  200 |
|  300 |
+------+
3 rows in set (0.00 sec)

mysql> show status like "Qcache_hits";
+---------------+-------+
| Variable_name | Value |
+---------------+-------+
| Qcache_hits   | 1     |
+---------------+-------+
1 row in set (0.00 sec)
```

```
mysql> SELECT SQL_NO_CACHE * FROM tbl1;
+------+
| a    |
+------+
|  100 |
|  200 |
|  300 |
+------+
3 rows in set (0.00 sec)

mysql> show status like "Qcache_hits";
+---------------+-------+
| Variable_name | Value |
+---------------+-------+
| Qcache_hits   | 1     |
+---------------+-------+
1 row in set (0.00 sec)

mysql> SELECT * FROM tbl1;
+------+
| a    |
+------+
|  100 |
|  200 |
|  300 |
+------+
3 rows in set (0.00 sec)

mysql> show status like "Qcache_hits";
+---------------+-------+
| Variable_name | Value |
+---------------+-------+
| Qcache_hits   | 2     |
+---------------+-------+
1 r
mysql>
```

Cache and Buffers

The caching and buffers subsystem is responsible for ensuring that the most frequently used data (or structures, as you will see) are available in the most efficient manner possible. In other words, the data must be resident, or ready to read, at all times. The caches dramatically increase the response time for requests for that data, because the data are in memory, and thus no additional disk access is necessary to retrieve it. The cache subsystem was created to encapsulate all of the caching and buffering into a loosely coupled set of library functions. Although you will find the caches implemented in several different source-code files, they are considered part of the same subsystem.

A number of caches are implemented in this subsystem. Most cache mechanisms use the same or similar concept of storing data as structures in a linked list. The caches are implemented in different portions of the code to tailor the implementation to the type of data that is being cached. Let's look at each of the caches.

Table Cache

The table cache was created to minimize the overhead in opening, reading, and closing tables (the .FRM files on disk). For this reason, it is designed to store metadata about the tables in memory. It does so by utilizing a data-chunking mechanism called Unireg. Unireg, a format created by a founder of MySQL, was once used for writing TTY applications. It stores data in segments called screens that originally were designed to be used to display data on a monitor. Unireq made it easier to store data and formulate displays (screens) for faster data refresh. As you may have surmised, this is an antiquated technology, and it shows the age of the MySQL source code. The good news is there are plans under way to redesign the table cache and eventually replace or remove the Unireg mechanism.

A WORD ABOUT FRM FILES

If you examine the data directory of a MySQL installation, you will see a folder named `data` that contains subfolders named for each database created. In these folders, you will see files named with the table names and a file extension of `.frm`. Many MySQL developers call these files "FRM files". Thus, a table named table1 in database1 has an FRM file named `/data/database1/table1.frm`.

When you attempt to open these files, you will see that they are binary files, not readable by normal means. Indeed, the format of the files have been a mystery for many years. Since the FRM files contain the metadata for the table, all of the column definitions and table options, including index definitions, are stored in the file. This means it should be possible to extract the data needed to reconstruct the `CREATE TABLE` statement from a FRM file. Unfortunately, given the interface and uniqueness of Unireg, it is not easy to parse these files for the information. Fortunately, there are efforts under way to decipher the FRM files via a Python utility that is part of the MySQL Utilities plugin for MySQL Workbench. If you need to read an FRM file to recover a table, see the online MySQL Utilities documentation for more details:
`http://dev.mysql.com/doc/workbench/en/mysql-utilities.html`

This makes it much faster for a thread to read the schema of the table without having to reopen the file every time. Each thread has its own list of table cache structures. This permits the threads to maintain their own views of the tables so that if one thread is altering the schema of a table (but has not committed the changes) another thread may use that table with the original schema. The structure used is a simple one that includes all of the metadata information for a table. The structures are stored in a linked list in memory and associated with each thread.

Buffer Pool

The buffer pool is a special cache used by the InnoDB storage engine. It caches table and index data, allowing data and indexes that are used most often to be read from memory instead of rereading from disk. The buffer pool improves performance significantly. Depending on your access patterns, you can tune the buffer pool to allocate more physical memory. It is one of the key parameters used to tune InnoDB storage-engine performance.

InnoDB uses several other caches. If you require additional performance from your InnoDB installation, consult the "InnoDB Performance Tuning and Troubleshooting" section in the online reference manual for InnoDB tuning best practices.

Record Cache

The record cache was created to enhance sequential reads from the storage engines. Thus, the record cache usually is used only during table scans. It works like a read-ahead buffer by retrieving one block of data at a time, thus resulting in fewer disk accesses during the scan. Fewer disk accesses generally equate to improved performance. Interestingly, the record cache is also used in writing data sequentially by writing the new (or altered) data to the cache first and then writing the cache to disk when full. In this way, write performance is improved as well. This sequential behavior (called locality of reference) is the main reason the record cache is most often used with the MyISAM storage engine, although it is not limited to MyISAM. The record cache is implemented in an agnostic manner that doesn't interfere with the code used to access the storage engine API. Developers don't have to do anything to take advantage of the record cache, as it is implemented within the layers of the API.

Key Cache

The key cache is a buffer for frequently used index data. In this case, it is a block of data for the index file (B-tree) and is used exclusively for MyISAM tables (the .MYI files on disk). The indexes themselves are stored as linked lists within the key cache structure. A key cache is created when a MyISAM table is opened for the first time. The key cache is accessed on every index read. If an index is found in the cache, it is read from there; otherwise, a new index block must be read from disk and placed into the cache. The cache has a limited size and is tunable by changing the key_cache_block_size configuration variable. Thus, not all blocks of the index file will fit into memory. So how does the system keep track of which blocks have been used?

The cache implements a monitoring system to keep track of how frequently the index blocks are used. The key cache has been implemented to keep track of how "warm" the index blocks are. Warm, in this case, refers to how many times the index block has been accessed over time. Values for warm include BLOCK_COLD, BLOCK_WARM, and BLOCK_HOT. As the blocks cool off and new blocks become warm, the cold blocks are purged and the warm blocks added. This strategy is a least recently used (LRU) page-replacement strategy—the same algorithm used for virtual memory management and disk buffering in operating systems—that has been proven to be remarkably efficient even in the face of much more sophisticated page-replacement algorithms. In a similar way, the key cache keeps track of the index blocks that have changed (called getting "dirty"). When a dirty block is purged, its data are written back to the index file on disk before being replaced. Conversely, when a clean block is purged, data are simply removed from memory.

■ **Note**   Practice has shown that the LRU algorithm performs within 80 percent of the best algorithms. In a world in which time is precious and simplicity ensures reliability, the 80 percent solution is a win-win.

Privilege Cache

The privilege cache is used to store grant data on a user account. This data are stored in the same manner as an access control list (ACL), which lists all of the privileges a user has for an object in the system. The privilege cache is implemented as a structure stored in a first-in, last-out (FILO) hash table. Data for the cache are gathered when the grant tables are read during user authentication and initialization. It is important to store this data in memory, because that saves a lot of time reading the grant tables.

Hostname Cache

The hostname cache is another helper cache, like the privilege cache. It, too, is implemented as a stack of a structure. It contains the hostnames of all the connections to the server. It may seem surprising, but this data are frequently requested and therefore in high demand and candidates for a dedicated cache.

Miscellaneous

A number of other small cache mechanisms are implemented throughout the MySQL source code. One is the join buffer cache, which is used during complex join operations. For example, some join operations require comparing one tuple to all the tuples in the second table. A cache in this case can store the tuples read so that the join can be implemented without having to reread the second table into memory multiple times.

File Access via Pluggable Storage Engines

One of the best features of MySQL is the ability to support different storage engines, or file types. This allows database professionals to tune their database performance by selecting the storage engine that best meets their application needs. Examples include using storage engines that provide transaction control for highly active databases for which transaction processing is required or using the memory storage engine whenever a table is read many times but seldom updated (e.g., a lookup table).

Oracle added a new architectural design in version 5.1 that makes it easier to add new storage types. The new mechanism is called the MySQL pluggable storage engine. Oracle has worked hard to make the server extensible via the pluggable storage engine. The pluggable storage engine was created as an abstraction of the file-access layer and built as an API that Oracle (or anyone) can use to build specialized file-access mechanisms called storage engines. The API provides a set of methods and access utilities for reading and writing data. These methods combine to form a standardized modular architecture that permits storage engines to use the same methods for every storage engine (this is the essence of why it is called pluggable—the storage engines all plug into the server using the same API). It also enables the use of storage-engine plugins.

PLUGGABLE VS PLUGIN

Pluggable is the concept that there may be several different implementations of a common interface allowing the exchange of the implementations while other portions of the system to remain unchanged. A plugin is a binary form of a module (a compiled module) that implements a pluggable interface. A plugin is therefore something that can be changed at runtime. The InnoDB storage engine is also a plugin, as are several of the modules in MySQL with plans to make other portions of the server into plugins.

To enable a plugin storage engine, use the INSTALL PLUGIN command. For example, to load the example plugin storage engine, issue the following command (example is for Linux OS):

```
mysql> INSTALL PLUGIN example SONAME 'ha_example.so';
```

Similarly, to unplug a storage engine, use the UNINSTALL PLUGIN command:

```
mysql> UNINSTALL PLUGIN example;
```

Alternatively, you can use the mysql_plugin client tool to enable and disable a storage engine plugin.

Perhaps most interesting of all is the fact that database implementers (you!) can assign a different storage engine to each table in a given database and even change storage engines after a table is created. This flexibility and modularity permits you to create new storage engines as the need arises. To change storage engines for a table, issue a command such as the following:

```
ALTER TABLE MyTable
ENGINE = InnoDB;
```

The pluggable storage engine is perhaps the most unusual feature of MySQL. No other database system comes close to having this level of flexibility and extensibility for the file-access layer of the architecture. The following sections describe all of the storage engines available in the server and present a brief overview of how you can create your own storage engine. I show you how to create your own storage engine in Chapter 10.

The strengths and weaknesses of the storage engines are many and varied. For example, some storage engines offered in MySQL support concurrency. As of version 5.6, the default storage engine for MySQL is InnoDB. The InnoDB tables support record locking (sometimes called row-level locking) for concurrency control; when an update is in progress, no other processes can access that row in the table until the operation is complete. Thus, the InnoDB table type provides an advantage for use in situations in which many concurrent updates are expected. Any of these storage engines, however, will perform well in read-only environments. such as web servers or kiosk applications.

■ **Tip**   You can change the default storage engine by setting the STORAGE_ENGINE configuration server variable.

Previous versions of MySQL had the MyISAM storage engine as the default. MyISAM supports table-level locking for concurrency control. That is, when an update is in progress, no other processes can access any data from the same table until the operation is completed. The MyISAM storage engine is also the fastest of the available types due to optimizations made using indexed sequential access method (ISAM) principles. The Berkeley Database (BDB) tables support page-level locking for concurrency control; when an update is in progress, no other processes can access any data from the same page as that of the data being modified until the operation is complete.

Concurrency operations such as those we've discussed are implemented in database systems using specialized commands that form a transaction subsystem. Currently, only three of the storage engines listed support transactions: InnoDB and NDB. Transactions provide a mechanism that permits a set of operations to execute as a single atomic operation. For example, if a database were built for a banking institution, the macro operations of transferring money from one account to another would preferably be executed completely (money removed from one account and placed in another) without interruption. Transactions permit these operations to be encased in an atomic operation that will back out any changes should an error occur before all operations are complete, thus avoiding data being removed from one table and never making it to the next table. A sample set of operations in the form of SQL statements encased in transactional commands is:

```
START TRANSACTION;
UPDATE SavingsAccount SET Balance=Balance - 100
WHERE AccountNum=123;
UPDATE CheckingAccount SET Balance=Balance+100
WHERE AccountNum=345;
COMMIT;
```

In practice, most database professionals specify the MyISAM table type if they require faster access and InnoDB if they need transaction support. Fortunately, MySQL provides facilities to specify a table type for each table in a database. In fact, tables within a database do not have to be the same type. This variety of storage engines permits the tuning of databases for a wide range of applications.

Interestingly, you can extend this list of storage engines by writing your own table handler. MySQL provides examples and code stubs to make this feature accessible to the system developer. The ability to extend this list of storage engines makes it possible to add support to MySQL for complex, proprietary data formats and access layers.

InnoDB

InnoDB is an Oracle storage engine that predates Oracles' acquisition of MySQL via the purchase of Sun MicroSystems. InnoDB was originally a third-party storage engine licensed from Innobase (www.innodb.com) and distributed under the GNU Public License (GPL) agreement. Innobase was acquired by Oracle, and until the acquisition of MySQL it was licensed for use by MySQL. Hence, now that Oracle owns both MySQL and InnoDB, it removes any licensing limitations and enables the two product-development teams to coordinate development. Gains from this relationship have been seen most recently in the significant performance improvements in the latest releases of MySQL.

InnoDB is most often used when you need to use transactions. InnoDB supports traditional ACID transactions (see the accompanying sidebar) and foreign key constraints. All indexes in InnoDB are B-trees where the index records are stored in the leaf pages of the tree. InnoDB improves the concurrency control of MyISAM by providing row-level locking. InnoDB is the storage engine of choice for high reliability and transaction processing environments.

WHAT IS ACID?

ACID stands for atomicity, consistency, isolation, and durability. Perhaps one of the most important concepts in database theory, it defines the behavior that database systems must exhibit to be considered reliable for transaction processing.

- Atomicity means that the database must allow modifications of data on an "all or nothing" basis for transactions that contain multiple commands. That is, each transaction is atomic. If a command fails, the entire transaction fails, and all changes up to that point in the transaction are discarded. This is especially important for systems that operate in highly transactional environments, such as the financial market. Consider for a moment the ramifications of a money transfer. Typically, multiple steps are involved in debiting one account and crediting another. If the transaction fails after the debit step and doesn't credit the money back to the first account, the owner of that account will be very angry. In this case, the entire transaction from debit to credit must succeed, or none of it does.

- Consistency means that only valid data will be stored in the database. That is, if a command in a transaction violates one of the consistency rules, the entire transaction is discarded, and the data is returned to the state they were in before the transaction began. Conversely, if a transaction completes successfully, it will alter the data in a manner that obeys the database consistency rules.

- Isolation means that multiple transactions executing at the same time will not interfere with one another. This is where the true challenge of concurrency is most evident. Database systems must handle situations in which transactions cannot violate the data (alter, delete, etc.) being used in another transaction. There are many ways to handle this. Most systems use a mechanism called locking that keeps the data from being used by another transaction until the first one is done. Although the isolation property does not dictate which transaction is executed first, it does ensure they will not interfere with one another.

- Durability means that no transaction will result in lost data nor will any data created or altered during the transaction be lost. Durability is usually provided by robust backup-and-restore maintenance functions. Some database systems use logging to ensure that any uncommitted data can be recovered on restart.

MyISAM

The MyISAM storage engine is used by most LAMP stacks, data warehousing, e-commerce, and enterprise applications. MyISAM files are an extension of ISAM built with additional optimizations, such as advanced caching and indexing mechanisms. These tables are built using compression features and index optimizations for speed. Additionally, the MyISAM storage engine provides for concurrent operations by providing table-level locking. The MyISAM storage mechanism offers reliable storage for a wide variety of applications while providing fast retrieval of data. MyISAM is the storage engine of choice when read performance is a concern.

ISAM

The ISAM file-access method has been around a long time. ISAM was originally created by IBM and later used in System R, IBM's experimental RDBMS that is considered by many to be the seminal work and the ancestor to all RDBMSs today. (Some have cited Ingres as the original RDBMS.)

ISAM files store data by organizing them into tuples of fixed-length attributes. The tuples are stored in a given order. This was done to speed access from tape. Yes, back in the day, that was a database implementer's only choice of storage except, of course, punch cards! (It is usually at this point that I embarrass myself by showing my age. If you, too, remember punch cards, then you and I probably share an experience few will ever have again—dropping a deck of cards that hadn't been numbered or printed (printing the data on the top of the card used to take a lot longer and was often skipped).

The ISAM files also have an external indexing mechanism that was normally implemented as a hash table that contained pointers (tape block numbers and counts), allowing you to fast-forward the tape to the desired location. This permitted fast access to data stored on tape—well, as fast as the tape drive could fast-forward.

While created for tape, the ISAM mechanism can be (and often is) used for disk file systems. The greatest asset of the ISAM mechanism is that the index is normally very small and can be searched quickly, because it can be searched using an in-memory search mechanism. Some later versions of the ISAM mechanisms permitted the creation of alternative indexes, thus enabling the file (table) to be accessed via several search mechanisms. This external indexing mechanism has become the standard for all modern database-storage engines.

MySQL included an ISAM storage engine (referred to then as a table type), but the ISAM storage engine has been replaced by the MyISAM storage engine. Future plans include replacing the MyISAM storage engine with a more modern transactional storage engine.

■ **Note** Older versions of MySQL supported an ISAM storage engine. With the introduction of MyISAM, Oracle has deprecated the ISAM storage engine.

Memory

The memory storage engine (sometimes called HEAP tables) is an in-memory table that uses a hashing mechanism for fast retrieval of frequently used data. Thus, these tables are much faster than those that are stored and referenced from disk. They are accessed in the same manner as the other storage engines, but the data is stored in-memory and is valid only during the MySQL session. The data is flushed and deleted on shutdown (or a crash). Memory storage engines are typically used in situations in which static data are accessed frequently and rarely ever altered. Examples of such situations include zip code, state, county, category, and other lookup tables. HEAP tables can also be used in databases that utilize snapshot techniques for distributed or historical data access.

■ **Tip** You can automatically create memory-based tables using the --init-file=file startup option. In this case, the file specified should contain the SQL statements to re-create the table. Since the table was created once, you can omit the CREATE statement, because the table definition is not deleted on system restart.

Merge

The merge storage engine is built using a set of MyISAM tables with the same structure (tuple layout or schema) that can be referenced as a single table. Thus, the tables are partitioned by the location of the individual tables, but no additional partitioning mechanisms are used. All tables must reside on the same machine (accessed by the same server). Data is accessed using singular operations or statements, such as SELECT, UPDATE, INSERT, and DELETE. Fortunately, when a DROP is issued on a merge table, only the merge specification is removed. The original tables are not altered.

The biggest benefit of this table type is speed. It is possible to split a large table into several smaller tables on different disks, combine them using a merge-table specification, and access them simultaneously. Searches and sorts will execute more quickly because there is less data in each table to manipulate. For example, if you divide the data by a predicate, you can search only those specific portions that contain the category you are searching for. Similarly, repairs on tables are more efficient because it is faster and easier to repair several smaller individual files than a single large table. Presumably, most errors will be localized to an area within one or two of the files and thus will not require rebuilding and repair of all the data. Unfortunately, this configuration has several disadvantages:

- You can use only identical MyISAM tables, or schemas, to form a single merge table. This limits the application of the merge storage engine to MyISAM tables. If the merge storage engine were to accept any storage engine, the merge storage engine would be more versatile.

- The replace operation is not permitted.

- Indexed access has been shown to be less efficient than for a single table.

- Merge storage mechanisms are best used in very large database (VLDB) applications, such as data warehousing where data resides in more than one table in one or more databases.

Archive

The archive storage engine is designed for storing large amounts of data in a compressed format. The archive storage mechanism is best used for storing and retrieving large amounts of seldom-accessed archival or historical data. Such data include security-access-data logs. While not something that you would want to search or even use daily, it is something a database professional who is concerned about security would want to have should a security incident occur.

No indexes are provided for the archive storage mechanism, and the only access method is via a table scan. Thus, the archive storage engine should not be used for normal database storage and retrieval.

Federated

The federated storage engine is designed to create a single table reference from multiple database systems. The federated storage engine therefore works like the merge storage engine, but it allows you to link data (tables) together across database servers. This mechanism is similar in purpose to the linked data tables available in other database systems. The federated storage mechanism is best used in distributed or data mart environments.

The most interesting aspect of the federated storage engine is that it does not move data, nor does it require the remote tables to be the same storage engine. This illustrates the true power of the pluggable-storage-engine layer. Data are translated during storage and retrieval.

Cluster/NDB

The cluster storage engine (called NDB to distinguish it from the cluster product[14]) was created to handle the cluster server capabilities of MySQL. The cluster storage mechanism is used almost exclusively when clustering multiple MySQL servers in a high-availability and high-performance environment. The cluster storage engine does not store any data. Instead, it delegates the storage and retrieval of the data to the storage engines used in the databases in the cluster. It manages the control of distributing the data across the cluster, thus providing redundancy and performance enhancements. The NDB storage engine also provides an API for creating extensible cluster solutions.

CSV

The CSV storage engine is designed to create, read, and write comma-separated value (CSV) files as tables. While the CSV storage engine does not copy the data into another format, the sheet layout, or metadata, is stored along with the filename specified on the server in the database folder. This permits database professionals to rapidly export structured business data that is stored in spreadsheets. The CSV storage engine does not provide any indexing mechanisms.

Due to the simplicity of the CSV storage engine, its source code provides an excellent starting point for developers who want or need to develop their own storage engines. You can find the source code for the CSV storage engine in the /storage/csv/ha_tina.h and /storage/csv/ha_tina.cc files in the source code tree.

WHO IS TINA?

An interesting factoid concerning the source code for the CSV storage engine is that it was named after a friend of the original author and was intended to be a special, and not a general, solution. Fortunately, the storage engine has proved to be useful for a much wider audience. Unfortunately, once the source files were introduced there has not been any incentive to change the file names.

Blackhole

The blackhole storage engine, an interesting feature with surprising utility, is designed to permit the system to write data, but the data are never saved. If binary logging is enabled, hwoever, the SQL statements are written to the logs. This permits database professionals to temporarily disable data ingestion in the database by switching the table type. This can be handy in situations in which you want to test an application to ensure it is writing data that you don't want to store, such as when creating a relay slave for the purpose of filtering replication.

Custom

The custom storage engine represents any storage engine you create to enhance your database server. For example, you may want to create a storage engine that reads XML files. While you could convert the XML files into tables, you

---

[14] For more information about the NDB API, see http://dev.mysql.com/doc/ndbapi/en/overview-ndb-api.html.

may not want to do that if you have a large number of files you need to access. The following is an overview of how you would create such an engine.

If you were considering using the XML storage engine to read a particular set of similar XML files, the first thing you would do is analyze the format, or schema, of your XML files and determine how you want to resolve the self-describing nature of XML files. Let's say that all the files contain the same basic data types but have differing tags and ordering of the tags. In this case, you decide to use style sheets to transform the files to a consistent format.

Once you've decided on the format, you can begin developing your new storage engine by examining the sample storage engine included with the MySQL source code in a folder named .\storage\example on the main source code tree. You'll find a makefile and two source code files (ha_example.h, ha_example.cc) with a stubbed-out set of code that permits the engine to work, but the code isn't really interesting, because it doesn't do anything. You can read the comments that the programmers left describing the features you will need to implement for your own storage engine, however. For example, the method for opening the file is called ha_example::open. When you examine the sample storage-engine files, you find this method in the ha_example.cpp file. Listing 2-2 shows an example of the open method.

Listing 2-2. Open Tables Method

```
/**
  @brief
  Used for opening tables. The name will be the name of the file.

  @details
  A table is opened when it needs to be opened; e.g. when a request comes in
  for a SELECT on the table (tables are not open and closed for each request,
  they are cached).

  Called from handler.cc by handler::ha_open(). The server opens all tables by
  calling ha_open() which then calls the handler specific open().

  @see
  handler::ha_open() in handler.cc
*/
int ha_example::open(const char *name, int mode, uint test_if_locked)
{
  DBUG_ENTER("ha_example::open");

  if (!(share = get_share()))
    DBUG_RETURN(1);
  thr_lock_data_init(&share->lock,&lock,NULL);

  DBUG_RETURN(0);
}
```

■ **Tip** You can also create storage engines in the Microsoft Windows environment. In this case, the files are in a Visual Studio project.

The example in Listing 2-2 explains what the method ha_example::open does and gives you an idea of how it is called and what return to expect. Although the source code may look strange to you now, it will become clearer the more you read it and the more familiar you become with the MySQL coding style.

■ **Note** Previous versions of MySQL (prior to version 5.1) permit the creation of custom storage engines but require you to recompile the server executable in order to pick up the changes. With the new version 5.1 pluggable architecture, the modular API permits the storage engines to have diverse implementation and features and allows them to be built independently of the MySQL system code. Thus, you need not modify the MySQL source code directly. Your new storage-engine project allows you to create your own custom engine and then compile and link it with an existing running server.

Once you are comfortable with the example storage engine and how it works, you can copy and rename the files to something more appropriate to your new engine and then begin modifying the files to read from XML files. Like all good programmers, you begin by implementing one method at a time and testing your code until you are satisfied it works properly. Once you have all the functionality you want, and you compile the storage engine and link it to your production server, your new storage engine becomes available for anyone to use.

Although this may sound like a difficult task, it isn't really, and it can be a good way to get started learning the MySQL source code. I return to creating a custom storage engine with detailed step-by-step instructions in Chapter 7.

Summary

In this chapter, I presented the architecture of a typical RDBMS. While short of being a complete database-theory lesson, this chapter gave you a look inside the relational-database architecture, and you should now have an idea of what goes on inside the box. I also examined the MySQL server architecture and explained where in the source code all of the parts that make up the MySQL server architecture reside.

The knowledge of how an RDBMS works and the examination of the MySQL server architecture will prepare you for an intensive journey into extending the MySQL database system. With knowledge of the MySQL architecture, you're now armed (but not very dangerous).

In the next chapter, I lead you on a tour of the MySQL source code that will enable you to begin extending the MySQL system to meet your own needs. So roll up your sleeves and get your geek on;[15] we're headed into the source code!

---

[15]Known best by the characteristic reclined-computer-chair, caffeine-laden-beverage-at-the-ready, music-blasting, hands-on-keyboard pose many of us enter while coding.

■ ■ ■

## CHAPTER 3

A Tour of the MySQL Source Code

This chapter presents a complete introduction to the MySQL source, along with an explanation of how to obtain and build the system. I introduce you to the mechanics of the source code as well as coding guidelines and best practices for how to maintain the code. I focus on the parts of the code that deal with processing queries; this will set the stage for topics introduced in Chapter 11 and beyond. I also give you a short overview of the plugin system for dynamically loading libraries containing features.

Getting Started

In this section, I examine the principles behind modifying the MySQL source code and how you can obtain the source code. Let's begin with a review of the available licensing options.

Understanding the Licensing Options

When planning your modifications to open-source software, consider how you're going to use those modifications. More specifically, how are you going to acquire the source code and work with it? Depending on your intentions for the modifications, your choices will be very different from others. There are three principal ways you may want to modify the source code:

- To gain insight on how MySQL is constructed; therefore, you are following the examples in this book or working on your own experiments.

- To develop a capability for you or your organization that will not be distributed outside your organization.

- To build an application or extension that you plan to share or market to others.

In the first chapter, I discussed the responsibilities of an open-source developer who is modifying software under an open-source license. Since MySQL released under GPLv2 and also under a commercial license (a *dual license*), we must consider these uses of the source code under *both* licenses. I'll begin our discussion with the GPLv2.

Modifying the source code in a purely academic session is permissible under the GPL, which clearly gives you the freedom to change the source code and experiment with it. The value of your contribution may determine whether your code is released under the GPL. For example, if your code modifications are considered singular in focus (they only apply to a limited set of users for a special purpose), the code may not be included in the source-code base. In a similar way, if your code was focused on the exploration of an academic exercise, the code may not be of value to anyone other than yourself. Few would consider an academic exercise in which you test options and features implemented in the source code as adding value to the MySQL system. On the other hand, if your experiments lead to a successful and meaningful addition to the system, most would agree that you're obligated to share your findings. For the purposes of this book, you'll proceed with modifying the source code as if you will not be sharing your modifications. Although I hope that you find the experiments in this book enlightening and entertaining, I don't think they would be considered for adoption into the MySQL system without further development. If you take these examples and make something wonderful out of them, you have my blessing. Just be sure to tell everyone where you got the idea.

■ **Caution**   If you are planning a project that you plan to share in any way with anyone, contact Oracle's MySQL Sales for clarification of your current license and the availability of licensing options to support your goals.

If you're modifying the MySQL source code for use by you or your organization, and you do not want to share your modifications, you should purchase the appropriate MySQL commercial license. MySQL's commercial-licensing terms allow you to make modifications (and even getting Oracle to help you) and keep them to yourself.

Similarly, if you're modifying the source code and intend to distribute the modifications, you're required by the GPL to distribute the modified source code free of charge (but you may charge a media fee). You should consult Oracle before doing so.

Furthermore, your changes cannot be made proprietary, and you cannot own the rights to the modifications under the GPL. If you choose not to publish your changes yourself, you should contribute the code to Oracle for consideration. If it is accepted, it becomes the property of Oracle. On the other hand, if you want to make proprietary changes to MySQL for use in an embedded system or similar installation, contact Oracle and discuss your plans before launching your project.

Getting the Source Code

You can obtain the MySQL source code by downloading it from the MySQL developers' Web site (http://dev.mysql.com/downloads). At that site, you'll see links to download all MySQL open-source products. (For use with this book, you need the MySQL Community Edition.) You will also see several links for downloading different versions of the server, including:

- The current release (also called the generally available or GA) for production use

- Older releases of the software

- Documentation for each version

If you scroll down, you will see a dropdown box that permits you to choose your platform. This will download a binary version of the server, including everything you need to install and run it on your system. You will also see an entry named "Source Code." This is the link you will use to download the source code.

You can also download the source code for newer versions of the server, called "Development Releases." You can click on the tab and see a similar list for selecting the platform or the source code. As a reminder, development releases are cutting-edge feature previews that may or may not contain final production code and, as such, they should not be considered for use in a production environment. For the purposes of this book, you can use development release versions 5.6.5 or later.

To follow the examples in this book, download version 5.6.5 or higher from the Web site. I provide instructions for installing MySQL in the next section. The site contains all the binaries and source code for all of the environments supported. Many different platforms are supported. You'll find the source code located near the bottom of the page. Download both the source code and the binaries (two downloads) for your platform. In this book, I'll use examples from both Ubuntu and Microsoft Windows 7.

■ **Tip**   If you're using Windows, download the MSI installer. In fact, consider downloading the MySQL Windows installer instead. This contains all of the MySQL components and makes installing MySQL on Windows a simple and fast process. It is the best way to install MySQL on your Windows system.

OLDER PLATFORM SUPPORT

If you do not see your platform listed for the binary distribution of your choice, it is likely your platform is either too new, is no longer supported, or has yet to be included. If this happens, you can still download the source code and build it yourself.

■ **Note**   Unless otherwise stated, the examples in this book are taken from the Linux source-code distribution (mysql-5.6.5. While most of the code is the same for Linux and Windows distributions, I highlight differences as they occur. Most notably, the Windows platform has a slightly different vio implementation.

The MySQL Source Code

Once you have downloaded the source code, unpack the files into a folder on your system. You can unpack them into the same directory if you want. When you do this, notice that there are a lot of folders and many source files. The main folder you'll need to reference is the /sql folder. This contains the main source files for the server. Table 3-1 lists the most commonly accessed folders and their contents.

Table 3-1. *MySQL Source Folders*

Folder	Contents
/BUILD	The compilation configuration and make files for all platforms supported.
/client	The MySQL command-line client tools.
/cmake	The configuration files for the CMake cross-platform build system.
/dbug	Utilities for use in debugging (see Chapter 5 for more details).
/include	The base system include files and headers.
/libmysql	The C client API used for MySQL client applications as well as creating embedded systems. (See Chapter 6 for more details.)
/libmysqld	The core server API files. Also used in creating embedded systems. (See Chapter 6 for more details.)
/mysql-test	The MySQL system test suite. (See Chapter 4 for more details.)
/mysys	The majority of the core-operating-system API wrappers and helper functions.
/plugin	A folder containing the source code for all of the provided plugins.
/regex	A regular expression library. Used in the query optimizer and execution to resolve expressions.
/scripts	A set of shell script-based utilities.
/sql	The main system code. You should start your exploration from this folder.
/sql-bench	A set of benchmarking utilities.
/storage	The MySQL pluggable-storage-engine source code is located inside this folder. Also included is the storage engine example code. (See Chapter 7 for more details.)

(continued)

Table 3-1. (*continued*)

Folder	Contents
/strings	The core string-handling wrappers. Use these for all of your string-handling needs.
/support-files	A set of preconfigured configuration files for compiling with different options.
/tests	A set of test programs and test files.
/vio	The network and socket layer code.
/zlib	Data compression tools.

I recommend taking some time now to dig your way through some of the folders and acquaint yourself with the location of the files. You will find many types of files and a variety of Perl scripts dispersed among the folders. While not overly simplistic, the MySQL source code is logically organized around the functions of the source code rather than the core subsystems. Some subsystems, such as the storage engines and plugins, are located in a folder hierarchy, but most are located in several places in the folder structure. For each subsystem discussed while examining the source code, I list the associated source files and their locations.

Getting Started

The best way to understand the flow and control of the MySQL system is to follow the source code along from the standpoint of a typical query. I presented a high-level view of each of the major MySQL subsystems in Chapter 2. I use the same subsystem view now as I show you how a typical SQL statement is executed. The sample SQL statement I use is:

```
SELECT lname, fname, DOB FROM Employees WHERE Employees.department = 'EGR'
```

This query selects the names and dates of birth for everyone in the engineering department. While not very interesting, the query will be useful in demonstrating almost all subsystems in the MySQL system. Let's begin with the query arriving at the server for processing.

Figure 3-1 shows the path the example query would take through the MySQL source code. I have pulled out the major lines of code that you should associate with the subsystems identified in Chapter 2. I have also abbreviated and omitted some of the parameter lists to make the graphic easier to read. Although not part of a specific subsystem, the mysqld_main() function is responsible for initializing the server and setting up the connection listener. The mysqld_main() function is in the file /sql/mysqld.cc.

■ **Note** Windows systems execute the win_main() method, also located in mysqld.cc.

```
int main(int argc, char **argv)
```

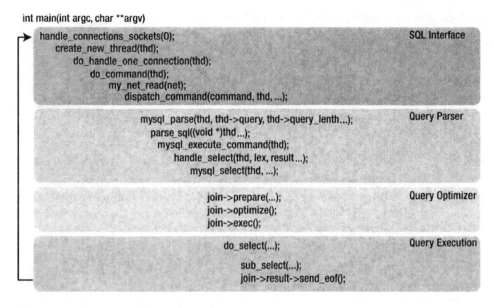

Figure 3-1. *Overview of the query path*

The path of the query, once it arrives at the server, begins in the SQL Interface subsystem (like most of the MySQL subsystems, the SQL Interface functions are distributed over a loosely associated set of source files). I tell you which files the methods are in as you go through this and the following sections. The handle_connections_socket() method (located in /sql/mysqld.cc) implements the listener loop, creating a thread for every connection detected. Once the thread is created, control flows to the do_handle_one_connection() function. The do_handle_one_connection() function identifies the command, then passes control to the do_command switch (located in /sql/sql_parse.cc). The do_command switch routes control to the proper network reading calls to read the query from the connection and passes the query to the parser via the dispatch_command() function (located in /sql/sql_parse.cc).

The query passes to the query parser subsystem, where the query is parsed and routed to the correct portion of the optimizer. The query parser is built in with Lex and YACC. Lex is used to identify tokens and literals as well as syntax of a language. YACC is used to build the code to interact with the MySQL source code. It captures the SQL commands storing the portions of the commands in an internal query representation and routes the command to a command processor called mysql_execute_command() (somewhat misnamed). This method then routes the query to the proper subfunction, in this case, mysql_select(). These methods are located in /sql/sql_parse.cc and /sql/sql_select.cc. This portion of the code enters the SELECT-PROJECT parts of the SELECT-PROJECT-JOIN query optimizer.

■ **Tip**   A project or projection is a relational database term describing the query operation that limits the result set to those columns defined in the column list on a SQL command. For example, the SQL command SELECT fname, lname FROM employee would "project" only the fname and lname columns from the employee table to the result set.

It is at this point that the query optimizer is invoked to optimize the execution of the query via the functions join->prepare() located in /sql/sql_resolver.cc and join->optimize() located in /sql/sql_optimizer.cc. Query execution occurs next in join->exec() located in /sql/sql_executor.cc, with control passing to the lower-level do_select() function located in /sql/sql_executor.cc that carries out the restrict and projection operations. Finally, the sub_select() function invokes the storage engine to read the tuples, process them, and return results to the client. These methods are located in /sql/sql_executor.cc. After the results are written to the network, control returns to the handle_connections_sockets loop (located in /sql/mysqld.cc).

■ **Tip** Classes, structures, classes, structures—it's all about classes and structures! Keep this in mind while you examine the MySQL source code. For just about any operation in the server, there is at least one class or structure that either manages the data or drives the execution. Learning the commonly used MySQL classes and structures is the key to understanding the source code, as you'll see in "Important Classes and Structures" later in this chapter.

You may be thinking that the code isn't as bad as you may have heard. That is largely true for simple SELECT statements such as the example I am using, but as you'll soon see, it can become more complicated than that. Now that you have seen this path and have had an introduction to where some of the major functions fall in the path of the query and the subsystems, open the source code and look for those functions. You can begin your search in /sql/mysqld.cc.

OK, so that was a whirlwind introduction, yes? From this point on, I slow things down a bit (OK, a lot) and navigate the source code in more detail. I also list the specific source files where the examples reside, in the form of a table at the end of each section. So tighten those safety belts, we're going in!

I leave out sections that are not relevant to our tour. These could include conditional compilation directives, ancillary code, and other system-level calls. I annotate the missing sections with the following: .... I have left many of the original comments in place, because I believe that they will help you follow the source code and offer you a glimpse into the world of developing a world-class database system. Finally, I highlight the important parts of the code in bold so that you can find them more easily while reading.

The mysqld_main() Function

The mysqld_main() function, where the server begins execution, is located in /sql/mysqld.cc. It is the first function called when the server executable is loaded into memory. Several hundred lines of code in this function are devoted to operating-system-specific startup tasks, and there's a good amount of system-level initialization code. Listing 3-1 shows a condensed view of the code, with the essential points in bold.

Listing 3-1. The main() Function

```
int mysqld_main(int argc, char **argv)
{
  ...

  if (init_common_variables())

  ...

  if (init_server_components())

  ...
  /*
   Initialize my_str_malloc() and my_str_free()
  */
  my_str_malloc= &my_str_malloc_mysqld;
  my_str_free= &my_str_free_mysqld;
```

```
...

if (mysql_rm_tmp_tables() || acl_init(opt_noacl) ||
    my_tz_init((THD *)0, default_tz_name, opt_bootstrap))

...

create_shutdown_thread();

...

handle_connections_sockets();

...

(void) mysql_mutex_lock(&LOCK_thread_count);

...

(void) mysql_mutex_unlock(&LOCK_thread_count);

...
}
```

The first interesting function is init_common_variables(). This uses the command-line arguments to control how the server will perform; it is where the server interprets the arguments and starts the server in a variety of modes. This function takes care of setting up the system variables and places the server in the desired mode. The init-server-components() function initializes the database logs for use by any of the subsystems. These are the typical logs you see for events, statement execution, and so on.

Two of the most important my_ library functions are my_str_malloc() and my_str_free(). It is at this point in the server startup code (near the beginning) that these two function pointers are set. You should always use these functions in place of the traditional C/C++ malloc() functions, because the MySQL functions have additional error handling and therefore are safer than the base methods. The acl_init() function's job is to start the authentication-and-access-control subsystem. This key system appears early in the server startup code.

Now you're getting to what makes MySQL tick: threads. Two important helper threads are created. The create-shutdown-thread() function creates a thread whose job is to shut down the server on signal. I discuss threads in more detail in the "Process vs. Thread" sidebar.

At this point in the startup code, the system is just about ready to accept connections from clients. To do that, the handle-connections-sockets() function implements a listener that loops through the code waiting for connections. I discuss this function in more detail next.

The last thing I want to point out to you in the code is an example of the critical-section protection code for mutually exclusive access during multithreading. A critical section is a block of code that must execute as a set and can be accessed only by a single thread at a time. Critical sections are usually areas that write to a shared memory variable, and they therefore must complete before another thread attempts to read the memory. Oracle has created an abstract of a common concurrency protection mechanism called a *mutex* (short for mutually exclusive). If you find an area in your code that you need to protect during concurrent execution, use the following functions to protect the code.

The first function you should call is mysql_mutex_lock([resource reference]. This places a lock on the code execution at this point in the code. It will not permit another thread to access the memory location specified until your code calls the unlocking function mysql_mutex_unlock([resource reference]). In the example from the mysqld_main() function, the mutex calls are locking the thread-count global variable.

Well, that's your first dive under the hood. How did it feel? Do you want more? Keep reading—you've only just begun. In fact, you haven't seen where our example query enters the system. Let's do that next.

PROCESS VS. THREAD

The terms *process* and *thread* are often used interchangeably. This is incorrect, because a *process* is an organized set of computer instructions that has its own memory and execution path. A *thread* is also a set of computer instructions, but threads execute in a host's execution path and do not have their own memory. (Some call threads lightweight processes. While a good description, calling them that doesn't help make the distinction.) They do store state (in MySQL, it is via the THD class). Thus, when talking about large systems that support processes, I mean systems that permit sections of the system to execute as separate processes and have their own memory. When talking about large systems that support threads, I mean systems that permit sections of the system to execute concurrently with other sections of the system, and they all share the same memory space as the host.

Most database systems use the process model to manage concurrent connections and helper functions. MySQL uses the multithreaded model. There are a number of advantages to using threads over processes. Most notably, threads are easier to create and manage (no overhead for memory allocation and segregation). Threads also permit very fast switching, because no context switching takes place. Threads do have one severe drawback, however. If things go *wonky* (a highly technical term used to describe strange, unexplained behavior; in the case of threading, they are often very strange and harmful events) during a thread's execution, it is likely that if the trouble is severe, the entire system could be affected. Fortunately, Oracle and the global community of developers have worked very hard to make MySQL's threading subsystem robust and reliable. This is why it is important for your modifications to be thread safe.

Handling Connections and Creating Threads

You saw in the previous section how the system is started and how the control flows to the listener loop that waits for user connections. The connections begin life at the client and are broken down into data packets, placed on the network by the client software, then flow across the network communications pathways, where they are picked up by the server's network subsystems and re-formed into data on the server. (A complete description of the communication packets is available in the MySQL Internals Manual.) This flow can be seen in Figure 3-2. I show more details about network-communication methods in the next chapter. I also include examples of how to write code that returns results to the client using these functions.

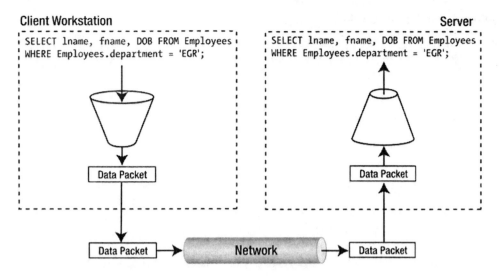

Figure 3-2. *Network communications from client to server*

At this point the system is in the SQL interface subsystem. That is, the data packets (containing the query) have arrived at the server and are detected via the handle_connections_sockets() function. This function enters a loop that waits until the variable abort_loop is set to TRUE. Table 3-2 shows the location of the files that manage the connection and threads.

Table 3-2. *Connections and Thread Management*

Source File	Description
/sql/net_serv.cc	Contains all of the network communications functions. Look here for information on how to communicate with the client or server via the network.
/include/mysql_com.h	Contains most of the structures used in communications.
/sql/sql_parse.cc	Contains the majority of the query routing and parsing functions except for the lexical parser.
/sql/mysqld.cc	Besides the mysqld_main and server startup functions, this file also contains the methods for creating threads.

Listing 3-2 offers a condensed view of the connection-handling code. When a connection is detected (I've hidden that part of the code, because it isn't helpful in learning how the system works), the function creates a new thread calling the aptly named create_new_thread() function. It is in this function that the first of the major structures is created. The THD class is responsible for maintaining all of the information for the thread. Although not allocated to the thread in a private memory space, the THD class allows the system to control the thread during execution. I'll expose some of the THD class in a later section.

Listing 3-2. The Handle-Connection-Sockets Functions

```
void handle_connections_sockets()
{

  ...

  DBUG_PRINT("general",("Waiting for connections."));

  ...

  while (!abort_loop)
  {

  ...

    /*
    ** Don't allow too many connections
    */

    if (!(thd= new THD))

  ...

    create_new_thread(thd);
  }

  ...
}
```

OK, the client has connected to the server. What happens next? Let's see what happens inside the `create_new_thread()` function. Listing 3-3 shows a condensed view of that function. The first thing you see is the mutex call to lock the thread count. As you saw in the `mysqld_main()` function, this is necessary to keep other threads from potentially competing for write access to the variable. When the thread is created, the associated unlock mutex call is made to unlock the resource.

Listing 3-3. The create_new_thread() Function

```
static void create_new_thread(THD *thd)
{

...

  /*
    Don't allow too many connections. We roughly check here that we allow
    only (max_connections + 1) connections.
  */
  mysql_mutex_lock(&LOCK_connection_count);
  if (connection_count >= max_connections + 1 || abort_loop)
  {
    mysql_mutex_unlock(&LOCK_connection_count);
...
```

```
        close_connection(thd, ER_CON_COUNT_ERROR);
        delete thd;
...
  }

  ++connection_count;

  if (connection_count > max_used_connections)
     max_used_connections= connection_count;
  mysql_mutex_unlock(&LOCK_connection_count);
  /* Start a new thread to handle connection. */
  mysql_mutex_lock(&LOCK_thread_count);
...

  thd->thread_id= thd->variables.pseudo_thread_id= thread_id++;
  MYSQL_CALLBACK(thread_scheduler, add_connection, (thd));
...

}
```

A very interesting thing occurs early in the function. Notice the MYSQL_CALLBACK() macro. The macro is designed to reuse a thread that may be residing in the connection pool. This helps speed things up a bit, because creating threads, while faster than creating processes, can take some time. Having a thread ready to go is a sort of caching mechanism for connections. The saving of threads for later use is called a *connection pool*.

If there isn't a connection (thread) ready for to reuse, the system creates one with the pthread_create() function call. Something really strange happens here. Notice the third parameter for this function call. What seems like a variable is actually the starting address of a function (a function pointer). pthread_create() uses this function pointer to associate the location in the server where execution should begin for the thread.

Now that the query has been sent from the client to the server and a thread has been created to manage the execution, control passes to the do_handle_one_connection() function. Listing 3-4 shows a condensed view of the do_handle_one_connection() function. In this view, I have commented out a large section of the code that deals with initializing the THD class for use. If you're interested, take a look at the code more closely later (located in /sql/ sql_connect.cc). For now, let's look at the essential work that goes on inside this function.

Listing 3-4. The do_handle_one_connection() Function

```
void do_handle_one_connection(THD *thd_arg)
{
  THD *thd= thd_arg;

...

    while (thd_is_connection_alive(thd))
    {
      mysql_audit_release(thd);
      if (do_command(thd))
        break;
    }
    end_connection(thd);

...

}
```

In this case, the only function call of interest for our exploration is the do_command(thd) function. It is inside a loop that is looping once for each command read from the networking-communications code. Although somewhat of a mystery at this point, this is of interest to those of us who have entered stacked SQL commands (more than one command on the same line). As you see here, this is where MySQL handles that eventuality. For each command read, the function passes control to the function that begins reads in the query from the network.

It is at this point that the system reads the query from the network and places it in the THD class for parsing. This takes place in the do_command() function. Listing 3-5 shows a condensed view of the do_command() function. I left some of the more interesting comments and code bits in to demonstrate the robustness of the MySQL source code.

Listing 3-5. The do_command() Function

```
bool do_command(THD *thd)
{
  bool return_value;
  char *packet = 0;
  ulong packet_length;
  NET *net= &thd->net;
  enum enum_server_command command;

...

  net_new_transaction(net);

...

  packet_length= my_net_read(net);

...

  if (packet_length == packet_error)
  {
    DBUG_PRINT("info",("Got error %d reading command from socket %s",
                       net->error,
                       vio_description(net->vio)));

...

  command= (enum enum_server_command) (uchar) packet[0];

  if (command >= COM_END)
    command= COM_END;                            // Wrong command

  DBUG_PRINT("info",("Command on %s = %d (%s)",
                     vio_description(net->vio), command,
                     command_name[command].str));

...

  my_net_set_read_timeout(net, thd->variables.net_read_timeout);

  DBUG_ASSERT(packet_length);
```

```
    return_value= dispatch_command(command, thd, packet+1,
                                   (uint) (packet_length-1));

    ...

}
```

The first thing to notice is the creation of a packet buffer and a NET structure. This packet buffer is a character array and stores the raw query string as it is read from the network and stored in the NET structure. The next item that is created is a command structure, which will be used to route control to the appropriate parser functions. The my_net_read() function reads the packets from the network and stores them in the NET structure. The length of the packet is also stored in the packet_length variable of the NET structure. The last thing you see occurring in this function is a call to dispatch_command(), the point at which you can begin to see how commands are routed through the server code.

OK, you're starting to get somewhere. The job of the dispatch_command() function is to route control to a portion of the server that can best process the incoming command. Since you have a normal SELECT query on the way, the system has identified it as a query by setting the command variable to COM_QUERY. Other command types are used to identify statements, change user, generate statistics, and many other server functions. For this chapter, I will only look at query commands (COM_QUERY). Listing 3-6 shows a condensed view of the function. I have omitted the code for all of the other commands in the switch for the sake of brevity (I'm omitting the comment break too) but I'm leaving in the case statements for most of the commands. Take a moment and scan through the list. Most of the names are self-explanatory. If you were to conduct this exploration for another type of query, you could find your way by looking in this function for the type identified and following the code along in that case statement. I have also included the large function comment block that appears before the function code. Take a moment to look at that. I'll be getting more into that later in this chapter.

Listing 3-6. The dispatch_command() Function

```
/**
  Perform one connection-level (COM_XXXX) command.

  @param command          type of command to perform
  @param thd              connection handle
  @param packet           data for the command, packet is always null-terminated
  @param packet_length    length of packet + 1 (to show that data is
                          null-terminated) except for COM_SLEEP, where it
                          can be zero.

  ...

  @retval
    0   ok
  @retval
    1   request of thread shutdown, i. e. if command is
        COM_QUIT/COM_SHUTDOWN
*/
bool dispatch_command(enum enum_server_command command, THD *thd,
                      char* packet, uint packet_length)
{
```

```
...
switch (command) {
  case COM_INIT_DB:
  ...
  case COM_REGISTER_SLAVE:
  ...
  case COM_TABLE_DUMP:
  ...
  case COM_CHANGE_USER:
  ...
  case COM_STMT_EXECUTE:
  ...
  case COM_STMT_FETCH:
  ...
  case COM_STMT_SEND_LONG_DATA:
  ...
  case COM_STMT_PREPARE:
  ...
  case COM_STMT_CLOSE:
  ...
  case COM_STMT_RESET:
  ...
  case COM_QUERY:
  {
    if (alloc_query(thd, packet, packet_length))
      break;          // fatal error is set

  ...

    if (opt_log_raw)
      general_log_write(thd, command, thd->query(), thd->query_length());

  ...

    mysql_parse(thd, thd->query(), thd->query_length(), &parser_state);

  ...
  }
  case COM_FIELD_LIST:        // This isn't actually needed
  ...
  case COM_QUIT:
  ...
  case COM_BINLOG_DUMP_GTID;
  ...
  case COM_BINLOG_DUMP:
  ...
  case COM_REFRESH:
  ...
  case COM_SHUTDOWN:
  ...
```

```
      case COM_STATISTICS:
      ...
      case COM_PING:
      ...
      case COM_PROCESS_INFO:
      ...
      case COM_PROCESS_KILL:
      ...
      case COM_SET_OPTION:
      ...
      case COM_DEBUG:
      ...
      case COM_SLEEP:
      ...
      case COM_DELAYED_INSERT:
      ...
      case COM_CONNECT;
      case COM_TIME;
      ...
      case COM_END:
      ...
      default:
      ...
}
```

The first thing that happens when control passes to the COM_QUERY handler is that the query is copied from the packet array to the thd->query member variable via the alloc_query() function. In this way, the thread now has a copy of the query, which will stay with it all through its execution. Notice also that the code writes the command to the general log. This will help with debugging system problems and query issues later on. The last function call of interest in Listing 3-6 is the mysql_parse() function call. At this point, the code can officially transfer from the SQL Interface subsystem to the Query Parser subsystem. As you can see, this distinction is one of semantics rather than syntax.

Parsing the Query

Finally, the parsing begins. This is the heart of what goes on inside the server when it processes a query. The parser code, like so much of the rest of the system, is located in a couple of places. It isn't that hard to follow if you realize that while it is highly organized, the code is not structured to match the architecture.

The function you're examining now is the mysql_parse() function (located in /sql/sql_parse.cc). Its job is to check the query cache for the results of a previously executed query that has the same result set, then pass control to the lexical parser (parse_sql()), and finally, route the command to the query optimizer. Listing 3-7 shows a condensed view of the mysql_parse() function.

Listing 3-7. The mysql_parse() Function

```
/**
  Parse a query.

  @param         thd     Current thread
  @param         rawbuf  Begining of the query text
  @param         length  Length of the query text
  @param[out]    found_semicolon For multi queries, position of the character of
```

```
                            the next query in the query text.
*/

void mysql_parse(THD *thd, char *rawbuf, uint length,
                 Parser_state *parser_state)
{
  int error __attribute__((unused));

  ...

  if (query_cache_send_result_to_client(thd, rawbuf, length) <= 0)
  {
    LEX *lex= thd->lex;

  ...

    bool err= parse_sql(thd, parser_state, NULL);

  ...

      error= mysql_execute_command(thd);

  ...

    }

  ...

  }
  else
  {
    /*
      Query cache hit. We need to write the general log here.
      Right now, we only cache SELECT results; if the cache ever
      becomes more generic, we should also cache the rewritten
      query string together with the original query string (which
      we'd still use for the matching) when we first execute the
      query, and then use the obfuscated query string for logging
      here when the query is given again.
    */
    thd->m_statement_psi= MYSQL_REFINE_STATEMENT(thd->m_statement_psi,
                                        sql_statement_info[SQLCOM_SELECT].m_key);
    if (!opt_log_raw)
      general_log_write(thd, COM_QUERY, thd->query(), thd->query_length());
    parser_state->m_lip.found_semicolon= NULL;
  }
  ...
}
```

The first thing to notice is the call to check the query cache. The query cache stores all the most frequently requested queries, complete with the results. If the query is already in the query cache, we skip to the else and you're done! All that is left is to return the results to the client. No parsing, optimizing, or even executing is necessary. How cool is that?

For the sake of our exploration, let's assume the query cache does not contain a copy of the example query. In this case, the function creates a new LEX structure to contain the internal representation of the query. This structure is filled out by the Lex/YACC parser, shown in Listing 3-8. This code is in the sql/sql_yacc.yy.

Listing 3-8. The SELECT Lex/YACC Parsing Code Excerpt

```
/*
  Select : retrieve data from table
*/

select:
          select_init
          {
            LEX *lex= Lex;
            lex->sql_command= SQLCOM_SELECT;
          }
        ;

/* Need select_init2 for subselects. */
select_init:
          SELECT_SYM select_init2
        | '(' select_paren ')' union_opt
        ;

select_paren:
          SELECT_SYM select_part2
          {
            if (setup_select_in_parentheses(Lex))
              MYSQL_YYABORT;
          }
        | '(' select_paren ')'
        ;

/* The equivalent of select_paren for nested queries. */
select_paren_derived:
          SELECT_SYM select_part2_derived
          {
            if (setup_select_in_parentheses(Lex))
              MYSQL_YYABORT;
          }
        | '(' select_paren_derived ')'
        ;

select_init2:
```

```
            select_part2
            {
              LEX *lex= Lex;
              SELECT_LEX * sel= lex->current_select;
              if (lex->current_select->set_braces(0))
              {
                my_parse_error(ER(ER_SYNTAX_ERROR));
                MYSQL_YYABORT;
              }
              if (sel->linkage == UNION_TYPE &&
                  sel->master_unit()->first_select()->braces)
              {
                my_parse_error(ER(ER_SYNTAX_ERROR));
                MYSQL_YYABORT;
              }
            }
            union_clause
          ;

select_part2:
            {
              LEX *lex= Lex;
              SELECT_LEX *sel= lex->current_select;
              if (sel->linkage != UNION_TYPE)
                mysql_init_select(lex);
              lex->current_select->parsing_place= SELECT_LIST;
            }
            select_options select_item_list
            {
              Select->parsing_place= NO_MATTER;
            }
            select_into select_lock_type
          ;

select_into:
            opt_order_clause opt_limit_clause {}
          | into
          | select_from
          | into select_from
          | select_from into
          ;

select_from:
            FROM join_table_list where_clause group_clause having_clause
            opt_order_clause opt_limit_clause procedure_analyse_clause
            {
              Select->context.table_list=
                Select->context.first_name_resolution_table=
                  Select->table_list.first;
            }
          | FROM DUAL_SYM where_clause opt_limit_clause
```

```
            /* oracle compatibility: oracle always requires FROM clause,
               and DUAL is system table without fields.
               Is "SELECT 1 FROM DUAL" any better than "SELECT 1" ?
            Hmmm :) */
        ;

select_options:
          /* empty*/
        | select_option_list
          {
            if (Select->options & SELECT_DISTINCT && Select->options & SELECT_ALL)
            {
              my_error(ER_WRONG_USAGE, MYF(0), "ALL", "DISTINCT");
              MYSQL_YYABORT;
            }
          }
        ;

select_option_list:
          select_option_list select_option
        | select_option
        ;

select_option:
          query_expression_option
        | SQL_NO_CACHE_SYM
          {
            /*
              Allow this flag only on the first top-level SELECT statement, if
              SQL_CACHE wasn't specified, and only once per query.
            */
            if (Lex->current_select != &Lex->select_lex)
            {
              my_error(ER_CANT_USE_OPTION_HERE, MYF(0), "SQL_NO_CACHE");
              MYSQL_YYABORT;
            }
            else if (Lex->select_lex.sql_cache == SELECT_LEX::SQL_CACHE)
            {
              my_error(ER_WRONG_USAGE, MYF(0), "SQL_CACHE", "SQL_NO_CACHE");
              MYSQL_YYABORT;
            }
            else if (Lex->select_lex.sql_cache == SELECT_LEX::SQL_NO_CACHE)
            {
              my_error(ER_DUP_ARGUMENT, MYF(0), "SQL_NO_CACHE");
              MYSQL_YYABORT;
            }
            else
            {
              Lex->safe_to_cache_query=0;
              Lex->select_lex.options&= ~OPTION_TO_QUERY_CACHE;
              Lex->select_lex.sql_cache= SELECT_LEX::SQL_NO_CACHE;
```

```
          }
        }
      | SQL_CACHE_SYM
        {
          /*
            Allow this flag only on the first top-level SELECT statement, if
            SQL_NO_CACHE wasn't specified, and only once per query.
          */
          if (Lex->current_select != &Lex->select_lex)
          {
            my_error(ER_CANT_USE_OPTION_HERE, MYF(0), "SQL_CACHE");
            MYSQL_YYABORT;
          }
          else if (Lex->select_lex.sql_cache == SELECT_LEX::SQL_NO_CACHE)
          {
            my_error(ER_WRONG_USAGE, MYF(0), "SQL_NO_CACHE", "SQL_CACHE");
            MYSQL_YYABORT;
          }
          else if (Lex->select_lex.sql_cache == SELECT_LEX::SQL_CACHE)
          {
            my_error(ER_DUP_ARGUMENT, MYF(0), "SQL_CACHE");
            MYSQL_YYABORT;
          }
          else
          {
            Lex->safe_to_cache_query=1;
            Lex->select_lex.options|= OPTION_TO_QUERY_CACHE;
            Lex->select_lex.sql_cache= SELECT_LEX::SQL_CACHE;
          }
        }
      ;

select_lock_type:
        /* empty */
      | FOR_SYM UPDATE_SYM
        {
          LEX *lex=Lex;
          lex->current_select->set_lock_for_tables(TL_WRITE);
          lex->safe_to_cache_query=0;
        }
      | LOCK_SYM IN_SYM SHARE_SYM MODE_SYM
        {
          LEX *lex=Lex;
          lex->current_select->
            set_lock_for_tables(TL_READ_WITH_SHARED_LOCKS);
          lex->safe_to_cache_query=0;
        }
      ;

select_item_list:
```

```
        select_item_list ',' select_item
      | select_item
      | '*'
        {
          THD *thd= YYTHD;
          Item *item= new (thd->mem_root)
                        Item_field(&thd->lex->current_select->context,
                                    NULL, NULL, "*");
          if (item == NULL)
            MYSQL_YYABORT;
          if (add_item_to_list(thd, item))
            MYSQL_YYABORT;
          (thd->lex->current_select->with_wild)++;
        }
      ;

select_item:
        remember_name table_wild remember_end
        {
          THD *thd= YYTHD;

          if (add_item_to_list(thd, $2))
            MYSQL_YYABORT;
        }
      | remember_name expr remember_end select_alias
        {
          THD *thd= YYTHD;
          DBUG_ASSERT($1 < $3);

          if (add_item_to_list(thd, $2))
            MYSQL_YYABORT;
          if ($4.str)
          {
            if (Lex->sql_command == SQLCOM_CREATE_VIEW &&
                check_column_name($4.str))
            {
              my_error(ER_WRONG_COLUMN_NAME, MYF(0), $4.str);
              MYSQL_YYABORT;
            }
            $2->item_name.copy($4.str, $4.length, system_charset_info, false);
          }
          else if (!$2->item_name.is_set())
          {
            $2->item_name.copy($1, (uint) ($3 - $1), thd->charset());
          }
        }
      ;
```

I have included an excerpt from the Lex/YACC parser that shows how the SELECT token is identified and passed through the YACC code to be parsed. To read this code (in case you don't know Lex or YACC), watch for the keywords (or tokens) in the code (they are located flush left with a colon, such as select:). These keywords are used to direct flow of the parser. The placement of tokens to the right of these keywords defines the order of what must occur in order for the query to be parsed. For example, look at the select: keyword. To the right of that, you will see a select_init2 keyword, which isn't very informative. If you look down through the code, however, you will see the select_init: keyword on the left. This allows the Lex/YACC author to specify certain behaviors in a sort of macro-like form. Also, notice that there are curly braces under the select_init keyword. This is where the parser does its work of dividing the query into parts and placing the items in the LEX structure. Direct symbols, such as SELECT, are defined in a header file (/sql/lex.h) and appear in the parser as SELECT_SYM. Take a few moments now to skim through the code. You may want to run through this several times. It can be confusing if you haven't studied compiler construction or text parsing.

If you're thinking, "What a monster," then you can rest assured that you're normal. The Lex/YACC code is a challenge for most developers. I've highlighted a few of the important code statements that should help explain how the code works. Let's go through it. I've repeated the example SELECT statement again here for convenience:

```
SELECT lname, fname, DOB FROM Employees WHERE Employees.department = 'EGR'
```

Look at the first keyword again. Notice how the select_init code block sets the LEX structure's sql_command to SQLCOM_SELECT. This is important, because the next function in the query path uses this in a large switch statement to further control the flow of the query through the server. The example SELECT statement has three fields in the field list. Let's try and find them in the parser code. Look for the add_item_to_list() function call. That is where the parser detects the fields and places them in the LEX structure. You will also see a few lines up from that call the parser code that identifies the * option for the field list. Now you've got the sql_command member variable set and the fields identified. So where does the FROM clause get detected? Look for the code statement that begins with FROM join_table_list where_clause. This code is the part of the parser that identifies the FROM and WHERE clause (and others). The code for the parser that processes these clauses is not included in Listing 3-8, but I think you get the idea. If you open the sql_yacc.yy source file (located in /sql), you should now be able to find all those statements and see how the rest of the LEX structure is filled in with the table list in the FROM clause and the expression in the WHERE clause.

I hope that this tour of the parser code has helped mitigate the shock and horror that usually accompanies examining this part of the MySQL system. I return to this part of the system later on when I demonstrate how to add your own commands the MySQL SQL lexicon (see Chapter 8 for more details). Table 3-3 lists the source files associated with the MySQL parser.

Table 3-3. *The MySQL Parser*

Source File	Description
/sql/lex.h	The symbol table for all of the keywords and tokens supported by the parser
/sql/lex_symbol.h	Type definitions for the symbol table
/sql/sql_lex.h	Definition of LEX structure
/sql/sql_lex.cc	Definition of Lex classes
/sql/sql_yacc.yy	The Lex/YACC parser code
/sql/sql_parse.cc	Contains the majority of the query routing and parsing functions except for the lexical parser

■ **Caution** Do not edit the files sql_yacc.cc, sql_yacc.h, or lex_hash.h. These files are generated by other utilities. See Chapter 7 for more details.

Preparing the Query for Optimization

Although the boundary delineating where the parser ends and the optimizer begins is not clear from the MySQL documentation (there are contradictions), it is clear from the definition of the optimizer that the routing and control parts of the source code can be considered part of the optimizer. To avoid confusion, I am going to call the next set of functions the *preparatory* stage of the optimizer.

The first of these preparatory functions is the mysql_execute_command() function (located in /sql/sql_parse.cc). The name leads you to believe that you are actually executing the query, but that isn't the case. This function performs much of the setup steps necessary to optimize the query. The LEX structure is copied, and several variables are set to help the query optimization and later execution. You can see some of these operations in a condensed view of the function shown in Listing 3-9.

Listing 3-9. The mysql_execute_command() Function

```
/**
  Execute command saved in thd and lex->sql_command.

  @param thd                     Thread handle

  ...

  @retval
    FALSE       OK
  @retval
    TRUE        Error
*/

int
mysql_execute_command(THD *thd)
{
  int res= FALSE;
  int  up_result= 0;
  LEX  *lex= thd->lex;
  /* first SELECT_LEX (have special meaning for many of non-SELECTcommands) */
  SELECT_LEX *select_lex= &lex->select_lex;
  /* first table of first SELECT_LEX */
  TABLE_LIST *first_table= select_lex->table_list.first;
  /* list of all tables in query */
  TABLE_LIST *all_tables;
  /* most outer SELECT_LEX_UNIT of query */
  SELECT_LEX_UNIT *unit= &lex->unit;
#ifdef HAVE_REPLICATION
  /* have table map for update for multi-update statement (BUG#37051) */
  bool have_table_map_for_update= FALSE;
#endif
  DBUG_ENTER("mysql_execute_command");

  ...

  switch (lex->sql_command) {
```

...

```
  case SQLCOM_SHOW_STATUS_PROC:
  case SQLCOM_SHOW_STATUS_FUNC:
  case SQLCOM_SHOW_DATABASES:
  case SQLCOM_SHOW_TABLES:
  case SQLCOM_SHOW_TRIGGERS:
  case SQLCOM_SHOW_TABLE_STATUS:
  case SQLCOM_SHOW_OPEN_TABLES:
  case SQLCOM_SHOW_PLUGINS:
  case SQLCOM_SHOW_FIELDS:
  case SQLCOM_SHOW_KEYS:
  case SQLCOM_SHOW_VARIABLES:
  case SQLCOM_SHOW_CHARSETS:
  case SQLCOM_SHOW_COLLATIONS:
  case SQLCOM_SHOW_STORAGE_ENGINES:
  case SQLCOM_SHOW_PROFILE:
  case SQLCOM_SELECT:
  {
    thd->status_var.last_query_cost= 0.0;
    thd->status_var.last_query_partial_plans= 0;

    if ((res= select_precheck(thd, lex, all_tables, first_table)))
      break;

    res= execute_sqlcom_select(thd, all_tables);
    break;
  }
```

...

A number of interesting things happen in this function. You will notice another switch statement that has as its cases the SQLCOM keywords. In the case of the example query, you saw the parser set the lex->sql_command member variable to SQLCOM_SELECT. I have included a condensed view of that case statement for you in Listing 3-9. What I did not include are the many other SQLCOM case statements. This is a very large function. Since it is the central routing function for query processing, it contains a case for every possible command. Consequently, the source code is tens of pages long.

Let's see what this case statement does. Notice the select_precheck() method call. This method executes the privilege checking to see if the user can execute the command using the list of tables to verify access. If the user has access, processing continues to the execute_sqlcom_select() method, as shown in listing 3-10. I leave the part of the code concerning the DESCRIBE (EXPLAIN) command for you to examine and figure out how it works.

Listing 3-10. The execute_sqlcom_command() Function

```
static bool execute_sqlcom_select(THD *thd, TABLE_LIST *all_tables)
{
  LEX    *lex= thd->lex;
  select_result *result= lex->result;
  bool res;
  /* assign global limit variable if limit is not given */
  {
```

```
    SELECT_LEX *param= lex->unit.global_parameters;
    if (!param->explicit_limit)
      param->select_limit=
        new Item_int((ulonglong) thd->variables.select_limit);
  }
  if (!(res= open_and_lock_tables(thd, all_tables, 0)))
  {
    if (lex->describe)
    {
      /*
        We always use select_send for EXPLAIN, even if it's an EXPLAIN
        for SELECT ... INTO OUTFILE: a user application should be able
        to prepend EXPLAIN to any query and receive output for it,
        even if the query itself redirects the output.
      */
      if (!(result= new select_send()))
        return 1;                              /* purecov: inspected */
      res= explain_query_expression(thd, result);
      delete result;
    }
    else
    {
      if (!result && !(result= new select_send()))
        return 1;                              /* purecov: inspected */
      select_result *save_result= result;
      select_result *analyse_result= NULL;
      if (lex->proc_analyse)
      {
        if ((result= analyse_result=
                new select_analyse(result, lex->proc_analyse)) == NULL)
          return true;
      }
      res= handle_select(thd, result, 0);
      delete analyse_result;
      if (save_result != lex->result)
        delete save_result;
    }
  }
  return res;
}
```

■ **Note** Once when I was modifying the code, I needed to find all the locations of the EXPLAIN calls so that I could alter them for a specific need. I looked everywhere until I found them in the parser. There, in the middle of the Lex/YACC code, was a comment that said something to the effect that DESCRIBE was left over from an earlier Oracle compatibility issue and that the correct term was EXPLAIN. Comments are useful, if you can find them.

The next interesting function call is one to handle_select(). You may be thinking, "Didn't we just do the handle thing?" The handle_select() is a wrapper for another function, mysql_select(). Listing 3-11 shows the complete code for the handle_select() function. Near the top of the listing is the select_lex->next_select() operation, which is checking for the UNION command that appends multiple SELECT results into a single set of results. Other than that, the code just calls the next function in the chain, mysql_select(). It is at this point that you are finally close enough to transition to the query optimizer subsystem. Table 3-4 lists the source files associated with the query optimizer.

■ **Note**   This is perhaps the part of the code that suffers most from ill-defined subsystems. While the code is still very organized, the boundaries of the subsystems are fuzzy at this point in the source code.

Listing 3-11. The handle_select() Function

```
bool handle_select(THD *thd, select_result *result,
                   ulong setup_tables_done_option)
{
  bool res;
  LEX *lex= thd->lex;
  register SELECT_LEX *select_lex = &lex->select_lex;
  DBUG_ENTER("handle_select");
  MYSQL_SELECT_START(thd->query());

  if (lex->proc_analyse && lex->sql_command != SQLCOM_SELECT)
  {
    my_error(ER_WRONG_USAGE, MYF(0), "PROCEDURE", "non-SELECT");
    DBUG_RETURN(true);
  }

  if (select_lex->master_unit()->is_union() ||
      select_lex->master_unit()->fake_select_lex)
    res= mysql_union(thd, lex, result, &lex->unit, setup_tables_done_option);
  else
  {
    SELECT_LEX_UNIT *unit= &lex->unit;
    unit->set_limit(unit->global_parameters);
    /*
       'options' of mysql_select will be set in JOIN, as far as JOIN for
       every PS/SP execution new, we will not need reset this flag if
       setup_tables_done_option changed for next rexecution
    */
    res= mysql_select(thd,
                      select_lex->table_list.first,
                      select_lex->with_wild, select_lex->item_list,
                      select_lex->where,
                      &select_lex->order_list,
                      &select_lex->group_list,
                      select_lex->having,
                      select_lex->options | thd->variables.option_bits |
                      setup_tables_done_option,
                      result, unit, select_lex);
  }
```

```
DBUG_PRINT("info",("res: %d  report_error: %d", res,
                   thd->is_error()));
res|= thd->is_error();
if (unlikely(res))
  result->abort_result_set();

MYSQL_SELECT_DONE((int) res, (ulong) thd->limit_found_rows);
DBUG_RETURN(res);
}
```

Table 3-4. *The Query Optimizer*

Source File	Description
/sql/sql_parse.cc	The majority of the parser code resides in this file
/sql/sql_select.cc	Contains some of the optimization functions and the implementation of the select functions
/sql/sql_prepare.cc	Contains the preparation methods for the optimizer.
/sql/sql_executor.cc	Contains the execution methods for the optimizer.

Optimizing the Query

At last! You're at the optimizer. You won't find it if you go looking for a source file or class by that name, however. Although the JOIN class contains a method called optimize(), the optimizer is actually a collection of flow control and subfunctions designed to find the shortest path to executing the query. What happened to the fancy algorithms and query paths and compiled queries? Recall from our architecture discussion in Chapter 2 that the MySQL query optimizer is a nontraditional hybrid optimizer utilizing a combination of known best practices and cost-based path selection. It is at this point in the code that the best-practices part kicks in.

An example of one of those best practices is standardizing the parameters in the WHERE clause expressions. The example query uses a WHERE clause with an expression, Employees.department = 'EGR', but the clause could have been written as 'EGR' = Employees.department and still be correct (it returns the same results). This is an example of where a traditional cost-based optimizer could generate multiple plans—one for each of the expression variants. Just a few examples of the many best practices that MySQL uses are:

> *Constant propagation*—The removal of transitive conjunctions using constants. For example, if you have a=b='c', the transitive law states that a='c'. This optimization removes those inner equalities, thereby reducing the number of evaluations. For example, the SQL command SELECT * FROM table1 WHERE column1 = 12 AND NOT (column3 = 17 OR column2 = column1) would be reduced to SELECT * FROM table1 WHERE column1 = 12 AND column3 <> 17 AND column2 <> 12.

> *Dead code elimination*—The removal of always-true conditions. For example, if you have a=b AND 1=1, the AND 1=1 condition is removed. The same occurs for always- false conditions in which the false expression can be removed without affecting the rest of the clause. For example, the SQL command SELECT * FROM table1 WHERE column1 = 12 AND column2 = 13 AND column1 < column2 would be reduced to SELECT * FROM table1 WHERE column1 = 12 AND column2 = 13.

Range queries—The transformation of the IN clause to a list of disjunctions. For example, if you have an IN (1,2,3), the transformation would be a = 1 or a = 2 or a = 3. This helps simplify the evaluation of the expressions. For example, the SQL command SELECT * FROM table1 WHERE column1 = 12 OR column1 = 17 OR column1 = 21 would be reduced to SELECT * FROM table1 WHERE column1 IN (12, 17, 21).

I hope this small set of examples has given you a glimpse into the inner workings of one of the world's most successful nontraditional query optimizers. In short, it works really well for a surprising amount of queries.

Well, I spoke too fast. There isn't much going on in the mysql_select() function in the area of optimization, either. It seems the mysql_select() function just locks tables then calls the mysql_execute_select() function. Once again, you are at another fuzzy boundary. Listing 3-12 shows an excerpt of the mysql_select() function.

Listing 3-12. The mysql_select() Function

```
/**
  An entry point to single-unit select (a select without UNION).

  @param thd              thread handler
  @param tables           list of all tables used in this query.
                          The tables have been pre-opened.
  @param wild_num         number of wildcards used in the top level
                          select of this query.
                          For example statement
                          SELECT *, t1.*, catalog.t2.* FROM t0, t1, t2;
                          has 3 wildcards.
  @param fields           list of items in SELECT list of the top-level
                          select
                          e.g. SELECT a, b, c FROM t1 will have Item_field
                          for a, b and c in this list.
  @param conds            top level item of an expression representing
                          WHERE clause of the top level select
  @param order            linked list of ORDER BY agruments
  @param group            linked list of GROUP BY arguments
  @param having           top level item of HAVING expression
  @param select_options   select options (BIG_RESULT, etc)
  @param result           an instance of result set handling class.
                          This object is responsible for send result
                          set rows to the client or inserting them
                          into a table.
  @param unit             top-level UNIT of this query
                          UNIT is an artificial object created by the
                          parser for every SELECT clause.
                          e.g.
                          SELECT * FROM t1 WHERE a1 IN (SELECT * FROM t2)
                          has 2 unions.
  @param select_lex       the only SELECT_LEX of this query

  @retval
    false   success
  @retval
    true    an error
*/
```

```
bool
mysql_select(THD *thd,
             TABLE_LIST *tables, uint wild_num, List<Item> &fields,
             Item *conds, SQL_I_List<ORDER> *order, SQL_I_List<ORDER> *group,
             Item *having, ulonglong select_options,
             select_result *result, SELECT_LEX_UNIT *unit,
             SELECT_LEX *select_lex)
{
  bool free_join= true;
  uint og_num= 0;
  ORDER *first_order= NULL;
  ORDER *first_group= NULL;
  DBUG_ENTER("mysql_select");

  if (order)
  {
    og_num= order->elements;
    first_order= order->first;
  }
  if (group)
  {
    og_num+= group->elements;
    first_group= group->first;
  }

  if (mysql_prepare_select(thd, tables, wild_num, fields,
                           conds, og_num, first_order, first_group, having,
                           select_options, result, unit,
                           select_lex, &free_join))
  {
    if (free_join)
    {
      THD_STAGE_INFO(thd, stage_end);
      (void) select_lex->cleanup();
    }
    DBUG_RETURN(true);
  }

  if (! thd->lex->is_query_tables_locked())
  {
    /*
      If tables are not locked at this point, it means that we have delayed
      this step until after the prepare stage (i.e. this moment). This allows us to
      do better partition pruning and avoid locking unused partitions.
      As a consequence, in such a case, the prepare stage can rely only on
      metadata about tables used and not data from them.
      We need to lock tables now in order to proceed with the remaining
      stages of query optimization and execution.
    */
```

```
  if (lock_tables(thd, thd->lex->query_tables, thd->lex->table_count, 0))
  {
    if (free_join)
    {
      THD_STAGE_INFO(thd, stage_end);
      (void) select_lex->cleanup();
    }
    DBUG_RETURN(true);
  }

  /*
    Only register query in cache if it tables were locked above.

    Tables must be locked before storing the query in the query cache.
    Transactional engines must have been signalled that the statement started,
    which external_lock signals.
  */
  query_cache_store_query(thd, thd->lex->query_tables);
}

DBUG_RETURN(mysql_execute_select(thd, select_lex, free_join));
}
```

Where are all of those best practices? They are in the JOIN class! A detailed examination of the optimizer source code in the JOIN class would take more pages than this entire book to present in any meaningful depth. Suffice it to say that the optimizer is complex, and it is also difficult to examine. Fortunately, few will ever need to venture that far down into the bowels of MySQL. You're welcome to do so, however! I will focus on a higher-level review of the optimizer from the mysql_execute_select() function.

The next major function call in this function is the join->exec() method. First, though, let's take a look at what happens in the mysql_execute_select() method in Listing 3-13.

Listing 3-13. The mysql_execute_select() Function

```
/**
  Execute stage of mysql_select.

  @param thd                 thread handler
  @param select_lex          the only SELECT_LEX of this query
  @param free_join           if join should be freed

  @return Operation status
    @retval false  success
    @retval true   an error

  @note tables must be opened and locked before calling mysql_execute_select.
*/

static bool
mysql_execute_select(THD *thd, SELECT_LEX *select_lex, bool free_join)
{
  bool err;
  JOIN* join= select_lex->join;
```

```
  DBUG_ENTER("mysql_execute_select");
  DBUG_ASSERT(join);

  if ((err= join->optimize()))
  {
    goto err;                              // 1
  }

  if (thd->is_error())
    goto err;

  if (join->select_options & SELECT_DESCRIBE)
  {
    join->explain();
    free_join= false;
  }
  else
    join->exec();

err:
  if (free_join)
  {
    THD_STAGE_INFO(thd, stage_end);
    err|= select_lex->cleanup();
    DBUG_RETURN(err || thd->is_error());
  }
  DBUG_RETURN(join->error);
}
```

Now we can see entry to the optimizer code in the mysql_execute_select() function. We see a reference to an existing JOIN class that was created in the prepare methods. A little farther down in the code, we see the method we've expected—the optimize() call. Shortly after that, we see the exec() method that executes the query via the JOIN class. Table 3-5 lists the more-important source files associated with query optimization.

Table 3-5. *Query Optimization*

Source File	Description
/sql/abstract_query_plan.cc	Implements an abstract-query-plan interface for examining certain aspects of query plans without accessing mysqld internal classes (JOIN_TAB, SQL_SELECT, etc.) directly.
/sql/sql_optimizer.cc	Contains the optimizer-core functionality
/sql/sql_planner.cc	Contains classes to assist the optimizer in determining table order for retrieving rows for joins.
/sql/sql_select.h	The definitions for the structures used in the select functions to support the SELECT commands
/sql/sql_select.cc	Contains some of the optimization functions and the implementation of the select functions
/sql/sql_union.cc	Code for performing UNION operations.

Executing the Query

In the same way as the optimizer, the query execution uses a set of best practices for executing the query. For example, the query execution subsystem detects special clauses, such as ORDER BY and DISTINCT, and routes control of these operations to methods designed for fast sorting and tuple elimination.

Most of this activity occurs in the methods of the JOIN class. Listing 3-14 presents a condensed view of the join::exec() method. Notice that there is yet another function call to a function called by some name that includes select. Sure enough, there is another call that needs to be made to a function called do_select(). Take a look at the parameters for this function call. You are now starting to see things such as field lists. Does this mean you're getting close to reading data? Yes, it does. In fact, the do_select() function is a high-level wrapper for exactly that.

Listing 3-14. The join::exec() Function

```
void
JOIN::exec()
{
  Opt_trace_context * const trace= &thd->opt_trace;
  Opt_trace_object trace_wrapper(trace);
  Opt_trace_object trace_exec(trace, "join_execution");
  trace_exec.add_select_number(select_lex->select_number);
  Opt_trace_array trace_steps(trace, "steps");
  List<Item> *columns_list= &fields_list;
  DBUG_ENTER("JOIN::exec");

...

  THD_STAGE_INFO(thd, stage_sending_data);
  DBUG_PRINT("info", ("%s", thd->proc_info));
  result->send_result_set_metadata(*fields,
                          Protocol::SEND_NUM_ROWS | Protocol::SEND_EOF);
  error= do_select(this);
  /* Accumulate the counts from all join iterations of all join parts. */
  thd->inc_examined_row_count(examined_rows);
  DBUG_PRINT("counts", ("thd->examined_row_count: %lu",
                     (ulong) thd->get_examined_row_count()));

  DBUG_VOID_RETURN;
}
```

There is another function call that looks very interesting. Notice the code statement result->send_result_set_metadata (). This function does what its name indicates. It is the function that sends the field headers to the client. As you can surmise, there are also other methods to send the results to the client. I will look at these methods later in Chapter 4. Notice the thd->inc_examined_row_count= assignments. This saves the record-count values in the THD class. Let's take a look at that do_select() function.

You can see in the do_select() method shown in Listing 3-15 that something significant is happening. Notice the last highlighted code statement. The statement join->result->send_eof() looks as if the code is sending an end-of-file flag somewhere. It is indeed sending an end-of-file signal to the client. So where are the results? They are generated in the first_select() function (which is mapped to the sub_select()). Let's look at that function next.

Listing 3-15. The do_select() Function

```
static int
do_select(JOIN *join)
{
  int rc= 0;
  enum_nested_loop_state error= NESTED_LOOP_OK;
  DBUG_ENTER("do_select");

...

  else
  {
    JOIN_TAB *join_tab= join->join_tab + join->const_tables;
    DBUG_ASSERT(join->tables);
    error= join->first_select(join,join_tab,0);
    if (error >= NESTED_LOOP_OK)
      error= join->first_select(join,join_tab,1);
  }

  join->thd->limit_found_rows= join->send_records;
  /* Use info provided by filesort. */
  if (join->order)
  {
    // Save # of found records prior to cleanup
    JOIN_TAB *sort_tab;
    JOIN_TAB *join_tab= join->join_tab;
    uint const_tables= join->const_tables;

    // Take record count from first non constant table or from last tmp table
    if (join->tmp_tables > 0)
      sort_tab= join_tab + join->tables + join->tmp_tables - 1;
    else
    {
      DBUG_ASSERT(join->tables > const_tables);
      sort_tab= join_tab + const_tables;
    }
    if (sort_tab->filesort &&
        sort_tab->filesort->sortorder)
    {
      join->thd->limit_found_rows= sort_tab->records;
    }
  }

  {
    /*
      The following will unlock all cursors if the command wasn't an
      update command
    */
    join->join_free();                 // Unlock all cursors
  }
  if (error == NESTED_LOOP_OK)
```

```
{
  /*
    Sic: this branch works even if rc != 0, e.g. when
    send_data above returns an error.
  */
  if (join->result->send_eof())
    rc= 1;                                    // Don't send error
  DBUG_PRINT("info",("%ld records output", (long) join->send_records));
}

...

}
```

Now you're getting somewhere! Take a moment to scan through Listing 3-16. This listing shows a condensed view of the sub_select() function. Notice that the code begins with an initialization of a structure named READ_RECORD. The READ_RECORD structure contains the tuple read from the table. The system initializes the tables to begin reading records sequentially, and then it reads one record at a time until all the records are read.

Listing 3-16. The sub_select() Function

```
enum_nested_loop_state
sub_select(JOIN *join,JOIN_TAB *join_tab,bool end_of_records)
{
  DBUG_ENTER("sub_select");

  join_tab->table->null_row=0;
  if (end_of_records)
  {
    enum_nested_loop_state nls=
      (*join_tab->next_select)(join,join_tab+1,end_of_records);
    DBUG_RETURN(nls);
  }
  READ_RECORD *info= &join_tab->read_record;

...

  join->thd->get_stmt_da()->reset_current_row_for_warning();

  enum_nested_loop_state rc= NESTED_LOOP_OK;
  bool in_first_read= true;
  while (rc == NESTED_LOOP_OK && join->return_tab >= join_tab)
  {
    int error;
    if (in_first_read)
    {
      in_first_read= false;
      error= (*join_tab->read_first_record)(join_tab);
    }
    else
      error= info->read_record(info);

    DBUG_EXECUTE_IF("bug13822652_1", join->thd->killed= THD::KILL_QUERY;);
```

```
    if (error > 0 || (join->thd->is_error()))     // Fatal error
      rc= NESTED_LOOP_ERROR;
    else if (error < 0)
      break;
    else if (join->thd->killed)                    // Aborted by user
    {
      join->thd->send_kill_message();
      rc= NESTED_LOOP_KILLED;
    }
    else
    {
      if (join_tab->keep_current_rowid)
        join_tab->table->file->position(join_tab->table->record[0]);
      rc= evaluate_join_record(join, join_tab);
    }
  }

  if (rc == NESTED_LOOP_OK && join_tab->last_inner && !join_tab->found)
    rc= evaluate_null_complemented_join_record(join, join_tab);

  DBUG_RETURN(rc);
}
```

■ **Note**   The code presented in Listing 3-16 is more condensed than the other examples I have shown. The main reason is that this code uses a fair number of advanced programming techniques, such as recursion and function pointer redirection. The concept as presented is accurate for the example query, however.

Control returns to the JOIN class for evaluation of the expressions and execution of the relational operators. After the results are processed, they are transmitted to the client and then control returns to the sub_select() function, where the end-of-file flag is sent to tell the client there are no more results. I hope that this tour has satisfied your curiosity and, if nothing else, that it has boosted your appreciation for the complexities of a real-world database system. Feel free to go back through this tour again until you're comfortable with the basic flow. I discuss a few of the more important classes and structures in the next section.

Supporting Libraries

There are many additional libraries in the MySQL source tree. Oracle has long worked diligently to encapsulate and optimize many of the common routines used to access the supported operating systems and hardware. Most of these libraries are designed to render the code both operating system and hardware agnostic. These libraries make it possible to write code so that specific platform characteristics do not force you to write specialized code. Among these libraries are libraries for managing efficient string handling, hash tables, linked lists, memory allocation, and many others. Table 3-6 lists the purposes and location of a few of the more common libraries.

■ **Tip** The best way to discover if a library exists for a routine that you're trying to use is to look through the source-code files in the /mysys directory using a text search tool. Most of the wrapper functions have a name similar to their original function. For example, my_alloc.c implements the malloc wrapper.

Table 3-6. *Supporting Libraries*

Source File	Utilities
/mysys/array.c	Array operations
/include/hash.h and /mysys/hash.c	Hash tables
/mysys/list.c	Linked lists
/mysys/my_alloc.c	Memory allocation
/strings/*.c	Base memory and string manipulation routines
/mysys/string.c	String operations
/mysys/my_pthread.c	Threading

Important Classes and Structures

Quite a few classes and structures in the MySQL source code can be considered key elements to the success of the system. To become fully knowledgeable about the MySQL source code, learn the basics of all of the key classes and structures used in the system. Knowing what is stored in which class or what the structures contain can help you make your modifications integrate well. The following sections describe these key classes and structures.

The ITEM_ Class

One class that permeates throughout the subsystems is the ITEM_ class. I called it ITEM_ because a number of classes are derived from the base ITEM class and even classes derived from those. These derivatives are used to store and manipulate a great many data (items) in the system. These include parameters (as in the WHERE clause), identifiers, time, fields, function, num, string, and many others. Listing 3-17 shows a condensed view of the ITEM base class. The structure is defined in the /sql/item.h source file and implemented in the /sql/item.cc source file. Additional subclasses are defined and implemented in files named after the data it encapsulates. For example, the function subclass is defined in /sql/item_func.h and implemented in /sql/item_func.cc.

Listing 3-17. The ITEM_ Class

```
class Item
{
  Item(const Item &);                    /* Prevent use of these */
  void operator=(Item &);
  /* Cache of the result of is_expensive(). */
  int8 is_expensive_cache;
  virtual bool is_expensive_processor(uchar *arg) { return 0; }

public:
```

```
static void *operator new(size_t size) throw ()
{ return sql_alloc(size); }
static void *operator new(size_t size, MEM_ROOT *mem_root) throw ()
{ return alloc_root(mem_root, size); }
static void operator delete(void *ptr,size_t size) { TRASH(ptr, size); }
static void operator delete(void *ptr, MEM_ROOT *mem_root) {}

enum Type {FIELD_ITEM= 0, FUNC_ITEM, SUM_FUNC_ITEM, STRING_ITEM,
           INT_ITEM, REAL_ITEM, NULL_ITEM, VARBIN_ITEM,
           COPY_STR_ITEM, FIELD_AVG_ITEM, DEFAULT_VALUE_ITEM,
           PROC_ITEM,COND_ITEM, REF_ITEM, FIELD_STD_ITEM,
           FIELD_VARIANCE_ITEM, INSERT_VALUE_ITEM,
           SUBSELECT_ITEM, ROW_ITEM, CACHE_ITEM, TYPE_HOLDER,
           PARAM_ITEM, TRIGGER_FIELD_ITEM, DECIMAL_ITEM,
           XPATH_NODESET, XPATH_NODESET_CMP,
           VIEW_FIXER_ITEM};

enum cond_result { COND_UNDEF,COND_OK,COND_TRUE,COND_FALSE };

enum traverse_order { POSTFIX, PREFIX };

/* Reuse size, only used by SP local variable assignment, otherwize 0 */
uint rsize;

/*
  str_values's main purpose is to be used to cache the value in
  save_in_field
*/
String str_value;

Item_name_string item_name;  /* Name from select */
Item_name_string orig_name;  /* Original item name (if it was renamed)*/

/**
   Intrusive list pointer for free list. If not null, points to the next
   Item on some Query_arena's free list. For instance, stored procedures
   have their own Query_arena's.

   @see Query_arena::free_list
 */
Item *next;
uint32 max_length;                 /* Maximum length, in bytes */
/**
   This member has several successive meanings, depending on the phase we're
   in:
   - during field resolution: it contains the index, in the "all_fields"
   list, of the expression to which this field belongs; or a special
   constant UNDEF_POS; see st_select_lex::cur_pos_in_all_fields and
   match_exprs_for_only_full_group_by().
   - when attaching conditions to tables: it says whether some condition
```

```
      needs to be attached or can be omitted (for example because it is already
      implemented by 'ref' access)
      - when pushing index conditions: it says whether a condition uses only
      indexed columns
      - when creating an internal temporary table: it says how to store BIT
      fields
      - when we change DISTINCT to GROUP BY: it is used for book-keeping of
      fields.
  */
  int marker;
  uint8 decimals;
  my_bool maybe_null;                   /* If item may be null */
  my_bool null_value;                   /* if item is null */
  my_bool unsigned_flag;
  my_bool with_sum_func;
  my_bool fixed;                        /* If item fixed with fix_fields */
  DTCollation collation;
  Item_result cmp_context;              /* Comparison context */
protected:
  my_bool with_subselect;               /* If this item is a subselect or some
                                           of its arguments is or contains a
                                           subselect. Computed by fix_fields
                                           and updated by update_used_tables. */

  my_bool with_stored_program;          /* If this item is a stored program
                                           or some of its arguments is or
                                           contains a stored program.
                                           Computed by fix_fields and updated
                                           by update_used_tables. */

  /**
     This variable is a cache of 'Needed tables are locked'. True if either
     'No tables locks is needed' or 'Needed tables are locked'.
     If tables are used, then it will be set to
     current_thd->lex->is_query_tables_locked().

     It is used when checking const_item()/can_be_evaluated_now().
  */
  bool tables_locked_cache;
public:
  // alloc & destruct is done as start of select using sql_alloc
  Item();
  /*
     Constructor used by Item_field, Item_ref & aggregate (sum) functions.
     Used for duplicating lists in processing queries with temporary
     tables
     Also it used for Item_cond_and/Item_cond_or for creating
     top AND/OR structure of WHERE clause to protect it from
     optimization changes in prepared statements
  */
  Item(THD *thd, Item *item);
```

```
  virtual ~Item()
  {
#ifdef EXTRA_DEBUG
    item_name.set(0);
#endif
  }                  /*lint -e1509 */
  void rename(char *new_name);
  void init_make_field(Send_field *tmp_field,enum enum_field_types type);
  virtual void cleanup();
  virtual void make_field(Send_field *field);
  virtual Field *make_string_field(TABLE *table);
  virtual bool fix_fields(THD *, Item **);
  ...

};
```

The LEX Structure

The LEX structure is responsible for being the internal representation (in-memory storage) of a query and its parts. It is more than that, though. The LEX structure is used to store all parts of a query in an organized manner. There are lists for fields, tables, expressions, and all of the parts that make up any query.

The LEX structure is filled in by the parser as it discovers the parts of the query. Thus, when the parser is done, the LEX structure contains everything needed to optimize and execute the query. Listing 3-18 shows a condensed view of the LEX structure. The structure is defined in the /sql/sql_lex.h source file.

Listing 3-18. The LEX Structure

```
struct LEX: public Query_tables_list
{
  SELECT_LEX_UNIT unit;                    /* most upper unit */
  SELECT_LEX select_lex;                   /* first SELECT_LEX */
  /* current SELECT_LEX in parsing */
  SELECT_LEX *current_select;
  /* list of all SELECT_LEX */
  SELECT_LEX *all_selects_list;

  char *length,*dec,*change;
  LEX_STRING name;
  char *help_arg;
  char* to_log;                            /* For PURGE MASTER LOGS TO */
  char* x509_subject,*x509_issuer,*ssl_cipher;
  String *wild;
  sql_exchange *exchange;
  select_result *result;
  Item *default_value, *on_update_value;
  LEX_STRING comment, ident;
  LEX_USER *grant_user;
  XID *xid;
  THD *thd;

  /* maintain a list of used plugins for this LEX */
```

```
  DYNAMIC_ARRAY plugins;
  plugin_ref plugins_static_buffer[INITIAL_LEX_PLUGIN_LIST_SIZE];

  const CHARSET_INFO *charset;

...

};
```

The NET Structure

The NET structure is responsible for storing all information concerning communication to and from a client. Listing 3-19 shows a condensed view of the NET structure. The buff member variable is used to store the raw communication packets (that when combined form the SQL statement). As you will see in later chapters, helper functions fill in, read, and transmit the data packets to and from the client. Two examples are:

- my_net_write(),which writes the data packets to the network protocol from theNET structure

- my_net_read(), which reads the data packets from the network protocol into theNET structure

You can find the complete set of network communication functions in /include/mysql_com.h.

Listing 3-19. The NET Structure

```
typedef struct st_net {
#if !defined(CHECK_EMBEDDED_DIFFERENCES) || !defined(EMBEDDED_LIBRARY)
  Vio *vio;
  unsigned char *buff,*buff_end,*write_pos,*read_pos;
  my_socket fd;                                  /* For Perl DBI/dbd */
  /*
    The following variable is set if we are doing several queries in one
    command ( as in LOAD TABLE ... FROM MASTER ),
    and do not want to confuse the client with OK at the wrong time
  */
  unsigned long remain_in_buf,length, buf_length, where_b;
  unsigned long max_packet,max_packet_size;
  unsigned int pkt_nr,compress_pkt_nr;
  unsigned int write_timeout, read_timeout, retry_count;
  int fcntl;
  unsigned int *return_status;
  unsigned char reading_or_writing;
  char save_char;
  my_bool unused1; /* Please remove with the next incompatible ABI change */
  my_bool unused2; /* Please remove with the next incompatible ABI change */
  my_bool compress;
  my_bool unused3; /* Please remove with the next incompatible ABI change. */
  /*
    Pointer to query object in query cache, do not equal NULL (0) for
    queries in cache that have not stored its results yet
  */
#endif
  /*
    Unused, please remove with the next incompatible ABI change.
```

```
*/
unsigned char *unused;
unsigned int last_errno;
unsigned char error;
my_bool unused4; /* Please remove with the next incompatible ABI change. */
my_bool unused5; /* Please remove with the next incompatible ABI change. */
/** Client library error message buffer. Actually belongs to struct MYSQL. */
char last_error[MYSQL_ERRMSG_SIZE];
/** Client library sqlstate buffer. Set along with the error message. */
char sqlstate[SQLSTATE_LENGTH+1];
/**
   Extension pointer, for the caller private use.
   Any program linking with the networking library can use this pointer,
   which is handy when private connection specific data needs to be
   maintained.
   The mysqld server process uses this pointer internally,
   to maintain the server internal instrumentation for the connection.
*/
void *extension;
} NET;
```

The THD Class

In the preceding tour of the source code, you saw many references to the THD class. In fact, there is exactly one THD object for every connection. The thread class is paramount to successful thread execution, and it is involved in every operation from implementing access control to returning results to the client. As a result, the THD class shows up in just about every subsystem or function that operates within the server. Listing 3-20 shows a condensed view of the THD class. Take a moment and browse through some of the member variables and methods. As you can see, this is a large class (I've omitted a great many of the methods). The class is defined in the /sql/sql_class.h source file and implemented in the /sql/sql_class.cc source file.

Listing 3-20. The THD Class

```
class THD :public MDL_context_owner,
           public Statement,
           public Open_tables_state
{
private:

  ...

  String  packet;                  // dynamic buffer for network I/O
  String  convert_buffer;          // buffer for charset conversions
  struct  rand_struct rand;        // used for authentication
  struct  system_variables variables;  // Changeable local variables
  struct  system_status_var status_var; // Per thread statistic vars
  struct  system_status_var *initial_status_var; /* used by show status */
  THR_LOCK_INFO lock_info;         // Locking info of this thread
  /**
     Protects THD data accessed from other threads:
     - thd->query and thd->query_length (used by SHOW ENGINE
```

```
    INNODB STATUS and SHOW PROCESSLIST
  - thd->mysys_var (used by KILL statement and shutdown).
   Is locked when THD is deleted.
*/
mysql_mutex_t LOCK_thd_data;

...

};
```

The READ_RECORD structure

As we saw earlier, the READ_RECORD structure is used to contain a tuple from the storage engine once the optimizer has identified it as a row to be returned to the user. We leave discussion of the storage engine until Chapter 10. Listing 3-21 shows the READ_RECORD structure. Notice that there are function pointers to callback to the JOIN class methods as well as variables to reference the THD class, record length, as well as a pointer to the record buffer itself. Examine the many methods in this class if you are interesting in learning how rows are stored in the system.

Listing 3-21. The READ_RECORD Structure

```
struct READ_RECORD
{
  typedef int (*Read_func)(READ_RECORD*);
  typedef void (*Unlock_row_func)(st_join_table *);
  typedef int (*Setup_func)(JOIN_TAB*);

  TABLE *table;                            /* Head-form */
  TABLE **forms;                           /* head and ref forms */
  Unlock_row_func unlock_row;
  Read_func read_record;
  THD *thd;
  SQL_SELECT *select;
  uint cache_records;
  uint ref_length,struct_length,reclength,rec_cache_size,error_offset;
  uint index;
  uchar *ref_pos;                                /* pointer to form->refpos */
  uchar *record;
  uchar *rec_buf;              /* to read field values  after filesort */
  uchar *cache,*cache_pos,*cache_end,*read_positions;
  struct st_io_cache *io_cache;
  bool print_error, ignore_not_found_rows;

...

  Copy_field *copy_field;
  Copy_field *copy_field_end;
public:
  READ_RECORD() {}
};
```

MySQL Plugins

A tour of the MySQL system would not be complete without mentioning one of the most important and newest innovations in the architecture. MySQL now supports a plugin facility that permits dynamic loading of system features. Not only does this mean that the user can tailor her system by loading only what she needs, it also means the developers of MySQL can develop features in a more modular design. The storage-engine subsystem is an example of one subsystem redesigned to use the new plugin mechanism. There are many others. We will see how plugins work in more detail in later chapters. For now, let us discuss how plugins are loaded and unloaded as well as how to determine the status of your plugins.

The plugins table in the mysql database is used load plugins at startup. The table contains only two columns, name and dl, which store the plugin name and the library name. On startup, unless the user has turned off the plugin, the system loads each library specified in the dl column and initiates each plugin specified in the name column for its respective library. It is possible, then, to modify this table manually to manage plugins, but that is not recommended, because some libraries can contain more than one plugin. You will see this concept in action later, when we examine the mysql_plugin client application.

Some plugins are considered "built in" and are available by default and in some cases loaded (installed) automatically. This includes many of the storage engines as well as the standard authentication mechanism, binary log, and others. Other plugins can be made available by installing them, and likewise, they can be disabled by uninstalling them. You can find complete documentation on managing plugins in the "Server Plugins" section of the online reference manual.

Installing and Uninstalling Plugins

Plugins can be loaded and unloaded either with special SQL commands, as startup options, or via the mysql_plugin client application. To load a plugin, you first need to place the correct libraries into the plugin directory specified by the path in the system variable plugin_dir. You can find the current value of that variable from MySQL as:

```
mysql> SHOW VARIABLES LIKE 'plugin_dir';
+---------------+----------------------------+
| Variable_name | Value                      |
+---------------+----------------------------+
| plugin_dir    | /usr/local/mysql/lib/plugin/ |
+---------------+----------------------------+
1 row in set (0.00 sec)
```

You can see that the path is /usr/local/mysql/lib/plugin/. When you build your plugin or to install an existing plugin, you must first place your libraries into the plugin directory. Then you can execute an INSTALL PLUGIN command similar to:

```
mysql> INSTALL PLUGIN something_cool SONAME some_cool_feature.so;
```

Here, we are loading a plugin named something_cool that is contained in the compiled library module named some_cool_feature.so.

Uninstalling the plugin is easier and is shown next. Here, we are unloading the same plugin we just installed.

```
mysql> UNINSTALL PLUGIN something_cool;
```

Plugins can also be installed at startup using the `--plugin-load` option. This option can either be listed multiple times—once for each plugin—or, it can accept a semicolon separated list (no spaces). Examples of how to use this option include:

```
mysqld ... --plugin-load=something_cool=some_cool_feature.so
mysqld ... --plugin-load=something_cool=some_cool_feature.so;something_even_better=even_better.so
```

■ **Note** The MySQL documentation uses the terms *install* and *uninstall* for dynamically loading and unloading plugins. The documentation uses the term *load* for specifying a plugin to use via a startup option.

Plugins can also be loaded and unloaded using the `mysql_plugin` client application. This application requires the server to be down to work. It will launch the server in bootstrap mode, load or unload the plugin, and then shut down the bootstrapped server. The application is used primarily for maintenance of servers during downtime or as a diagnostic tool for attempts to restart a failed server by eliminating plugins (to simplify diagnosis).

The client application uses a configuration file to keep pertinent data about the plugin, such as the name of the library and all of the plugins contain within. Yes, it is possible that a plugin library can contain more than one plugin. The following is an example of the configuration file for the `daemon_example` plugin:

```
#
# Plugin configuration file. Place the following on a separate line:
#
# library binary file name (without .so or .dll)
# component_name
# [component_name] - additional components in plugin
#
libdaemon_example
daemon_example
```

To use the `mysql_plugin` application to install (enable) or uninstall (disable) plugins, specify the name of the plugin: `ENABLE` or `DISABLE`, `basedir`, `datadir`, `plugin-dir`, and `plugin-ini` options at a minimum. You may also need to specify the `my-print-defaults` option if the mysql_plugin application is not on your path. The application runs silently, but you can turn on verbosity to see the application in action. (Use the option: -vvv). The following shows how to load the daemon_example plugin using the mysql_plugin client application. The example is being run from the bin folder of the MySQL installation.

```
cbell$ sudo ./mysql_plugin --datadir=/mysql_path/data/ --basedir=/mysql_path/ --plugin-dir=../
plugin/daemon_example/ --plugin-ini=../plugin/daemon_example/daemon_example.ini --my-print-
defaults=../extra daemon_example ENABLE -vvv
# Found tool 'my_print_defaults' as '/mysql_path/bin/my_print_defaults'.
# Command: /mysql_path/bin/my_print_defaults mysqld > /var/tmp/txtdoaw2b
#     basedir = /mysql_path/
# plugin_dir = ../plugin/daemon_example/
#     datadir = /mysql_path/data/
# plugin_ini = ../plugin/daemon_example/daemon_example.ini
# Found tool 'mysqld' as '/mysql_path/bin/mysqld'.
# Found plugin 'daemon_example' as '../plugin/daemon_example/libdaemon_example.so'
# Enabling daemon_example...
# Query: REPLACE INTO mysql.plugin VALUES ('daemon_example','libdaemon_example.so');
# Command: /mysql_path/bin/mysqld --no-defaults
--bootstrap --datadir=/mysql_path/data/ --basedir=/mysql_path/ < /var/tmp/sqlft1mF7
# Operation succeeded.
```

Notice from the output that I had to rely upon super-user privileges. You will need to use such privileges if you are attempting to install or uninstall plugins from a server installed on platforms that isolate access to the mysql folders, such as Linux and Mac OS X.

Notice also that the verbose output shows you exactly what the application is doing. In this case, it is replacing any rows in the mysql.plugin table with the information for the plugin we specified. Similarly, delete queries would be issued for disabling a plugin.

Discovering Status of Available Plugins

You can discover the plugins available on your system by examining the INFORMATION_SCHEMA PLUGINS view. Listing 3-22 is an excerpt of the output from this view. Notice that there are entries for each storage engine, as well as for the version and status of each plugin. The view also contains fields for storing the plugin type version (the version of the system when the plugin was created), and the author. You can see all of the fields for this view by using the EXPLAIN command.

Listing 3-22. INFORMATION_SCHEMA.PLUGINS View

```
mysql> SELECT plugin_name, plugin_version, plugin_status, plugin_type
       FROM INFORMATION_SCHEMA.PLUGINS;
+-----------------------+----------------+---------------+--------------------+
| plugin_name           | plugin_version | plugin_status | plugin_type        |
+-----------------------+----------------+---------------+--------------------+
| binlog                | 1.0            | ACTIVE        | STORAGE ENGINE     |
| mysql_native_password | 1.0            | ACTIVE        | AUTHENTICATION     |
| mysql_old_password    | 1.0            | ACTIVE        | AUTHENTICATION     |
| CSV                   | 1.0            | ACTIVE        | STORAGE ENGINE     |
| MEMORY                | 1.0            | ACTIVE        | STORAGE ENGINE     |
| MyISAM                | 1.0            | ACTIVE        | STORAGE ENGINE     |
| MRG_MYISAM            | 1.0            | ACTIVE        | STORAGE ENGINE     |
| ARCHIVE               | 3.0            | ACTIVE        | STORAGE ENGINE     |
| BLACKHOLE             | 1.0            | ACTIVE        | STORAGE ENGINE     |
| FEDERATED             | 1.0            | DISABLED      | STORAGE ENGINE     |
| InnoDB                | 1.1            | ACTIVE        | STORAGE ENGINE     |
| INNODB_TRX            | 1.1            | ACTIVE        | INFORMATION SCHEMA |
| INNODB_LOCKS          | 1.1            | ACTIVE        | INFORMATION SCHEMA |
| INNODB_LOCK_WAITS     | 1.1            | ACTIVE        | INFORMATION SCHEMA |
| INNODB_CMP            | 1.1            | ACTIVE        | INFORMATION SCHEMA |
| INNODB_CMP_RESET      | 1.1            | ACTIVE        | INFORMATION SCHEMA |
| INNODB_CMPMEM         | 1.1            | ACTIVE        | INFORMATION SCHEMA |
| INNODB_CMPMEM_RESET   | 1.1            | ACTIVE        | INFORMATION SCHEMA |
| PERFORMANCE_SCHEMA    | 0.1            | ACTIVE        | STORAGE ENGINE     |
| partition             | 1.0            | ACTIVE        | STORAGE ENGINE     |
+-----------------------+----------------+---------------+--------------------+
20 rows in set (0.00 sec)
```

Now that you have had a tour of the source code and have examined some of the important classes and structures used in the system, I shift the focus to items that will help you implement your own modifications to the MySQL system. Let's take a break from the source code and consider the coding guidelines and documentation aspects of software development.

Coding Guidelines

If the source code I've described seems to have a strange format, it may be because you have a different style than the authors of the source code. Consider the case in which there are many developers writing a large software program such as MySQL, each with their own style. As you can imagine, the code would quickly begin to resemble a jumbled mass of statements. To avoid this, Oracle has published coding guidelines in various forms. As you will see when you begin exploring the code yourself, it seems that there are a few developers who aren't following the coding guidelines. The only plausible explanation is that the guidelines have changed over time, which can happen over the lifetime of a large project. Thus, some portions of the code were written using one set of rules, while others perhaps used a different version of the rules. Regardless of this consequence, the developers did strive to follow the guidelines.

The coding guidelines have a huge bulleted list containing the do's and don'ts of writing C/C++ code for the MySQL server. I have captured the most important guidelines and summarized them for you in the following paragraphs.

General Guidelines

One of the most stressed aspects of the guidelines is that you should write code that is as optimized as possible. This goal is counter to agile development methodologies, in which you code only what you need and leave refinement and optimization to refactoring. If you develop using agile methodologies, you may want to wait to check in your code until you have refactored it.

Another very important overall goal is to avoid the use of direct API or operating-system calls. You should always look in the associated libraries for wrapper functions. Many of these functions are optimized for fast and safe execution. For example, never use the C `malloc()` function. Instead, use the `sql_alloc()` or `my_alloc()` function.

All lines of code must be fewer than 80 characters long. If you need to continue a line of code onto another line, align the code so that parameters are aligned vertically or the continuation code is aligned with the indention space count.

Comments are written using the standard C-style comments, for example, `/* this is a comment */`. You should use comments liberally through your code.

■ **Tip** Resist the urge to use the C++ `//` `comment` option. The MySQL coding guidelines specifically discourage this technique.

Documentation

The language of choice for the source code is English. This includes all variables, function names, constants, and comments. The developers who write and maintain the MySQL source code are located throughout Europe and the United States. The choice of English as the default language in the source code is largely due to the influence of American computer science developments. English is also taught as a second language in many primary and secondary education programs in many European countries.

When writing functions, use a comment block that describes the function, its parameters, and the expected return values. The content of the comment block should be written in sections, with section names in all caps. You should include a short descriptive name of the function on the first line after the comment and, at a minimum, include the sections, synopsis, description, and return value. You may also include optional sections such as WARNING, NOTES, SEE ALSO, TODO, ERRORS, and REFERENCED_BY. The sections and content are described here:

- *SYNOPSIS* (required)—Presents a brief overview of the flow and control mechanisms in the function. It should permit the reader to understand the basic algorithm of the function. This helps readers understand the function and provide an at-a-glance glimpse of what it does. This section also includes a description of all of the parameters (indicated by IN for input, OUT for output, and IN/OUT for referenced parameters whose values may be changed).

- *DESCRIPTION* (required)—A narrative of the function. It should include the purpose of the function and a brief description of its use.

- *RETURN VALUE* (required)—Presents all possible return values and what they mean to the caller.

- *WARNING*—Include this section to describe any unusual side effects that the caller should be aware of.

- *NOTES*—Include this section to provide the reader with any information you feel is important.

- *SEE ALSO*—Include this section when you're writing a function that is associated with another function, or that requires specific outputs of another function, or that is intended to be used by another function in a specific calling order.

- *TODO*—Include this section to communicate any unfinished features of the function. Remove the items from this section as you complete them. I tend to forget to do this, and it often results in a bit of head scratching to figure out that I've already completed the TODO item.

- *ERRORS*—Include this section to document any unusual error handling that your function has.

- *REFERENCED_BY*—Include this section to communicate specific aspects of the relationship this function has with other functions or objects—for example, whenever your function is called by another function, the function is a primitive of another function, or the function is a friend method or even a virtual method.

■ **Tip** Oracle suggests that it isn't necessary to provide a comment block for short functions that have only a few lines of code, but I recommend writing a comment block for all of the functions you create. You will appreciate this advice as you explore the source code and encounter numerous small (and some large) functions with little or no documentation.

A sample of a function comment block is shown in Listing 3-23.

Listing 3-23. Example Function Comment Block

```
/**
  Find tuples by key.

  SYNOPSIS
    find_by_key()
    string key              IN    A string containing the key to find.
    Handler_class *handle IN    The class containing the table to be searched.
    Tuple *                 OUT   The tuple class containing the key passed.

  Uses B Tree index contained in the Handler_class. Calls Index::find()
```

```
    method then returns a pointer to the tuple found.

DESCRIPTION
    This function implements a search of the Handler_class index class to find
    a key passed.

RETURN VALUE
    SUCCESS (TRUE)                      Tuple found.
    != SUCCESS (FALES)                  Tuple not found.

WARNING
    Function can return an empty tuple when a key hit occurs on the index but
    the tuple has been marked for deletion.

NOTES
    This method has been tested for empty keys and keys that are greater or
    less than the keys in the index.

SEE ALSO
    Query:;execute(), Tuple.h

TODO
    * Change code to include error handler to detect when key passed in exceeds
    the maximum length of the key in the index.

ERRORS
    -1                                  Table not found.
    1                                   Table locked.

REFERENCED_BY
    This function is called by the Query::execute() method.
*/
```

Functions and Parameters

I want to call these items out specifically, because some inconsistencies exist in the source code. If you use the source code as a guide for formatting, you may wander astray of the coding guidelines. Functions and their parameters should be aligned so that the parameters are in vertical alignment. This applies to both defining the function and calling it from other code. In a similar way, variables should be aligned when you declare them. The spacing of the alignment isn't such an issue as the vertical appearance of these items. You should also add line comments about each of the variables. Line comments should begin in column 49 and not exceed the maximum 80-column rule. In the case in which a comment for a variable exceeds 80 columns, place that comment on a separate line. Listing 3-24 shows examples of the type of alignment expected for functions, variables, and parameters.

Listing 3-24. Variable, Function, and Parameter Alignment Examples

```
int     var1;                                 /* comment goes here */
long    var2;                                 /* comment goes here too */
/* variable controls something of extreme interest and is documented well */
bool    var3;

return_value *classname::classmethod(int  var1,
```

```
                         int  var2
                         bool var3);

if (classname->classmethod(myreallylongvariablename1,
                           myreallylongvariablename2,
                           myreallylongvariablename3) == -1)
{
  /* do something */
}
```

■ **Warning**   If you're developing on Windows, the line-break feature of your editor may be set incorrectly. Most editors in Windows issue a CRLF (/r/n) when you place a line break in the file. Oracle requires you to use a single LF (/n), not a CRLF. This is a common incompatibility between files created on Windows versus files created in UNIX or Linux. If you're using Windows, check your editor and make the appropriate changes to its configuration.

Naming Conventions

Oracle prefers that you assign your variables meaningful names using all lowercase letters with underscores instead of initial caps. The exception is the use of class names, which are required to have initial caps. Enumerations should be prefixed with the phrase enum_. All structures and defines should be written with uppercase letters. Examples of the naming conventions are shown in Listing 3-25.

Listing 3-25. Sample Naming Conventions

```
class My_classname;
int   my_integer_counter;
bool  is_saved;

#define CONSTANT_NAME 12;

int my_function_name_goes_here(int variable1);
```

Spacing and Indenting

The MySQL coding guidelines state that spacing should always be two characters for each indention level. Never use tabs. If your editor permits, change the default behavior of the editor to turn off automatic formatting and replace all tabs with two spaces. This is especially important when using documentation utilities such as Doxygen (which I'll discuss in a moment) or line-parsing tools to locate strings in the text.

When spacing between identifiers and operators, include no spaces between a variable and an operator and a single space between the operator and an operand (the right side of the operator). In a similar way, no space should follow the open parenthesis in functions, but include one space between parameters and no space between the last parameter name and the closing parenthesis. Last, include a single blank line to delineate variable declarations from control code, and control code from method calls, and block comments from other code, and functions from other declarations. Listing 3-26 depicts a properly formatted excerpt of code that contains an assignment statement, a function call, and a control statement.

Listing 3-26. Spacing and Indention

```
return_value= do_something_cool(i, max_limit, is_found);
if (return_value)
{
  int var1;
  int var2;

  var1= do_something_else(i);

  if (var1)
  {
    do_it_again();
  }
}
```

The alignment of the curly braces is also inconsistent in some parts of the source code. The MySQL coding guidelines state that the curly braces should align with the control code above it, as I have shown in all of our examples. If you need to indent another level, use the same column alignment as the code within the curly braces (two spaces). It is also not necessary to use curly braces if you're executing a single line of code in the code block.

An oddity of sorts in the curly braces area is the switch statement. A switch statement should be written to align the open curly brace after the switch condition and align the closing curly brace with the switch keyword. The case statements should be aligned in the same column as the switch keyword. Listing 3-27 illustrates this guideline.

Listing 3-27. Switch Statement Example

```
switch (some_var) {
case 1:
   do_something_here();
   do_something_else();
   break;
case 2:
   do_it_again();
   break;
}
```

■ **Note** The last break in the previous code is not needed. I usually include it in my code for the sake of completeness.

Documentation Utilities

Another useful method of examining source code is to use an automated documentation generator that reads the source code and generates function- and class-based lists of methods. These programs list the structures used and provide clues as to how and where they are used in the source code. This is important for investigating MySQL because of the many critical structures that the source code relies on to operate and manipulate data.

One such program is called Doxygen. The nice thing about Doxygen is that it, too, is open source and governed by the GPL. When you invoke Doxygen, it reads the source code and produces a highly readable set of HTML files that pull the comments from the source code preceding the function, and it also lists the function primitives. Doxygen can read programming languages such as C, C++, and Java, among several others. Doxygen can be a useful tool for investigating a complex system such as MySQL—especially when you consider that the base library functions are called from hundreds of locations throughout the code.

Doxygen is available for both UNIX and Windows platforms. To use the program on Linux, download the source code from the Doxygen Web site at `http://www.doxygen.com`.

Once you have downloaded the installation, follow the installation instructions (also on the Web site). Doxygen uses configuration files to generate the look and feel of the output as well as what gets included in the input. To generate a default configuration file, issue the command:

```
doxygen -s -g /path_to_new_file/doxygen_config_filename
```

The path specified should be the path you want to store the documentation in. Once you have a default configuration file, you can edit the file and change the parameters to meet your specific needs. See the Doxygen documentation for more information on the options and their parameters. You would typically specify the folders to process, the project name, and other project-related settings. Once you have set the configurations you want, you can generate documentation for MySQL by issuing this command:

```
doxygen </path_to_new_file/Doxygen_config_filename>
```

■ **Caution**   Depending on your settings, Doxygen could run for a long time. Avoid using advanced graphing commands if you want Doxygen to generate documentation in a reasonable time period.

The latest version of Doxygen can be run from Windows using a supplied GUI. The GUI allows you to use create the configuration file using a wizard that steps you through the process and creates a basic configuration file, an expert mode that allows you to set your own parameters, and the ability to load a config file. I found the output generated by using the wizard interface sufficient for casual to in-depth viewing.

I recommend spending some time running Doxygen and examining the output files prior to diving into the source code. It will save you tons of lookup time. The structures alone are worth tacking up on the wall next to your monitor or pasting into your engineering logbook. A sample of the type of documentation Doxygen can generate is shown in Figure 3-3.

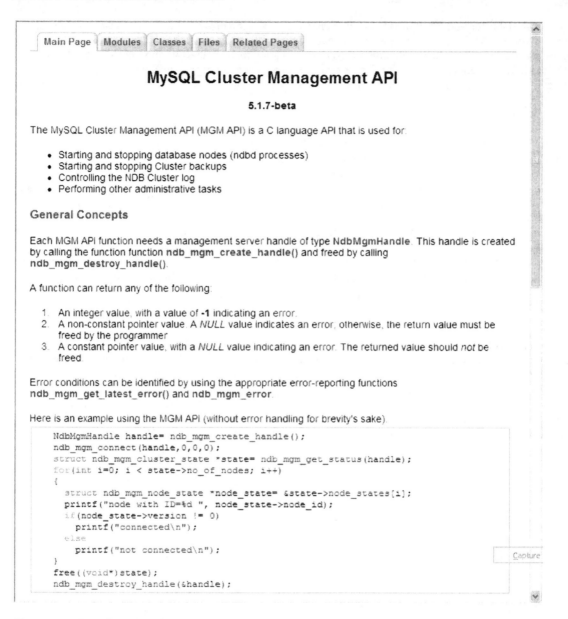

Figure 3-3. *Sample MySQL Doxygen output*

Keeping an Engineering Logbook

Many developers keep notes of their projects. Some are more detailed than others, but most take notes during meetings and phone conversations, thereby providing a written record for verbal communications. If you aren't in the habit of keeping an engineering logbook, you should consider doing so. I have found a logbook to be a vital tool in my work. Yes, it does require more effort to write things down, and the log can get messy if you try to include all of the various drawings and emails you find important (mine are often bulging with clippings from important documents taped in place like some sort of engineer's scrapbook). The payoff is potentially huge, however.

This is especially true when you're doing the sort of investigative work you will be doing while studying the MySQL source code. Keep a logbook of each discovery you make. Write down every epiphany, important design decision, snippets from important paper documents, and even the occasional *ah-ha*! Over time, you will build up a paper record of your findings (a former boss of mine called it her paper brain!) that will prove invaluable for reviews and your own documentation efforts. If you do use a logbook and make journal entries or paste in important document snippets, you will soon discover that logbooks of the journal variety do not lend themselves to being organized well. Most engineers (such as I) prefer lined, hardbound journals that cannot be reorganized (unless you use lots of scissors and glue). Others prefer loose-leaf logbooks that permit easy reorganization. If you plan to use a hardbound journal, consider building a "living" index as you go.

■ **Tip**   If your journal pages aren't numbered, take a few minutes and place page numbers on each page.

There are many ways to build the living index. You could write any interesting keywordsat the top of the page or in a specific place in the margin. This would allow you to quickly skim through your logbook and locate items of interest. What makes a living index is the ability to add references over time. The best way I have found to create the living index is to use a spreadsheet to list all of the terms you write on the logbook pages and to write the page number next to it. I update the spreadsheet every week or so, print it out, and tape it into my logbook near the front. I have seen some journals that have a pocket in the front, but the tape approach works too. Over time you can reorder the index items and reference page numbers to make the list easier to read; you can also place an updated list in the front of your logbook so you can locate pages more easily.

Consider using an engineering logbook. You won't be sorry when it comes time to give your report on your progress to your superiors. It can also save you tons of rework later, when you are asked to report on something you did six months or more ago.

Tracking Your Changes

Always use comments when you create code that is not intuitive to the reader. For example, the code statement `if (found)` is pretty self-explanatory. The code following the control statement will be executed if the variable evaluates to TRUE. The code `if (func_call_17(i, x, lp))` requires some explanation, however. Of course, you want to write all of your code to be self-explanatory, but sometimes that isn't possible. This is particularly true when you're accessing supporting library functions. Some names are not intuitive, and the parameter lists can be confusing. Document these situations as you code them, and your life will be enhanced.

When writing comments, you can use inline comments, single-line comments, or multiline comments. Inline comments are written beginning in column 49 and cannot exceed 80 columns. A single-line comment should be aligned with the code it is referring to (the indention mark) and also should not exceed 80 columns. Likewise, multiline comments should align with the code they are explaining and should not exceed 80 columns, but they should have the opening and closing comment markers placed on separate lines. Listing 3-28 illustrates these concepts.

Listing 3-28. Comment Placement and Spacing Examples

```
if (return_value)
{
  int     var1;                         /* comment goes here */
  long    var2;                         /* comment goes here too */

  /* this call does something else based on i */
  var1= do_something_else(i);
```

```
  if (var1)
  {
    /*
      This comment explains
      some really interesting thing
      about the following statement(s).
    */
    do_it_again();
  }
}
```

■ **Tip**   Never use repeating *s to emphasize portions of code. It distracts the reader from the code and makes for a cluttered look. Besides, it's too much work to get all those things to line up—especially when you edit your comments later.

If you are modifying the MySQL source code using a source-control application such as bazaar, you don't have to worry about tracking your changes. Bazaar provides several ways for you to detect and report on which changes are yours versus others. If you are not using a source-control application, you could lose track of which changes are yours, particularly if you make changes directly to existing system functions. In this case, it becomes difficult to distinguish what you wrote from what was already there. Keeping an engineering logbook helps immensely with this problem, but there is a better way.

You could add comments before and after your changes to indicate which lines of code are your modifications. For example, you could place a comment such as /* BEGIN CAB MODIFICATION */ before the code and a comment such as /* END CAB MODIFICATION */ after the code. This allows you to bracket your changes and helps you search for the changes easily using a number of text and line parsing utilities. An example of this technique is shown in Listing 3-29.

Listing 3-29. Commenting Your Changes to the MySQL Source Code

```
/* BEGIN CAB MODIFICATION */
/* Reason for Modification: */
/* This section adds my revision note to the MySQL version number. */
   /* original code:    */
   /*strmov(end, "."); */
   strmov(end, "-CAB Modifications");
/* END CAB MODIFICATION */
```

Notice that I have also included the reason for the modification and the commented-out lines of the original code (the example is fictional). Using this technique will help you quickly access your changes and enhance your ability to diagnose problems later.

This technique can also be helpful if you make modifications for use in your organization and you are not going to share the changes with Oracle. If you do not share the changes, you will be forced to make the modifications to the source code every time Oracle releases a new build of the system you want to use. Having comment markers in the source code will help you quickly identify which files need changes and what those changes should be. Chances are that if you create some new functionality, you will eventually want to share that functionality, if for no other reason than to avoid making the modifications every time a new version of MySQL is released.

■ **Caution** Although this technique isn't prohibited when using source code under configuration control (BitKeeper), it is usually discouraged. In fact, developers may later remove your comments altogether. Use this technique only when you make changes that you are not going to share with anyone.

Building the System for the First Time

Now that you've seen the inner workings of the MySQL source code and followed the path of a typical query through the source code, it is time for you to take a turn at the wheel. If you are already working with the MySQL source code, and you are reading this book to learn more about the source code and how to modify it, you can skip this section.

I recommend, before you get started, that you download the source code if you haven't already and then download and install the executables for your chosen platform. It is important to have the compiled binaries handy in case things go wrong during your experiments. Attempting to diagnose a problem with a modified MySQL source-code build without a reference point can be quite challenging. You will save yourself a lot of time if you can revert to the base compiled binary when you encounter a difficult debugging problem. I cover debugging in more detail in Chapter 5. If you ever find yourself with that system problem, you can always reinstall the binaries and return your MySQL system to normal.

Compiling the source is easy. If you are using Linux, open a command shell, change to the root of your source tree, and run the cmake and make commands. The cmake script will check the system for dependencies and create the appropriate makefiles. The following outlines a typical build process for building the source code on Linux for the first time:

```
$ cmake .

-- The C compiler identification is GNU
-- The CXX compiler identification is GNU
-- Check for working C compiler: /usr/bin/gcc
-- Check for working C compiler: /usr/bin/gcc -- works
-- Detecting C compiler ABI info
-- Detecting C compiler ABI info - done
-- Check for working CXX compiler: /usr/bin/c++
-- Check for working CXX compiler: /usr/bin/c++ -- works
-- Detecting CXX compiler ABI info
-- Detecting CXX compiler ABI info - done
-- Looking for SHM_HUGETLB
-- Looking for SHM_HUGETLB - found
-- Looking for sys/types.h
-- Looking for sys/types.h - found
-- Looking for stdint.h
-- Looking for stdint.h - found
-- Looking for stddef.h
-- Looking for stddef.h - found

...

-- Configuring done
-- Generating done
-- Build files have been written to: /source/mysql-5.6.6
```

```
$ make

[  0%] Built target INFO_BIN
[  0%] Built target INFO_SRC
[  0%] Built target abi_check
[  0%] Building C object zlib/CMakeFiles/zlib.dir/adler32.c.o
[  0%] Building C object zlib/CMakeFiles/zlib.dir/compress.c.o
[  0%] Building C object zlib/CMakeFiles/zlib.dir/crc32.c.o
[  0%] Building C object zlib/CMakeFiles/zlib.dir/deflate.c.o
[  0%] Building C object zlib/CMakeFiles/zlib.dir/gzio.c.o
[  0%] Building C object zlib/CMakeFiles/zlib.dir/infback.c.o
[  0%] Building C object zlib/CMakeFiles/zlib.dir/inffast.c.o
[  0%] Building C object zlib/CMakeFiles/zlib.dir/inflate.c.o
[  0%] Building C object zlib/CMakeFiles/zlib.dir/inftrees.c.o
[  0%] Building C object zlib/CMakeFiles/zlib.dir/trees.c.o
[  0%] Building C object zlib/CMakeFiles/zlib.dir/uncompr.c.o
[  1%] Building C object zlib/CMakeFiles/zlib.dir/zutil.c.o
Linking C static library libzlib.a
[  1%] Built target zlib
[  1%] Building CXX object extra/yassl/CMakeFiles/yassl.dir/src/buffer.cpp.o

...

Linking CXX executable my_safe_process
[100%] Built target my_safe_process

$
```

■ **Tip** For more information about setting conditionals for complication, see `http://www.cmake.org/cmake/help/documentation.html`. You can also use the `cmake-gui` application to set options with a graphical interface. You can download both `cmake` and `cmake-gui` from the cmake.org site. The online reference manual also contains some good examples of using conditionals for compiling MySQL.

You can compile the Windows platform source code using Microsoft Visual Studio. To compile the system on Windows, open a Visual Studio command window (to ensure the vcvarsall.bat batch file is run to load the paths needed), and then issue the `cmake .` command followed by `devenv mysql.sln /build debug`.

■ **Note** You must include the dot that tells cmake to start work in the current directory.

This will build a debug version of the server. If you wish to install the server from the source tree, see the "Source Installation Overview" section in the MySQL Reference Manual at `http://dev.mysql.com/doc/refman/5.6/en/source-installation.html`).

You can also open the `mysql.sln` project workspace in the root of the source distribution tree from Visual Studio after the cmake command is run. From there, you set the active project to `mysqld` classes and the project configuration to `mysqld - Win32 nt`. When you click Build mysqld, the project is designed to compile any necessary libraries and link them to the project that you specified. Take along a fresh beverage to entertain yourself, as it can take a while to build all the libraries the first time. Regardless of which platform you use, your compiled executable will be placed in the `client_release` or `client_debug` folder, depending on which compile option you chose.

___

■ **Caution**   Most compilation problems can be traced to improperly configured development tools or missing libraries. Consult the MySQL forums for details on how to resolve the most common compilation problems.

___

The first thing you will notice about your newly compiled binary (unless there were problems) is that you cannot tell that the binary is the one you compiled! You could check the date of the file to see that the executable is the one you just created, but there isn't a way to know that from the client side. Although this approach is not recommended by Oracle, and it is probably shunned by others as well, you could alter the version number of the MySQL compilation to indicate that it is the one you compiled.

Let's assume you want to identify your modifications at a glance. For example, you want to see in the client window some indication that the server is your modified version. You could change the version number to show that. Figure 3-4 is an example of such a modification.

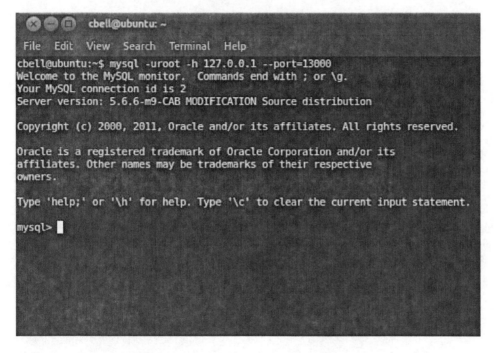

Figure 3-4. *Sample MySQL command cient with version modification*

Notice in both the header and the result of issuing the command, SELECT Version();, the version number returned is the same version number of the server you compiled plus an additional label that I placed in the string. To make this change yourself, simply edit the set_server_version() function in the mysqld.cpp file, as shown in Listing 3-30. In the example, I have bolded the one line of code you can add to create this effect.

Listing 3-30. Modified set_server_version Function

```
/*
  Create version name for running mysqld version
  We automaticly add suffixes -debug, -embedded and -log to the version
  name to make the version more descriptive.
  (MYSQL_SERVER_SUFFIX is set by the compilation environment)
*/

static void set_server_version(void)
{
  char *end= strxmov(server_version, MYSQL_SERVER_VERSION,
                     MYSQL_SERVER_SUFFIX_STR, NullS);
#ifdef EMBEDDED_LIBRARY
  end= strmov(end, "-embedded");
#endif
#ifndef DBUG_OFF
  if (!strstr(MYSQL_SERVER_SUFFIX_STR, "-debug"))
    end= strmov(end, "-debug");
#endif
  if (opt_log || opt_slow_log || opt_bin_log)
    strmov(end, "-log");                          // This may slow down system
  /* BEGIN CAB MODIFICATION */
  /* Reason for modification: */
  /* This section adds my revision note to the MySQL version number. */
  strmov(end, "-CAB MODIFICATION");
  /* END CAB MODIFICATION */
}
```

Note also that I have included the modification comments I referred to earlier. This will help you determine which lines of code you have changed. This change also has the benefit that the new version number will be shown in other MySQL tools, such as the MySQL Workbench. Figure 3-5 shows the results of running the SELECT @@version query in MySQL Workbench against the code compiled with this change.

Figure 3-5. *Accessing the modified MySQL server using MySQL Workbench*

■ **Caution**   Did I mention that this isn't an approved method? If you are using MySQL to conduct your own experiments or you are modifying the source code for your own use, you can get away with doing what I have suggested. If, however, you are creating modifications that will be added to the base source code at a later date, you should *not* implement this technique.

Summary

In this chapter, you learned several methods of getting the source code. Whether you choose to download a snapshot of the source tree or a copy of the GA release source code, or to use the developer-milestone releases to gain access to the latest and greatest version, you can get and start using the source code. That is the beauty of open source!

Perhaps the most intriguing aspect of this chapter is your guided tour of the MySQL source code. I hope that by following a simple query all the way through the system and back, you gained a lot of ground on your quest to understand the MySQL source code. I also hope that you haven't tossed the book down in frustration if you've encountered issues with compiling the source code. Much of what makes a good open-source developer is her ability to systematically diagnose and adapt her environment to the needs of the current project. Do not despair if you had issues come up. Solving issues is a natural part of the learning cycle.

You also explored the major elements from the MySQL Coding Guidelines document and saw examples of some code formatting and documentation guidelines. While not complete, the coding guidelines I presented are enough to give you a feel for how Oracle wants you to write the source code for your modifications. If you follow these simple guidelines, you should not be asked to conform later.

In the next two chapters, I take you through two very important concepts of software development that are often overlooked. The next chapter shows you how to apply a test-driven development methodology to exploring and extending the MySQL system, and the chapter that follows discusses debugging the MySQL source code.

CHAPTER 4

■ ■ ■

Test-Driven MySQL Development

Systems integrators must overcome the limitations of the systems they are integrating, but sometimes a system lacks certain functions or commands that are needed for the integration. Oracle recognizes this and includes flexible options in the MySQL server that add new functions and commands. This chapter introduces a key element in generating high-quality extensions to the MySQL system. I discuss software testing and explain some common practices for testing large systems, using specific examples to illustrate the accepted practices of testing the MySQL system.

Background

Why include a chapter about testing so early in the book? You need to learn about the testing capabilities available so that you can plan your own modifications by first planning how to test them. This is the premise of test-driven development: to develop and implement the tests from the requirements, write the code, and then immediately execute the tests. This may sound a tad counterintuitive to someone not familiar with this concept—after all, how do you write tests for code that hasn't been written?

In the following sections, I'll clarify by providing some background information about this increasingly popular concept.

Why Test?

When I lecture about software quality issues, I often get asked, "Why test?" Some students want to know how much testing is enough. I offer students who feel testing is largely a waste of time, or that it is highly overrated, the opportunity to complete their class projects[1] using a minimal- or no-testing strategy. The results are often interesting and enlightening.[2]

These same students often discuss how well they code their modules and classes and how careful they are to use good modeling practices. Many use Unified Modeling Language (UML) diagrams to assist their software development. While these are good practices, testing involves a lot more than making sure your source code matches your model. Students who insist that their highly honed coding skills are sufficient often produce project deliverables that have feature and functionality issues.

Although most of these projects do not suffer from fatal errors or crashes (which are often found during development), they often have issues with integration and how the software works. That is, the students fail to ensure that their software works the way the customer expects it to.

---

[1]Which normally include large group projects beginning with requirements elicitation.
[2]Especially when I announce the next project, in which teams pass their projects to other teams for software testing. It is amazing how many defects they find in other students' code while insisting their own coding is superior.

If this has happened to you, you now know the value of software testing. Choosing *which* technique to use *when* is the real nature of the science of software testing.

■ **Tip** Professional software testers (sometimes called quality control engineers or quality assurance engineers) have a very different view of software. If you ever work with a professional software tester, spend time learning to understand how they approach software testing. They often have incredible insight—which few developers ever hone successfully— into how software works. Don't be embarrassed if they break your code—that's their job, and most are very good at it!

Testing vs. Debugging

Although they often have the same goal—identifying defects, debugging and testing are not the same. Debugging is an interactive process designed to locate defects in the logic of the source code by exposing the internal workings of the source code. Testing, on the other hand, identifies defects in the execution of the source code without examining its inner workings.

Test-Driven Development

Test-driven development is often associated with agile programming and often used by organizations that adopt extreme programming (XP) methods. That may sound scary, but here's a secret about XP: you don't have to adopt XP to use agile practices!

I often encounter developers who are deeply concerned about adopting agile practices because of all the negative hype tossed about by uninformed people. Those who view traditional software engineering processes as cast in stone think that agile practices are designed to do more with less, and that, therefore, they are inferior. Others believe that agile practices "cut out the clutter" of requirements analysis and design to "focus on the code." None of this is true.

Agile practices are designed to streamline software development, to re-engage the customer, to produce only *what* is needed *when* it is needed, and to focus on the job at hand (what the customer wants). The customer, not the process, is the focus of agile methods Clearly, the emphasis is on analysis and design.

Furthermore, agile practices are designed to be used either as a set or selectively in an application. That is, organizations are encouraged to adopt agile practices as they see fit rather than jumping in with both feet and turning their engineers' world upside down. That is one reason behind the negative hype—that and the resulting failures reported by organizations that tried to do too much too soon.[3] If you would like to learn more about the debate about agile versus traditional methods, direct your browser to the Agile Alliance web site, http://www.agilealliance.org.

One profoundly useful agile practice is test-driven development. The philosophy of test-driven development is simple: start with a basic model of the solution, write the test, run the test (which will fail), code the solution, and validate it with the test (when the unaltered test passes). While that sounds really intuitive, it is amazing how complicated it can become. Creating the test before the code sounds backward. How can you test something that doesn't exist? How can that help?

Developing the test first allows you to focus on the design of your software rather than on the code. I'll explain a typical test-driven agile development process so that you can see how test-driven development complements the design and actually drives the source code. That sounds weird, but give it a chance and it will make sense.

---

[3]Yes, this is a bit of a dichotomy, considering agile practices are designed to reduce unnecessary work.

Test-driven development begins with a simple model of the system, usually a simple class diagram of the basic classes within the system. The class diagram is set with just the empty class blocks, annotated only with the *proposed* name of the class. I say *proposed* because this is usually the point at which developers who are used to traditional methods get stumped. In agile practices, nothing is set in stone, and anything can be a candidate for change (a practice known as *refactoring*)—It just has to make sense and to further the ultimate goal of producing the software that the customer wants.

WHAT IS REFACTORING?

Refactoring is a process of critical analysis that asks, "How can this be done better?" For example, when examining code for defect repair or adding new features, developers who practice refactoring look for better ways to reorganize the code to make it more efficient and easier to maintain. The goal of refactoring, therefore, is improve the nonfunctional aspects of the software.

While refactoring is often associated with source code, the premise applies to all areas of software development, from refining source code to refining tests for greater coverage.

Once an initial class diagram is created, it is copied, set aside, and referred to as the *domain model*, because it depicts the initial layout of your classes. From there, use case diagrams, and supplemental use-case scenarios (textual descriptions of the use case and alternative execution sequences) are created. Each use case is then augmented by a single sequence diagram that maps out the functions needed for the classes referenced.

As each class begins to take shape, you begin writing the tests. Even though the classes don't exist, you still must write the tests—they form a hybrid of integration, system, and interface testing (all white-box techniques) in which each test exercises one of the classes in the domain model.

■ **Note**   *White-box* testing is testing without knowledge of how the system is constructed. *Black-box* testing is testing the behavior of the system given knowledge of its internal structures.

For most agile practices, at this point the lessons learned from the first iteration of this sequence are incorporated into the appropriate parts of the design (use case, sequence diagram, etc.) and the appropriate changes are made.

■ **Note**   Some agile practitioners add another modeling step to the process by using robustness diagrams. This adaptation closely resembles the ICONIX process. For more information about the ICONIX process, see "*Agile Development with ICONIX Process.*"[4]

Sometimes these changes include the discovery of new classes, the reorganization of the existing class, and even the formulation of the methods and properties of the class. In other words, writing the test before the code helps validate the design. That is really cool, because once you complete the level of design you want for your iteration and begin writing the source code, your tests are completed! You can simply run them and demonstrate that your code is working as designed. Of course, if you need to change the test, and therefore the design—well, that's the beauty of agile development.

---

[4]D. Rosenberg, M. Stephens, M. Collins-Cope. *Agile Development with ICONIX Process* (Berkeley, CA: Apress, 2005).

Benchmarking

Benchmarking is designed to establish performance characteristics of software. You can use benchmarking to establish a known performance level (called a *baseline*) and then later run the benchmarks again after a change in the environment in which the software executes to determine the effects of those changes. This is the most common use of benchmarking. Others include identification of performance limits under load, managing change to the system or environment, and identifying conditions that may be causing performance problems.

You perform benchmarking by running a set of tests that exercise the system, and storing the performance counter results, called benchmarks. They are typically stored or archived and annotated with a description of the system environment. For example, savvy database professionals often include the benchmarks and a dump of the system configuration and environment in their archive. This permits them to compare how the system performed in the past with how it is currently performing and to identify any changes to the system or its environment.

The tests, normally of the functional variety, are targeted toward testing a particular feature or function of the system. Benchmarking tools include a broad range of tests that examine everything about the system, from the mundane to the most complex operations, under light, medium, and heavy loads.

Although most developers consider running benchmarks only when something odd happens, it can be useful to run the benchmarks at fixed intervals or even before and after major events, such as changes to the system or the environment. Remember to run your benchmarks the first time to create a baseline. Benchmarks taken after an event without a baseline will not be very helpful.

Guidelines for Good Benchmarks

Many good practices are associated with benchmarking. In this section, I take you through a few that I've found to be helpful in getting the most out of benchmarking.

First, always consider the concept of before-and-after snapshots. Don't wait until after you've made a change to the server to see how it compares to the baseline you took six months ago—a lot can happen in six months. Instead, measure the system before the change, make the change, and then measure the system again. This will give you three metrics to compare: how the system is expected to perform, how it performs before the change, and how it performs after the change. You may find that something has taken place that makes your change more or less significant. For example, let's say your benchmarks include a metric for query time. Your baseline established six months ago for a given test query was set at 4.25 seconds. You decide to modify the index of the table being tested. You run your before benchmark and get a value of 15.50, and your after benchmark produces a value of 4.5 seconds. If you had not taken the before picture, you wouldn't have known that your change increased performance dramatically. Instead, you might have concluded that the change caused the query to perform a bit slower—which might have led you to undo that change, thus resulting in a return to slower queries.

This example exposes several aspects that I want to warn you about. If you are conducting benchmarks on the performance of data retrieval on systems that are expected to grow in the amount of data stored, you need to run your benchmarks more frequently, so that you can map the effects of the growth of data with the performance of the system. In the previous example, you would have considered the before value to be "normal" for the conditions of the system, such as data load.

Also, be careful to ensure that your tests are valid for what you are measuring. If you are benchmarking the performance of a query for a table, your benchmarks are targeted at the application level and are not useful for predicting the performance of the system in the general sense. Segregate application-level benchmarks from the more general metrics to avoid skewing your conclusions.

Another good practice that is related to the before-and-after concept is to run your benchmarks several times over a constrained period of activity (under a consistent load) to ensure that they are not affected by localized activity, such as a rogue process or a resource-intensive task. I find that running the benchmark up to several dozen times permits me to determine mean values for the results. You can create these aggregates using many techniques.

For example, you could use a statistic package to create the basic statistics, or use your favorite statistical friendly spreadsheet application.[5]

■ **Note**   Some benchmark tools provide this feature for you. Alas, the MySQL Benchmark Suite does not.

Perhaps the most useful practice to adopt is changing one thing at a time. Don't go through your server with a wide brush of changes and expect to conclude anything meaningful from the results. What often happens in this case is that one of the six or so changes negatively affects the gains of several others, and the remaining ones have little or no effect on performance. Unless you made one change at a time, you would have no idea which affected the system in a negative, positive, or neutral way.

Use real data whenever possible. Sometimes manufactured data contain data that fall neatly into the ranges of the fields specified and that therefore never test certain features of the system (domain and range checking, etc.). If your data can change frequently, you may want to snapshot the data at some point and build your tests using the same set of data each time. While this will ensure you are testing the performance using real data, however, it may not test performance degradation over time with respect to growth.

Last, when interpreting the results of your benchmarks and managing your expectations, set realistic goals. If you are trying to improve the performance of the system under certain conditions, have a firm grasp of the known consequences before you set your goals. For example, if you are examining the effect of switching the network interface from a gigabit connection to an interface that performs network communication 100 times faster, your server will not perform its data transfer 100 times faster. In this case and ones similar to it, the value added by the hardware should be weighed against the cost of the hardware and the expected gains of using the new hardware. In other words, your server should perform some percentage faster, thereby saving you money (or increasing income).

If you estimate that you need to increase your network performance by 10 percent in order to meet a quarterly expense and income goal that will lead to a savings, use that value as your goal. If your benchmarks show that you have achieved the desired improvements (or, better yet, surpassed them), ask your boss for a raise. If the benchmarks show performance metrics that don't meet the goal, tell your boss you can save him money by returning the hardware (and then ask for a raise). Either way, you can back up your claims with empirical data: your benchmarks!

Benchmarking Database Systems

You might agree that benchmarking can be a very powerful tool in your arsenal, but what, exactly, do benchmarks have to do with database servers? The answer is—a lot. Knowing when your database server is performing its best allows you to set a bar for measuring performance degradation during heavy query-processing loads. More to the point, how would you decide whether a resource intensive query is the cause or the effect of a performance issue?

You can benchmark your database server on many levels. The most notable is benchmarking changes to your database schema. You would probably not create tests for a single table (although you can), but you are more likely to be interested in how the changes for a database schema affect performance.

This is especially true for new applications and databases. You can create several schemas, populate them with data, and write benchmark tests designed to mimic the proposed system. (Here's that test-driven thing again.) By creating the alternative schemas and benchmarking them, and perhaps even making several iterations of changes, you can quickly determine which schemas are best for the application you are designing.

You can also benchmark database systems for specialized uses. For example, you might want to check the performance of your database system under various loads or in various environments. What better way to say for sure

---

[5]Some statisticians consider the statistical engine in Microsoft Excel to be inaccurate. For the values you are likely to see, however, the inaccuracies are not a problem.

whether that new RAID device will improve performance than to run before-and-after benchmarks and know just how much of a difference the change to the environment makes? Yes, it *is* all about the cost, and benchmarking will help manage your database-system cost.

Profiling

Sometimes a defect doesn't manifest unless the system is under load. In these cases, the system may slow down but not produce any errors. How do you find those types of problems? You need a way to examine the system while it is running. This process is called *profiling*. Some authors group profiling with debugging, but profiling is more than just a debugging tool. Profiling allows you to identify performance bottlenecks and potential problems before they are detected in the benchmarks. Profiling is usually done after a problem is detected and sometimes as a means to determine its origins, however. You can discover or monitor memory and disk consumption, CPU usage, I/O usage, system response time, and many other system parameters using profiling.

The term *profile* (or *profiler*) is sometimes confused with performing the measurement of the targeted system parameters. The identification of the performance metric is called a *diagnostic operation* or *technique* (or sometimes a *trace*). A system that manages these diagnostic operations and permits you to run them against a system is called a profiler. Therefore, profiling is the application of diagnostic operations using a profiler.

Profilers typically produce reports that include machine-readable recordings of the system during a fixed time period. These types of performance measurements are commonly called traces, because they trace the path of the system over time. Other profilers are designed to produce human-readable printouts that detail specifics of what portion of the system executed the longest or, more commonly, where the system spent most of its time. This type of profiler is typically used to monitor resources such as I/O, memory, CPU, and threads or processes. For example, you can discover what commands or functions your threads and processes are performing. If your system records additional metadata in the thread or process headers, you may also discover performance issues with thread or process blocking and deadlocks.

■ **Note**   An example of deadlocking is when a process has a lock (exclusive access) to one resource and is waiting on another that is locked in turn by another process that is waiting for the first resource. Deadlock detection is a key attribute of a finely designed database system.

You can also use profiling to determine which queries are performing the poorest, and even which threads or processes are taking the longest to execute. In these situations, you may also discover that a certain thread or process is consuming a large number of resources (such as CPU or memory) and thus take steps to correct the problem. This situation is not uncommon in environments with a large community of users accessing central resources.

Sometimes certain requests of the system result in situations in which the actions of one user (legitimate or otherwise—let's hope the legitimate kind) may be affecting others. In this case, you can correctly identify the troublesome thread or process and its owner, and take steps to correct the problem.

Profiling can also be a powerful diagnostic aid when developing systems, hence the tendency to call them debugging tools. The types of reports you can obtain about your system can lead you to all manner of unexpected inefficiencies in your source code. Take care not to overdo it, however. You can spend a considerable amount of time profiling a piece of source code that takes a long time to execute such that you may never fully meet your expectations of identifying the bottleneck. Remember, some things take a while to execute. Such is the case for disk I/O or network latency. Usually you can't do a lot about it except redesign your architecture to become less dependent on slow resources. Of course, if you were designing an embedded real-time system, this may indeed be a valid endeavor, but it generally isn't worth the effort to try to improve something you cannot control.

You should always strive to make your code run as efficiently as possible, however. If you find a condition in which your code can be improved using profiling, then by all means do it. Just don't get carried away trying to identify or track the little things. Go after the big-ticket items first.

BENCHMARKING OR PROFILING?

The differences between benchmarking and profiling are sometimes confused. *Benchmarking* establishes a performance rating or measurement. Profiling identifies the behavior of the system in terms of its performance.

While benchmarking is used to establish known performance characteristics under given configurations, profiling is used to Identify where the system is spending most of its execution time. Benchmarking, therefore, is used to ensure the system is performing at or better than a given standard (baseline), whereas profiling is used to determine performance bottlenecks.

Introducing Software Testing

Software testing is increasingly vital to our industry, because it's long been clear that a significant contributor to the failure of software systems is the lack of sufficient testing or time to conduct it.

The means by which the testing is conducted and the goals of testing itself are sometimes debated, however. For example, the goal of a well-designed test is to detect the presence of defects. That sounds right, doesn't it? Think about that a moment—that means a successful test is one that has found a defect. So, what happens if the test doesn't find any defects? Did the test fail because it was incorrectly written, or did it just not produce any errors? These debates (and many others) are topics of interest for software-testing researchers.

Some software testers (let's just call them testers for short) consider a test successful if it doesn't find any defects, which isn't the same as stating that a successful test is one that finds defects. If you take the viewpoint of these testers, it is possible for a system to pass testing (all tests successful) and yet still have defects. In this case, the focus is on the test and not the software. Furthermore, if defects are found after testing, it is seldom considered a failure of the tests.

However, if you take the viewpoint that a successful test is one that finds defects, your tests fail only when the software has no defects. Thus, when no defects are found, the goal becomes making the tests more robust so that they can discover more defects.

Functional Testing vs. Defect Testing

Testers are often focused on ensuring the system performs the way the specification (also known as a requirements document) dictates. They often conduct tests that verify the functionality of the specification and therefore are not attempting to find defects. This type of testing is called *functional testing* and sometimes *system testing*. Tests are created with no knowledge of the internal workings of the system (called *black-box testing*) and are often written as a user-centric stepwise exercise of a feature of the software. For example, if a system includes a print feature, functional tests can be written to execute the print feature using the preferred and alternate execution scenarios. A successful test in this case would show that the print feature works without errors and the correct output is given. Functional testing is just one of the many types of testing that software engineers and testers can use to ensure they produce a high-quality product.

The first viewpoint, *defect testing, is* the purposeful intent of causing the system to fail given a set of valid and invalid input data. These tests are often written with knowledge of the internal workings of the software (often referred to as *white-box testing*). Defect tests are constructed to exercise all the possible execution scenarios (or paths) through the source code for a particular component of the software while testing all of its gate and threshold conditions. For instance, if you were to write defect tests for the print feature example, you would write tests that test not only the correct operation of the feature but also every known error handler and exception trigger. That is, you would write the test to purposefully try to break the code. In this case, the defect test that completes without identifying defects can be considered a failed test (or simply negative—"failed" gives the impression that there is something wrong, but there isn't; simply put, no errors were found in this case).[6]

For the purposes of this book, I present a combination of the functional and the defect testing viewpoints. That is, I show you how to conduct functional testing that has built-in features for detecting defects. The testing mechanism we'll use allows you to conduct functional tests against the MySQL server using tests that execute SQL statements. Although you can construct tests that simply test functionality, you can also construct tests to identify defects. Indeed, I recommend that you write all of your tests to test the error handlers and exceptions. Should your test fail to identify a defect, or a bug is reported to you later, you can create a test or modify an existing test to test for the presence of that bug. That way, you can repeat the bug before you fix it and later show that the bug has been fixed.

Types of Software Testing

Software testing is often conducted in a constrained process that begins with analyzing the system requirements and design. Tests are then created using the requirements and design to ensure the quality (correctness, robustness, usability, etc.) of the software. As I mentioned earlier, some tests are conducted to identify defects and others are used to verify functionality without errors (which is not the same as not having defects). The goal of some testing techniques is to establish a critique or assessment of the software. These tests are typically focused on qualitative factors rather than quantitative results.

Testing is part of a larger software engineering mantra that ensures the software meets its requirements and delivers the desired functionality. This process is sometimes referred to as *verification and validation*. It is easy to confuse these. Validation simply means you are ensuring that the software was built to its specifications. Verification simply means that you followed the correct processes and methodologies to create it. In other words, validation asks, "Did we build the right product?" and verification asks, "Did we build the product right?"

While many software-development processes include verification and validation activities, most developers refer to the portion of the process that validates that the specifications are met as *software testing*. Moreover, the validation process is typically associated with testing the functions of the system and the absence of defects in the functionality rather than the correctness of the software.

You can conduct many types of software testing. Indeed, there are often spirited discussions during early project planning about what type of testing should or should not be required. Fortunately, most developers agree that testing is a vital component of software development. In my experience, however, few understand the role of the different types of software testing. Only you can choose what is right for your project. My goal is to explain some of the more popular types of software testing so that you can apply the ones that make the most sense for your needs.

The following sections describe popular software-testing techniques, their goals and applications, and how they relate to continuous test-driven development. As you will see, the traditional stages of testing are milestones in the continuous testing effort.

Integration Testing

Integration testing is conducted as the system is assembled from its basic building blocks. Tests usually are written to test first a single component, then that component and another, and so on, until the entire system is integrated. This form of testing is most often used in larger development projects that are built using semi-independent components.

---

[6]For more information about software testing, see http://en.wikipedia.org/wiki/Software_testing.

Component Testing

Component testing is conducted on a semi-independent portion (or component) of the system in an isolated test run. That is, the component is exercised by calling all its methods and interrogating all its attributes. Component tests are usually constructed in the form of test harnesses that provide all the external communication necessary to test a component. This includes any dependent components, which are simulated using code scaffolding (sometimes called mock or stub components). These code scaffolds provide all the input and output necessary to communicate and exercise the component being tested.

Interface Testing

Interface testing is conducted on the interface of the component itself rather than on the component. The purpose is to show that the interface provides all the functionality required. This type of testing is usually done in coordination with component testing.

Regression Testing

Regression testing ensures that any addition or correction of the software does not affect other portions of it. In this case, tests that were run in the past are run again and the results compared to the previous run. If the results are the same, the change did not affect the functionality (insofar as the test is written). This type of testing normally uses automated testing software that permits developers (or testers) to run the tests unattended. The results are then compared after the bulk of tests are completed. Automated testing is a popular concept in the agile development philosophy.

Path Testing

Path testing ensures that all possible paths of execution are exercised. Tests are written with full knowledge of the source code (white-box testing) and are generally not concerned with conformance to specifications but rather with the system's ability to accurately traverse all of its conditional paths. Many times, though, these tests are conducted with functionality in mind.

Alpha-Stage Testing

Traditionally, alpha-stage testing begins once a stable development-quality system is ready. This is typically early in the process of producing software for production use. Testing at this stage is sometimes conducted to ensure the system has achieved a level of stability at which most of the functionality can be used (possibly with minor defects). This may include running a partial set of tests that validate that the system works under guarded conditions. Systems deemed alpha are normally mostly complete and may include some known defect issues, ranging from minor to moderate. Typically, passing alpha testing concludes the alpha stage, and the project moves on to the beta stage.

It is at this point that the system is complete enough so that all tests are running against actual code and no scaffolding (stubbed classes) are needed. When the test results satisfy the project parameters for what is considered a beta, the project moves on to the beta stage.

Beta-Stage Testing

A project is typically considered a stable production-quality system when it boasts a complete set of functionality but may include some features that have yet to be made efficient or may require additional robustness work (hardening). Tests run at this stage are generally the complete set of tests for the features being delivered. If defects are found, they are usually minor. This type of testing can include tests conducted by the target audience and the customer. These groups tend to be less scientific in their approach to testing, but they offer developers a chance to vet their system with the customer and make any minor course corrections to improve their product. Passing beta testing means the software is ready to be prepared for eventual release.

In a test-driven development environment, beta testing is another milestone in the continuing testing effort. A beta under a test-driven development is normally the point at which the majority of the features are performing well with respect to the test results. The level of stability of the system is usually judged as producing few defects.

Release, Functional, and Acceptance Testing

Release testing is usually functional testing by which the system is validated that it meets its specifications, and this testing is conducted prior to delivery of the system to the customer. As with the beta stage, some organizations choose to involve the customer in this stage of testing. In this case, the testing method is usually called *acceptance testing,* as it is the customers who decide that the software is validated to meet their specifications. A test-driven development environment would consider these milestones as the completion of the tests.

Usability Testing

Usability testing is conducted after or near the completion of the system and is sometimes conducted parallel to functional and release testing. The goal of usability testing is to determine how well a user can interact with the system. There is usually no pass-or-fail result but rather a list of likes and dislikes. Though very subjective and based solely on the users' preferences, usability testing can be helpful in creating software that can gain the loyalty of its users.

Usability testing is best completed in a laboratory designed to record the users' responses and suggestions for later review. This allows the users to focus on the software without distractions. Most usability testing, however, is done in an informal setting where the developer observes the user using the system or where the user is given the software to use for a period of time and then her comments are taken as part of a survey or interview.

Reliability Testing

Reliability tests are usually designed to vary the load on the system and to challenge the system with complex data and varying quantities of load (data), and they are conducted in order to determine how well the system continues to run over a period of time. Reliability is typically measured in the number of hours the system continues to function and the number of defects per hour or per test.

Performance Testing

Performance testing is conducted either to establish performance behaviors (benchmarking) or to ensure that the system performs within established guidelines. Aspects of the system being examined sometimes include reliability as well as performance. Performance under extreme loads (known as stress testing) is sometimes examined during this type of testing.

■ **Note**   Usability, reliability, and performance testing are forms of testing that can be conducted in either a traditional testing or a test-driven development environment.

Test Design

Now that you have had a brief introduction to software testing and the types of testing that you can conduct in your own projects, let's turn our attention to how tests are constructed. All the different philosophies for constructing tests ultimately intend to exercise, validate, or verify a certain aspect of the software or its process. Let's look at three of the most prominent basic philosophies.

Specification-Based Tests

Specification-based tests (sometimes called *functional tests*) exercise the software requirements and design. The focus is to validate that the software meets its specification. These tests are usually constructed (and based on) a given requirement or group of requirements. Tests are organized into functional sets (sometimes called *test suites*). As a system is being built, the test sets can be run whenever the requirements are completed or at any time later in the process to validate continued compliance with the requirement (also known as *regression testing*).

Partition Tests

Partition tests focus on the input and output data characteristics of the system. They test the outer, edge, and mean value ranges of the input or output data being tested. For example, suppose a system is designed to accept input of a positive integer value in the range of 1 to 10. You can form partitions (called equivalence partitions or domains) of this data by testing the values {0, 1, 5, 10, 11}. Some may take this further and include a negative value, such as –1. The idea is that if the system does perform range checking, it is more likely that the boundary conditions will exhibit defects than will the valid, or even wildly invalid, data.

In our earlier example, there is no need to test values greater than 11 unless you want to test the internal data-collection code (the part of the system that reads and interprets the input). Most modern systems use system-level calls to manage the data entry that by their nature are very reliable (e.g., Microsoft Windows Forms). What is most interesting is you can form partitions for the output data as well. In this case, the tests are designed to exercise how the system takes in known data (good or bad) and produces results (good or bad). In this case, tests are attempting to validate the robustness aspect as well as accuracy of the processing the input data. Partition testing is useful in demonstrating that the system meets performance and robustness aspects.

Structural Tests

Structural tests (sometimes called *architectural tests*) ensure that the system is built according to the layout (or architecture) specified—that is, to verify that the system conforms to a prescribed construction. Tests of this nature are designed to ensure that certain interfaces are available and are working, and that components are working together properly. These categories of tests include all manner of white-box testing, where the goal is to exercise every path through the system (known as *path testing*). These tests can be considered of the verification variety, because they establish whether the architecture was built correctly and that it followed the prescribed process.

MySQL Testing

You can test the MySQL system in many ways. You can test the server connectivity and basic functionality using the `mysqlshow` command, run tests manually using the client tools, use the benchmarking tools to establish performance characteristics, and even conduct profiling on the server. The tools of choice for most database professionals are the MySQL Test Suite and the MySQL Benchmarking tool. The following sections describe each of these facilities and techniques.

Using the MySQL Test Suite

Oracle has provided a capable testing facility called the MySQL Test Suite, an executable named mysqltest and a collection of Perl modules and scripts designed to exercise the system and compare the results. Table 4-1 lists some of the pertinent directories and their contents. The test suite comes with the Unix/Linux binary and source distributions, although it is included in some Mac and Windows distributions.

Table 4-1. *Directories under the* mysql-test *Directory*

Directory	Contents
/collections	Groups of tests executed during integration and release testing
/r	Main suite of result files
/std_data	Test data for the test suite
/suite	Also called "suites," a subfolder containing feature-specific tests, such as binlog, (storage) engines, and replication
/t	The main suite tests

■ **Note** The MySQL Test Suite does not currently run in the Windows environment. This would be an excellent project to take on if you wanted to contribute to the development of MySQL through the MySQL code-contribution program. It can be run in the Cygwin environment if the Perl environment is set up and the Perl DBI modules are installed. See "Perl Installation Notes" in the MySQL Reference Manual for more details.

When MySQL is installed, you will find the mysql-test-run.pl Perl script in the mysql-test directory under the installation directory. Best of all, the test suite is extensible. You can write your own tests and conduct testing for your specific application or need. The tests are designed as regression tests in the sense that the tests are intended to be run to ensure all the functionality works as it has in the past.

The tests are located in a directory under the mysql-test directory named simply /t. This directory contains nearly 740 tests along with more than 3,400 tests among all of the suites. While that may sound comprehensive, the MySQL documentation states that the test suite does not cover all the features or nuances of the system. The current set of tests is designed to detect bugs in most SQL commands, the operating system and library interactions, and cluster and replication functionality. Oracle hopes to ultimately accumulate enough tests to provide test coverage for the entire system. The goal is to establish a set of tests that test 100 percent of the features of the MySQL system. If you create additional tests that you feel cover a feature that isn't already covered by one of the tests in the mysql-test/t directory, feel free to submit your tests to Oracle.

■ **Tip** You can find more information about the MySQL Test Suite by visiting the MySQL Internals mailing list (see http://lists.mysql.com/ for more details and to see the available lists). You can also submit your tests for inclusion by sending an e-mail message to the list. If you decide to send your tests to Oracle for inclusion in the test suite, be sure you are using data that you can show the world. The tests are available to everyone. For example, I am sure your friends and relatives would not want their phone numbers showing up in every installation of MySQL!

For each test, a corresponding result file is stored in the `mysql-test/r` directory. The result file contains the output of the test run and is used to compare (using the diff command) the results of the test as it is run. In many ways, the result file is the benchmark for the output of the test. This enables you to create tests and save the expected results, then run the test later and ensure that the system is producing the same output.

You must use this premise with some caution. Data values that, by their nature, change between executions can be used, but they require additional commands to handle properly. Unfortunately, data values such as these are ignored by the test suite rather than compared directly. Thus, time and date fields are data types that could cause some issues if used in a test. I discuss more on this topic and other commands later.

Running Tests

Running tests using the test suite is easy. Simply navigate to the `mysql-test` directory and execute the command `./mysql-test-run.pl`. This will launch the test executable, connect to the server, and run all the tests in the `/t` directory. Because running all the tests could take some time, Oracle has written the test suite to allow you to execute several tests in order. For example, the following command will run just the tests named t1, t2, and t3:

```
%> ./mysql-test-run.pl t1 t2 t3
```

The test suite will run each test in order but will stop if any test fails. To override this behavior, use the `--force` command-line parameter to force the test suite to continue.

The test suite is designed to execute its own instance of the `mysqld` executable. This may conflict with another instance of the server running on your machine. You may want to shut down other instances of the MySQL server before running the test suite. If you use the test suite from the source directory, you can create the `mysqld` executable by compiling the source code. This is especially handy if you want to test something you've changed in the server but do not want to or cannot take your existing server down to do so.

■ **Caution**   You can run the test suite alongside an existing server as long as the server is not using port 13000 and above. If it is, the test suite may not run correctly, and you may need to stop the server or change it to use other ports.

If you want to connect to a specific server instance, you can use the `--extern` command-line parameter to tell the test suite to connect to the server. If you have additional startup commands or want to use a specific user to connect to the server, you can add those commands as well. For more information about the available command-line parameters to the `mysql-test-run` script, enter the command `%>./mysql-test-run.pl --help`.

Visit `http://dev.mysql.com/doc/mysql/en/mysql-test-suite.html` for more details.

■ **Note**   Using the `--extern` command-line parameter requires that you also include the name of the tests you want to execute. Some tests require a local instance of the server to execute. For example, the following command connects to a running server and executes the alias and analyze tests: `perl mysql-test-run.pl --extern alias analyze`.

Creating a New Test

To create your own test, use a standard text editor to create the test in the `/t` directory in a file named `mytestname.test`. For example, I created a sample test named cab.test (see Listing 4-1).

Listing 4-1. Sample Test

```
#
# Sample test to demonstrate MySQL Test Suite
#
--disable_warnings
SHOW DATABASES;
--enable_warnings
CREATE TABLE characters (ID INTEGER PRIMARY KEY,
                        LastName varchar(40),
                        FirstName varchar(20),
                        Gender varchar(2)) ENGINE = MYISAM;
EXPLAIN characters;
#
INSERT INTO characters (ID, LastName, FirstName, Gender)
            VALUES (3, 'Flintstone', 'Fred', 'M');
INSERT INTO characters (ID, LastName, FirstName, Gender)
            VALUES (5, 'Rubble', 'Barney', 'M');
INSERT INTO characters (ID, LastName, FirstName, Gender)
            VALUES (7, 'Flintstone', 'Wilma', 'F');
INSERT INTO characters (ID, LastName, FirstName, Gender)
            VALUES (9, 'Flintstone', 'Dino', 'M');
INSERT INTO characters (ID, LastName, FirstName, Gender)
            VALUES (4, 'Flintstone', 'Pebbles', 'F');
INSERT INTO characters (ID, LastName, FirstName, Gender)
            VALUES (1, 'Rubble', 'Betty', 'F');
INSERT INTO characters (ID, LastName, FirstName, Gender)
            VALUES (6, 'Rubble', 'Bam-Bam', 'M');
INSERT INTO characters (ID, LastName, FirstName, Gender)
            VALUES (8, 'Jetson', 'George', 'M');
#
SELECT * FROM characters;
#
EXPLAIN (SELECT DISTINCT LASTNAME from characters);
#
SELECT DISTINCT LASTNAME from characters;
#
# Cleanup
#
DROP TABLE characters;
# ...and we're done.
```

Notice that the contents of the test are simply SQL commands that create a table, insert some data, and then do a few simple selects. Most tests are a bit more complex than this, but you get the idea. You create your test to exercise some set of commands (or data handling). Notice the first six lines. The first three are comment lines and they begin with a # symbol. Always document your tests with a minimal explanation at the top of the file to indicate what the test is doing. Use comments in the body of the test to explain any commands that aren't easily understood (e.g., complex joins or user-defined functions). The fourth and sixth lines are interesting because they are issuing commands to the test suite. Test-suite commands always begin on a line with -- in front of them. These lines are directing the test suite to temporarily disable and then enable any warning messages from the server. This is necessary in case the table (characters) does not already exist. If I had left the warnings enabled, the test would have failed under this condition because:

- The server would have issued a warning, or

- The output would not match the expected results.

The general layout of your tests should include a cleanup section at the beginning to remove any tables or views that may exist as a result of a failed test. The body of the test should include all the necessary statements to complete the test, and the end of the test should include cleanup statements to remove any tables or views you've created in the test.

■ **Tip** When writing your own tests, Oracle requests that you use table names such as t1, t2, t3, etc. and view names such as v1, v2, or v3, etc., so that your test tables do not conflict with existing ones.

Running the New Test

Once the test is created, you need to execute the test and create the baseline of expected results. Execute the following commands to run the newly created test named cab.test from the mysql-test directory:

```
%> touch r/cab.result
%> ./mysql-test-run.pl cab
%> cp r/cab.reject r/cab.result
%> ./mysql-test-run.pl cab
```

The first command creates an empty result file. This ensures that the test suite has something to compare to. The next command runs the test for the first time. Listing 4-2 depicts a typical first-run test result. Notice that the test suite indicated that the test failed and generated a difference report. This is because there were no results to compare to. I have omitted a number of the more mundane statements for brevity.

Listing 4-2. Running a New Test for the First Time

```
Logging: ./mysql-test-run.pl  cab.test
120620  9:48:44 [Note] Plugin 'FEDERATED' is disabled.
120620  9:48:44 [Note] Binlog end
120620  9:48:44 [Note] Shutting down plugin 'CSV'
120620  9:48:44 [Note] Shutting down plugin 'MyISAM'
MySQL Version 5.6.6
Checking supported features...
 - skipping ndbcluster
 - SSL connections supported
 - binaries are debug compiled
Collecting tests...
Checking leftover processes...
Removing old var directory...
Creating var directory '/source/mysql-5.6/mysql-test/var'...
Installing system database...
Using server port 49261
```

```
================================================================================

TEST                                    RESULT    TIME (ms) or COMMENT
--------------------------------------------------------------------------

main.cab                            [ fail ]
        Test ended at 2012-06-20 09:48:49

CURRENT_TEST: main.cab
--- /source/mysql-5.6/mysql-test/r/cab.result    2012-06-20 16:48:40.000000000 +0300
+++ /source/mysql-5.6/mysql-test/r/cab.reject    2012-06-20 16:48:49.000000000 +0300
@@ -0,0 +1,52 @@
+SHOW DATABASES;
+Database
+information_schema

[...]

+DROP TABLE characters;

mysqltest: Result length mismatch

 - saving '/source/mysql-5.6/mysql-test/var/log/main.cab/' to '/source/mysql-5.6/mysql-test/var/log/
main.cab/'
--------------------------------------------------------------------------
The servers were restarted 0 times
Spent 0.000 of 5 seconds executing testcases

Completed: Failed 1/1 tests, 0.00 % were successful.

Failing test(s): main.cab

The log files in var/log may give you some hint of what went wrong.

If you want to report this error, please read first the documentation
at http://dev.mysql.com/doc/mysql/en/mysql-test-suite.html

mysql-test-run: *** ERROR: there were failing test cases
```

The difference report shows the entire test result because our result file was empty. Had we run a test that was modified, the difference report would show only those portions that differ. This is a very powerful tool that developers use to run regression tests whenever they make changes to the code. It shows them exactly how their code affects the known outcome of the system operation.

The next command copies the newest results from the cab.reject file over the cab.result file. You only do this step once you are certain that the test runs correctly and that there are no unexpected errors. One way to ensure this is to run the test statements manually and verify that they work correctly. Only then should you copy the reject file to a result file. Listing 4-3 depicts the result file for the new test. Notice that the output is exactly what you would expect to see from a manual execution, minus the usual pretty printout and column spacing.

Listing 4-3. The Result File

```
SHOW DATABASES;
Database
information_schema
mtr
mysql
performance_schema
test
CREATE TABLE characters (ID INTEGER PRIMARY KEY,
LastName varchar(40),
FirstName varchar(20),
Gender varchar(2)) ENGINE=MYISAM;
EXPLAIN characters;
Field   Type    Null    Key     Default Extra
ID      int(11) NO      PRI     NULL
LastName        varchar(40)     YES             NULL
FirstName       varchar(20)     YES             NULL
Gender  varchar(2)      YES             NULL
INSERT INTO characters (ID, LastName, FirstName, Gender)
VALUES (3, 'Flintstone', 'Fred', 'M');
INSERT INTO characters (ID, LastName, FirstName, Gender)
VALUES (5, 'Rubble', 'Barney', 'M');
INSERT INTO characters (ID, LastName, FirstName, Gender)
VALUES (7, 'Flintstone', 'Wilma', 'F');
INSERT INTO characters (ID, LastName, FirstName, Gender)
VALUES (9, 'Flintstone', 'Dino', 'M');
INSERT INTO characters (ID, LastName, FirstName, Gender)
VALUES (4, 'Flintstone', 'Pebbles', 'F');
INSERT INTO characters (ID, LastName, FirstName, Gender)
VALUES (1, 'Rubble', 'Betty', 'F');
INSERT INTO characters (ID, LastName, FirstName, Gender)
VALUES (6, 'Rubble', 'Bam-Bam', 'M');
INSERT INTO characters (ID, LastName, FirstName, Gender)
VALUES (8, 'Jetson', 'George', 'M');
SELECT * FROM characters;
ID      LastName        FirstName       Gender
3       Flintstone      Fred            M
5       Rubble          Barney          M
7       Flintstone      Wilma           F
9       Flintstone      Dino            M
4       Flintstone      Pebbles         F
1       Rubble          Betty           F
6       Rubble          Bam-Bam         M
8       Jetson          George          M
EXPLAIN (SELECT DISTINCT LASTNAME from characters);
id      select_type     table   type    possible_keys   key     key_len ref     rows    Extra
1       SIMPLE  characters      ALL     NULL    NULL    NULL    NULL    8       Using temporary
```

133

```
SELECT DISTINCT LASTNAME from characters;
LASTNAME
Flintstone
Rubble
Jetson
DROP TABLE characters;
```

Last, we rerun the test using the expected results, and the test suite reports that the test passed. Listing 4-4 depicts a typical test result.

Listing 4-4. A Successful Test Run

```
Logging: ./mysql-test-run.pl  cab.test
120620   9:53:19 [Note] Plugin 'FEDERATED' is disabled.
120620   9:53:19 [Note] Binlog end
120620   9:53:19 [Note] Shutting down plugin 'CSV'
120620   9:53:19 [Note] Shutting down plugin 'MyISAM'
MySQL Version 5.6.6
Checking supported features...
 - skipping ndbcluster
 - SSL connections supported
 - binaries are debug compiled
Collecting tests...
Checking leftover processes...
Removing old var directory...
Creating var directory '/source/mysql-5.6/mysql-test/var'...
Installing system database...
Using server port 49273


===============================================================================

TEST                                  RESULT    TIME (ms) or COMMENT
-------------------------------------------------------------------------------
main.cab                              [ pass ]    28
-------------------------------------------------------------------------------
The servers were restarted 0 times
Spent 0.028 of 7 seconds executing testcases

Completed: All 1 tests were successful.
```

Creating your own tests and running them is easy. You can repeat the process I just described as many times as you want for as many tests as you want. This process follows the spirit of test-driven development by first creating the test, running it without proof of results, creating the solution (the expected results), and then executing the test and verifying successful test completion. I encourage you to adopt the same philosophy when creating your own MySQL applications and especially when extending the MySQL server.

For example, say you want to create a new SHOW command. In this case, you should create a new test to execute the new command, run it, and establish the test results. Naturally, the test will fail every time until you actually create the new command. The benefit is that it allows you to focus on the results of the command and how the command syntax should be prior to actually writing the code. If you adopt this practice for all your development, you won't regret it and will see dividends in the quality of your code. Once you have implemented the command and verified that it works by running the test again and examining the reject file (or running the command manually), you can copy the reject file to the result file, which the test suite will use for verification (pass/fail) in later test runs.

Advanced Tests

The MySQL Test Suite provides a rich set of commands you can use to create powerful tests. This section introduces some of the more popular and useful commands. Unfortunately, no comprehensive document explains all the available commands. The following are those that I found by exploring the supplied tests and online posts.

■ **Tip** If you use the advanced test-suite commands, you can create the result file using the `--record` command-line parameter to record the proper results. For example, you can run the command `./mysql-test-run.pl --record cab` to record the results of the cab test file.

If you're expecting a certain error to occur (say you're testing the presence of errors rather than the absence of detecting them), you can use the `--error num` command. This command tells the test suite that you expect the error specified and that it should not fail the test when that error occurs. This command is designed to precede the command that produces the error. You can also specify additional error numbers, separated by commas. For example, `--error 1550, 1530` indicates these (fictional) errors are permitted for the command that follows.

You can also use flow of control code inside your test. For example, you can use a loop to execute something for a fixed number of times. The following code executes a command 100 times:

```
let $1 = 100;
while ($1)
{
  # Insert your commands here
  dec($1)
}
```

Another useful command is sleep. The sleep command takes as a parameter the number of seconds to pause before executing the next command. For example, `--real_sleep 3.5` tells the test suite to pause for 3.5 seconds before executing the next command. This command can help if there is unexpected latency in the network or if you're experiencing tests failing due to heavy traffic. Using the sleep command will allow you to slow down the test, thereby reducing any interference due to poor performance by external factors.

Using sleeps for making tests deterministic by overcoming timing issues within the server code is a poor practice, however. For example, inserting sleeps to test queries run from multiple connections is a bad idea. Given the nature of multithreaded execution, coordinating the results using sleeps alone is insufficient, and while using sleeps may enable a test to be deterministic on one machine, (in this case, connection 1 returning results before connection 2), it may not work on another machine.

If you are interested in seeing additional information about a command, use the `--enable_metadata` command. This produces and displays internal metadata that may assist you in debugging commands for a complex test. Similarly, if you want to suppress the recording of the output, use `--disable_result_log` to turn off recording and `--enable_result_log` to turn it back on.

If you have commands that result in data that may change between runs (such as date or time fields), tell the test suite to ignore those values by substituting another character string using the `--replace_column column string` command. For example, if your output produces the current time in the second column (column counting begins at 1, not 0), you can use the command `--replace_column 2 CURTIME`. This tells the test suite that the output from the next command is to have column 2 replaced with the string "CURTIME." While this does suppress the actual value in the output, it provides a way to ignore those values that cannot be predicted because they change between test runs.

Finally, if you need to include additional test commands within a test, you can use the `--source include/filetoinclude.inc` to include a file from the `mysql-test/include` directory. This practice is typical in tests that form a test suite with a set of commonly used commands.

Reporting Bugs

You could find a bug as the result of running one of the tests or in the creation of your own test. Oracle welcomes feedback on the test suite and has provided a means of reporting bugs. Before you fire up your e-mail and crank out an intensive report of the failure, however, be sure to confirm the bug thoroughly.

Oracle asks that you run the test on its own and discover the exact command and error codes behind the failure. First determine if the errors are the result of your environment (see "Operating System-Specific Notes" in the MySQL Reference Manual for potential issues; visit http://dev.mysql.com/doc/refman/5.6/en/ installing.html for more details) by running the test either on a fresh installation or on another known-good installation. You should also run the commands in the test manually to confirm the error and error codes. Sometimes running the commands manually will reveal additional information you could not get otherwise. It may also help to run the server in de-bug mode. Last, if the test and error conditions can be repeated, include the test file, test results, test reject file, and any test data to MySQL when you submit your bug report.

MySQL Benchmarking

Oracle has provided a capable benchmarking facility called the MySQL Bench-marking Suite. This is a collection of Perl modules and scripts designed to exercise the system saving the performance metrics. The benchmarking suite comes with most binary and source distributions and can be run on Windows.[7] When MySQL is installed, you will find the `run-all-tests` script in the `sql-bench` directory under the installation directory. The tests are designed in the regression-test sense in that they are intended to record the performance of the system under current conditions. The benchmarking suite is also available as a separate download for most operating systems from the MySQL developer web site (http://dev.mysql.com).

■ **Note** You will need to install the dbi and DBD::mysql module to use the benchmarking tools. You can download these from the MySQL download page http://dev.mysql.com/downloads/dbi.html.

Like most benchmarking tools, the MySQL Benchmarking Suite is best used to determine the effects of changes to the system and the environment. The benchmarking suite differs somewhat from the testing suite in that the benchmarking suite has the ability to run benchmarks against other systems—you can use the benchmarking suite to run the same benchmarks against your MySQL, Oracle, and Microsoft SQL Server installations. As you can imagine, doing so can help you to determine how much better MySQL performs in your environment than your existing database system. To run the benchmarks against the other servers, use the `--server = 'server'` command-line switch. Values for this parameter include MySQL, Oracle, Informix, and MS-SQL.

A host of command-line parameters control the benchmarking suite. Table 4-2 lists a few popular ones and an explanation of each. See the `README` file in the `sql-bench` directory for more information about the command-line parameters.

To run the benchmarking suite of tests, simply navigate to the `sql-bench` directory under your installation and run the command `run-all-tests`. Notice one important characteristic of the benchmarking suite: all tests are run serially. Thus, the tests are run one at a time. To test the performance of multiple processes, or threads, use a third-party benchmarking suite, such as Sysbench and DBT2.

---

[7]Requires ActivePerl, the official Perl distribution for Windows. See http://www.activestate.org for details and to download the latest version.

Table 4-2. Command-Line Parameters for the MySQL Benchmarking Suite

Command-Line Parameter	Explanation
--log	Saves the results of the benchmarks to a file. Use with the --dir option to specify a directory to store the results in. Result files are named using the same output of the Unix command uname –a.
--user	Specifies the user to log into the server.
--password	Specifies the password of the user for logging in to the server.
--host	Specifies the hostname of the server.
--small-test	Specifies running the minimal benchmarking tests. Omitting this parameter executes the entire benchmarking suite of tests. For most uses, the small tests are adequate for determining the more common performance metrics.

Another limitation of the benchmarking suite is that it is not currently extensible. That is, there is no facility to create your own tests for your own application. The source code is freely distributed, however, so those of you well versed in Perl can have at it. If you do create your own tests, be sure to share them with the global community of developers. You never know—someone might need the test you create.

SYSBENCH AND DBT2

SysBench and DBT2 are benchmarking suites designed to test the system under load. They are available at http://sourceforge.net/projects/sysbench/, and http://osdldbt.sourceforge.net/#dbt2.

■ **Tip** For best results, disable the MySQL query cache before running benchmarks. Turn off the query cache by issuing the command SET GLOBALS query_cache_size=0; in the MySQL client interface. This will allow your benchmarks to record the actual time of the queries rather than the time the system takes to retrieve the query from the cache. You'll get a more accurate reading of the performance of your system.

If the base set of benchmarks is all that you need, you can run the command run-all-tests --small-test and generate the results for the basic set of tests. While running all of the tests ensures a more thorough measurement of the performance, it can also take a long time to complete. If, on the other hand, you identify a particular portion of the system you want to measure, you can run an individual test by executing the test independently. For example, to test the connection to the server, you can run the command test-connect. Table 4-3 lists a few of the independent tests available.

Table 4-3. *Partial List of Benchmarking Tests*

Test	Description
test-ATIS.sh	Creates a number of tables and several selects on them
test-connect.sh	Tests the connection speed to the server
test-create.sh	Tests how quickly a table is created
test-insert.sh	Tests create and fill operations of a table
test-wisconsin.sh	Runs a port of the PostgreSQL version of this benchmark

■ **Note** The benchmarking suite runs the tests in a single thread. Oracle has plans to add multi-threaded tests to the benchmark suite in the future.

For more information about other forms of benchmarking available for MySQL, see Michael Kruckenberg and Jay Pipes's *Pro MySQL*.[8] It is an excellent reference for all things MySQL.

Running the Small Tests

Let's examine what you can expect when you run the benchmarking tools on your system. In this example, I ran the benchmarking suite using the small tests on my Linux system. Listing 4-5 shows the top portion of the output file generated.

Listing 4-5. Excerpt of Small Tests Benchmark

```
$ ./run-all-tests --small-test --password=XXX --user=root
Benchmark DBD suite: 2.15
Date of test:        2012-06-20 10:39:38
Running tests on:    Linux 2.6.38-15-generic x86_64
Arguments:           --small-test
Comments:
Limits from:
Server version:      MySQL 5.1.63 0ubuntu0.11.04.1
Optimization:        None
Hardware:

alter-table: Total time:  1 wallclock secs ( 0.02 usr  0.01 sys +  0.00 cusr  0.00 csys =  0.03 CPU)
ATIS: Total time:  2 wallclock secs ( 0.75 usr  0.23 sys +  0.00 cusr  0.00 csys =  0.98 CPU)
big-tables: Total time:  0 wallclock secs ( 0.06 usr  0.01 sys +  0.00 cusr  0.00 csys =  0.07 CPU)
connect: Total time:  1 wallclock secs ( 0.39 usr  0.14 sys +  0.00 cusr  0.00 csys =  0.53 CPU)
create: Total time:  1 wallclock secs ( 0.02 usr  0.01 sys +  0.00 cusr  0.00 csys =  0.03 CPU)
insert: Total time:  3 wallclock secs ( 1.22 usr  0.24 sys +  0.00 cusr  0.00 csys =  1.46 CPU)
```

---

[8] M. Kruckenberg and J. Pipes. *Pro MySQL* (Berkeley, CA: Apress, 2005).

```
select: Total time:  3 wallclock secs ( 1.27 usr  0.21 sys +  0.00 cusr  0.00 csys =  1.48 CPU)
transactions: Test skipped because the database doesn't support transactions
wisconsin: Total time:  4 wallclock secs ( 1.40 usr  0.49 sys +  0.00 cusr  0.00 csys =  1.89 CPU)

All 9 test executed successfully
```

At the top of the listing, the benchmarking suite gives the metadata describing the tests run, including the date the tests were run, the version of the operating system, the version of the server, and any special optimization or hardware installed (in this case, none). Look at what follows the metadata. You see the results of each of the tests run reporting the wall clock elapsed seconds. The times indicated in the parentheses are the times recorded during the execution of the benchmark suite itself and should be deducted from the actual wall clock seconds for accurate times. Don't be too concerned about this, as this section is mostly used for a brief look at the tests in groups. The next section is the most interesting of all because it contains the actual data collected during each test. The results of the example benchmark tests are shown in Table 4-4. Notice there are a lot of operations being tested.

Table 4-4. *Specific Test Result Data of the Small Tests Run (Totals per Operation)*

Operation	seconds	usr	sys	cpu	tests
alter_table_add	1.00	0.01	0.00	0.01	92
alter_table_drop	0.00	0.00	0.01	0.01	46
connect	0.00	0.04	0.01	0.05	100
connect+select_1_row	0.00	0.05	0.00	0.05	100
connect+select_simple	0.00	0.03	0.02	0.05	100
count	0.00	0.02	0.00	0.02	100
count_distinct	0.00	0.01	0.00	0.01	100
count_distinct_2	0.00	0.01	0.00	0.01	100
count_distinct_big	0.00	0.02	0.00	0.02	30
count_distinct_group	0.00	0.02	0.00	0.02	100
count_distinct_group_on_key	1.00	0.00	0.01	0.01	100
count_distinct_group_on_key_parts	0.00	0.00	0.01	0.01	100
count_distinct_key_prefix	0.00	0.00	0.00	0.00	100
count_group_on_key_parts	0.00	0.01	0.00	0.01	100
count_on_key	0.00	0.55	0.08	0.63	5100
create+drop	0.00	0.00	0.00	0.00	10
create_MANY_tables	0.00	0.00	0.00	0.00	10
create_index	0.00	0.00	0.00	0.00	8

(continued)

Table 4-4. (*continued*)

Operation	seconds	usr	sys	cpu	tests
create_key + drop	1.00	0.02	0.00	0.02	100
create_table	0.00	0.00	0.00	0.00	31
delete_all_many_keys	0.00	0.00	0.00	0.00	1
delete_big	0.00	0.00	0.00	0.00	1
delete_big_many_keys	0.00	0.00	0.00	0.00	128
delete_key	0.00	0.01	0.00	0.01	100
delete_range	0.00	0.00	0.00	0.00	12
drop_index	0.00	0.00	0.00	0.00	8
drop_table	0.00	0.00	0.00	0.00	28
drop_table_when_MANY_tables	0.00	0.00	0.01	0.01	10
insert	5.00	1.50	0.77	2.27	44768
insert_duplicates	0.00	0.05	0.02	0.07	1000
insert_key	0.00	0.00	0.00	0.00	100
insert_many_fields	0.00	0.01	0.01	0.02	200
insert_select_1_key	0.00	0.00	0.00	0.00	1
insert_select_2_keys	0.00	0.00	0.00	0.00	1
min_max	0.00	0.01	0.00	0.01	60
min_max_on_key	1.00	0.42	0.09	0.51	7300
multiple_value_insert	0.00	0.00	0.00	0.00	1000
once_prepared_select	0.00	0.07	0.02	0.09	1000
order_by_big	0.00	0.06	0.00	0.06	10
order_by_big_key	0.00	0.04	0.01	0.05	10
order_by_big_key2	1.00	0.06	0.00	0.06	10
order_by_big_key_desc	0.00	0.06	0.00	0.06	10
order_by_big_key_diff	0.00	0.05	0.00	0.05	10
order_by_big_key_prefix	0.00	0.05	0.00	0.05	10
order_by_key2_diff	0.00	0.00	0.00	0.00	10
order_by_key_prefix	0.00	0.00	0.00	0.00	10
order_by_range	0.00	0.00	0.00	0.00	10

(*continued*)

Table 4-4. (*continued*)

Operation	seconds	usr	sys	cpu	tests
outer_join	0.00	0.00	0.00	0.00	10
outer_join_found	0.00	0.00	0.00	0.00	10
outer_join_not_found	0.00	0.00	0.00	0.00	10
outer_join_on_key	0.00	0.01	0.00	0.01	10
prepared_select	0.00	0.13	0.03	0.16	1000
select_1_row	0.00	0.04	0.02	0.06	1000
select_1_row_cache	1.00	0.04	0.01	0.05	1000
select_2_rows	0.00	0.04	0.02	0.06	1000
select_big	0.00	0.06	0.00	0.06	17
select_big_str	0.00	0.02	0.00	0.02	100
select_cache	0.00	0.08	0.00	0.08	1000
select_cache2	1.00	0.13	0.01	0.14	1000
select_column+column	0.00	0.04	0.02	0.06	1000
select_diff_key	0.00	0.00	0.00	0.00	10
select_distinct	0.00	0.06	0.00	0.06	80
select_group	1.00	0.06	0.00	0.06	391
select_group_when_MANY_tables	0.00	0.00	0.00	0.00	10
select_join	0.00	0.02	0.00	0.02	10
select_key	0.00	0.00	0.00	0.00	20
select_key2	0.00	0.00	0.00	0.00	20
select_key2_return_key	0.00	0.00	0.00	0.00	20
select_key2_return_prim	0.00	0.00	0.00	0.00	20
select_key_prefix	0.00	0.00	0.00	0.00	20
select_key_prefix_join	0.00	0.10	0.00	0.10	10
select_key_return_kcy	0.00	0.01	0.00	0.01	20
select_many_fields	0.00	0.05	0.00	0.05	200
select_range	0.00	0.05	0.00	0.05	41
select_range_key2	0.00	0.03	0.03	0.06	505
select_range_prefix	0.00	0.06	0.00	0.06	505
select_simple	0.00	0.04	0.02	0.06	1000

(*continued*)

141

Table 4-4. (*continued*)

Operation	seconds	usr	sys	cpu	tests
select_simple_cache	0.00	0.04	0.01	0.05	1000
select_simple_join	0.00	0.03	0.00	0.03	50
update_big	0.00	0.00	0.00	0.00	10
update_of_key	0.00	0.01	0.01	0.02	500
update_of_key_big	0.00	0.00	0.00	0.00	13
update_of_primary_key_many_keys	0.00	0.01	0.00	0.01	256
update_with_key	1.00	0.07	0.01	0.08	3000
update_with_key_prefix	0.00	0.02	0.05	0.07	1000
wisc_benchmark	1.00	0.56	0.01	0.57	34
TOTALS	**15.00**	**4.99**	**1.32**	**6.31**	**78237**

When performing benchmarks, I like to convert the latter part of the listing to a spreadsheet so that I can perform statistical analysis on the results. This also allows me to perform calculations using the expected, before, and after results. Table 4-4 shows the time spent for each operation in total seconds, the time spent in the benchmarking tools (usr, sys, cpu), and the number of tests run for each operation.

Notice that at the bottom of Table 4-4 the columns are summed, giving you the total time spent executing the benchmark tests. This information, combined with that in Listing 4-1, forms the current baseline of the performance of my Windows system. I encourage you to create and archive your own benchmarks for your database servers.

Running a Single Test

Suppose you are interested in running the benchmark for creating tables. As shown in Table 4-3 the test is named test-create. To run this command, I navigated to the sql-bench directory and entered the command perl test-create. Listing 4-6 shows the results of running this command on my Windows system.

Listing 4-6. Output of Test—Create Benchmark Test

```
$ ./test-create --user=root --password=XXXX
Testing server 'MySQL 5.1.63 0ubuntu0.11.04.1' at 2012-06-20 10:40:59

Testing the speed of creating and dropping tables
Testing with 10000 tables and 10000 loop count

Testing create of tables
Time for create_MANY_tables (10000): 85 wallclock secs ( 0.87 usr  0.18 sys +  0.00 cusr  0.00 csys
=  1.05 CPU)

Accessing tables
Time to select_group_when_MANY_tables (10000):  2 wallclock secs ( 0.22 usr  0.12 sys +  0.00 cusr
0.00 csys =  0.34 CPU)
```

```
Testing drop
Time for drop_table_when_MANY_tables (10000):  1 wallclock secs ( 0.18 usr  0.09 sys +  0.00 cusr
0.00 csys =  0.27 CPU)

Testing create+drop
Time for create+drop (10000): 83 wallclock secs ( 1.18 usr  0.50 sys +  0.00 cusr  0.00 csys =
1.68 CPU)
Time for create_key+drop (10000): 86 wallclock secs ( 1.45 usr  0.43 sys +  0.00 cusr  0.00 csys =
1.88 CPU)
Total time: 257 wallclock secs ( 3.90 usr  1.32 sys +  0.00 cusr  0.00 csys =  5.22 CPU)
```

In Listing 4-6, you see the typical parameters captured for each test run. Notice that the test is designed to run many iterations of the same test. This is necessary to ensure that the timings aren't dependent on any single event and have more meaning when used as a set.

I chose this example so that you can consider another use of benchmarking. Suppose you want to create a new CREATE SQL command. In this case, you can modify the test-create script to include tests of your new command. Then, later ,run the benchmark tests to establish the baseline performance of your new command. This is a powerful tool to use in your extension of the MySQL system. I encourage you to explore this option if you have any performance or even scalability requirements or concerns about your extensions.

Applied Benchmarking

I return to this topic before moving on as it is important to understand and appreciate the benefits of benchmarking. The only way benchmarking will be useful to you is if you archive your results. I find the best solution is to tuck the results away in individual directories named by the date the benchmarks were taken. I recommend placing the output files (from the --log parameter) along with a short description of the current configuration of the system and the environment (use your favorite system inspection software to do this) into a separate directory for each set of benchmarking tests.

If I need to compare the performance of the system to a known state—for example, whenever I change a server variable and want to see its effect on performance—I can run the benchmarking tools before and after I make the change. Then I can look back through the history of the benchmarks and compare these results with the most stable state. This approach also allows me to track changes in system performance over time.

Benchmarking used in this way will enable you to manage your systems on a level few have achieved otherwise.

MySQL Profiling

Although no formal profiling tool or suite is included in the MySQL server suite of tools (or the source distribution), a number of diagnostic utilities available can be used as a simple set of profiling techniques. For example, you can check the status of thread execution, examine the server logs, and even examine how the optimizer will execute a query.

To see a list of the current threads, use the MySQL SHOW FULL PROCESSLIST command. This command shows all the current processes, or threads, running; the user running them; the host the connection was issued from; the database being used; current command; execution time; state parameters; and additional information provided by the thread. For example, if I ran the command on my system, the results would be something like what is shown in Listing 4-7.

Listing 4-7. Output of the SHOW FULL PROCESSLIST Command

```
mysql > SHOW FULL PROCESSLIST \G
*************************** 1. row ***************************
     Id: 7
   User: root
   Host: localhost:1175
     db: test
Command: Query
   Time: 0
  State: NULL
   Info: SHOW FULL PROCESSLIST
1 row in set (0.00 sec)
```

This example shows that I am the only user connected and running from the local host. The example shows the connection executed a query with an execution time of 0. The example also shows the command issued. The downside to this command is that it is a snapshot in time and must be run many times to detect patterns of performance bottlenecks. Fortunately, you can use a tool called mytop that repeatedly calls the command and displays several useful views of the data. For more information or to download mytop, see Jeremy Zawodny's web site (http://jeremy.zawodny.com/mysql/mytop).

■ **Note** The mytop application has had limited success on the Windows platform.

Another useful command for displaying server information is SHOW STATUS. This command displays all the server and status variables. As you can imagine, that is a very long list. Fortunately, you can limit the display by passing the command a LIKE clause. For example, to see the thread information, enter the command SHOW STATUS LIKE "thread%";. Listing 4-8 shows the results of this command.

Listing 4-8. The SHOW STATUS Command

```
mysql > SHOW STATUS LIKE "threads%";
+-------------------+-------+
| Variable_name     | Value |
+-------------------+-------+
| Threads_cached    | 0     |
| Threads_connected | 1     |
| Threads_created   | 6     |
| Threads_running   | 1     |
+-------------------+-------+
4 rows in set (0.00 sec)
```

To examine the slow-query log, you can set the log-slow-queries variable and set the query timeout using the long-query-time variable. Typical values for the long query timeout vary, but they should be set to your own concept of what constitutes a long query. To display the slow queries, use the mysqldumpslow command to display the slow queries. This command groups the slow queries by similarity (also called *bucket*s). Additional metadata provided include information on locks, expected rows and actual rows generated, and the timing data.

The general query log can be examined using the MySQL Workbench software. You can view all of the logs provided you are connected to the server locally. If you have never used the MySQLAdminstrator software, download it from http://dev.mysql.com/downloads and give it a try.

■ **Tip**   You can use the MySQL Workbench software to control almost every aspect of the server, including startup set-tings, logging, and variables.

You can also examine resources used during a session by using the SHOW PROFILES command. To use this command, profiling must be turned on and is controlled with the profiling session variable. To turn profiling on, issue the SET PROFILING = ON; command.

■ **Note**   Profiling is only partially supported on some platforms. Platforms that do not support the getrusage() method return NULL. Also, profiling is per-process and may be affected by activity on other threads.

Once profiling is on, issuing the SHOW PROFILES command will display a list of the fifteen most recent queries issued in the current session. You can change the size of the list by modifying the value for the profiling_history_size variable. This list will show the query id (sequential), duration, and command.

To see specifics for a particular query, use the SHOW PROFILE FOR QUERY N command. This will display the state and duration of the query as it was executed. You can add options such as BLOCK IO, CONTEXT SWITCHES, CPU, etc. or ALL to show more details. For a complete listing of the options for the SHOW PROFILE FOR QUERY N command, see the syntax from the online MySQL Reference Manual http://dev.mysql.com/doc/refman/5.6/en/show-profiles.html. An example use of these commands is shown in listing 4-9.

Listing 4-9. The SHOW PROFILES and SHOW PROFILE commands

```
mysql> SHOW VARIABLES LIKE 'profiling';
+---------------+-------+
| Variable_name | Value |
+---------------+-------+
| profiling     | OFF   |
+---------------+-------+
1 row in set (0.00 sec)

mysql> SET profiling=ON;
Query OK, 0 rows affected (0.00 sec)

mysql> SHOW VARIABLES LIKE 'profiling';
+---------------+-------+
| Variable_name | Value |
+---------------+-------+
| profiling     | ON    |
+---------------+-------+
1 row in set (0.00 sec)

mysql> use sakila;
Reading table information for completion of table and column names
    You can turn off this feature to get a quicker startup with -A
```

```
Database changed
mysql> show full tables;
+----------------------------+------------+
| Tables_in_sakila           | Table_type |
+----------------------------+------------+
| actor                      | BASE TABLE |
| actor_info                 | VIEW       |
| address                    | BASE TABLE |
| category                   | BASE TABLE |
| city                       | BASE TABLE |
| country                    | BASE TABLE |
| customer                   | BASE TABLE |
| customer_list              | VIEW       |
| film                       | BASE TABLE |
| film_actor                 | BASE TABLE |
| film_category              | BASE TABLE |
| film_list                  | VIEW       |
| film_text                  | BASE TABLE |
| inventory                  | BASE TABLE |
| language                   | BASE TABLE |
| nicer_but_slower_film_list | VIEW       |
| payment                    | BASE TABLE |
| rental                     | BASE TABLE |
| sales_by_film_category     | VIEW       |
| sales_by_store             | VIEW       |
| staff                      | BASE TABLE |
| staff_list                 | VIEW       |
| store                      | BASE TABLE |
+----------------------------+------------+
23 rows in set (0.00 sec)

mysql> select * from sales_by_store;
+---------------------+---------------+-------------+
| store               | manager       | total_sales |
+---------------------+---------------+-------------+
| Woodridge,Australia | Jon Stephens  |    33726.77 |
| Lethbridge,Canada   | Mike Hillyer  |    33679.79 |
+---------------------+---------------+-------------+
2 rows in set (0.05 sec)

mysql> show profiles;
+----------+------------+---------------------------------+
| Query_ID | Duration   | Query                           |
+----------+------------+---------------------------------+
|        1 | 0.00039000 | SHOW VARIABLES LIKE 'profiling' |
|        2 | 0.00008800 | SELECT DATABASE()               |
|        3 | 0.00023600 | show databases                  |
|        4 | 0.00020100 | show tables                     |
|        5 | 0.00078500 | show full tables                |
|        6 | 0.04890200 | select * from sales_by_store    |
+----------+------------+---------------------------------+
6 rows in set (0.00 sec)
```

146

```
mysql> show profile for query 6;
+----------------------+----------+
| Status               | Duration |
+----------------------+----------+
| starting             | 0.000034 |
| checking permissions | 0.000006 |
| Opening tables       | 0.000200 |
| checking permissions | 0.000004 |
| checking permissions | 0.000002 |
| checking permissions | 0.000001 |
| checking permissions | 0.000002 |
| checking permissions | 0.000001 |
| checking permissions | 0.000002 |
| checking permissions | 0.000001 |
| checking permissions | 0.000047 |
| init                 | 0.000011 |
| System lock          | 0.000010 |
| optimizing           | 0.000003 |
| optimizing           | 0.000016 |
| statistics           | 0.000064 |
| preparing            | 0.000020 |
| Creating tmp table   | 0.000013 |
| Sorting for group    | 0.000006 |
| Sorting result       | 0.000003 |
| statistics           | 0.000004 |
| preparing            | 0.000004 |
| executing            | 0.000007 |
| Sending data         | 0.000006 |
| executing            | 0.000002 |
| Sending data         | 0.048299 |
| Creating sort index  | 0.000033 |
| removing tmp table   | 0.000006 |
| Creating sort index  | 0.000010 |
| end                  | 0.000003 |
| query end            | 0.000006 |
| closing tables       | 0.000002 |
| removing tmp table   | 0.000003 |
| closing tables       | 0.000018 |
| freeing items        | 0.000038 |
| cleaning up          | 0.000015 |
+----------------------+----------+
36 rows in set (0.00 sec)

mysql> show profile CPU for query 6;
+----------------------+----------+----------+------------+
| Status               | Duration | CPU_user | CPU_system |
+----------------------+----------+----------+------------+
| starting             | 0.000034 | 0.000030 | 0.000004   |
| checking permissions | 0.000006 | 0.000005 | 0.000001   |
| Opening tables       | 0.000200 | 0.000150 | 0.000050   |
| checking permissions | 0.000004 | 0.000001 | 0.000003   |
```

```
| checking permissions | 0.000002 | 0.000001 |    0.000000 |
| checking permissions | 0.000001 | 0.000001 |    0.000001 |
| checking permissions | 0.000002 | 0.000001 |    0.000001 |
| checking permissions | 0.000001 | 0.000001 |    0.000000 |
| checking permissions | 0.000002 | 0.000001 |    0.000001 |
| checking permissions | 0.000001 | 0.000000 |    0.000001 |
| checking permissions | 0.000047 | 0.000047 |    0.000001 |
| init                 | 0.000011 | 0.000009 |    0.000001 |
| System lock          | 0.000010 | 0.000010 |    0.000001 |
| optimizing           | 0.000003 | 0.000001 |    0.000001 |
| optimizing           | 0.000016 | 0.000015 |    0.000000 |
| statistics           | 0.000064 | 0.000059 |    0.000006 |
| preparing            | 0.000020 | 0.000018 |    0.000002 |
| Creating tmp table   | 0.000013 | 0.000012 |    0.000001 |
| Sorting for group    | 0.000006 | 0.000005 |    0.000001 |
| Sorting result       | 0.000003 | 0.000002 |    0.000001 |
| statistics           | 0.000004 | 0.000004 |    0.000001 |
| preparing            | 0.000004 | 0.000003 |    0.000000 |
| executing            | 0.000007 | 0.000006 |    0.000001 |
| Sending data         | 0.000006 | 0.000005 |    0.000001 |
| executing            | 0.000002 | 0.000001 |    0.000001 |
| Sending data         | 0.048299 | 0.048286 |    0.000025 |
| Creating sort index  | 0.000033 | 0.000027 |    0.000006 |
| removing tmp table   | 0.000006 | 0.000005 |    0.000001 |
| Creating sort index  | 0.000010 | 0.000010 |    0.000000 |
| end                  | 0.000003 | 0.000002 |    0.000001 |
| query end            | 0.000006 | 0.000005 |    0.000001 |
| closing tables       | 0.000002 | 0.000001 |    0.000000 |
| removing tmp table   | 0.000003 | 0.000003 |    0.000001 |
| closing tables       | 0.000018 | 0.000018 |    0.000001 |
| freeing items        | 0.000038 | 0.000012 |    0.000025 |
| cleaning up          | 0.000015 | 0.000013 |    0.000001 |
+----------------------+----------+----------+-------------+
36 rows in set (0.00 sec)

mysql>
```

The last profiling technique included in the MySQL system is the ability to examine how the optimizer performs queries. While not strictly a performance-measuring device, it can be used to diagnose tricky queries that show up in the slow-query log. As a simple example, let's see what the optimizer predicts about how the following query will be executed:

```
select * from customer where phone like "%575 %"
```

This query is not very interesting, and using the LIKE clause with %s surrounding the value is not efficient and almost sure to result in an indexless access method. If you run the command preceded by the EXPLAIN keyword, you see the results of the proposed query optimization. Listing 4-10 shows the results of using the EXPLAIN command.

Listing 4-10. Output of EXPLAIN Command

```
mysql> explain select * from customer where email like "%575 %" \G
*************************** 1. row ***************************
           id: 1
  select_type: SIMPLE
        table: customer
         type: ALL
possible_keys: NULL
          key: NULL
      key_len: NULL
          ref: NULL
         rows: 541
        Extra: Using where
1 row in set (0.00 sec)
```

The output shows that the command is a simple select on the customer table, there are no possible keys to use, there are 541 rows in the table, and the optimizer is using the WHERE clause. In this case, it is telling us that the execution will be a simple table scan without indexes—perhaps one of the slowest possible select statements.

Summary

In this chapter, I've presented a number of software-testing techniques and strategies. You learned about the benefits of software testing and how to leverage test-driven development in your software projects. I also presented the testing facilities available to you for testing MySQL. I showed you the MySQL test and benchmark suites and introduced you to the profiling scripts for MySQL.

The knowledge of these testing facilities will prepare you to ensure your modifications to the MySQL source code are of the highest quality possible. With this knowledge, you are now ready to begin creating extensions and enhancements of the MySQL system that will meet the same high-quality standards that Oracle adheres to.[9] Now that you have this information, you can begin to design your solution and include testing early in your design phase.

The next chapter, which begins the second part of this book, introduces you to the most important tool in a developer's toolbox: debugging!

---

[9]Why else would they have created and made available to you testing, benchmarking, and profiling tools?

PART 2

■ ■ ■

Extending MySQL

Using a hands-on approach, this section provides the tools you need to explore and extend the MySQL system. It introduces you to how the MySQL code can be modified and explains how you can use the system as an embedded database system. Chapter 5 reviews debugging skills and techniques that help make development easy and less prone to failure. It presents several debugging techniques, along with the pros and cons of each. Chapter 6 contains a tutorial on how to embed the MySQL system in enterprise applications. Chapter 7 presents the most popular modification to the MySQL code. You'll learn how to modify SQL commands to add new parameters and functions, and how to add new SQL commands. Chapter 8 is a tour of the high availability components of MySQL. You'll learn how to extend MySQL for use in your own custom, high-availability solution. Chapter 9 presents a tutorial on building authentication plugins for creating your own authentication mechanism for connecting to MySQL. Chapter 10 examines the MySQL pluggable storage-engine capability, complete with examples and projects that permit you to build a sample storage engine.

CHAPTER 5

■ ■ ■

Debugging

This chapter discusses one of the most powerful tools any developer can wield: debugging. Good debugging skills help ensure that your software projects are easy to develop and less prone to failure. I'll also explore the most common techniques for debugging the MySQL system. If you have already developed solid debugging skills, feel free to skim the following sections and move on to the section "Debugging MySQL."

Debugging Explained

Anyone who has written anything more substantial than a "Hello world" program has encountered defects (bugs) in his software. Although most defects are easily found, others can be difficult to locate and correct.

If you wanted to explain the concept of debugging to a novice developer, you'd probably tell her that it's largely a process of troubleshooting in an effort to discover what went wrong. You might also note that developing good debugging skills comes from mastering the appropriate debugging techniques and tools. While this may be an adequate introductory definition, take the time to better understand debugging nuances.

For starters, it's important to properly frame the sort of defect you're trying to locate and correct. There are two basic types of defects: *syntax errors* and *logic errors*. Syntax errors are naturally found during the code compilation process, and although they, too, may be difficult to correct, we must correct them to build the software. Logic errors are those types of errors not found during compilation, and, thus, they are usually manifested as defects during the execution of the software. Debugging, therefore, is the act of finding and fixing errors in your program.

■ **Note**   Available tools that you can run at compile time (or earlier) help minimize the risk of logic errors. They range from simple flow-control analyzers that detect dead code to more sophisticated range and type checkers that walk your code to locate possible data mismatches. Other tools check for proper error handling using best practices for code hardening.

When a logic error is found, the system usually does something odd or produces erroneous data. In the more extreme cases, the system may crash. Well-structured systems that include code hardening best practices tend to be more robust than others, because they are designed to capture and handle errors as they occur. Even then, some errors are so severe that the system crashes (or the operating system terminates it) in order to protect the data and the system state.

The art of debugging software is the ability to quickly locate the error, either by observing the system as its state changes or by direct inspection of the code and its data. We call the tools that we use to debug *system debuggers*. In the following sections, I'll examine some common debugging techniques and related debuggers.

The origins of debugging

You have no doubt heard stories about how the term *computer bug* was coined, and I'd like to tell my favorite one. I have the pleasure of working near the location where Rear Admiral Grace Hopper discovered the first computer bug. Legend has it that Hopper was working with a large computational computer called a Mark II Aiken Relay Calculator in 1945. To call it a large computer today would be a stretch, but it was the size of a semi back then. When a troublesome electronic problem was traced to a failed relay that had a moth trapped in it, Hopper noted that the source of the error was a "bug" and that the system had been "debugged" and was now operational. To this day, we refer to the removal of defective code as *debugging*.

Debugging Techniques

There are almost as many debugging techniques as there are developers. It seems as if everyone debugs his code in a slightly different way. These approaches, however, can generally be grouped into several categories.

The most basic of these approaches are included in the source code and become part of the executable. These include inline debugging statements (statements that print messages or values of variables during execution (e.g., `printf("Code is at line 199. my_var = %d\n", my_var);`) and error handlers. Most developers use these techniques either as a last resort (when a defect cannot be found easily) or during the development phase (to test the code as it is being written). While you may think that error handlers have more to do with robustness and hardening than with debugging, they can also be powerful debugging tools. Since this approach embeds the debugging code into the program, you can use conditional compilation directives to omit the code when debugging is complete. Most developers leave the debugging statements in the code, and, thus, they become part of the program. When using this technique, take care to ensure that the added debugging code does not adversely affect the program.

The debugging technique most of you know best is the use of external debuggers. *External debuggers* are tools designed to either monitor the system in real time or permit you to watch the execution of the code with the ability to stop and start the code at any point. These techniques are described in detail in the following sections. First, though, let's look at the basic process for debugging.

Basic Process

Every debugging session will be unique, but the process should always follow the same basic steps. Being consistent in your debugging process can help make the experience more effective and more rewarding. There's no better feeling than crushing a particularly nasty bug after chasing it for hours. While you may have long established a preferred debugging method, chances are it consists of at least these steps:

1. Identify the defect (bug reporting, testing).

2. Reproduce the defect.

3. Create a test to confirm the defect.

4. Isolate the cause of the defect.

5. Create a corrective patch and apply it.

6. Run a test to confirm that the defect was repaired: Yes—continue, No—Go back to 4.

7. Run regression tests to confirm that the patch does not affect other parts of your system.

Identifying the defect can sometimes be hard. When faced with a defect report, be it an official bug report or a failed system test, you may be tempted to dismiss the defect as spurious, especially when the defect is not obvious. Those defects that cause the system to crash or damage data naturally get your attention right away. But what about those that happen once in a while or only under certain conditions? For those, you have to first assume that the defect exists.

If you are fortunate enough to have a complete bug report that contains a description of how to re-create the defect, you can create a test from the defect and run it to confirm the presence of the defect. If you don't have a complete description of how to reproduce the defect, it can take some effort to get to that point.

Once you are able to re-create the defect, create a test that encompasses all of the steps in reproducing the problem. This test will be important later when you need to confirm that you've fixed the problem.

The next step is the one in which the real debugging begins: isolating the defect. This is the point at which you must employ one or more of the techniques discussed in this chapter to isolate and diagnose the cause of the defect. This is the most important and most challenging aspect of debugging software.

Creating a *patch* (sometimes called a *diff* or *fix*) for the defect is usually an iterative process much like coding itself. You should apply your corrections one step at a time. Make one change at a time and test its effects on the defect and the rest of the system. When you think you have a viable patch, rerun your defect test to confirm it. If you have corrected the problem, the test will fail. As a reminder, a test designed to find defects that doesn't find the defect is considered a failed test—but that's exactly what you want! If the test passes, return to inspection and repair, repeating the iteration until your defect test fails.

CREATING AND USING A PATCH

A little-known software-development technique is called a patch. A patch is simply a file that contains the differences between an original file and its modified form. When you create a patch, you run a GNU program called `diff` and save the output to a file. (You can find `diff` at www.gnu.org/software/diffutils/diffutils.html. Unfortunately, the code is available only for Linux and Unix, but it can be run on Windows using Cygwin.) For example, if you were modifying the `mysqld` file and added a line of code to change the version number, you could create a patch for the code change by running the command `diff -Naur mysqld.cc.old mysqld.cc > mysqld.patch`. This would create a file that looks like:

```
--- mysqld.cc.old   2006-08-19 15:41:09.000000000 -0400
+++ mysqld.cc   2006-08-19 15:41:30.000000000 -0400
@@ -7906,6 +7906,11 @@
 #endif
    if (opt_log || opt_update_log || opt_slow_log || opt_bin_log)
      strmov(end, "-log");                      // This may slow down system
+/* BEGIN DBXP MODIFICATION */
+/* Reason for Modification: */
+/* This section adds the DBXP version number to the MySQL version number. */
+  strmov(end, "-DBXP 1.0");
+/* END DBXP MODIFICATION */
  }
```

You can also use `diff` when you want to create a difference file for an entire list of files or an entire directory. You can then use the resulting file to patch another installation of the files somewhere else.

When you use the patch, you use the GNU program called `patch`. (You can find `patch` at www.gnu.org/software/patch/. Unfortunately, once again the code is available only for Linux and Unix, but can be run on Windows using Cygwin.) The `patch` program reads the patch file from the `diff` program and applies it to the file as specified in the top of the patch. For example, to patch a `mysqld.cc` file that doesn't have the change you created with `diff`, you can run the command `patch < mysqld.patch`. The `patch` program applies the changes to the `mysqld.cc` file and merges the changes into the file.

CHAPTER 5 ■ DEBUGGING

Creating and applying patches is a handy way of distributing small changes to files—such as those encountered when fixing defects. Whenever you fix a bug, you can create a patch and use it to track and apply the same changes to older files.

Many open-source projects use the patch concept to communicate changes. In fact, patches are the primary way in which the global community of developers makes changes to the MySQL source code. Instead of uploading whole files, developers can send a patch to Oracle. From there, Oracle can examine the patch for correctness and either accept the changes (and apply the patch) or reject them. If you have never used the `diff` and `patch` programs, feel free to download them and experiment with them as you work through the examples.

Last, when the defect has been repaired, you should perform a regression-testing step to confirm that no other defects have been introduced. If you are fortunate to be working on a system that is built using a component or modular architecture, and the system is documented well, you may be able to easily identify the related components or modules by examining the requirements matrix. A *requirements matrix* tracks the requirements from use case, class, and sequence diagrams and identifies the tests created for each. Thus, when one part of a class (module) changes, you can easily find the set of tests you need to run for your regression testing. If you do not have a requirements matrix, you can either create one using a simple document or spreadsheet or annotate the source code files with the requirements they satisfy.

Approaches to Debugging

You can take various approaches to debugging. These include simply displaying or printing values of interest or tracing suspect sections of code using interactive debuggers. You can even add special commands to your code ahead of time to facilitate debugging down the road—a practice termed *instrumentation*.

Inline Debugging Statements

Most novice developers start out placing print statements in their code. It is a common form of testing variables that permits them to learn the art of programming. You may think that any debugging technique that uses inline debugging statements is rudimentary or cumbersome, and you'd be partially correct. Inline debugging statements are cumbersome, but they can be a powerful tool. Inline debugging statements are any code that is used to document or present the data or state of the system at a point in time.

Before I present an example of inline debugging statements, let's consider the impact of using them. The first thing that comes to mind is that the debugging statements are code! Therefore, if the debugging statement does anything other than writing to the standard error stream (window), it could result in further unintended consequences. It should also be noted that inline debugging statements are usually stripped out or ignored (using conditional compilation) prior to building the system. If you were a tried-and-true validation-and-verification proponent, you'd argue that this process introduces additional unwarranted risk. That is, the system being compiled for use is different than the one used to debug.

Inline debugging statements, however, can be helpful in situations in which either you cannot use an external debugger or the defect seems to occur at random intervals.[1] These situations could occur, for example, in real-time systems, multiprocess and multithreaded systems, and large systems operating on large amounts of data.

---

[1]Personally, I don't believe in random intervals. Until computers can think for themselves, they are just machines following the instructions humans gave them.

INSTRUMENTATION

Many developers consider inline debugging statements to be a form of instrumentation. This includes code designed to track performance, data, user, client, and execution metrics. Instrumentation is usually implemented by placing statements in the code to display data values, warnings, errors, and so forth, but it may also be implemented using wrapper code that monitors the execution in a sandbox-like environment. One example of a software instrumentation suite is Pin by Intel. For more information about software instrumentation and Pin, see `http://www.pintool.org/`.

There are two types of inline debugging statements. The first is concerned with inspection. Lines of code are added to present the state of memory or the value of variables. This type of debugging statement is used during development and is typically commented out or ignored using conditional compilation. The second concerns tracing the path of the system as it executes. This type of debugging statement can be used at any time and is usually enabled or disabled by a switch at runtime. Since the first type is familiar to most developers (most of us learned debugging this way), I'll discuss the second with an example.

Suppose you have a large system that is running in a multithreaded model, and you're trying to determine what is causing a defect. Using inline debugging statements that present memory and variable values may help, but defects are rarely that easy to find. In this case, you may need to discover the state of the system leading up to the defect. If you had code in your system that simply wrote a log entry whenever it entered a function and another when it left (perhaps with some additional information about the data), you could determine what state the system was in by examining the log. Listing 5-1 depicts an excerpt from the MySQL source code that includes inline debugging statements. I've highlighted the debugging code in bold. In this case, each inline debugging statement writes an entry in a trace file that can be examined after the system executes (or crashes).

Listing 5-1. Example of Inline Debugging Statements

```
/**************************************************************************
** List all Authors.
** If you can update it, you get to be in it :)
**************************************************************************/

bool mysqld_show_authors(THD *thd)
{
  List<Item> field_list;
  Protocol *protocol= thd->protocol;

  DBUG_ENTER("mysqld_show_authors");

  field_list.push_back(new Item_empty_string("Name",40));
  field_list.push_back(new Item_empty_string("Location",40));
  field_list.push_back(new Item_empty_string("Comment",80));

  if (protocol->send_result_set_metadata(&field_list,
                        Protocol::SEND_NUM_ROWS | Protocol::SEND_EOF))

    DBUG_RETURN(TRUE);
```

```
show_table_authors_st *authors;
for (authors= show_table_authors; authors->name; authors++)
{
  protocol->prepare_for_resend();
  protocol->store(authors->name, system_charset_info);
  protocol->store(authors->location, system_charset_info);
  protocol->store(authors->comment, system_charset_info);
  if (protocol->write())

    DBUG_RETURN(TRUE);

}
my_eof(thd);

DBUG_RETURN(FALSE);

}
```

Notice in Listing 5-1 that the first inline-debugging-statements code documents the arrival of the system at this function, or its state, by indicating the name of the function. Notice also that each exit point of the function is documented along with the return value of the function. An excerpt from a trace file running the SHOW AUTHORS command is shown in Listing 5-2. I've omitted a large section of the listing in order to show you how the trace file works for a successful execution of the SHOW AUTHORS command.

Listing 5-2. Sample Trace File

```
T@3     : | | | | >mysqld_show_authors

...

T@3     : | | | | | >send_result_set_metadata
T@3     : | | | | | | packet_header: Memory: 0x7f889025c610  Bytes: (4)
01 00 00 01
T@3     : | | | | | | >alloc_root
T@3     : | | | | | | | enter: root: 0x270af88
T@3     : | | | | | | | exit: ptr: 0x287f9c0
T@3     : | | | | | | <alloc_root 247
T@3     : | | | | | | >Protocol::write
T@3     : | | | | | | <Protocol::write 820
T@3     : | | | | | | packet_header: Memory: 0x7f889025c5c0  Bytes: (4)
1A 00 00 02
T@3     : | | | | | | >Protocol::write
T@3     : | | | | | | <Protocol::write 820
T@3     : | | | | | | packet_header: Memory: 0x7f889025c5c0  Bytes: (4)
1E 00 00 03
T@3     : | | | | | | >Protocol::write
T@3     : | | | | | | <Protocol::write 820
T@3     : | | | | | | packet_header: Memory: 0x7f889025c5c0  Bytes: (4)
1D 00 00 04
T@3     : | | | | | | packet_header: Memory: 0x7f889025c5b0  Bytes: (4)
```

```
05 00 00 05
T@3     : | | | | | <send_result_set_metadata 807
T@3     : | | | | | info: Protocol_text::store field 0 (3): Brian (Krow) Aker
T@3     : | | | | | info: Protocol_text::store field 1 (3): Seattle, WA, USA
T@3     : | | | | | info: Protocol_text::store field 2 (3): Architecture, archive, federated,
bunch of little stuff :)
T@3     : | | | | | >Protocol::write
T@3     : | | | | | <Protocol::write 820
T@3     : | | | | | packet_header: Memory: 0x7f889025ca70  Bytes: (4)
5E 00 00 06
T@3     : | | | | | info: Protocol_text::store field 0 (3): Marc Alff
T@3     : | | | | | info: Protocol_text::store field 1 (3): Denver, CO, USA
T@3     : | | | | | info: Protocol_text::store field 2 (3): Signal, Resignal, Performance schema
T@3     : | | | | | >Protocol::write

...

47 00 00 55
T@3     : | | | | | info: Protocol_text::store field 0 (3): Peter Zaitsev
T@3     : | | | | | info: Protocol_text::store field 1 (3): Tacoma, WA, USA
T@3     : | | | | | info: Protocol_text::store field 2 (3): SHA1(), AES_ENCRYPT(), AES_DECRYPT(), bug
fixing
T@3     : | | | | | >Protocol::write
T@3     : | | | | | <Protocol::write 820
T@3     : | | | | | packet_header: Memory: 0x7f889025ca70  Bytes: (4)
4F 00 00 56
T@3     : | | | | | >set_eof_status
T@3     : | | | | | <set_eof_status 483
T@3     : | | | | <mysqld_show_authors 279
```

■ **Note**   These inline debug statements are turned off by default. You can turn them on by compiling the server with `debug` and running the server in debug mode using the `--debug` command-line switch. This creates a trace file with all of the debug statements. On Linux, the trace file is stored in `/tmp/mysqld.trace` and on Windows, the file is stored in `c:\mysqld.trace`. These files can become quite large as all of the functions in MySQL are written using inline debugging statements.

This technique, while simple, is a versatile tool. When you examine the flow of the system by inspecting the trace file, you can easily discover a starting point for further investigation. Sometimes just knowing where to look can be the greatest challenge.

Error Handlers

Have you ever encountered an error message while using software? Whether you're using something created in the Pacific Northwest or created by the global community of developers, chances are you've seen the end result of an error handler.

You may be wondering why I would include error handlers as a debugging technique. That's because a good error handler presents the cause of the problem along with any possible corrective options. Good error handlers provide developers with enough information to understand what went wrong and how they might overcome the problem, and in some cases, they include additional information that can help developers diagnose the problem. That last bit can sometimes go too far. Too many of us have seen dialog boxes containing terse error messages with confusing resolution options, such as the one shown in Figure 5-1.

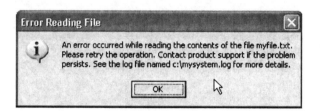

Figure 5-1. *Poor error handler example*

As humorous as this example may be, users see messages like it every day. Developers who write error messages like this are not making themselves clear. Statements that may be perfectly understandable to developers of a system can be gibberish to its users. The best policy is to create error messages that explain what has gone wrong and offer the user a resolution, if one exists, or at least a means to report the problem. It is also a good idea to provide a way to record the information that a developer needs to diagnose the problem. This could be done via logging, a system state dump, or an auto-generated report. Figure 5-2 depicts a better example of how to present errors to the user.

Figure 5-2. *Better error handler example*

Error handlers aren't just for reporting errors. There is another construct that is also called an error handler. This construct is simply the code used to trap and process (handle) errors. Perhaps you are familiar with the C++ `try...catch` block. This is an excellent example of an error handler, as the language has been modified to include the construct in its syntax. Listing 5-3 depicts a typical `try...catch` block. The example shows the basic syntax for the C++ error handler (also called an exception handler).

Listing 5-3. Example C++ Error Handler try ... catch Block

```
try
{
  //attempt file operation here
}
catch (CFileException* e)
{
  //handle the exception here
}
```

While Listing 5-3 is less sophisticated than the C++ construct, you can create error handlers in just about any language that supports conditional statements. For example, Listing 5-4 shows an example from the C language. Here, we see that the return code is checked and, depending on the failure, the code handles the problem. Take care when creating error handlers from scratch. You want to be sure to cover all possible conditions so that you can successfully recover or at least process the error in a way that does not affect the performance of the system and (more important) loss or corruption of data.

Listing 5-4. Example C Error Handler

```c
if (!(azopen(&frm_stream, az_file, O_RDONLY|O_BINARY)))
{
  if (errno == EROFS || errno == EACCES)
    DBUG_RETURN(my_errno= errno);
  DBUG_RETURN(HA_ERR_CRASHED_ON_USAGE);
}
```

Error handlers cover more than simply reporting errors. They are also a front line of defense for debugging. Good error handlers are written to not only trap and process the error but also to store or display diagnostic information.

Take another look at Listing 5-4. This code was taken from the ha_archive.cc file of the MySQL source code. Notice the line of code that is highlighted. This line is one of the numerous inline debugging statements found throughout the code, but its use in this error handler shows how you can record the diagnostic information necessary to troubleshoot a problem with this part of the system. If I were debugging a session about this code, I could run the server in debug mode and look to the trace file to read the diagnostic information recorded by this error handler.

I encourage you to consider writing all of your error-handling code in this manner. You can always display an appropriate error message to the user, but you should also always trap the error codes (return values) and record them and any other pertinent diagnostic information. Using error handlers in this manner will greatly enhance your debugging skills and make your system much easier to diagnose. I have found that sometimes I don't even need to run a debugger at all. A study of the trace files containing the diagnostic information can be enough to lead me directly to the source of the problem.

External Debuggers

A debugger is a software tool designed to analyze a set of executing code and trace the flow of the system as it executes. Most tools that we consider debuggers are actually executed in conjunction with the software being debugged, hence the name *external debugger*. For brevity and conformity, I'll refer to all the tools discussed in this section as simply debuggers.

There are several types of debuggers, but most fit into one of three categories. The debuggers you may be most familiar with are those that run as separate tools that you can attach to a running process and use to control the system. There are also debuggers designed to run as an interactive process, combining control with inspection capabilities. Others include specialized debuggers offering more advanced control of the system. I'll examine each of these types in the following sections.

Stand-alone Debuggers

The most common debugger is a stand-alone debugger. These run as a separate process and permit you to attach to a system that has been compiled to include the appropriate debug information (for mapping to source code, especially linking to the symbols in the code). Unless you're debugging code that contains the source files (such as some forms of interpreted languages), you usually must have the source-code files available and use those to complete the connection to the running process.

Once you've attached to the system (or process) you want to debug, stand-alone debuggers permit you to stop, start, and step through the execution. Stepping through refers to three basic operations:

1. Execute the current line of code and step into the next line of code.

2. Skip over the next line of code (execute function calls and return to the next line).

3. Execute until a particular line of code comes into focus.

The last operation usually refers to lines of code that have been tagged as the lines to stop on (called *breakpoints*) or the lines that are currently highlighted (called run to cursor).

Stand-alone debuggers provide tools for inspecting memory, the call stack, and even sometimes the heap. The ability to inspect variables is perhaps the most important diagnostic tool that debuggers can provide. After all, almost everything you will want to inspect is stored somewhere.

■ **Note** A *heap* is a structure that stores available memory addresses in a tree structure for fast allocation and de-allocation of memory blocks. A *stack* is a structure that allows developers to place items on the stack in a first-in, last-out method (much like a stack of plates at a buffet).

Stand-alone debuggers are not typically integrated with the development environment. That is, they are not part of the compiler suite of tools. Thus, many operate outside the development environment. The advantage of using stand-alone debuggers is that there are many to choose from, each with a slightly different feature set. This allows you to choose the stand-alone debugger that best meets your needs.

A popular example of this type of debugger is the GNU Debugger (gdb). (For more information, visit www.gnu.org/software/gdb/documentation.) The gdb debugger, which on Linux, provides a way to control and inspect a system that has been compiled in debug mode. Listing 5-5 shows a sample program I wrote to calculate factorials. Those of you with a keen eye will spot the logic error, but let's assume the program was run as written. When I enter a value of 3, I should get the value 6 returned. Instead, I get 18.

Listing 5-5. Sample Program (sample.c)

```c
#include <stdio.h>
#include <stdlib.h>

static int factorial(int num)
{
  int i;
  int fact = num;

  for (i = 1; i < num; i++)
  {
    fact += fact * i;
  }
  return fact;
}

int main(int argc, char *argv[])
{
  int num;
  int fact = 0;

  num = atoi(argv[1]);
  fact = factorial(num);
  printf("%d! = %d\n", num, fact);
  return 0;
}
```

If I want to debug this program using gdb, I first have to compile the program in debug mode using the command:

```
gcc -g -o sample sample.c
```

Once the program is compiled, I launch gdb using the command:

```
gdb sample
```

When the gdb debugger issues its command prompt, I issue breakpoints using the break command (supplying the source file and line number for the break) and run the program, providing the necessary data. I can also print out any variables using the print command. If I want to continue the execution, I can issue the continue command. Finally, when done, I can exit gdb with the quit command. Listing 5-6 shows a sample debug session using these commands.

Listing 5-6. Sample gdb Session

```
cbell@ubuntu:~/source/sample$ gcc -g -o sample sample.c
cbell@ubuntu:~/source/sample$ gdb sample
GNU gdb (Ubuntu/Linaro 7.2-1ubuntu11) 7.2
Copyright (C) 2010 Free Software Foundation, Inc.
License GPLv3+: GNU GPL version 3 or later <http://gnu.org/licenses/gpl.html>
This is free software: you are free to change and redistribute it.
There is NO WARRANTY, to the extent permitted by law.  Type "show copying"
and "show warranty" for details.
This GDB was configured as "x86_64-linux-gnu".
For bug reporting instructions, please see:
<http://www.gnu.org/software/gdb/bugs/>...
Reading symbols from /home/cbell/source/sample/sample...done.
(gdb) break sample.c:10
Breakpoint 1 at 0x40055a: file sample.c, line 10.
(gdb) run 3
Starting program: /home/cbell/source/sample/sample 3

Breakpoint 1, factorial (num=3) at sample.c:11
11              fact += fact * i;
(gdb) print i
$1 = 1
(gdb) print num
$2 = 3
(gdb) print fact
$3 = 3
(gdb) continue
Continuing.

Breakpoint 1, factorial (num=3) at sample.c:11
11              fact += fact * i;
(gdb) continue
Continuing.
3! = 18
```

```
Program exited normally.
(gdb) quit
cbell@ubuntu:
```

Do you see the logic error? I'll give you a hint. What should the first value be for calculating the factorial of the number 3? Take a look at the variable declarations for the factorial method. Something smells with that int fact = num; declaration.

■ **Note**   Some folks may want to call debuggers such as gdb interactive debuggers, because they interact with the system while it is running, thus allowing the user to observe the execution. While this is true, keep in mind that gdb is controlling the system externally, and you cannot see or interact with the source code other than through very simplistic methods (e.g., the list command, list, lists the source code). If gdb provided a graphical user interface that presented the source code and allowed you to see the data and interact with the source code, it would be an interactive debugger. But wait, that's what the ddd debugger does.

Interactive Debuggers

These are debuggers that are part of the development environment, either as part of the compile-link-run tools or as an integrated part of the interactive development environment. Unlike stand-alone debuggers, interactive debuggers use the same or a very similar interface as the development tools. An excellent example of a well-integrated interactive debugger is the debugging facilities in Microsoft Visual Studio .NET. In Visual Studio, the interactive debugger is simply a different mode of the rapid-application-development process. You dress up a form, write a bit of code, and then run it in debug mode.

Figure 5-3 depicts a sample Visual Studio .NET 2005 debug session using a Windows variant of the sample program shown earlier.

Figure 5-3. *Sample Visual Studio debugging (sample.c)*

Interactive debuggers have all of the same features as stand-alone debuggers. You can stop, start, step into, step over, and run to breakpoints or cursor. Interactive debugger are most useful when you detect the cause of a defect; you can stop the execution, make any necessary changes, and run the system again. Table 5-1 provides a brief description of these commands. While most debuggers have all of these commands and more, some use different names. Consult the documentation for your debugger for the precise names of the commands.

Table 5-1. *Basic Debugger Control Commands*

Command	Description
Start (Run)	Executes the system.
Stop (Break)	Temporarily halts execution of the code.
Step Into	Runs the next code statement, changing focus to the following statement. If the statement being executed is a function, this command will change focus to the first executable statement in the function being called.
Step Over	Runs the next code statement changing focus to the following statement. If the statement being executed is a function, this command will execute the function and change focus to the next executable statement following the function call.
Breakpoint	The debugger stops when code execution reaches the statement wherethe breakpoint has been issued. Many debuggers allow the use of conditional breakpoints where you can set the breakpoint to occur based on an expression.
Run to Cursor	The debugger resumes execution but halts the execution when control reaches the code statement where the cursor is placed. This is a form of a one-use breakpoint.

The compilation and linking in this scenario happens in the background; it often takes no longer than a moment to complete, and you're back in the debugger. As you can imagine, interactive debuggers are real time savers. If you have never used a stand-alone debugger, you may be dismayed at the apparent lack of integration that stand-alone debuggers have with the source-code projects. What may seem like "old school" is really the state of most development. It is only through the relatively recent development of rapid-application-development tools that interactive debuggers have become the preferred tool for debugging.

GNU Data Display Debugger

Another example of an interactive debugger is the GNU Data Display Debugger (ddd), which is available at http://www.gnu.org/software/ddd. The ddd debugger permits you to run your program and see the code while it is running. It is similar in concept to the rapid-application-development debuggers such as Visual Studio. Figure 5-4 shows our sample program run in ddd.

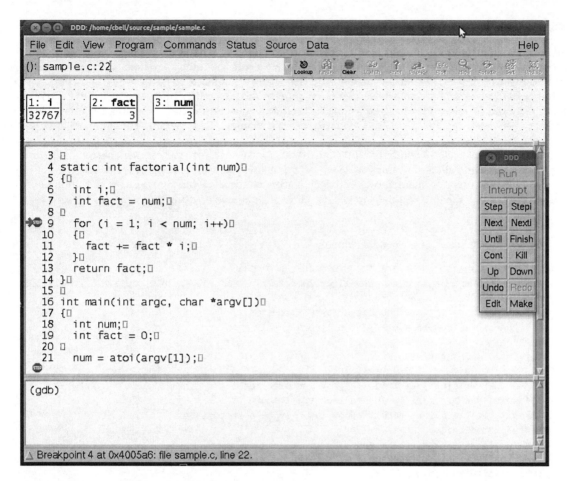

Figure 5-4. Sample ddd session debugging "sample.c"

Notice that the same variables are displayed in the upper portion of the window. With ddd, I can set breakpoints in the code by pointing and clicking on the line of code rather than having to remember the line number in the file I want to break on. I can also view the contents of any variable by double-clicking on the variable. I can even change values in a similar fashion. This allows me to experiment with how the code would perform with different values. This is a powerful feature that can allow the discovery of "off by one" errors (e.g., starting a list iterator index at 1 instead of 0).

■ **Note** Some would call the ddd tool a stand-alone debugger, because it essentially operates in a stand-alone mode. Because of its sophisticated user interface and development-like layout, however, I consider the ddd tool a hybrid that matches the interactive type a bit better than most stand-alone debuggers. Besides, it really does kick gdb up a notch!

Bidirectional Debuggers

Despite all of the power that today's debuggers have to offer, work is under way to make debugging even more efficient. Most interesting, researchers are investigating ways to both execute and undo operations in order to observe what each operation affected. This gives the person doing the debugging the ability to roll back the execution to discover the source of the defect. This is called *backwards reasoning* by the researchers who promote it. They contend that the most efficient way to determine what went wrong is the ability to observe the code executing and to be able to rewind the events when a defect is found and replay them to see what changed. Tools that implement this technique are called *bidirectional debuggers*.

One commercial product, called UndoDB by Undo Ltd. (http://undo-software.com), is available for the Linux platform for a modest fee. Undo offers an evaluation download that allows you to evaluate its product. UndoDB is a stand-alone debugger that uses gdb information. Unlike gdb, its commands allow you to reverse the execution to go back and undo the last statement. Listing 5-7 shows a sample debugging session using UndoDB with our sample program.

Listing 5-7. Sample UndoDB Session Debugging (sample.c)

```
cbell@ubuntu:~/source/sample$ ~/undodb-3.5.205/undodb-gdb sample
undodb-gdb: Reversible debugging system.  Copyright 2006, 2007, 2008, 2009, 2010, 2011, 2012 Undo Ltd.
undodb-gdb: undodb-3.5.205
undodb-gdb: By running this software you agree to the terms in:
undodb-gdb:     /home/cbell/undodb-3.5.205/demo_license.html
undodb-gdb: starting gdb
GNU gdb (Ubuntu/Linaro 7.2-1ubuntu11) 7.2
Copyright (C) 2010 Free Software Foundation, Inc.
License GPLv3+: GNU GPL version 3 or later <http://gnu.org/licenses/gpl.html>
This is free software: you are free to change and redistribute it.
There is NO WARRANTY, to the extent permitted by law.  Type "show copying"
and "show warranty" for details.
This GDB was configured as "x86_64-linux-gnu".
For bug reporting instructions, please see:
<http://www.gnu.org/software/gdb/bugs/>...
Reading symbols from /home/cbell/source/sample/sample...done.
(undodb-gdb) break sample.c:9
Breakpoint 1 at 0x400551: file sample.c, line 9.
(undodb-gdb) run 3
undodb-gdb: debug-server pid 2561, port 35605
Starting program: /home/cbell/source/sample/sample 3
undodb: license type: UndoDB version 3.5, demo, user: Charles Bell

Breakpoint 1, factorial (num=3) at sample.c:9
9           for (i = 1; i < num; i++)
(undodb-gdb) next
11              fact += fact * i;
(undodb-gdb) bnext

Breakpoint 1, factorial (num=3) at sample.c:9
9           for (i = 1; i < num; i++)
(undodb-gdb) next
undodb-gdb: Have switched to record mode.
11              fact += fact * i;
```

```
(undodb-gdb) break sample.c:13
Breakpoint 2 at 0x400575: file sample.c, line 13.
(undodb-gdb) continue
Continuing.

Breakpoint 2, factorial (num=3) at sample.c:13
13          return fact;
(undodb-gdb) print fact
$1 = 18
(undodb-gdb) bnext
9           for (i = 1; i < num; i++)
(undodb-gdb) print fact
$2 = 18
(undodb-gdb) bnext
11              fact += fact * i;
(undodb-gdb) print fact
$3 = 6
(undodb-gdb) print i
$4 = 2
(undodb-gdb) next
9           for (i = 1; i < num; i++)
(undodb-gdb) print i
$5 = 2
(undodb-gdb) print fact
$6 = 18
(undodb-gdb) print num
$7 = 3
(undodb-gdb) next
undodb-gdb: Have switched to record mode.

Breakpoint 2, factorial (num=3) at sample.c:13
13          return fact;
(undodb-gdb) continue
Continuing.
3! = 18

(undodb-gdb) quit
A debugging session is active.

        Inferior 1 [Remote target] will be killed.

Quit anyway? (y or n) y
cbell@ubuntu:~/source/sample$
```

Notice the commands bnext in Listing 5-7. The bnext command is one of the unique UndoDB commands that allows for the back trace (bidirectional) of the execution. All the UndoDB back-trace commands are mirrors of the gdb commands. That makes this debugger very friendly to developers who use gdb. Its greatest power is being able to rollback statements to rerun portions of the code without starting over.

THERE IS NO WRONG WAY

You may be wondering why I have included debugging methods that some may suggest are "old school" and not the latest interactive-development trend. I submit that it is possible to argue that one debugging method is better than another in certain circumstances or even in the general case. It is true, however, that any method presented here, and potentially many others, can lead to successful results. Organizations should not force developers into a particular mold of "do it this way" (which applies to more than just debugging), because what works well for one instance or person may not work for others. My recommendation is to adopt whatever debugging tools or methods you feel best meet your needs and project. If that means using a trace-like method or an interactive method, it doesn't matter, as long as you can efficiently and effectively debug your project. If you develop good troubleshooting skills and can get the information you need to discover the problem, how you get there shouldn't matter.

Debugging MySQL

You may have excellent debugging skills when debugging your own applications, some of which may indeed be quite large. Few, however, have the opportunity to attempt to debug a large system, such as MySQL. While it isn't difficult, I have found many challenges during my work with the source code. I hope the following sections give you the knowledge that I gained through my many trials. I encourage you to read through this section at least once and then follow my examples when you have time.

I'll begin by examining a debugging session with an example of debugging MySQL using inline debugging statements. I'll then move on to an error handler example, followed by an in-depth look at debugging MySQL on both Linux and Windows. If you have been waiting for a chance to get your hands dirty with the MySQL source code, this section is for you. Roll up those sleeves and grab some of your favorite caffeine-laden beverage, because we're going in!

Inline Debugging Statements

Oracle has provided their customers with a robust inline-debugging-statements debugging tool based on the debugger originally created by Fred Fish and later modified by one of MySQL's founders, Michael "Monty" Widenius, for thread safety. This tool is actually a collection of C macros called DBUG.

Using DBUG is easy, because the macros provided allow you to simply place a single code statement where you want to record something. The Oracle developers have many good examples throughout the code. They record a great many aspects of the execution of the server. The individual macros are referred to as debug tags (called DBUG tags in the MySQL documentation). The tags currently used in the MySQL source code include:

DBUG_ENTER: Identify entry into a function using function specification.

DBUG_EXIT: Record return results from function.

DBUG_INFO: Record diagnostic information.

DBUG_WARNING: Record an unusual event or unexpected event.

DBUG_ERROR: Record error codes (used in error handlers mainly).

DBUG_LOOP: Record entry or exit from a loop.

DBUG_TRANS: Record transaction information.

DBUG_QUIT: Record a failure resulting in premature system shutdown.

DBUG_QUERY: Record query statement.

DBUG_ASSERT: Record the error on a failed test of an expression.

Listing 5-8 shows how some of these tags are used in the `mysqld_show_privileges()` function. The highlighted code statements are some of the more commonly used DBUG tags.

Listing 5-8. Example DBUG Tags

```
bool mysqld_show_privileges(THD *thd)
{
  List<Item> field_list;
  Protocol *protocol= thd->protocol;

  DBUG_ENTER("mysqld_show_privileges");

  field_list.push_back(new Item_empty_string("Privilege",10));
  field_list.push_back(new Item_empty_string("Context",15));
  field_list.push_back(new Item_empty_string("Comment",NAME_CHAR_LEN));

  if (protocol->send_result_set_metadata(&field_list,
                        Protocol::SEND_NUM_ROWS | Protocol::SEND_EOF))

    DBUG_RETURN(TRUE);

  show_privileges_st *privilege= sys_privileges;
  for (privilege= sys_privileges; privilege->privilege ; privilege++)
  {
    protocol->prepare_for_resend();
    protocol->store(privilege->privilege, system_charset_info);
    protocol->store(privilege->context, system_charset_info);
    protocol->store(privilege->comment, system_charset_info);
    if (protocol->write())

      DBUG_RETURN(TRUE);

  }
  my_eof(thd);

  DBUG_RETURN(FALSE);

}
```

The list of debug tags is quite comprehensive. The `DBUG_ENTER` and `DBUG_RETURN` tags are some of the most useful, because they allow you to record a trace of the execution of the system throughout all of the functions called. It is especially important to point out that all the functions in the MySQL source code include these tags on entry and exit, respectively. Should you add your own functions, do the same, and record the entry and exit(s) of your functions. These tags are written to a trace file stored in `/tmp/mysqld.trace` on Linux and `c:\mysqld.trace` on Windows.

The trace file created can become very large. Fortunately, you can control which tags are written to the trace file by supplying them on the command line. For example, to limit the trace file to display the more interesting debug tags, you can use a command like the following. The general format of the switches is `a:b:c` for turning on switches a, b, and c. Any switches that take parameters are separated by commas.

```
mysqld-debug --debug=d,info,error,query,general,where:t:L:g:O,
/tmp/mysqd.trace -u root
```

The previous command runs the MySQL server that is compiled with debug enabled (mysqld-debug). The command line parameter --debug=d,info,error,query,general, where:t:L:g:O,/tmp/mysqd.trace instructs the DBUG system to enable output from the DBUG_INFO, DBUG_ERROR, DBUG_QUERY, and DBUG_WHERE macros, turns on the trace lines for enter/exit of functions, includes the line number of the source code for the debug statement, enables profiling, and writes the file to /tmp/mysqld.trace. The -u root parameter passes the username root to the server for execution. Many more options are available; some common options are shown in Table 5-2.[2]

Table 5-2. *List of Commonly Used DBUG Switches*

Switch	Description
d	Turns on the output for the DBUG tags specified in the parameters. An empty list causes output for all tags.
D	Performs a delay after each output. The parameter specifies the number of tenths of seconds to delay. For example, D,40 will cause a delay of 4 seconds.
f	Limits the recording of debugging, tracing, and profiling to the list specified with d.
F	Outputs the name of the source file for every line of debug or trace recorded.
I	Outputs the process ID or thread ID for every line of debug or trace recorded.
g	Turns on profiling. The parameters specify the keywords for those items to be profiled. An empty list implies all keywords are profiled.
L	Outputs the source code line number for each line recorded.
n	Sets the nesting depth for each line of output. This can help make the outputmore readable.
N	Places sequential numbers on each line recorded.
o	Saves the output to the file specified in the parameter. The default is written to stderr.
O	Saves the output to the file specified in the parameter. The default is written to stderr. Flushes the file between each write.
P	Outputs the current process name for each line recorded.
t	Turns on function call/exit trace lines (represented as a vertical bar).

Listing 5-9 shows an excerpt of a trace run while executing the show authors; command. You can see the entire trace of the system as it runs the command and returns data (I have omitted many lines as this list was generated with the default debug switches). I've highlighted the most interesting lines. Notice also the trace lines that run down the lines of output. This allows you to follow the flow of the execution more easily.

If you write your own functions in MySQL, you can use the DBUG tags to record your own information to the trace file. This file can be helpful in the event that your code causes unpredictable or unexpected behavior.

---

[2]A complete list of the commonly used DBUG switches can be found in the MySQL reference manual in the appendix titled "Porting to Other Systems," under the subheading "The DBUG Package."

Listing 5-9. Sample Trace of the Show Privileges Command

```
T@3     : | | | | >mysqld_show_privileges
T@3     : | | | | | >alloc_root
T@3     : | | | | | | enter: root: 0x2264f88
T@3     : | | | | | | exit: ptr: 0x23d97b0
T@3     : | | | | | <alloc_root 247
T@3     : | | | | | >alloc_root
T@3     : | | | | | | enter: root: 0x2264f88
T@3     : | | | | | | exit: ptr: 0x23d9850
T@3     : | | | | | <alloc_root 247
T@3     : | | | | | >alloc_root
T@3     : | | | | | | enter: root: 0x2264f88
T@3     : | | | | | | exit: ptr: 0x23d9860
T@3     : | | | | | <alloc_root 247
T@3     : | | | | | >alloc_root
T@3     : | | | | | | enter: root: 0x2264f88
T@3     : | | | | | | exit: ptr: 0x23d9900
T@3     : | | | | | <alloc_root 247
T@3     : | | | | | >alloc_root
T@3     : | | | | | | enter: root: 0x2264f88
T@3     : | | | | | | exit: ptr: 0x23d9910
T@3     : | | | | | <alloc_root 247
T@3     : | | | | | >alloc_root
T@3     : | | | | | | enter: root: 0x2264f88
T@3     : | | | | | | exit: ptr: 0x23d99b0
T@3     : | | | | | <alloc_root 247
T@3     : | | | | | >send_result_set_metadata
T@3     : | | | | | | packet_header: Memory: 0x7f61f196f610  Bytes: (4)
01 00 00 01
T@3     : | | | | | | >alloc_root
T@3     : | | | | | | | enter: root: 0x2264f88
T@3     : | | | | | | | exit: ptr: 0x23d99c0
T@3     : | | | | | | <alloc_root 247
T@3     : | | | | | | >Protocol::write
T@3     : | | | | | | <Protocol::write 820
T@3     : | | | | | | packet_header: Memory: 0x7f61f196f5c0  Bytes: (4)
1F 00 00 02
T@3     : | | | | | | >Protocol::write
T@3     : | | | | | | <Protocol::write 820
T@3     : | | | | | | packet_header: Memory: 0x7f61f196f5c0  Bytes: (4)
1D 00 00 03
T@3     : | | | | | | >Protocol::write
T@3     : | | | | | | <Protocol::write 820
T@3     : | | | | | | packet_header: Memory: 0x7f61f196f5c0  Bytes: (4)
1D 00 00 04
T@3     : | | | | | | packet_header: Memory: 0x7f61f196f5b0  Bytes: (4)
05 00 00 05
T@3     : | | | | | <send_result_set_metadata 807
T@3     : | | | | | info: Protocol_text::store field 0 (3): Alter
T@3     : | | | | | info: Protocol_text::store field 1 (3): Tables
T@3     : | | | | | info: Protocol_text::store field 2 (3): To alter the table
```

```
T@3      : | | | | | >Protocol::write
T@3      : | | | | | <Protocol::write 820
T@3      : | | | | | packet_header: Memory: 0x7f61f196fa70  Bytes: (4)
20 00 00 06
T@3      : | | | | | info: Protocol_text::store field 0 (3): Alter routine
T@3      : | | | | | info: Protocol_text::store field 1 (3): Functions,Procedures
T@3      : | | | | | info: Protocol_text::store field 2 (3): To alter or drop stored
functions/procedures
T@3      : | | | | | >Protocol::write
T@3      : | | | | | <Protocol::write 820
T@3      : | | | | | packet_header: Memory: 0x7f61f196fa70  Bytes: (4)
50 00 00 07
T@3      : | | | | | info: Protocol_text::store field 0 (3): Create
T@3      : | | | | | info: Protocol_text::store field 1 (3): Databases,Tables,Indexes
T@3      : | | | | | info: Protocol_text::store field 2 (3): To create new databases and tables
T@3      : | | | | | >Protocol::write
T@3      : | | | | | <Protocol::write 820
T@3      : | | | | | packet_header: Memory: 0x7f61f196fa70  Bytes: (4)
43 00 00 08
T@3      : | | | | | info: Protocol_text::store field 0 (3): Create routine
T@3      : | | | | | info: Protocol_text::store field 1 (3): Databases
T@3      : | | | | | info: Protocol_text::store field 2 (3): To use CREATE FUNCTION/PROCEDURE
T@3      : | | | | | >Protocol::write
T@3      : | | | | | <Protocol::write 820
T@3      : | | | | | packet_header: Memory: 0x7f61f196fa70  Bytes: (4)
3A 00 00 09
T@3      : | | | | | info: Protocol_text::store field 0 (3): Create temporary tables
T@3      : | | | | | info: Protocol_text::store field 1 (3): Databases
T@3      : | | | | | info: Protocol_text::store field 2 (3): To use CREATE TEMPORARY TABLE
T@3      : | | | | | >Protocol::write
T@3      : | | | | | <Protocol::write 820
T@3      : | | | | | packet_header: Memory: 0x7f61f196fa70  Bytes: (4)
40 00 00 0A
T@3      : | | | | | info: Protocol_text::store field 0 (3): Create view
T@3      : | | | | | info: Protocol_text::store field 1 (3): Tables
T@3      : | | | | | info: Protocol_text::store field 2 (3): To create new views
T@3      : | | | | | >Protocol::write
T@3      : | | | | | <Protocol::write 820
T@3      : | | | | | packet_header: Memory: 0x7f61f196fa70  Bytes: (4)
27 00 00 0B
T@3      : | | | | | info: Protocol_text::store field 0 (3): Create user
T@3      : | | | | | info: Protocol_text::store field 1 (3): Server Admin
T@3      : | | | | | info: Protocol_text::store field 2 (3): To create new users
T@3      : | | | | | >Protocol::write
T@3      : | | | | | <Protocol::write 820
T@3      : | | | | | packet_header: Memory: 0x7f61f196fa70  Bytes: (4)
2D 00 00 0C
T@3      : | | | | | info: Protocol_text::store field 0 (3): Delete
T@3      : | | | | | info: Protocol_text::store field 1 (3): Tables
T@3      : | | | | | info: Protocol_text::store field 2 (3): To delete existing rows
T@3      : | | | | | >Protocol::write
```

```
T@3      : | | | | | <Protocol::write 820
T@3      : | | | | | packet_header: Memory: 0x7f61f196fa70  Bytes: (4)
26 00 00 0D
T@3      : | | | | | info: Protocol_text::store field 0 (3): Drop
T@3      : | | | | | info: Protocol_text::store field 1 (3): Databases,Tables
T@3      : | | | | | info: Protocol_text::store field 2 (3): To drop databases, tables, and views
T@3      : | | | | | >Protocol::write
T@3      : | | | | | <Protocol::write 820
T@3      : | | | | | packet_header: Memory: 0x7f61f196fa70  Bytes: (4)
3B 00 00 0E
T@3      : | | | | | info: Protocol_text::store field 0 (3): Event
T@3      : | | | | | info: Protocol_text::store field 1 (3): Server Admin
T@3      : | | | | | info: Protocol_text::store field 2 (3): To create, alter, drop and execute events
T@3      : | | | | | >Protocol::write
T@3      : | | | | | <Protocol::write 820
T@3      : | | | | | packet_header: Memory: 0x7f61f196fa70  Bytes: (4)
3D 00 00 0F
T@3      : | | | | | info: Protocol_text::store field 0 (3): Execute
T@3      : | | | | | info: Protocol_text::store field 1 (3): Functions,Procedures
T@3      : | | | | | info: Protocol_text::store field 2 (3): To execute stored routines
T@3      : | | | | | >Protocol::write
T@3      : | | | | | <Protocol::write 820
T@3      : | | | | | packet_header: Memory: 0x7f61f196fa70  Bytes: (4)
38 00 00 10
T@3      : | | | | | info: Protocol_text::store field 0 (3): File
T@3      : | | | | | info: Protocol_text::store field 1 (3): File access on server
T@3      : | | | | | info: Protocol_text::store field 2 (3): To read and write files on the server
T@3      : | | | | | >Protocol::write
T@3      : | | | | | <Protocol::write 820
T@3      : | | | | | packet_header: Memory: 0x7f61f196fa70  Bytes: (4)
41 00 00 11
T@3      : | | | | | info: Protocol_text::store field 0 (3): Grant option
T@3      : | | | | | info: Protocol_text::store field 1 (3): Databases,Tables,Functions,Procedures
T@3      : | | | | | info: Protocol_text::store field 2 (3): To give to other users those privileges
you possess
T@3      : | | | | | >Protocol::write
T@3      : | | | | | <Protocol::write 820
T@3      : | | | | | packet_header: Memory: 0x7f61f196fa70  Bytes: (4)
67 00 00 12
T@3      : | | | | | info: Protocol_text::store field 0 (3): Index
T@3      : | | | | | info: Protocol_text::store field 1 (3): Tables
T@3      : | | | | | info: Protocol_text::store field 2 (3): To create or drop indexes
T@3      : | | | | | >Protocol::write
T@3      : | | | | | <Protocol::write 820
T@3      : | | | | | packet_header: Memory: 0x7f61f196fa70  Bytes: (4)
27 00 00 13
T@3      : | | | | | info: Protocol_text::store field 0 (3): Insert
T@3      : | | | | | info: Protocol_text::store field 1 (3): Tables
T@3      : | | | | | info: Protocol_text::store field 2 (3): To insert data into tables
T@3      : | | | | | >Protocol::write
```

```
T@3     : | | | | | <Protocol::write 820
T@3     : | | | | | packet_header: Memory: 0x7f61f196fa70  Bytes: (4)
29 00 00 14
T@3     : | | | | | info: Protocol_text::store field 0 (3): Lock tables
T@3     : | | | | | info: Protocol_text::store field 1 (3): Databases
T@3     : | | | | | info: Protocol_text::store field 2 (3): To use LOCK TABLES (together with SELECT
privilege)
T@3     : | | | | | >Protocol::write
T@3     : | | | | | <Protocol::write 820
T@3     : | | | | | packet_header: Memory: 0x7f61f196fa70  Bytes: (4)
4A 00 00 15
T@3     : | | | | | info: Protocol_text::store field 0 (3): Process
T@3     : | | | | | info: Protocol_text::store field 1 (3): Server Admin
T@3     : | | | | | info: Protocol_text::store field 2 (3): To view the plain text of currently
executing queries
T@3     : | | | | | >Protocol::write
T@3     : | | | | | <Protocol::write 820
T@3     : | | | | | packet_header: Memory: 0x7f61f196fa70  Bytes: (4)
4B 00 00 16
T@3     : | | | | | info: Protocol_text::store field 0 (3): Proxy
T@3     : | | | | | info: Protocol_text::store field 1 (3): Server Admin
T@3     : | | | | | info: Protocol_text::store field 2 (3): To make proxy user possible
T@3     : | | | | | >Protocol::write
T@3     : | | | | | <Protocol::write 820
T@3     : | | | | | packet_header: Memory: 0x7f61f196fa70  Bytes: (4)
2F 00 00 17
T@3     : | | | | | info: Protocol_text::store field 0 (3): References
T@3     : | | | | | info: Protocol_text::store field 1 (3): Databases,Tables
T@3     : | | | | | info: Protocol_text::store field 2 (3): To have references on tables
T@3     : | | | | | >Protocol::write
T@3     : | | | | | <Protocol::write 820
T@3     : | | | | | packet_header: Memory: 0x7f61f196fa70  Bytes: (4)
39 00 00 18
T@3     : | | | | | info: Protocol_text::store field 0 (3): Reload
T@3     : | | | | | info: Protocol_text::store field 1 (3): Server Admin
T@3     : | | | | | info: Protocol_text::store field 2 (3): To reload or refresh tables, logs and
privileges
T@3     : | | | | | >Protocol::write
T@3     : | | | | | <Protocol::write 820
T@3     : | | | | | packet_header: Memory: 0x7f61f196fa70  Bytes: (4)
45 00 00 19
T@3     : | | | | | info: Protocol_text::store field 0 (3): Replication client
T@3     : | | | | | info: Protocol_text::store field 1 (3): Server Admin
T@3     : | | | | | info: Protocol_text::store field 2 (3): To ask where the slave or master servers are
T@3     : | | | | | >Protocol::write
T@3     : | | | | | <Protocol::write 820
T@3     : | | | | | packet_header: Memory: 0x7f61f196fa70  Bytes: (4)
4D 00 00 1A
T@3     : | | | | | info: Protocol_text::store field 0 (3): Replication slave
T@3     : | | | | | info: Protocol_text::store field 1 (3): Server Admin
```

```
T@3     : | | | | | info: Protocol_text::store field 2 (3): To read binary log events from the master
T@3     : | | | | | >Protocol::write
T@3     : | | | | | <Protocol::write 820
T@3     : | | | | | packet_header: Memory: 0x7f61f196fa70  Bytes: (4)
49 00 00 1B
T@3     : | | | | | info: Protocol_text::store field 0 (3): Select
T@3     : | | | | | info: Protocol_text::store field 1 (3): Tables
T@3     : | | | | | info: Protocol_text::store field 2 (3): To retrieve rows from table
T@3     : | | | | | >Protocol::write
T@3     : | | | | | <Protocol::write 820
T@3     : | | | | | packet_header: Memory: 0x7f61f196fa70  Bytes: (4)
2A 00 00 1C
T@3     : | | | | | info: Protocol_text::store field 0 (3): Show databases
T@3     : | | | | | info: Protocol_text::store field 1 (3): Server Admin
T@3     : | | | | | info: Protocol_text::store field 2 (3): To see all databases with SHOW DATABASES
T@3     : | | | | | >Protocol::write
T@3     : | | | | | <Protocol::write 820
T@3     : | | | | | packet_header: Memory: 0x7f61f196fa70  Bytes: (4)
45 00 00 1D
T@3     : | | | | | info: Protocol_text::store field 0 (3): Show view
T@3     : | | | | | info: Protocol_text::store field 1 (3): Tables
T@3     : | | | | | info: Protocol_text::store field 2 (3): To see views with SHOW CREATE VIEW
T@3     : | | | | | >Protocol::write
T@3     : | | | | | <Protocol::write 820
T@3     : | | | | | packet_header: Memory: 0x7f61f196fa70  Bytes: (4)
34 00 00 1E
T@3     : | | | | | info: Protocol_text::store field 0 (3): Shutdown
T@3     : | | | | | info: Protocol_text::store field 1 (3): Server Admin
T@3     : | | | | | info: Protocol_text::store field 2 (3): To shut down the server
T@3     : | | | | | >Protocol::write
T@3     : | | | | | <Protocol::write 820
T@3     : | | | | | packet_header: Memory: 0x7f61f196fa70  Bytes: (4)
2E 00 00 1F
T@3     : | | | | | info: Protocol_text::store field 0 (3): Super
T@3     : | | | | | info: Protocol_text::store field 1 (3): Server Admin
T@3     : | | | | | info: Protocol_text::store field 2 (3): To use KILL thread, SET GLOBAL, CHANGE
MASTER, etc.
T@3     : | | | | | >Protocol::write
T@3     : | | | | | <Protocol::write 820
T@3     : | | | | | packet_header: Memory: 0x7f61f196fa70  Bytes: (4)
47 00 00 20
T@3     : | | | | | info: Protocol_text::store field 0 (3): Trigger
T@3     : | | | | | info: Protocol_text::store field 1 (3): Tables
T@3     : | | | | | info: Protocol_text::store field 2 (3): To use triggers
T@3     : | | | | | >Protocol::write
T@3     : | | | | | <Protocol::write 820
T@3     : | | | | | packet_header: Memory: 0x7f61f196fa70  Bytes: (4)
1F 00 00 21
T@3     : | | | | | info: Protocol_text::store field 0 (3): Create tablespace
T@3     : | | | | | info: Protocol_text::store field 1 (3): Server Admin
T@3     : | | | | | info: Protocol_text::store field 2 (3): To create/alter/drop tablespaces
```

```
T@3    : | | | | | >Protocol::write
T@3    : | | | | | <Protocol::write 820
T@3    : | | | | | packet_header: Memory: 0x7f61f196fa70  Bytes: (4)
40 00 00 22
T@3    : | | | | | info: Protocol_text::store field 0 (3): Update
T@3    : | | | | | info: Protocol_text::store field 1 (3): Tables
T@3    : | | | | | info: Protocol_text::store field 2 (3): To update existing rows
T@3    : | | | | | >Protocol::write
T@3    : | | | | | <Protocol::write 820
T@3    : | | | | | packet_header: Memory: 0x7f61f196fa70  Bytes: (4)
26 00 00 23
T@3    : | | | | | info: Protocol_text::store field 0 (3): Usage
T@3    : | | | | | info: Protocol_text::store field 1 (3): Server Admin
T@3    : | | | | | info: Protocol_text::store field 2 (3): No privileges - allow connect only
T@3    : | | | | | >Protocol::write
T@3    : | | | | | <Protocol::write 820
T@3    : | | | | | packet_header: Memory: 0x7f61f196fa70  Bytes: (4)
36 00 00 24
T@3    : | | | | | >set_eof_status
T@3    : | | | | | <set_eof_status 483
T@3    : | | | | <mysqld_show_privileges 390
```

Error Handlers

There are no specific tools to demonstrate concerning error handlers in MySQL. You should strive to generate code that handles all possible errors. The best way to show you how to do this is with an example of an error handler from an older, unsupported release of MySQL that does not properly manage errors. Listing 5-10 shows an excerpt from the MySQL source code that has an issue with a particular type of error.

Listing 5-10. Sample of Error Handler in MySQL

```
int my_delete(const char *name, myf MyFlags)
{
  int err;
  DBUG_ENTER("my_delete");
  DBUG_PRINT("my",("name %s MyFlags %d", name, MyFlags));

  if ((err = unlink(name)) == -1)
  {
    my_errno=errno;
    if (MyFlags & (MY_FAE+MY_WME))
      my_error(EE_DELETE,MYF(ME_BELL+ME_WAITTANG+(MyFlags & ME_NOINPUT)),
          name,errno);
  }
  DBUG_RETURN(err);
} /* my_delete */
```

Can you see the defect? I'll give you a hint. The return value for the unlink() function in Windows has several important values that need to be checked. One of those is missing from the error handler shown in Listing 5-10. The defect resulted in the optimize() function improperly copying an intermediate file during its operation. Fortunately, this defect was fixed some time ago. Listing 5-11 shows the corrected form of this function.

Listing 5-11. Sample of Error Handler in MySQL

```
int my_delete(const char *name, myf MyFlags)
{
  int err;
  DBUG_ENTER("my_delete");
  DBUG_PRINT("my",("name %s MyFlags %d", name, MyFlags));

  if ((err = unlink(name)) == -1)
  {
    my_errno=errno;
    if (MyFlags & (MY_FAE+MY_WME))
    {
      char errbuf[MYSYS_STRERROR_SIZE];
      my_error(EE_DELETE, MYF(ME_BELL+ME_WAITTANG+(MyFlags & ME_NOINPUT)),
               name, errno, my_strerror(errbuf, sizeof(errbuf), errno));
    }
  }
  else if ((MyFlags & MY_SYNC_DIR) &&
           my_sync_dir_by_file(name, MyFlags))
    err= -1;
  DBUG_RETURN(err);
} /* my_delete */
```

Oracle has provided a well-designed error-message mechanism that can make your error handlers more robust. To add your own error messages, add them to the `sql/share/errmsg-utf8.txt` file. See the internal documentation on `dev.mysql.com` for more details on adding your own error messages.

I cannot stress enough the importance of forming error handlers that handle all possible errors and take the appropriate actions to rectify and report the errors. Adding the DBUG macros to trace and record the error messages will ensure that all of your debugging sessions are more efficient.

Debugging in Linux

Linux excels in the quality of its advanced development tools (primarily the GNU tools). These tools include excellent debuggers capable of handling not only single-threaded but also multithreaded systems.

Many debuggers are available for Linux. The most popular are gdb and ddd. The following sections present an example of each tool debugging the MySQL system. The scenario for these examples is to inspect what happens when the SHOW AUTHORS command is issued. I'll begin with the gdb debugger, and then show you the same scenario using ddd.

Using gdb

Let's begin by re-examining the show_authors() function. Refer back to Listing 5-1 for the complete code for the function. The first thing I need to do is make sure I have built my server with the debugger turned on. Do this by issuing these commands from the root of the source folder:

```
cmake . -DWITH_DEBUG=ON
make
```

These commands will cause the system to be compiled with the appropriate debugging information so that I can use the debugger. I can now launch the server in debug mode using the command `mysqld-debug`. Listing 5-12 shows the startup statements presented when the server starts.

> ■ **Caution** Ensure all installations of the MySQL server have been shut down prior to launching the server in debug mode. While not strictly necessary, this should allow you to avoid attempting to debug the wrong process.

Listing 5-12. Starting MySQL Server in Debug Mode

```
cbell@ubuntu:~/source/mysql-5.6/mysql-test$ ./mysql-test-run.pl --start-and-exit --debug
Logging: ./mysql-test-run.pl  --start-and-exit --debug
120707 18:10:11 [Note] Plugin 'FEDERATED' is disabled.
120707 18:10:11 [Note] Binlog end
120707 18:10:11 [Note] Shutting down plugin 'CSV'
120707 18:10:11 [Note] Shutting down plugin 'MyISAM'
MySQL Version 5.6.6
Checking supported features...
 - skipping ndbcluster
 - SSL connections supported
 - binaries are debug compiled
Using suites: main,sys_vars,binlog,federated,rpl,innodb,innodb_fts,perfschema,funcs_1,opt_trace
Collecting tests...
Checking leftover processes...
 - found old pid 7375 in 'mysqld.1.pid', killing it...
   process did not exist!
Removing old var directory...
Creating var directory '/home/cbell/source/mysql-5.6/mysql-test/var'...
Installing system database...
Using server port 49434

==============================================================================

TEST                                    RESULT   TIME (ms) or COMMENT
------------------------------------------------------------------------------

worker[1] Using MTR_BUILD_THREAD 300, with reserved ports 13000..13009
worker[1]
Started [mysqld.1 - pid: 7506, winpid: 7506]
worker[1] Using config for test main.1st
worker[1] Port and socket path for server(s):
worker[1] mysqld.1  13000  /home/cbell/source/mysql-5.6/mysql-test/var/tmp/mysqld.1.sock
worker[1] Server(s) started, not waiting for them to finish
```

Notice that in this case, I am using the socket specified as /var/lib/mysql/mysql.sock. This allows me to run a copy of the server in debug mode without affecting a running server. I need to tell the client to use the same socket, however. First, though, I need to determine the process ID for my server. I can do this by issuing the ps -A command to list all of the running processes. Alternatively, I could issue the command ps -A| grep mysql and get the process IDs of all of the processes that include mysql in the name. The following demonstrates this command:

```
7506 pts/2    00:00:00 mysqld
```

Now that I have my process ID, I can launch gdb and attach to the correct process using the `attach 10592` command. I also want to set a breakpoint in the `show_authors()` function. An examination of the source file shows that the first line that I'm interested in is line 260. I issue the command break /home/cbell/source/bzr/mysql-5.6/ sql/sql_show.cc:260. The format of this command is `file:line#`. Now that I have a breakpoint, I issue the command `continue` to tell the process to execute, and gdb will halt the program when the breakpoint is encountered. Listing 5-13 shows the complete debugging session.

Listing 5-13. Running gdb

```
cbell@ubuntu:~/source/bzr/mysql-5.6/mysql-test$ gdb
GNU gdb (Ubuntu/Linaro 7.2-1ubuntu11) 7.2
Copyright (C) 2010 Free Software Foundation, Inc.
License GPLv3+: GNU GPL version 3 or later <http://gnu.org/licenses/gpl.html>
This is free software: you are free to change and redistribute it.
There is NO WARRANTY, to the extent permitted by law.  Type "show copying"
and "show warranty" for details.
This GDB was configured as "x86_64-linux-gnu".
For bug reporting instructions, please see:
<http://www.gnu.org/software/gdb/bugs/>.
(gdb) attach 7506
Attaching to process 7506
Reading symbols from /home/cbell/source/bzr/mysql-5.6/sql/mysqld...done.
Reading symbols from /lib/x86_64-linux-gnu/libpthread.so.0...(no debugging symbols found)...done.
[Thread debugging using libthread_db enabled]
[New Thread 0x7f7ba8e57700 (LWP 7524)]
[New Thread 0x7f7ba4a26700 (LWP 7523)]
[New Thread 0x7f7ba5227700 (LWP 7522)]
[New Thread 0x7f7ba5a28700 (LWP 7521)]
[New Thread 0x7f7ba6229700 (LWP 7520)]
[New Thread 0x7f7ba6a2a700 (LWP 7519)]
[New Thread 0x7f7ba722b700 (LWP 7518)]
[New Thread 0x7f7ba7a2c700 (LWP 7517)]
[New Thread 0x7f7ba822d700 (LWP 7516)]
[New Thread 0x7f7ba8a2e700 (LWP 7515)]
[New Thread 0x7f7ba9658700 (LWP 7513)]
[New Thread 0x7f7ba9e59700 (LWP 7512)]
[New Thread 0x7f7baa65a700 (LWP 7511)]
[New Thread 0x7f7baae5b700 (LWP 7510)]
[New Thread 0x7f7bab65c700 (LWP 7509)]
[New Thread 0x7f7bb085f700 (LWP 7508)]
Loaded symbols for /lib/x86_64-linux-gnu/libpthread.so.0
Reading symbols from /lib/x86_64-linux-gnu/librt.so.1...(no debugging symbols found)...done.
Loaded symbols for /lib/x86_64-linux-gnu/librt.so.1
Reading symbols from /lib/x86_64-linux-gnu/libcrypt.so.1...(no debugging symbols found)...done.
Loaded symbols for /lib/x86_64-linux-gnu/libcrypt.so.1
Reading symbols from /lib/x86_64-linux-gnu/libdl.so.2...(no debugging symbols found)...done.
Loaded symbols for /lib/x86_64-linux-gnu/libdl.so.2
Reading symbols from /usr/lib/x86_64-linux-gnu/libstdc++.so.6...(no debugging symbols found)...done.
Loaded symbols for /usr/lib/x86_64-linux-gnu/libstdc++.so.6
Reading symbols from /lib/x86_64-linux-gnu/libm.so.6...(no debugging symbols found)...done.
Loaded symbols for /lib/x86_64-linux-gnu/libm.so.6
```

```
Reading symbols from /lib/x86_64-linux-gnu/libgcc_s.so.1...(no debugging symbols found)...done.
Loaded symbols for /lib/x86_64-linux-gnu/libgcc_s.so.1
Reading symbols from /lib/x86_64-linux-gnu/libc.so.6...(no debugging symbols found)...done.
Loaded symbols for /lib/x86_64-linux-gnu/libc.so.6
Reading symbols from /lib64/ld-linux-x86-64.so.2...(no debugging symbols found)...done.
Loaded symbols for /lib64/ld-linux-x86-64.so.2
0x00007f7bb0939ae3 in poll () from /lib/x86_64-linux-gnu/libc.so.6
(gdb) break /home/cbell/source/bzr/mysql-5.6/sql/sql_show.cc:260
Breakpoint 1 at 0x7cee94: file /home/cbell/source/bzr/mysql-5.6/sql/sql_show.cc, line 260.
(gdb) continue
Continuing.

Note: Here, you can run the mysql client and issue the SHOW AUTHORS command.

[New Thread 0x7f7ba8e16700 (LWP 7536)]
[Switching to Thread 0x7f7ba8e16700 (LWP 7536)]

Breakpoint 1, mysqld_show_authors (thd=0x3a62ca0) at
/home/cbell/source/bzr/mysql-5.6/sql/sql_show.cc:260
260         field_list.push_back(new Item_empty_string("Name",40));
(gdb) next
261         field_list.push_back(new Item_empty_string("Location",40));
(gdb) next
262         field_list.push_back(new Item_empty_string("Comment",80));
(gdb) next
265                                 Protocol::SEND_NUM_ROWS | Protocol::SEND_EOF))
(gdb) next
264         if (protocol->send_result_set_metadata(&field_list,
(gdb) next
269         for (authors= show_table_authors; authors->name; authors++)
(gdb) next
271            protocol->prepare_for_resend();
(gdb) print authors->name
$1 = 0xec70c2 "Brian (Krow) Aker"
(gdb) quit
A debugging session is active.

        Inferior 1 [process 7506] will be detached.

Quit anyway? (y or n) y
Detaching from program: /home/cbell/source/bzr/mysql-5.6/sql/mysqld, process 7506
```

Listing 5-14 shows the initialization of the client specifying the desired socket on the command line. I then launch the SHOW AUTHORS command.

Listing 5-14. Starting MySQL Client to Attach to Server

```
cbell@ubuntu:~$ mysql -uroot -h 127.0.0.1 --port=13000
Welcome to the MySQL monitor.  Commands end with ; or \g.
Your MySQL connection id is 1
Server version: 5.6.6-m9-debug-CAB MODIFICATION Source distribution
```

Type 'help;' or '\h' for help. Type '\c' to clear the current input statement.

mysql> show authors;

The first thing I notice when I enter the command is that the client stops. The reason is that the gdb debugger has encountered the breakpoint and has halted execution. When I switch back to the debugger, I can issue commands to step through the execution using the next command. I can also display the values of variables using the print command. (Listing 5-13 shows these commands in action.) Once I've finished my debugging session, I can shut down the server and exit the debugger.

The gdb debugger is a powerful tool, but it lacks the sophistication of debuggers found in most integrated development environments (IDEs). The ddd debugger makes up for this limitation by providing a robust graphical environment.

Using ddd

The GNU ddd debugger is an excellent example of an integrated debugger. Though not exclusively built around an IDE, the ddd debugger provides a similar experience. You can launch the program you wish to debug and view the source code. Using the integrated tools, you can set breakpoints, stop and start the program being debugged, set watches on variables, view the stack trace, and even edit variable values.

Several windows are associated with the debugger. The *data window* displays all of the data items you have set watches on. The *source window* (the main display area) displays the current source code for the program being debugged. The *debugger console* displays the host debugger (gdb) output. This window is handy for developers who use gdb, because it permits you to enter your own gdb commands. Thus, you can use either the menu system to control the program or the debugger console to issue commands to the debugger directly.

The ddd debugger is actually a wrapper around the GNU gdb stand-alone debugger. In typical open-source fashion, the developers of ddd reused what was already built (gdb) and instead of re-inventing the wheel (the symbolic debugger code), they augmented it with a new set of functionality. Furthermore, ddd can support several stand-alone debuggers, making it very versatile. Indeed, it can support any language its host debugger can support. In many ways, ddd exemplifies what an integrated debugger should be. It has all the tools you need to debug just about any program written in a host of languages.

One of the features I find most appealing about the ddd debugger is the ability to save a debugging session and recall it later. This gives you the advantage of not having to re-create a scenario to demonstrate or repeat a defect. I recommend that, to use it most effectively, you debug your program up to the point of defect discovery (say in the start of the function in question), set all of your watches and breakpoints, and then save the session. This will allow you to restart the debugging session again later should you need to retrace your steps. While not as efficient as a bidirectional debugger, saving a debugging session saves you a lot of time.

You can use the ddd debugger to examine core dumps. This allows you to examine the data in the core dump to determine the state of the program and the last few operations prior to the crash. That's really handy if the defect that caused the crash also causes the debugger to crash.[3] There is also support for remote debugging and examining memory directly. This allows you to debug a system running on another computer (typically a server) and to manipulate the debugger on your development workstation. For more information about the ddd debugger, see the excellent documentation available at www.gnu.org/software/ddd/ddd.html#Doc.

---

[3]This is a most annoying situation that can be tricky to overcome. In these situations, I usually resort to inline debugging statements and core dumps for debugging.

Debugging MySQL using ddd can be accomplished using these steps:

1. Stop any running MySQL servers. Use the command mysqladmin -uroot -p shutdown and enter your root password.

2. Change to the directory that contains your source code. If you are debugging the server (mysqld), you want to change to the sql directory.

3. Launch the ddd debugger using the command ddd mysqld-debug.

4. Open the source code file you want to debug. In the following example, I use sql_show.cc.

5. Set any breakpoints you want the code to stop at. In the following example, I set a breakpoint at line 207 in the show_authors() function.

6. Use the Program ➤ Run menu to run the server, specifying the server is to run as the root user by supplying the parameters u root in the dialog box.

7. Launch your MySQL client. In the following example, I use the normal MySQL command-line client.

8. Issue your commands in the client. The debugger will temporarily halt execution and stop on any breakpoints defined. From here, you can begin your debugging.

9. When you have finished debugging, exit the client and shut down the server using the command mysqladmin -uroot -p shutdown and enter your root password.

■ **Tip** You might need to extend the timeout duration for your test MySQL client. Debugging can take some time if you are stepping through a series of breakpoints or you are examining a lot of variables. The system is essentially in a zombie state while you are debugging. This may cause the server and the client to cease communication. Some clients are designed to terminate if they cannot communicate with the server after a period of time. If you are using the MySQL command-line client, you will need to extend the timeout. You can do this by specifying the value on the command line using --connection-timeout=600. This gives you about 10 minutes to work with the debugger before the client drops the connection.

Listing 5-15 shows how you can use the ddd debugger to debug the MySQL server. I chose the same function from earlier, the show_authors() function in the sql_show.cc source file. In this scenario, I was interested in seeing how the server handled sending information to the client. You may recall from Chapter 3 that I mentioned having an example that showed the process of returning data to the client.

Listing 5-15. The show_authors Function with Highlights

```
/************************************************************************
** List all Authors.
** If you can update it, you get to be in it :)
************************************************************************/

bool mysqld_show_authors(THD *thd)
{
  List<Item> field_list;
  Protocol *protocol= thd->protocol;
  DBUG_ENTER("mysqld_show_authors");
```

```
field_list.push_back(new Item_empty_string("Name",40));
field_list.push_back(new Item_empty_string("Location",40));
field_list.push_back(new Item_empty_string("Comment",40));

if (protocol->send_result_set_metadata(&field_list,
                        Protocol::SEND_NUM_ROWS | Protocol::SEND_EOF))
    DBUG_RETURN(TRUE);

show_table_authors_st *authors;
for (authors= show_table_authors; authors->name; authors++)
{
  protocol->prepare_for_resend();
  protocol->store(authors->name, system_charset_info);
  protocol->store(authors->location, system_charset_info);
  protocol->store(authors->comment, system_charset_info);
  if (protocol->write())
    DBUG_RETURN(TRUE);
}
my_eof(thd);
DBUG_RETURN(FALSE);
}
```

The statements in bold are the methods used to send data back to the client. The show_authors() function is perfect for demonstrating the process, because it is the simplest of implementations (no complex operations—just sending data). The first highlighted statement shows the declaration of a pointer to the existing threads protocol class. The protocol class encapsulates all of the lower-level communication methods (such as networking and socket control). The next set of statements builds a field list. You always send a field list to the client first. Once the field list is built, you can send it to the client with the protocol->send_fields() method. In the loop, the code is looping through a list of authors defined in a linked list of show_table_authors_st. Inside the loop are the three principal methods used to send the data to the client. The first is protocol->prepare_for_resend(), which clears the appropriate buffers and variables for sending data. The next is protocol->store(), which places information in the send buffer. You should send each field as a separate call to this method. The protocol->write() method issues the appropriate action to send the data to the client. Finally, the send_eof() method instructs the communication mechanism to send the end-of-file marker to mark the end of the data. At this point, the client displays the data.

Let's see how this function works using the ddd debugger. I have built my server using the debug switches by issuing the commands:

```
cmake . -DWITH_DEBUG=ON
make
```

These commands will cause the system to be compiled with the debugging information so that I can use the debugger. Once I confirm that no other servers are running, I launch the ddd debugger, load my source file (sql_show.cc), set a breakpoint in the show_authors() function at line 207, and then run the program. At that point, I launch my MySQL client program, setting the connection timeout to 10 minutes, and issue the SHOW AUTHORS command. Refer back to Listing 5-13 to see the server startup sequence; Listing 5-16 shows the client startup sequence.

Listing 5-16. Starting the MySQL Client for Use with the ddd Debugger

```
cbell@ubuntu:~$ mysql -uroot -h 127.0.0.1 --port=13000
Welcome to the MySQL monitor.  Commands end with ; or \g.
Your MySQL connection id is 1
Server version: 5.6.6-m9-debug-CAB MODIFICATION Source distribution
```

Copyright (c) 2000, 2011, Oracle and/or its affiliates. All rights reserved.

Oracle is a registered trademark of Oracle Corporation and/or its
affiliates. Other names may be trademarks of their respective
owners.

Type 'help;' or '\h' for help. Type '\c' to clear the current input statement.

mysql> show authors;

When execution reaches the breakpoint in the debugger, the server will stop, and the ddd debugger will display the code with an arrow pointing to the breakpoint. You'll also notice that the client has stopped. If you take too long debugging, the client may time out. This is why I used the connection-timeout override.

Once the debugger has halted execution, you can begin to explore the code and examine the values of any variable, the stack, or memory. I have set the debugger to examine the authors structure to see the data as it is being written to the client. Figure 5-5 depicts the ddd debugger with the authors structure displayed in the data window.

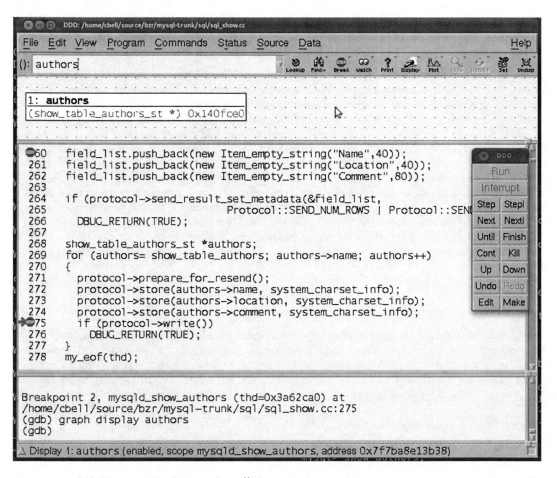

Figure 5-5. ddd *debugging the* show_authors() *function*

I can also expand the authors structure and see the current contents. Figure 5-6 shows the contents of the authors structure displayed in the data window.

Figure 5-6. *The authors structure data in the ddd debugger*

Notice that the values and the addresses are displayed in the data window. The ddd debugger also allows you to modify the contents of memory. Let's say I am debugging this method, and I want to change the values in the authors structure. I could do that simply by right-clicking on each of the items in the authors structure, choosing Set Value from the right-click menu, and then changing the value. Figure 5-7 shows that I've changed the contents of the authors structure.

Figure 5-7. *The authors structure data changed*

You might be wondering if this actually works. Well, it does! Listing 5-17 shows the output from the client (I omitted many lines for clarity). Notice that the data I changed were indeed sent to the client.

Listing 5-17. Resulting Output from Data Modifications

```
mysql> show authors;
+---------------+--------------+-------------------------------------+
| Name          | Location     | Comment                             |
+---------------+--------------+-------------------------------------+
| Chuck Bell    | Anytown, USA | Replication, Backup, MySQL Utilities |
...
+---------------+--------------+-------------------------------------+
80 rows in set (48.35 sec)

mysql>
```

Once I've finished my debugging session, I issue the command to shut down the server and then exit ddd:

```
mysqladmin -uroot -p shutdown
```

As you can see from this simple example, debugging with ddd can be a useful experience, and it allows you to see the code as it executes. The power of being able to see the data as they are associated with the current execution is an effective means of discovering and correcting defects. I encourage you to try the example and play around with ddd until you are comfortable using it.

Debugging in Windows

The main method of debugging in Windows is using Microsoft Visual Studio .NET. Some developers have had success using other tools, such as external debuggers, but most will use the debugger that is integrated with Visual Studio .NET. Using an integrated debugger is convenient, because you can compile and debug from the same interface.

I will use the same scenario as the ddd example earlier. While the steps are similar, you'll see some differences. Specifically, I begin my debugging session by launching Visual Studio and opening the mysql.sln solution file in the root of the source-code directory. I make sure my session is set to compile the program in debug for the win32 platform. This will ensure that the proper debug information is compiled into the executable. Once Visual Studio is launched and the correct compilation mode is set, I can set my breakpoint (again, on line 207 in the show_authors() function). Figure 5-8 shows Visual Studio properly configured with the breakpoint set.

Figure 5-8. *Visual Studio debugger setup*

To debug the server, I have to launch the server in debug mode. On Windows, use the switch to run the server stand-alone so that it doesn't run as a service. While this isn't strictly necessary, it allows you to see any messages from the server in the command window that would otherwise be suppressed. You can issue the following command to accomplish this:

```
mysqld-debug --debug –standalone
```

■ **Note** I renamed the `mysqld.exe` server to `mysqld-debug.exe` to make it easier to find in the Windows task manager.

Once the server is running, I can attach to the process from Visual Studio using the Debug ➤ Attach to Process menu selection. Figure 5-9 shows the Attach to Process dialog box. I choose to run and attach to the `mysqld-debug` process so that I can also generate a trace file during the debugging session.

Figure 5-9. *Attaching to a process in Visual Studio .NET*

The next thing I need to do is launch the client. I once again use the `connect-timeout` parameter to set the timeout to a longer delay. The command I use to launch the client from a command window is:

```
mysql -uroot -p --connect-timeout=600
```

With the client running, I can issue the `show authors;` command, which Visual Studio will intercept when the breakpoint is encountered. I can then use the step over (F10) and step into (F11) commands to step through the code. I stop the code inside the loop, which sends data, and inspect the authors structure. Figure 5-10 shows the state of the debugger after I have stepped into the loop.

Figure 5-10. *Displaying variable values in Visual Studio .NET*

As with ddd, you can also change values of variables. Doing so in Visual Studio is a bit more complicated, however. While there may be other options, the best way to change values in Visual Studio is to edit the values in the watch window. If the values in the watch window are pointers to memory locations, however, you have to change the memory location. Do this by opening the memory debug window and use the watch window to locate the memory location and edit it in place. Figure 5-11 shows the memory window open and the values edited.

Figure 5-11. *Editing values in memory using Visual Studio .NET*

After the values in memory are edited, I can continue the execution and see the results in the client window. Listing 5-18 shows an excerpt of the sample output.

Listing 5-18. Output of Debugging Session

```
mysql> show authors;
+-------------+------------------+--------------------------+
| Name        | Location         | Comment                  |
+-------------+------------------+--------------------------+
| Aker, Brian | Seattle, WA, USA | bunch of little stuff :)|
| JonJon      | Hometown, USA    | Companion, Best Friend   |
...
+-------------+------------------+--------------------------+
80 rows in set (1 min 55.64 sec)

mysql>
```

To stop the debugging session, I issue the `shutdown` command in a command window and then detach from the process using the Debug ➤ Detach All menu selection in Visual Studio.

```
mysqladmin -uroot -p shutdown
```

Now that you've seen how to debug the MySQL system using Visual Studio on Windows, I encourage you to read through this example again and try it out on your own Windows development machine.

Summary

In this chapter, I explained debugging, showed you some basic debugging techniques, and provided examples of how to use them. These techniques include inline debugging statements, error handling, and external debuggers.

You learned how to use the inline debugging statements DBUG tool provided by Oracle to create trace files of the system execution, write out pertinent data, and record errors and warnings. You also learned about debugging in Linux and Windows using gdb, ddd, and Visual Studio .NET.

Developing good debugging skills is essential to becoming a good software developer. I hope that this chapter has provided you with a foundation for perfecting your own debugging skills.

In the next chapter, I examine one popular uses of the MySQL system by system integrators: embedded MySQL. This permits the MySQL system to become a part of another system. As you can imagine, the process could require some serious debugging to figure out what went wrong at what level of the embedding.

CHAPTER 6

■ ■ ■

Embedded MySQL

The MySQL server is well known for its lightweight and high-performance features, but did you know it can also be used as an embedded database for your enterprise applications? This chapter explains the concepts of embedded applications and how to use the MySQL C API for creating your own embedded MySQL applications. I'll introduce you to the techniques for compiling the embedded server and writing applications for both Linux and Windows.

Building Embedded Applications

Numerous applications have been built using lightweight database systems as internal data storage. If you use Microsoft Windows as your primary desktop operating system, the chances are you have seen or used at least one application that uses the Microsoft Access database engine. Even if the application doesn't advertise the use of Access, you can usually tell with just a cursory peek at the installation directory.

Some embedded applications use existing database systems on the host computer (such as Access), while others use dedicated installations of larger database systems. Less obvious are those applications that include database systems compiled into the software itself.

What Is an Embedded System?

An *embedded system* is one that is contained within another system. Simply put, the embedded system is a slave to the host system. The purpose of the embedded system is to provide some functionality that the host system requires. This could be communication mechanisms, data storage and retrieval, or even graphical user displays.

Embedded systems have traditionally been thought of as dedicated hardware or electronics. For example, an automated teller machine (ATM) is an embedded system that contains dedicated hardware. Today, embedded systems include not only dedicated hardware but also dedicated software systems. Unlike embedded hardware that is difficult or impossible to modify, embedded software is often modified to work in the specific environment. Embedded hardware and software share the qualities of being self-contained and providing some service to the host system.

Embedded software systems are not typically the same applications as those you see and use on a daily basis. Some, such as those that use the embedded MySQL library, are adaptations of existing functionality rebuilt in order to work more efficiently inside another software system. Unlike its stand-alone server version, however, the embedded MySQL server is designed to operate at a programmatic level. That is, the calls to the server are done via a programming language and not as ad hoc queries. Methods are exposed in the embedded server to take ad hoc queries as parameters and to initiate the server to execute them.

This means that the embedded MySQL server can be accessed only via another application. As you will see in the next few sections, embedded software can exist in a number of applications ranging in their level of integration from a closed programmatic-only access to a fully functional system that is "hidden" by the host application. Let's first look at the most common types of embedded systems.

Types of Embedded Systems

The many types of embedded systems can be difficult to classify because of the unique nature of their use. They generally fall into one (or more) of these categories:

Real-time: A system that is used in installations that require a response and action within a given threshold on the part of the host system. The feature most common to this set of systems is timing. The execution time of every command process must be minimized to achieve the goals of the system. Often, these systems are required to perform within events that occur externally rather than any internal-processing speed. An example of a real-time system would be a router or a telecommunications switch.

Reactive: A system that responds solely to external events. These events tend to be recurring and cyclical in nature, but they may also be in the form of user input (interactive systems are reactive systems). Reactive systems are designed to always be available for operation. Timing is usually secondary and limited only by the frequency of the cyclic operations. An example of a reactive system would be a safety-monitoring system designed to page or alert service personnel when certain events or thresholds occur.

Process control: A system designed to control other systems. These tend to be those designed to monitor and control hardware devices, such as robots and processing machinery. These systems are typically programmed to repeat a series of actions and generally do not vary from their intended programming or respond to external events or the threshold of status variables or conditions. An example of a process control system is the robot used on an automotive assembly line that assembles a specific component of the automobile.

Critical: A system that is used in installations that have a high cost factor, such as safety, medical, or aviation. These systems are designed so that they cannot fail (or should never fail). Often these systems include variants of the embedded systems described earlier. Examples of a critical system would include medical systems, such as a respirator or artificial circulatory system.

Embedded Database Systems

An *embedded database system* is a system designed to provide data to a host application or environment. This data is usually requested in-process, and therefore the database must respond to the request and return any information without delay. Embedded database systems are considered vital to the host application and the system as a whole. Thus, embedded database systems must also meet the timing requirements of the user. These requirements mean that embedded database systems are generally classified as reactive systems.

All but the most trivial applications that individuals and businesses use produce, consume, and store data. Many applications have data that is well structured and has intrinsic value to the customer. Indeed, in many cases, the data are persisted automatically, and the customer expects the data to be available whenever she needs it. Such applications have as a subsystem either access methods or connectivity to external file or data-handling systems, such as database servers.

Embedded systems that use files to access the data are faced with a number of problems, not the least of which is whether the data is accessible outside of the host application. In this case, the access restrictions may have to be created from scratch or added as yet another layer in the system. File systems often have very good performance and offer faster access times, but they are not as flexible as database systems. Database systems offer more flexibility in the form of the data being stored (as tables versus structured files) but usually incur slower access speeds.

While the reasons for protecting the data may be many and varied, the fundamental requirement is to store and retrieve the data in the most efficient manner possible without exposing the data to others. Many times this is simply a need for a database system. For example, an application such as Adobe Bridge manages a lot of data about the files, projects, photos, and so forth that are used in the Adobe Production suite of tools. These files need to be organized in a way that makes them easy to search for and retrieve. Adobe uses an embedded database (MySQL) to manage the metadata about the files stored by Adobe Bridge. In this case, the application uses the database system to handle the more difficult job of storing, searching, and retrieving the metadata about the objects it manages.

Since the data must be protected, the options for using an external database system become limiting, because it is not always easy or possible to fully protect (or hide) the data. An embedded database system allows applications to use the full power of a database system while hiding the mechanisms and data from external sources.

Embedding MySQL

MySQL engineers recognized early in the development of MySQL that many of its customers are systems integrators with a need for a robust, efficient, and programmatically accessible database system. They responded with not just an embedded library but also a fully functional client library. The client library allows you to create your own MySQL clients. For example, you could create your own version of the MySQL command-line client. The client library is named libmysql. If you would like to see how a typical MySQL client uses this library, check out the mysql project source files.

The MySQL embedded library is named libmysqld after the name of the server executable. You may see the library referred to as the embedded server or simply the C API. This chapter is dedicated to the embedded library (libmysqld), but, much of the access and connectivity is similar between the client and embedded-server libraries.

The embedded library provides numerous functions for accessing the database system via an application programming interface (API). The API provides a number of features that permit systems to take advantage of the MySQL server (programmatically). These features include:

- Connecting to and establishing a server instance

- Disconnecting from the server

- Shutting down the server using a controlled (safe) mechanism

- Manipulating server startup options

- Handling errors

- Generating DBUG trace files

- Issuing queries and retrieving the results

- Managing data

- Accessing the (near) full feature set of the MySQL server

This last point is one of the most significant differences between the stand-alone server and the embedded server. The embedded server does not use the full authentication mechanism and is disabled by default. This is one of the reasons an embedded MySQL system could be challenging to secure (see the later section "Security Concerns" for more details). You can turn on the authentication using the configuration option --with-embedded-privilege-control and recompile the embedded server, however. Other than that, the server behaves nearly identically to the stand-alone server with respect to features and capabilities.

What is really cool is that since the embedded library uses the same access methods as the stand-alone server, all of the databases and tables you create using the stand-alone server can be used with the embedded server. This allows you to create tables and test them using the stand-alone server, and then move them to the embedded system later. Although it is possible to have both servers access the same data directory, it is strictly discouraged and can result in loss of data and unpredictable behavior (you should never "share" data directories among MySQL server instances).

Does this mean you can have a stand-alone server executing on the same machine as an embedded server? Not only yes, but how many embedded servers would you like? As long as the embedded-server instances aren't using the same data directory, you can have several running at the same time. The data each manages is separate from the data the others manage—no data is shared. I tried this out on my own system and it works. I've a 5.6.9 embedded application running right alongside my 5.1 (Generally Available) GA stand-alone server. At the time of this writing, MySQL 5.5 is the latest GA release. I didn't have to stop or even interrupt the stand-alone to interact with the embedded server. How cool is that?

Methods of Embedding MySQL

There are many types of embedded applications. Embedded database applications typically fall into one of three categories. They are either partially hidden behind another interface (bundled embedding), or a system that wraps or contains the database server (deep embedding). The following sections describe each of these types with respect to embedding the MySQL system.

Bundled Server Embedding

Bundled server embedding is a system that is built with a stand-alone installation of the MySQL server. Instead of making MySQL available to anyone on the system or network, the server-level embedded system hides the MySQL server by turning off external (network) access. Thus, this form of an embedded MySQL system is simply a stand-alone server that has had its network access (TCP/IP) turned off.

This type of embedded MySQL system has the advantage that the server can be maintained using locally installed (and properly configured) client applications. So, rather than having to load data using external applications, the system integrators, administrators, and developers can use the normal set of administration and development tools to maintain the embedded MySQL server.

One example of a server-level embedded MySQL system is the LeapTrack software produced by LeapFrog (www.leapfrogschoolhouse.com/do/findsolution?detailPage=overview&name=ReadingPro). MySQL reports that LeapFrog chose MySQL for its cross-platform support, allowing LeapFrog to offer its product on a variety of platforms without changing the core database capabilities. Until then, LeapFrog had been using different proprietary database solutions for its various platforms.

Deep Embedding (libmysqld)

Deep embedding is even more restrictive than bundled embedding. This type of embedded system uses the MySQL system as an integral component. That means that not only is the MySQL system inaccessible from the network, but it is also inaccessible from the normal set of client applications. Rather, the system is built using the special embedded library provided by Oracle called libmysqld. Most embedded MySQL systems will fall into this category.

Since this type of embedded system still uses a MySQL mechanism for data access, it provides the same set of database functionality with only a few limitations (which I'll discuss in a moment). Developers gain the ability to use the deeply embedded MySQL system on a wide variety of platforms through a broad spectrum of development languages (as I explained earlier). Furthermore, it provides developers with a code-level solution that few if any relational database systems provide.

The biggest advantage of using a deeply embedded MySQL system is that it provides an almost completely isolated MySQL system that serves the purpose of the embedded application alone.

One example of a deeply embedded MySQL application is Adobe Bridge by Adobe (www.adobe.com/products/bridge.html). Adobe Bridge is part of the larger Adobe Creative Suite and is used for managing aspects of the data supported by the Creative Suite all while the end user is blissfully unaware they are running a dedicated MySQL system.[1] Most deeply embedded systems are desktop applications that users install on their local computers.

Resource Requirements

The requirements for running an embedded server depend on the type of embedding. If you are using bundled embedding, the requirements are the same as those for a stand-alone installation. A deeply embedded MySQL system

---

[1] Well, until now it seems.

is different, however. A deeply embedded system should require approximately 2MB of memory to run in addition to the needs of the application. The compiled embedded server adds quite a bit more space to the executable memory size, but it isn't onerous or unmanageable.

Disk space is the most unpredictable resource to consider. This is true because it really depends on how much data the embedded system is using. Disk space and time are also concerns for high-throughput systems or systems that process a large number of changes to the data. Processing large numbers of changes to the data can often impact response time more than the space that is used. In these cases, the maintenance of the database may require special access to the server or special interfaces to allow administrator access to the data. This is an excellent case in which having access to the database server in bundled embedding forms would be easier than that of one using deep embedding.

Security Concerns

Security is another area that depends on the type of embedding performed. If the system is built using server embedding, addressing security concerns can be quite challenging. This is true because the MySQL system is still accessible from the local server using the normal set of tools. It may be very difficult to lock this type of embedded system down completely.

Bundled embedding is a lot easier, because the embedded stand-alone MySQL system is accessible only through the embedded application. Unless the embedded-application developers have a maladjusted ethical compass, they will have taken steps to ensure proper credentials are necessary to access the administration capabilities.

Deeply embedded systems present the most difficult case for protecting the data. The embedded MySQL system may not have any password set for it (they typically do not), because, like bundled embedding, they require the user to use the interface provided to access the data. Unfortunately, it isn't that simple. In many cases, the data is placed in directories that are accessible by the user. Indeed, the data needs to be accessible to the user; otherwise, how would she be able to read the data?

That's the problem. The data files are unprotected and could be copied and accessed using another MySQL installation. This isn't limited to just the embedded server; it is also a problem for the stand-alone server. Is that shocking? It could be, if your organization has a limitation of tight control on the use of open-source software. Imagine the look on your information-assurance officer's face when he finds out. OK, so you might want to break it to him gently. Therefore, it may require additional security features included in the embedded application to protect the embedded MySQL system and its data appropriately.

Advantages of MySQL Embedding

The MySQL embedded API enables developers to use a full-featured MySQL server inside another application. The most important benefits are increased speed of data access (since the server is either part of or runs on the same hardware as the application), built-in database management tools, and a very flexible storage and retrieval mechanism. These benefits allow developers the opportunity to incorporate all of the benefits of using MySQL while hiding its implementation from the users. This means that developers can increase the capabilities of their own products by leveraging the features of MySQL.

Limitations of MySQL Embedding

There are some limitations of using the embedded MySQL server. Fortunately, it is a short list. Most of the limitations make sense and are not normally an issue for system integrators. Table 6-1 lists the known limitations of using an embedded MySQL system. Included with each is a brief description.

Table 6-1. *Limitations of Using Embedded MySQL*

Limitation	Description
Security	Access control is turned off by default. The privilege system is inactive.
Replication	No replication or logging facilities.
External Access	No external network communications permitted (unless you build them).
Installation	Deeply embedded applications (such as `libmysqld`) may require additional libraries for deployment.
Events	Event scheduler is not available.
Data	The embedded server stores data just like the stand-alone server, using a folder for each database and set of files for each table.
Version	The embedded server does not work with some releases of MySQL 5.1.
UDF	No user-defined functions are permitted.
Debug/Trace	No stack trace is generated with the core dump.
Connectivity	You cannot connect to an embedded server from network protocols. Note that you can provide this external access via your embedded application.
Resources	May be heavy if using bundled embedding and supporting large amounts of data and/or many simultaneous connections.

The MySQL C API

A first glance at the MySQL C API documentation (a chapter entitled "APIs and Libraries" in the MySQL Reference Manual) may seem intimidating. Well, it is. The C API is designed to encapsulate all of the functionality of the stand-alone server. That's not a simple or easy task. Fortunately, Oracle provides ready access to the MySQL documentation online at `http://dev.mysql.com/doc`. Look for the online reference manual for the subsection "libmysqld, the Embedded MySQL Server Library".

■ **Note** The documentation available online is usually the most up-to-date version available. If you have downloaded a copy for convenience, you may want to check the online documentation periodically. I've found answers to several stumbling blocks by re-examining the documentation online.

Ironically, perhaps the most intimidating aspect of the C API is the documentation itself. Simply stated, it is a bit terse and requires reading through several times before the concepts become clear. It is my goal to provide you a look into the C API in the form of a short tutorial and a couple of examples to help jumpstart your embedded application project.

Getting Started

The first recommendation I make to developers who want to learn how to build embedded applications is to read the documentation. Present text and chapter notwithstanding, it is always a good idea to read through the product documentation before you begin using an API, even if you don't take to the information right away. I often find tidbits of information in the MySQL documentation that on the surface seem insignificant but that later turn out to be the missing key between a successful compilation and a frustrating search for the source of the error.

I also recommend logging on to the MySQL Web site and looking through the Forum (there is a dedicated embedded forum at `http://forums.mysql.com`) and Mailing List (`http://lists.mysql.com`) repositories. You don't have to read everything, but chances are some of your questions can be answered by reading the entries in these repositories. I also sometimes check out the MySQL blogs (`www.planetmysql.org`). Various authors have posted information about the embedded server and many other items of interest. There is so much interesting information out there that sometimes I find myself reading for over an hour at a time. Many MySQL experts consider this tactic the key to becoming a MySQL guru. Information is power.

The online documentation and the various lists and blogs are definitely the best source of the very latest about MySQL. The most important reading you should do is contained in the following sections. I'll present the major C API functions and walk through a simple example of an embedded application. Later, I'll demonstrate a more complex embedded application, complete with an abstracted data access class and written in .NET.

The best way to learn how to create an embedded application is by coding one yourself. Feel free to open your favorite source code editor and follow along with me as I demonstrate a couple of examples. I first walk through each function you need to call in the order it needs to be called. Then, in a later section, I show you how to build the library and write your first embedded-server application.

Most Commonly Used Functions

A quick glance at the documentation shows the C API supports more than 65 functions. Some of these have been deprecated, but Oracle is very good at pointing this out in the documentation (another good reason to read it). Only a few functions are used frequently.

Most of the functions in the library provide connection and server-manipulation functions. Some are dedicated to gathering information about the server and the data, while others are designed to provide calls to perform queries and other manipulations of the data. There are also functions for retrieving error information.

Table 6-2 lists the most commonly used functions. Included are the names of the functions, a brief description, and the source file where it is defined. The functions are listed in roughly the order they would be called in a simple embedded-server example.

■ **Note**   I encourage you to take some time, after you have read through this chapter and understand the examples, to read through the list of functions in the C API portion of the MySQL reference manual. You may find some interesting functions that meet your special database needs.

Table 6-2. *Most Commonly Used Functions*

Function	Description	Source
mysql_server_init()	Initializes the embedded server library.	libmysql.c
mysql_init()	Starts the server.	client.c
mysql_options()	Allows you to change or set the server options.	client.c
mysql_debug()	Turns the debugging trace file on (DBUG).	libmysql.c
mysql_real_connect()	Establishes connection to the embedded server.	client.c
mysql_query()	Issues a query statement (SQL). Statement is passed as a null terminated string.	libmysql.c

(continued)

Table 6-2. (*continued*)

Function	Description	Source
mysql_store_result()	Retrieves the results from the last query.	client.c
mysql_fetch_row()	Returns a single row from the result set.	client.c
mysql_num_fields()	Returns the number of fields in the result set.	client.c
mysql_num_rows()	Returns the number of rows (records) in the result set.	client.c
mysql_error()	Returns a formatted error message (string) describing the last error.	client.c
mysql_errno()	Returns the error number of the last error.	client.c
mysql_free_result()	Frees the memory allocated to the result set. Note: don't forget to use this function often. It will not generate an error to call this on an empty result set.	client.c
mysql_close()	Closes the connection to the server.	client.c
mysql_server_end()	Finalizes the embedded server library and shuts down the server.	libmysql.c

For a complete description of these functions, including the return values and usage, see the MySQL reference manual.

Creating an Embedded Server

The embedded server is established as an instance during the initialization function calls. Most of the functions require a pointer to the instance of the server as a required parameter. When you create an embedded MySQL application, you need to create a pointer to the MYSQL object. You also need to create instances for a result set and a row from the result set (known as a record). Fortunately, the definition of the server and the major structures are defined in the MySQL header files. The header files you need to use (for most applications) are:

```
#include <stdio.h>
#include <stdlib.h>
#include <stdarg.h>
#include <mysql.h>
```

Creating pointer variables to the embedded server and the result set and record structure can be done by using the statements:

```
MYSQL *mysql;              // the embedded server class
MYSQL_RES *results;        // stores results from queries
MYSQL_ROW record;          // a single row in a result set
```

These statements allow you to have access to the embedded server (MYSQL), a result structure (MYSQL_RES), and a record (MYSQL_ROW). You can use global variables to define these pointers. Some of you may not like to use global variables, and there's no reason you have to. The result set and record can be created and destroyed however you like. Just be sure to keep the MYSQL pointer variable the same instance throughout your application.

We're not done with the setup. We still need to establish some strings to use during connection. I've seen many different ways to accomplish this, but the most popular method is to create an array of character strings.

At a minimum, you need to create character strings for the location of the my.cnf (my.ini in Windows) file and the location of the data. A typical set of initialization character strings is:

```
static char *server_options[] = {"mysql_test",
  "--defaults-file=c:\\mysql_embedded\\my.ini",
  "--datadir=c:\\mysql_embedded\\data", NULL };
```

The examples in this chapter depict the server options for a Windows compilation. If you use Linux, you will need to use the appropriate paths and change the my.ini to my.cnf. In this example, I use the label "mysql_test" (which is ignored by mysql_server_init()), the location of my.cnf (my.ini) file to the normal installation directory, and the data directory to the normal MySQL installation. If you want to establish both a stand-alone and an embedded server, you should use a different data location for each server. You would also want to use a different configuration file just to keep things tidy.

To help keep errors to a minimum, I also use an integer variable to identify the number of elements in my array of strings (I'll discuss this in a moment). This allows me to write bounds-checking code without having to remember how many elements are permitted. I can allow the number of elements to change at runtime, thereby allowing the bounds-checking code to adapt to changes as necessary.

```
int num_elements=(sizeof(server_options) / sizeof(char *)) - 1;
```

The last setup step is to create another array of character strings that identify the server groups that contain any additional server options in my configuration file (my.cnf). This defines the sections that will be read when the server is started.

```
static char *server_groups[] = {"libmysqld_server", "libmysqld_client", NULL };
```

Initializing the Server

The embedded server must be initialized, or started, before you can connect to it. This usually involves two initialization calls followed by any number of calls to set additional options. The first initialization function you need to call to start an embedded server is mysql_server_init()[2]. This function is defined as:

```
int mysql_server_init(int argc, char **argv, char **groups)
```

The function is called only once before calling any other function. It takes as parameters argc and argv, much the same as the normal arguments for a program (the same as the main function). In addition, the group labels from the configuration are passed to allow the server to read runtime server options. The return values are either a 0 for success or 1 for failure. This allows you to call the function inside a conditional statement and act if a failure occurs. Here's an example call of this function using the declarations from the startup section:

```
mysql_server_init(num_elements, server_options, server_groups);
```

■ **Note**   In order to keep the example short and easily understood, I refrain from using error handling in the example source code. I revisit error handling in a later example.

---

[2]This function may be changed to mysql_library_init(). At the time of this writing, both functions are supported.

The second initialization function you need to call is mysql_init(). This function allocates the MYSQL object for you in connecting to the server. This function is defined as;

```
MYSQL *mysql_init(MYSQL *mysql)
```

Here is an example call of this function using the global variable defined earlier:

```
mysql = mysql_init(NULL);
```

Notice I use NULL to pass into the function. This is because it is the first call of the function requesting a new instance of the MYSQL object. In this case, a new object is allocated and initialized. If you called the function passing in an existing instance of the object, the function just initializes the object.

The function returns NULL if there was an error or the address of the object if successful. This means you can place this call in a conditional statement to process errors on failure or simply interrogate the MYSQL pointer variable to detect NULL.

■ **Tip**   Almost all of the mysql_XXX functions return 0 for success and non-zero for failure. Only those that return pointers return non-zero for success and 0 (NULL) for failure.

Setting Options

The embedded server allows you to set additional connection options prior to connecting to the server. The function you use to set connection options is defined as:

```
int mysql_options(MYSQL *mysql, enum mysql_option, const char *arg)
```

The first parameter is the instance of the embedded-server object. The second parameter is an enumerated value from the possible options, and the last parameter is used to pass in a parameter value for the option selected using an optional character string. There is a long list of possible values for the option list. Some of the more commonly used options and their values are shown in Table 6-3. The complete set of options is listed in the MySQL reference manual.

Table 6-3. *Partial List of Connection Options*

Option	Value	Description
MYSQL_OPT_USE_REMOTE_CONNECTION	N/A	Forces the connection to use a remote server to connect to
MYSQL_OPT_USE_EMBEDDED_CONNECTION	N/A	Forces the connection to the embedded server
MYSQL_READ_DEFAULT_GROUP	Group	Instructs the server to read server configuration options from the specified group in the configuration file
MYSQL_SET_CLIENT_IP	IP address	Provides the IP address for embedded servers configuredto use authentication

The following example calls to this function instruct the server to read configuration options from the [libmysqld_client] section of the configuration file and tell the server to use an embedded connection:

```
mysql_options(mysql, MYSQL_READ_DEFAULT_GROUP, "libmysqld_client");
mysql_options(mysql, MYSQL_OPT_USE_EMBEDDED_CONNECTION, NULL);
```

The return values are 0 for success and non-zero for any option that is invalid or has an invalid value.

Connecting to the Server

Now that the server is initialized and all of the options are set, you can connect to the server. The function you use to do this is called mysql_real_connect(). It has a large number of parameters that allow for fine-tuning of the connection. The function is declared as;

```
MYSQL *mysql_real_connect(MYSQL *mysql, const char *host, const char *user, const
char *passwd, const char *db, unsigned int port, const char *unix_socket,
unsigned long client_flag)
```

This function must complete without errors. If it fails (in fact, if any of the previous functions fail), you cannot use the server and should either reattempt to connect to the server or gracefully abort the operation.

The parameters for the function include the MYSQL instance, a character string that defines the hostname (either an IP address or fully qualified name), a username, a password, the name of the initial database to use, the port number you want to use, the Unix socket number you want to use, and finally, a flag to enable special client behavior. See the MySQL reference manual for more details on the client flags. Any parameter value specified as NULL will signal the function to use the default value for that parameter. Here is an example call to this function that connects using all defaults except the database:

```
mysql_real_connect(mysql, NULL, NULL, NULL, "information_schema", 0, NULL, 0);
```

The function returns a connection handle if successful and NULL if there is a failure. Most applications do not trap the connection handle. Rather, they check the return value for NULL. Notice that I do not use any of the authentication parameters. This is because the authentication is turned off by default. If I had compiled the embedded server with the authentication switch on, these parameters would have to be provided. Last, the fourth parameter is the name of the default database you want to connect to. This database must exist or you may encounter errors.

At this point, you should have all of the code necessary to set up variables to call the embedded server, initialize, set options, and connect to the embedded server. The following shows these operations as represented by the previous code samples:

```
#include <stdio.h>
#include <stdlib.h>
#include <stdarg.h>
#include "mysql.h"

MYSQL *mysql;                    //the embedded server class
MYSQL_RES *results;              //stores results from queries
MYSQL_ROW record;                //a single row in a result set

static char *server_options[] = {"mysql_test",
  "--defaults-file=c:\\mysql_embedded\\my.ini",
  "--datadir=c:\\mysql_embedded\\data", NULL };
```

```c
int num_elements = (sizeof(server_options) / sizeof(char *)) - 1;
static char *server_groups[] = {"libmysqld_server", "libmysqld_client", NULL };

int main(void)
{
  mysql_server_init(num_elements, server_options, server_groups);
  mysql = mysql_init(NULL);
  mysql_options(mysql, MYSQL_READ_DEFAULT_GROUP, "libmysqld_client");
  mysql_options(mysql, MYSQL_OPT_USE_EMBEDDED_CONNECTION, NULL);
  mysql_real_connect(mysql, NULL, NULL, NULL, "INFORMATION_SCHEMA",
    0, NULL, 0);

...

  return 0;
}
```

Running Queries

At last, we get to the good stuff—the meat of what makes a database system a database system: the processing of ad hoc queries. The function that permits you to issue a query is the mysql_query() function. The function is declared as;

```c
int mysql_query(MYSQL *mysql, const char *query)
```

The parameters for the function are the MYSQL object instance and a character string containing the SQL statement (null terminated). The SQL statement can be any valid query, including data-manipulation statements (SELECT, INSERT, UPDATE, DELETE, DROP, etc.). If the query produces results, the results can be bound to a pointer variable for access by using the methods mysql_store_result() and mysql_fetch_row(). If no results are returned, the result set will be NULL.

An example call to this function to retrieve the list of databases on the server is:

```c
mysql_query(mysql, " SELECT SCHEMA_NAME FROM INFORMATION_SCHEMA.SCHEMATA;")
```

The return value for this function is 0 if successful and non-zero if there is a failure.

Retrieving Results

Once you have issued a query, the next steps are to fetch the result set and store a reference to it in the result pointers' variable. You can then fetch the next row (record) and store it in the record structure (which happens to be a named array). The functions to accomplish this process are mysql_store_result() and mysql_fetch_row(), which are defined as;

```c
MYSQL_RES *mysql_store_result(MYSQL *mysql)
MYSQL_ROW mysql_fetch_row(MYSQL_RES *result)
```

The mysql_store_result() function accepts the MYSQL object as its parameter and returns an instance of the result set for the most recently run query. The function returns NULL if either an error has occurred or the last query did not return any results. You have to take care at this point to check for errors by calling the mysql_errno() function. If there was an error, you will have to call the error functions and compare the result to the list of known errors. The known error values generated from this function are CR_OUT_OF_MEMORY (no memory available to store the results),

CR_SERVER_GONE_ERROR or CR_SERVER_LOST (the connection was lost to the server), and CR_UNKNOWN_ERR (a catchall error indicating the server is in an unpredictable state).

▪ **Note** There are a number of possible conditions for using the mysql_store_result() function. The most common uses are described here. To explore the function usage in more detail, or if you have problems diagnosing a problem with using the function, see the MySQL reference manual for more details.

The mysql_fetch_row() function accepts the result set as the only parameter. The function returns NULL if there are no more rows in the result set. This is handy, because it allows you to use this feature in your loops or iterators. If this function fails, the return value of NULL is still set. It is up to you to check the mysql_errno() function to see if any of the defined errors have occurred. These errors include CR_SERVER_LOST, which indicates the connection has failed, and CR_UNKOWN_ERROR, which is a ubiquitous "something is wrong" error indicator.

Examples of these calls used together to query a table and print the results to the console are:

```
mysql_query(mysql, "SELECT ItemNum, Description FROM tblTest");
results = mysql_store_result(mysql);
while(record=mysql_fetch_row(results))
{
  printf("%s\t%s\n", record[0], record[1]);
}
```

Notice that after the query is run, I call the mysql_store_result() function to get the results; then I placed the mysql_fetch_row() function inside my loop evaluation. Since mysql_fetch_row() returns NULL when no more rows are available (at the end of the record set), the loop will terminate at that point. While there are rows, I access each of the columns in the row using the array subscripts (starting at 0).

This example demonstrates the basic structure for all queries made to the embedded server. You can wrap this process and include it inside a class or abstracted set of functions. I demonstrate this in the second example embedded application.

Cleanup

The data returned from the query and placed into the result set required the allocation of resources. Since we are good programmers, we strive to free up the memory no longer needed to avoid memory leaks.[3] Oracle provides the mysql_free_result() function to help free those resources. This function is defined as:

```
void mysql_free_result(MYSQL_RES *result)
```

This function is call-safe, meaning that you can call it using a result set that has already been freed without producing an error. That's just in case you get happy and start flinging "free" code everywhere. Don't laugh—I've seen programs with more "free" than "new" calls. Most of the time this isn't a problem, but if the free calls are not used properly, having too many of them could result in freeing something you don't want freed. As with the new operation, you should use the free operation with deliberate purpose and caution.

Here is an example call to this function to free a result set:

```
mysql_free_result(results);
```

---

[3]It isn't actually leaking as much as it is no longer referenced but still allocated, making that portion of memory unusable.

Disconnecting from and Finalizing the Server

When you are finished with the embedded server, you need to disconnect and shut it down. This can be accomplished by using the mysql_close() and mysql_server_end()[4] functions. The close function closes the connection and the other finalizes the server and deallocates memory. These functions are defined as:

```
void mysql_close(MYSQL *mysql);
void mysql_server_end();
```

Example calls for these functions are shown here. Note that these are the last function calls you need to make, and they are normally called when shutting down your application.

```
mysql_close(mysql);
mysql_server_end();
```

Putting It All Together

Now, let's see all of this code together. Listing 6-1 shows a completed embedded server that lists the databases accessible from the given data directory. I go through the process of building and running this example in a later section.

■ **Note** The following example is written for Windows. A Linux example is discussed in a later section.

Listing 6-1. An Example Embedded Server Application

```
#include <stdio.h>
#include <stdlib.h>
#include <stdarg.h>
#include "mysql.h"

MYSQL *mysql;                       //the embedded server class
MYSQL_RES *results;                 //stores results from queries
MYSQL_ROW record;                   //a single row in a result set

static char *server_options[] = {"mysql_test",
  "--defaults-file=c:\\mysql_embedded\\my.ini",
  "--datadir=c:\\mysql_embedded\\data", NULL };
int num_elements = (sizeof(server_options) / sizeof(char *)) - 1;
static char *server_groups[] = {"libmysqld_server", "libmysqld_client", NULL };

int main(void)
{
  mysql_server_init(num_elements, server_options, server_groups);
  mysql = mysql_init(NULL);
  mysql_options(mysql, MYSQL_READ_DEFAULT_GROUP, "libmysqld_client");
```

---

[4]This may be changed to mysql_library_end() in later releases of MySQL. At the time of this writing, both functions are supported.

```
mysql_options(mysql, MYSQL_OPT_USE_EMBEDDED_CONNECTION, NULL);
mysql_real_connect(mysql, NULL, NULL, NULL, "information_schema",
  0, NULL, 0);
mysql_query(mysql, "SHOW DATABASES");              // issue query
results = mysql_store_result(mysql);               // get results
printf("The following are the databases supported:\n");
while(record=mysql_fetch_row(results))             // fetch row
{
  printf("%s\n", record[0]);                       // process row
}
mysql_query(mysql, "CREATE DATABASE testdb1;");
mysql_query(mysql, "SHOW DATABASES;");             // issue query
results = mysql_store_result(mysql);               // get results
printf("The following are the databases supported:\n");
while(record=mysql_fetch_row(results))             // fetch row
{
  printf("%s\n", record[0]);                       // process row
}
mysql_free_result(results);
mysql_query(mysql, "DROP DATABASE testdb1;");      // issue query
mysql_close(mysql);
mysql_server_end();
return 0;
}
```

Error Handling

You may be wondering what happened to all of the error handling that you read about in a previous chapter. Well, the facilities are there in the C API. Oracle has provided for error handling using two functions. The first, msyql_errno(), retrieves the error number from the most recent error. The second, mysql_error(), retrieves the associated error message for the most recent error. These functions are defined as:

```
unsigned int mysql_errno(MYSQL *mysql)
const char *mysql_error(MYSQL *mysql)
```

The parameter passed for both functions is the MYSQL object. Since these methods are error handlers, they are not expected to fail. If they are called when no error has occurred, however, mysql_errno() returns 0 and mysql_error() returns an empty character string.

Here are some example calls to these functions:

```
if(somethinggoeshinkyhere)
{
  printf("There was an error! Error number : %d = $s\n",
    mysql_errno(&mysql), mysql_error(&mysql));
}
```

Whew! That's all there is to it. I hope that my explanations clear the fog from the reference manual. I wrote this section primarily because I feel that there aren't any decent examples out there that help you learn how to use the embedded server—at least none that capture what is needed in a few short pages.

Building Embedded MySQL Applications

The previous sections walked you through the basic functions used in an embedded MySQL application. This section will show you how to actually build one. I begin by showing you how to compile the application and move on to discuss methods of constructing the embedded library calls. I also present two example applications for you to use to experiment with your own system.

I've also included a brief foray into modifying the core MySQL source code. Yes, I know that may be a bit scary, but I show you all the details step by step. Fortunately, it is an easy modification that requires changing only two files.

I encourage you to read the source code that I've included. I know there is a lot of it, but I've trimmed it down to what I think is a manageable hunk. I've learned a lot of interesting things about the MySQL source code simply from reading through it. It is my goal that you gain additional insight into building your own embedded MySQL applications by studying the source code for these examples.

Compiling the Library (libmysqld)

Before you can work with the embedded library (libmysqld), you need to compile it. Some distributions of the MySQL binaries may not include a precompiled embedded library. The embedded library is included in most source-code distributions and can be found in the /libmysqld directory off the root of the source tree. The library is usually built without debug information. You will want to have a debug-enabled version for your development.

Compiling libmysqld on Linux

To compile the library under Linux, set the configuration using the configure script and then perform a normal make and make install step. The configuration parameters that you will need are --with-debug and --with-embedded-server. The following shows the complete process. Run this from the root of your source-code directory. The compilation process can take a while, so feel free to start that now while you read ahead. You can expect the compilation to take anywhere from a few minutes to about an hour, depending on the speed of your machine and whether you have built the system previously with debug information.

■ **Note**   The following commands build the server and install it into the default location. These operations require root privileges.

```
cmake . -DWITH_EMBEDDED_SERVER=ON -DWITH_DEBUG=ON
make
sudo make install
```

■ **Tip**   You can also use the cmake-gui . command to set the parameters using the graphical interface. Once the options are set, click Configure and then Generate.

Compiling libmysqld on Windows

To compile the library under Windows, launch Visual Studio and open the main solution file in the root source-code directory (mysql.sln). Turning debug on is simply a matter of selecting the libmysqld project and setting the build configuration to Debug Win32. You can compile the library in the usual manner by first clicking on the project to select it at the current project then selecting Build ➤ Build or by building the complete solution. Any dependent projects will be built as needed. The compilation process can take a while, so feel free to start that now while you read ahead. You can expect the compilation to take anywhere from a few minutes to about half an hour depending on the speed of your machine and whether you have built the system previously with debug information.

What About Debugging?

You may be wondering if debugging in the embedded library works the same as in the stand-alone server. Well, it does! In fact, you can use the same debugging methods. Debugging the embedded server at runtime is a bit of a challenge, but since the server is supposed to be embedded, you are not likely to need to debug down to that level. You may need to create a trace file in order to help debug your application.

I explained several debugging techniques in the last chapter. One of the most powerful and simple to use is the DBUG package. While the embedded server has all of that plumbing hooked up and indeed follows the same debugging practice of marking all entries and exits of functions, the DBUG package is not exposed via the embedded library.

You could create your own instance of the DBUG package and use that to write your own trace file. You may opt to do this for large applications using the embedded server. Most applications are small enough so that the added work isn't helpful. In this case, it would be really cool if the embedded library offered a debugging option.

The DBUG package can be turned on either via the configuration file or through a direct call to the embedded library. This assumes, of course, that your embedded library was compiled with debug enabled.

Turning on the trace file at runtime requires a call to the embedded library. The method is mysql_debug(), and it takes one character string parameter that specifies the debug options. The following example turns the trace file on at runtime, specifying the more popular options and directing the library to write the trace file to the root directory. This method should be called before you have connected to the server.

```
mysql_debug("debug=d:t:i:O,\\mysqld_embedded.trace");
```

■ **Tip** Use a different filename for your embedded-server trace. This will help distinguish the embedded-server trace from any other stand-alone server you may have running.

You can also turn debugging on using the configuration file. Simply place the string from the previous example into the my.cnf (my.ini) file that your source code specifies at startup (more on that in a moment).

What if you want to use the DBUG package from your embedded application but don't want to include the DBUG package in your own code? Are you simply out of luck? The embedded library doesn't expose the DBUG methods, but it could! The following paragraphs explain the procedure to modify the embedded server to include a simple DBUG method. I'm using a simple example, because I do not want to throw you into the deep end just yet.

The first thing you need to do is to make a backup of the original source code. If you downloaded a tarred or zipped file, you're fine. If you do find yourself struggling with getting the server to compile after you've added some code, returning to the original copy can have profound effects on your stress level (and sanity). This is especially true if you've removed your changes and it still doesn't compile!

Adding a new method is really easy. Edit the mysql.h file in the /include directory and add the definition. I chose to create a method that exposes the DBUG_PRINT function. I named it simply mysql_dbug_print(). Listing 6-2 shows the function definition for this method. Note that the function accepts a single character pointer. I use this to pass in a string I've defined in my embedded application. This allows me to write a string to the trace file as sort of a marker for where my embedded application synchronizes with the trace from the embedded server.

Listing 6-2. Modifications to mysql.h

```
/* BEGIN CAB MODIFICATION */
/* Reason for Modification: */
/* Adds a method to permit embedded applications to call DBUG_PRINT */
void STDCALL mysql_dbug_print(const char *a);
/* END CAB MODIFICATION */
```

To create the function, edit the /libmysqld/libmysqld.c and add the function to the rest of the source code. The location doesn't matter as long as it is in the main body of the source code somewhere. I chose to locate it near the other exposed library functions (near line number 89). Listing 6-3 shows the code for this method. Notice that the code simply echoes the string to the DBUG_PRINT method. Notice that I also add a string to the end of the string passed. This helps me locate all of the trace lines that came from my application regardless of what I pass in to be printed.

Listing 6-3. Modifications to libmysqld.c

```
/* BEGIN CAB MODIFICATION */
/* Reason for Modification: */
/* Adds a method to permit embedded applications to call DBUG_PRINT */
void STDCALL mysql_dbug_print(const char *a)
{
  DBUG_PRINT(a, (" -- Embedded application."));
}
/* END CAB MODIFICATION */
```

To add a method to the embedded library in Windows, you also must modify the libmysqld_exports.def file to include the new method. Listing 6-4 shows an abbreviated listing as an example. Here, I've added the mysql_dbug_print() statement to the file. Note that the file is maintained in alphabetical order.

Listing 6-4. Modifications to libmysqld_exports.def

```
LIBRARY     LIBMYSQLD
DESCRIPTION 'MySQL 5.6 Embedded Server Library'
VERSION     5.6
EXPORTS
  _dig_vec_upper
  _dig_vec_lower
...
  mysql_dbug_print
  mysql_debug
  mysql_dump_debug_info
  mysql_eof
...
```

That's it! Now just recompile the embedded server, and your new method can be used in your application. I've done this to my installation of the embedded server. The examples that follow use this method to write a string to the trace file. This helps me greatly in finding the synchronization points in the trace file with my source code.

■ **Tip** In the previous listings, I use the same commenting strategy that I presented in Chapter 3. This will help you identify any differences with the source code whenever you need to migrate to a newer version.

What About the Data?

Before you launch into creating and running your first embedded MySQL application, consider the data that you want to use. If you plan to create an embedded application that provides an administration interface that allows you to create tables and populate them, you're all set. If you have not planned such an interface or similar facilities, you will need to get the database configured using other tools.

Fortunately, as long as you use the simpler table types (like MyISAM), you can use a stand-alone server and your favorite utilities to create the database and tables and populate them. If you use InnoDB, you should either start the server with the `--innodb_file_per_table` option or create a clean installation of MySQL, add your data, then copy the data directory and the InnoDB files to the new location. Once the data have been created, you can copy the directories from the data directory of the stand-alone server installation to another location. Remember, it is important that you separate the embedded server data locations from that of the stand-alone server. Take note of where you place the data, as you will need that for your embedded application.

I use this technique with all of my examples and my own embedded applications. It gives me the ability to shape and populate the data I want to use first without having to worry about creating an administration interface. Most embedded MySQL applications are built this way.

Creating a Basic Embedded Server

The previous sections showed you all the necessary functions needed to use the embedded library. I show you a simple example using all of the functions I've described. I've included both a Linux and Windows example. While they are nearly identical, there are some minor differences in the source code. The biggest difference is in how the programs are compiled. The examples in this chapter assume that you are using an embedded library that has been compiled with debug information.

The example program reads the list of databases in the data directory for the embedded server printing the list to the console, creates a new database called `testdb1`, reads the list of databases again printing the list to the console, and, finally, deletes the database `testdb1`. While not very complicated, all the example function calls are exercised. I've also included the calls to turn the trace file on (DBUG) and to print information to the trace file using the new `mysql_dbug_print()` function in the embedded library.

Linux Example

The first file you need to create is the configuration file (`my.cnf`). You can use an existing configuration file, but I recommend copying it to the location of your embedded server. For example, if you created a directory named `/var/lib/mysql_embedded`, you would place the configuration file there and copy all of your data directories (the database files and folders) to that directory as well. Those are the only files that need to be in that directory. The only exception is if you wanted to use a different language for your embedded server. In this case, I recommend copying the appropriate files from a stand-alone installation to your embedded-server directory and referencing them from the configuration file. Listing 6-5 shows the configuration file for the example program.

Listing 6-5. Sample my.cnf File for Linux

```
[libmysqld_server]
basedir=/var/lib/mysql_embedded
datadir=/var/lib/mysql_embedded
#slow query log#=
#tmpdir#=
#port=3306
#set-variable=key_buffer=16M
```

```
[libmysqld_client]
#debug=d:t:i:O,\\mysqld_embedded.trace
```

Notice that I've disabled most of the options (by using the # symbol at the start of the line). I usually do this so that I can easily and quickly turn them on should I need to. Debugging is turned off so that I can show you how to turn it on programmatically.

The next file you need to create is the source code for the application. If you have followed along with the tutorial on the C API from earlier, it should look very familiar. Listing 6-6 shows the complete source code for a simple embedded MySQL application.

Listing 6-6. Embedded Example 1 (Linux: example1_linux.c)

```c
#include <stdio.h>
#include <stdlib.h>
#include <stdarg.h>
#include "mysql.h"

MYSQL *mysql;                       //the embedded server class
MYSQL_RES *results;                 //stores results from queries
MYSQL_ROW record;                   //a single row in a result set

/*
  These variables set the location of the ini file and data stores.
*/
static char *server_options[] = {"mysql_test",
  "--defaults-file=/var/lib/mysql_embedded/my.cnf",
  "--datadir=/var/lib/mysql_embedded", NULL };
int num_elements = (sizeof(server_options) / sizeof(char *)) - 1;
static char *server_groups[] = {"libmysqld_server", "libmysqld_client", NULL };

int main(void)
{
  /*
    This section initializes the server and sets server options.
  */
  mysql_server_init(num_elements, server_options, server_groups);
  mysql = mysql_init(NULL);
  mysql_options(mysql, MYSQL_READ_DEFAULT_GROUP, "libmysqld_client");
  mysql_options(mysql, MYSQL_OPT_USE_EMBEDDED_CONNECTION, NULL);
  /*
    The following call turns debugging on programmatically.
    Comment out to turn off debugging.
  */
  //mysql_debug("d:t:i:O,\\mysqld_embedded.trace");
  /*
    Connect to embedded server.
  */
  mysql_real_connect(mysql, NULL, NULL, NULL, "information_schema",
    0, NULL, 0);
  /*
```

This section executes the following commands and demonstrates
how to retrieve results from a query.

```
    SHOW DATABASES;
    CREATE DATABASE testdb1;
    SHOW DATABASES;
    DROP DATABASE testdb1;
*/
mysql_dbug_print("Showing databases.");              //record trace
mysql_query(mysql, "SHOW DATABASES;");               //issue query
results = mysql_store_result(mysql);                 //get results
printf("The following are the databases supported:\n");
while(record=mysql_fetch_row(results))               //fetch row
{
  printf("%s\n", record[0]);                         //process row
}
mysql_dbug_print("Creating the database testdb1.");  //record trace
mysql_query(mysql, "CREATE DATABASE testdb1;");
mysql_dbug_print("Showing databases.");
mysql_query(mysql, "SHOW DATABASES;");               //issue query
results = mysql_store_result(mysql);                 //get results
printf("The following are the databases supported:\n");
while(record=mysql_fetch_row(results))               //fetch row
{
  printf("%s\n", record[0]);                         //process row
}
mysql_free_result(results);
mysql_dbug_print("Dropping database testdb1.");      //record trace
mysql_query(mysql, "DROP DATABASE testdb1;");        //issue query
/*
  Now close the server connection and tell server we're done (shutdown).
*/
mysql_close(mysql);
mysql_server_end();

  return 0;
}
```

I've added comments (some would say overkill) to help you follow along in the code. The first thing I do is create my global variables and set up my initialization arrays. I then initialize the server with the array options, set a few more options, and connect to the server. The body of the example application reads data from the database and prints it out. The last portion of the example closes and finalizes the server.

When compiling the example, you can use the mysql_config script to identify the location of the libraries. The script returns to the command line the actual path each of the options passed to it. You can also run the script from a command line and see all of the options and their values. A sample command to compile the example is:

```
gcc example1_linux.c -g -o example1_linux -lstdc++ -I./include -L./lib -lmysqld -lpthread -ldl
-lcrypt -lm -lrt
```

This command should work for most Linux systems, but in some cases this could be a problem. If your MySQL installation is at another location, you may need to alter the phrase with the mysql_config script. If you have multiple installations of MySQL on your system or you have installed the embedded library in another location, you may not be able to use the mysql_config script, because it will return the wrong library paths. This is also true for cases in which you have multiple versions of the MySQL source code installed. You certainly want to avoid the case of using the include files from one version of the server to compile an embedded library from another. You could also run into problems if you do not have the earlier glibc libraries.

■ **Note**   If you are compiling the embedded server from a source tree and you are using mysql_config, you must set the cmake option -DCMAKE_INSTALL_PREFIX=ON.

To correct these problems, first run the mysql_config script from the command line and note the paths for the libraries. You should also locate the correct paths to the libraries and header files you want to use. An example of how I overcame these problems is shown here (I have all of these situations on my SUSE machine):

```
g++ example1_linux.c -g -o example1_linux -lz -I/usr/include/mysql
-L/usr/lib/mysql -lmysqld -lz -lpthread -lcrypt -lnsl -lm -lpthread -lc
-lnss_files -lnss_dns -lresolv -lc -lnss_files -lnss_dns -lresolv -lrt
```

Notice that I used the newer g++ compiler instead of the normal gcc. This is because my system has the latest GNU libraries and does not have the older ones. I could, of course, have loaded the older libraries and fixed this problem but typing g++ is much easier. OK, so we programmers are lazy.

Listing 6-7 shows the sample output of running this example under a typical installation of MySQL. In this case, I copied all of the data from the stand-alone server directory to my embedded-server directory.

Listing 6-7. Sample Output

```
linux:/home/Chuck/source/Embedded # ./example1_linux
The following are the databases supported:
information_schema
mysql
test
The following are the databases supported:
information_schema
mysql
test
testdb1
linux:/home/Chuck/source/Embedded #
```

Please take some time and explore this example application on your own machine. I recommend that you experiment with the body of the application and run a few queries of your own to get a feel for how you might write your own embedded MySQL application. If you implemented the mysql_dbug_print() function in your embedded library, try it out with the example by either removing the comments on the mysql_debug() function call or by removing the comments for the debug option in the configuration file.

The next example will show you how to encapsulate the embedded library calls; it demonstrates their use in a more realistic application.

Windows Example

The first file you need to create is the configuration file (my.ini). You can use an existing configuration file, but I recommend copying it to the location of your embedded server. For example, if you created a directory named c:/mysql_embedded, you would place the configuration file there and copy all of your data directories to that directory as well. Those are the only files that need to be in that directory. The only exception is if you wanted to use a different language for your embedded server. In this case, I suggest copying the appropriate files from a stand-alone installation to your embedded-server directory and referencing them from the configuration file. Listing 6-8 shows the configuration file for the example program. Included are the most commonly used options and where they are specified in the file.

Listing 6-8. Sample my.ini File for Windows

```
[mysqld]
basedir=C:/mysql_embedded
datadir=C:/mysql_embedded/data
language=C:/mysql_embedded/share/english

[libmysqld_client]
#debug=d:t:i:O,\\mysqld_embedded.trace
```

Creating the project file is a little trickier. To get the most out of using Visual Studio, I recommend opening the master solution file (mysql.sln) from the root of the source-code directory and adding your new application as a new project to that solution. You do not have to store your source code in the same source tree, but you should store it in such a way as to know what version of the source code it applies to.

You can create the project using the project wizard. You should select the C++ ➤ Win32 Console project template (Templates ➤ Visual C++ ➤ Win32 in Visual Studio 2012) and name the project. This creates a new folder under the root of the folder specified in the wizard with the same name as the project. You should create an empty project and add your own source files.

Creating a project file as a subproject of the solution gives you some really cool advantages. To take advantage of the automated build process (no make files—yippee!), add the libmysqld project to your projects dependencies. You can open the project dependencies tool from the Project ➤ Project Dependencies menu. Set the build configuration to Active(Debug) by using the solution's Configuration drop-down box and setting the platform to Active(Win32) using the solution's Platform drop-down box on the standard toolbar.

You also need to set some switches in the project properties. Open the project-properties dialog box by selecting Project ➤ Properties or by right-clicking on the project and choosing Properties. The first item you want to check is the runtime library generation. Set this switch to Multi-threaded Debug DLL (/MDd) by expanding the C/C++ label in the tree and clicking on the Code Generation label in the tree and selecting it from the Runtime Library drop-down list. This option causes your application to use the debug multithread- and DLL-specific version of the runtime library. Figure 6-1 shows the project properties dialog box and the location of this option.

Figure 6-1. *Project properties dialog box, with the Code Generation page displayed*

Next, add the MySQL include directory to your project properties. The easiest way to do this is to expand the C/C++ label and click on the Command Line label. This will display the command-line parameters. To add a new parameter, type it in the Additional Options text box. In this case, you need to add an option such as:

```
/I ../include.
```

If you located your project somewhere other than under the MySQL source tree, you may need to alter the parameter accordingly. Figure 6-2 shows the project properties dialog box and the location of this option.

Figure 6-2. *Project properties dialog box: Command Line page*

You can also remove the precompiled header option if you do not want (or need) to use precompiled headers. This option is on the C/C++ Precompile Headers page in the project properties dialog box.

Add the libmysqld project to the example1_win32 project using the Project ➤ Add Reference menu selection. A dialog will open (shown in Figure 6-3) allowing you to choose a project among the solutions to use as a reference. Choose the libmysqld project. Figure 6-4 shows the resulting project-properties dialog with the libmysqld project reference added. Failure to do this step will result in numerous undefined symbol errors when you compile.

Figure 6-3. *Choose a project reference*

Figure 6-4. *Project properties dialog box: reference*

Now that you have the project configured correctly, add your source file or paste in the example code if you chose to create the base project files when you created the project. Listing 6-9 shows the complete Windows version.

Listing 6-9. Embedded Example 1 (Windows: example1_win32.cpp)

```cpp
#include <stdio.h>
#include <stdlib.h>
#include <stdarg.h>
#include "mysql.h"

MYSQL *mysql;                    //the embedded server class
MYSQL_RES *results;              //stores results from queries
MYSQL_ROW record;                //a single row in a result set

/*
  These variables set the location of the ini file and data stores.
*/
static char *server_options[] = {"mysql_test",
  "--defaults-file=c:\\mysql_embedded\\my.ini",
  "--datadir=c:\\mysql_embedded\\data", NULL };
int num_elements = (sizeof(server_options) / sizeof(char *)) - 1;
static char *server_groups[] = {"libmysqld_server", "libmysqld_client", NULL };

int main(void)
{
  /*
    This section initializes the server and sets server options.
  */
  mysql_server_init(num_elements, server_options, server_groups);
  mysql = mysql_init(NULL);
  mysql_options(mysql, MYSQL_READ_DEFAULT_GROUP, "libmysqld_client");
  mysql_options(mysql, MYSQL_OPT_USE_EMBEDDED_CONNECTION, NULL);
  /*
    The following call turns debugging on programmatically.
    Comment out to turn off debugging.
  */
  mysql_debug("d:t:i:O,\\mysqld_embedded.trace");
  /*
    Connect to embedded server.
  */
  mysql_real_connect(mysql, NULL, NULL, NULL, "information_schema",
    0, NULL, 0);
  /*
    This section executes the following commands and demonstrates
    how to retrieve results from a query.

    SHOW DATABASES;
    CREATE DATABASE testdb1;
    SHOW DATABASES;
    DROP DATABASE testdb1;
  */
```

```
mysql_dbug_print("Showing databases.");              //record trace
mysql_query(mysql, "SHOW DATABASES;");               //issue query
results = mysql_store_result(mysql);                 //get results
printf("The following are the databases supported:\n");
while(record=mysql_fetch_row(results))               //fetch row
{
  printf("%s\n", record[0]);                         //process row
}
mysql_dbug_print("Creating the database testdb1.");  //record trace
mysql_query(mysql, "CREATE DATABASE testdb1;");
mysql_dbug_print("Showing databases.");
mysql_query(mysql, "SHOW DATABASES;");               //issue query
results = mysql_store_result(mysql);                 //get results
printf("The following are the databases supported:\n");
while(record=mysql_fetch_row(results))               //fetch row
{
  printf("%s\n", record[0]);                         //process row
}
mysql_free_result(results);
mysql_dbug_print("Dropping database testdb1.");      //record trace
mysql_query(mysql, "DROP DATABASE testdb1;");        //issue query
/*
  Now close the server connection and tell server we're done (shutdown).
*/
mysql_close(mysql);
mysql_server_end();

  return 0;
}
```

I've added comments (some would say overkill) to help you follow along in the code. The first thing I do is create my global variables and set up my initialization arrays. I then initialize the server with the array options, set a few more options if necessary, and connect to the server. The body of the example application reads data from the database and prints them out. The last portion of the example closes and finalizes the server.

Compiling the example is really easy. Just select the project, then choose Project ➤ Build, or right-click on the project and choose build. If you have already compiled the libmysqld project, all you should see is the compilation of the example. If for some reason the object files are out of date for libmysqld or any of its dependencies, Visual Studio will compile those as well.

■ **Caution** You may encounter some really strange errors found in the mysql_com.h or similar header files. The most likely cause of this may be an optimization strategy. Microsoft automatically includes the #define WIN32_LEAN_AND_MEAN statement in the stdafx.h file. If you have that turned on, it tells the compiler to ignore a host of includes and links that are not needed (normally). You will want to delete that line altogether (or comment it out). Your program should now compile without errors. If you opted to not use the stdafx files, you should not encounter this problem.

When the compilation is complete, you can either run the program from the debug menu commands or open a command window and run it from the command line. If this is your first time, you should see an error message such as:

```
This application has failed to start because LIBMYSQLD.dll was not found.
Re-installing the application may fix this problem.
```

The reason for this error has nothing to do with the second sentence in the error message. It means that the embedded library isn't in the search path. If you have worked with .NET or COM applications and never used C libraries, you may never have encountered the error. Unlike .NET and COM, C libraries are not registered in a Global Assembly Cache (GAC) or registry. These libraries (DLLs) should be collocated with applications that call them or at least on an execution path. Most developers place a copy of the DLL in the execution directory.

To fix this problem, copy the libmysqld.dll file from the lib_debug directory to the directory where the example1_win32.exe file resides (or add lib_debug to the execution path). Once you get past that hurdle, you should see an output like that shown in Listing 6-10.

Listing 6-10. Example Output

```
c:\source\mysql-5.6\example1_win32\Debug>example1_win32
The following are the databases supported:
information_schema
cluster
mysql
test
The following are the databases supported:
information_schema
cluster
mysql
test
testdb1
```

Please take some time and explore this example application on your own machine. I recommend you experiment with the body of the application and run a few queries of your own to get a feel for how you might write your own embedded MySQL application. If you implemented the mysql_dbug_print() function in your embedded library, try it out with the example by either removing the comments on the mysql_debug() function call or by removing the comments for the debug option in the configuration file.

What About Error Handling?

Some of you may be wondering about error handling. Specifically, how can you detect problems with the embedded server and handle them gracefully? A number of the embedded library calls have error codes that you can interrogate and act on. The previous sections described the return values for the functions I'll be using. Although I didn't include much error handling in the first embedded MySQL examples, I will in the next example. Note how I capture the errors and handle sending the errors to the client.

Embedded Server Application

The previous examples showed how to create a basic embedded MySQL application. While the examples showed how to connect and read data from a dedicated MySQL installation, they aren't good models for building your own embedded application, because they lack enough coverage for all but the most trivial requirements. Oh, and they don't have any error handling! The example in this chapter, while fictional, is all about providing you with the tools you need to build a real embedded application.

This application, called the Book Vending Machine (BVM), is an embedded system designed to run on a dedicated Microsoft Windows–based PC with a touch screen. The system and its other input devices are housed in a specialized mechanical vending machine designed to dispense books. The idea behind the BVM is to allow publishers to offer their most popular titles in a semi-mobile package that the vendor can configure and replenish as needed. The BVM would allow publishers to install their vending machine in areas where space is at a premium, such as trade shows, airports, and shopping malls. These areas usually have high traffic consisting of customers interested in purchasing printed books. The BVM saves publishers money by reducing the need for a storefront and personnel to staff it.

■ **Note** I've often found myself wondering if this idea has ever been given consideration. I've read several articles predicting the continued rise of print-on-demand, but seldom have I seen anything written about how a book-vending machine would work. I understand there are a few prototype installations by some publishers, but these trials have not generated much enthusiasm. I chose to use this example as a means to add some realism. I, too, read technical books and often find myself bored with unrealistic or trivial examples. Here is an example that I hope you agree is at least plausible.

The Interface

This application has a need for a dual interface; one for the normal vending-machine activity and one to allow vendors to restock the vending machine, adjusting the information as needed. The vending-machine interface is designed to provide the customer with an array of buttons that provide a thumbnail of books for specific slots in the vending machine. Since most modern vending machines use product buttons that are illuminated when the product is available and dimmed or turned off when the product is depleted, the BVM interface enables the button when the product in that slot is available and disables it when the product is depleted.

When the customer clicks a product button, the screen changes to a short, detailed display that describes the book and gives its price. If the customer wants to purchase the book, she can click Purchase and is prompted for payment. This application is written to simulate those activities. A real implementation would call the appropriate hardware-control library to receive payment, validate the payment, and engage the mechanical part of the vending machine to disperse the product from the indicated slot. Figure 6-5 shows the main interface for the book vending machine. Figure 6-6 shows the effect of low quantity for some of the books.

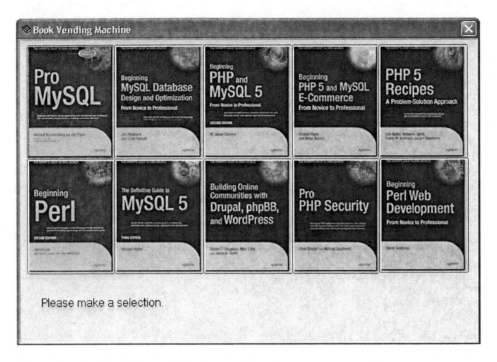

Figure 6-5. *Book vending machine customer interface*

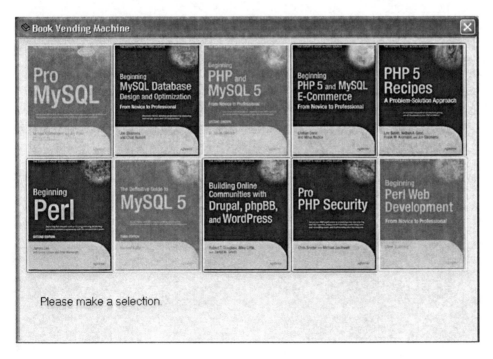

Figure 6-6. *Resulting "Product Depleted" view of the customer interface*

Figure 6-7 shows a sample of the details for one of the books.

Figure 6-7. Book details interface

A vending machine wouldn't be very useful if there were not any way to replenish the product. The BVM provides this via an administration interface. When the vendor needs to replenish the books or change the details to match a different set of books, the vendor opens the machine and closes the embedded application (this feature would have to be added to the example). The vendor would then restart the application, providing the administrator switch on the command line, like this:

```
C:\>Books BookVendingMachine -admin
```

The administration interface allows the vendor to enter an ad hoc query and execute it. Figure 6-8 shows the administration interface. The example shows a typical update operation to reset the quantity of the products. This interface allows the vendor to enter any query she needs to reset the data for the embedded application.

Figure 6-8. *Administration interface*

The Data and Database

The data for this example was created on a stand-alone MySQL server and copied to the embedded MySQL directory. When I created this application, I designed the data structures and the database to hold the data first. This is always a good idea.

■ **Note**   Some developers may disagree, believing it is better to start with the user-interface design and allow the data requirements to evolve. Neither practice is better than the other. The important point is that the data must be a focus of your design.

Most of your projects will come with either requirements for the data or actual data in existing repositories. For new applications, such as this example, always design the database by designing the tables in such a way as to represent the items and the relationships among them. This is usually a single step in a small project, but it may be an iterative process in which you use the initial tables and relationships as input to the design and planning of the user interfaces using UML drawings and modeling techniques. Changes to the database (the organization of the data) are often discovered during the later steps, which you then use as the starting point for going through the process again.

The data for this example consists of a short list of descriptive fields about the books in the machine. This includes the title, author, price, and description. I added the ISBN to use as a key for the table (since it is unique by definition and used by the publishing industry as a primary means of identifying the book). I also added some other fields that I would want to see before I decide to purchase a book. These include publication date and number of pages. I also needed to store a thumbnail image. (I chose an external method, storing the path and filename to the file and reading it from the file system. I could have used a binary large object (BLOB) to store the thumbnail, but this is easier—although admittedly error prone.) Last, I projected what I would need to run the user interface and decided to add a field to record the slot number where the book is located and dispensed, and a field to measure the quantity on hand. I named the table books and placed it in a database named bvm. The CREATE SQL statement for the table is shown here. Listing 6-11 shows the layout of the table using the EXPLAIN command.

```
CREATE DATABASE BVM;
CREATE TABLE Books (
  ISBN varchar(15) NOT NULL,
```

```
  Title varchar(125) NOT NULL,
  Authors varchar(100) NOT NULL,
  Price float NOT NULL,
  Pages int NOT NULL,
  PubDate date NOT NULL,
  Quantity int DEFAULT 0,
  Slot int NOT NULL,
  Thumbnail varchar(100) NOT NULL,
  Description text NOT NULL
);
```

Listing 6-11. Table Structure

```
mysql> USE bvm
mysql> explain Books;
```

Field	Type	Null	Key	Default	Extra
ISBN	varchar(15)	NO			
Title	varchar(125)	NO			
Authors	varchar(100)	NO			
Price	float	NO			
Pages	int(11)	NO			
PubDate	date	NO			
Quantity	int(11)	YES		0	
Slot	int(11)	NO			
Thumbnail	varchar(100)	NO			
Description	text	NO			

```
10 rows in set (0.08 sec)
```

To manage the thumbnail images, I stored the thumbnail filename in the thumbnail field and use a system-level option for the path. One way to do this is to create a command-line switch. Another is to place it in the MySQL configuration file and read it from there. You can also read it from the database. I used a database table named settings that contains only two fields: FieldName, which stores the name of the option (e.g., "ImagePath"), and Value, which store its value (e.g., "c:\images\mypic.tif"). This method allows me to create any number of system options and control them externally. The CREATE SQL command for the settings table is shown here, followed by a sample INSERT command to set the ImagePath option for the example application:

```
CREATE TABLE settings (FieldName varchar(20), Value varchar(255));
INSERT INTO settings VALUES ("ImagePath", "c:\\mysql_embedded\\images\\");
```

Creating the Project

The best way to create the project is to use the wizard to create a new Windows project. I recommend opening the master-solution file from the root of the source-code directory and adding your new application as a new project to that solution. You don't have to store your source code in the same source tree, but you should store it in such a way as to know what version of the source code it applies to.

You can create the project using the project wizard. Select the CLR Windows Forms Application project template and name the project. This creates a new folder under the root of the folder specified in the wizard with the same name as the project.

Creating a project file as a subproject of the solution gives you some really cool advantages. To take advantage of the automated build process (no make files—yippee!), you need to add the `libmysqld` project to your project's dependencies. You can open the project dependencies tool from the Project ➤ Project Dependencies menu. Set the build configuration to Active(Debug) by using the solution's Configuration drop-down box and set the platform to Active(Win32) using the solution's Platform drop-down box on the standard toolbar.

You also need to set some switches in the project properties. Open the project-properties dialog box. The first item to check is the runtime library generation. Set this switch to Multi-threaded Debug DLL (/MDd) by expanding the C/C++ label in the tree and clicking on the Code Generation label in the tree and selecting it from the Runtime Library drop-down list. Figure 6-1 earlier in this chapter shows the project properties dialog box and the location of this option.

Then, add the MySQL include directory to your project properties. The easiest way to do this is to expand the C/C++ label and click on the Command Line label. This will display the command-line parameters. To add a new parameter, type it in the Additional Options text box. In this case, you need to add something like `/I ../include`. If you located your project somewhere other than under the MySQL source tree, you may need to alter the parameter accordingly. Figure 6-2 earlier in this chapter shows the project properties dialog box and the location of this option.

You can also remove the precompiled header option if you do not want (or need) to use precompiled headers. This option is on the C/C++ Precompile Headers page in the project-properties dialog box.

As in the previous example, you also need to add the libmysqld project as a reference using the Project->Add Reference menu item. Figures 6-3 and 6-4 depict the dialogs for this operation.

Last, set the common language-runtime setting to `/clr`. You can set this in the project-properties dialog box by clicking on General in the tree and selecting Common Language Runtime Support (/clr) from the Common Language Runtime support option. Figure 6-9 shows the project dialog box and the location of this option.

Figure 6-9. *Project properties dialog box: General page*

Design

I had to meet two important requirements to design the application. Not only did I need to design a user interface that is easy to use and free from errors, I also needed to be able to call a C API from a .NET application. If you do some searching in the MySQL forums and lists, you will see that several poor souls have struggled with getting this to work. If you follow along with my example, you should not encounter those problems. The main cause of the problems seems to be the inability to call the C API functions in the embedded library. I get around this by writing my application in C++ using managed C++ code. You cannot use C API calls in a managed application, but C++ allows you to temporarily turn that off and back on by using the #pragma unmanaged and #pragma managed directives.

The need to call unmanaged code is also a great motivator for encapsulation of the library calls. Unmanaged code enables the developer to write a DLL that can be used in programs that are not written in .NET. For this example, I use a C++ class to encapsulate the C API calls wrapped in the #pragma unmanaged directive. This allows me to show you an example of a .NET application that calls the embedded library C API directly. Cool, eh?

I also wanted to keep the user interface completely separate from anything to do with the embedded library. I wanted to do this so that I can provide you with an encapsulated database access class that you can reuse as the basis for your own applications. It also permits me to present to you one example (Windows) of a realistic application without long lists of source code for you to read through. The data-access design for this example is therefore a single unmanaged C++ class that encapsulates the embedded library C API calls. The design also includes two forms: one for each of the user interfaces (Customer and Administrator).

Managed vs. unmanaged code

Managed code is .NET applications that run under the control of the common language runtime (CLR). These applications can take advantage of all the features of the CLR, specifically garbage collection and better program-execution control. Unmanaged code is Windows applications that do not run under the CLR and therefore do not benefit from the .NET enhancements.

Database Engine Class

I began by designing the database engine class using just pen and paper. I could have used a UML drawing application, but since the class is small, I just listed the methods that I needed. For example, I needed methods to initialize, connect to, and shut down the embedded MySQL server. These methods are easy to encapsulate, because they don't need any parameters from the form.

One of the first challenges I encountered was error handling. How can I communicate the errors to the client form without requiring the client to know anything about the embedded library? There are probably dozens of ways to do this, but I chose to implement an error-check method that allows the client to check for the presence of errors after an operation, and then another method to retrieve the error message. This allows me to once again separate the database access from the forms.

The class methods having to do with issuing queries and retrieving results are a design from a choice of implementations. I chose to implement an access iterator that permits the client to issue the query and then iterate through the results. I also needed a method that tells the database that a book has been vended, so that the database can reduce the quantity on hand value for that book.

Data retrieval is accomplished using three methods that return a character string, an integer, or a large text field. I also added helper methods for getting a setting from the settings table, getting a field from the database (for the administrator interface), and a quick method to retrieve the quantity on hand.

Listing 6-12 shows the complete source code for the database class header. I named the class DBEngine. Table 6-4 includes a description and use for each method in the class.

Listing 6-12. Database Engine Class Header (DBEngine.h)

```
#pragma once
#pragma unmanaged
#include <stdio.h>

class DBEngine
{
private:
  bool mysqlError;
public:
  DBEngine(void);
  const char *GetError();
  bool Error();

  void Initialize();
  void Shutdown();
  char *GetSetting(char *Field);
  char *GetBookFieldStr(int Slot, char *Field);
  char *GetBookFieldText(int Slot, char *Field);
  int GetBookFieldInt(int Slot, char *Field);
  int GetQty(int Slot);
  void VendBook(char *ISBN);
  void StartQuery(char *QueryStatement);
  void RunQuery(char *QueryStatement);
  int GetNext();
  char *GetField(int fldNum);
  ~DBEngine(void);
};
#pragma managed
```

Table 6-4. *Database Engine Class Methods*

Method	Return	Description
GetError()	char *	Returns the error message for the last error generated.
Error()	int	Returns 1 if the server has detected an error condition.
Initialize()	void	Encapsulates the embedded-server initialization and connection operations.
Shutdown()	void	Encapsulates the embedded-server finalization and shutdown operations.
GetSetting()	char *	Returns the value for the setting named. Looks up information in the settings table.
GetBookFieldStr()	char *	Returns a character-string value from the books table for the field passed in the specified slot.
GetBookFieldText()	char *	Returns a character-string value from the books table for the field passed in the specified slot.
GetBookFieldInt()	int	Returns an integer value from the books table for the field passed in the specified slot.
GetQty()	int	Returns the quantity on hand for the book in the specified slot.

(continued)

Table 6-4. (*continued*)

Method	Return	Description
VendBook()	void	Reduces the quantity on hand for the book in the specified slot.
StartQuery()	void	Initializes the query iterator by executing the query and retrieving the result set.
RunQuery()	void	A helper method designed to run a query that does not return results.
GetNext()	int	Retrieves the next record in the result set. Returns 0 if there are no more records in result set or non-zero for success.
GetField	char *	Returns the field name for the field number passed.

Defining the class was the easy part. Completing the code for all of these methods is a little harder. Instead of starting from scratch, I used the code from the first example and changed it into the database-class source code. Listing 6-13 shows the complete source code for the database class. Notice that I've used the same global (well, local to this source) variables and arrays of characters for the initialization and startup options. This part should look very familiar to you. Take some time to read through this code. When you are done, I explain some of the grittier details.

Listing 6-13. *Database Engine Class (DBEngine.cpp)*

```
#pragma unmanaged

#include "DBEngine.h"
#include <stdio.h>
#include <stdlib.h>
#include <stdarg.h>
#include "mysql.h"

MYSQL *mysql;                        //the embedded server class
MYSQL_RES *results;                  //stores results from queries
MYSQL_ROW record;                    //a single row in a result set
bool IteratorStarted;                //used to control iterator
MYSQL_RES *ExecQuery(char *Query);

/*
  These variables set the location of the ini file and data stores.
*/
static char *server_options[] = {"mysql_test",
  "--defaults-file=c:\\mysql_embedded\\my.ini",
  "--datadir=c:\\mysql_embedded\\data", NULL };
int num_elements = (sizeof(server_options) / sizeof(char *)) - 1;
static char *server_groups[] = {"libmysqld_server", "libmysqld_client", NULL };

DBEngine::DBEngine(void)
{
  mysqlError = false;
}

DBEngine::~DBEngine(void)
{
}
```

```cpp
const char *DBEngine::GetError()
{
  return (mysql_error(mysql));
  mysqlError = false;
}

bool DBEngine::Error()
{
  return(mysqlError);
}

char *DBEngine::GetBookFieldStr(int Slot, char *Field)
{
  char *istr = new char[10];
  char *str = new char[128];

  _itoa_s(Slot, istr, 10, 10);
  strcpy_s(str, 128, "SELECT ");
  strcat_s(str, 128, Field);
  strcat_s(str, 128, " FROM books WHERE Slot = ");
  strcat_s(str, 128, istr);
  mysqlError = false;
  results=ExecQuery(str);
  strcpy_s(str, 128, "");
  if (results)
  {
    mysqlError = false;
    record=mysql_fetch_row(results);
    if(record)
    {
      strcpy_s(str, 128, record[0]);
    }
    else
    {
      mysqlError = true;
    }
  }
  return (str);
}

char *DBEngine::GetBookFieldText(int Slot, char *Field)
{
  char *istr = new char[10];
  char *str = new char[128];

  _itoa_s(Slot, istr, 10, 10);
  strcpy_s(str, 128, "SELECT ");
  strcat_s(str, 128, Field);
  strcat_s(str, 128, " FROM books WHERE Slot = ");
  strcat_s(str, 128, istr);
  mysqlError = false;
```

```
  results=ExecQuery(str);
  delete str;
  if (results)
  {
    mysqlError = false;
    record=mysql_fetch_row(results);
    if(record)
    {
      return (record[0]);
    }
    else
    {
      mysqlError = true;
    }
  }
  return ("");
}

int DBEngine::GetBookFieldInt(int Slot, char *Field)
{
  char *istr = new char[10];
  char *str = new char[128];
  int qty = 0;

  _itoa_s(Slot, istr, 10, 10);
  strcpy_s(str, 128, "SELECT ");
  strcat_s(str, 128, Field);
  strcat_s(str, 128, " FROM books WHERE Slot = ");
  strcat_s(str, 128, istr);
  results=ExecQuery(str);
  if (results)
  {
    record=mysql_fetch_row(results);
    if(record)
    {
      qty = atoi(record[0]);
    }
    else
    {
      mysqlError = true;
    }
  }
  delete str;
  return (qty);
}

void DBEngine::VendBook(char *ISBN)
{
  char *str = new char[128];
  char *istr = new char[10];
  int qty = 0;
```

```
    strcpy_s(str, 128, "SELECT Quantity FROM books WHERE ISBN = '");
    strcat_s(str, 128, ISBN);
    strcat_s(str, 128, "'");
    results=ExecQuery(str);
    record=mysql_fetch_row(results);
    if (record)
    {
      qty = atoi(record[0]);
      if (qty >= 1)
      {
        _itoa_s(qty - 1, istr, 10, 10);
        strcpy_s(str, 128, "UPDATE books SET Quantity = ");
        strcat_s(str, 128, istr);
        strcat_s(str, 128, " WHERE ISBN = '");
        strcat_s(str, 128, ISBN);
        strcat_s(str, 128, "'");
        results=ExecQuery(str);
      }
    }
    else
    {
      mysqlError = true;
    }
}

void DBEngine::Initialize()
{
  /*
    This section initializes the server and sets server options.
  */
  mysql_server_init(num_elements, server_options, server_groups);
  mysql = mysql_init(NULL);
  if (mysql)
  {
    mysql_options(mysql, MYSQL_READ_DEFAULT_GROUP, "libmysqld_client");
    mysql_options(mysql, MYSQL_OPT_USE_EMBEDDED_CONNECTION, NULL);
    /*
      The following call turns debugging on programmatically.
      Comment out to turn off debugging.
    */
    //mysql_debug("d:t:i:O,\\mysqld_embedded.trace");
    /*
      Connect to embedded server.
    */
    if(mysql_real_connect(mysql, NULL, NULL, NULL, "INFORMATION_SCHEMA",
      0, NULL, 0) == NULL)
    {
      mysqlError = true;
    }
```

```
      else
      {
        mysql_query(mysql, "use bvm");
      }
    }
    else
    {
      mysqlError = true;
    }
    IteratorStarted = false;
}

void DBEngine::Shutdown()
{
  /*
    Now close the server connection and tell server we're done (shutdown).
  */
  mysql_close(mysql);
  mysql_server_end();
}

char *DBEngine::GetSetting(char *Field)
{
  char *str = new char[128];
  strcpy_s(str, 128, "SELECT * FROM settings WHERE FieldName = '");
  strcat_s(str, 128, Field);
  strcat_s(str, 128, "'");
  results=ExecQuery(str);
  strcpy_s(str, 128, "");
  if (results)
  {
    record=mysql_fetch_row(results);
    if (record)
    {
      strcpy_s(str, 128, record[1]);
    }
  }
  else
  {
    mysqlError = true;
  }
  return (str);
}


void DBEngine::StartQuery(char *QueryStatement)
{
  if (!IteratorStarted)
  {
    results=ExecQuery(QueryStatement);
    if (results)
```

```
    {
      record=mysql_fetch_row(results);
    }
  }
  IteratorStarted=true;
}

void DBEngine::RunQuery(char *QueryStatement)
{
  results=ExecQuery(QueryStatement);
  if (results)
  {
    record=mysql_fetch_row(results);
    if(!record)
    {
      mysqlError = true;
    }
  }
}

int DBEngine::GetNext()
{
  //if EOF then no more records
  IteratorStarted=false;
  record=mysql_fetch_row(results);
  if (record)
  {
    return (1);
  }
  else
  {
    return (0);
  }
}

char *DBEngine::GetField(int fldNum)
{
  if (record)
  {
    return (record[fldNum]);
  }
  else
  {
    return ("");
  }
}
MYSQL_RES *ExecQuery(char *Query)
{
  mysql_dbug_print("ExecQuery.");
  mysql_free_result(results);
```

```
    mysql_query(mysql, Query);
    return (mysql_store_result(mysql));
}
#pragma managed
```

One thing you should notice about this code is all of the error handling that I've added to make the code more robust, or hardened. While I do not have all possible error handlers implemented, the most important ones are.

The get methods are all implemented using the same process. I first generate the appropriate query (and thereby hide the SQL statement from the client), execute the query, retrieve the result set and then the record from the query, and return the value.

One method of interest is VendBook(). Take a moment and look through that one again. You'll see that I've followed a similar method of generating the query, but this time I don't get the results, because there aren't any. Actually, there is a result—it is the number of records affected. This could be handy if you want to do some additional process or rule checking in your application.

The rest of the methods should look familiar to you, because they are all copies of the original example I showed you, except this time they have error handling included. Now, let's take a look at how the user-interface code calls the database class.

Customer Interface (Main Form)

The source code for the customer interface is very large. This is because of the auto-generated code that Microsoft places in the form.h file. I'm including only those portions that I wrote. I've included this section to show you how you can write your own .NET (or other) user interfaces. Aside from the code in the button events, I use only four additional methods that I need to complete the user interface. The first method, DisplayError(), is defined as:

```
void DisplayError()
```

I use this function to detect errors in the database class and to present the error message to the user. The implementation of the method is a typical call to the MessageBox::Show() function.

The second method is a helper method that completes the detail view of the book selected. The function is named LoadDetails(). I abstracted this method because I realized I would be repeating the code for all ten buttons.[5] Abstracting in this manner minimizes the code and permits easier debugging. This method is defined as:

```
void LoadDetails(int Slot)
```

The method takes as a parameter the slot number (which corresponds to the button number). It queries the database using the database-class methods and populates the detail-interface elements. This is where most of the heavy lifting of communicating with the database-engine class occurs.

■ **Note** You may be wondering what all that gnarly code is surrounding the character strings. It turns out that the .NET string class is not compatible with the C-style character strings. The extra code I included is designed to marshal the strings between these formats.

---

[5]There was only one feature of Visual Basic I found really cool: control arrays. Alas, they are a thing of the past.

The third method, a helper method named Delay(), is defined as:

```
void Delay(int secs)
```

The function causes a delay in processing for the number of seconds passed as a parameter. While not something you would want to include in your own application, I added it to simulate the vending process. This is an excellent example of how you can use stubbed functionality to demonstrate an application. This can be especially helpful in prototyping a new interface.

The fourth method, CheckAvailability(), is used to turn the buttons on the interface on or off depending on whether there is sufficient quantity of the product available. This method is defined as:

```
void CheckAvailability()
```

The function makes a series of calls to the database engine to check the quantity for each slot. If the slot is empty (quantity == 0), the button is disabled.

Listing 6-14 shows an excerpt of the source code for the customer interface. I've omitted a great deal of the auto-generated code (represented as . . .). Notice that at the top of the file I reference the database-engine header using the #include "DBEngine.h" directive. Also notice that I've defined a variable of type DBEngine. I use this object throughout the code. Since it is local to the form, I can use it in any event or method. I use the . . . to indicate portions of the auto-generated code and comments omitted from the listing.

Listing 6-14. Main Form Source Code (MainForm.h)

```
#include <stdio.h>
#include <stdlib.h>
#include <string>
#include "vcclr.h"
#include <time.h>
#include "DBEngine.h"

namespace BookVendingMachine {

  const char GREETING[] = "Please make a selection.";

  DBEngine  *Database = new DBEngine();

. . .

#pragma endregion
  void DisplayError()
  {
    String ^str = gcnew String("There was an error with the database system.\n" \
                        "Please contact product support.\nError = ");
    str = str + gcnew String(Database->GetError());
    MessageBox::Show(str, "Internal System Error", MessageBoxButtons::OK,
                  MessageBoxIcon::Information);
  }

  void LoadDetails(int Slot)
  {
    int Qty = Database->GetBookFieldInt(Slot, "Quantity");
    if (Database->Error()) DisplayError();
    pnlButtons->Visible = false;
```

```
    pnlDetail->Visible = true;
    lblStatus->Visible = false;
    lblTitle->Text = gcnew String(Database->GetBookFieldStr(Slot, "Title"));
    if (Database->Error()) DisplayError();
    lblAuthors->Text =
      gcnew String(Database->GetBookFieldStr(Slot, "Authors"));
    if (Database->Error()) DisplayError();
    lblISBN->Text = gcnew String(Database->GetBookFieldStr(Slot, "ISBN"));
    if (Database->Error()) DisplayError();
    txtDescription->Text =
      gcnew String(Database->GetBookFieldText(Slot, "Description"));
    if (Database->Error()) DisplayError();
    lblPrice->Text = gcnew String(Database->GetBookFieldStr(Slot, "Price"));
    if (Database->Error()) DisplayError();
    lblNumPages->Text =
      gcnew String(Database->GetBookFieldStr(Slot, "Pages"));
    if (Database->Error()) DisplayError();
    lblPubDate->Text =
      gcnew String(Database->GetBookFieldStr(Slot, "PubDate"));
    if (Database->Error()) DisplayError();
    if(Qty < 1)
    {
      btnPurchase->Enabled = false;
    }
  }
  void CheckAvailability()
  {
    btnBook1->Enabled = (Database->GetBookFieldInt(1, "Quantity") >= 1);
    if (Database->Error()) DisplayError();
    btnBook2->Enabled = (Database->GetBookFieldInt(2, "Quantity") >= 1);
    if (Database->Error()) DisplayError();
    btnBook3->Enabled = (Database->GetBookFieldInt(3, "Quantity") >= 1);
    if (Database->Error()) DisplayError();
    btnBook4->Enabled = (Database->GetBookFieldInt(4, "Quantity") >= 1);
    if (Database->Error()) DisplayError();
    btnBook5->Enabled = (Database->GetBookFieldInt(5, "Quantity") >= 1);
    if (Database->Error()) DisplayError();
    btnBook6->Enabled = (Database->GetBookFieldInt(6, "Quantity") >= 1);
    if (Database->Error()) DisplayError();
    btnBook7->Enabled = (Database->GetBookFieldInt(7, "Quantity") >= 1);
    if (Database->Error()) DisplayError();
    btnBook8->Enabled = (Database->GetBookFieldInt(8, "Quantity") >= 1);
    if (Database->Error()) DisplayError();
    btnBook9->Enabled = (Database->GetBookFieldInt(9, "Quantity") >= 1);
    if (Database->Error()) DisplayError();
    btnBook10->Enabled = (Database->GetBookFieldInt(10, "Quantity") >= 1);
    if (Database->Error()) DisplayError();
  }

  void Delay(int secs)
  {
    time_t start;
```

```
    time_t current;

    time(&start);
    do
    {
      time(&current);
    } while(difftime(current,start) < secs);
  }

private: System::Void btnCancel_Click(System::Object^  sender,
                                      System::EventArgs^  e)
  {
    lblStatus->Visible = true;
    pnlDetail->Visible = false;
    pnlButtons->Visible = true;
    btnPurchase->Enabled = true;
    lblStatus->Text = gcnew String(GREETING);
  }

private: System::Void btnPurchase_Click(System::Object^  sender,
                                        System::EventArgs^  e)
  {
    String ^orig = gcnew String(lblISBN->Text->ToString());
    pin_ptr<const wchar_t> wch = PtrToStringChars(orig);

    // Convert to a char*
    size_t origsize = wcslen(wch) + 1;
    const size_t newsize = 100;
    size_t convertedChars = 0;
    char nstring[newsize];
    wcstombs_s(&convertedChars, nstring, origsize, wch, _TRUNCATE);

    lblStatus->Visible = true;
    pnlDetail->Visible = false;
    pnlButtons->Visible = true;
    btnPurchase->Enabled = true;
    Database->VendBook(nstring);
    //
    // Simulate buying the book.
    //
    lblStatus->Text = "Please Insert your credit card.";
    this->Refresh();
    Delay(3);
    lblStatus->Text = "Thank you. Processing card number ending in 4-1234.";
    this->Refresh();
    Delay(3);
    lblStatus->Text = "Vending....";
    this->Refresh();
    Delay(5);
    this->Refresh();
```

```
      CheckAvailability();
      lblStatus->Text = gcnew String(GREETING);
  }

private: System::Void MainForm_Load(System::Object^  sender,
                                    System::EventArgs^  e)
  {
      String ^imageName;
      String ^imagePath;

      Database->Initialize();
      if (Database->Error()) DisplayError();
      //
      //For each button, check to see if there are sufficient qty and load
      //the thumbnail for each.
      //
      imagePath = gcnew String(Database->GetSetting("ImagePath"));

      imageName = imagePath +
        gcnew String(Database->GetBookFieldStr(1, "Thumbnail"));
      if (Database->Error()) DisplayError();
      btnBook1->Image = btnBook1->Image->FromFile(imageName);
      imageName = imagePath +
        gcnew String(Database->GetBookFieldStr(2, "Thumbnail"));
      if (Database->Error()) DisplayError();
      btnBook2->Image = btnBook2->Image->FromFile(imageName);
      imageName = imagePath +
        gcnew String(Database->GetBookFieldStr(3, "Thumbnail"));
      if (Database->Error()) DisplayError();
      btnBook3->Image = btnBook3->Image->FromFile(imageName);
      imageName = imagePath +
        gcnew String(Database->GetBookFieldStr(4, "Thumbnail"));
      if (Database->Error()) DisplayError();
      btnBook4->Image = btnBook4->Image->FromFile(imageName);
      imageName = imagePath +
        gcnew String(Database->GetBookFieldStr(5, "Thumbnail"));
      if (Database->Error()) DisplayError();
      btnBook5->Image = btnBook5->Image->FromFile(imageName);
      imageName = imagePath +
        gcnew String(Database->GetBookFieldStr(6, "Thumbnail"));
      if (Database->Error()) DisplayError();
      btnBook6->Image = btnBook6->Image->FromFile(imageName);
      imageName = imagePath +
        gcnew String(Database->GetBookFieldStr(7, "Thumbnail"));
      if (Database->Error()) DisplayError();
      btnBook7->Image = btnBook7->Image->FromFile(imageName);
      imageName = imagePath +
        gcnew String(Database->GetBookFieldStr(8, "Thumbnail"));
      if (Database->Error()) DisplayError();
      btnBook8->Image = btnBook8->Image->FromFile(imageName);
      imageName = imagePath +
```

```
      gcnew String(Database->GetBookFieldStr(9, "Thumbnail"));
    if (Database->Error()) DisplayError();
    btnBook9->Image = btnBook9->Image->FromFile(imageName);
    imageName = imagePath +
      gcnew String(Database->GetBookFieldStr(10, "Thumbnail"));
    if (Database->Error()) DisplayError();
    btnBook10->Image = btnBook10->Image->FromFile(imageName);
    CheckAvailability();

  }

private: System::Void btnBook1_Click(System::Object^  sender,
                                     System::EventArgs^  e)
  {
    LoadDetails(1);
  }

private: System::Void btnBook2_Click(System::Object^  sender,
                                     System::EventArgs^  e)
  {
    LoadDetails(2);
  }

private: System::Void btnBook3_Click(System::Object^  sender,
                                     System::EventArgs^  e)
  {
    LoadDetails(3);
  }

private: System::Void btnBook4_Click(System::Object^  sender,
                                     System::EventArgs^  e)
  {
    LoadDetails(4);
  }

private: System::Void btnBook5_Click(System::Object^  sender,
                                     System::EventArgs^  e)
  {
    LoadDetails(5);
  }

private: System::Void btnBook6_Click(System::Object^  sender,
                                     System::EventArgs^  e)
  {
    LoadDetails(6);
  }

private: System::Void btnBook7_Click(System::Object^  sender,
                                     System::EventArgs^  e)
  {
    LoadDetails(7);
  }
```

```
private: System::Void btnBook8_Click(System::Object^  sender,
                                     System::EventArgs^  e)
  {
    LoadDetails(8);
  }
private: System::Void btnBook9_Click(System::Object^  sender,
                                     System::EventArgs^  e)
  {
    LoadDetails(9);
  }

private: System::Void btnBook10_Click(System::Object^  sender,
                                      System::EventArgs^  e)
  {
    LoadDetails(10);
  }

private: System::Void MainForm_FormClosing(System::Object^  sender,
    System::Windows::Forms::FormClosingEventArgs^  e)
  {
    Database->Shutdown();
  }

};
}
```

The `MainForm_Load()` event is where the database engine is initialized and the buttons are loaded with the appropriate thumbnails. I follow each call to the database with the statement.

```
if (Database->Error()) DisplayError();
```

This statement allows me to detect when an error occurs and inform the user. Although I don't act on the error in this event, I could and do act on it in other events. If a severe database error occurs here, the worst case is that the buttons will not be populated with the thumbnails. I use this concept throughout the source code.

The `btnBook1_Click()` through `btnBook10_Click()` events are implemented to call the `LoadDetails()` method and populate the details interface components with the proper data.As you can see, abstracting the loading of the details has saved me lots of code!

On the detail portion of the interface are two buttons. The `btnCancel_Click()` event returns the interface to the initial vending machine view. The `btnPurchase_Click()` event is a bit more interesting. It is here where the vending part occurs. Notice I first call the `VendBook()` method and then run the simulation for the vending process and return the interface to the vending view.

That's it! The customer interface is very straightforward—as most vending machines are. Just a row of buttons and a mechanism for taking in the money (in this case I assume the machine accepts credit cards as payment but a real vending machine would probably take several forms of payment).

Administration Interface (Administration Form)

The customer interface is uncomplicated and easy to use. But what about maintaining the data? How can a vendor replenish the stock of the vending machine or even change the list of books offered? One way to do that is to use an administration interface that is separate from the customer interface. You could also create another separate embedded application to handle this, or possibly create the data on another machine and copy to the vending machine. I've chosen to build a simple administration form, as shown in Figure 6-10.

```
Book Vending Machine Administration                                    _ □ X

(ISBN, Slot, Quantity, Price, Pages, PubDate, Title, Authors, Thumbnail, Description)
1-59059-505-X    1      10       49.99    768    2005-07-28   Pro MySQL        Michae
1-59059-332-4    2      10       44.99    520    2004-10-28   Beginning MySQL Databa
1-893115-51-8    3      10       39.99    952    2004-06-28   Beginning PHP 5 and My
1-59059-392-8    4      10       44.99    568    2004-11-12   Beginning PHP 5 and My
1-59059-509-2    5      10       44.99    672    2005-09-08   PHP 5 Recipes: A Probl
1-59059-391-X    6      10       39.99    464    2004-08-05   Beginning Perl, Second
1-59059-535-1    7      10       49.99    784    2005-09-28   The Definitive Guide t
1-59059-562-9    8      10       49.99    560    2005-12-20   Building Online Commun
1-59059-508-4    9      10       44.99    528    2005-08-11   Pro PHP Security
1-59059-531-9   10      10       49.99    376    2005-11-02   Beginning Perl Web Dev


UPDATE books SET Quantity = 10



                                                            [ Execute ]
```

Figure 6-10. *Example administration form*

As with the customer interface, I need to create a helper function. This function, LoadList(), is used to populate a list that displays all the data in the books table. This is handy because it allows the vendor to see what the database contains.

Listing 6-15 shows an excerpt of the administration-form source code. I've omitted the auto-generated Windows form code (represented as . . .). At the top of the source code, I've defined the pointer variable as AdminDatabase instead of Database. This is mainly for clarity and isn't meant to distract you from the usage of the database-engine class. I use the . . . to indicate portions of the auto-generated code and comments omitted from the listing.

Listing 6-15. Administration Form Source Code (AdminForm.h)

```
#pragma once
#include "DBEngine.h"

using namespace System;
using namespace System::ComponentModel;
using namespace System::Collections;
using namespace System::Windows::Forms;
using namespace System::Data;
using namespace System::Drawing;

namespace BookVendingMachine {

  DBEngine   *AdminDatabase = new DBEngine();
...
#pragma endregion
  void LoadList()
  {
    int i = 0;
    int j = 0;
    String^ str;
```

```cpp
    lstData->Items->Clear();
    AdminDatabase->StartQuery("SELECT ISBN, Slot, Quantity, Price," \
        " Pages, PubDate, Title, Authors, Thumbnail," \
        " Description FROM books");
    do
    {
      str = gcnew String("");
      for (i = 0; i < 10; i++)
      {
        if (i != 0)
        {
          str = str + "\t";
        }
        str = str + gcnew String(AdminDatabase->GetField(i));
      }
      lstData->Items->Add(str);
      j++;
    }while(AdminDatabase->GetNext());
  }

private: System::Void btnExecute_Click(System::Object^  sender,
                                       System::EventArgs^  e)
  {
    String ^orig = gcnew String(txtQuery->Text->ToString());
    pin_ptr<const wchar_t> wch = PtrToStringChars(orig);

    // Convert to a char*
    size_t origsize = wcslen(wch) + 1;
    const size_t newsize = 100;
    size_t convertedChars = 0;
    char nstring[newsize];
    wcstombs_s(&convertedChars, nstring, origsize, wch, _TRUNCATE);
    AdminDatabase->RunQuery(nstring);
    LoadList();
  }

private: System::Void Admin_Load(System::Object^  sender,
                                 System::EventArgs^  e)
  {
    AdminDatabase->Initialize();
    LoadList();
  }

private: System::Void AdminForm_FormClosing(System::Object^  sender,
    System::Windows::Forms::FormClosingEventArgs^  e)
  {
    AdminDatabase->Shutdown();
  }
};
}
```

I've included the usual initialize and shutdown method calls to the database engine in the form load and closing events.

This interface is designed to accept an ad hoc query and execute it when the Execute button is clicked. Thus, the btnExecute_Click() is the only other method in this source code. The method calls the database engine and requests that the query be run, but it is not checking for any results. That is because this interface is used to adjust things in the database, not select data. The last call in this method is the LoadList() helper method, which repopulates the list.

Detecting Interface Requests

You might be wondering how I plan to detect which interface to execute. The answer is, I use a command-line parameter to tell the code which interface to run. The switch is implemented in the main() function in the BookVendingMachine.cpp source file. The source code for processing command-line parameters is self-explanatory. Listing 6-16 contains the entire source code for the main() function for the embedded application.

Listing 6-16. The BookVendingMachine Main Function (BookVendingMachine.cpp)

```
// BookVendingMachine.cpp : main project file.

#include "MainForm.h"
#include "AdminForm.h"

using namespace BookVendingMachine;

[STAThreadAttribute]
int main(array<System::String ^> ^args)
{
  // Enabling Windows XP visual effects before any controls are created
  Application::EnableVisualStyles();
  Application::SetCompatibleTextRenderingDefault(false);

  // Create the main window and run it
  if ((args->Length == 1) && (args[0] == "-admin"))
  {
    Application::Run(gcnew AdminForm());
  }
  else
  {
    Application::Run(gcnew MainForm());
  }
  return 0;
}
```

You should now be able to re-create this example from this text or by downloading the information from the book Web site. I encourage you to become comfortable with the client source code (the forms) so that you can see and understand how the database engine is used. When you're ready, you can compile and run the example.

Compiling and Running

Compiling this example is just a matter of clicking on Build ➤ Build BookVendingMachine. If you have already compiled the libmysqld project, all you should see is the compilation of the example. If for some reason the object files are out of date for libmysqld or any of its dependencies, Visual Studio will compile those as well.

> ■ **Note** I used Visual Studio 2010 for the following examples. Newer versions of Visual Studio may change the location of some of the menu commands. All the changes described can be set in the newer version.

When the compilation is complete, you can either run the program from the debug menu commands or open a command window and run it from the command line by entering the command debug\BookVendingMachine from the project directory. If this is your first time, you should see an error message like:

This application has failed to start because LIBMYSQLD.dll was not found.
Re-installing the application may fix this problem.

The reason for this error has nothing to do with the second sentence in the error message. It means that the embedded library isn't in the search path. If you have worked with .NET or COM applications and never used C libraries, you may have never encountered the error. Unlike .NET and COM, C libraries are not registered in a GAC or registry. These libraries (DLLs) should be collocated with application that calls them, or at least on an execution path. Most developers place a copy of the DLL in the execution directory.

To fix this problem, copy the libmysqld.dll file from the lib_debug directory to the directory where the bookvendingmachine.exe file resides (or add lib_debug to the execution path). Once you have copied the library to the execution directory, you should see the application run as shown in Figures 6-3, 6-4, and 6-5.

Take some time and play around with the interface. If the time delay is too annoying, you can reduce the number of seconds in the delay or comment out the delay method calls.

If you want to access the administration interface, run the program using the -admin command-line switch. If you are running the example from the command line, you can enter the command:

```
BookVendingMarchine -admin
```

If you want to run the example from Visual Studio using the debugger, set the command-line switch in the project properties. Open the dialog box by selecting Project ➤ Project Properties and click on the Debugging label in the tree. You can add any number of command-line parameters by typing them into the Command Arguments option. Figure 6-11 shows the location of this option in the project properties.

Figure 6-11. *Setting command-line arguments from Visual Studio*

I encourage you to try out the example. If you are not running Windows, you can still use the database-engine class and provide your own interface for the application. This shouldn't be difficult now that you have seen one example of how that interface works with the abstracted `libmysqld` system calls. If you find yourself building unique vending machines using an embedded MySQL system, send me a photo!

Summary

In this chapter, you learned how to create embedded MySQL applications. The MySQL embedded library is often overlooked, but it has been highly successful in permitting systems integrators to add robust data-management facilities to their enterprise applications and products.

Perhaps the most intriguing aspect of this chapter is your guided tour of the MySQL embedded library C API. I hope that by following the examples in this chapter, you can appreciate the power of embedded MySQL applications. I also hope that you haven't tossed the book down in frustration if you've encountered issues with compiling the source code. Much of what makes a good open-source developer is her ability to systematically diagnose and adapt her environment to the needs of the current project. Do not despair if you had issues come up. Solving issues is a natural part of the learning cycle.

You also explored the concepts of turning on debug tracing for your embedded applications. I also took you on a brief journey into modifying the MySQL server source code by exposing a DBUG method through the embedded library that allows you to add your own strings to the DBUG trace output. You saw some interesting error-handling situations and how to handle them. Finally, I showed you an encapsulated database-access class that you can use in your own embedded applications.

In the next chapter, I'll examine one of the more popular extensions of the MySQL system. This includes adding your own user-defined functions (UDFs), extending an existing SQL command, and adding your own SQL commands to the server. These techniques permit the MySQL system to evolve even further to meet your specific needs for your environment.

## CHAPTER 7

Adding Functions and Commands to MySQL

One of the greatest challenges facing systems integrators is overcoming the limitations of the systems being integrated. This is usually a result of the system having limitations with, or not having certain functions or commands that are needed for, the integration. Often, this means getting around the problem by creating more "glue" programs to translate or augment existing functions and commands.

MySQL developers recognized this need and added flexible options in the MySQL server to add new functions and commands. For example, you may need to add functions to perform some calculations or data conversions, or you may need a new command to provide specific data for administration.

This chapter introduces you to the options available for adding functions and shows you how to add your own SQL commands to the server. We will explore user-defined functions, native functions, and new SQL commands. Much of the background material for this chapter has been covered in previous chapters. Feel free to refer back to those chapters as you follow along.

Adding User-Defined Functions

User-defined functions (UDF) have been supported by MySQL for some time. A UDF is a new function (calculation, conversion, etc.) that you can add to the server, thereby expanding the list of available functions that can be used in SQL commands. The best thing about UDFs is that they can be dynamically loaded at runtime. Furthermore, you can create your own libraries of UDFs and use them in your enterprise or even give them away for free (as open source). This is perhaps the first place systems integrators look for extending the MySQL server. MySQL engineers had another genius-level idea with the UDF mechanism.

User-defined functions can be used anywhere the SQL language permits an expression. For example, you can use UDFs in stored procedures and SELECT statements. They are an excellent way to expand your server without having to modify the server source code. In fact, you can define as many UDFs as you please and even group them together to form libraries of functions. Each library is a single file containing source code that is compiled into a library (.so in Linux or .dll in Windows).

The mechanism is similar to the plug-in interface and, in fact, predates it. The UDF interface utilizes external, dynamically loadable object files to load and unload UDFs. The mechanism uses a CREATE FUNCTION command to establish a connection to the loadable object file on a per-function basis and a DROP FUNCTION command to remove the connection for a function. Let's take a look at the syntax for these commands.

CREATE FUNCTION Syntax

The CREATE FUNCTION command registers the function with the server, placing a row in the mysql.func table. The syntax is:

```
CREATE FUNCTION function_name RETURNS [STRING | INTEGER | REAL | DECIMAL] SONAME "mylib.so";
```

The function_name parameter represents the name of the function you are creating. The return type can be one of STRING, INTEGER, REAL, or DECIMAL and the SONAME refers to the name of the library. The CREATE FUNCTION command tells the MySQL server to create a mapping of the function name in the command (function_name) to the object file. When the function is invoked, the server calls the function in the library for execution.

DROP FUNCTION Syntax

The DROP FUNCTION command unregisters the function with the server by removing the associated row from the func table in the selected database. The syntax is shown here. The function_name parameter represents the name of the function you are creating.

```
DROP FUNCTION function_name;
```

Let's take a look at how you can create a UDF library and use it in your own MySQL server installations. We will start off by modifying the existing sample UDF library. Once you are familiar with how the functions are coded, it is an elementary exercise to create a new source file and add it to the server build files (CMakeLists.txt).

Creating a User-Defined Library

There are two types of user-defined functions:

- You can create functions that operate as a single call that evaluates a set of parameters and returns a single result.

- You can create functions that operate as aggregates being called from within grouping functions. For instance, you can create a UDF that converts one data type into another, such as a function that changes a date field from one format to another, or you can create a function that performs advanced calculations for a group of records, such as a sum of squares function. UDFs can return only integers, strings, or real values.

- You can create functions that provide values used in SELECT statements.

The single-call UDF is the most common. They are used to perform an operation on one or more parameters. In some cases, no parameters are used. For example, you could create a UDF that returns a value for a global status or like SERVER_STATUS(). This form of UDF is typically used in field lists of SELECT statements or in stored procedures as helper functions.

Aggregate UDF functions are used in GROUP BY clauses. When they are used, they are called once for each row in the table and again at the end of the group.

The process for creating a UDF library is to create a new project that exposes the UDF load/unload methods (xxx_init and xxx_deinit, where xxx is the name of the function) and the function itself. The xxx_init and xxx_deinit functions are called once per statement. The XXX function would be called once per row. If you are creating an aggregate function, you also need to implement the grouping functions xxx_clear and xxx_add. The xxx_clear function is called to reset the value (at the start of a group). The xxx_add function is called for each row in the grouping, and the function itself is called at the end of the group processing. Thus, the aggregate is cleared, then data are added for each call to add. Finally, the function itself is called to return the value.

Once the functions are implemented, you compile the file and copy it to the plugin directory of your server installation. You can load and use the functions using the CREATE FUNCTION command. Listing 7-1 shows a sample set of methods for a UDF.

Listing 7-1. Sample UDF Methods

```
/*
  Simple example of how to get a sequences starting from the first
  argument or 1 if no arguments have been given
*/

my_bool sequence_init(UDF_INIT *initid, UDF_ARGS *args, char *message)
{
  if (args->arg_count > 1)
  {
    strmov(message,"This function takes none or 1 argument");
    return 1;
  }
  if (args->arg_count)
    args->arg_type[0]= INT_RESULT;              /* Force argument to int */

  if (!(initid->ptr=(char*) malloc(sizeof(longlong))))
  {
    strmov(message,"Couldn't allocate memory");
    return 1;
  }
  memset(initid->ptr, 0, sizeof(longlong));
  /*
    sequence() is a non-deterministic function : it has different value
    even if called with the same arguments.
  */
  initid->const_item=0;
  return 0;
}

void sequence_deinit(UDF_INIT *initid)
{
  if (initid->ptr)
    free(initid->ptr);
}

longlong sequence(UDF_INIT *initid __attribute__((unused)), UDF_ARGS *args,
                  char *is_null __attribute__((unused)),
                  char *error __attribute__((unused)))
{
  ulonglong val=0;
  if (args->arg_count)
    val= *((longlong*) args->args[0]);
  return ++*((longlong*) initid->ptr) + val;
}
```

Oracle has provided an example UDF project, named `udf_example.cc` and located in the `/sql` folder, that contains samples of all the types of functions you may want to create. This provides an excellent starting point for adding your own functions. The sample functions include:

- A metaphon function that produces a soundex-like operation on strings

- A sample function that returns a double value that is the sum of the character-code values of the arguments divided by the sum of the length of all the arguments

- A sample function that returns an integer that is the sum of the lengths of the arguments

- A sequence function that returns the next value in a sequence based on the value passed

- An example aggregate function that returns the average cost from the list of integer arguments (quantity) and double arguments (cost)

Depending on your needs, you may find some of these examples useful.

Let's begin by modifying the example UDF project. Locate the `udf_example.cc` file located in the `/sql` directory off the root of your source-code tree and open it in your favorite editor. Since the udf_example library is included in the cmake files, compiling it is very easy. You simply execute make once you've finished your edits. On Windows, you can rebuild the mysql.sln file using Visual Studio.

■ **Caution** Windows users will have to remove the networking UDFs from the library. These are not supported directly on Windows. Comment out the functions if you encounter errors about missing header files or external functions.

If you encounter errors during the compilation, go back and correct them, and try the compile again. The most likely cause is a mistyped name, incorrect code replacement, or incorrect path.

Now that the library is compiled, let's test the load and unload operations. This will ensure that the library has been properly compiled and is located in the correct location. Open a MySQL client window and issue the `CREATE FUNCTION` and `DROP FUNCTION` commands to load all of the functions in the library. Listing 7-2 shows the commands for loading and unloading the first five functions. The listing shows the commands for Windows; replace `udf_example.dll` with `udf_example.so` on Linux. The output will be the same on any platform on which you execute the functions.

Listing 7-2. Sample CREATE and DROP FUNCTION Commands

```
CREATE FUNCTION metaphon RETURNS STRING SONAME "udf_example.dll";
CREATE FUNCTION myfunc_double RETURNS REAL SONAME "udf_example.dll";
CREATE FUNCTION myfunc_int RETURNS INTEGER SONAME "udf_example.dll";
CREATE FUNCTION sequence RETURNS INTEGER SONAME "udf_example.dll";
CREATE AGGREGATE FUNCTION avgcost RETURNS REAL SONAME "udf_example.dll";

DROP FUNCTION metaphon;
DROP FUNCTION myfunc_double;
DROP FUNCTION myfunc_int;
DROP FUNCTION sequence;
DROP FUNCTION avgcost;
```

Listings 7-3 and 7-4 show the correct results when you run the `CREATE FUNCTION` and `DROP FUNCTION` commands shown earlier.

Listing 7-3. *Installing the Functions*

```
mysql> CREATE FUNCTION metaphon RETURNS STRING SONAME "udf_example.dll";
Query OK, 0 rows affected (0.00 sec)

mysql> CREATE FUNCTION myfunc_double RETURNS REAL SONAME "udf_example.dll";
Query OK, 0 rows affected (0.00 sec)

mysql> CREATE FUNCTION myfunc_int RETURNS INTEGER SONAME "udf_example.dll";
Query OK, 0 rows affected (0.00 sec)

mysql> CREATE FUNCTION sequence RETURNS INTEGER SONAME "udf_example.dll";
Query OK, 0 rows affected (0.00 sec)

mysql> CREATE AGGREGATE FUNCTION avgcost RETURNS REAL SONAME "udf_example.dll";
Query OK, 0 rows affected (0.00 sec)
```

Listing 7-4. *Uninstalling the Functions*

```
mysql> DROP FUNCTION metaphon;
Query OK, 0 rows affected (0.00 sec)

mysql> DROP FUNCTION myfunc_double;
Query OK, 0 rows affected (0.00 sec)

mysql> DROP FUNCTION myfunc_int;
Query OK, 0 rows affected (0.00 sec)

mysql> DROP FUNCTION sequence;
Query OK, 0 rows affected (0.00 sec)

mysql> DROP FUNCTION avgcost;
Query OK, 0 rows affected (0.00 sec)
```

Now, let's run the commands and see if they work. Go back to your MySQL client window and run the CREATE FUNCTION commands again to load the UDFs. Listing 7-5 shows sample execution of each of the first five UDFs in the library. Feel free to try out the commands as shown. Your results should be similar.

Listing 7-5. *Example Execution of UDF Commands*

```
mysql> SELECT metaphon("This is a test.");
+---------------------------+
| metaphon("This is a test.") |
+---------------------------+
| OSSTS                     |
+---------------------------+
1 row in set (0.00 sec)
```

```
mysql> SELECT myfunc_double(5.5, 6.1);
+-------------------------+
| myfunc_double(5.5, 6.1) |
+-------------------------+
| 50.17                   |
+-------------------------+
1 row in set (0.01 sec)

mysql> SELECT myfunc_int(5, 6, 8);
+---------------------+
| myfunc_int(5, 6, 8) |
+---------------------+
| 19                  |
+---------------------+
1 row in set (0.00 sec)

mysql> SELECT sequence(8);
+-------------+
| sequence(8) |
+-------------+
| 9           |
+-------------+
1 row in set (0.00 sec)

mysql> CREATE TABLE testavg (order_num int key auto_increment, cost double, qty int);
Query OK, 0 rows affected (0.02 sec)

mysql> INSERT INTO testavg (cost, qty) VALUES (25.5, 17);
Query OK, 1 row affected (0.00 sec)

mysql> INSERT INTO testavg (cost, qty) VALUES (0.23, 5);
Query OK, 1 row affected (0.00 sec)

mysql> INSERT INTO testavg (cost, qty) VALUES (47.50, 81);
Query OK, 1 row affected (0.00 sec)

mysql> SELECT avgcost(qty, cost) FROM testavg;
+--------------------+
| avgcost(qty, cost) |
+--------------------+
| 41.5743            |
+--------------------+
1 row in set (0.03 sec)
```

The last few commands show a very basic use of the avgcost() aggregate function. You would typically use aggregate functions when using the GROUP BY clause.

Adding a New User-Defined Function

Let's now add a new UDF to the library. What if you are working on an integration project and the requirements call for expressing dates in the Julian format? The Julian conversion simply takes the day of the year (number of days elapsed since December 31 of the previous year) and adds the year to form a numeric value, such as DDDYYYY. In this case, you need to add a function that takes a month, date, and year value and returns the date expressed as a Julian date. The function should be defined as:

```
longlong julian(int month, int day, int year);
```

I kept the function simple and used three integers. The function could be implemented in any number of ways (e.g., accepting a date or string value). Now let's add the JULIAN function to the UDF library that you just built.

This is what makes creating your own UDF library so valuable. Any time you encounter a need for a new function, you can just add it to the existing library without having to create a new project from scratch.

The process for adding a new UDF begins with adding the function declarations to the extern section of the UDF library source code and then implementing the functions. You can then recompile the library and deploy it to the plugin directory of your MySQL server installation. Let's walk through that process with the JULIAN function.

■ **Note** Use SHOW VARIABLES LIKE 'plugin%'; to discover the plugin directory.

Open the udf_example.cc file and add the function declarations. Recall that you need definitions for the julian_init(), julian_deinit(), and julian() functions. The julian_init() function takes three arguments:

- UDF_INIT, a structure that the method can use to pass information among the methods
- UDF_ARGS, a structure that contains the number of arguments, the type of arguments, and the arguments themselves
- A string that the method should return if an error occurs

The julian() method takes four arguments:

- The UDF_INIT structure completed by the julian_init() function
- A UDF_ARGS structure that contains the number of arguments, the type of arguments, and the arguments
- A char pointer to a variable that is set to 1 if the result is null
- The message that is sent to the caller if an error occurs

The julian_deinit() function uses the UDF_INIT structure completed by the julian_init() function.

When a UDF is called from the server, a new UDF_INIT structure is created and passed to the function, the arguments are placed in the UDF_ARGS structure, and the julian_init() function is called. If that function returns without errors, the julian() function is called with the UDF_INIT structure from the julian_init() function. After the julian() function completes, the julian_deinit() function is called to clean up the values saved in the UDF_INIT structure. Listing 7-6 shows an excerpt of the declaration section of the file with the JULIAN functions added. This section is denoted with the C_MODE_START and C_MODE_END macros, and it is located at the top of the file. We include out modification markers to ensure that others (or ourselves in the future) know that we modified this file intentionally.

Listing 7-6. The Declarations for JULIAN (udf_example.cc)

```
C_MODE_START;
...

/* BEGIN CAB MODIFICATION */
/* Reason for Modification: */
/* This section declares the methods for the Julian function */
my_bool julian_init(UDF_INIT *initid, UDF_ARGS *args, char *message);
longlong julian(UDF_INIT *initid, UDF_ARGS *args,
                char *is_null, char *error);
void julian_deinit(UDF_INIT *initid);
/* END CAB MODIFICATION */
...
C_MODE_END;
```

■ **Note**   We show the macros delineated with the ellipse to indicate where these statements should be placed.

You can now add the implementation for these functions. I find it helpful to copy the example functions that match my return types and then modify them to match my needs. The julian_init() function is responsible for initializing variables and checking correct usage. Since the JULIAN function requires three integer parameters, you need to add appropriate error handling to enforce this. Listing 7-7 shows the implementation of the julian_init() function. You can insert this method near the end of the udf_example.cc fle.

Listing 7-7. Implementation for the julian_init() Function (udf_example.cc)

```
/* BEGIN CAB MODIFICATION */
/* Reason for Modification: */
/* This section implements the Julian initialization function */
my_bool julian_init(UDF_INIT *initid, UDF_ARGS *args, char *message)
{
  if (args->arg_count != 3) /* if there are not three arguments */
  {
    strcpy(message, "Wrong number of arguments: JULIAN() requires 3 arguments.");
    return 1;
  }
  if ((args->arg_type[0] != INT_RESULT) ||
      (args->arg_type[1] != INT_RESULT) ||
      (args->arg_type[2] != INT_RESULT))
  {
    strcpy(message, "Wrong type of arguments: JULIAN() requires 3 integers.");
    return 1;
  }
  return 0;
}
/* END CAB MODIFICATION */
```

Notice in Listing 7-7 that the argument count is checked first, followed by type checking of the three parameters. This ensures that they are all integers. Savvy programmers will note that the code should also check for ranges of the values. Since the code does not check ranges of the parameters, this could lead to unusual or invalid return values. I leave this to you to complete should you decide to implement the function in your library. It is always a good practice to check range values when the domain and range of the parameter values is known.

The julian_deinit() function isn't really needed, because there are no memory or variables to clean up. You can implement an empty function just to complete the process. It is always a good idea to code this function even if you don't need it. Listing 7-8 shows the implementation for this function. Since we didn't use any new variables or structures, the implementation is simply an empty function. If there had been variables or structures created, you would deallocate them in this function.

Listing 7-8. Implementation for the julian_deinit() Function (udf_example.cc)

```
/* BEGIN CAB MODIFICATION */
/* Reason for Modification: */
/* This section implements the Julian deinitialization function */
void julian_deinit(UDF_INIT *initid)
{
}
/* END CAB MODIFICATION */
```

The real work of the JULIAN function occurs in the julian() implementation. Listing 7-9 shows the completed julian() function.

■ **Note** Some sophisticated Julian-calendar methods calculate the value as elapsed days since a start date (usually in the 18th or 19th century). This method assumes that the need is for a Julian day/year value.

Listing 7-9. Implementation for the julian() Function (udf_example.cc)

```
/* BEGIN CAB MODIFICATION */
/* Reason for Modification: */
/* This section the Julian function */
longlong julian(UDF_INIT *initid, UDF_ARGS *args,
                char *is_null, char *error)
{
  longlong jdate = 0;
  static int DAYS_IN_MONTH[] = {31, 28, 31, 30, 31, 30, 31,
                                31, 30, 31, 30, 31};
  longlong month = 0;
  longlong day = 0;
  longlong year = 0;
  int i;

  /* copy memory from the arguments */
  month = *(longlong *)args->args[0];
  day = *(longlong *) args->args[1];
  year = *(longlong *) args->args[2];
```

```
/* add the days in the month for each prior month */
for (i = 0; i < month - 1; i++)
  jdate += DAYS_IN_MONTH[i];

/* add the day of this month */
jdate += day;

/* find the year */
if (((year % 100) != 0) && ((year % 4) == 0))
  jdate++;  /*leap year!*/

/* shift day of year to left */
jdate *= 10000;

/* add the year */
jdate += year;
return jdate;
}
/* END CAB MODIFICATION */
```

Notice the first few lines after the variable declarations. This is an example of how you can marshal the values from the args array to your own local variables. In this case, I copied the first three parameters to integer values. The rest of the source code is the calculation of the Julian-date value that is returned to the caller.

■ **Note** The calculation for a leap year is intentionally naïve. I leave a more correct calculation for you as an exercise. Hint: When should the jdate variable be incremented?

If you are using Windows, you also need to modify the udf_example.def file and add the methods for the JULIAN function. Listing 7-10 shows the updated udf_example.def file.

Listing 7-10. The udf_example.def Source Code

```
LIBRARY       MYUDF
DESCRIPTION   'MySQL Sample for UDF'
VERSION       1.0
EXPORTS
  metaphon_init
  metaphon_deinit
  metaphon
  myfunc_double_init
  myfunc_double
  myfunc_int
  myfunc_int_init
  sequence_init
  sequence_deinit
  sequence
  avgcost_init
  avgcost_deinit
  avgcost_reset
  avgcost_add
```

```
avgcost_clear
avgcost
julian_init
julian_deinit
julian
```

Now you can compile the library. Once the library is compiled, copy the library to the plugin directory of your MySQL server installation. If you are running Linux, you will be copying the file udf_example.so; if you are running Windows, you will be copying the file udf_example.dll from the /udf_example/debug directory.

I recommend stopping the server before you copy the file and restarting it after the copy is complete. This is because it is possible (depending on where you placed your new function) that the object file could be different from the previous compilation. It is always a good practice to follow any time you make changes to the executable code.

Go ahead and copy the library and install the function, then enter the CREATE FUNCTION command and try out the new function. Listing 7-11 shows an example of installing and running the JULIAN function on Windows.

Listing 7-11. Sample Execution of the julian() Function

```
mysql> CREATE FUNCTION julian RETURNS INTEGER SONAME "udf_example.dll";
Query OK, 0 rows affected (0.00 sec)

mysql> SELECT JULIAN(8, 13, 2012);

+---------------------+
| JULIAN(8, 13, 2012) |
+---------------------+
| 2262012             |
+---------------------+
1 row in set (0.00 sec)
```

WHAT IF I WANT TO CREATE MY OWN LIBRARY?

You can use the udf_example library as the start of your own library or copy it and create your UDF libraries. To compile your own UDF library in the /sql folder, edit the /sql/CMakeLists.txt file and copy the following block, replacing udf_example for the name of your library. You will need to re-run the cmake command before the make command.

```
IF(WIN32 OR HAVE_DLOPEN AND NOT DISABLE_SHARED)
  ADD_LIBRARY(udf_example MODULE udf_example.cc)
  SET_TARGET_PROPERTIES(udf_example PROPERTIES PREFIX "")
  # udf_example depends on strings
  IF(WIN32)
    IF(MSVC)
SET_TARGET_PROPERTIES(udf_example PROPERTIES LINK_FLAGS
"/DEF:${CMAKE_CURRENT_SOURCE_DIR}/udf_example.def")
    ENDIF()
    TARGET_LINK_LIBRARIES(udf_example strings)
  ELSE()
    # udf_example is using safemutex exported by mysqld
    TARGET_LINK_LIBRARIES(udf_example mysqld)
  ENDIF()
ENDIF()
```

UDF libraries can help you expand the capabilities of your server to meet almost any computational need. The libraries are easy to create and require only a small number of functions for implementation. Except for the need to have the dynamically loaded version for Linux, UDFs work very well with few special configuration requirements.

Adding Native Functions

Native functions are those that are compiled as part of the MySQL server. They can be used without having to load them from a library, and they are therefore always available. They also have direct access to the server internals, which UDFs do not, permitting the native functions to respond to or initiate system operations. There is a long list of available native functions ranging from ABS() to UCASE(), and many more. For more information about the currently supported set of native functions, consult the online MySQL reference manual.

If the function that you want to use isn't available (it's not one of the built-in native functions), you can add your own native function by modifying the server source code. Now that you have a JULIAN function, wouldn't it be best if there were an equivalent function to convert a Julian date back to a Gregorian date? I'll show you how to add a new native function in this section.

The process for adding a new native function involves changing the mysqld source-code files. We need to create two classes: Item_func_gregorian and Create_func_gregorian. The server instantiates Item_func_gregorian once for each SQL statement that invokes the function; then it calls a member function of this class to do the actual computation, once for each row of the result set. Create_func_gregorian is instantiated only once, when the server starts. This class contains only a factory member function that the server calls when it needs to create an object of Item_func_gregorian..The files that you need to change are summarized in Table 7-1.

Table 7-1. *Changes to mysqld Source-code Files for Adding a New Native Function*

File	Description of Changes
item_create.cc	Add the function-class definition for registering the function, helper methods, and symbol definition.
item_str_func.h	Add the function class definition.
item_str_func.cc	Add the implementation for the Gregorian function.

■ **Note** Files are located in the /sql directory off the root of the source-code tree.

WHAT HAPPENED TO THE LEX[1] FILES?

Readers familiar with earlier versions of MySQL prior to version 5.6.5 may recall the lexical analyzer files lex* and sql_parse.yy. These files are still in the source-code files, but the MySQL developers have made it much easier to add new functions and commands by almost completely eliminating the need to modify the lex and yacc code. As we will see in a future section, we still must do this for SQL commands, but for functions and similar extensions, the code was changed to make it easier to modify and remove the restriction of creating new reserved words. The new reserved words could impose restrictions on users who may want to use the reserved words in the SQL statements.

---

[1] The lexical analyzer and yacc files—not to be confused with the often-quirky science fiction program named Lexx. (NOTE: UC YACC?)

Let's get started adding the Gregorian-function registration code. Open the `item_create.cc` file and add the instantiation as shown in Listing 7-12. You can add this near line number 2000, right after one of the other `Create_func_*` class definitions.

Listing 7-12. Add the Create_func_gregorian class

```
/* BEGIN CAB MODIFICATION */
/* Reason for Modification: */
/* Add gregorian class definition */
class Create_func_gregorian : public Create_func_arg1
{
public:
  virtual Item *create(THD *thd, Item *arg1);

  static Create_func_gregorian s_singleton;

protected:
  Create_func_gregorian() {}
  virtual ~Create_func_gregorian() {}
};
/* END CAB MODIFICATION */
```

The code from Listing 7-12 creates a class that the parser can use to associate the Gregorian function (defined later) with the GREGORIAN symbol (see Listing 7-14). The Create function here creates a singleton (a single instantiation of the class that all threads use) of the `Create_func_gregorian` class that the parser can use to execute the Gregorian function.

Next, we add the code for the `Create_function_gregorian` method itself. Listing 7-13 shows the modifications for this code. You can place this code in the file around line number 4700 after another `Create_func_` method. This code is used to return the instance of the singleton and execute the Gregorian function and return its result. Here, then, is where the Gregorian function is called and the result returned to the user.

Listing 7-13. Add the Create_func_gregorian method

```
/* BEGIN CAB MODIFICATION */
/* Reason for Modification: */
/* Add gregorian singleton create method */
Create_func_gregorian Create_func_gregorian::s_singleton;

Item*
Create_func_gregorian::create(THD *thd, Item *arg1)
{
  return new (thd->mem_root) Item_func_gregorian(arg1);
}
/* END CAB MODIFICATION */
```

Last, we must add the GREGORIAN symbol. Listing 7-14 shows the code needed to define the symbol. You must place this in the section where the following array is defined.

```
static Native_func_registry func_array[] = {
```

I placed the code after the GREATEST symbol definition because the array is intended to define symbols alphabetically.

Listing 7-14. Add the GREGORIAN symbol

```
/* BEGIN CAB MODIFICATION */
/* Reason for Modification: */
/* Add gregorian symbol */
  { { C_STRING_WITH_LEN("GREGORIAN") }, BUILDER(Create_func_gregorian)},
/* END CAB MODIFICATION */
```

Take a look at the symbol definition. Notice how Listing 7-14 calls the macro BUILDER with the Create_func_gregorian class. Calling the macro is how the parser associates our Gregorian code with the GREGORIAN symbol. You may be wondering how that association is used to tell the parser what to do when the symbol is detected. The mechanism used is called a *lexical hash*.

The lexical hash is an implementation of an advanced hashing lookup procedure from the works of Knuth.[2] It is generated using a command-line utility that implements the algorithm. The utility, gen_lex_hash, has one source-code file named gen_lex_hash.cc. This program produces a file that you will use to replace the existing lexical-hash header file (lex_hash.h). I leave exploration of the BUILDER macro to you for further study.

Now that the create function is implemented, you need to create a new class to implement the code for the function. This is where most developers get very confused. Oracle has provided a number of the Item_xxx_func base (and derived) classes for you to use. For example, derive your class from Item_str_func for functions that return a string and Item_int_func for those that return an integer. Similarly, there are other classes for functions that return other types. This is a departure from the dynamically loadable UDF interface and is the main reason you would choose to create a native function versus a dynamically loadable one. For more information about what Item_xxx_func classes there are, see the item_func.h file in the /sql directory off the root of the source-code tree.

Since the Gregorian function will return a string, you need to derive from the Item_str_func class, define the class in item_strfunc.h, and implement the class in item_strfunc.cc. Open the item_strfunc.h file and add the class definition to the header file, as shown in Listing 7-15.

Listing 7-15. Modifications to the item_strfunc.h File

```
/* BEGIN CAB MODIFICATION */
/* Reason for Modification: */
/* Add gregorian Item function code */
class Item_func_gregorian :public Item_str_func
{
  String tmp_value;
public:
  Item_func_gregorian(Item *a) :Item_str_func(a) {}
  const char *func_name() const { return "gregorian"; }
  String *val_str(String *);
  void fix_length_and_dec()
  {
   max_length=30;
  }
};
/* END CAB MODIFICATION */
```

---

[2]Knuth, D. E., *The Art of Computer Programming. 2nd ed.* (Addison-Wesley, 1997).

Notice that the class in Listing 7-15 has only four functions that must be declared. The minimal functions needed are the constructor (Item_func_gregorian), a function that contains the code that performs the conversion (val_str), a function that returns the name (func_name), and a function to set the maximum length of the string argument (fix_length_and_dec). You can add any others that you might need, but these four are required for functions that return strings.

Other item base (and derived) classes may require additional functions, such as val_int(), val_double(), and so on. Check the definition of the class you need to derive from in order to identify the methods that must be overridden; these are known as virtual functions.

Notice also that we implement in Listing 7-15 a fix_length_and_dec() method, which is used by the server to set the maximum length. In this case, we choose 30, which is largely arbitrary but large enough to not be an issue with the values we return.

Let's add the class implementation. Open the item_strfunc.cc file and add the implementation of the Gregorian-class functions as shown in Listing 7-16. You need to implement the main function, val_str(), which does the work of the Julian-to-Gregorian operation. You can place this in the file around line 4030 after another val_str() implementation.

Listing 7-16. Modifications to the item_strfunc.cc File

```
/* BEGIN CAB MODIFICATION */
/* Reason for Modification: */
/* Add gregorian function code */
String *Item_func_gregorian::val_str(String *str)
{
  static int DAYS_IN_MONTH[] = {31, 28, 31, 30, 31, 30, 31, 31, 30, 31, 30, 31};
  longlong jdate = args[0]->val_int();
  int year = 0;
  int month = 0;
  int day = 0;
  int i;
  char cstr[30];
  cstr[0] = 0;
  str->length(0);

  /* get date from value (right 4 digits */
  year = jdate - ((jdate / 10000) * 10000);

  /* get value for day of year and find current month*/
  day = (jdate - year) / 10000;
  for (i = 0; i < 12; i++)
    if (DAYS_IN_MONTH[i] < day)
      day = day - DAYS_IN_MONTH[i]; /* remainder is day of current month */
    else
    {
      month = i + 1;
      break;
    }

  /* format date string */
  sprintf(cstr, "%d", month);
  str->append(cstr);
```

```
  str->append("/");
  sprintf(cstr, "%d", day);
  str->append(cstr);
  str->append("/");
  sprintf(cstr, "%d", year);
  str->append(cstr);
  if (null_value)
    return 0;
  return str;
}
/* END CAB MODIFICATION */
```

Compiling and Testing the New Native Function

Recompile your server and restart it. If you encounter errors during compile, go back and check the statements you entered for errors. Once the errors are corrected and you have a new executable, stop your server, copy the new executable to the location of your MySQL installation, and restart the server. You can now execute the native function Gregorian, as shown in Listings 7-17 and 7-18. To test the Gregorian function for correctness, run the julian() command first and use that value as input to the gregorian() function.

Listing 7-17. Running the julian() Function

```
mysql> select julian(8,15,2012);

+-------------------+
| julian(8,15,2012) |
+-------------------+
| 2272012           |
+-------------------+
1 row in set (0.00 sec)
```

Listing 7-18. Running the gregorian() Function

```
mysql> select gregorian(2272012);

+--------------------+
| gregorian(2272012) |
+--------------------+
| 8/15/2012          |
+--------------------+
1 row in set (0.00 sec)
```

That's about it for adding native functions. Now that you have had an introduction to creating native functions, you can further plan your integration with MySQL to include customizations to the server source code.

As an exercise, consider adding a new function that calculates the number years, months, weeks, days, and hours until a given date and time. This function could be used to tell you how long you need to wait for the event to occur. In many ways, this function will be a sort of countdown, such as a countdown until your next birthday, anniversary, or perhaps to your retirement.

Adding SQL Commands

If the native SQL commands do not meet your needs and you cannot solve your problems with user-defined functions, you may have to add a new SQL command to the server. This section shows you how to add your own SQL commands to the server.

Many consider adding new SQL commands to be the most difficult extension of all to the MySQL server source code. As you will see, the process isn't as complicated as it is tedious. To add new SQL commands, you must modify the parser (in `sql/ql_yacc.yy`) and add the commands to the SQL command-processing code (in `sql/sql_parse.cc`), sometimes called the "big switch."

When a client issues a query, a new thread is created, and the SQL statement is forwarded to the parser for syntactic validation (or rejection due to errors). The MySQL parser is implemented using a large Lex-YACC script that is compiled with Bison, and the symbols are converted to a hash for use in C code with a MySQL utility named gen_lex_hash. The parser constructs a query structure used to represent the query statement (SQL) in memory as a data structure that can be used to execute the query. Thus, to add a new command to the parser, you will need a copy of GNU Bison. You can download Bison from the GNU Web site[3] and install it.

WHAT IS LEX AND YACC AND WHO'S BISON?

Lex stands for "lexical analyzer generator" and is used as a parser to identify tokens and literals as well as syntax of a language. YACC stands for "yet another compiler compiler" and is used to identify and act on the semantic definitions of the language. The use of these tools together with Bison (a YACC-compatible parser generator that generates C source code from the Lex/YACC code) provides a rich mechanism of creating subsystems that can parse and process language commands. Indeed, that is exactly how MySQL uses these technologies.

Let's assume that you want to add a command to the server to show the current disk usage of all of the databases in the server. Although external tools can retrieve this information[4], you desire a SQL equivalent function that you can easily use in your own database-driven applications. Let's also assume you want to add this as a SHOW command. Specifically, you want to be able to execute the command SHOW DISK_USAGE and retrieve a result set that has each database listed as a row along with the total size of all of the files (tables) listed in kilobytes.

Adding a new SQL command involves adding symbols to the lexical analyzer and adding the SHOW DISK_USAGE command syntax to the YACC parser (`sql_yacc.yy`). The new parser must be compiled into a C program by Bison and then a new lexical hash created using the gen_lex_hash utility described earlier. The code for the parser to direct control to the new command is placed in the large case statement in `sql_parse.cc` with a case for the new command symbol.

Let's begin with adding the symbols to the lexical analyzer. Open the `lex.h` file and locate the `static SYMBOL symbols[]` array. You can make the symbol anything you want, but it should be something meaningful (like all good variable names). Be sure to choose a symbol that isn't already in use. In this case, use the symbol DISK_USAGE. This acts like a label to the parser, identifying it as a token. Place a statement in the array to direct the lexical analyzer to generate the symbol and call it DISK_USAGE_SYM. The list is in (roughly) alphabetic order, so place it in the proper location. Listing 7-19 shows an excerpt of the array with the symbols added.

---

[3]Linux/Unix users can either use their package manager and install it or download it from the GNU Web site (`www.gnu.org/software/bison`). Windows users can download a Win32 version from `http://gnuwin32.sourceforge.net/packages/bison.htm`.
[4]For example, the MySQL Utilities utility mysqldiskusage. MySQL Utilities is a subproject of the MySQL Workbench. You can download the MySQL Workbench from `dev.mysql.com`.

Listing 7-19. Updates to the lex.h File for the SHOW DISK_USAGE Command

```
static SYMBOL symbols[] = {
  { "&&",      SYM(AND_AND_SYM)},
...
  { "DISK",    SYM(DISK_SYM)},
/* BEGIN CAB MODIFICATION */
/* Reason for Modification: */
/* This section identifies the tokens for the SHOW DISK_USAGE command*/
  { "DISK_USAGE",          SYM(DISK_USAGE_SYM)},
/* END CAB MODIFICATION */
  { "DISTINCT",   SYM(DISTINCT)},
...
```

The next thing you need to do is add a mnemonic to identify the command. This mnemonic will be used in the parser to assign to the internal-query structure and to control the flow of execution via a case in the large switch statement in the `sql_parse.cc` file. Open the `sql_cmd.h` file and add the new command to the enum_sql_command enumeration. Listing 7-20 shows the modifications with the new command mnemonic.

Listing 7-20. Changes to the sql_cmd.h File for the SHOW DISK_USAGE Command

```
enum enum_sql_command {
...
  SQLCOM_SHOW_SLAVE_HOSTS, SQLCOM_DELETE_MULTI, SQLCOM_UPDATE_MULTI,
  SQLCOM_SHOW_BINLOG_EVENTS, SQLCOM_DO,
  SQLCOM_SHOW_WARNS, SQLCOM_EMPTY_QUERY, SQLCOM_SHOW_ERRORS,
  SQLCOM_SHOW_STORAGE_ENGINES, SQLCOM_SHOW_PRIVILEGES,
/* BEGIN CAB MODIFICATION */
/* Reason for Modification: */
/* Add SQLCOM_SHOW_DISK_USAGE reference */
  SQLCOM_SHOW_STORAGE_ENGINES, SQLCOM_SHOW_PRIVILEGES, SQLCOM_SHOW_DISK_USAGE,
/* END CAB MODIFICATION */
  SQLCOM_HELP, SQLCOM_CREATE_USER, SQLCOM_DROP_USER, SQLCOM_RENAME_USER,
  SQLCOM_REVOKE_ALL, SQLCOM_CHECKSUM,
  SQLCOM_CREATE_PROCEDURE, SQLCOM_CREATE_SPFUNCTION, SQLCOM_CALL,
...
```

Now that you have the new symbol and the command mnemonic, add code to the `sql_yacc.yy` file to define the new token that you used in the `lex.h` file, and add the source code for the new SHOW DISK_USAGE SQL command. Open the `sql_yacc.yy` file and add the new token to the list of tokens (near the top). These are defined (roughly) in alphabetical order, so place the new token in the proper order. Listing 7-21 shows the modifications to the `sql_yacc.yy` file.

Listing 7-21. Adding the Token to the sql_yacc.yy File

```
...
%token  DISK_SYM
/* BEGIN CAB MODIFICATION */
/* Reason for Modification: */
/* Add DISK_USAGE symbol */
%token  DISK_USAGE_SYM
/* END CAB MODIFICATION */
```

```
%token  DISTINCT                        /* SQL-2003-R */
%token  DIV_SYM
%token  DOUBLE_SYM                      /* SQL-2003-R */
...
```

You also need to add the command syntax to the parser YACC code (also in `sql_yacc.yy`). Locate the `show:` label and add the command as shown in Listing 7-22.

Listing 7-22. Parser Syntax Source Code for the SHOW DISK_USAGE Command

```
/* Show things */

show:
/* BEGIN CAB MODIFICATION */
/* Reason for Modification: */
/* Add show disk usage symbol parsing */
      SHOW DISK_USAGE_SYM
        {
            LEX *lex=Lex;
            lex->sql_command= SQLCOM_SHOW_DISK_USAGE;
        }
        |
/* END CAB MODIFICATION */
        SHOW
        {
```

■ **Caution**   Don't forget the | before the original SHOW statement.

You're probably wondering what this code does. It looks rather benign, and yet it is important to get this part right. In fact, this is the stage at which most developers give up and fail to add new commands.

The set of code identified by the `show:` label is executed whenever the `SHOW` token is identified by the parser. YACC code is almost always written this way.[5] The `SHOW DISK_USAGE_SYM` statement indicates the only valid syntax that has the `SHOW` and `DISK_USAGE` tokens appearing (in that order). If you look through the code, you'll find other similar syntactical arrangements. The code block following the syntax statement gets a pointer to the `lex` structure and sets the `command` attribute to the new command token `SQLCOM_SHOW_DISK_USAGE`. This code matches the `SHOW` and `DISK_USAGE_SYM` symbols to the `SQLCOM_SHOW_DISK_USAGE` command so that the SQL command switch in the `sql_parse.cc` file can correctly route the execution to the implementation of the `SHOW DISK_USAGE` command.

Notice also that I placed this code at the start of the `show:` definition and used the vertical bar symbol (|) in front of the previous `SHOW` syntax statement. The vertical bar is used as an "or" for the syntax switch. Thus, the statement is valid if, and only if, it meets one of the syntax statement definitions. Feel free to look around in this file and get a feel for how the code works. Don't sweat over learning every nuance. What I have shown you is the minimum of what you need to know to create a new command. If you decide to implement more complex commands, study the examples of similar commands to see how they handle tokens and variables.

Next, add the source code to the large command statement switch in `sql_parse.cc`. Open the file and add a new case to the switch statement, as shown in Listing 7-23.

---

[5]To learn more about the YACC parser and how to write YACC code, see `http://dinosaur.compilertools.net/`.

Listing 7-23. Adding a Case for the New Command

```
...
  case SQLCOM_SHOW_AUTHORS:
    res= mysqld_show_authors(thd);
    break;
/* BEGIN CAB MODIFICATION */
/* Reason for Modification: */
/* Add SQLCOM_SHOW_DISK_USAGE case statement */
 case SQLCOM_SHOW_DISK_USAGE:
   res = show_disk_usage_command(thd);
   break;
/* END CAB MODIFICATION */
  case SQLCOM_SHOW_CONTRIBUTORS:
    res= mysqld_show_contributors(thd);
    break;
...
```

Notice that I just added a call to a new function named show_disk_usage_command(). You will add this function to the sql_show.cc file. The name of this function matches the tokens in the lex.h file, the symbols identified in the sql_yacc.yy file, and the command switch in the sql_parse.cc file. Not only does this make it clear what is going on, it also helps to keep the already-large switch statement within limits. Feel free to look around in this file, because it is the heart of the command-statement flow of execution. You should be able to find all of the commands, such as SELECT, CREATE, and so on.

Now, let's add the code to execute the command. Open the sql_show.h file and add the function declaration for the new command, as shown in Listing 7-24. I have placed the function declaration near the same functions as defined in the sql_parse.cc file. This isn't required, but it helps organize the code a bit.

Listing 7-24. Function Declaration for the New Command

```
...
int mysqld_show_variables(THD *thd,const char *wild);
bool mysqld_show_storage_engines(THD *thd);
bool mysqld_show_authors(THD *thd);
/* BEGIN CAB MODIFICATION */
/* Reason for Modification: */
/* Add show disk usage method reference */
bool show_disk_usage_command(THD *thd);
/* END CAB MODIFICATION */
bool mysqld_show_contributors(THD *thd);
bool mysqld_show_privileges(THD *thd);
...
```

The last modification is to add the implementation for the show_disk_usage_command() function (Listing 7-25). Open the sql_show.cc file and add the function implementation for the new command. The code in Listing 7-25 is stubbed out. This is to ensure that the new command was working before I added any code. This practice is a great one to follow if you have to implement complex code. Implementing just the basics helps to establish that your code changes are working and that any errors encountered are not related to the stubbed code. This practice is especially important to follow whenever modifying or adding new SQL commands.

Listing 7-25. The show_disk_usage_command() Implementation

```
/* BEGIN CAB MODIFICATION */
/* Reason for Modification: */
/* Add show disk usage method */
bool show_disk_usage_command(THD *thd)
{
  List<Item> field_list;
  Protocol *protocol= thd->protocol;
  DBUG_ENTER("show_disk_usage");

  /* send fields */
  field_list.push_back(new Item_empty_string("Database",50));
  field_list.push_back(new Item_empty_string("Size_in_bytes",30));

  if (protocol->send_result_set_metadata(&field_list,
                         Protocol::SEND_NUM_ROWS |
                         Protocol::SEND_EOF))
    DBUG_RETURN(TRUE);

  /* send test data */
  protocol->prepare_for_resend();
  protocol->store("test_row", system_charset_info);
  protocol->store("1024", system_charset_info);
  if (protocol->write())
    DBUG_RETURN(TRUE);

  my_eof(thd);
  DBUG_RETURN(FALSE);
}

/* END CAB MODIFICATION */
```

I want to call your attention to the source code for a moment. If you recall, in a previous chapter, I mentioned that there are low-level network functions that allow you to build a result set and return it to the client. Look at the lines of code indicated by the /* send fields */ comment. This code creates the fields for the result set. In this case, I'm creating two fields (or columns), named Database and Size_in_bytes. These will appear as the column headings in the MySQL client utility when the command is executed.

Notice the protocol->XXX statements. This is where I use the Protocol class to send rows to the client. I first call prepare_for_resend() to clear the buffer, then make as many calls to the overloaded store() method setting the value for each field (in order). Finally, I call the write() method to write the buffer to the network. If anything goes wrong, I exit the function with a value of true (which means errors were generated). The last statement that ends the result set and finalizes communication to the client is the my_eof() function, which sends an end-of-file signal to the client. You can use these same classes, methods, and functions to send results from your commands.

COMPILE ERRORS FOR DISK_USAGE_SYM

If you want to compile the server, you can, but you may encounter errors concerning the DISK_USAGE_SYM symbol. This can happen if you built the server without cmake or skipped the cmake step. The following will help you resolve these issues.

If you've been studying the MySQL source code, you've probably noticed that there are `sql_yacc.cc` and `sql_yacc.h` files. These files are generated from the `sql_yacc.yy` file by Bison. Let's use Bison to generate these files. Open a command window and navigate to the `/sql` directory off the root of your source-code tree. Run the command:

```
bison -y -p MYSQL -d sql_yacc.yy
```

This generates two new files: `y.tab.c` and `y.tab.h`. These files will replace the `sql_yacc.cc` and `sql_yacc.h` files, respectively. Before you copy them, make a backup of the original files. After you have made a backup of the files, copy `y.tab.c` to `sql_yacc.cc` and `y.tab.h` to `sql_yacc.h`.

Once the `sql_yacc.cc` and `sql_yacc.h` files are correct, generate the lexical hash by running this command:

```
gen_lex_hash > lex_hash.h
```

Everything is now set for you to compile the server. Since you have modified a number of the key header files, you may encounter longer-than-normal compilation times. Should you encounter compilation errors, please correct them before you proceed.

If you compile the code using debug, however, you may encounter a compilation error in `mysqld.cc`. If this occurs, it is likely the call to a `compile_time_assert()` macro. If that is the case, change the code as follows to compensate for the difference in number of `com_status_vars` enumerations.

```
compile_time_assert(sizeof(com_status_vars)/
                              sizeof(com_status_vars[0]) - 1 == SQLCOM_END + 8-1);
```

Once the server is compiled and you have a new executable, stop your server, copy the new executable to the location of your MySQL installation, and restart the server. You can now execute the new command in a MySQL client utility. Listing 7-26 shows an example of the SHOW DISK_USAGE command.

Listing 7-26. Example Execution of the SHOW DISK_USAGE Command

```
mysql> SHOW DISK_USAGE;

+----------+---------------+
| Database | Size_in_bytes |
+----------+---------------+
| test_row | 1024          |
+----------+---------------+
1 row in set (0.00 sec)
```

Now that everything is working, open the `sql_show.cc` file and add the actual code for the SHOW DISK_USAGE command ,as shown in Listing 7-27.

Listing 7-27. The Final show_disk_usage_command Source Code

```
/* This section adds the code to call the new SHOW DISK_USAGE command. */
/* BEGIN CAB MODIFICATION */
/* Reason for Modification: */
/* Add show disk usage method */
bool show_disk_usage_command(THD *thd)
{
  List<Item> field_list;
```

```
  List<LEX_STRING> dbs;
  LEX_STRING *db_name;
  char *path;
  MY_DIR *dirp;
  FILEINFO *file;
  longlong fsizes = 0;
  longlong lsizes = 0;
  Protocol *protocol= thd->protocol;
  DBUG_ENTER("show_disk_usage");

  /* send the fields "Database" and "Size" */
  field_list.push_back(new Item_empty_string("Database",50));
  field_list.push_back(new Item_return_int("Size_in_bytes", 7,
                      MYSQL_TYPE_LONGLONG));
  if (protocol->send_result_set_metadata(&field_list,
                                  Protocol::SEND_NUM_ROWS |
                                  Protocol::SEND_EOF))
    DBUG_RETURN(TRUE);

  /* get database directories */
  find_files_result res = find_files(thd, &dbs, 0, mysql_data_home,0,1);
  if (res != FIND_FILES_OK)
    DBUG_RETURN(1);

  List_iterator_fast<LEX_STRING> it_dbs(dbs);
  path = (char *)my_malloc(PATH_MAX, MYF(MY_ZEROFILL));
  dirp = my_dir(mysql_data_home, MYF(MY_WANT_STAT));
  fsizes = 0;
  for (int i = 0; i < (int)dirp->number_off_files; i++)
  {
    file = dirp->dir_entry + i;
    if (strncasecmp(file->name, "ibdata", 6) == 0)
      fsizes = fsizes + file->mystat->st_size;
    else if (strncasecmp(file->name, "ib", 2) == 0)
      lsizes = lsizes + file->mystat->st_size;
  }

  /* send InnoDB data to client */
  protocol->prepare_for_resend();
  protocol->store("InnoDB TableSpace", system_charset_info);
  protocol->store((longlong)fsizes);
  if (protocol->write())
    DBUG_RETURN(TRUE);
  protocol->prepare_for_resend();
  protocol->store("InnoDB Logs", system_charset_info);
  protocol->store((longlong)lsizes);
  if (protocol->write())
    DBUG_RETURN(TRUE);

  /* now send database name and sizes of the databases */
  while ((db_name = it_dbs++))
```

```
  {
    fsizes = 0;
    strcpy(path, mysql_data_home);
    strcat(path, "/");
    strcat(path, db_name->str);
    dirp = my_dir(path, MYF(MY_WANT_STAT));
    for (int i = 0; i < (int)dirp->number_off_files; i++)
    {
      file = dirp->dir_entry + i;
      fsizes = fsizes + file->mystat->st_size;
    }

    protocol->prepare_for_resend();
    protocol->store(db_name->str, system_charset_info);
    protocol->store((longlong)fsizes);
    if (protocol->write())
      DBUG_RETURN(TRUE);
  }
  my_eof(thd);

  /* free memory */
  my_free(path);
  my_dirend(dirp);
  DBUG_RETURN(FALSE);
}

/* END CAB MODIFICATION */
```

■ **Note**   On Windows, you may need to substitute MAX_PATH for PATH_MAX in the my_malloc() calls and use strnicmp in place of the strncasecmp.

When you compile and load the server, and then run the command, you should see something similar to the example shown in Listing 7-28.

Listing 7-28. Example Execution of the new SHOW DISK_USAGE Command

```
mysql> show disk_usage;
+--------------------+---------------+
| Database           | Size_in_bytes |
+--------------------+---------------+
| InnoDB TableSpace  |      77594624 |
| InnoDB Logs        |      10485760 |
| mtr                |         33423 |
| mysql              |        844896 |
| performance_schema |        493595 |
| test               |          8192 |
+--------------------+---------------+
6 rows in set (0.00 sec)

mysql>
```

The list shows you the cumulative size of each database on your server in the MySQL data directory. One thing you might want to do is add a row that returns the grand total of all disk space used (much like a WITH ROLLUP clause). I leave this modification for you to complete as you experiment with implementing the function.

I hope that this short section on creating new SQL commands has helped eliminate some of the confusion and difficulty surrounding the MySQL SQL command-processing source code. Now that you have this information, you can plan your own extensions to the MySQL commands to meet your own unique needs.

Adding to the Information Schema

The last area I want to cover in this chapter is adding information to the information schema. The *information schema* is an in-memory collection of logical tables that contain status and other pertinent data (also known as *metadata*) about the server and its environment. Introduced in version 5.0.2, the information schema has become an important tool for administration and debugging the MySQL server, its environment, and databases.[6] For example, the information schema makes it easy to display all the columns for all the tables in a database by using this SQL command:

```
SELECT table_name, column_name, data_type FROM information_schema.columns
WHERE table_schema = 'test';
```

The metadata is grouped into logical tables that permit you to issue SELECT commands against them. One of the greatest advantages of creating an INFORMATION_SCHEMA view is the use of the SELECT command. Specifically, you can use a WHERE clause to restrict the output to matching rows. This provides a unique and useful way to get information about the server. Table 7-2 lists some of the logical tables and their uses.

Table 7-2. *Information Schema Logical Tables*

Name	Description
SCHEMATA	Provides information about databases.
TABLES	Provides information about the tables in all the databases.
COLUMNS	Provides information about the columns in all the tables.
STATISTICS	Provides information about indexes for the tables.
USER_PRIVILEGES	Provides information about the database privileges. It encapsulates the mysql.db grant table.
TABLE_PRIVILEGES	Provides information about the table privileges. It encapsulates the mysql.tables_priv grant table.
COLUMN_PRIVILEGES	Provides information about the column privileges. It encapsulates the mysql.columns_priv grant table.
COLLATIONS	Provides information about the collations for the character sets.
KEY_COLUMN_USAGE	Provides information about the key columns.
ROUTINES	Provides information about the procedures and functions (does not include user-defined functions).
VIEWS	Provides information about the views from all the databases.
TRIGGERS	Provides information about the triggers from all the databases.

---

[6]For more information about the information schema, see the online MySQL reference manual.

Since the disk-usage command falls into the category of metadata, I'll show you how to add it to the information-schema mechanism in the server. The process is actually pretty straightforward, with no changes to the sql_yacc.yy code or lexical hash. Instead, you add an enumeration and a case for the switch statement in the function that creates the data (rows) for the disk usage function, define a structure to hold the columns for the table, and then add the source code to execute it.

Let's begin with modifying the header files for the new enumeration. Open the handler.h file and locate the enum_schema_tables enumeration. Add a new enumeration named SCH_DISKUSAGE to the list. Listing 7-29 shows an excerpt of the enumerations with the new enumeration added.

Listing 7-29. Changes to the enum_schema_tables Enumeration

```
enum enum_schema_tables
{
...
  SCH_COLLATION_CHARACTER_SET_APPLICABILITY,
  SCH_COLUMNS,
  SCH_COLUMN_PRIVILEGES,
/* BEGIN CAB MODIFICATION */
/* Reason for Modification: */
/* Add case enum for the new SHOW DISK_USAGE view. */
  SCH_DISKUSAGE,
/* END CAB MODIFICATION */
  SCH_ENGINES,
  SCH_EVENTS,
  SCH_FILES,
...
```

Now you need to add the case for the switch command in the prepare_schema_tables() function that creates the new schema table. Open the sql_parse.cc file and add the case statement shown in Listing 7-30. Notice that I just added the case without a break statement. This allows the code to fall through to code that satisfies all of the case. This is an elegant alternative to lengthy if-then-else-if statements that you see in most source code.

Listing 7-30. Modifications to the prepare_schema_table Function

```
int prepare_schema_table(THD *thd, LEX *lex, Table_ident *table_ident,
                         enum enum_schema_tables schema_table_idx)
{
...
  DBUG_ENTER("prepare_schema_table");

  switch (schema_table_idx) {
/* BEGIN CAB MODIFICATION */
/* Reason for Modification: */
/* Add case statement for the new SHOW DISK_USAGE view. */
  case SCH_DISKUSAGE:
/* END CAB MODIFICATION */
  case SCH_SCHEMATA:
#if defined(DONT_ALLOW_SHOW_COMMANDS)
    my_message(ER_NOT_ALLOWED_COMMAND,
...
```

You may have noticed I refer to the disk-usage schema table as DISKUSAGE. I do this because the DISK_USAGE token has already been defined in the parser and lexical hash. If I had used DISK_USAGE and issued the command SELECT * FROM DISK_USAGE, I'd have gotten an error. This is because the parser associates the DISK_USAGE token with the SHOW command and not with the SELECT command.

Now we're at the last set of code changes. You need to add a structure that the information-schema functions can use to create the field list for the table. Open the sql_show.cc file and add a new array of type ST_FIELD_INFO as shown in Listing 7-31. Notice that the columns are named the same and have the same types as in the show_disk_usage_command().

Listing 7-31. New Field Information Structure for the DISKUSAGE Schema Table

```
/* BEGIN CAB MODIFICATION */
/* Reason for Modification: */
/* This section adds the code to call the new SHOW DISK_USAGE command. */
ST_FIELD_INFO disk_usage_fields_info[]=
{
  {"DATABASE", 40, MYSQL_TYPE_STRING, 0, 0, NULL, SKIP_OPEN_TABLE},
  {"Size_in_bytes", 21 , MYSQL_TYPE_LONG, 0, 0, NULL, SKIP_OPEN_TABLE },
  {0, 0, MYSQL_TYPE_STRING, 0, 0, 0, SKIP_OPEN_TABLE}
};
/* END CAB MODIFICATION */
```

The next change you need to make is to add a row in the schema_tables array (also in sql_show.cc). Locate the array and add a statement like that shown in Listing 7-32. This declares that the new table is called DISKUSAGE, that the column definitions are specified by disk_usage_fields_info, that Create_schema_table will be used to create the table, and that fill_disk_usage will be used to populate the table. The make_old_format tells the code to make sure that the column names are shown. The last four parameters are a pointer to a function to do some additional processing on the table, two index fields, and a bool variable to indicate that it is a hidden table. In the example, I set the pointer to the function to NULL (0); -1 indicates the indexes aren't used, and 0 indicates the table is not hidden.

Listing 7-32. Modifications to the schema_tables Array

```
ST_SCHEMA_TABLE schema_tables[]=
{
...
  {"ENGINES", engines_fields_info, create_schema_table,
   fill_schema_engines, make_old_format, 0, -1, -1, 0, 0},
/* BEGIN CAB MODIFICATION */
/* Reason for Modification: */
/* This section adds the code to call the new SHOW DISK_USAGE command. */
  {"DISKUSAGE", disk_usage_fields_info, create_schema_table,
   fill_disk_usage, make_old_format, 0, -1, -1, 0, 0},
/* END CAB MODIFICATION */
 #ifdef HAVE_EVENT_SCHEDULER
 {"EVENTS", events_fields_info, create_schema_table,
   fill_schema_events, make_old_format, 0, -1, -1, 0, 0},
...
```

OK, we're on the home stretch. All that is left is to implement the fill_disk_usage() function. Scroll up from the schema_tables array[7] and insert the implementation for the fill_disk_usage() function, as shown in Listing 7-33.

---

[7]Remember, if you do not use function declarations, you must locate the code for functions in front of the code that references it.

Listing 7-33. The fill_disk_usage Function Implementation

```
/* BEGIN CAB MODIFICATION */
/* Reason for Modification: */
/* Add code to fill the output for the new SHOW DISK_USAGE view. */
int fill_disk_usage(THD *thd, TABLE_LIST *tables, Item *cond)
{
  TABLE *table= tables->table;
  CHARSET_INFO *scs= system_charset_info;
  List<Item> field_list;
  List<LEX_STRING> dbs;
  LEX_STRING *db_name;
  char *path;
  MY_DIR *dirp;
  FILEINFO *file;
  longlong fsizes = 0;
  longlong lsizes = 0;
  DBUG_ENTER("fill_disk_usage");

  find_files_result res = find_files(thd, &dbs, 0, mysql_data_home,0,1);
  if (res != FIND_FILES_OK)
    DBUG_RETURN(1);

  List_iterator_fast<LEX_STRING> it_dbs(dbs);
  path = (char *)my_malloc(PATH_MAX, MYF(MY_ZEROFILL));
  dirp = my_dir(mysql_data_home, MYF(MY_WANT_STAT));
  fsizes = 0;
  for (int i = 0; i < (int)dirp->number_off_files; i++)
  {
    file = dirp->dir_entry + i;
    if (strncasecmp(file->name, "ibdata", 6) == 0)
      fsizes = fsizes + file->mystat->st_size;
    else if (strncasecmp(file->name, "ib", 2) == 0)
      lsizes = lsizes + file->mystat->st_size;
  }

  /* send InnoDB data to client */
  table->field[0]->store("InnoDB TableSpace",
                         strlen("InnoDB TableSpace"), scs);
  table->field[1]->store((longlong)fsizes, TRUE);
  if (schema_table_store_record(thd, table))
    DBUG_RETURN(1);
  table->field[0]->store("InnoDB Logs", strlen("InnoDB Logs"), scs);
  table->field[1]->store((longlong)lsizes, TRUE);
  if (schema_table_store_record(thd, table))
    DBUG_RETURN(1);

  /* now send database name and sizes of the databases */
  while ((db_name = it_dbs++))
```

```
  {
    fsizes = 0;
    strcpy(path, mysql_data_home);
    strcat(path, "/");
    strcat(path, db_name->str);
    dirp = my_dir(path, MYF(MY_WANT_STAT));
    for (int i = 0; i < (int)dirp->number_off_files; i++)
    {
      file = dirp->dir_entry + i;
      fsizes = fsizes + file->mystat->st_size;
    }
    restore_record(table, s->default_values);

    table->field[0]->store(db_name->str, db_name->length, scs);
    table->field[1]->store((longlong)fsizes, TRUE);
    if (schema_table_store_record(thd, table))
      DBUG_RETURN(1);
  }

  /* free memory */
  my_free(path);
  DBUG_RETURN(0);
}
/* END CAB MODIFICATION */
```

■ **Note**   On Windows, substitute MAX_PATH for PATH_MAX in the my_malloc() calls and use strnicmp in place of the strncasecmp.

I copied the code from the previous DISK_USAGE command, removing the calls for creating fields (that's handled via the disk_usage_fields_info array) and the code for sending rows to the client. Instead, I use an instance of the TABLE class/structure to store values in the fields array, starting at zero for the first column. The call to the function schema_table_store_record() function dumps the values to the network protocols.

Everything is now set for you to compile the server. Since you have modified one of the key header files (handler.h), you may encounter longer-than-normal compilation times as some of the dependencies for the mysqld project may have to be compiled. Should you encounter compilation errors, please correct them before you proceed.

Once the server is compiled and you have a new executable, stop your server, copy the new executable to the location of your MySQL installation, and restart the server. You can now execute the new command in a MySQL client utility. Listing 7-34 shows an example of using the information schema, displaying all of the available schema tables, and dumping the contents of the new DISKUSAGE table.

Listing 7-34. *Example Information Schema Use with the new DISKUSAGE Schema Table*

```
mysql> use INFORMATION_SCHEMA;
Database changed

mysql> SHOW TABLES LIKE 'DISK%';
+---------------------------------------+
| Tables_in_information_schema (DISK%)  |
+---------------------------------------+
| DISKUSAGE                             |
+---------------------------------------+
1 row in set (0.00 sec)

mysql> SELECT * from DISKUSAGE;
+---------------------+---------------+
| DATABASE            | Size_in_bytes |
+---------------------+---------------+
| InnoDB TableSpace   |    77594624   |
| InnoDB Logs         |    10485760   |
| mtr                 |       33423   |
| mysql               |      844896   |
| performance_schema  |      493595   |
| test                |        8192   |
+---------------------+---------------+
6 rows in set (0.00 sec)

mysql>
```

Now that you know how to add to the information schema, the sky is the limit for what you can add to enable your database professionals to more closely monitor and tune your MySQL servers.

Summary

In this chapter, I've shown you how to extend the capabilities of the MySQL server by adding your own new functions and commands.

You learned how to build a UDF library that can be loaded and unloaded at runtime, how to add a native function to the server source code, and how to add a new SHOW command to the parser and the query-execution code. You also learned how to add a view to the information schema.

The ability to extend the server in this manner makes MySQL very flexible. The UDF mechanism is one of the easiest to code, and it far surpasses the competition in sophistication and speed of development. The fact that the server is open source means that you can also get right into the source code and add your own SQL commands for your specific environment. Regardless of whether you use these facilities, you can appreciate knowing that you aren't limited by the "out-of-the-box" functions and commands.

The next chapter will explore one of the most popular features of MySQL that enables high availability – MySQL replication. I will introduce the basics of replication and take you on a tour of the replication source code. This is followed by example extensions to replication that you can use to learn the internals of replication as well as get an idea for extensions that you can use to enhance your own high availability solutions.

CHAPTER 8

■ ■ ■

Extending MySQL High Availability

One advanced feature of MySQL is its ability to provide high-availability database solutions. The server component responsible for obtaining high availability is replication. Some would include other features, such as partitioning and a host of smaller features, but the most important feature that enables high availability is replication.

In this chapter, you will learn what replication is and the basics of its configuration through a brief tutorial on MySQL replication. With those basic skills and the skills we learned from previous chapters, you will journey through the replication source code and learn how to extend replication through example projects. First, let's find out what replication is and how it works.

What is Replication?

MySQL replication is the ability to duplicate data changes that occur on one server to another. Rather than copying the data directly (which could be slow and complicated when it comes to applying UPDATE or DELETE statements), the changes are transferred in the form of metadata and commands, hence events, that are copied to the second server and executed there.

These events are written to an ordered, sequential file called a binary log on the original server, and the second server reads those events via a remote connection, storing them in a file of the same format called a relay log. Events are then read one at a time on the second server from the relay log and executed.

This provides the ability to duplicate exactly the data changes from the original server, because it preserves the order of the events and ensures the same path through the server is used. We therefore call the process replication, because it replicates the changes as they occur. We call the connection among the servers involved a replication topology.

There are several roles[1] a server can perform. The following briefly describes each.

- Master—this server is the original server to which all write and DML statements are sent.

- Slave—this server is the server that maintains a copy of the data through the events replicated.

- Relay slave—this server performs the role of a slave as well as being the master to one or more slaves.

---

[1]Some feel that the names of these roles are derogatory and have suggested they may be offensive in some cultures. Thus, in the future, these names may change, but the role or job of the server is not likely to change.

Slaves are intended to be read-only by practice. This is to ensure there is only one location from which events (data changes) can originate. The master, therefore, is the location to which all of your writes should be directed. The slave uses two threads[2]: an input/output (IO) thread for reading events from the master and a SQL thread for executing events from its relay log. I will explain the details of how these threads work in a later section.

■ **Note**   The latest release of MySQL includes a multithreaded slave that uses a single IO thread to read the masters binary log entries and multiple SQL threads to execute events. For replication installations that permit events to run in parallel (.e.g., isolated by database), a multithreaded slave can improve replication performance. See the online reference manual for more details on multithreaded slaves (MTS).

The following sections will explain why you would want to use replication, what capabilities it provides beyond making a duplicate of the date, and what is required to use replication. A complete explanation of every aspect and nuance of the replication system would require an entire volume itself. Rather than attempt to explain everything there is to know about replication, I present a broader view of replication that will enable you to get started quickly.

If you plan to experiment with replication, the coverage in this chapter should be sufficient. If you plan to use replication for advanced high availability solutions, you should read this chapter and bolster it with a careful study of the replication chapters in the online reference manual.

Why use Replication?

There are many reasons to use replication. What I have described above—one master and a single slave—is the most basic building block for constructing topologies. This simple master–slave topology provides a redundant copy of the data on the slave, enabling you to keep a copy in case something happens to the master or if you want to separate your writes and reads for better application performance.

But there is far more that you can do. You can use the slave as a hot standby in case the master fails, and you can use the slave to run backup and maintenance operations that would normally require taking the server offline. In this case, you temporarily stop the slave from processing events (once conditions permit), take the backup, and then restart the slave. The slave would start reading events, starting with the next event from the master's binary log.

Applications with many clients can see a dramatic improvement in read operations by using multiple slaves to permit simultaneous reads. This process, called scale-out, is a building block for high-availability solutions.

These are just a few of the uses of replication. Table 8-1 summarizes the major capabilities that can be realized with replication.

---

[2]MySQL has a multithreaded slave feature that implements multiple threads to read the relay log, thereby improving performance of the slave for certain use cases. A deeper discussion of this feature is beyond the scope of this work but can be found in the online reference manual.

Table 8-1. *The Many Uses of Replication*

Use	Description
Backup	Run backup operations that require taking the server offline (or not).
Scale Out	Add more slaves to improve read throughput.
Hot Standby	Provide a replacement for the master to reduce downtime significantly.
Data Analysis	Perform resource-intensive operations on a slave instead of the master to avoid conflicts with other active applications.
Debugging	Conduct potentially invasive diagnoses of complex queries, and refine database design without risking effects to the production databases.
Development	Provide near-production-quality data for development of new applications to help avoid manufactured data that may not represent actual data values, ranges, and size.

As you can surmise, replication places a bit more demand on resources. Happily, replication can run on any machine that supports MySQL. In larger installations, employing multiple tiers of masters and many slaves, masters are typically installed on machines with increased memory, networking connections, and faster disk systems. This is because of the high number of writes that are performed on masters (writes take more time than reads in most cases).

Slaves, on the other hand, are typically installed on machines optimized for read operations. In cases in which you may want to use a slave as a hot standby for the master, you would use the same hardware as the master. This makes changing roles less likely to experience performance issues.

This section presented a brief look at MySQL replication in its barest, simplest terms. For more in-depth coverage of replication and all of its nuances, see the online reference manual.

How Does Replication Achieve High Availability?

You may be wondering how replication relates to high availability, given that most think of high availability as being a state with very little downtime (other than short, deliberately planned events). Replication enables high availability by providing the capability to switch the role of master from the master to another, capable slave. We say capable because not all slaves may be suitable to take on the role of master. If the hardware for the slave is vastly different (slower) from the master, you would not want to choose that slave as the new master. There are many ways to use a save as a standby for the master, and several ways to switch the role. Generally, we consider there to be two methods of changing the role: switchover and failover.

If the master is healthy but you need to change the role because you need to perform maintenance on the master or something has happened on the master but not completely disabled it, we call this switchover, because you are switching the role from a master to a slave.

If the master has crashed or is otherwise offline, we have to choose a slave to make the new master. In this case, we call this failover, because a failure is the impetus for changing the role.

This is where high availability comes into play. If you have several slaves capable of taking over for the master, especially if there is a failure on the master, you can avoid potentially long downtime and, more important, loss of data, by switching the role of the master quickly to one of the slaves.

Some effort of late has been put into trying to achieve near zero downtime even in the event of complete loss of the master. Oracle has added new features to replication that enable administrators to set up automatic failover. This is achieved with a combination of a feature in the server called Global Transaction Identifiers (GTID) and a script from the MySQL Utilities suite (see below) called mysqlfailover. While an in-depth look at GTIDs and automatic failover is beyond the scope of this book, see the sidebar "What's a GTID?" for an overview of the process.

WHAT'S A GTID?

GTIDs enable servers to assign a unique identifier to each set or group of events, thereby making it possible to know which events have been applied on each slave. To perform failover with GTIDs, one takes the best slave (the one with the fewest missing events and the hardware that matches the master best) and makes it a slave of every other slave. We call this slave the candidate slave. The GTID mechanism will ensure that only those events that have not been executed on the candidate slave are applied. In this way, the candidate slave becomes the most up-to-date, and therefore a replacement for the master.

The `mysqlfailover` command-line tool monitors the original master and performs automatic failover by executing the above sequence of events and takes care of redirecting the remaining slaves to the new master.

Thus, GTIDs make replication even more capable of providing high-availability database solutions. For more information about GTIDs and using the automatic solution with MySQL Utilities, visit:

`http://dev.mysql.com/doc/refman/5.6/en/replication-gtids.html`

`http://dev.mysql.com/doc/workbench/en/mysqlfailover.html`

`http://drcharlesbell.blogspot.com/2012/04/mysql-utilities-and-global-transaction.html`

Before GTIDs, replication events executed on the slave and stored on the slave's local binary log would be reapplied and, therefore, cause errors if a companion slave that had not read and executed those events were to attempt to set up replication. While this may sound a little strange, the online reference manual discusses this topic in much greater detail.

As you can tell, you can accomplish a lot with replication. What I have discussed thus far is really just the basics. You can find more in-depth information about replication in the online reference manual. If you would like to explore the advanced features of replication and configure your systems for maximum high availability, I recommend my book *MySQL High Availability,* published by O'Reilly Media.

In the next section, I demonstrate how to set up replication, and I discuss some of the general principles and commands needed to establish a replication topology.

Basic Replication Setup

You may be thinking that replication may be difficult to setup or complicated. Neither is the case. Replication is very easy to set up, and the commands are few. Furthermore, replication is very stable when set up correctly and very rarely has issues unrelated to data configuration, user-induced problems (e.g. an accidental DROP TABLE), or data corruption. Nevertheless, Oracle is constantly improving replication with additional features for more reliable replication, such as checking for data corruption during transmission using checksums.

In this section, I present the requirements for replication, explain the commands used in setting up replication, and present the standard method for establishing replication between a master and a slave.

Requirements for Replication

In order to set up replication, you need at least two servers: one to be the master for the original data where applications apply changes (the master), and one to be location where your applications read the data (the slave).

The most restrictive requirement is that each server in the topology must have a unique server identifier. This can be set in the option file with server-id=N, as a command line with --server-id=N or set with the SET GLOBAL server_id=N SQL command. You can also use an alternative form of the command; SET @@GLOBAL.server_id=N.

The master must have binary logging enabled. The easiest way to do this is to use the `--log-bin` option. This option allows you to specify a path and file name to use for the binary log. Include just the file name and no extension. The replication system will append an extension made up of six digits representing the sequence number of the binary log. This number is increased each time the binary logs are rotated.

Rotation of the binary log (and the relay log) can be accomplished using the `FLUSH BINARY LOGS` command. When this command is issued, the current file is closed (after transactions complete), and a new file is created with an incremented sequence number.

You can find an example of how to turn on binary logging in the standard my.cnf (my.ini for Windows) file. I include an example below that shows turning on binary logging and setting the binary log format.

```
# Uncomment the following if you want to log updates
log-bin=mysql-bin

# binary logging format - mixed recommended
binlog_format=mixed
```

Rotation means that the logs are flushed (cached events are written to disk) and closed, and a new log file is opened. Rotating the binary logs can be accomplished manually using the command:

```
mysql> FLUSH BINARY LOGS;
```

You also need to set up a special user that has the privilege to replicate events. More specifically, it is used to read events from the master's binary log. You can do this using the following command on the master. You need only run this command once. This user and password are used in a special command on the slave to connect to the master.

```
mysql> GRANT REPLICATION SLAVE ON *.* TO 'rpl'@'%' IDENTIFIED BY 'secret';
```

You also need what are called the coordinates of the master's binary log. These include the name of the current binary log and the position of the latest event, discovered through the use of the `SHOW MASTER STATUS` command, as shown below.

```
mysql> SHOW MASTER STATUS;
+------------------+----------+--------------+------------------+-------------------+
| File             | Position | Binlog_Do_DB | Binlog_Ignore_DB | Executed_Gtid_Set |
+------------------+----------+--------------+------------------+-------------------+
| mysql-bin.000001 |      245 |              |                  |                   |
+------------------+----------+--------------+------------------+-------------------+
1 row in set (0.00 sec)
```

Notice the columns displayed in this view. You can see the current binary log file and the current position. There are also two columns that display any binary log filters in action. The use of binary log filters is discouraged, because when activated, the events that do not pass through the filter are not written to the binary log. See the online reference manual for more information about binary log filters and replication filters on the slave.

Last, if you have any data on the master, copy the data in their current state to the slave; this is normally done via a backup and restore process. If binary logging is turned on, you need to lock the tables while you make a copy so that no events get written to the binary log while you are copying the data. If you use the InnoDB storage engine exclusively, you can use a consistent read lock to lock the tables but still permit reads. The basic process for copying data from a master that contains data to a slave is:.

1. Lock tables on the master with `FLUSH TABLES WITH READ LOCK`.

2. Copy the data. You can use any method you wish. For small amounts of data, you can use mysqldbexport (from MySQL Utilities) or the mysqldump client application.

3. Record the masters log file and position with SHOW MASTER STATUS.

4. Unlock the tables on the master with UNLOCK TABLES.

5. Import the data to the slave. For example, use mysqldbimport to import the file generated by msyqldbexport or read the mysqldump output via the source command in the mysql client.

6. Start replication using the values from (3).

Now that I have explained the requirements for setting up replication, let's see how we can configure a master and slave. The following sections assume that you have two servers of compatible hardware with MySQL installed. The examples are not using GTIDs, but I make note of the differences below.

It is also assumed that you have copied any existing data from the server to be configured as the master to the server to be configured as a slave and that the master is not experiencing writes (changes to data) either by locking the tables or because there are no clients connected. This is important, because having writes occurring while you are establishing replication could mean you choose the wrong master log file and position (coordinates) for the slave.

Configuring the Master

If the server is running, check to see if it has binary logging turned on. Execute a SHOW VARIABLES LIKE 'log_bin'. You should see a similar result as:

```
mysql> SHOW VARIABLES LIKE 'log_bin';
+-----------------------------------+---------------------+
| Variable_name                     | Value               |
+-----------------------------------+---------------------+
| log_bin                           | ON                  |
+-----------------------------------+---------------------+
1 rows in set (0.00 sec)
```

Notice the value for the variable log_bin. In this example, it is turned on (ON). If this value is OFF for your server, shut down the server and turn binary logging on, either via the command line, if you started your server this way, or via the option file. It is best for servers that you intend to use for applications to place the setting in the configuration file.

To set the variable via the command line, add the following options when starting your server. The first option tells the server to use row format for the events (this is optional but recommended), the second is to turn on binary logging and to use mysql_bin as the file name (without extension), and the third is used to set a unique server_id. Be sure to check your slave to ensure it has a different value for server_id.

```
--binlog-format=row --log-bin=mysql_bin --server-id=5
```

■ **Note** You can set the server_id dynamically, but this will not save the value to the option file. Thus, when the server is restarted, the value reverts to the default or as read from the option file.

To set the variables in the configuration file, open the configuration file named my.cnf (or whatever you named your file) and add the following lines. For installations of MySQL that use predefined configuration files you may see these entries commented out. Just uncomment them in that case. Place these values in the [mysqld] section.

```
binlog_format=row
log_bin=mysql_bin
server_id = 5
```

▓ **Note**   Be sure to locate the option file that your server is using. This is normally found in /etc./my.cnf, /etc./mysql/
my.cnf, /usr/local/mysql/etc./my.cnf, or ~/.my.cnf for Mac, Linux, and Unix systems. Windows systems may name
the file my.ini, and it is normally located in c:\windows\my.ini, c:\my.ini, <installation directory>\my.ini, or <application
data for user>\.mylogin.cnf. Consult the online reference manual section "Using Option Files" for more information.

Once the changes are made to the configuration file, restart your server and check again to ensure that binary logging is turned on.

To permit a slave to connect to the master and read events, you must define a replication and issue the appropriate permissions. This user must have the REPLICATION SLAVE privilege and can be created with the GRANT statement as follows. Be sure to set the host name according to your domain or use IP addresses. Also, set the password according to your information-security policies.

```
mysql> GRANT REPLICATION SLAVE ON *.* TO 'rpl'@'%.mydomain.com' IDENTIFIED BY 'secret';
```

We will use these credentials later when we connect the slave to the master and start replication.

▓ **Tip**   If you have configured your server to not allow automatic creation of user accounts with the GRANT statement,
you must issue a CREATE USER command before the GRANT command.

One more thing you need to do on the master is to discover the name of the binary log file and its current position. If you have not done so already or have not taken steps to ensure there are no writes occurring on the master, lock the tables as shown below.

```
mysql> FLUSH TABLES WITH READ LOCK;
```

Once you are sure there are no more writes occurring, you can use the SHOW MASTER STATUS command as shown below. We will use this information when we connect the slave to the master.

```
mysql> SHOW MASTER STATUS;
+------------------+----------+--------------+------------------+-------------------+
| File             | Position | Binlog_Do_DB | Binlog_Ignore_DB | Executed_Gtid_Set |
+------------------+----------+--------------+------------------+-------------------+
| mysql-bin.000152 |      243 |              |                  |                   |
+------------------+----------+--------------+------------------+-------------------+
1 row in set (0.00 sec)
```

Notice in this example that the binary log has been incremented a number of times. This is not uncommon for a server that has been running for an extended period. If you are following along and setting up a new master, you are likely to see a much lower value for the binary log number and possibly a smaller value for the position. This is perfectly normal. Just record the values for use later.

If you locked the tables before issuing the SHOW MASTER STATUS command, you can now unlock them with the command:

```
mysql> UNLOCK TABLES;
```

■ **Note** If you are using GTIDs, you do not need to know the coordinates of the master. The GTID feature will automatically resolve the starting location in the binary log for you.

Configuring the Slave

Configuring the slave is a bit easier. You only need to set the server_id for the slave. As with the master, you can set this value via the command line if you start your server that way (--server-id=7), but the best method is to change the value in the configuration file. Open the option file for the slave and add or uncomment the following. Place these values in the [mysqld] section.

```
[mysqld]
...
server_id = 7
```

Connecting the Slave to the Master

Now that you have configured your master with binary logging and set the server_id for both servers to a unique value, you are ready to connect the slave to the master. This requires two commands issued in order. The first is used to instruct the slave as to how to connect to which master and the second is to initiate the startup of the IO and SQL threads on the slave.

The CHANGE MASTER command makes the connection from the slave to the master. You can specify several options and forms of connections, including SSL connections. For this example, we use the most basic and essential options, and use normal MySQL authentication to connect to the slave. For more information about SSL connections and the many options, see the online reference manual.

The following is an example of the CHANGE MASTER command that would be used to connect a slave to a master using the information from the SHOW MASTER STATUS above. the values from your master when you set up your own master and slave.

```
mysql> CHANGE MASTER TO MASTER_HOST='localhost', MASTER_USER='rpl',
       MASTER_PASSWORD='pass', MASTER_LOG_FILE='mysql_bin.000152',
       MASTER_LOG_POS=243;
```

If you are using GTIDs, you can omit the master binary log coordinates and use a special option, as follows. This tells the servers to begin negotiating the starting transactions to be executed on the slave.

```
mysql> CHANGE MASTER TO MASTER_HOST='localhost', MASTER_USER='rpl',
       MASTER_PASSWORD='pass', MASTER_AUTO_POSITION = 1;
```

The next command is used to start the threads on the slave and begin replicating events from the master.

```
mysql> START SLAVE;
```

A companion command, STOP SLAVE, stops the slave threads, thereby stopping replication. There is also a command, RESET SLAVE, for removing all replication files on the slave and resetting the slave connection information for the master. The reset command is rarely used in cases in which it is necessary to purge the connection information from the slave. An equivalent RESET MASTER command removes all binary log files and clears the binary log index.

> ■ **Caution** Be sure you really want to destroy the replication information (RESET SLAVE) or the binary log information (RESET MASTER) and that there are no slaves connected to the master (RESET MASTER). Inadvertently issuing these commands can cause your replication topologies to incur errors and replication of data to cease.

You may see warnings, or in some cases an error ,when issuing the START SLAVE command. Unfortunately, this isn't always that informative. Savvy database administrators use a special command—the SHOW SLAVE STATUS command—to check the status of a slave that is similar in syntax to the SHOW MASTER command. This command will generate a very long (wide) view of a single row with lots of information about exactly what is going on inside the slave concerning replication. The best way to view this information is to show it in a vertical format (use \G). Listing 8-1 shows a typical output for a slave without errors. I highlight the more important attributes to check in bold.

Listing 8-1. SHOW SLAVE STATUS report

```
mysql> SHOW SLAVE STATUS \G
*************************** 1. row ***************************
               Slave_IO_State: Waiting for master to send event
                  Master_Host: localhost
                  Master_User: rpl
                  Master_Port: 3306
                Connect_Retry: 60
              Master_Log_File: my_log.000152
          Read_Master_Log_Pos: 243
               Relay_Log_File: clone-relay-bin.000002
                Relay_Log_Pos: 248
        Relay_Master_Log_File: my_log.000152
             Slave_IO_Running: Yes
            Slave_SQL_Running: Yes
              Replicate_Do_DB:
          Replicate_Ignore_DB:
           Replicate_Do_Table:
       Replicate_Ignore_Table:
      Replicate_Wild_Do_Table:
  Replicate_Wild_Ignore_Table:
                   Last_Errno: 0
                   Last_Error:
                 Skip_Counter: 0
          Exec_Master_Log_Pos: 243
              Relay_Log_Space: 403
              Until_Condition: None
               Until_Log_File:
                Until_Log_Pos: 0
           Master_SSL_Allowed: No
           Master_SSL_CA_File:
           Master_SSL_CA_Path:
              Master_SSL_Cert:
            Master_SSL_Cipher:
               Master_SSL_Key:
        Seconds_Behind_Master: 0
Master_SSL_Verify_Server_Cert: No
```

```
          Last_IO_Errno: 0
          Last_IO_Error:
         Last_SQL_Errno: 0
         Last_SQL_Error:
1 row in set (0.00 sec)
```

Get into the habit of always issuing this command when setting up replication. It will provide a wealth of information, including more detail about any problems and errors.

Next Steps

If you have issued all of the commands above and there were no errors either in the output of SHOW SLAVE STATUS or the commands themselves, congratulations! You have just set up your first replication topology.

If you want to test your replication setup, create a new database and table on the master and check the slave to ensure that these events were repeated there. Check the slave with SHOW SLAVE STATUS until it reports that it is waiting on the master for new events. Otherwise, you could be checking the slave before it has finished reading events from the relay log. Rather than show you this by example, I leave testing your replication setup as an exercise.

In the next section, I delve a little deeper into the most important enabling feature for replication—the binary log.

BUT WAIT, ISN'T THERE A BETTER WAY?

If you've read over the previous sections and performed the steps on your own servers, you may think that while the process is simple there are a lot of steps to perform and things to check. You may wonder why there isn't a simple command to "just do it" for replication.

I have good news. There is such a command, but it is in the form of a Python utility that is bundled with MySQL Workbench. Called MySQL Utilities, it includes two very useful commands: mysqlreplicate, which automates the setup of a master and slave; and mysqlrplcheck, which checks the prerequisites of a master and slave either prior to or after replication is set up. I explain these and MySQL Utilities in more detail below.

The Binary Log

No discussion about replication would be complete without a detailed look at the binary log. In this section, we discover more about how the binary log works and how to read the binary log and relay log using an external client as well as a special SHOW command.

Some may believe the binary log is replication, but that is not entirely true. Any server, including one performing the role of a slave, can have binary logging enabled. In the case of a slave, the server would contain both a relay log and a binary log. This makes it possible for a slave that has other servers as its slaves to perform the role of master and slave (sometimes called an intermediate slave).

The binary log originally had another purpose. It can be used for recovery of data in the event of loss. For example, if a server has the binary log enabled, it is possible to replay the binary logs to recover data up to the point of loss. This is called point in time recovery, and it is made possible because the mysql client can read the events and execute them. You can either source the file or copy and paste individual events (or a range of events) into a mysql client. See the online reference manual for more information about point in time recovery.

▪ **Tip** To discover all the variables used for binary logging, issue the command SHOW VARIABLES LIKE '%binlog%'. Similarly, to discover the variables used for the relay log, issue the command SHOW VARIABLES LIKE '%relay%'.

As mentioned previously, the name of the binary log can be set by the user with the `--log-bin` option, with which you specify a file name to be used for all binary log files. When a binary log is rotated, a new file with an incremented six-digit number is appended as the file extension. There is also an index file with the name specified for the binary log and the extension `.index`. This file maintains the current binary-log file. The server uses this file at startup to know where to begin appending events. Thus, the binary log is a collection of files rather than a single file. Whenever you perform maintenance or wish to archive the binary log (or relay log), include all the files associated, including the index file.

■ **Tip**   You can change the name of the relay log with the --relay-log startup option.

The binary log is the mechanism that makes replication possible and the place that administrators focus on when things go wonky. But first, let's examine the format of the binary log.

Row Formats

The binary log is a sequential file in which events (changes to the data) are written to the end of the file. A file position is used to determine the offset into the file for the next binary-log event. The server therefore maintains the name of the current binary log and the next position pointer (as seen in SHOW MASTER STATUS above). In this way, the server can know where to write the next event.

While somewhat of a misnomer, the binary log can be considered one of two primary formats: statement based or row based. There is also a hybrid version called mixed format. While this may sound like the file is formatted differently, it is the events themselves that the format refers. The binary-log file itself is still a sequential file, regardless of the format of the events, and it is written and read using the simple concept of file name plus offset. The different formats are:

- Statement-based replication (SBR)—the events contain the actual SQL statements that were executed on the master. These are packaged without change, shipped to the slave, and executed there.

- Row-based replication (RBR)—the events contain the resulting binary row after the changes. This permits the slave to simply apply the event to the row rather than executing the statement via the SQL interface.

- Mixed format—this combination of SBR and RBR is governed by the storage engine and other elements of the server, as well as the type of command being executed. Mixed format uses SBR by default. For example, if the storage engine supports RBR, the event will be in RBR format. Similarly, if there is a reason to not use RBR, SBR will be used for that event instead.

See the online reference manual for a complete list of which commands force SBR versus RBR format for the event.

The mysqlbinlog Client

All MySQL installations include a special client for reading the binary log. The client is convincingly named mysqlbinlog. The purpose of the client is to display the contents of the binary log in a human-readable form. For SBR format, the actual query is included in the payload of the event, thereby making it easy to read. RBR format events are in binary form. For RBR events, the client will display any information that can be made human readable, displaying the row format in ASCII form.

The mysqlbinlog client has a number of options for controlling the output. You can display the output in hexadecimal format, skip the first N events, display events in a range of positions, or use many more options. To read a range of events in the binary log, you can specify a start datetime and end datetime or a start and a stop position.

Perhaps the most powerful feature for the client is the ability to connect to a remote server and read its binary log. This feature makes managing multiple servers easier.

Listing 8-2 shows an example of running the mysqlbinlog client against a typical binary log file. In this case, the file is from a master that has had its logs rotated once. We can tell this by the sequence number used for the binary-log file extension. This value is incremented each time the log is rotated. Recall that this process is initiated by FLUSH LOGS and results in the existing binary-log file being closed, a new file opened, and a new header written to the new file.

Listing 8-2. The mysqlbinlog Client Example Output

```
$ mysqlbinlog /usr/local/mysql/data/mysql-bin.000002
/*!40019 SET @@session.max_insert_delayed_threads=0*/;
/*!50003 SET @OLD_COMPLETION_TYPE=@@COMPLETION_TYPE,COMPLETION_TYPE=0*/;
DELIMITER /*!*/;
# at 4
#121016 20:50:47 server id 1  end_log_pos 107   Start: binlog v 4, server v 5.6.7-log created 121016
20:50:47 at startup
ROLLBACK/*!*/;
BINLOG '
5wB+UA8BAAAAZwAAAGsAAAABAAQANS41LjIzLWxvZwAAAAAAAAAAAAAAAAAAAAAAAAAAAAAAA
AAAAAAAAAAAAAAAAADnAH5QEzgNAAgAEgAEBAQEEgAAVAAEGggAAAAICAgCAA==
'/*!*/;
# at 107
#121016 20:54:23 server id 1  end_log_pos 198   Query   thread_id=108   exec_time=0     error_code=0
SET TIMESTAMP=1350435263/*!*/;
SET @@session.pseudo_thread_id=108/*!*/;
SET @@session.foreign_key_checks=1, @@session.sql_auto_is_null=0, @@session.unique_checks=1, @@
session.autocommit=1/*!*/;
SET @@session.sql_mode=0/*!*/;
SET @@session.auto_increment_increment=1, @@session.auto_increment_offset=1/*!*/;
/*!\C utf8 *//*!*/;
SET @@session.character_set_client=33,@@session.collation_connection=33,@@session.collation_
server=8/*!*/;
SET @@session.lc_time_names=0/*!*/;
SET @@session.collation_database=DEFAULT/*!*/;
CREATE DATABASE example1
/*!*/;
# at 198
#121016 20:54:42 server id 1  end_log_pos 303   Query   thread_id=108   exec_time=0     error_code=0
SET TIMESTAMP=1350435282/*!*/;
CREATE TABLE example1.t1(a int, b varchar(20))
/*!*/;
# at 303
#121016 20:55:05 server id 1  end_log_pos 367   Query   thread_id=108   exec_time=0     error_code=0
SET TIMESTAMP=1350435305/*!*/;
BEGIN
/*!*/;
# at 367
#121016 20:55:05 server id 1  end_log_pos 493   Query   thread_id=108   exec_time=0     error_code=0
SET TIMESTAMP=1350435305/*!*/;
insert into example1.t1 values (1, 'one'), (2, 'two'), (3, 'three')
/*!*/;
```

```
# at 493
#121016 20:55:05 server id 1  end_log_pos 520    Xid = 141
COMMIT/*!*/;
# at 520
#121016 20:55:17 server id 1  end_log_pos 584    Query   thread_id=108   exec_time=0    error_code=0
SET TIMESTAMP=1350435317/*!*/;
BEGIN
/*!*/;
# at 584
#121016 20:55:17 server id 1  end_log_pos 682    Query   thread_id=108   exec_time=0    error_code=0
SET TIMESTAMP=1350435317/*!*/;
DELETE FROM example1.t1 where b = 'two'
/*!*/;
# at 682
#121016 20:55:17 server id 1  end_log_pos 709    Xid = 148
COMMIT/*!*/;
DELIMITER ;
# End of log file
ROLLBACK /* added by mysqlbinlog */;
/*!50003 SET COMPLETION_TYPE=@OLD_COMPLETION_TYPE*/;
```

Notice that in the output we see a lot of metadata about each event as well as a header with information about the binary-log file. Also, notice that each event (SBR format in this example) shows the log position as well as the thread id and other pertinent information. The timestamp entries are a special form of event that the server uses to maintain timestamp data in the log (and hence on the slave).

■ **Tip** The binary log and the relay log have the same layout, and therefore both can be read by the `mysqlbinlog` client.

Reading events from the binary or relay log using the mysqlbinlog client is powerful, but there is also a convenient SHOW command that shows the events in a tabular form.

SHOW BINLOG EVENTS Command

The MySQL server contains a special SHOW command, SHOW BINLOG EVENTS, that permits you to see the latest events located in the binary log. Let's see this command in action. Listing 8-3 shows the results of the SHOW BINLOG EVENTS run on the same server that was used for the mysqlbinlog example in the previous section. I use the vertical format to make it easier to read.

Listing 8-3. SHOW BINLOG EVENTS Example 1

```
cbell$ mysql -uroot
Welcome to the MySQL monitor.  Commands end with ; or \g.
Your MySQL connection id is 508
Server version: 5.6.7-m9 MySQL Community Server (GPL)

Copyright (c) 2000, 2012, Oracle and/or its affiliates. All rights reserved.
```

```
Oracle is a registered trademark of Oracle Corporation and/or its
affiliates. Other names may be trademarks of their respective
owners.

Type 'help;' or '\h' for help. Type '\c' to clear the current input statement.

mysql> SHOW BINLOG EVENTS \G
*************************** 1. row ***************************
   Log_name: mysql-bin.000001
        Pos: 4
 Event_type: Format_desc
  Server_id: 1
End_log_pos: 107
       Info: Server ver: 5.6.7-m9, Binlog ver: 4
*************************** 2. row ***************************
   Log_name: mysql-bin.000001
        Pos: 107
 Event_type: Query
  Server_id: 1
End_log_pos: 245
       Info: SET PASSWORD FOR 'root'@'localhost'='*81F5E21E35407D884A6CD4A731AEBFB6AF209E1B'
*************************** 3. row ***************************
   Log_name: mysql-bin.000001
        Pos: 245
 Event_type: Stop
  Server_id: 1
End_log_pos: 264
       Info:
3 rows in set (0.00 sec)
```

You may be wondering what happened to the events from the previous example. This reveals an often mistaken assumption on the part of users new to binary logging. The SHOW BINLOG EVENTS command displays events from the first binary log by default. In the previous section, I used the second binary log. To see events from a binary log other than the first, use the IN clause, as shown below. I use the vertical format to make it easier to read.

Listing 8-4. SHOW BINLOG EVENTS Example 2

```
mysql> SHOW BINLOG EVENTS IN 'mysql-bin.000002' \G
*************************** 1. row ***************************
   Log_name: mysql-bin.000002
        Pos: 4
 Event_type: Format_desc
  Server_id: 1
End_log_pos: 107
       Info: Server ver: 5.6.7-m9, Binlog ver: 4
*************************** 2. row ***************************
   Log_name: mysql-bin.000002
        Pos: 107
 Event_type: Query
  Server_id: 1
End_log_pos: 198
       Info: CREATE DATABASE example1
```

```
*************************** 3. row ***************************
    Log_name: mysql-bin.000002
         Pos: 198
  Event_type: Query
   Server_id: 1
 End_log_pos: 303
        Info: CREATE TABLE example1.t1(a int, b varchar(20))
*************************** 4. row ***************************
    Log_name: mysql-bin.000002
         Pos: 303
  Event_type: Query
   Server_id: 1
 End_log_pos: 367
        Info: BEGIN
*************************** 5. row ***************************
    Log_name: mysql-bin.000002
         Pos: 367
  Event_type: Query
   Server_id: 1
 End_log_pos: 493
        Info: insert into example1.t1 values (1, 'one'), (2, 'two'), (3, 'three')
*************************** 6. row ***************************
    Log_name: mysql-bin.000002
         Pos: 493
  Event_type: Xid
   Server_id: 1
 End_log_pos: 520
        Info: COMMIT /* xid=141 */
*************************** 7. row ***************************
    Log_name: mysql-bin.000002
         Pos: 520
  Event_type: Query
   Server_id: 1
 End_log_pos: 584
        Info: BEGIN
*************************** 8. row ***************************
    Log_name: mysql-bin.000002
         Pos: 584
  Event_type: Query
   Server_id: 1
 End_log_pos: 682
        Info: DELETE FROM example1.t1 where b = 'two'
*************************** 9. row ***************************
    Log_name: mysql-bin.000002
         Pos: 682
  Event_type: Xid
   Server_id: 1
 End_log_pos: 709
        Info: COMMIT /* xid=148 */
9 rows in set (0.00 sec)

mysql>
```

The command displays the log name, the starting and ending position of the event in the log (file offset), the event type, and the payload (the query for SBR events).

It may seem as if these tools—the msyqlbinlog client and the SHOW BINLOG EVENTS command—are like a limited set, but the truth is that they are the key to becoming a good administrator of servers that run binary logging and replication topologies. Make learning these tools a priority. The following lists several resources (in addition to the online reference manual) that you can use to learn more about binary logging and replication of events.

Additional Resources

Some rather obscure resources may be of interest to anyone wanting to know more about the details of the binary log and its format. Of course, the online reference manual has considerable documentation and should be your primary source, but the following contain some key information not found in other sources.

- `http://dev.mysql.com/doc/internals/en/index.html`

- `http://dev.mysql.com/doc/internals/en/replication-protocol.html`

- `http://dev.mysql.com/doc/internals/en/row-based-replication.html`

In the next sections, I dive into the finer points of replication, starting with an overview of the replication architecture, followed by a brief tour of the replication source code.

Replication Architecture

The replication source code is quite large, and indeed, it is one of the largest portions of the server code. Since replication permeates so many levels of the server code, and it has grown over the years, it is sometimes difficult to see how it fits into the other portions of the server.

It is helpful, therefore, to take a moment and look at a high-level view of the architecture itself to see how the parts work within replication. This is also a good way to introduce the major sections of the replication source code. Figure 8-1 shows a simplified block diagram of the replication architecture. The sections following the figure explain the components in more detail.

Figure 8-1. *Replication Architecture*

The numbered arrows in the figure above show the simplified sequence of events that describe the replication architecture. First, the master writes an event to the binary log. Second, the slave's IO_THREAD reads the event from the master's binary log via a dedicate network connection and writes it to its relay log. Third, the slave's SQL_THREAD reads the event from the relay log and applies (executes) it to the database.

Lets slow that down a bit and examine the sequence in more detail. What follows is a generalization of the code sequence. Some events follow a slightly different path in the master, but generally, this is how events are shipped to the slave.

When a user or application issues a SQL statement on the master that is of the type that is written to the binary log (a SHOW command is one that is not recorded), the server code calls the code for writing to the binary log in binlog.cc, which in turn calls code in rpl_master.cc to create an instance of a log-event class. When written to the binary log, the pack_info() method of the log-event class is called to format a block of data for storing in the binary log. Of particular interest here is that the binary-log-class updates its log position so that the server and the user know the location of the next event in the binary-log file.

When the slave requests more events from the master, via the code in rpl_slave.cc, it connects to the master and issues a special command, COM_BINLOG_DUMP, which is executed via the big switch in sql_parse.cc and results in the code in the rpl_master.cc sending any events in the binary log since the last position read from the slave. As these events are read, they are written to the slave's binary-log file via the code in rpl_slave.cc. This process is executed by the slave via the IO thread. Meanwhile, the slave has another thread, the SQL thread, which reads events from the relay log and executes them. This code is also inside rpl_slave.cc.

While this explanation leaves many of the details out, it is an accurate description of how the replication architecture achieves its goals. Many lines of code are involved in this process, so to generalize it as simple would be a gross understatement. The replication source code is far from simplistic, yet it has an elegance of execution that belies its complexity.

In the next section, I give you a brief tour of the replication source code. Because of the large number of elements that make up the replication feature, I concentrate on one of the key areas that will help you understand what makes replication work—the log events.

A Brief Tour of the Replication Source Code

As I mentioned earlier, the replication source touches many pieces of the server code. Consider for a moment all that is involved with recording an event in the binary log. Clearly, every command we wish to replicate must make calls to the replication code (in this case, the binary-logging code) to initiate the event and record it in the binary log. Shipping that event to the slave and executing it there introduces code that places the event in the server for execution—either by executing the query (SBR) or by applying the resulting row (RBR).

In the following sections, I take you on a tour of the replication source code, concentrating on the code surrounding the log events. Before we take that journey, let us take a look at the source-code files for replication.

Replication Source Code Files

Furthermore, more than 48 separate source-code files comprise the replication source code. As you can imagine, this is a huge amount of code, and as a result, it is difficult to remember (or learn) what all the files do and where each piece of code resides.

I recently interviewed a number of developers (who will remain nameless) and discovered an interesting trend. While some were knowledgeable about most of the source files and what they do, even the most experienced had to search their memories to recall what each file contains. It is safe to say that only the Oracle replication developers themselves can be considered experts in this area.

What I present here is a private tour of one of the most important aspects of the replication code. A complete tour of all of the code and what each class and method does would consume an entire book and would require the coordinated efforts of the author and the replication developers.

The good news here is that I have arranged this tour to provide you with a working knowledge of what log events are, how they are coded, where they are coded, and how they work to enable replication.

Before we journey down that thorny path, read through Table 8-2 for an overview of the 48 replication source files and what each contains. I am sure you will agree it is a formidable list. Most of these files are in the /sql folder of the source tree.

Table 8-2. *List of Replication Source Files*

Source Files	Description
binlog.h/.cc	Contains the binary log code
log_event.h/.cc	Defines log events and operations for each
rpl_constants.h/.cc	Global constants and definitions for replication
rpl_filter.h/.cc	Implements the filters for binary logging and replication
rpl_gtid_cache.cc	Class Gtid_cache, holds the GTIDs in the transaction currently being committed by the thread.
rpl_gtid_execution.cc	Logic for how the slave re-executes GTIDs.
rpl_gtid.h	Class definitions for all GTID things.
rpl_gtid_misc.cc	Convert GTID to string and vice versa.
rpl_gtid_mutex_cond_array.cc	The data structure 'class Mutex_cond_array', which is a growable array in which each element holds a mutex and a condition variable associated with that mutex.
rpl_gtid_owned.cc	The data structure 'class Gtid_owned', which holds the current status of GTID ownership.
rpl_gtid_set.cc	The data structure 'class Gtid_set', which holds a set of GTIDs.
rpl_gtid_sid_map.cc	The data structure 'class Sid_map', which holds a bidirectional map between SIDs and numbers.
rpl_gtid_specification.cc	The data structure 'class Gtid_specification', which holds the datatype for GTID_NEXT, i.e., either a GTID or 'ANONYMOUS' or 'AUTOMATIC'.
rpl_gtid_state.cc	The data structure 'class Gtid_state', which holds the global state of GTIDs, that is, the set of committed GTIDs (@@global.gtid_done / Gtid_state::logged_gtids), the GTID ownership status (@@global.gtid_owned / Gtid_state::owned_gtids), the lost GTIDs (@@global.gtid_lost / Gtid_state::lost_gtids)
rpl_handler.h/.cc	Helper functions for the handler interface
rpl_info.h/.cc	Base classes for storing the slave's master information
rpl_info_dummy.h/.cc	Dummy version of rpl_info.h
rpl_info_factory.h/.cc	Factory for generating worker threads and references to classes for manipulating the slave's master information
rpl_info_file.h/.cc	Master information file operations
rpl_info_handler.h/.cc	Memory, file flushing, and similar operations for the slave's master information
rpl_info_table_access.h/.cc	Table level access to the slave's master information
rpl_info_table.h/.cc	Table-level I/O operations for the slave's master information
rpl_info_values.h/.cc	Class for handling values read from slave's master information

(continued)

Table 8-2. (*continued*)

Source Files	Description
rpl_injector.h/.cc	Used by NDB (Cluster) storage engine for injecting events into binary log
rpl_master.h/.cc	Defines replication operations for the master role
rpl_mi.h/.cc	Encapsulates the master information for slaves
rpl_record.h/.cc	Row record methods
rpl_record_old.h/.cc	Row record methods for old format in pre-GA of 5.1 row-based events
rpl_reporting.h/.cc	Base class for reporting errors in binary log file and show slave status output
rpl_rli.h/.cc	Relay log information handling
rpl_rli_pdb.h/.cc	Relay log helper classes including hash and queues
rpl_slave.h/.cc	Defines replication operations for the slave role
rpl_tblmap.h/.cc	Implements the table map event type
rpl_utility.h/.cc	Contains miscellaneous helper methods for replication
sql_binlog.h/.cc	The SQL statement BINLOG, generated by mysqlbinlog to execute row events and format description log events.

The main files you will be working in are the log_event.h/.cc files. These contain all of the code for the log events. I explain the major log-event classes in the next section. Also of interest to study are the rpl_master.h/.cc files. This is where the code for the master role resides, including code to write events to the binary log. If you are working on a solution to extend replication for the master role, begin your research in these files. You may also want to examine the rpl_slave.h/.cc files. This is where the code resides for executing events on the slave. When working on extensions to the slave role, begin your research in these files. Now lets get on with the tour of the log events.

Log Events Explained

We begin our tour by examining the base class for all log events - Log_event. This class contains all of the methods and attributes needed to store, ship, and execute events via the binary log and relay log. Open the file /sql/log_event.h and scroll down to around line 962 to the start of the Log_event class. Listing 8-5 shows an excerpt of the log-event class in the log_event.h file.

I omit some details to make it easier to read. There is a lot of documentation inside the code from an explanation of the enumerations to a description of the byte layout for a log event. If you are interested in more details about these and similar details, see the excellent documentation in the source code. Take a moment to look through this code. Later in this chapter, I explain some of the details about the key methods one would use when creating your own log event class. As you can see from the listing above, this class is quite complex.

■ **Note**   There are two log_event* header and class files. The log_event_old* files are those log-event classes that are for older formats of the RBR-event format. We focus on the newer log-event format in this chapter. You are free to examine the older format as an exercise.

Listing 8-5. Log_event Class Declaration

```
class Log_event
{
public:
enum enum_skip_reason {
    EVENT_SKIP_NOT,
    EVENT_SKIP_IGNORE,
    EVENT_SKIP_COUNT
  };

protected:
  enum enum_event_cache_type
  {
    EVENT_INVALID_CACHE= 0,
    EVENT_STMT_CACHE,
    EVENT_TRANSACTIONAL_CACHE,
    EVENT_NO_CACHE,
    EVENT_CACHE_COUNT
  };

  enum enum_event_logging_type
  {
    EVENT_INVALID_LOGGING= 0,
    EVENT_NORMAL_LOGGING,
    EVENT_IMMEDIATE_LOGGING,
    EVENT_CACHE_LOGGING_COUNT
  };

public:
  typedef unsigned char Byte;
  my_off_t log_pos;
  char *temp_buf;
  struct timeval when;
  ulong exec_time;
  ulong data_written;
  uint32 server_id;
  uint32 unmasked_server_id;
  uint16 flags;
  ulong slave_exec_mode;
  enum_event_cache_type event_cache_type;
  enum_event_logging_type event_logging_type;
  ha_checksum crc;
  ulong mts_group_idx;
  Relay_log_info *worker;
  ulonglong future_event_relay_log_pos;

#ifdef MYSQL_SERVER
  THD* thd;
  db_worker_hash_entry *mts_assigned_partitions[MAX_DBS_IN_EVENT_MTS];
  Log_event(enum_event_cache_type cache_type_arg= EVENT_INVALID_CACHE,
            enum_event_logging_type logging_type_arg= EVENT_INVALID_LOGGING);
```

```
  Log_event(THD* thd_arg, uint16 flags_arg,
            enum_event_cache_type cache_type_arg,
            enum_event_logging_type logging_type_arg);
  static Log_event* read_log_event(IO_CACHE* file,
                                   mysql_mutex_t* log_lock,
                                   const Format_description_log_event
                                   *description_event,
                                   my_bool crc_check);
  static int read_log_event(IO_CACHE* file, String* packet,
                            mysql_mutex_t* log_lock, uint8 checksum_alg_arg);

  static void init_show_field_list(List<Item>* field_list);
#ifdef HAVE_REPLICATION
  int net_send(Protocol *protocol, const char* log_name, my_off_t pos);

  virtual int pack_info(Protocol *protocol);
#endif /* HAVE_REPLICATION */
  virtual const char* get_db()
  {
    return thd ? thd->db : 0;
  }
#else // ifdef MYSQL_SERVER
  Log_event(enum_event_cache_type cache_type_arg= EVENT_INVALID_CACHE,
            enum_event_logging_type logging_type_arg= EVENT_INVALID_LOGGING)
  : temp_buf(0), event_cache_type(cache_type_arg),
    event_logging_type(logging_type_arg)
  { }
    /* avoid having to link mysqlbinlog against libpthread */
  static Log_event* read_log_event(IO_CACHE* file,
                                   const Format_description_log_event
                                   *description_event, my_bool crc_check);
  /* print*() functions are used by mysqlbinlog */
  virtual void print(FILE* file, PRINT_EVENT_INFO* print_event_info) = 0;
  void print_timestamp(IO_CACHE* file, time_t* ts);
  void print_header(IO_CACHE* file, PRINT_EVENT_INFO* print_event_info,
                    bool is_more);
  void print_base64(IO_CACHE* file, PRINT_EVENT_INFO* print_event_info,
                    bool is_more);
#endif // ifdef MYSQL_SERVER ... else
  uint8 checksum_alg;

  static void *operator new(size_t size)
  {
    return (void*) my_malloc((uint)size, MYF(MY_WME|MY_FAE));
  }

  static void operator delete(void *ptr, size_t)
  {
    my_free(ptr);
  }
```

```cpp
  static void *operator new(size_t, void* ptr) { return ptr; }
  static void operator delete(void*, void*) { }
  bool wrapper_my_b_safe_write(IO_CACHE* file, const uchar* buf,
                               ulong data_length);

#ifdef MYSQL_SERVER
  bool write_header(IO_CACHE* file, ulong data_length);
  bool write_footer(IO_CACHE* file);
  my_bool need_checksum();

  virtual bool write(IO_CACHE* file)
  {
    return(write_header(file, get_data_size()) ||
           write_data_header(file) ||
           write_data_body(file) ||
           write_footer(file));
  }
  virtual bool write_data_header(IO_CACHE* file)
  { return 0; }
  virtual bool write_data_body(IO_CACHE* file __attribute__((unused)))
  { return 0; }
  inline time_t get_time()
  {
    if (!when.tv_sec && !when.tv_usec) /* Not previously initialized */
    {
      THD *tmp_thd= thd ? thd : current_thd;
      if (tmp_thd)
        when= tmp_thd->start_time;
      else
        my_micro_time_to_timeval(my_micro_time(), &when);
    }
    return (time_t) when.tv_sec;
  }
#endif
  virtual Log_event_type get_type_code() = 0;
  virtual bool is_valid() const = 0;
  void set_artificial_event() { flags |= LOG_EVENT_ARTIFICIAL_F; }
  void set_relay_log_event() { flags |= LOG_EVENT_RELAY_LOG_F; }
  bool is_artificial_event() const { return flags & LOG_EVENT_ARTIFICIAL_F; }
  bool is_relay_log_event() const { return flags & LOG_EVENT_RELAY_LOG_F; }
  bool is_ignorable_event() const { return flags & LOG_EVENT_IGNORABLE_F; }
  bool is_no_filter_event() const { return flags & LOG_EVENT_NO_FILTER_F; }
  inline bool is_using_trans_cache() const
  {
    return (event_cache_type == EVENT_TRANSACTIONAL_CACHE);
  }
  inline bool is_using_stmt_cache() const
  {
    return(event_cache_type == EVENT_STMT_CACHE);
  }
```

```cpp
  inline bool is_using_immediate_logging() const
  {
    return(event_logging_type == EVENT_IMMEDIATE_LOGGING);
  }
  Log_event(const char* buf, const Format_description_log_event
            *description_event);
  virtual ~Log_event() { free_temp_buf();}
  void register_temp_buf(char* buf) { temp_buf = buf; }
  void free_temp_buf()
  {
    if (temp_buf)
    {
      my_free(temp_buf);
      temp_buf = 0;
    }
  }
  virtual int get_data_size() { return 0;}
  static Log_event* read_log_event(const char* buf, uint event_len,
                                   const char **error,
                                   const Format_description_log_event
                                   *description_event, my_bool crc_check);
  static const char* get_type_str(Log_event_type type);
  const char* get_type_str();

#if defined(MYSQL_SERVER) && defined(HAVE_REPLICATION)

private:

  enum enum_mts_event_exec_mode
  {
    EVENT_EXEC_PARALLEL,
    EVENT_EXEC_ASYNC,
    EVENT_EXEC_SYNC,
    EVENT_EXEC_CAN_NOT
  };

  bool is_mts_sequential_exec()
  {
    return
      get_type_code() == START_EVENT_V3          ||
      get_type_code() == STOP_EVENT              ||
      get_type_code() == ROTATE_EVENT            ||
      get_type_code() == LOAD_EVENT              ||
      get_type_code() == SLAVE_EVENT             ||
      get_type_code() == CREATE_FILE_EVENT       ||
      get_type_code() == DELETE_FILE_EVENT       ||
      get_type_code() == NEW_LOAD_EVENT          ||
      get_type_code() == EXEC_LOAD_EVENT         ||
      get_type_code() == FORMAT_DESCRIPTION_EVENT||

      get_type_code() == INCIDENT_EVENT;
  }
```

```
  enum enum_mts_event_exec_mode get_mts_execution_mode(ulong slave_server_id,
                                                       bool mts_in_group)
  {
    if ((get_type_code() == FORMAT_DESCRIPTION_EVENT &&
         ((server_id == (uint32) ::server_id) || (log_pos == 0))) ||
        (get_type_code() == ROTATE_EVENT &&
         ((server_id == (uint32) ::server_id) ||
          (log_pos == 0     /* very first fake Rotate (R_f) */
           && mts_in_group /* ignored event turned into R_f at slave stop */))))
      return EVENT_EXEC_ASYNC;
    else if (is_mts_sequential_exec())
      return EVENT_EXEC_SYNC;
    else
      return EVENT_EXEC_PARALLEL;
  }

  Slave_worker *get_slave_worker(Relay_log_info *rli);

  virtual List<char>* get_mts_dbs(MEM_ROOT *mem_root)
  {
    List<char> *res= new List<char>;
    res->push_back(strdup_root(mem_root, get_db()));
    return res;
  }

  virtual void set_mts_isolate_group()
  {
    DBUG_ASSERT(ends_group() ||
                get_type_code() == QUERY_EVENT ||
                get_type_code() == EXEC_LOAD_EVENT ||
                get_type_code() == EXECUTE_LOAD_QUERY_EVENT);
    flags |= LOG_EVENT_MTS_ISOLATE_F;
  }
public:

  bool contains_partition_info(bool);
  virtual uint8 mts_number_dbs() { return 1; }
  bool is_mts_group_isolated() { return flags & LOG_EVENT_MTS_ISOLATE_F; }
  virtual bool starts_group() { return FALSE; }
  virtual bool ends_group()   { return FALSE; }
  int apply_event(Relay_log_info *rli);
  int update_pos(Relay_log_info *rli)
  {
    return do_update_pos(rli);
  }
  enum_skip_reason shall_skip(Relay_log_info *rli)
  {
    return do_shall_skip(rli);
  }
```

```
  virtual int do_apply_event(Relay_log_info const *rli)
  {
    return 0;                      /* Default implementation does nothing */
  }
  virtual int do_apply_event_worker(Slave_worker *w);

protected:

  enum_skip_reason continue_group(Relay_log_info *rli);
  virtual int do_update_pos(Relay_log_info *rli);
  virtual enum_skip_reason do_shall_skip(Relay_log_info *rli);
#endif
};
```

First, notice the conditional compilation directives in this code. These are necessary because other portions of the greater MySQL source code use the log-event class. For example, the mysqlbinlog client application will compile against this code. Thus, there are portions marked specifically for use in a server (MYSQL_SERVER), portions marked for elimination if replication is not used (HAVE_REPLICATION).[3] Those sections where these directives are not met (the #else) are used when compiling the external code such as mysqlbinlog.

The class includes many helper functions, such as methods for getting the database for the event, creating and destroying an instance (new, delete), and more. Some of the more interesting helper methods are the write_*() methods. These are used to write the event (also known as serialization) to the binary log in conjunction with the pack_info() method that is responsible for embedding the payload the event.

Similarly, there are methods for reading the event from the binary log file. Notice the reoccurrence of the read_event() method. Several of these are located in this class. This is because, depending on where or how you are reading the event, you may need different forms of this method. Thus, this method is overloaded, and which is called depends on the context of the parameters. The one we are most interested in is the version that returns an instance of the event once it is read from the binary log. We will see this in action a little later in this section.

Last, the server uses the do_apply_event() to execute the event. Each log-event type has a specific implementation of this method—hence the need to make it and a number of other methods virtual.

Notice the other methods that are marked as virtual. When you examine the different log events, you will see the class implementation of those events is a lot smaller and generally includes only those methods marked as virtual here.

In the next section, I describe some types of log events and what each is designed to perform. This is followed by a brief look at the execution path of log events.

Types of Log Events

There are more than 30 log events defined for replicating commands from the master to the slave. It is likely that if you examine your binary logs or relay logs, you will not find all of these events. Indeed, some classes are defined for a specific format (SBR or RBR), and unless you used mixed binary-log format, you will not find both classes of events.

The basic staple of SBR events is the Query_log_event. This contains the SQL statement issued by the user on the master. When this event is applied, the SQL statement is executed as written. Any variables used by the query—including user-defined variables, random number, or time-related values—are written to the binary log prior to the Query_log_event and therefore executed on the slave before the query itself. This is how replication keeps items such as timestamps, random numbers, incremental columns, and similar special events or codes the same on the master and slave. For example, in the case of random numbers, the seed that was used on the master is transmitted to the slave, resulting in the RAND function returning the same values on the slave as the master.

---

[3]The HAVE_REPLICATION conditional compilation is used primarily for the embedded server.

The events for RBR are a little different. These use a base class, Rows_log_event to encapsulate the base functionality for all RBR events. Because the RBR events contain only the row images or the results of applying a query on the master, there are unique log events for each type. There are log events for inserts, updates (with a before image event), and deletes.

Of special note is the Incident_log_event. This event stores any unusual condition or state encountered on the master, such as an error generating an event, or another error, or warnings, ranging from minor to serious. This event was created so that should something extraordinary occur on the master, the slave, when it applies (executes) the event, can decide if the incident is serious enough to warrant stopping replication. When troubleshooting replication, examine the incident events for more details.

Table 8-3 shows a list of the more frequently encountered log events. I include a description of each along with the binary log format used where these events are likely to appear.

Table 8-3. *Important Log Event Types*

Event Type	Description	Format
Ignorable_log_event	Ignore the event on the slave and do not write it to the relay log for execution.	All
Incident_log_event	Records an extraordinary event, such as an error or warning that occurred on the master. Can result in the slave stopping replication. Examine these events when troubleshooting replication.	All
Intvar_log_event	Created prior to a Query_log_event to include any variables used by the query such as LAST_INSERT_ID.	SBR
User_var_log_event	Created prior to a Query_log_event to include any user variables defined and used by the query.	SBR
Query_log_event	The query issued by the user on the master.	SBR
Rand_log_event	Calculate or transport a random seed from the master.	SBR
Rotate_log_event	Initiate a rotate of the logs.	All
Rows_log_event	Base class for RBR events.	RBR
Write_rows_log_event	Includes one or more insert or update rows for a table.	RBR
Update_rows_log_event	Includes one or more row updates before image for the row.	RBR
Delete_rows_log_event	Includes row images for deletion.	RBR
Table_map_log_event	Informative event that contains information regarding the table currently being modified or acted on by the proceeding events. The information includes the database name, table name, and column definitions.	RBR
Unknown_log_event	Dummy event for catching events that are unknown or defined in later versions.	All

In the upcoming sections, we will be working with a new log event designed to embed information in the binary log for diagnostic purposes. This event is not pertinent to the slave, so we will create an event similar to the Ignorable_log_event.

Now that we have seen some of the more important event types, let us examine how events are executed on the slave.

Execution of Log Events

Log events are executed by the slave by first reading them from the relay log and instantiating the class instance. This is where the type of log event is paramount. The slave must know what type of log event it is reading. As you will see when we explore extending replication, each log event is assigned a special enumeration (code). This is how the slave knows which class to instantiate. The code that reads log events and instantiates them is located in rpl_slave.cc in the `Log_event::next_event()` method.

The method contains an endless loop whose job is to read an event, check for prerequisites, errors, and special commands to manage the relay log (such as purge and rotate), and instantiate the event.

Events are instantiated via the `Log_event::read_log_event()` method. This method will also conduct error checking (like checksum validation) before creating the event instance. The code is located near line number 1386 in `log_event.cc`. If you open that file and scroll down through the method, you will see the switch statement used to instantiate the events. Listing 8-6 shows an excerpt of the method highlighting the switch statement

Listing 8-6. Log_event::read_log_event() Method

```
Log_event* Log_event::read_log_event(const char* buf, uint event_len,
                                     const char **error,
                                      const Format_description_log_event *description_event,
                                      my_bool crc_check)
{
  Log_event* ev;
...

    if (alg != BINLOG_CHECKSUM_ALG_UNDEF &&
        (event_type == FORMAT_DESCRIPTION_EVENT ||
         alg != BINLOG_CHECKSUM_ALG_OFF))
      event_len= event_len - BINLOG_CHECKSUM_LEN;

    switch(event_type) {
    case QUERY_EVENT:
      ev  = new Query_log_event(buf, event_len, description_event,
                                QUERY_EVENT);
      break;
    case LOAD_EVENT:
      ev = new Load_log_event(buf, event_len, description_event);
      break;
    case NEW_LOAD_EVENT:
      ev = new Load_log_event(buf, event_len, description_event);
      break;
    case ROTATE_EVENT:
      ev = new Rotate_log_event(buf, event_len, description_event);
      break;
    case CREATE_FILE_EVENT:
      ev = new Create_file_log_event(buf, event_len, description_event);
      break;
    case APPEND_BLOCK_EVENT:
      ev = new Append_block_log_event(buf, event_len, description_event);
      break;
    case DELETE_FILE_EVENT:
      ev = new Delete_file_log_event(buf, event_len, description_event);
      break;
```

```
    case EXEC_LOAD_EVENT:
      ev = new Execute_load_log_event(buf, event_len, description_event);
      break;
    case START_EVENT_V3: /* this is sent only by MySQL <=4.x */
      ev = new Start_log_event_v3(buf, description_event);
      break;
    case STOP_EVENT:
      ev = new Stop_log_event(buf, description_event);
      break;
    case INTVAR_EVENT:
      ev = new Intvar_log_event(buf, description_event);
      break;
    case XID_EVENT:
      ev = new Xid_log_event(buf, description_event);
      break;
    case RAND_EVENT:
      ev = new Rand_log_event(buf, description_event);
      break;
    case USER_VAR_EVENT:
      ev = new User_var_log_event(buf, description_event);
      break;
    case FORMAT_DESCRIPTION_EVENT:
      ev = new Format_description_log_event(buf, event_len, description_event);
      break;
#if defined(HAVE_REPLICATION)
    case PRE_GA_WRITE_ROWS_EVENT:
      ev = new Write_rows_log_event_old(buf, event_len, description_event);
      break;
    case PRE_GA_UPDATE_ROWS_EVENT:
      ev = new Update_rows_log_event_old(buf, event_len, description_event);
      break;
    case PRE_GA_DELETE_ROWS_EVENT:
      ev = new Delete_rows_log_event_old(buf, event_len, description_event);
      break;
    case WRITE_ROWS_EVENT_V1:
      ev = new Write_rows_log_event(buf, event_len, description_event);
      break;
    case UPDATE_ROWS_EVENT_V1:
      ev = new Update_rows_log_event(buf, event_len, description_event);
      break;
    case DELETE_ROWS_EVENT_V1:
      ev = new Delete_rows_log_event(buf, event_len, description_event);
      break;
    case TABLE_MAP_EVENT:
      ev = new Table_map_log_event(buf, event_len, description_event);
      break;
#endif
    case BEGIN_LOAD_QUERY_EVENT:
      ev = new Begin_load_query_log_event(buf, event_len, description_event);
      break;
```

```
        case EXECUTE_LOAD_QUERY_EVENT:
          ev= new Execute_load_query_log_event(buf, event_len, description_event);
          break;
        case INCIDENT_EVENT:
          ev = new Incident_log_event(buf, event_len, description_event);
          break;
        case ROWS_QUERY_LOG_EVENT:
          ev= new Rows_query_log_event(buf, event_len, description_event);
          break;
        case SLAVE_CONNECT_LOG_EVENT:
          ev= new Slave_connect_log_event(buf, event_len, description_event);
          break;
        case GTID_LOG_EVENT:
        case ANONYMOUS_GTID_LOG_EVENT:
          ev= new Gtid_log_event(buf, event_len, description_event);
          break;
        case PREVIOUS_GTIDS_LOG_EVENT:
          ev= new Previous_gtids_log_event(buf, event_len, description_event);
          break;
#if defined(HAVE_REPLICATION)
        case WRITE_ROWS_EVENT:
          ev = new Write_rows_log_event(buf, event_len, description_event);
          break;
        case UPDATE_ROWS_EVENT:
          ev = new Update_rows_log_event(buf, event_len, description_event);
          break;
        case DELETE_ROWS_EVENT:
          ev = new Delete_rows_log_event(buf, event_len, description_event);
          break;
#endif
        default:
          /*
            Create an object of Ignorable_log_event for unrecognized sub-class.
            So that SLAVE SQL THREAD will only update the position and continue.
          */
          if (uint2korr(buf + FLAGS_OFFSET) & LOG_EVENT_IGNORABLE_F)
          {
            ev= new Ignorable_log_event(buf, description_event);
          }
          else
          {
            DBUG_PRINT("error",("Unknown event code: %d",
                              (int) buf[EVENT_TYPE_OFFSET]));
            ev= NULL;
          }
          break;
      }
  }
...
  DBUG_RETURN(ev);
}
```

Once the event is read, the slave code calls the `Log_event::apply_event()` method, which in turn calls the `*_log_event::do_apply_event()` for the log-event-class instance. This method is responsible for executing the event. As seen in a previous section, all log event classes have an `*_log_event::apply_event()` method. An example implementation of this event is shown in Listing 8-7 below. This shows the code that is executed when an `Intvar_log_event` is executed.

Listing 8-7. Example do_apply_event() Method

```
/*
  Intvar_log_event::do_apply_event()
*/

int Intvar_log_event::do_apply_event(Relay_log_info const *rli)
{
  /*
    We are now in a statement until the associated query log event has
    been processed.
  */
  const_cast<Relay_log_info*>(rli)->set_flag(Relay_log_info::IN_STMT);

  if (rli->deferred_events_collecting)
    return rli->deferred_events->add(this);

  switch (type) {
  case LAST_INSERT_ID_EVENT:
    thd->stmt_depends_on_first_successful_insert_id_in_prev_stmt= 1;
    thd->first_successful_insert_id_in_prev_stmt= val;
    break;
  case INSERT_ID_EVENT:
    thd->force_one_auto_inc_interval(val);
    break;
  }
  return 0;
}
```

Notice how the code is designed to manipulate attributes for auto-increment values. This is how the slave ensures that it sets auto-increment values correctly for the queries executed. This is primarily used for SBR because RBR contains an image of the resulting row from the master.

Now that we understand how log events are executed on the slave, now is a good time to roll up our sleeves and once again dive into the source code to conduct experiments on modifying the replication source code. The next sections show you some basic ways that you can extend replication to meet your unique high-availability needs.

Extending Replication

This section presents a number of example projects you can use to explore the MySQL replication source code. While some may consider the examples academic in nature, you may find them informative for using as templates for practical applications for your environment.

> ■ **Caution** Modifying the replication code should be taken very seriously. It is one of the most complex subsystems, as well as one of the most robust and reliable. Be sure that your modifications are sound. If your code introduces side effects—or, worse, causes the server to crash—the replicated data could become out of date or corrupt. It is best to plan your modifications carefully and test them extensively before attempting to use them in any production environment.

If the above caution scares, you that is good, because the replication subsystem is well designed, with a long history of solid stability. Clearly, if you want to use replication or are relying on replication for standby, backups, or high availability, it is reasonable to be cautious.

Do not let that stop you from exploring these examples. Indeed, sometimes the best way to learn about something is to break it first. If you have worked through the examples from the earlier chapters, you have probably already experienced this.

Now that the requisite admonishments have been stated, let's modify some code!

Global Slave Stop Command

I will start with a less complicated extension. Suppose that you have a replication topology with many slaves, and there arises a time when you need to stop replication. In this case, you must visit each slave and issue the STOP SLAVE command. Wouldn't it be a lot easier to have a command on the master that you can use to tell all of the slaves to stop replication?

That is not to say there isn't a way to do this—there are several. You could lock all of the tables on the master, thereby stopping the flow of events. You could also turn off the binary log, but this could cause the slaves to throw an error.

Visiting each slave still may not be enough, however. Consider for a moment an active master that is continuously receiving updates from clients. Consider also that it is unlikely one could issue the STOP SLAVE command to every slave at the same time. You would still need to stop the replication of events on the master before visiting each slave.

If there were a command on the master that is replicated to each slave at the same time, it would ensure that the slaves are all stopped at the same point in the replication process.

Thus, if there were a SQL command—say, STOP ALL SLAVES—that replicated the STOP SLAVE command to all slaves, you could be sure that all slaves are stopped at the same time. Let's see how we can go about making such a command.

Code Modifications

This extension requires modifying the parser and adding the case statement for the big switch in sql_parse.cc. Table 8-4 includes a list of the files that need to be modified.

Table 8-4. *Files Changed for STOP ALL SLAVES Command*

File	Summary of Changes
sql/lex.h	Add the new symbols for the new command
sql/sql_cmd.h	Add new enumerations
sql/sql_yacc.yy	Add new parser rules for new command
sql/sql_parse.cc	Add new case for the big switch to send the SLAVE STOP command

Now that we know what files need to change, let's dive into the modifications. First, open the `sql/lex.h` file and add the following code. We are adding the new symbol for the command. This file contains the symbol array stored in alphabetical order. Thus, we will add the SLAVES symbol near line number 523. Listing 8-8 depicts the modifications in context.

Listing 8-8. Adding SLAVES Symbol to sql/lex.h

```
{ "SIGNED",              SYM(SIGNED_SYM)},
{ "SIMPLE",              SYM(SIMPLE_SYM)},
{ "SLAVE",             SYM(SLAVE)},
/* BEGIN CAB MODIFICATION */
/* Reason for Modification: */
/* Add SLAVES keyword */
{ "SLAVES",           SYM(SLAVES)},
/* END CAB MODIFICATION */
{ "SLOW",             SYM(SLOW)},
{ "SNAPSHOT",           SYM(SNAPSHOT_SYM)},
{ "SMALLINT",            SYM(SMALLINT)},
```

Next, we need to modify the sql_cmd.h file to add a new enumeration for the big switch. Open the sql_cmd.h file and locate the enum enum_sql_command definition near the top of the file. Listing 8-9 shows the code to add a new enumeration for the new command.

Listing 8-9. Adding the Enumeration for the STOP ALL SLAVES Command

```
SQLCOM_FLUSH, SQLCOM_KILL, SQLCOM_ANALYZE,
SQLCOM_ROLLBACK, SQLCOM_ROLLBACK_TO_SAVEPOINT,
SQLCOM_COMMIT, SQLCOM_SAVEPOINT, SQLCOM_RELEASE_SAVEPOINT,
/* BEGIN CAB MODIFICATION */
/* Reason for Modification: */
/* Add SQLCOM_STOP_SLAVES enum */
SQLCOM_SLAVE_START, SQLCOM_SLAVE_STOP, SQLCOM_STOP_SLAVES,
/* END CAB MODIFICATION */
SQLCOM_BEGIN, SQLCOM_CHANGE_MASTER,
SQLCOM_RENAME_TABLE,
SQLCOM_RESET, SQLCOM_PURGE, SQLCOM_PURGE_BEFORE, SQLCOM_SHOW_BINLOGS,
```

Next we need to add a new token to be used in the new rule. Once again, the list of tokens is arranged in alphabetical order. Open the sql_yacc.yy file and locate the section where new tokens are defined. In this case, we need to add a definition for a token for the new command. We will name it SLAVES. Listing 8-10 shows the code in context to be added. You can find this code near line number 1497.

Listing 8-10. Adding the Tokens

```
%token  SIGNED_SYM
%token  SIMPLE_SYM                   /* SQL-2003-N */
%token  SLAVE
/* BEGIN CAB MODIFICATION */
/* Reason for Modification: */
/* Add SLAVES token */
%token  SLAVES
/* END CAB MODIFICATION */
```

```
%token  SLOW
%token  SMALLINT                        /* SQL-2003-R */
%token  SNAPSHOT_SYM
```

Next, modify the section where the %type <NONE> definition resides. We need to add the new token to this definition. You can find this section near line number 1813. Listing 8-11 shows the code in context.

Listing 8-11. Adding the Token to the Type None Definition

```
/* BEGIN CAB MODIFICATION */
/* Reason for Modification: */
/* Add stop to list of NONE types */
    repair analyze check start stop checksum
/* END CAB MODIFICATION */
        field_list field_list_item field_spec kill column_def key_def
        keycache_list keycache_list_or_parts assign_to_keycache
        assign_to_keycache_parts
```

...

We're almost done. Next, we add a new command definition to the list of commands so that the parser can direct control to the new rule. Once again, this list is in alphabetical order. You can find the location to be modified around line number 2035. Listing 8-12 shows the modification. Notice we add a new 'or' condition mapping to a new rule to be evaluated. In this case, we name the rule stop.

Listing 8-12. Adding a New Rule Definition

```
        | show
        | slave
        | start
/* BEGIN CAB MODIFICATION */
/* Reason for Modification: */
/* Add stop to list of statement targets */
        | stop
/* END CAB MODIFICATION */
        | truncate
        | uninstall
        | unlock
```

Last, we will add the new rule to process the STOP ALL SLAVES command. I place this code near the existing start rule around line 8027. Listing 8-13 shows the new rule. The rule simply saves the new enumeration to the lex->sql_command attribute. This is how the code maps the result of the rule (and the processing of the command) to the big switch to a case equal to the enumeration value.

Listing 8-13. Adding the STOP ALL SLAVES Rule to the Parser

```
}
    ;

/* BEGIN CAB MODIFICATION */
/* Reason for Modification: */
```

```
/* Add rule for STOP ALL SLAVES command */
stop:
        STOP_SYM ALL SLAVES
        {
          LEX *lex= Lex;
          lex->sql_command= SQLCOM_STOP_SLAVES;
        }
        ;
/* END CAB MODIFICATION */
```

```
start:
        START_SYM TRANSACTION_SYM opt_start_transaction_option_list
        {
```

With the changes to the YACC file complete, we can add a new case for the big switch to ensure the command, once captured by the parser, is directed to code to written the event to the binary log. Normally, the STOP SLAVE command is not replicated. Our code would also need to override this restriction. Let us add that case statement. Open the sql_parse.cc file and locate the section with the replication statements. This is near line number 3054. Listing 8-14 shows the new case statement.

Listing 8-14. Adding the Case for the Big Switch

```
mysql_mutex_unlock(&LOCK_active_mi);
  break;
}

/* BEGIN CAB MODIFICATION */
/* Reason for Modification: */
/* Add case statement for STOP ALL SLAVES command */
case SQLCOM_STOP_SLAVES:
{
  if (!lex->no_write_to_binlog)
    res= write_bin_log(thd, TRUE, "STOP SLAVE IO_THREAD", 20);
 break;
}
/* END CAB MODIFICATION */

#endif /* HAVE_REPLICATION */

case SQLCOM_RENAME_TABLE:
```

Take a moment to examine this code. The first statement is designed to check to see if the server is able to write to the binary log. If so, we add a new log event, passing it the STOP SLAVE SQL command. Notice that we use a specific version of the STOP SLAVE command. In this case, we are stopping only the IO thread. This is for two reasons. First, we need only stop the IO thread to stop replicating events to the slave. This would still permit the slave to process any events read from the master to this point (as done by the SQL thread). Second, the STOP SLAVE command is more complicated in that it stops both threads, and in doing so, it has several critical sections that need to be protected by mutexes. Executing a STOP SLAVE command in the middle of executing a log event (the log event itself is the STOP SLAVE) will lead to conflicts with the mutexes. Thus, stopping only the IO thread is the only way to successfully execute the command on the slave.

Compiling the Code

To compile the new code, simply execute make from the root of the source tree. Since there are no new files or changes to the cmake files, we only need to rebuild the executables. If there are errors, go back and fix them until the server code compiles successfully.

Example Execution

Execution of the global slave-stop command requires a replication topology with at least one slave. To illustrate how well the command works, I will create a topology that uses three slaves.

The first step is to set up a simple replication topology. Rather than go through all the steps outlined above to set up the master and slave, I use the MySQL Utilities commands to quickly set up my test conditions.

I begin by cloning an instance of a running server once for the master and once for each slave. The utility, mysqlserverclone, is designed to create a new instance of either a downed or a running slave. We simply connect to the server using the server option, pass in any options for the new server (mysqld), and define a new data directory, port, and server_id. Listing 8-15 shows the results of these steps.

Listing 8-15. Setting up a Simple Replication Topology

```
cbell@ubuntu:$ mysqlserverclone.py --basedir=/source/mysql-5.6 \
  --mysqld="--log-bin=mysql-bin"  --new-port=3310 –new-data=/source/temp_3310 \
  --new-id=100 --delete-data
# WARNING: Root password for new instance has not been set.
# Cloning the MySQL server located at /source/mysql-5.6.
# Creating new data directory...
# Configuring new instance...
# Locating mysql tools...
# Setting up empty database and mysql tables...
# Starting new instance of the server...
# Testing connection to new instance...
# Success!
# Connection Information:
#  -uroot --socket=/source/temp_3310/mysql.sock
#...done.

cbell@ubuntu:$ mysqlserverclone.py --basedir=/source/mysql-5.6 \
  --mysqld="--log-bin=mysql-bin --report-port=3311 --report-host=localhost" \
  --new-port=3311 –new-data=/source/temp_3311 \
  --new-id=101 --delete-data
# WARNING: Root password for new instance has not been set.
# Cloning the MySQL server located at /source/mysql-5.6.
# Creating new data directory...
# Configuring new instance...
# Locating mysql tools...
# Setting up empty database and mysql tables...
# Starting new instance of the server...
# Testing connection to new instance...
# Success!
# Connection Information:
#  -uroot --socket=/home/cbell/source/temp_3311/mysql.sock
#...done.
```

```
cbell@ubuntu:$ mysqlserverclone.py --basedir=/source/mysql-5.6 \
   --mysqld="--log-bin=mysql-bin --report-port=3312 --report-host=localhost" \
   --new-port=3312 -new-data=/source/temp_3312 \
   --new-id=102 --delete-data
# WARNING: Root password for new instance has not been set.
# Cloning the MySQL server located at /source/mysql-5.6.
# Creating new data directory...
# Configuring new instance...
# Locating mysql tools...
# Setting up empty database and mysql tables...
# Starting new instance of the server...
# Testing connection to new instance...
# Success!
# Connection Information:
#   -uroot --socket=/home/cbell/source/temp_3311/mysql.sock
#...done.

cbell@ubuntu:$ mysqlserverclone.py --basedir=/source/mysql-5.6 \
   --mysqld="--log-bin=mysql-bin --report-port=3313 --report-host=localhost" \
   --new-port=3313 -new-data=/source/temp_3313 \
   --new-id=103 --delete-data
# WARNING: Root password for new instance has not been set.
# Cloning the MySQL server located at /source/mysql-5.6.
# Creating new data directory...
# Configuring new instance...
# Locating mysql tools...
# Setting up empty database and mysql tables...
# Starting new instance of the server...
# Testing connection to new instance...
# Success!
# Connection Information:
#   -uroot --socket=/home/cbell/source/temp_3311/mysql.sock
#...done.
```

Once we have the master and slaves running, we then set up replication between the master and each slave. The utility, mysqlreplicate, makes connecting a slave to a master one step. Listing 8-16 shows the results. Notice that the utility simply requires a connection to the master and a connection to the slave.

Listing 8-16. Setting up Replication

```
cbell@ubuntu:$ mysqlreplicate.py --master=root@localhost:3310 \
   --slave=root@localhost:3311
# master on localhost: ... connected.
# slave on localhost: ... connected.
# Checking for binary logging on master...
# Setting up replication...
# ...done.

cbell@ubuntu:$ mysqlreplicate.py --master=root@localhost:3310 \
   --slave=root@localhost:3312
```

```
# master on localhost: ... connected.
# slave on localhost: ... connected.
# Checking for binary logging on master...
# Setting up replication...
# ...done.

cbell@ubuntu:$ mysqlreplicate.py --master=root@localhost:3310 \
  --slave=root@localhost:3313
# master on localhost: ... connected.
# slave on localhost: ... connected.
# Checking for binary logging on master...
# Setting up replication...
# ...done.
```

WHAT ARE MYSQL UTILITIES?

MySQL Utilities is a subproject of the MySQL Workbench tool. MySQL Utilities contains a number of helpful command-line tools for managing MySQL servers with emphasis on replication.

When you download Workbench, you will also get MySQL Utilities. You can access the utilities via the plugin in Workbench. You can also download MySQL Utilities directly from Launchpad.

MySQL Workbench download: `http://dev.mysql.com/downloads/workbench/5.2.html`

MySQL Utilities download from Launchpad: `https://launchpad.net/mysql-utilities`

For more information about MySQL Utilities, see the online documentation:

`http://dev.mysql.com/doc/workbench/en/mysql-utilities.html`

Let us review the setup thus far. The commands above allow me to create a running instance of a server from a source-code tree (specified by `--basedir`), passing it parameters such as the port to use and the location of its data directory. The mysqlserverclone utility will do all of the work for me and then tell me how to connect to the server. I do this twice: once for the master and once for the slave, using different ports and data directories. I then use the automated-replication setup utility, `mysqlreplicate`, to set up replication between the master and three slaves. Notice that I set the `--report-port` and `--report-host` for each slave in the `--mysqld` option. This option allows you to specify options for server startup.

As you can see, this is very easy and very quick to set up. You can even put these commands in a script so that you can create the test topology at any time.

Now that we have our test topology, let's check the status of each slave's IO thread and then issue the command and check the status again. The first step is to see a list of the slaves attached to the master. For this, I use the mysqlrplshow command. Listing 8-17 shows the output of this command; it prints a nice graph of our topology. While we are at it, we also show the slave status for each slave to ensure that each is actively replicating data from the master. I include excerpts of the output for brevity.

Listing 8-17. Checking the Topology

```
cbell@ubuntu:$ mysqlrplshow.py --master=root@localhost:3310
# master on localhost: ... connected.
# Finding slaves for master: localhost:3310

# Replication Topology Graph
localhost:3310 (MASTER)
```

```
     |
     +--- localhost:3311 - (SLAVE)
     |
     +--- localhost:3312 - (SLAVE)
     |
     +--- localhost:3313 - (SLAVE)
```

```
cbell@ubuntu: $ mysql -uroot -h 127.0.0.1 --port=3311
Welcome to the MySQL monitor.  Commands end with ; or \g.
Your MySQL connection id is 5
Server version: 5.6.6-m9-log Source distribution

Copyright (c) 2000, 2011, Oracle and/or its affiliates. All rights reserved.

Oracle is a registered trademark of Oracle Corporation and/or its
affiliates. Other names may be trademarks of their respective
owners.

Type 'help;' or '\h' for help. Type '\c' to clear the current input statement.

mysql> SHOW SLAVE STATUS \G
*************************** 1. row ***************************
               Slave_IO_State: Waiting for master to send event
                  Master_Host: localhost
                  Master_User: rpl
                  Master_Port: 3310
                Connect_Retry: 60
              Master_Log_File: mysql-bin.000001
          Read_Master_Log_Pos: 325
               Relay_Log_File: clone-relay-bin.000002
                Relay_Log_Pos: 283
        Relay_Master_Log_File: mysql-bin.000001
             Slave_IO_Running: Yes
            Slave_SQL_Running: Yes
...
1 row in set (0.00 sec)

cbell@ubuntu: $ mysql -uroot -h 127.0.0.1 --port=3312
Welcome to the MySQL monitor.  Commands end with ; or \g.
Your MySQL connection id is 3
Server version: 5.6.6-m9-log Source distribution

Copyright (c) 2000, 2011, Oracle and/or its affiliates. All rights reserved.

Oracle is a registered trademark of Oracle Corporation and/or its
affiliates. Other names may be trademarks of their respective
owners.

Type 'help;' or '\h' for help. Type '\c' to clear the current input statement.
```

```
mysql> SHOW SLAVE STATUS \G
*************************** 1. row ***************************
               Slave_IO_State: Waiting for master to send event
                  Master_Host: localhost
                  Master_User: rpl
                  Master_Port: 3310
                Connect_Retry: 60
              Master_Log_File: mysql-bin.000001
          Read_Master_Log_Pos: 325
               Relay_Log_File: clone-relay-bin.000002
                Relay_Log_Pos: 283
        Relay_Master_Log_File: mysql-bin.000001
             Slave_IO_Running: Yes
            Slave_SQL_Running: Yes
...
1 row in set (0.00 sec)

cbell@ubuntu: $ mysql -uroot -h 127.0.0.1 --port=3313
Welcome to the MySQL monitor.  Commands end with ; or \g.
Your MySQL connection id is 2
Server version: 5.6.6-m9-log Source distribution

Copyright (c) 2000, 2011, Oracle and/or its affiliates. All rights reserved.

Oracle is a registered trademark of Oracle Corporation and/or its
affiliates. Other names may be trademarks of their respective
owners.

Type 'help;' or '\h' for help. Type '\c' to clear the current input statement.

mysql> SHOW SLAVE STATUS \G
*************************** 1. row ***************************
               Slave_IO_State: Waiting for master to send event
                  Master_Host: localhost
                  Master_User: rpl
                  Master_Port: 3310
                Connect_Retry: 60
              Master_Log_File: mysql-bin.000001
          Read_Master_Log_Pos: 325
               Relay_Log_File: clone-relay-bin.000002
                Relay_Log_Pos: 283
        Relay_Master_Log_File: mysql-bin.000001
             Slave_IO_Running: Yes
            Slave_SQL_Running: Yes
...
1 row in set (0.00 sec)
```

Now that we have set up the new topology and verified that all is well, we can test the new STOP ALL SLAVES command. Listing 8-18 shows the results.

Listing 8-18. Demonstration of the STOP ALL SLAVES Command

```
cbell@ubuntu$ mysql -uroot -h 127.0.0.1 --port=3310
Welcome to the MySQL monitor.  Commands end with ; or \g.
Your MySQL connection id is 10
Server version: 5.6.6-m9-log Source distribution

Copyright (c) 2000, 2011, Oracle and/or its affiliates. All rights reserved.

Oracle is a registered trademark of Oracle Corporation and/or its
affiliates. Other names may be trademarks of their respective
owners.

Type 'help;' or '\h' for help. Type '\c' to clear the current input statement.

mysql> STOP ALL SLAVES;
Query OK, 0 rows affected (0.00 sec)
```

You may be thinking, "Is that it?" For the master, it is. Nothing happens, because (recall the code for the big switch) we only write the command to the binary log. Nothing else is done on the master, and it keeps executing without interruption.

The desired effect, of course, is for the slaves to stop. Let us check the slave status on the slaves to see if this indeed has occurred. Remember, we are stopping the IO thread, so we should look for that in the slave-status output. Listing 8-19 shows the output of each slave status excerpted for brevity. Notice that in each case the slaves IO thread has indeed stopped (Slave_IO_Running = No).

Listing 8-19. Result of the STOP ALL SLAVES Command on the Slaves

```
cbell@ubuntu: $ mysql -uroot -h 127.0.0.1 --port=3311
Welcome to the MySQL monitor.  Commands end with ; or \g.
Your MySQL connection id is 6
Server version: 5.6.6-m9-log Source distribution

Copyright (c) 2000, 2011, Oracle and/or its affiliates. All rights reserved.

Oracle is a registered trademark of Oracle Corporation and/or its
affiliates. Other names may be trademarks of their respective
owners.

Type 'help;' or '\h' for help. Type '\c' to clear the current input statement.

mysql> SHOW SLAVE STATUS \G
*************************** 1. row ***************************
               Slave_IO_State:
                  Master_Host: localhost
                  Master_User: rpl
                  Master_Port: 3310
                Connect_Retry: 60
              Master_Log_File: mysql-bin.000001
          Read_Master_Log_Pos: 408
               Relay_Log_File: clone-relay-bin.000002
                Relay_Log_Pos: 366
```

```
         Relay_Master_Log_File: mysql-bin.000001
               Slave_IO_Running: No
              Slave_SQL_Running: Yes
...
1 row in set (0.00 sec)

cbell@ubuntu: $ mysql -uroot -h 127.0.0.1 --port=3312
Welcome to the MySQL monitor.  Commands end with ; or \g.
Your MySQL connection id is 6
Server version: 5.6.6-m9-log Source distribution

Copyright (c) 2000, 2011, Oracle and/or its affiliates. All rights reserved.

Oracle is a registered trademark of Oracle Corporation and/or its
affiliates. Other names may be trademarks of their respective
owners.

Type 'help;' or '\h' for help. Type '\c' to clear the current input statement.

mysql> SHOW SLAVE STATUS \G
*************************** 1. row ***************************
               Slave_IO_State:
                  Master_Host: localhost
                  Master_User: rpl
                  Master_Port: 3310
                Connect_Retry: 60
              Master_Log_File: mysql-bin.000001
          Read_Master_Log_Pos: 408
               Relay_Log_File: clone-relay-bin.000002
                Relay_Log_Pos: 366
        Relay_Master_Log_File: mysql-bin.000001
             Slave_IO_Running: No
            Slave_SQL_Running: Yes
...
1 row in set (0.00 sec)

cbell@ubuntu: $ mysql -uroot -h 127.0.0.1 --port=3313
Welcome to the MySQL monitor.  Commands end with ; or \g.
Your MySQL connection id is 6
Server version: 5.6.6-m9-log Source distribution

Copyright (c) 2000, 2011, Oracle and/or its affiliates. All rights reserved.

Oracle is a registered trademark of Oracle Corporation and/or its
affiliates. Other names may be trademarks of their respective
owners.
Type 'help;' or '\h' for help. Type '\c' to clear the current input statement.
```

```
mysql> SHOW SLAVE STATUS \G
*************************** 1. row ***************************
               Slave_IO_State:
                  Master_Host: localhost
                  Master_User: rpl
                  Master_Port: 3310
                Connect_Retry: 60
              Master_Log_File: mysql-bin.000001
          Read_Master_Log_Pos: 408
               Relay_Log_File: clone-relay-bin.000002
                Relay_Log_Pos: 366
        Relay_Master_Log_File: mysql-bin.000001
             Slave_IO_Running: No
            Slave_SQL_Running: Yes
...
1 row in set (0.00 sec)
```

This example demonstrates how to create a unique replication command that can be executed on the master and sent to all of the slaves for the purpose of stopping the flow of replication events. As you can see, this extension is easy to add and shows the power of the binary log events. If you use your imagination, you can think of other useful commands that you may want to send to all of your slaves.

In the next example, the difficultly level increases considerably. I show you how to create a new log event that records information in the binary log. In this case, we create a new log event that documents when a slave connects to the master. This could be useful if you need to determine when or if a new slave joined the topology.

Slave Connect Logging

Savvy administrators know to check replication topologies periodically for errors. This can range from checking the result of SHOW SLAVE STATUS and examining the values for errors, slave lag, and similar events. Administrators who encounter errors or who have to diagnose replication problems are missing a key data point. Replication in large topologies with many slaves that are brought online for scale out may be taken offline. This process may occur several times a week, and in some cases, it may occur multiple times a day. Administrators of smaller or even medium replication topologies might keep a log (at least mentally) when slaves are connected and disconnected, but this may not be possible for larger replication topologies. In that case, it may be impossible to determine when a slave was connected to a master, just that a slave is connected to the master.

In the case of diagnosing and repairing replication, it helps to know when a slave was connected in order to map the timing of that event to other events that occurred at the same time. Perhaps the events are related. If you don't know when the slave connected to the master, you may never know.

In this section, we create a new log event that records when a slave connects to a master. This is written to the binary log as a permanent entry. While it is also sent to the slaves, we make the event an ignorable event that permits the slaves to skip the event. The slaves, therefore, will take no action and will not write the event to its relay log, nor will they write the event to their binary logs, if binary logging is engaged.

Let us begin by reviewing the source files that need to be modified. While the event itself is simplistic in design and purpose, the code needed to create the new event is extensive and dispersed throughout the replication source files. As you will see, there are a number of places where an event gets processed in both the master and slave.

Code Modifications

This extension will require modifying a number of the replication source files. Table 8-5 includes a list of the files that need to be modified. All these files are located in the /sql folder.

Table 8-5. *Files Changed for Slave Connect Event*

File	Summary of Changes
log_event.h	New Slave_connect_log_event class declaration
log_event.cc	New Slave_connect_log_event class definition
binlog.h	New MYSQL_BIN_LOG::write_slave_connect() method declaration
binlog.cc	New MYSQL_BIN_LOG::write_slave_connect() definition
rpl_master.cc	Modifications to register_slave() to call write_slave_connect()
rpl_rli.h	Add reference to Slave_connect_log_event class
rpl_rli.cc	Add code to delete Slave_connect_log_event class to discard it
rpl_rli_pdb.cc	Add code to delete Slave_connect_log_event class to discard it
rpl_slave.cc	Add code to delete Slave_connect_log_event class to discard it
sql_binlog.cc	Add code to delete Slave_connect_log_event class to discard it

The list of modifications may seem daunting at first glance. Fortunately, most source files require small changes. The major effort is creating the new log-event class and connecting it to the register_slave() method for the master. To make it easier, and to keep the same general isolation as the server code (the main source files for the server), do not create log events directly; instead use a method defined in the MYSQL_BIN_LOG class. I will create a new method to do just that.

There are several places in the source code where we need to discard the new event. We mirror the Rows_query_log_event action so that we can be sure to cover all cases in which the event needs to be ignored and deleted.

Now that we know what files need to change, let's dive into the modifications. We start with the new log event. Open the log_event.h file located in the ./sql folder. First, add a new enumeration for the new event to the enum Log_event_type list. We need to add the enumeration to the end of the list prior to the ENUM_END_EVENT marker. Name the new entry SLAVE_CONNECT_LOG_EVENT and assign it the next value in the list. Listing 8-20 shows the modification in context.

■ **Tip** This is a standard mechanism seen in most enumerated lists in the source code. The use of an end marker allows for loop constricts as well as out of bounds checking.

Listing 8-20. Adding a New Enumeration for the New Event in log_event.h

```
enum Log_event_type
{
  /*
    Every time you update this enum (when you add a type), you have to
    fix Format_description_log_event::Format_description_log_event().
  */
  UNKNOWN_EVENT= 0,
  START_EVENT_V3= 1,
  QUERY_EVENT= 2,
  STOP_EVENT= 3,
  ROTATE_EVENT= 4,
```

```
  INTVAR_EVENT= 5,
  LOAD_EVENT= 6,

...

/* BEGIN CAB MODIFICATION */
/* Reason for Modification: */
/* Add new log event enumeration */
  SLAVE_CONNECT_LOG_EVENT= 36,
/* END CAB MODIFICATION */
  ENUM_END_EVENT /* end marker */
};
```

Also in the log_event.h file, we need to add a new class declaration for the new event. Name the event Slave_connect_log_event and derive it from the Log_event base class. Add this code to the section of the file that contains declarations for the other log-event classes.

You can copy any of the other log-event declarations and change the name according. Be careful if you use search and replace, because you don't want to change the original log event. Listing 8-21 shows the completed class declaration. I describe each element in more detail later in this section.

Listing 8-21. The Slave_connect_log_event Class Declaration in log_event.h

```
/* BEGIN CAB MODIFICATION */
/* Reason for Modification: */
/* Add new log event class declaration */
class Slave_connect_log_event : public Log_event {
public:
#ifndef MYSQL_CLIENT
  Slave_connect_log_event(THD *thd_arg, const char * query, ulong query_len)
      : Log_event(thd_arg, LOG_EVENT_IGNORABLE_F,
                  Log_event::EVENT_STMT_CACHE,
                  Log_event::EVENT_IMMEDIATE_LOGGING)
  {
    DBUG_ENTER("Slave_connect_log_event::Slave_connect_log_event");
    if (!(m_slave_connect= (char*) my_malloc(query_len + 1, MYF(MY_WME))))
      return;
    my_snprintf(m_slave_connect, query_len + 1, "%s", query);
    DBUG_PRINT("enter", ("%s", m_slave_connect));
    DBUG_VOID_RETURN;
  }
#endif

#ifndef MYSQL_CLIENT
  int pack_info(Protocol*);
#endif

  Slave_connect_log_event(const char *buf, uint event_len,
                          const Format_description_log_event *descr_event);

  virtual ~Slave_connect_log_event();
  bool is_valid() const { return 1; }
```

```
#ifdef MYSQL_CLIENT
  virtual void print(FILE *file, PRINT_EVENT_INFO *print_event_info);
#endif
  virtual bool write_data_body(IO_CACHE *file);

  virtual Log_event_type get_type_code() { return SLAVE_CONNECT_LOG_EVENT; }

  virtual int get_data_size()
  {
    return IGNORABLE_HEADER_LEN + 1 + (uint) strlen(m_slave_connect);
  }
#if defined(MYSQL_SERVER) && defined(HAVE_REPLICATION)
  virtual int do_apply_event(Relay_log_info const *rli);
#endif

private:

  char *m_slave_connect;
};
/* END CAB MODIFICATION */
```

Notice that some portions are protected with conditional compilation flags. This is because this code is shared with other parts of the server source code. For example, it is used in the mysqlbinlog client tool. Clearly, some of the code is not needed for that application. Thus, we mask out the portions that are not needed with conditional compilation.

I want to call your attention to a very important, but obscure, flag. Notice the LOG_EVENT_IGNORABLE_F flag is the second argument to the base-class constructor. As evident by its name, this flag is what tells the server to ignore the event. The binary-log and relay-log code are designed to ignore any event with this flag. This means that we need only handle the normal methods for writing to the binary log (and printing events). In a number of places, we must also add code to skip destroying the event instance, but fortunately, we have a model to follow. I describe these later in this section.

At the bottom of the class declaration, I placed a pointer to contain the message that will be added to the log event as the payload. The key methods that need to be defined in the class include the constructor and destructor, pack_info(), print(), write_body(), and apply_event(). Most remaining methods are self-explanatory. Notice the get_type_code() and get_data_size() methods. I will explain each of these when we add the code to the log_event.cc file.

Now that we have the class declaration, open the log_event.cc file located in the ./sql folder. First, locate the Log_event::get_type_str() method and add a new case statement for the Slave_connect_log_event. The case statement uses the enumeration we created earlier. This method is used in various places to describe the event in views such as SHOW BINLOG EVENTS. Listing 8-22 shows the change in context. This code is located near line number 686.

Listing 8-22. Case Statement for Log_event::get_type_str() in log_event.cc

```
  case INCIDENT_EVENT: return "Incident";
  case IGNORABLE_LOG_EVENT: return "Ignorable";
  case ROWS_QUERY_LOG_EVENT: return "Rows_query";
/* BEGIN CAB MODIFICATION */
/* Reason for Modification: */
/* Add case to return name of new log event */
  case SLAVE_CONNECT_LOG_EVENT: return "Slave_connect";
/* END CAB MODIFICATION */
  case WRITE_ROWS_EVENT: return "Write_rows";
  case UPDATE_ROWS_EVENT: return "Update_rows";
  case DELETE_ROWS_EVENT: return "Delete_rows";
```

We also need to add a case statement for the new event to the Log_event::read_log_event(). This method is responsible for creating a new event. It also uses the new enumeration defined earlier. Add a new case statement to create a new instance of the Slave_connect_log_event class. Listing 8-23 shows the changes in context. This code is located near line number 1579. Notice that except for the class name, it is the same code as other events.

Listing 8-23. Case Statement for Log_event::read_log_event() in log_event.cc

```
      case ROWS_QUERY_LOG_EVENT:
        ev= new Rows_query_log_event(buf, event_len, description_event);
        break;
/* BEGIN CAB MODIFICATION */
/* Reason for Modification: */
/* Add case to create new log event */
      case SLAVE_CONNECT_LOG_EVENT:
        ev= new Slave_connect_log_event(buf, event_len, description_event);
        break;
/* END CAB MODIFICATION */
      case GTID_LOG_EVENT:
      case ANONYMOUS_GTID_LOG_EVENT:
```

One more method needs modification. The Format_description_log_event() returns the header length for each log event. In this case, we need to return the header length for the new log event. Listing 8-24 shows this code in context. This code is located near line number 5183. In this case, we return the length of the ignorable log event header already defined in the code.

Listing 8-24. New lookup for Format_description_log_event() in log_event.cc

```
      post_header_len[HEARTBEAT_LOG_EVENT-1]= 0;
      post_header_len[IGNORABLE_LOG_EVENT-1]= IGNORABLE_HEADER_LEN;
      post_header_len[ROWS_QUERY_LOG_EVENT-1]= IGNORABLE_HEADER_LEN;
/* BEGIN CAB MODIFICATION */
/* Reason for Modification: */
/* Return header length for the new log event */
      post_header_len[SLAVE_CONNECT_LOG_EVENT-1]= IGNORABLE_HEADER_LEN;
/* END CAB MODIFICATION */
      post_header_len[WRITE_ROWS_EVENT-1]=  ROWS_HEADER_LEN_V2;
      post_header_len[UPDATE_ROWS_EVENT-1]= ROWS_HEADER_LEN_V2;
      post_header_len[DELETE_ROWS_EVENT-1]= ROWS_HEADER_LEN_V2;
```

Now we can add the code for the class methods themselves. I list all of the code in Listing 8-25 and then explain each method.

Listing 8-25. The Slave_connect_log_event Methods in log_event.cc

```
/* BEGIN CAB MODIFICATION */
/* Reason for Modification: */
/* Class method definitions for the new log event */
Slave_connect_log_event::Slave_connect_log_event(const char *buf,
                              uint event_len,
                              const Format_description_log_event *descr_event)
  : Log_event(buf, descr_event)
```

```
{
  DBUG_ENTER("Slave_connect_log_event::Slave_connect_log_event");
  uint8 const common_header_len= descr_event->common_header_len;
  uint8 const post_header_len=
    descr_event->post_header_len[SLAVE_CONNECT_LOG_EVENT-1];

  DBUG_PRINT("info",
             ("event_len: %u; common_header_len: %d; post_header_len: %d",
                  event_len, common_header_len, post_header_len));

  /*
   m_slave_connect length is stored using only one byte, but that length is
   ignored and the complete query is read.
  */
  int offset= common_header_len  post_header_len  1;
  int len= event_len - offset;
  if (!(m_slave_connect= (char*) my_malloc(len1, MYF(MY_WME))))
    return;
  strmake(m_slave_connect, buf  offset, len);
  DBUG_PRINT("info", ("m_slave_connect: %s", m_slave_connect));
  DBUG_VOID_RETURN;
}

Slave_connect_log_event::~Slave_connect_log_event()
{
  my_free(m_slave_connect);
}

#ifndef MYSQL_CLIENT
int Slave_connect_log_event::pack_info(Protocol *protocol)
{
  char *buf;
  size_t bytes;
  ulong len= sizeof("# SLAVE_CONNECT = ")  (ulong) strlen(m_slave_connect);
  if (!(buf= (char*) my_malloc(len, MYF(MY_WME))))
    return 1;
  bytes= my_snprintf(buf, len, "# SLAVE_CONNECT = %s", m_slave_connect);
  protocol->store(buf, bytes, &my_charset_bin);
  my_free(buf);
  return 0;
}
#endif

#ifdef MYSQL_CLIENT
void
Slave_connect_log_event::print(FILE *file,
                               PRINT_EVENT_INFO *print_event_info)
{
  IO_CACHE *const head= &print_event_info->head_cache;
  IO_CACHE *const body= &print_event_info->body_cache;
```

```
  char *slave_connect_copy= NULL;
  if (!(slave_connect_copy= my_strdup(m_slave_connect, MYF(MY_WME))))
    return;

  my_b_printf(head, "# Slave Connect:\n# %s\n", slave_connect_copy);
  print_header(head, print_event_info, FALSE);
  my_free(slave_connect_copy);
  print_base64(body, print_event_info, true);
}
#endif

bool
Slave_connect_log_event::write_data_body(IO_CACHE *file)
{
  DBUG_ENTER("Slave_connect_log_event::write_data_body");
  /*
   m_slave_connect length will be stored using only one byte, but on read
   that length will be ignored and the complete query will be read.
  */
  DBUG_RETURN(write_str_at_most_255_bytes(file, m_slave_connect,
           (uint) strlen(m_slave_connect)));
}

#if defined(MYSQL_SERVER) && defined(HAVE_REPLICATION)
int Slave_connect_log_event::do_apply_event(Relay_log_info const *rli)
{
  DBUG_ENTER("Slave_connect_log_event::do_apply_event");
  DBUG_ASSERT(rli->info_thd == thd);
  /* Set query for writing Slave_connect log event into binlog later.*/
  thd->set_query(m_slave_connect, (uint32) strlen(m_slave_connect));

  DBUG_ASSERT(rli->slave_connect_ev == NULL);

  const_cast<Relay_log_info*>(rli)->slave_connect_ev= this;

  DBUG_RETURN(0);
}
#endif
```

The following sections describe each method in more detail. I explain why we need the method and how the method is used, along with any particulars implemented in the code.

Slave_connect_log_event::Slave_connect_log_event()

This is the constructor for the class instance. Of particular note here is that we allocate memory for the message or payload for the event when written to the binary log. It also has code to set up the header length.

Slave_connect_log_event::~Slave_connect_log_event()

This is the destructor for the class instance. Here, we simply free the string that we allocated in the constructor.

Slave_connect_log_event::pack_info()

This method is used to store the event data for writing to the binary log. We format a string to include a label that describes the event along with a string that contains the hostname, port, and server_id of the slave that connected to the master.

Slave_connect_log_event::print()

This method is used by clients to print the event in a human-readable form. Notice the conditional compilation directives that ensure the code is compiled only with clients. This tells us this method is very different from the pack_info() event.

In this method, the header is printed, followed by a similar format for the event data containing the hostname, port, and server_id. In this method, we also duplicate the string from the class so that it can be used outside of the class by the client application.

Slave_connect_log_event::write_data_body()

This method is used in conjunction with the pack_info() method. It will write the event data to the binary log.

Slave_connect_log_event::do_apply_event()

This method is used to write the event to the relay log. Since this event is ignored, it won't be written to the relay log. Rather than leave this method empty, I complete it as an example in case you wish to create custom events. In that case, you can use the code here as an example.

Now that we have the class defined, we can add a method to the binary log class that can be called from the main code more easily. We begin by adding a new method declaration to the class. Open the binlog.h file and locate write_incident() event near line number 541. Add a new method named write_slave_connect() with parameters for the current thread instance, hostname, port, and server_id. We will use the last three parameters to for the informational message or payload of the Slave_connect_log_event class. Listing 8-26 shows the new method declaration.

Listing 8-26. Method Declaration for write_slave_connect() in binlog.h

```
    bool write_incident(Incident_log_event *ev, bool need_lock_log,
                        bool do_flush_and_sync= true);

/* BEGIN CAB MODIFICATION */
/* Reason for Modification: */
/* Method declaration for writing the slave connect event to the binlog */
    bool write_slave_connect(THD *thd, char *host, int port, int server_id);
/* END CAB MODIFICATION */

    void start_union_events(THD *thd, query_id_t query_id_param);
    void stop_union_events(THD *thd);
    bool is_query_in_union(THD *thd, query_id_t query_id_param);
```

Now we can add the method definition to the binlog.cc file. As with the header file, we will place the new method near the write_incident() method. Open this file and location this method near line number 5154. Listing 8-27 shows the completed method.

Listing 8-27. The write_slave_connect() Method Definition in binlog.cc

```
/* BEGIN CAB MODIFICATION */
/* Reason for Modification: */
/* Add new method definition to write slave connect event to binlog */
bool MYSQL_BIN_LOG::write_slave_connect(THD *thd, char *host, int port, int server_id)
{
  char buffer[255];
  binlog_cache_data* cache_data= NULL;
  DBUG_ENTER("MYSQL_BIN_LOG::write_slave_connect");

  /* Record slave connection in the binary log */
  sprintf(buffer, "Host: %s Port: %d Server_Id: %d", host, port, server_id);
  Slave_connect_log_event ev(thd, buffer, (int)strlen(buffer));

  if (thd->binlog_setup_trx_data())
    DBUG_RETURN(1);
  cache_data= &thd_get_cache_mngr(thd)->trx_cache;
  if (cache_data->write_event(thd, &ev))
    DBUG_RETURN(1);
  cache_data->finalize(thd, NULL);
  ordered_commit(thd, true);

  DBUG_RETURN(0);
}
/* END CAB MODIFICATION */
```

In the method, we first create a new instance of the new event and then call methods to set up a transaction, retrieve the cache manager (the device used to write events to the cache for the binary log), and write the event. The finalize() method ensures that the correct flags are set for the event and that the ordered_commit() method completes the transaction, ensuring that the event is written to the binary log when the cache is flushed to disk.

Next, we will change the code for the master that will call the new binary-log method. The rpl_master.cc file contains the code for the master, including the code used whenever a slave connects. The register_slave() method is called when the slave connects. We will use this method as our starting point for initiating the Slave_connect_log_event via the write_slave_connect() method.

Open the rpl_master.cc file and locate the register_slave() method near line number 147. Add the code shown in listing 8-28. This code should appear right after the mutex lock call and before the unregister_slave() call.

Listing 8-28. Changes to register_slave() in rpl_master.cc

```
  mysql_mutex_lock(&LOCK_slave_list);
/* BEGIN CAB MODIFICATION */
/* Reason for Modification: */
/* Write a new Slave_connect_log_event to binary log when slave connects */
  /* If this is a new slave registration, log the slave connect message. */
  if (my_hash_search(&slave_list, (uchar*)&thd->server_id, 4) == NULL)
  {
    DBUG_PRINT("info", ("Logging slave connect for host: %s", si->host));
    mysql_bin_log.write_slave_connect(thd, si->host, si->port, si->server_id);
  }
```

```
/* END CAB MODIFICATION */
    unregister_slave(thd, false, false/*need_lock_slave_list=false*/);
    res= my_hash_insert(&slave_list, (uchar*) si);
    mysql_mutex_unlock(&LOCK_slave_list);
```

You might notice something odd about this code. If you are like me, when I first looked at the `register_slave()` method, I concluded that the method was called once each time the slave connects to the master. What I didn't realize, however, is that this method is called every time the slave requests data from the master. Thus, the `register_slave()` method can be called many times. If we want to record the slave-connect event only when the slave connects the first time, we must search the slave hash first. If we don't find it, we can call `write_slave_connect()`.

Now that we have the new event class and a new method in the binary-log class to write the event, and have linked it to the master code, we can work on the minor parts of the extension to complete the feature.

We begin with the relay-log code. Open the `rpl_rli.h` file and add a new member variable to contain an instance of the class. While the event is ignored, it is still read by the slave's IO thread and interrogated by the relay log code. Thus, the relay log code will need to create an instance in order to determine if it is ignorable. Listing 8-29 shows the code to add the new variable. This is located near line number 480, but anywhere in the `Relay_log_info` class is fine.

Listing 8-29. Add New Variable for the Slave_connect_log_event class in rpl_rli.h

```
    bool deferred_events_collecting;

/* BEGIN CAB MODIFICATION */
/* Reason for Modification: */
/* Add a new variable for a Slave_connect_log_event instance */

  Slave_connect_log_event* slave_connect_ev;

/* END CAB MODIFICATION */
  /**************************************************************************
```

Next, we add code to initialize the new variable when the event is read by the IO thread. Open the rpl_rli.cc file and locate the constructor Relay_log_info::Relay_log_info(). Add an initialization of the new variable and set it to NULL. We do this to protect against calling methods or attributes on a class instance that has not been initialized (instantiated). This works well but requires that you always check the variable for NULL prior to calling any method or attribute. Listing 8-30 shows the code to add to the constructor.

Listing 8-30. Initialization of slave_connect_ev Variable in rpl_rli.cc

```
    retried_trans(0),
    tables_to_lock(0), tables_to_lock_count(0),
    rows_query_ev(NULL), last_event_start_time(0), deferred_events(NULL),
/* BEGIN CAB MODIFICATION */
/* Reason for Modification: */
/* Initialize the slave_connect_ev variable */
    slave_connect_ev(NULL), slave_parallel_workers(0),
/* END CAB MODIFICATION */
    recovery_parallel_workers(0), checkpoint_seqno(0),
    checkpoint_group(opt_mts_checkpoint_group),
    recovery_groups_inited(false), mts_recovery_group_cnt(0),
```

The next few files to be changed are mostly to add the new event to existing destroy instance and error handling code. I chose to place this code in the same locations as Rows_query_log_event. This is a good choice because the Rows_query_log_event is also an ignorable event.

Also in the rpl_rli.cc file, we need to add code to destroy the instance if it is was instantiated earlier. We do this in the cleanup_context() method. Listing 8-31 shows the code to delete (destroy) the instance. Notice we first check to see that the instance has been instantiated. This avoids a particularly nasty error when attempting to destroy a class instance that does not exist.

Listing 8-31. Code to Destroy the Variable in cleanup_context() in rpl_rli..cc

```
    rows_query_ev= NULL;
    info_thd->set_query(NULL, 0);
  }
/* BEGIN CAB MODIFICATION */
/* Reason for Modification: */
/* Destroy the Slave_connect_log_event instance */
  if (slave_connect_ev)
  {
    delete slave_connect_ev;
    slave_connect_ev= NULL;
    info_thd->set_query(NULL, 0);
  }
/* END CAB MODIFICATION */
  m_table_map.clear_tables();
  slave_close_thread_tables(thd);
```

The next file to change is rpl_rli_pdb.cc. Open the file and locate the last method in the file, slave_worker_exec_job(). We need to add another exclusion in that method's error-handling code. Listing 8-32 shows the new changes. Notice that we add another condition in the same manner as the Rows_query_log_event event.

Listing 8-32. Add Condition to Delete Slave_connect_log_event in rpl_rli_pdb.cc

```
  // todo: simulate delay in delete
/* BEGIN CAB MODIFICATION */
/* Reason for Modification: */
/* Destroy the Slave_connect_log_event instance */
  if (ev && ev->worker && ev->get_type_code() != ROWS_QUERY_LOG_EVENT &&
      ev->get_type_code() != SLAVE_CONNECT_LOG_EVENT)
/* END CAB MODIFICATION */
  {
    delete ev;
  }
```

Next, we add the new event to another exclusion in the rpl_slave.cc code. Open the file and locate the condition that destroys the event after execution in the exec_relay_log_event() method. This is located near line number 3654. Listing 8-33 shows the changes needed for this condition. Notice that we add another condition to the if statement.

Listing 8-33. Exclude Slave_connect_log_event from Destroy Condition in rpl_slave.cc

```
        clean-up routine.
    */
/* BEGIN CAB MODIFICATION */
/* Reason for Modification: */
/* Exclude the Slave_connect_log_event from destruction */
    if (ev->get_type_code() != FORMAT_DESCRIPTION_EVENT &&
        ev->get_type_code() != ROWS_QUERY_LOG_EVENT &&
        ev->get_type_code() != SLAVE_CONNECT_LOG_EVENT)
/* END CAB MODIFICATION */
    {
        DBUG_PRINT("info", ("Deleting the event after it has been executed"));
        delete ev;
```

The last file to change is sql_binlog.cc. There are two places where we need to change the code. First, we must add the SLAVE_CONNECT_LOG_EVENT to the exclusion for deleting an event that has been executed. Second, we must add code to destroy the new event instance in the case of an error.

Open the sql_binlog.cc file, locate the error condition for the Rows_query_log_event around line number 292, and make the changes shown in listing 8-34. Notice that we simply add another condition to the if statement.

Listing 8-34. Exclude Slave_connect_log_event from Destroy Condition in sql_binlog.cc

```
        of the event.
    */
/* BEGIN CAB MODIFICATION */
/* Reason for Modification: */
/* Exclude the Slave_connect_log_event from destruction */
    if (ev->get_type_code() != FORMAT_DESCRIPTION_EVENT &&
        ev->get_type_code() != ROWS_QUERY_LOG_EVENT &&
        ev->get_type_code() != SLAVE_CONNECT_LOG_EVENT)
/* END CAB MODIFICATION */
    {
        delete ev;
        ev= NULL;
```

We must add a condition to the error condition that destroys the new event in case there is an error. As with previous cases, we will mimic the code for the Rows_query_log_event. This is located near line number 320. Listing 8-35 shows the new code. We check for an error, and if there is an error and the new event exists (the pointer is not NULL or 0), we delete the instance.

Listing 8-35. Destroy Slave_connect_log_event if Error Condition in sql_binlog.cc

```
        delete rli->rows_query_ev;
        rli->rows_query_ev= NULL;
    }
/* BEGIN CAB MODIFICATION */
/* Reason for Modification: */
/* Destroy the Slave_connect_log_event instance if there is an error */
    if ((error || err) && rli->slave_connect_ev)
```

```
    {
      delete rli->slave_connect_ev;
      rli->slave_connect_ev= NULL;
    }
/* END CAB MODIFICATION */
    rli->slave_close_thread_tables(thd);
  }
  thd->variables.option_bits= thd_options;
```

This completes the modifications to the code to add a new ignorable event to the list of events in the binary log. Clearly, this is not a trivial change, and log events touch several source-code files.

You are now ready to compile the code. Check all the files you modified for correctness. You should also compile the server from the root of the source tree so that all components are built with the changes. This is necessary so that the mysqlbinlog client application can decipher the new event.

Compiling the Code

Now, compile the server code. If all modifications were made as shown in the listings, the code should compile. If it does not, go back and check the modifications. The next section demonstrates the new event in action.

Example Execution

In this section, we see a demonstration of the new log event in action. There isn't much to see in the form of output on either the master or the slave, because log events live under the hood of replication. There is, however, a SQL command, SHOW BINLOG EVENTS, that can be used to display an excerpt of the binary-log events on a server. A client tool, mysqlbinlog, which we previously discussed, can be used to examine the contents of the binary or relay log.

We being by setting up a test environment. Instead of using the utilities, like I did with the first example in this chapter, I show you an interesting trick in setting up a master and slave quickly using the existing server test environment.

The test environment described in Chapter 4, mysql-test-run, can be used to setup a master and slave. We do this by using two key options;: --start-and-exit and --suite. The --start-and-exit option tells mysql-test-run to start a new server and exit. This has the same effect as the mysqlserverclone utility, but unlike the utility, mysql-test-run uses predefined options for the mysqld process. In most cases, this is fine, but the utility allows you to create specialized server instances.

We also want to start a slave at the same time. If you provide a test suite, specifically the replication suite, mysql-test-run will create additional servers. For --suite=rpl, mysql-test-run will create two servers that are preconfigured for replication.

Clearly, this is easier than starting a new instance for the master and slave. Rather than two commands—which is already easier than launching mysqld instance manually—for the case of needing a master and a single slave, we can use one command. Listing 8-36 shows an example of using mysql-test-run to launch a master and slave.

Listing 8-36. Starting a new Master and Slave Using MTR

```
cbell@ubuntu:$ ./mysql-test-run.pl --start-and-exit --suite=rpl
Logging: ./mysql-test-run.pl  --start-and-exit --suite=rpl
121003 18:26:01 [Note] Plugin 'FEDERATED' is disabled.
121003 18:26:01 [Note] Binlog end
121003 18:26:01 [Note] Shutting down plugin 'CSV'
121003 18:26:01 [Note] Shutting down plugin 'MyISAM'
MySQL Version 5.6.6
```

```
Checking supported features...
 - skipping ndbcluster
 - SSL connections supported
 - binaries are debug compiled
Using suites: rpl
Collecting tests...
Checking leftover processes...
Removing old var directory...
Creating var directory '/mysql-test/var'...
Installing system database...
Using server port 54781


==============================================================================

TEST                                    RESULT   TIME (ms) or COMMENT
------------------------------------------------------------------------------

worker[1] Using MTR_BUILD_THREAD 300, with reserved ports 13000..13009
worker[1]
Started [mysqld.1 - pid: 2300, winpid: 2300] [mysqld.2 - pid: 2330, winpid: 2330]
worker[1] Using config for test rpl.rpl_000010
worker[1] Port and socket path for server(s):
worker[1] mysqld.1   13000   /mysql-test/var/tmp/mysqld.1.sock
worker[1] mysqld.2   13001   /mysql-test/var/tmp/mysqld.2.sock
worker[1] Server(s) started, not waiting for them to finish
```

We can now use the mysqlreplicate utility to quickly attach the slave to the master and begin replicating data. Listing 8-37 shows the output of running this utility.

Listing 8-37. Setting up Replication

```
cbell@ubuntu:$ python ./scripts/mysqlreplicate.py   --master=root@localhost:13000
--slave=root@localhost:13001
# master on localhost: ... connected.
# slave on localhost: ... connected.
# Checking for binary logging on master...
# Setting up replication...
# ...done.
```

Were you expecting something? Perhaps a message or the ubiquitous "bing" sound? None of those are supposed to happen. The code behind replication is extensive but stable, and for the most part completely silent. To find out what is going on with replication, and in this case what has just transpired, you must either query the master or the slave for status.

If you recall, the extension is supposed to write a single log event to the binary log on the master recording when the slave connects. Since we set up replication with mysqlreplicate, nothing was displayed or otherwise presented there. We must go to the master to see if the event actually occurred.

■ **Tip** If you started the servers in console mode, you would have seen any messages and errors in the console. This includes errors and warnings from replication. For instance, the slave would display messages pertaining to connecting to the master and an error if there is a problem reading or executing events from the master. You can start a server in console mode on Linux and Mac systems by starting the mysqld executable directly. On Windows, you must use the --console option.

It might be a good idea to check the slave for errors. Execute SHOW SLAVE STATUS on the slave and check for errors. I leave this to you as an exercise. What you should see is a normal, healthy slave.

Let's return to the master. The SHOW BINLOG EVENTS command will display the most recent events written to the binary log. If the Slave_connect_log_event worked correctly, you should see it in the view. Listing 8-38 shows the results of the SHOW BINLOG EVENTS run on the master. Remember, this command only shows the events from the first binary log. Use the IN clause to specify a particular binary log.

■ **Note** Running SHOW BINLOG EVENTS on any server that does not have binary logging enabled will result in an empty result set. If you see this when running your test on this code, check to be sure that you are not running on the slave.

Listing 8-38. Binary Log Events on the Master

```
cbell@ubuntu:$ mysql -uroot -h 127.0.0.1 --port=13000
Welcome to the MySQL monitor.  Commands end with ; or \g.
Your MySQL connection id is 4
Server version: 5.6.6-m9-debug-log Source distribution

Copyright (c) 2000, 2011, Oracle and/or its affiliates. All rights reserved.

Oracle is a registered trademark of Oracle Corporation and/or its
affiliates. Other names may be trademarks of their respective
owners.

Type 'help;' or '\h' for help. Type '\c' to clear the current input statement.

mysql> show binlog events \G
*************************** 1. row ***************************
   Log_name: master-bin.000001
        Pos: 4
 Event_type: Format_desc
  Server_id: 1
End_log_pos: 121
       Info: Server ver: 5.7.0-m10-debug-log, Binlog ver: 4
*************************** 2. row ***************************
   Log_name: master-bin.000001
        Pos: 121
 Event_type: Query
  Server_id: 1
End_log_pos: 326
       Info: GRANT REPLICATION SLAVE ON *.* TO 'rpl'@'localhost'
```

```
*************************** 3. row ***************************
    Log_name: master-bin.000001
         Pos: 326
  Event_type: Slave_connect
   Server_id: 2
 End_log_pos: 390
        Info: # SLAVE_CONNECT = Host: 127.0.0.1 Port: 13001 Server_Id: 2
3 rows in set (0.00 sec)

mysql>
```

Notice that the listing above shows the new log event in the output. We see that the payload (Info field) of the event includes the hostname, port, and server_id of the slave. It is showing the loopback address because the replication topology (master and slave) runs on the local machine (localhost = 127.0.0.1).

Now, let us examine the output of the mysqlbinlog client application. Run the application with only the binary log of the master as the only argument. Since I set up the servers using mysql-test-run, I find the files under the /mysql-test/var folder. In this case, I am looking for the binary file for the master, which is the first server and, therefore, the folder is named mysqld.1, and the data directory, named data. Thus, the relative path from mysql-test is ./var/mysqld.1/data.

Listing 8-39 shows the output of the mysqlbinlog client application dumping the binary log of the master in the test topology.

Listing 8-39. Examining the Binary Log on the Master with mysqlbinlog

```
cbell@ubuntu:$ ../client/mysqlbinlog ./var/mysqld.1/data/master-bin.000001
/*!40019 SET @@session.max_insert_delayed_threads=0*/;
/*!50003 SET @OLD_COMPLETION_TYPE=@@COMPLETION_TYPE,COMPLETION_TYPE=0*/;
DELIMITER /*!*/;
# at 4
#121003 16:03:59 server id 1  end_log_pos 121 CRC32 0x83c06bae  Start: binlog v 4, server v
5.6.6-m9-debug-log created 121003 16:03:59 at startup
# Warning: this binlog is either in use or was not closed properly.
ROLLBACK/*!*/;
BINLOG '
X8RsUA8BAAAAdQAAAHkAAAABAAQANS43LjAtbTEwLWRlYnVnLWxvZwAAAAAAAAAAAAAAAAAAAA
AAAAAAAAAAAAAAAAAABfxGxQEzgNAAgAEgAEBAQEEgAAXQAEGggAAAAICAgCAAAACgoKGRkAAAGu
a8CD
'/*!*/;
# at 121
#121003 16:05:23 server id 1  end_log_pos 326 CRC32 0x559a612a  Query    thread_id=1      exec_time=0
error_code=0
SET TIMESTAMP=1349305523/*!*/;
SET @@session.pseudo_thread_id=1/*!*/;
SET @@session.foreign_key_checks=1, @@session.sql_auto_is_null=0, @@session.unique_checks=1,
@@session.autocommit=1/*!*/;
SET @@session.sql_mode=1073741824/*!*/;
SET @@session.auto_increment_increment=1, @@session.auto_increment_offset=1/*!*/;
/*!\C latin1 *//*!*/;
SET @@session.character_set_client=8,@@session.collation_connection=8,@@session.collation_
server=8/*!*/;
```

```
SET @@session.lc_time_names=0/*!*/;
SET @@session.collation_database=DEFAULT/*!*/;
GRANT REPLICATION SLAVE ON *.* TO 'rpl'@'localhost'
/*!*/;
# at 326
# Slave Connect:
# Host: 127.0.0.1 Port: 13001 Server_Id: 2
#121003 16:05:23 server id 2  end_log_pos 390 CRC32 0x262bb144 DELIMITER ;
# End of log file
ROLLBACK /* added by mysqlbinlog */;
/*!50003 SET COMPLETION_TYPE=@OLD_COMPLETION_TYPE*/;
```

The output may seem like a bunch of random, magical strings and bits, but trust me, it all makes sense. Near the bottom of the list you can see the result of the Slave_connect_log_event. Remember, the Slave_connect_log_event::print() method is used to display binary-log events by the mysqlbinlog client application. The print() method was designed to print two lines for the event: a title and the payload displaying the hostname, port, and server_id of the slave.

If this binary log was from a master with many slaves, some of which have been added, removed, and added again, the output of running the mysqlbinlog client application would show all of the slave-connection events. In fact, you can pipe the output to a program such as grep to find all of the locations in the file for the '# Slave Connect:' lines.

Aside from this utility, this extension of the replication features has demonstrated the location of the log-event code and how log events are written to and read from the binary log. I hope that this exercise has given you some ideas for solving your own unique and advanced replication challenges.

Summary

In this chapter, I've presented a brief tutorial of MySQL replication, including why you would use it, a look at its architecture, and a tour of the replication source code. You learned how to setup replication as well as several ways to extend the MySQL replication feature set.

In the next chapter, I present another powerful feature of MySQL – the pluggable architecture. I explore the architecture through an exploration of another advanced feature - pluggable authentication. I present a short introduction into the pluggable facility in MySQL and present a sample authentication plugin that uses RFID tags for user validation.

CHAPTER 9

■ ■ ■

Developing MySQL Plugins

During our tour of the MySQL source code and architecture in Chapter 3, we touched on a special feature of MySQL called plugins. MySQL plugins are specially designed dynamic libraries that allow you to add new functionality to the server without taking the server offline. There are several forms of plugins supported today, but as the server continues to evolve, expect to see more features offered using this architecture.

This chapter examines the MySQL plugin architecture in more detail. You will learn more about how plugins work, how they are constructed, and what types of plugins are supported by the server. I will also demonstrate how to create a plugin by creating a unique authentication plugin.

MySQL Plugins Explained

MySQL plugins are contained in dynamically loadable modules called libraries. A library can contain one or more plugins and can be installed (loaded) or uninstalled (unloaded) individually. Plugins provide extensions to the server in the form of specialized features. Aside from the feature itself, plugins can also contain their own status and system variables. A plugin is developed using a standardized architecture called an application programming interface (API).

The plugin architecture (called the MySQL Plugin API) uses a special set of structures that contain information as well as function pointers to common methods. Using a common structure allows the server to call specific methods whereby the function pointers remap the calls to the specific implementation of the method for that plugin. I will explain the plugin architecture in more detail in a later section.

Types of Plugins

The MySQL server currently supports several types of plugins. We have already seen an example of a very early form of plugin—user defined functions[1] (UDF). Chapter 7 presented this form of plugin in great detail. Some would say UDFs are not true plugins, despite the fact they are dynamically loadable and use the same commands to install and uninstall. This is because they do not use the standard plugin architecture.

Table 9-1 lists the types of plugins that are supported using this architecture, including the name of the plugin, the type name, a short description, and the location of an example in the source code, if one exists.

---

[1] UDFs predate the plugin architecture, first appearing in version 3.21.24. They have not been changed to use the new architecture.

Table 9-1. Plugins Supported by the MySQL Plugin API

Type	Description	Example
UDF	Special functions for use in SQL commands.	/sql/udf_example.cc
Storage Engine	Storage engines for reading and writing data.	/storage/*
Full Text Parser	Full text parser for searching text columns in tables.	/plugin/fulltext
Daemon	Permits the loading of discrete code modules into the server without interacting with the server itself, such as replication heartbeat and monitoring	/plugin/daemon_example
Information Schema	Permits the creation of new INFORMATION_SCHEMA views for communicating information to the user.	
Audit	Enables server auditing. An audit log plugin exists in the commercial release of MySQL.	/plugin/audit_null
Replication	Specialized replication features, such as changing the synchronization method of event execution.	/plugin/semisync
Authentication	Change the authentication method for logging into the server.	/plugin/auth
Validate Password	Enforce password rules for more secure passwords.	/plugin/password_validation

As you can see, there are many types of plugins, and they provide a wide range of features. With emphasis on more modular design, we are likely to see more plugin types in the future.

Using MySQL Plugins

Plugins can be loaded and unloaded either with special SQL commands, as startup options, or via the `mysql_plugin` client application.

To load a plugin using an SQL command, use the `LOAD PLUGIN` command as follows. Here, we are loading a plugin named `something_cool` that is contained in the compiled-library module named `some_cool_feature.so`. These libraries need to be placed in the `plugin_dir` path so that the server can find them.

```
mysql> SHOW VARIABLES LIKE 'plugin_dir';
+---------------+------------------------------+
| Variable_name | Value                        |
+---------------+------------------------------+
| plugin_dir    | /usr/local/mysql/lib/plugin/ |
+---------------+------------------------------+
1 row in set (0.00 sec)
```

■ **Note** The MySQL documentation uses the terms *install* and *uninstall* for dynamically loading and unloading plugins. The documentation uses the term *load* for specifying a plugin to use via a startup option.

```
mysql> INSTALL PLUGIN something_cool SONAME some_cool_feature.so;
```

Uninstalling the plugin is easier and is shown below. Here we are unloading the same plugin we just installed.

```
mysql> UNINSTALL PLUGIN something_cool;
```

Plugins can also be installed at startup using the --plugin-load option. This option can either be listed multiple times—once for each plugin—or can accept a semicolon-separated list (no spaces). Examples of how to use this option include:

```
mysqld ... --plugin-load=something_cool ...
mysqld ... --plugin-load=something_cool;something_even_better ...
```

Plugins can also be loaded and unloaded using the mysql_plugin client application. This application requires the server to be down to work. It will launch the server in bootstrap mode, load or unload the plugin, and then shut down the bootstrapped server. The application is used primarily for maintenance of servers during downtime or as a diagnostic tool for attempts to restart a failed server by eliminating plugins (to simplify diagnosis).

The client application uses a configuration file to keep pertinent data about the plugin, such as the name of the library and all of the plugins contain within. A plugin library can contain more than one plugin. The following is an example of the configuration file for the daemon_example plugin.

```
#
# Plugin configuration file. Place on a separate line:
#
# library binary file name (without .so or .dll)
# component_name
# [component_name] - additional components in plugin
#
libdaemon_example
daemon_example
```

To use the mysql_plugin application to install (enable) or uninstall (disable) plugins, specify the name of the plugin, ENABLE or DISABLE, basedir, datadir, plugin-dir, and plugin-ini options at a minimum. You may also need to specify the my-print-defaults option if that application is not on your path. The application runs silently, but you can turn on verbosity to see the application in action (–vvv). The following depicts an example of loading the daemon_example plugin using the client application.

```
cbell$ sudo ./mysql_plugin --datadir=/mysql_path/data/ --basedir=/mysql_path/ --plugin-dir=../
plugin/daemon_example/ --plugin-ini=../plugin/daemon_example/daemon_example.ini --my-print-
defaults=../extra daemon_example ENABLE -vvv
# Found tool 'my_print_defaults' as '/mysql_path/bin/my_print_defaults'.
# Command: /mysql_path/bin/my_print_defaults mysqld > /var/tmp/txtdoaw2b
#     basedir = /mysql_path/
# plugin_dir = ../plugin/daemon_example/
#     datadir = /mysql_path/data/
# plugin_ini = ../plugin/daemon_example/daemon_example.ini
# Found tool 'mysqld' as '/mysql_path/bin/mysqld'.
# Found plugin 'daemon_example' as '../plugin/daemon_example/libdaemon_example.so'
# Enabling daemon_example...
# Query: REPLACE INTO mysql.plugin VALUES ('daemon_example','libdaemon_example.so');
# Command: /mysql_path/bin/mysqld --no-defaults --bootstrap --datadir=/mysql_path/data/
--basedir=/mysql_path/ < /var/tmp/sqlft1mF7
# Operation succeeded.
```

Notice in the output that I had to use super-user privileges. You will need to use this if you are attempting to install or uninstall plugins from a server installed on platforms that isolate access to the mysql folders, such as Linux and Mac OS X. Notice also that the verbose output shows you exactly what this application is doing. In this case, it is replacing any rows in the mysql.plugin table with the information for the plugin we specified. Similar delete queries would be issued for disabling a plugin.

You can discover which plugins are loaded or have been loaded in one of three ways. You can use a special SHOW command, select information from the mysql.plugin table, or select information from the INFORMATION_SCHEMA.plugins view. Each of these displays slightly different information. The following demonstrates each of these commands. I use excerpts of the output for brevity.

```
mysql> show plugins;
+----------------------------+----------+-----------------+---------+---------+
| Name                       | Status   | Type            | Library | License |
+----------------------------+----------+-----------------+---------+---------+
| binlog                     | ACTIVE   | STORAGE ENGINE  | NULL    | GPL     |
| mysql_native_password      | ACTIVE   | AUTHENTICATION  | NULL    | GPL     |
| mysql_old_password         | ACTIVE   | AUTHENTICATION  | NULL    | GPL     |
| sha256_password            | ACTIVE   | AUTHENTICATION  | NULL    | GPL     |
| CSV                        | ACTIVE   | STORAGE ENGINE  | NULL    | GPL     |
| MEMORY                     | ACTIVE   | STORAGE ENGINE  | NULL    | GPL     |
| MyISAM                     | ACTIVE   | STORAGE ENGINE  | NULL    | GPL     |
| MRG_MYISAM                 | ACTIVE   | STORAGE ENGINE  | NULL    | GPL     |
| ARCHIVE                    | ACTIVE   | STORAGE ENGINE  | NULL    | GPL     |
| BLACKHOLE                  | ACTIVE   | STORAGE ENGINE  | NULL    | GPL     |
| FEDERATED                  | DISABLED | STORAGE ENGINE  | NULL    | GPL     |
| InnoDB                     | ACTIVE   | STORAGE ENGINE  | NULL    | GPL     |
...
| PERFORMANCE_SCHEMA         | ACTIVE   | STORAGE ENGINE  | NULL    | GPL     |
| partition                  | ACTIVE   | STORAGE ENGINE  | NULL    | GPL     |
+----------------------------+----------+-----------------+---------+---------+
41 rows in set (0.00 sec)
```

Notice the information shown in the SHOW PLUGINS command output. This view is a list of all known plugins, some of which are loaded automatically via either command-line options or from special compilation directives. It shows the plugin type as well as the license type. Now, let's see the output of the mysql.plugin table.

```
mysql> select * from mysql.plugin;
Empty set (0.00 sec)
```

But wait, there is no output! This is because the mysql.plugin table stores only those dynamic plugins that have been installed—more specifically, those that were installed with the INSTALL PLUGIN command. Since we did not install any plugins, there is nothing to display. The following shows the output when a plugin has been installed.

```
mysql> install plugin daemon_example soname 'libdaemon_example.so';
Query OK, 0 rows affected (0.00 sec)

mysql> select * from mysql.plugin;
+----------------+----------------------+
| name           | dl                   |
+----------------+----------------------+
| daemon_example | libdaemon_example.so |
+----------------+----------------------+
1 row in set (0.00 sec)
```

Now let's see the output of the INFORMATION_SCHEMA.plugins view. The following shows the output of the view.

```
mysql> select * from information_schema.plugins \G
*************************** 1. row ***************************
           PLUGIN_NAME: binlog
        PLUGIN_VERSION: 1.0
         PLUGIN_STATUS: ACTIVE
           PLUGIN_TYPE: STORAGE ENGINE
   PLUGIN_TYPE_VERSION: 50606.0
        PLUGIN_LIBRARY: NULL
PLUGIN_LIBRARY_VERSION: NULL
         PLUGIN_AUTHOR: MySQL AB
    PLUGIN_DESCRIPTION: This is a pseudo storage engine to represent the binlog in a transaction
        PLUGIN_LICENSE: GPL
           LOAD_OPTION: FORCE
*************************** 2. row ***************************
           PLUGIN_NAME: mysql_native_password
        PLUGIN_VERSION: 1.0
         PLUGIN_STATUS: ACTIVE
           PLUGIN_TYPE: AUTHENTICATION
   PLUGIN_TYPE_VERSION: 1.0
        PLUGIN_LIBRARY: NULL
PLUGIN_LIBRARY_VERSION: NULL
         PLUGIN_AUTHOR: R.J.Silk, Sergei Golubchik
    PLUGIN_DESCRIPTION: Native MySQL authentication
        PLUGIN_LICENSE: GPL
           LOAD_OPTION: FORCE
*************************** 3. row ***************************
           PLUGIN_NAME: mysql_old_password
        PLUGIN_VERSION: 1.0
         PLUGIN_STATUS: ACTIVE
           PLUGIN_TYPE: AUTHENTICATION
   PLUGIN_TYPE_VERSION: 1.0
        PLUGIN_LIBRARY: NULL
PLUGIN_LIBRARY_VERSION: NULL
         PLUGIN_AUTHOR: R.J.Silk, Sergei Golubchik
    PLUGIN_DESCRIPTION: Old MySQL-4.0 authentication
        PLUGIN_LICENSE: GPL
           LOAD_OPTION: FORCE
...

*************************** 41. row ***************************
           PLUGIN_NAME: partition
        PLUGIN_VERSION: 1.0
         PLUGIN_STATUS: ACTIVE
           PLUGIN_TYPE: STORAGE ENGINE
   PLUGIN_TYPE_VERSION: 50606.0
        PLUGIN_LIBRARY: NULL
PLUGIN_LIBRARY_VERSION: NULL
         PLUGIN_AUTHOR: Mikael Ronstrom, MySQL AB
    PLUGIN_DESCRIPTION: Partition Storage Engine Helper
```

```
            PLUGIN_LICENSE: GPL
               LOAD_OPTION: ON
*************************** 42. row ***************************
               PLUGIN_NAME: daemon_example
            PLUGIN_VERSION: 1.0
             PLUGIN_STATUS: ACTIVE
               PLUGIN_TYPE: DAEMON
       PLUGIN_TYPE_VERSION: 50606.0
            PLUGIN_LIBRARY: libdaemon_example.so
    PLUGIN_LIBRARY_VERSION: 1.4
             PLUGIN_AUTHOR: Brian Aker
        PLUGIN_DESCRIPTION: Daemon example, creates a heartbeat beat file in mysql-heartbeat.log
            PLUGIN_LICENSE: GPL
               LOAD_OPTION: ON
42 rows in set (0.01 sec)

mysql>
```

We see the similar information as with the SHOW PLUGINS command, but with additional information. Aside from the name, type, and license information, we also see the author, version, and description of the plugin. Notice also that the dynamically loaded plugin, the daemon_example, is also displayed in the view.

Now that you know what each of these commands does, you can use the appropriate command for working with plugins. For example, if you want to see which plugins are available at a glance, use the SHOW PLUGINS command. If you want to see which plugins are loaded, query the mysql.plugin table. If you want to see the metadata about the available plugins, query the INFORMATION_SCHEMA.plugins view.

The MySQL Plugin API

The plugin architecture is defined in /include/mysql/plugin.h. There are many elements in this file, including specialized code for some of the plugin types. A complete explanation of every line of code is beyond the scope of this work; rather, in this section, we focus on the key elements you need to be familiar with in order to build your own plugins.

Near the top of the file, you will find the defines for the symbols and values used in creating plugins. Listing 9-1 shows the definitions of the most frequently used symbols. There are definitions for each plugin type as well as definitions for license type.

Listing 9-1. Definitions from plugin.h

```
/*
  The allowable types of plugins
*/
#define MYSQL_UDF_PLUGIN                0  /* User-defined function      */
#define MYSQL_STORAGE_ENGINE_PLUGIN     1  /* Storage Engine             */
#define MYSQL_FTPARSER_PLUGIN           2  /* Full-text parser plugin    */
#define MYSQL_DAEMON_PLUGIN             3  /* The daemon/raw plugin type */
#define MYSQL_INFORMATION_SCHEMA_PLUGIN 4  /* The I_S plugin type */
#define MYSQL_AUDIT_PLUGIN              5  /* The Audit plugin type      */
#define MYSQL_REPLICATION_PLUGIN        6  /* The replication plugin type */
#define MYSQL_AUTHENTICATION_PLUGIN     7  /* The authentication plugin type */
#define MYSQL_VALIDATE_PASSWORD_PLUGIN  8   /* validate password plugin type */
#define MYSQL_MAX_PLUGIN_TYPE_NUM       9  /* The number of plugin types  */
```

```
/* We use the following strings to define licenses for plugins */
#define PLUGIN_LICENSE_PROPRIETARY 0
#define PLUGIN_LICENSE_GPL 1
#define PLUGIN_LICENSE_BSD 2

#define PLUGIN_LICENSE_PROPRIETARY_STRING "PROPRIETARY"
#define PLUGIN_LICENSE_GPL_STRING "GPL"
#define PLUGIN_LICENSE_BSD_STRING "BSD"
```

There are definitions for the type of license the plugin supports. For most standard MySQL plugins, the license is GPL. For those plugins that are available only with the commercial license of MySQL, the license is set to PROPRIETARY. If you need to add more license types, add them to the file, increment the value, and provide a text string to identify it in the plugin views.

The mechanism used by the MySQL Plugin API to communicate with the server is the st_mysql_structure, also defined in the /include/mysql/plugin.h file. Listing 9-2 shows the definition of the st_mysql_structure.

Listing 9-2. The st_mysql_plugin Structure in plugin.h

```
/*
  Plugin description structure.
*/

struct st_mysql_plugin
{
  int type;              /* the plugin type (a MYSQL_XXX_PLUGIN value)  */
  void *info;            /* pointer to type-specific plugin descriptor  */
  const char *name;      /* plugin name                                 */
  const char *author;    /* plugin author (for I_S.PLUGINS)             */
  const char *descr;     /* general descriptive text (for I_S.PLUGINS)  */
  int license;           /* the plugin license (PLUGIN_LICENSE_XXX)     */
  int (*init)(MYSQL_PLUGIN);  /* the function to invoke when plugin is loaded */
  int (*deinit)(MYSQL_PLUGIN);/* the function to invoke when plugin is unloaded */
  unsigned int version; /* plugin version (for I_S.PLUGINS)             */
  struct st_mysql_show_var *status_vars;
  struct st_mysql_sys_var **system_vars;
  void * __reserved1;    /* reserved for dependency checking            */
  unsigned long flags;  /* flags for plugin */
};
```

The first six attributes in the structure contain metadata information about the plugin, including the type, description, name, author information, and license information. The next two attributes are function pointers to functions for loading and unloading the plugin. Following that are structures to contain status and system variables defined for the plugin. Last, there is an attribute for setting flags for communicating the plugin capabilities to the server.

Of special note is the info attribute. This is a pointer to a structure dedicated to each type of plugin. These are defined in header files in /include/mysql with the name plugin_* where * represents the plugin type. For example, the plugin_auth.h file contains the structure definition for the authentication plugin type.

The structure defined is named for the plugin as well. Each structure contains attributes and function pointers for specific methods for each plugin type. In this way, the server can successfully navigate and call the specific methods for each plugin type. The following shows the st_mysql_auth structure from the plugin_auth.h file.

```
/**
  Server authentication plugin descriptor
*/
struct st_mysql_auth
{
  int interface_version;                      /** version plugin uses */
  /**
    A plugin that a client must use for authentication with this server
    plugin. Can be NULL to mean "any plugin".
  */
  const char *client_auth_plugin;
  /**
    Function provided by the plugin which should perform authentication (using
    the vio functions if necessary) and return 0 if successful. The plugin can
    also fill the info.authenticated_as field if a different username should be
    used for authorization.
  */
  int (*authenticate_user)(MYSQL_PLUGIN_VIO *vio, MYSQL_SERVER_AUTH_INFO *info);
};
```

A special version number located in the file is unique for each plugin type. It defines the version number for the plugin type and is used to help identify and confirm architecture compatibility with the server when installed.

```
#define MYSQL_AUTHENTICATION_INTERFACE_VERSION 0x0100
```

PLUGINS AND VERSION NUMBERS

The st_mysql_plugin structure contains a version attribute. This is not used directly by the server other than to display it in the plugin views. There are two other version numbers that we should know. The first is PLUGIN_LIBRARY_VERSION, the version number set by the server that indicates the version of the plugin API. This permits the server to know if a plugin has compatible architecture. The second, PLUGIN_VERSION_TYPE, is specific to each plugin type. We can see these in /library/mysql/plugin.h as:

```
#define MYSQL_PLUGIN_INTERFACE_VERSION 0x0104
```

The value for the 5.6.6 server is 1.4. You can see this in the output of the INFORMATION_SCHEMA.plugins view above.

```
#define MYSQL_DAEMON_INTERFACE_VERSION (MYSQL_VERSION_ID << 8)
```

The above shows the specific plugin type for the daemon_example. In this case, the version of the server is placed in the higher-order bytes to help further identify the plugin. For server version 5.6.6, this value would be calculated as 50606.0. You can see this in the output of the INFORMATION_SCHEMA.plugins view above.

■ **Note** As we see above, most plugin types have specific values. The daemon_example, being an early example, has version number 0.

To create a plugin, first create a new folder in the /plugin folder named something easily associated with your plugin. Place in this folder, at a minimum, a source file containing an implementation of the st_mysql_plugin structure along with a specific implementation for the information structure associated with the plugin type. You should populate the plugin structure with the correct metadata, implement the methods for initialization and deinitialization, and implement the specific methods for the plugin type.

As an alternative, you could create a folder outside of the source tree, compile it, and link it with the server libraries. Advanced developers may want to explore this option if they desire to keep the plugin code separate from the server source code.

You would also create an ini file containing the information about the plugin as described in the section "Using MySQL Plugins." If you have specific structures, variables, definitions, etc., for your plugin, you can create the appropriate files and place them in the same folder.

Now that we have seen the building blocks for creating a plugin, we will see how to compile the plugin and then begin creating a plugin of our own.

Compiling MySQL Plugins

You may be thinking that there is some arcane mechanism used to make your plugins compile. I have good news for you—there isn't. The only thing you need is a CMakeList.txt file containing the cmake directives to compile your plugin. For simple plugins that have only a single plugin in the library, the content of the file is short. Listing 9-3 shows the complete contents for the example authentication plugin.

Listing 9-3. CMakeLists.txt for Authentication Plugin Example

```
# Copyright (c) 2010, Oracle and/or its affiliates. All rights reserved.
#
# This program is free software; you can redistribute it and/or
# modify it under the terms of the GNU General Public License as
# published by the Free Software Foundation; version 2 of the
# License.
#
# This program is distributed in the hope that it will be useful,
# but WITHOUT ANY WARRANTY; without even the implied warranty of
# MERCHANTABILITY or FITNESS FOR A PARTICULAR PURPOSE. See the
# GNU General Public License for more details.
#
# You should have received a copy of the GNU General Public License
# along with this program; if not, write to the Free Software
# Foundation, Inc., 51 Franklin St, Fifth Floor, Boston, MA 02110-1301  USA

MYSQL_ADD_PLUGIN(auth dialog.c
  MODULE_ONLY)

MYSQL_ADD_PLUGIN(auth_test_plugin test_plugin.c
  MODULE_ONLY)

MYSQL_ADD_PLUGIN(qa_auth_interface qa_auth_interface.c
  MODULE_ONLY)

MYSQL_ADD_PLUGIN(qa_auth_server qa_auth_server.c
  MODULE_ONLY)
```

```
MYSQL_ADD_PLUGIN(qa_auth_client qa_auth_client.c
  MODULE_ONLY)

CHECK_CXX_SOURCE_COMPILES(
"#define _GNU_SOURCE
#include <sys/socket.h>
int main() {
  struct ucred cred;
  getsockopt(0, SOL_SOCKET, SO_PEERCRED, &cred, 0);
}" HAVE_PEERCRED)

IF(HAVE_PEERCRED)
  MYSQL_ADD_PLUGIN(auth_socket auth_socket.c
    MODULE_ONLY)
ENDIF()
```

This example has five plugins defined. For each, the MYSQL_ADD_PLUGIN directive is used to define the plugin name and associate it with a source file. At the top of the file there is defined a module that is not associated with a plugin. This is how you would specify additional source files to compile if your plugin code were to use special methods, functions, or classes that you defined in other source files.

Now that we know what the building blocks are for building a plugin, where to find plugin-type-specific structures and definitions, and how to build a plugin, we can build a new plugin.

In the following sections, I show you how to build an authentication plugin that uses a hardware device to further secure your server by restricting login to users who must possess a special key card as well as a personal identification code (PIN).

The RFID Authentication Plugin

To illustrate how to create a MySQL plugin, I show you how to create an authentication plugin, because it is likely one of the most useful, and also one of the areas that developers seeking to customize their MySQL installations may want to create. I chose to make the project more interesting by introducing a hardware device to make the solution more secure than a typical user-name and password pair. In this case, the hardware device reads a special identification card that an administrator would give to a user that contains a unique number read only by the hardware device. This provides one-level-greater security than a simple password.[2]

The keycard device I chose to use is a radio frequency identification card (RFID).[3] A RFID tag is typically a credit-car- sized plastic card, label, or something similar, that contains a special antenna, typically in the form of a coil, thin wire, or foil layer that is "tuned" to a specific frequency, so that when the reader emits a radio signal, the tag can use the electromagnet energy to transmit a nonvolatile message embedded in the embedded coil, which is then converted to an alphanumeric string. This form of RFID tag is a passive device, because it contains no battery. RFID systems with a need for greater range or power typically include a battery in the RFID tag itself. These are called active tags.

Tags and readers must be tuned to the same frequency. There are many RFID tag manufacturers and numerous frequencies. Thus, when choosing to incorporate a RFID system into your project, ensure that you purchase tags that are tuned to the same frequency as the reader. I recommend purchasing a kit that includes both the reader and several tags to be sure you avoid issues with compatibility.

For this project, we will use that string as part of the authentication mechanism. If we also include a prompt for the user to remember a PIN it further secures the solution because no one other than the intended user can use the card to login (unless, of course, they shared their PIN but in that case you've got a more serious problem).

---

[2] I will describe some modifications that make the example even more secure.
[3] http://en.wikipedia.org/wiki/Radio-frequency_identification

The solution is more secure because instead of relying only on something the user must know, such as a password, the user must also have a physical item that they must present to complete the authentication. Thus, the solution provides two of the three elements considered to be very secure authentication. The third element is a biometric such as a finger or palm print that further identifies the user.

In the next section, I will describe how this authentication mechanism works. As you will see, it involves a client software component, a client hardware component, and a server software component. The software component is a special authentication plugin.

Concept of Operations

This project uses a RFID reader and a tag or keycard in place of the traditional user password. The setup on the server side involves using a variant of the CREATE USER command to create the user and associate with her account the RFID authentication plugin. The user is also assigned or allowed to choose a special personal identification number (PIN) using a short numeric string (I use 4 digits like most banks and credit cards). We use the RFID code with the PIN concatenated to form the passcode for that user.

When the user desires to login to the server, she starts her mysql client and is then prompted to swipe her card and once read correctly asked to enter her PIN. This information is then transmitted to the server to validate the combined code and PIN. Once validated, the user is logged into the server and the client proceeds. If the codes do not match, the user is given the appropriate error message indicating that her login attempt has failed.

If this sounds familiar to some of you, it isn't an accident. I have used several similar systems to gain access to resources I was assigned. Not only are these systems more secure, they are also easier for the user because, unless they loose their keycard,[4] she only has to remember a short PIN number.

Now that you are familiar with how the system operates, lets see how to build the system.

RFID Module

The first component you will need is a RFID reader (module). I chose to purchase a starter kit that contains a RFID tag reader that reads 125kHz tags and three tags (keycards). I am a Maker, so I often turn to electronics vendors who cater to the Maker community. One is SparkFun Electronics (`http://www.sparkfun.com`).

▨ **Note**   If you have purchased a different RFID system, follow the vendor's setup guide, but read the following in case your system is similar.

SparkFun's RFID starter kit (item# RTL-09875 $49.95 USD) was a great choice because it is USB based and therefore will work on all modern platforms. It is relatively inexpensive and exposes pins on the module that permit you to explore the hardware features of the RFID module should you want to make a more complex solution. While it does not contain a case (more on this later), it does provide a no-solder solution complete with an audible read chime. Last, the kit includes three keycards with unique RFID codes.

Figure 9-1 shows the RFID Starter Kit in its retail package. It contains a RFID module, the module board, and three keycards. You will have to supply your own USB to mini-USB cable (also available from SparkFun). Figure 9-2 shows a detail of the module board itself with the extra pins for developers (show to the right). Figure 9-3 shows a sample keycard included with the kit.

---

[4] While it is still possible to lose a keycard, having one avoids the much more frequent forgotten-password event.

Figure 9-1. *RFID Start Kit from SparkFun Electronics*

Figure 9-2. *RFID module board*

Figure 9-3. *Keycard*

I recommend reading through this chapter and following along with the walk through of the code. Once you have ordered your own RFID kit, you can return to the chapter and complete the example.

One reason I like to buy from electronics vendors who cater to hobbyists and professionals alike is that they typically include a wealth of information about their products. Their Web sites have everything from datasheets (detailed specifications including everything an electronics professional would need to use the component in a project) and schematics to links to example projects and, in some cases, tutorials and quick-start guides.

SparkFun is an excellent vendor in this regard. For example, the RFID Starter Kit contains links to the datasheet, schematics, Eagle files for creating your own module board, and a quick-start guide to using the kit (http://www.sparkfun.com/tutorials/243).

I will not reproduce the quick-start guide in this book, but I will walk you through the things you need to do to use the RFID module for this example project in the following sections. I recommend reading the quick-start guide once you've read through this chapter to see an alternative presentation of the setup.

■ **Note** The quick-start guide is written for use with Windows, so if you use Windows, you may find the guide more useful than if you use another platform.

Installing a Driver

If you want to use the RFID module to read the codes via a serial interface[5] like a modem reads from a COM port, you will need a special driver called an FTDI chip driver. Fortunately, the folks at SparkFun included a link for that too (http://www.ftdichip.com/FTDrivers.htm).

---

[5] While a USB port is by definition a serial connection, most people associate the older ports with nine or more pins as a "serial port." It is this type of port to which I refer.

This driver is required for most platforms so that existing software can read from the device via those standardized COM ports. Once the driver is installed and the RFID module is connected, the driver will map the USB port to a COM port (Windows) or to a tty device (Linux and Mac OS X). You can discover the USB device in Linux and Mac OS X platforms by listing the contents of the /dev folder as shown below.

```
Chucks-iMac:~ cbell$ ls /dev/tty.usb*
/dev/tty.usbserial-A501D94V
```

In the above output, we see a single device named so that it gives you a clue as to what it is. The FTDI driver will take care of interfacing the USB port with the standard communication-port protocols.

On Windows, you can discover the COM port assigned by opening the device manager, expanding the tree for COM and LPT ports, right-clicking on a port, and then choosing the advanced-settings dialog. Not only can you see the COM port assigned, you can also change it if you need to. Figure 9-4 shows an example of this dialog.

Figure 9-4. *COM Port advanced settings on Windows*

■ **Tip** I found it necessary to change the COM port from COM13 to COM1 on my Windows laptop. The RFID module was not working with any terminal client on Windows until I changed the mapping. Once changed, it worked flawlessly in a terminal client as well as the authentication plugin.

Once you have the driver installed and the module connected via the USB cable, open a terminal client and change the settings to connect to the COM port. The SparkFun RFID Starter Kit uses a configuration of 9600,8,N,1 for baud rate, bits, parity, and stop bits. This is a typical default for most terminal clients. If your client has a connect button or switch, click that now, and then try swiping a card. If everything works, you should hear a loud beep from the RFID module indicating that it has read the keycard, and you should see a string of 12 characters or more appear in the terminal client. If it doesn't, go back and diagnose the settings for the COM port, your USB port, and the terminal client.

Discovering the Card Identification Numbers

If you looked at the keycards carefully (perhaps trying to see the antenna), you may have noticed that they do not have any codes written on them. So how do you find out what the codes are? If you setup your RFID module as described in the previous section, you would have seen the code for that keycard.

Thus, you will need to read each keycard and note the code returned. Take a moment now to discover all of the codes and make a mark on each card so that you can discover (recall) the code associated with the keycard. Figure 9-5 shows an example of a terminal client reading the code from a connected RFID module.

Figure 9-5. *Terminal client reading RFID code*

Depending on your terminal clients settings (some have a hexadecimal view option), you may see several extra characters that may appear as dots or other strange symbols. These are the control codes sent by the RFID module and for our uses they can be safely ignore. What you are looking for are the 12 characters that represent the RFID code.

Now that you know the codes associated with the keycards, let's take a short detour and talk about how to make that bare printed circuit board (the RFID module board) a bit more secure, rugged, and user friendly.

Securing the RFID Module

Aside from the lack of protection for the RFID reader itself, a criticism of a solution such as this could be the lack of security for the RFID reader itself. As you have seen, it would be very easy for a savvy reader to pluck the reader out of its USB tether and use it on another computer to discover his or others' keycard numbers.

Fortunately, this will get the errand user only so far. He would also have to discover another user's PIN. In this way, securing the RFID reader itself may be considered a lesser concern. If you are concerned about securing the reader, I offer some possible solutions.

If you are experienced with hardware development or electronics, you could incorporate the RFID module into the user's computer case. One possible location is behind an empty drive bay. Many PC manufacturers have additional USB connectors on the motherboard, and some vendors do not connect these additional ports. In some cases, the motherboard may have dedicated internal USB connections. If one such is available, you could route the RFID readers' USB cable to the internal port. Finally, you can use special security locks to secure the case from tampering.

I chose to use a small project case from Radio Shack (item# 270–1801 $3.99) to mount the RFID module. Figure 9-6 shows the project case. I began by drilling a small hole in one end of the case so that the read tone would not be stifled (it won't be nearly as loud), and I cut a slot in the other end to allow the USB cable to fit snuggly.

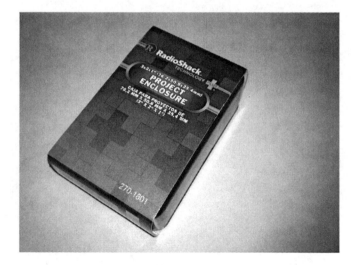

Figure 9-6. *RFID case unmodified*

I then used a piece of double-sided tape to secure the RFID module to the metal lid. I oriented the module so that the reader would face upward and the plastic case would sit upside down (lid down) on the desk. I then closed the case with the provided screws, placing a nonskip, self-adhesive foot to conceal each screw. Figure 9-7 shows the case unassembled, and Figure 9-8 shows the completed solution. Let's call the completed unit simply the RFID reader.

Figure 9-7. *Assembling the RFID reader unit*

Figure 9-8. *Assembled RFID reader*

Now that we have a working RFID reader, let's dive into the code for making this work with MySQL. In the next section, I explain how authentication plugins are constructed and show you the details for constructing an authentication plugin that uses the RFID reader to validate user logins.

Architecture of Authentication Plugins

Now that we have seen how the solution will work, and how to configure the RFID reader and discover the key card identification strings, let's look at the composition and architecture of an authentication plugin.

Authentication plugins contain two components: a client-side plugin and a server-side plugin. For convenience, both of these can reside in the same code module.

As with all plugins, you must configure the plugin on the server before you can use it. The procedure described earlier in this chapter and in Chapter 7 is the same for authentication plugins. Specifically, you must place the compiled library in the folder designated by the `plugin-dir` variable and use the `INSTALL PLUGIN` command to install the plugin. The following is an example command to install the plugin we are about to build on Linux.

```
INSTALL PLUGIN rfid_auth SONAME 'rfid_auth.so';
```

To associate a user with an authentication plugin, use the IDENTIFIED WITH clause of the CREATE USER command (see below). This tells the server to replace normal MySQL authentication with a request to the client to initiate the client-side component of the plugin specified.

```
CREATE USER 'test'@'localhost' IDENTIFIED WITH rfid_auth AS 'XXXXXXXPPPPP';
```

In the two example commands above, I refer to the plugin as rfid_auth, the name I have chosen to name the RFID authentication plugin. You will need to have the same consistency for any authentication plugin you may wish to create.

Notice also the AS clause. This clause allows you to specify a phrase that the server-side authentication plugin can use to help identify the user. For the purposes of illustration, brevity, and ease to develop, I chose to use this string to store the user's keycard code appended with her PIN. While this is stored in the `mysql.user` table as clear text, it is still safe, because most users will not have read access to this table. I offer some more secure ways of storing this value in a later section. Now let's turn our attention to how an authentication plugin works.

How Does an Authentication Plugin Work?

When a user is associated with an authentication plugin, and the user attempts to connect to the server, the server will request a packet from the server that contains a response that will be used by the server to complete the validation. This mechanism mirrors the challenge-and-response sequence of the traditional MySQL server-authentication protocol.

In this case, the client is designed to attempt to load the corresponding client-side plugin by the same name as the server-side plugin. The client knows this because the name of the plugin is returned in a special area of the packet sent from the server. In this way, we are assured the authentication-plugin segments (server and client) communicate only to each other.

You may be wondering, "How can this work? Wouldn't the client need to know how to load the plugin?" The answer to the second question is, "Yes." The client must be capable of loading client-side plugins. Thus, you cannot use an older version of the mysql client application to log into a server via a user account that is associated with a server-side authentication plugin.

The MySQL client applications will attempt to load the plugin from the --plugin-dir specified in the MySQL configuration file. You can also specify its location by providing the --plugin-dir option like:

```
cbell@ubuntu $ ../client/mysql -utest -h 127.0.0.1 --port=13000 --plugin-dir=../lib/plugin
```

Now that we have an idea for how the authentication plugin works, let's take a moment to see how each is constructed.

Creating an Authentication Plugin

To create an authentication plugin, you need to create the following three files.

- CMakeLists.txt – cmake configuration file
- rfid_auth.cc – source file
- rfid_auth.ini – plugin ini file (described above and used by the `mysql_plugin` client application)

That's it! Easy, eh? Go ahead and create the folder now.

Building the RFID Authentication Plugin

Let's begin our coding effort with the CMakeLists.txt file. Open a text editor of your choice and enter the directives shown in Listing 9-4. The first line calls a macro that set ups up everything needed to correctly compile a MySQL plugin (hence the name). The macro takes as parameters the name of the plugin, the name of the source file(s), and any special directives. In this case, we use MODULE_ONLY[6] to build the module but not to link it to the server and MODULE_OUTPUT_NAME to set the name of the compiled plugin.

Listing 9-4. CMakeLists.txt File

```
# cmake configuration file for the RFID Authentication Plugin

MYSQL_ADD_PLUGIN(rfid_auth rfid_auth.cc
  MODULE_ONLY MODULE_OUTPUT_NAME "rfid_auth")

INSTALL(FILES rfid_auth.ini DESTINATION ${INSTALL_PLUGINDIR})
```

This is another example of the tireless efforts of the Oracle MySQL engineers to make the server code more modular and easier to extend via the plugin interface.

Now we are ready to start coding the solution. Open your favorite code editor, start a new file, and name it rfid_auth.cc. Place it in the /plugin/rfid_auth folder. Rather than list the entire contents of the rfid_auth.cc file, I will walk through the code a portion at a time. I start with the include file section, then describe and list the client-side plugin code, and later describe and list the server-side plugin code. All of the code in Listings 9-5 through 9-10 should be placed in the same source file.

Include Files and Definitions

First, list all include files and any definitions you want to make for the code. Listing 9-5 shows the include files needed for the RFID authentication plugin. These are the include files needed for both plugins.

Listing 9-5. Include and Definition Code

```
#include <my_global.h>
#include <mysql/plugin_auth.h>
#include <mysql/client_plugin.h>
#include <string.h>
#include <stdio.h>
#include <stdlib.h>
#include <stdio.h>
#include <fcntl.h>
#include <errno.h>
#include <mysql.h>

#ifndef __WIN__

#include <unistd.h>
#include <pwd.h>

#else
```

---

[6] These directives are defined in the cmake/plugin.cmake file.

```cpp
#include <windows.h>
#include <conio.h>
#include <iostream>
#include <string>
using namespace std;

/*
 Get password with no echo.
*/
char *getpass(const char *prompt)
{
  string pass ="";
  char ch;
  cout << prompt;
  ch = _getch();
  while(ch != 13) //character 13 is enter key
  {
    pass.push_back(ch);
    ch = _getch();
  }
  return (char *)pass.c_str();
}

#endif

#define MAX_RFID_CODE  12
#define MAX_BUFFER     255
#define MAX_PIN         16
```

Notice that there is a conditional compilation statement. This is because the Windows platform has different mechanisms for reading from serial ports. Also, the Windows platform does not have a native getpass() method.

Now that the preamble for the source file is done, let's see how the code looks for the client-side plugin.

Client-side Plugin

A client-side authentication plugin is constructed using a specific structure that resembles the st_mysql_plugin structure described above. Fortunately, there are macros that you can use to simplify the creation.

The client-side plugin is responsible for sending the user's credentials to the server for validation. For the RFID-authentication plugin, this means prompting the user to swipe her card, reading the keycard, ask the user to enter her PIN, and then sending the concatenated RFID code and PIN to the server.

Let's start by looking at the code to read the keycode. Once again, we need to use a conditional compile, because the code to read the COM port on Windows is very different from that of Linux and Mac OS X. Listing 9-6 shows the code for reading the RFID code from the RFID reader.

Listing 9-6. Reading RFID Code

```cpp
/*
 * Read a RFID code from the serial port.
 */
#ifndef __WIN__
unsigned char *get_rfid_code(char *port)
```

```
{
  int fd;
  unsigned char *rfid_code= NULL;
  int nbytes;
  unsigned char raw_buff[MAX_BUFFER];
  unsigned char *bufptr = NULL;

  fd = open(port, O_RDWR | O_NOCTTY | O_NDELAY);
  if (fd == -1)
  {
    printf("Unable to open port: %s.\n", port);
    return NULL;
  }
  else
    fcntl(fd, F_SETFL, 0);

  bufptr = raw_buff;
  while ((nbytes = read(fd, bufptr, raw_buff + sizeof(raw_buff) - bufptr - 1)) > 0)
  {
    bufptr += nbytes;
    if (bufptr[-1] == '\n' || bufptr[-2] == '\n' || bufptr[-3] == '\n' ||
        bufptr[-1] == '\r' || bufptr[-2] == '\r' || bufptr[-3] == '\r' ||
        bufptr[-1] == 0x03 || bufptr[-2] == 0x03 || bufptr[-3] == 0x03)
    break;
  }
  *bufptr = '\0';

  rfid_code = (unsigned char *)strdup((char *)raw_buff);
  return rfid_code;
}

#else

unsigned char *get_rfid_code(char *port)
{
  HANDLE com_port;
  DWORD nbytes;
  unsigned char raw_buff[MAX_BUFFER];
  unsigned char *rfid_code= NULL;

    /* Open the port specified. */
    com_port = CreateFile(port, GENERIC_READ, 0, 0, OPEN_EXISTING,

    FILE_ATTRIBUTE_NORMAL, 0);
    if (com_port == INVALID_HANDLE_VALUE)
    {
      int error = GetLastError();
      if (error == ERROR_FILE_NOT_FOUND)
      {
        printf("Unable to open port: %s.\n", port);
        return NULL;
      }
```

```
    printf("Error opening port: %s:%d.\n", port, error);
    return NULL;
  }

  /* Configure the port. */
  DCB com_config = {0};
  com_config.DCBlength = sizeof(com_config);
  if (!GetCommState(com_port, &com_config))
  {
    printf("Unable to get port state.\n");
    return NULL;
  }
  com_config.BaudRate = CBR_9600;
  com_config.ByteSize = 8;
  com_config.Parity = NOPARITY;
  com_config.StopBits = ONESTOPBIT;
  if (!SetCommState(com_port, &com_config))
  {
    printf("Unable to set port state.\n");
    return NULL;
  }

  /* Set timeouts. */
  COMMTIMEOUTS timeouts = {0};
  timeouts.ReadIntervalTimeout=50;
  timeouts.ReadTotalTimeoutConstant=50;
  timeouts.ReadTotalTimeoutMultiplier=10;
  if (!SetCommTimeouts(com_port, &timeouts))
  {
    printf("Cannot set timeouts for port.\n");
    return NULL;
  }

  /* Read from the port. */
  if (!ReadFile(com_port, raw_buff, MAX_BUFFER, &nbytes, NULL))
  {
    printf("Unable to read from the port.\n");
    return NULL;
  }

  /* Close the port. */
  CloseHandle(com_port);

  rfid_code = (unsigned char *)strdup((char *)raw_buff);
  return rfid_code;
}

#endif /* __WIN__ */
```

I leave the details of the Windows portion to those familiar with Windows programming, because this code is a well-proven and frequently duplicated section of code.

> **Note** The non-Windows code is easy to write, but it has a particularly interesting wrinkle. In testing the RFID reader on several platforms, I discovered that the RFID code returned from the reader can contain a number of different patterns of control codes. Thus, I had to write the code to take into consideration all of the permutations I encountered. Your own experience with your platform may result in similar observations.

Now, let's turn our attention to the core method of this plugin. Listing 9-7 shows the code used to control the client-side plugin. This method is mapped to the client-side plugin structure (described below) and called when the client detects that the server is requesting data from the rfid_auth plugin.

Listing 9-7. Sending RFID Code to the Server

```
static int rfid_send(MYSQL_PLUGIN_VIO *vio, st_mysql *mysql)
{
  char *port= 0;
  char pass[MAX_PIN];
  int len, res;
  unsigned char buffer[MAX_BUFFER];
  unsigned char *raw_buff= NULL;
  int start= 0;

  /* Get the port to open. */
  port= getenv("MYSQL_RFID_PORT");
  if (!port)
  {
    printf("Environment variable not set.\n");
    return CR_ERROR;
  }

  printf("Please swipe your card now...\n");

  raw_buff = get_rfid_code(port);
  if (raw_buff == NULL)
  {
    printf("Cannot read RFID code.\n");
    return CR_ERROR;
  }
  len = strlen((char *)raw_buff);

  // Strip off leading extra bytes.
  for (int j= 0; j < 2; j++)
    if (raw_buff[j] == 0x02 || raw_buff[j] == 0x03)
      start++;

  strncpy((char *)buffer, (char *)raw_buff+start, len-start);
  len = strlen((char *)buffer);
```

```
  /* Check for valid read. */
  if (len >= MAX_RFID_CODE)
  {
    // Strip off extra bytes at end (CR, LF, etc.)
    buffer[MAX_RFID_CODE] = '\0';
        len = MAX_RFID_CODE;
  }
  else
  {
    printf("RFID code length error. Please try again.\n");
    return CR_ERROR;
  }

  strncpy(pass, getpass("Please enter your PIN: "), sizeof(pass));
  strcat((char *)buffer, pass);
  len = strlen((char *)buffer);

  res= vio->write_packet(vio, buffer, len);

  return res ? CR_ERROR : CR_OK;
}
```

The above method begins with checking which port to use to read from the RFID reader. I use an environment variable named MYSQL_RFID_PORT for the user to specify the text string for the port to open. Examples include COM1, COM2, /dev/ttyUSB0, etc. There may be other, more elegant ways to specify the port, but this is the easiest to code and the easiest to deploy (simply add it to the user's login script).

After the environment variable containing the port is read, the method prompts the user to swipe her keycard and calls the get_rfid_code() method defined above to read the RFID code. Some simple error handling is included to ensure that the code was read correctly (all 12 characters are available). Once the code is read, the method prompts the user for her PIN and then reads the PIN from standard input (keyboard).

This information is then concatenated and sent to the server using the vio class method write_packet(). That's it! The client-side authentication plugin has turned control over to the server-side plugin to validate the string. If it is validated, the write_packet() returns CR_OK otherwise it returns CR_ERROR. If the server-side validation succeeds, the client application takes over to complete the handshake with the server and completes the login.

The last item to discuss and code is the client-side plugin definition structure. There are macros that make this definition easier. Listing 9-8 shows the use of the prefix macro mysql_declare_client_plugin and the mysql_end_client_plugin postfix macro. The contents of the structure begins with the name of the plugin, the author, a description of the plugin, the version array, and the license. Following this are function pointers to the MySQL API (internal use only), initialization, de-initialization, and option-handling helper methods. Since the RFID authentication plugin is rather simple, we don't use any of these methods, and therefore, we set them to NULL. The last entry is the function pointer to the method called when the server requests the validation data from the client. As you can see, this is the rfid_send() method described above.

Listing 9-8. Defining the Client-side Plugin

```
mysql_declare_client_plugin(AUTHENTICATION)
  "rfid_auth",
  "Chuck Bell",
  "RFID Authentication Plugin - Client",
  {0, 0, 1},
  "GPL",
  NULL,
```

```
  NULL,
  NULL,
  NULL,
  rfid_send
mysql_end_client_plugin;
```

■ **Caution**   The name you assign to the client-side plugin (the first entry in the structure) **must** match the name of the server-side plugin (see below). If it does not match, you will encounter some unusual error messages from the client or the server.

As you can see, the client-side plugin isn't that complicated (aside from reading from the serial port). Now let's look at the server-side plugin code.

Server-side Plugin

The server-side plugin code is simpler. This is because it only has to validate the RFID code received from the client. Listing 9-9 shows the validation code.

Listing 9-9. Validating the RFID Code

```
/*
 * Server-side plugin
 */
static int rfid_auth_validate(MYSQL_PLUGIN_VIO *vio,
                    MYSQL_SERVER_AUTH_INFO *info)
{
  unsigned char *pkt;
  int pkt_len, err= CR_OK;

  if ((pkt_len= vio->read_packet(vio, &pkt)) < 0)
    return CR_ERROR;

  info->password_used= PASSWORD_USED_YES;

  if (strcmp((const char *) pkt, info->auth_string))
    return CR_ERROR;

  return err;
}
```

The above code only has to read a packet from the client via the vio->read_packet() class method and match it to the code stored in the mysql.user table.

The server-side definition also uses macros to define the structure. It requires the definition of two structures, however. We have a similar structure for defining the plugin, but there is also a special structure, the plugin handler structure, to store the version, text string descriptor, and a function pointer to the server-side validation code (also called the authentication method in some documentation). The handler structure is also used to present the information about the plugin via the plugin utility commands. Listing 9-10 shows both structures used to define the server-side plugin.

Listing 9-10. Defining the Server-side Plugin

```
static struct st_mysql_auth rfid_auth_handler=
{
  MYSQL_AUTHENTICATION_INTERFACE_VERSION,
  "rfid_auth",
  rfid_auth_validate
};

mysql_declare_plugin(rfid_auth_plugin)
{
  MYSQL_AUTHENTICATION_PLUGIN,
  &rfid_auth_handler,
  "rfid_auth",
  "Chuck Bell",
  "RFID Authentication Plugin - Server",
  PLUGIN_LICENSE_GPL,
  NULL,
  NULL,
  0x0100,
  NULL,
  NULL,
  NULL,
  0,
}
mysql_declare_plugin_end;
```

The second structure is the same structure used to define any server plugin. The macros `mysql_declare_plugin` and `mysql_declare_plugin_end` help simplify the code. As you can see, it contains the type of the plugin, the address to the handler structure, name of the plugin, the author, the description string, the type of license, the function pointers to initialization and deinitialization, the version (in hex), function pointers to status variables, system variables, an internal use-only position, and finally, a set of flags used to further describe the plugin's capabilities. See the online reference manual for more details about this structure.

■ **Caution** The name you assign to the server-side plugin (the first entry in the structure) **must** match the name of the client-side plugin (see above). If it does not, you will encounter some unusual error messages from the client or the server.

Now that we have all of the code for the RFID authentication plugin, we can compile the plugin and test it. First, let's look at the last file—the `rfid_auth.ini` file.

The rfid_auth.ini File

To complete our plugin, we also need to create the initialization file for use with the mysql_plugin client application. If you do not plan to bundle the plugin with a special build of the server or to initiate the make install command from the source tree, you need not create this file. Listing 9-11 shows the contents of the file.

Listing 9-11. The rfid_auth.ini file

```
#
# Plugin configuration file. Place the following on a separate line:
#
# library binary file name (without .so or .dll)
# component_name
# [component_name] - additional components in plugin
#
librfid_auth
rfid_auth
```

Now that the source files are complete, lets compile the plugin.

Compiling the Plugin

Compiling the plugin is even easier. The base cmake files for the server code contain all the macros needed to ensure that any plugin placed in the /plugin folder that has the correctly formatted CMakeLists.txt file will be automatically configured when the following commands are issued from the root of the source tree.

```
cmake .
make
```

That's right. No special, complicated, or convoluted commands are needed. Just create a folder, say /plugin/rfid_auth, and place your files in it. When ready to compile, navigate to the root of the tree and enter the commands above.

Go ahead and compile the plugin, and then copy it to the plugin directory of your server. If you encounter errors, go back and fix those until the plugin code compiles without errors or warnings.

RFID Authentication in Action

Before you rush off to buy a RFID reader and start coding, let's take a look at this example executing on a real server. Recall that once compiled, we need to copy the plugin (e.g. rfid_auth.so or rfid_auth.dll) to the location on the server that corresponds with the setting for --plugin-dir.

The server does not need to be restarted, but if you are attempting to copy an existing, installed plugin, you may encounter some unusual and potentially damaging behavior by the server. For example, on Windows, the server may crash, but on Ubuntu, the server is not affected.

For authentication plugins, the plugin must also be placed in a location that the clients can find (or specified via the --plugin-dir option for the client applications).

Once the plugin is in the correct locations, we must go to the server and install the plugin as shown below.

```
INSTALL PLUGIN rfid_auth SONAME 'rfid_auth.so';
```

The command should return without errors. You can verify that the plugin is loaded by issuing a query against the INFORMATION_SCHEMA.plugins view, as shown in Listing 9-12. Notice the name, type, description, author, and versions of the plugin. Compare these to those defined in the code above.

Listing 9-12. Verifying the Plugin is Installed

```
mysql> select * from information_schema.plugins where plugin_name like 'rfid%' \G
*************************** 1. row ***************************
           PLUGIN_NAME: rfid_auth
        PLUGIN_VERSION: 1.0
         PLUGIN_STATUS: ACTIVE
           PLUGIN_TYPE: AUTHENTICATION
   PLUGIN_TYPE_VERSION: 1.0
        PLUGIN_LIBRARY: rfid_auth.so
PLUGIN_LIBRARY_VERSION: 1.4
         PLUGIN_AUTHOR: Chuck Bell
    PLUGIN_DESCRIPTION: RFID Authentication Plugin - Server
       PLUGIN_LICENSE: GPL
           LOAD_OPTION: ON
1 row in set (0.00 sec)
```

Once we know that the plugin is installed, we can create users that are associated with the plugin. The following shows an example of creating a user to authenticate with the RFID authentication plugin.

```
CREATE USER 'test'@'localhost' IDENTIFIED WITH rfid_auth AS '51007BB754C91234';
```

Now we can go to the client and attempt to log in using the plugin. Listing 9-13 shows the user attempting to log in to the server. Notice the use of the --plugin-dir option to specify the location of the RFID authentication plugin. Notice also the prompts from the client-side plugin to swipe the keycard and to enter the PIN. When prompted to swipe my card, I simply placed the card on top of the RFID reader case until I heard it signal a correct read with a beep. The process took less than two seconds (I had my card on my desk ready to use,) and typing the PIN was a simple matter of typing a four-digit number.

Listing 9-13. Logging in with the RFID Authentication Plugin

```
cbell@ubuntu:$ ../client/mysql -utest -h 127.0.0.1 --port=13000 --plugin-dir=../lib/plugin
Please swipe your card now...
Please enter your PIN:
Welcome to the MySQL monitor.  Commands end with ; or \g.
Your MySQL connection id is 2
Server version: 5.6.6-m9 Source distribution

Copyright (c) 2000, 2012, Oracle and/or its affiliates. All rights reserved.

Oracle is a registered trademark of Oracle Corporation and/or its
affiliates. Other names may be trademarks of their respective
owners.

Type 'help;' or '\h' for help. Type '\c' to clear the current input statement.

mysql>
```

You may be wondering if only the mysql client application is client-side plugin enabled. The good news is that all of the supplied client applications are plugin enabled for use with authentication plugins. Listing 9-14 shows an example of the mysqladmin client application using the authentication plugin.

Listing 9-14. Logging in with the mysqladmin Client Application

```
cbell@ubuntu:$ mysqladmin processlist -utest -h 127.0.0.1 --port=13000 --plugin-dir=../lib/plugin
Please swipe your card now...
Please enter your PIN:
+----+------+-----------------+----+---------+------+-------+------------------+
| Id | User | Host            | db | Command | Time | State | Info             |
+----+------+-----------------+----+---------+------+-------+------------------+
| 3  | test | localhost:46374 |    | Query   | 0    | init  | show processlist |
+----+------+-----------------+----+---------+------+-------+------------------+
```

▨ **Note**   Using the authentication plugin does not violate or circumvent the user-security layer in the MySQL server.

As you can see, using an authentication plugin changes the way that users log in to the server. In this example, I created a unique method of logging in to the server that requires the use of a special keycard and does not use passwords (PIN code excluded).

In the next section, I present some suggestions for improving and hardening the plugin for use in production environments or for creating your own professional RFID reader based authentication mechanism.

Further Work

If you find the RFID authentication plugin a worthwhile model for building your own, more-secure user-login mechanism, you can improve the solution in a number of ways. You could change the size of the PIN, use the validate_password plugin to help create more secure PINs, or add an additional hardware element, such as the MAC address of the client workstation. In this case, the MAC address would further restrict login to a user with a specific keycard and a matching PIN read from a specific machine.

Perhaps the best and most secure option is to use SHA1 or MD% algorithms to encrypt the keycode stored in the mysql.plugin table. The client-side plugin would have to use the same seed to form the encrypted string, so using the MySQL methods may be problematic. A simple hash or even a scramble, however, should be sufficient to protect the code from accidental discover. Even then, the use of the code is limited, since the infiltrator would have to construct a facsimile of the client-side plugin, and that, I hope you agree, is beyond the skills of the average user.

Another option is to use the RFID code itself as the seed and encrypt a known phrase. I would recommend the use of a random byte stream, so that someone reading the code—or if an extremely persistent snoop attempts to read the binary code for the plugin—will not discover the passcode in clear text. Either way, encrypting what is stored in the mysql.user table should be considered a vital requirement for production use.

Beyond securing the RFID reader itself, you could also incorporate a biometric element, such as a fingerprint reader. Implementing such a device may require a bit more programming that you may expect, but if you are after a highly secure solution, a biometric device will complete your quest.

Summary

You may be thinking, "Wow, that's a lot to take in." That may be true, but once you have worked with the code and seen it in action, I hope that you will see this as a good example of how to build a plugin for authentication that you can use as a boilerplate for your own authentication plugin.

In this chapter, I discussed the most import feature of the MySQL server—he ability to add new features without stopping or reconfiguring the server. You were introduced to the types of plugins available and how they form the basis for future expansion of server features. I then examined the architecture of MySQL plugins and how they are installed and uninstalled, as well as demonstrated how to create a plugin through the creation of an authentication plugin using a RFID reader.

The next chapter will explore the most complex type of plugin, a MySQL storage engine. You will see how to create your own storage engines. You should be impressed with the ease of extending the MySQL system to meet your needs. Just the embedded server library alone opens up a broad realm of possibilities. Add to that the ability to create your own storage engines and even (later) your own functions in MySQL, and it is easy to see why MySQL is the "world's most popular open-source database."

■ ■ ■

## CHAPTER 10

Building Your Own Storage Engine

The MySQL pluggable architecture that enables the use of multiple storage engines is one of the most important features of the MySQL system. Many database professionals have refined advanced skills for tuning the logical structure of relational database systems to meet the needs of the data and their applications. With MySQL, database professionals can also tune the physical layer of their database systems by choosing the storage method that best optimizes the access methods for the database. That is a huge advantage over relational database systems that use only a single storage mechanism.[1]

This chapter guides you through the process of creating your own storage engine. I begin by explaining the details of building a storage engine plugin in some detail and then walk you through a tutorial for building a sample storage engine. If you've been itching to get your hands on the MySQL source code and make it do something really cool, now is the time to roll up your sleeves and refill that beverage. If you're a little wary of making these kinds of modifications, read through the chapter and follow the examples until you are comfortable with the process.

MySQL Storage Engine Overview

A storage-engine plugin is a software layer in the architecture of the MySQL server. It is responsible for abstracting the physical data layer from the logical layers of the server, and it provides the low-level input/output (I/O) operations for the server. When a system is developed in a layered architecture, it provides a mechanism for streamlining and standardizing the interfaces between the layers. This quality measures the success of a layered architecture. A powerful feature of layered architectures is the ability to modify one layer and, provided the interfaces do not change, not alter the adjacent layers.

Oracle has reworked the architecture of MySQL (starting in version 5.0) to incorporate this layered-architecture approach. The plugin architecture was added in version 5.1, and pluggable storage engines are the most visible form of that endeavor. The storage-engine plugin empowers systems integrators and developers to use MySQL in environments in which the data requires special processing to read and write. Furthermore, the plugin architecture allows you to create your own storage engine.

One reason for doing this rather than convert the data to a format that can be ingested by MySQL is the cost of doing that conversion. For example, suppose you have a legacy application that your organization has been using for a long time. The data that the application has used are valuable to your organization and cannot be duplicated. Furthermore, you may need to use the old application. Rather than converting the data to a new format, you can create a storage engine that can read and write the data in the old format. Other examples include cases in which the data and their access methods are such that you require special data handling to ensure the most efficient means of reading and writing the data.

Furthermore, and perhaps most important, the storage-engine plugin can connect data that are not normally connected to database systems. That is, you can create storage engines to read streaming data (e.g., RSS) or other

---

[1]The use of clustered indexes and other data-file optimizations notwithstanding.

nontraditional, non-disk-stored data. Whatever your needs, MySQL can meet them by allowing you to create your own storage engines that will enable you to create an efficient, specialized relational-database system for your environment.

You can use the MySQL server as your relational-database-processing engine and wire it directly to your legacy data by providing a special storage engine that plugs directly into the server. This may not sound like an easy thing to do, but it really is.

The most important architectural element is the use of an array of single objects to access the storage engines (one object per storage engine). The control of these single objects is in the form of a complex structure called a handlerton (as in singleton—see the sidebar on singletons). A special class called a handler is a base class that uses the handlerton to complete the interface and provide the basic connectivity to enable a storage engine. I demonstrate this in Figure 10-1 later in this chapter.

Figure 10-1. *Pluggable storage-engine-class derivation*

All storage engines are derived from the base-handler class, which acts as a police officer, marshaling the common access methods and function calls to the storage engine and from the storage engine to the server. In other words, the handler and handlerton structure act as an intermediary (or black box) between the storage engine and the server. As long as your storage engine conforms to the handler interface and the pluggable architecture, you can plug it into the server. All of the connection, authentication, parsing, and optimization is still performed by the server in the usual way. The different storage engines merely pass the data to and from the server in a common format, translating them to and from the specialized storage medium.

Oracle has documented the process of creating a new storage engine fairly well. As of this writing, Chapter 14 of the MySQL reference manual contains a complete explanation of the storage engine and all functions supported and required by the handler interface. I recommend reading the MySQL reference manual after you have read this chapter and worked through building the example storage engine. The MySQL reference manual in this case is best used as just that—a reference.

WHAT IS A SINGLETON?

In some situations in object-oriented programming, you may need to limit object creation so that only one object instantiation is made for a given class. One reason for this may be that the class protects a shared set of operations or data. For example, if you had a manager class designed to be a gatekeeper for access to a specific resource or data, you might be tempted to create a static or global reference to this object and therefore permit only one instance in the entire application. The use of global instances and constant structures or access functions flies in the face of the object-oriented mantra, however. Instead of doing that, you can create a specialized form of the object that restricts creation to only one instance so that it can be shared by all areas (objects) in the application. These special, one-time-creation objects are called singletons. (For more information on singletons, see http://www.codeproject.com/Articles/1921/Singleton-Pattern-its-implementation-with-C). There are a variety of ways to create singletons:

- Static variables

- Heap-registration

- Runtime type information (RTTI)

- Self-registering

- Smart singletons (like smart pointers)

Now that you know what a singleton is, you're probably thinking that you've been creating these your entire career but didn't know it!

Storage Engine Development Process

One process for developing a new storage engine can be described as a series of stages. After all, a storage engine does not merely consist of a few lines of code; therefore, the most natural way to develop something of this size and complexity is through an iterative process, in which a small part of the system is developed and tested prior to moving on to another, more complicated portion. In the tutorial that follows, I start with the most basic functions and gradually add functionality until a fully functional storage engine emerges.

The first few stages create and add the basic data read and write mechanisms. Later stages add indexing and transaction support. Depending on what features you want to add to your own storage engine, you may not need to complete all the stages. A functional storage engine should support, at a minimum, the functions defined in the first four stages.[2] The stages are:

1. *Stubbing the engine*—The first step in the process is creating the basic storage engine that can be plugged into the server. The basic source-code files are created, the storage engine is established as a derivative of the handler-base class, and the storage engine itself is plugged into the server source code.

2. *Working with tables*—A storage engine would not be very interesting if it didn't have a means of creating, opening, closing, and deleting files. This stage is the one in which you set up the basic file-handling routines and establish that the engine is working with the files correctly.

3. *Reading and writing data*—To complete the most basic of storage engines, you must implement the read and write methods to read and write data from and to the storage medium.[3] This stage is the one in which you add those methods to read data in the storage-medium format and translate them to the MySQL internal-data format. Likewise, you write out the data from the MySQL internal-data format to the storage medium.

4. *Updating and deleting data*—To make the storage engine something that can be used in applications, you must also implement those methods that allow for altering data in the storage engine. This stage is the one in which the resolution of updates and deletion of data is implemented.

5. *Indexing the data*—A fully functional storage engine should also include the ability to permit fast random reads and range queries. This stage is the one in which you implement the secondmost complex operation of file access methods—indexing. I have provided an index class that should make this step easier for you to explore on your own.

6. *Adding transaction support*—The last stage of the process involves adding transaction support to the storage engine. At this stage, the storage engine becomes a truly relational-database storage mechanism suitable for use in transactional environments. This is the most complex operation of file-access methods.

---

[2] Some special storage engines may not need to write data at all. For example, the BLACKHOLE storage engine does not actually implement any write functions. Hey, it's a blackhole!

[3] It is more correct to refer to the data the storage engine is reading and writing as a storage medium, because there is nothing that stipulates that the data must reside on traditional data-storage mechanisms.

Throughout this process, you should test and debug at every stage. In the sections that follow, I show you examples of debugging a storage engine and writing tests to test the various stages. All normal debugging and trace mechanisms can be used in the storage engine. You can also use the interactive debuggers and get in to see the code in action!

Source Files Needed

The source files you will be working with are typically created as a single code (or class) file and a header file. These files are named ha_<engine name>.cc and ha_<engine name>.h, respectively.[4] The storage-engine source code is located in the storage directory off the main source-code tree. Inside that folder are the source code files for the various storage engines. Aside from those two files, that's all you need to get started!

Unexpected Help

The MySQL reference manual mentions several source-code files that can be helpful in learning about storage engines. Indeed, much of what I'm including here has come from studying those resources. Oracle provides an example storage engine (called example) that provides a great starting point for creating a storage engine at stage 1. In fact, I use it to get you started in the tutorial.

The archive engine is an example of a Stage 3 engine that provides good examples of reading and writing data. If you want to see more examples of how to do the file reading, writing, and updating, the CSV engine is a good place to look. The CSV engine is an example of a Stage 4 engine (CSV can read and write data as well as update and delete data). The CSV engine differs from the naming convention, because it was one of the first to be implemented. The source files are named ha_tina.cc and ha_tina.h. Finally, to see examples of Stage 5 and 6 storage engines, examine the MyISAM and InnoDB storage engines.

Before moving on to creating your own storage engine, take time to examine these storage engines in particular. because embedded in the source code are some golden nuggets of advice and instruction on how storage engines should work. Sometimes the best way to learn and extend or emulate a system is by examining its inner workings.

The Handlerton

As I mentioned earlier, the standard interface for all storage engines is the handlerton structure. It is implemented in the handler.cc and handler.h files in the sql directory, and it uses many other structures to provide organization of all of the elements needed to support the plug-in interface and the abstracted interface.

You might be wondering how concurrency is ensured in such a mechanism. The answer is—another structure! Each storage engine is responsible for creating a shared structure that is referenced from each instance of the handler among all the threads. Naturally, this means that some code must be protected. The good news is that not only are there mutual exclusion (mutex) protection methods available, but the handlerton source code has been designed to minimize the need for these protections.

The handlerton structure is a large structure with many data items and methods. Data items are represented as their normal data types defined in the structure, but methods are implemented using function pointers. The use of function pointers is one of those brilliantly constructed mechanisms that advanced developers use to permit runtime polymorphism. It is possible to use function pointers to redirect execution to a different (but equivalent interface) function. This is one of the techniques that make the handlerton so successful.

---

[4] The MyISAM and InnoDB storage engines contain additional source files. These are the oldest of the storage engines, and they are the most complex.

Listing 10-1 is an abbreviated listing of the handlerton structure definition, and Table 10-1 includes a description of the more important elements.

Listing 10-1. The MySQL Handlerton Structure

```
struct handlerton
{
  SHOW_COMP_OPTION state;
  enum legacy_db_type db_type;
  uint slot;
  uint savepoint_offset;
  int  (*close_connection)(handlerton *hton, THD *thd);
  int  (*savepoint_set)(handlerton *hton, THD *thd, void *sv);
  int  (*savepoint_rollback)(handlerton *hton, THD *thd, void *sv);
  int  (*savepoint_release)(handlerton *hton, THD *thd, void *sv);
  int  (*commit)(handlerton *hton, THD *thd, bool all);
  int  (*rollback)(handlerton *hton, THD *thd, bool all);
  int  (*prepare)(handlerton *hton, THD *thd, bool all);
  int  (*recover)(handlerton *hton, XID *xid_list, uint len);
  int  (*commit_by_xid)(handlerton *hton, XID *xid);
  int  (*rollback_by_xid)(handlerton *hton, XID *xid);
  void *(*create_cursor_read_view)(handlerton *hton, THD *thd);
  void (*set_cursor_read_view)(handlerton *hton, THD *thd, void *read_view);
  void (*close_cursor_read_view)(handlerton *hton, THD *thd, void *read_view);
  handler *(*create)(handlerton *hton, TABLE_SHARE *table, MEM_ROOT *mem_root);
  void (*drop_database)(handlerton *hton, char* path);
  int (*panic)(handlerton *hton, enum ha_panic_function flag);
  int (*start_consistent_snapshot)(handlerton *hton, THD *thd);
  bool (*flush_logs)(handlerton *hton);
  bool (*show_status)(handlerton *hton, THD *thd, stat_print_fn *print, enum ha_stat_type stat);
  uint (*partition_flags)();
  uint (*alter_table_flags)(uint flags);
  int (*alter_tablespace)(handlerton *hton, THD *thd, st_alter_tablespace *ts_info);
  int (*fill_is_table)(handlerton *hton, THD *thd, TABLE_LIST *tables,
                       class Item *cond,
                       enum enum_schema_tables);
  uint32 flags;                            /* global handler flags */
  int (*binlog_func)(handlerton *hton, THD *thd, enum_binlog_func fn, void *arg);
  void (*binlog_log_query)(handlerton *hton, THD *thd,
                      enum_binlog_command binlog_command,
                      const char *query, uint query_length,
                      const char *db, const char *table_name);
  int (*release_temporary_latches)(handlerton *hton, THD *thd);
  enum log_status (*get_log_status)(handlerton *hton, char *log);
  enum handler_create_iterator_result
    (*create_iterator)(handlerton *hton, enum handler_iterator_type type,
                      struct handler_iterator *fill_this_in);
  int (*discover)(handlerton *hton, THD* thd, const char *db,
                  const char *name,
                  uchar **frmblob,
                  size_t *frmlen);
  int (*find_files)(handlerton *hton, THD *thd,
                    const char *db,
```

```
                     const char *path,
                     const char *wild, bool dir, List<LEX_STRING> *files);
   int (*table_exists_in_engine)(handlerton *hton, THD* thd, const char *db,
                            const char *name);
   int (*make_pushed_join)(handlerton *hton, THD* thd,
                       const AQP::Join_plan* plan);
   const char* (*system_database)();
   bool (*is_supported_system_table)(const char *db,
                             const char *table_name,
                             bool is_sql_layer_system_table);

   uint32 license; /* Flag for Engine License */
   void *data; /* Location for engines to keep personal structures */
};
```

Table 10-1. *The Handlerton-structure Definition*

Element	Description
SHOW_COMP_OPTION state	Determines whether the storage engine is available.
const char *comment	A comment that describes the storage engine and also returned by the SHOW command.
enum legacy_db_type db_type	An enumerated value saved in the .frm file that indicates which storage engine created the file. This value is used to determine the handler class associated with the table.
uint slot	The position in the array of handlers that refers to this handlerton.
uint savepoint_offset	The size of memory needed to create savepoints for the storage engine.
int (*close_connection)(...)	The method used to close the connection.
int (*savepoint_set)(...)	The method that sets the savepoint to the savepoint offset specified in the savepoint_offset element.
int (*savepoint_rollback)(...)	The method to roll back (undo) a savepoint.
int(*savepoint_release)(...)	The method to release (ignore) a savepoint.
int(*commit)(...)	The commit method that commits pending transactions.
int(*rollback)(...)	The rollback method that rolls back pending transactions.
int(*prepare)(...)	The prepare method for preparing a transaction for commit.
int(*recover)(...)	The method to return a list of transactions being prepared.
int(*commit_by_xid)(...)	The method that commits a transaction by transaction ID.
int(*rollback_by_xid)(...)	The method that rolls back a transaction by transaction ID.
void *(*create_cursor_read_view)()	The method used to create a cursor.
void (*set_cursor_read_view)(void *)	The method used to switch to a specific cursor view.
void (*close_cursor_read_view)(void *)	The method used to close a specific cursor view.

(continued)

Table 10-1. (*continued*)

Element	Description
handler *(*create)(TABLE_SHARE *table)	The method used to create the handler instance of this storage engine.
int (*panic)(enum ha_panic_function flag)	The method that is called during server shutdown and crashes.
int (*start_consistent_snapshot)(...)	The method called to begin a consistent read (concurrency).
bool (*flush_logs)()	The method used to flush logs to disk.
bool (*show_status)(. . .)	The method that returns status information for the storage engine.
uint (*partition_flags)()	The method used to return the flag used for partitioning.
uint (*alter_table_flags)(. . .)	The method used to return flag set for the ALTER TABLE command.
int (*alter_tablespace)(. . .)	The method used to return flag set for the ALTER TABLESPACE command.
int (*fill_is_table)(. . .)	The method used by the server mechanisms to fill INFORMATION_SCHEMA views (tables).
uint32 flags	Flags that indicate what features the handler supports.
int (*binlog_func)(. . .)	The method to call back to the binary-log function.
void (*binlog_log_query)(. . .)	The method used to query the binary log.
int (*release_temporary_latches)(. . .)	InnoDB specific use (see the documentation for the InnoDB engine).

■ **Note** I have omitted the comments from the code to save space. I have also skipped the less-important items of the structure for brevity. Please see the `handler.h` file for additional information about the handlerton structure.

The Handler Class

The other part of the equation for understanding the storage-engine plugin interface is the handler class. The handler class is derived from Sql_alloc, which means that all of the memory-allocation routines are provided through inheritance. The handler class is designed to be the implementation of the storage handler. It provides a consistent set of methods for interfacing with the server via the handlerton structure. The handlerton and handler instances work as a unit to achieve the abstraction layer for the storage-engine architecture. Figure 10-1 depicts these classes and how they are derived to form a new storage engine. The drawing shows the handlerton structure as an interface between the handler and the new storage engine.

A complete detailed investigation of the handler class is beyond the scope of this book. Instead, I demonstrate the most important and most frequently used methods of the handler class implementing the stages of the sample storage engine. I explain each of the methods implemented and called in a more narrative format later in this chapter.

As a means of introduction to the handler class, I've provided an excerpt of the handler class definition in Listing 10-2. Take a few moments now to skim through the class. Notice the many methods available for a wide variety of tasks, such as creating, deleting, altering tables, and methods to manipulate fields and indexes. There are even methods for crash protection, recovery, and backup.

Although the handler class is quite impressive and covers every possible situation for a storage engine, most storage engines do not use the complete list of methods. If you want to implement a storage engine with some of the advanced features provided, spend some time exploring the excellent coverage of the handler class in the MySQL reference manual. Once you become accustomed to creating storage engines, you can use the reference manual to take your storage engine to the next level of sophistication.

Listing 10-2. The Handler-class Definition

```
class handler :public Sql_alloc
{
...
  const handlerton *ht;                   /* storage engine of this handler */
  uchar *ref;                             /* Pointer to current row */
  uchar *dupp_ref;                        /* Pointer to dupp row */
...

  handler(const handlerton *ht_arg, TABLE_SHARE *share_arg)
    :table_share(share_arg), ht(ht_arg),
    ref(0), data_file_length(0), max_data_file_length(0), index_file_length(0),
    delete_length(0), auto_increment_value(0),
    records(0), deleted(0), mean_rec_length(0),
    create_time(0), check_time(0), update_time(0),
    key_used_on_scan(MAX_KEY), active_index(MAX_KEY),
    ref_length(sizeof(my_off_t)), block_size(0),
    ft_handler(0), inited(NONE), implicit_emptied(0),
    pushed_cond(NULL)
    {}
...
  int ha_index_init(uint idx, bool sorted)
...
  int ha_index_end()
...
  int ha_rnd_init(bool scan)
...
  int ha_rnd_end()
...
  int ha_reset()
...
...
  virtual int exec_bulk_update(uint *dup_key_found)
...
  virtual void end_bulk_update() { return; }
...
  virtual int end_bulk_delete()
...
  virtual int index_read(uchar * buf, const uchar * key,
      uint key_len, enum ha_rkey_function find_flag)
...
```

```
  virtual int index_read_idx(uchar * buf, uint index, const uchar * key,
          uint key_len, enum ha_rkey_function find_flag);
  virtual int index_next(uchar * buf)
   { return  HA_ERR_WRONG_COMMAND; }
  virtual int index_prev(uchar * buf)
   { return  HA_ERR_WRONG_COMMAND; }
  virtual int index_first(uchar * buf)
   { return  HA_ERR_WRONG_COMMAND; }
  virtual int index_last(uchar * buf)
   { return  HA_ERR_WRONG_COMMAND; }
  virtual int index_next_same(uchar *buf, const uchar *key, uint keylen);
  virtual int index_read_last(uchar * buf, const uchar * key, uint key_len)
...

virtual int read_range_first(const key_range *start_key,
                             const key_range *end_key,
                             bool eq_range, bool sorted);
  virtual int read_range_next();
  int compare_key(key_range *range);
  virtual int ft_init() { return HA_ERR_WRONG_COMMAND; }
  void ft_end() { ft_handler=NULL; }
  virtual FT_INFO *ft_init_ext(uint flags, uint inx,String *key)
    { return NULL; }
  virtual int ft_read(uchar *buf) { return HA_ERR_WRONG_COMMAND; }
  virtual int rnd_next(uchar *buf)=0;
  virtual int rnd_pos(uchar * buf, uchar *pos)=0;
  virtual int read_first_row(uchar *buf, uint primary_key);
...
  virtual int restart_rnd_next(uchar *buf, uchar *pos)
    { return HA_ERR_WRONG_COMMAND; }
  virtual int rnd_same(uchar *buf, uint inx)
    { return HA_ERR_WRONG_COMMAND; }
  virtual ha_rows records_in_range(uint inx, key_range *min_key,
                                   key_range *max_key);
    { return (ha_rows) 10; }
  virtual void position(const uchar *record)=0;
  virtual void info(uint)=0; // see my_base.h for full description
  virtual void get_dynamic_partition_info(PARTITION_INFO *stat_info,
                                          uint part_id);
  virtual int extra(enum ha_extra_function operation)
  { return 0; }
  virtual int extra_opt(enum ha_extra_function operation, ulong cache_size)
  { return extra(operation); }
...
  virtual int delete_all_rows()
...
  virtual ulonglong get_auto_increment();
  virtual void restore_auto_increment();
...
```

```
  virtual int reset_auto_increment(ulonglong value)
...
  virtual void update_create_info(HA_CREATE_INFO *create_info) {}
...
  int ha_repair(THD* thd, HA_CHECK_OPT* check_opt);
...
  virtual bool check_and_repair(THD *thd) { return TRUE; }
  virtual int dump(THD* thd, int fd = -1) { return HA_ERR_WRONG_COMMAND; }
  virtual int disable_indexes(uint mode) { return HA_ERR_WRONG_COMMAND; }
  virtual int enable_indexes(uint mode) { return HA_ERR_WRONG_COMMAND; }
  virtual int indexes_are_disabled(void) {return 0;}
  virtual void start_bulk_insert(ha_rows rows) {}
  virtual int end_bulk_insert() {return 0; }
  virtual int discard_or_import_tablespace(my_bool discard)
...
  virtual uint referenced_by_foreign_key() { return 0;}
  virtual void init_table_handle_for_HANDLER()
...
  virtual void free_foreign_key_create_info(char* str) {}
...
  virtual const char *table_type() const =0;
  virtual const char **bas_ext() const =0;
...
  virtual uint max_supported_record_length() const { return HA_MAX_REC_LENGTH; }
  virtual uint max_supported_keys() const { return 0; }
  virtual uint max_supported_key_parts() const { return MAX_REF_PARTS; }
  virtual uint max_supported_key_length() const { return MAX_KEY_LENGTH; }
  virtual uint max_supported_key_part_length() const { return 255; }
  virtual uint min_record_length(uint options) const { return 1; }
...
  virtual bool is_crashed() const  { return 0; }
...
  virtual int rename_table(const char *from, const char *to);
  virtual int delete_table(const char *name);
  virtual void drop_table(const char *name);

  virtual int create(const char *name, TABLE *form, HA_CREATE_INFO *info)=0;
...
  virtual int external_lock(THD *thd __attribute__((unused)),
                            int lock_type __attribute__((unused)))
...
  virtual int write_row(uchar *buf __attribute__((unused)))
...
  virtual int update_row(const uchar *old_data __attribute__((unused)),
                         uchar *new_data __attribute__((unused)))
...
  virtual int delete_row(const uchar *buf __attribute__((unused)))
...
};
```

A Brief Tour of a MySQL Storage Engine

The best way to see the handler work is to watch it in action. Therefore, let's examine a real storage engine in use before we start building one. Follow along by compiling your server with debug if you haven't already. Go ahead and start your server and debugger, and then attach your debugging tool to the running server, as described in Chapter 5.

I want to show you a simple storage engine in action. In this case, I use the archive storage engine. With the debugger open and the server running, open the ha_archive.cc file and place a breakpoint on the first executable line for the methods:

```
int ha_archive::create(...)
static ARCHIVE_SHARE *ha_archive::get_share(...)
int ha_archive::write_row(...)int ha_tina::rnd_next(...)
int ha_archive::rnd_next(...)
```

Once the breakpoints are set, launch the command-line MySQL client, change to the test database, and issue this command:

```
CREATE TABLE testarc (a int, b varchar(20), c int) ENGINE=ARCHIVE;
```

You should immediately see the debugger halt in the create() method. This method is where the base-data table is created. Indeed, it is one of the first things to execute. The my_create() method is called to create the file. Notice that the code is looking for a field with the AUTO_INCREMENT_FLAG set (at the top of the method); if the field is found, the code sets an error and exits. This is because the archive storage engine doesn't support auto-increment fields. You can also see that the method is creating a meta file and checking to see that the compression routines are working properly.

Step through the code and watch the iterator. You can continue the execution at any time or, if you're really curious, continue to step through the return to the calling function.

Now, let's see what happens when we insert data. Go back to your MySQL client and enter this command:

```
INSERT INTO testarc VALUES (10, "test", -1);
```

This time, the code halts in the get_share() method. This method is responsible for creating the shared structure (which is stored as the .frm file) for all instances of the archive handler. As you step through this method, you can see where the code is setting the global variables and other initialization-type tasks. Go ahead and let the debugger continue execution.

The next place the code halts is in the write_row() method. This method is where the data that are passed through the buf parameter are written to disk. The record buffer (uchar *buf) is the mechanism that MySQL uses to pass rows through the system. It is a binary buffer containing the data for the row and other metadata. It is what the MySQL documentation refers to as the "internal format." As you step through this code, you will see the engine set some statistics, do some more error checking, and eventually write the data using the method real_write_row() at the end of the method. Go ahead and step through that method as well.

In the real_write_row() method, you can see another field iterator. This iterator is iterating through the binary large objects (BLOB) fields and writing those to disk using the compression method. If you need to support BLOB fields, this is an excellent example of how to do so—just substitute your low-level IO call for the compression method. Go ahead and let the code continue; then return to your MySQL client and enter the command:

```
SELECT * FROM testarc;
```

The next place the code halts is in the rnd_next() method. This is where the handler reads the data file and returns the data in the record buffer (uchar *buf). Notice again that the code sets some statistics, does error checking, and then reads the data using the get_row() method. Step through this code a bit and then let it continue.

What a surprise! The code halts again at the rnd_next() method. This is because the rnd_next() method is one of a series of calls for a table scan. The method is responsible not only for reading the data but also for detecting the end of the file. Thus, in the example you're working through, there should be two calls to the method. The first retrieves the first row of data and the second detects the end of the file (you inserted only one row). The following lists the typical sequence of calls for a table scan using the example you've been working through:

```
ha_spartan::info
ha_spartan::rnd_init
ha_spartan::extra
ha_spartan::rnd_next
ha_spartan::rnd_next
ha_spartan::extra
```

```
+------+------+------+
| a    | b    | c    |
+------+------+------+
| 10   | test | -1   |
+------+------+------+
1 row in set (26.25 sec)
```

■ **Note**   The time returned from the query is actual elapsed time as recorded by the server and not execution time. Thus, the time spent in debugging counts.

Take some time and place breakpoints on other methods that may interest you. You can also spend some time reading the comments in this storage engine ,as they provide excellent clues to how some of the handler methods are used.

The Spartan Storage Engine

I chose for the tutorial on storage engines the concept of a basic storage engine that has all the features that a normal storage engine would have. This includes reading and writing data with index support. That is to say, it is a Stage 5 engine. I call this sample storage engine the Spartan storage engine, because in many ways it implements only the basic necessities for a viable database-storage mechanism.

I guide you through the process of building the Spartan storage using the example (ha_example) MySQL storage engine. I refer you to the other storage engines for additional information as I progress through the tutorial. While you may find areas that you think could be improved upon (and indeed there are several), refrain from making any enhancements to the Spartan engine until you have it successfully implemented to the Stage 5 level.

Let's begin by examining the supporting class files for the Spartan storage engine.

Low-Level I/O Classes

A storage engine is designed to read and write data using a specialized mechanism that provides some unique benefits to the user. This means that the storage engines, by nature, are not going to support the same features.

Most storage engines either use C functions defined in other source files or C++ classes defined in class header and source files. For the Spartan engine, I elected to use the latter method. I created a data-file class as well as an index-file class. Holding true to the intent of this chapter and the Spartan-engine project, neither of the classes is optimized for performance. Rather, they provide a means to create a working storage engine and demonstrate most of the things you will need to do to create your own storage engine.

This section describes each of the classes in a general overview. You can follow along with the code and see how the classes work. Although the low-level classes are just the basics and could probably use a bit of fine-tuning, I think you'll find these classes beneficial to use, and perhaps you'll even base your own storage engine I/O on them.

The Spartan_data Class

The primary low-level I/O class for the Spartan storage engine is the Spartan_data class. This class is responsible for encapsulating the data for the Spartan storage engine. Listing 10-3 includes the complete header file for the class. As you can see from the header, the methods for this class are simplistic. I implement just the basic open, close, read, and write operations.

Listing 10-3. Spartan_data Class Header

```
/*
  Spartan_data.h

  This header defines a simple data file class for writing and reading raw
  data to and from disk. The data written is in uchar format so it can be
  anything you want it to be. The write_row and read_row accept the
  length of the data item to be written/read.
*/
#include "my_global.h"
#include "my_sys.h"

class Spartan_data
{
public:
  Spartan_data(void);
  ~Spartan_data(void);
  int create_table(char *path);
  int open_table(char *path);
  long long write_row(uchar *buf, int length);
  long long update_row(uchar *old_rec, uchar *new_rec,
                       int length, long long position);
  int read_row(uchar *buf, int length, long long position);
  int delete_row(uchar *old_rec, int length, long long position);
  int close_table();
  long long cur_position();
  int records();
  int del_records();
  int trunc_table();
  int row_size(int length);
private:
  File data_file;
  int header_size;
  int record_header_size;
  bool crashed;
  int number_records;
  int number_del_records;
```

```
  int read_header();
  int write_header();
};
```

Listing 10-4 includes the complete source code for the Spartan-storage-engine data class. Notice that in the code I have included the appropriate DBUG calls to ensure my source code can write to the trace file should I wish to debug the system using the --with-debug switch. Notice also that the read and write methods used are the my_xxx platform-safe utility methods provided by Oracle.

Listing 10-4. Spartan_data Class Source Code

```
/*
  Spartan_data.cc

  This class implements a simple data file reader/writer. It
  is designed to allow the caller to specify the size of the
  data to read or write. This allows for variable length records
  and the inclusion of extra fields (like blobs). The data are
  stored in an uncompressed, unoptimized fashion.
*/
#include "spartan_data.h"
#include <my_dir.h>
#include <string.h>

Spartan_data::Spartan_data(void)
{
  data_file = -1;
  number_records = -1;
  number_del_records = -1;
  header_size = sizeof(bool) + sizeof(int) + sizeof(int);
  record_header_size = sizeof(uchar) + sizeof(int);
}

Spartan_data::~Spartan_data(void)
{
}

/* create the data file */
int Spartan_data::create_table(char *path)
{
  DBUG_ENTER("SpartanIndex::create_table");
  open_table(path);
  number_records = 0;
  number_del_records = 0;
  crashed = false;
  write_header();
  DBUG_RETURN(0);
}
```

```
/* open table at location "path" = path + filename */
int Spartan_data::open_table(char *path)
{
  DBUG_ENTER("Spartan_data::open_table");
  /*
    Open the file with read/write mode,
    create the file if not found,
    treat file as binary, and use default flags.
  */
  data_file = my_open(path, O_RDWR | O_CREAT | O_BINARY | O_SHARE, MYF(0));
  if(data_file == -1)
    DBUG_RETURN(errno);
  read_header();
  DBUG_RETURN(0);
}

/* write a row of length uchars to file and return position */
long long Spartan_data::write_row(uchar *buf, int length)
{
  long long pos;
  int i;
  int len;
  uchar deleted = 0;

  DBUG_ENTER("Spartan_data::write_row");
  /*
    Write the deleted status uchar and the length of the record.
    Note: my_write() returns the uchars written or -1 on error
  */
  pos = my_seek(data_file, 0L, MY_SEEK_END, MYF(0));
  /*
    Note: my_malloc takes a size of memory to be allocated,
    MySQL flags (set to zero fill and with extra error checking).
    Returns number of uchars allocated -- <= 0 indicates an error.
  */
  i = my_write(data_file, &deleted, sizeof(uchar), MYF(0));
  memcpy(&len, &length, sizeof(int));
  i = my_write(data_file, (uchar *)&len, sizeof(int), MYF(0));
  /*
    Write the row data to the file. Return new file pointer or
    return -1 if error from my_write().
  */
  i = my_write(data_file, buf, length, MYF(0));
  if (i == -1)
    pos = i;
  else
    number_records++;
  DBUG_RETURN(pos);
}
```

```
/* update a record in place */
long long Spartan_data::update_row(uchar *old_rec, uchar *new_rec,
                                   int length, long long position)
{
  long long pos;
  long long cur_pos;
  uchar *cmp_rec;
  int len;
  uchar deleted = 0;
  int i = -1;

  DBUG_ENTER("Spartan_data::update_row");
  if (position == 0)
    position = header_size; //move past header
  pos = position;
  /*
    If position unknown, scan for the record by reading a row
    at a time until found.
  */
  if (position == -1) //don't know where it is...scan for it
  {
    cmp_rec = (uchar *)my_malloc(length, MYF(MY_ZEROFILL | MY_WME));
    pos = 0;
    /*
      Note: my_seek() returns pos if no errors or -1 if error.
    */
    cur_pos = my_seek(data_file, header_size, MY_SEEK_SET, MYF(0));
    /*
      Note: read_row() returns current file pointer if no error or
      -1 if error.
    */
    while ((cur_pos != -1) && (pos != -1))
    {
      pos = read_row(cmp_rec, length, cur_pos);
      if (memcmp(old_rec, cmp_rec, length) == 0)
      {
        pos = cur_pos;        //found it!
        cur_pos = -1;         //stop loop gracefully
      }
      else if (pos != -1)   //move ahead to next rec
        cur_pos = cur_pos + length + record_header_size;
    }
    my_free(cmp_rec);
  }
  /*
    If position found or provided, write the row.
  */
  if (pos != -1)
```

```
  {
    /*
      Write the deleted uchar, the length of the row, and the data
      at the current file pointer.
      Note: my_write() returns the uchars written or -1 on error
    */
    my_seek(data_file, pos, MY_SEEK_SET, MYF(0));
    i = my_write(data_file, &deleted, sizeof(uchar), MYF(0));
    memcpy(&len, &length, sizeof(int));
    i = my_write(data_file, (uchar *)&len, sizeof(int), MYF(0));
    pos = i;
    i = my_write(data_file, new_rec, length, MYF(0));
  }
  DBUG_RETURN(pos);
}

/* delete a record in place */
int Spartan_data::delete_row(uchar *old_rec, int length,
                             long long position)
{
  int i = -1;
  long long pos;
  long long cur_pos;
  uchar *cmp_rec;
  uchar deleted = 1;

  DBUG_ENTER("Spartan_data::delete_row");
  if (position == 0)
    position = header_size; //move past header
  pos = position;
  /*
    If position unknown, scan for the record by reading a row
    at a time until found.
  */
  if (position == -1) //don't know where it is...scan for it
  {
    cmp_rec = (uchar *)my_malloc(length, MYF(MY_ZEROFILL | MY_WME));
    pos = 0;
    /*
      Note: my_seek() returns pos if no errors or -1 if error.
    */
    cur_pos = my_seek(data_file, header_size, MY_SEEK_SET, MYF(0));
    /*
      Note: read_row() returns current file pointer if no error or
      -1 if error.
    */
    while ((cur_pos != -1) && (pos != -1))
    {
      pos = read_row(cmp_rec, length, cur_pos);
      if (memcmp(old_rec, cmp_rec, length) == 0)
```

```
      {
        number_records--;
        number_del_records++;
        pos = cur_pos;
        cur_pos = -1;
      }
      else if (pos != -1)    //move ahead to next rec
        cur_pos = cur_pos + length + record_header_size;
    }
    my_free(cmp_rec);
  }
  /*
    If position found or provided, write the row.
  */
  if (pos != -1)             //mark as deleted
  {
    /*
      Write the deleted uchar set to 1 which marks row as deleted
      at the current file pointer.
      Note: my_write() returns the uchars written or -1 on error
    */
    pos = my_seek(data_file, pos, MY_SEEK_SET, MYF(0));
    i = my_write(data_file, &deleted, sizeof(uchar), MYF(0));
    i = (i > 1) ? 0 : i;
  }
  DBUG_RETURN(i);
}

/* read a row of length uchars from file at position */
int Spartan_data::read_row(uchar *buf, int length, long long position)
{
  int i;
  int rec_len;
  long long pos;
  uchar deleted = 2;

  DBUG_ENTER("Spartan_data::read_row");
  if (position <= 0)
    position = header_size; //move past header
  pos = my_seek(data_file, position, MY_SEEK_SET, MYF(0));
  /*
    If my_seek found the position, read the deleted uchar.
    Note: my_read() returns uchars read or -1 on error
  */
  if (pos != -1L)
  {
    i = my_read(data_file, &deleted, sizeof(uchar), MYF(0));
    /*
      If not deleted (deleted == 0), read the record length then
      read the row.
    */
```

```
    if (deleted == 0) /* 0 = not deleted, 1 = deleted */
    {
      i = my_read(data_file, (uchar *)&rec_len, sizeof(int), MYF(0));
      i = my_read(data_file, buf,
                  (length < rec_len) ? length : rec_len, MYF(0));
    }
    else if (i == 0)
      DBUG_RETURN(-1);
    else
      DBUG_RETURN(read_row(buf, length, cur_position() +
                           length + (record_header_size - sizeof(uchar))));
  }
  else
    DBUG_RETURN(-1);
  DBUG_RETURN(0);
}

/* close file */
int Spartan_data::close_table()
{
  DBUG_ENTER("Spartan_data::close_table");
  if (data_file != -1)
  {
    my_close(data_file, MYF(0));
    data_file = -1;
  }
  DBUG_RETURN(0);
}

/* return number of records */
int Spartan_data::records()
{
  DBUG_ENTER("Spartan_data::num_records");
  DBUG_RETURN(number_records);
}

/* return number of deleted records */
int Spartan_data::del_records()
{
  DBUG_ENTER("Spartan_data::num_records");
  DBUG_RETURN(number_del_records);
}

/* read header from file */
int Spartan_data::read_header()
{
  int i;
  int len;
```

```
  DBUG_ENTER("Spartan_data::read_header");
  if (number_records == -1)
  {
    my_seek(data_file, 0l, MY_SEEK_SET, MYF(0));
    i = my_read(data_file, (uchar *)&crashed, sizeof(bool), MYF(0));
    i = my_read(data_file, (uchar *)&len, sizeof(int), MYF(0));
    memcpy(&number_records, &len, sizeof(int));
    i = my_read(data_file, (uchar *)&len, sizeof(int), MYF(0));
    memcpy(&number_del_records, &len, sizeof(int));
  }
  else
    my_seek(data_file, header_size, MY_SEEK_SET, MYF(0));
  DBUG_RETURN(0);
}

/* write header to file */
int Spartan_data::write_header()
{
  DBUG_ENTER("Spartan_data::write_header");
  if (number_records != -1)
  {
    my_seek(data_file, 0l, MY_SEEK_SET, MYF(0));
    i = my_write(data_file, (uchar *)&crashed, sizeof(bool), MYF(0));
    i = my_write(data_file, (uchar *)&number_records, sizeof(int), MYF(0));
    i = my_write(data_file, (uchar *)&number_del_records, sizeof(int), MYF(0));
  }
  DBUG_RETURN(0);
}

/* get position of the data file */
long long Spartan_data::cur_position()
{
  long long pos;

  DBUG_ENTER("Spartan_data::cur_position");
  pos = my_seek(data_file, 0L, MY_SEEK_CUR, MYF(0));
  if (pos == 0)
    DBUG_RETURN(header_size);
  DBUG_RETURN(pos);
}

/* truncate the data file */
int Spartan_data::trunc_table()
{
  DBUG_ENTER("Spartan_data::trunc_table");
  if (data_file != -1 )
  {
    my_chsize(data_file, 0, 0, MYF(MY_WME));
    write_header();
  }
  DBUG_RETURN(0);
}
```

```
/* determine the row size of the data file */
int Spartan_data::row_size(int length)
{
  DBUG_ENTER("Spartan_data::row_size");
  DBUG_RETURN(length + record_header_size);
}
```

Note the format that I use to store the data. The class is designed to support reading data from disk and writing the data in memory to disk. I use a uchar pointer to allocate a block of memory for storing the rows. This really useful, because it provides the ability to write the rows in the table to disk using the internal MySQL row format. Likewise, I can read the data from disk, write them to a memory buffer, and simply point the handler class to the block of memory to be returned to the optimizer.

I may not be able to predict the exact amount of memory needed to store a row, however. Some uses of the storage engine may have tables that have variable fields or even binary large objects (BLOBs). To overcome this problem, I chose to store a single integer length field at the start of each row. This allows me to scan a file and read variable-length rows by first reading the length field and then reading the number of uchars specified into the memory buffer.

■ **Tip** Whenever coding an extension for the MySQL server, always use the my_xxx utility methods. The my_xxx utility methods are encapsulations of many of the base-operating-systems functions and provide a better level of cross-platform support.

The data class is rather straightforward and can be used to implement the basic read and write operations needed for a storage engine. I want to make the storage engine more efficient, however. To achieve good performance from my data file, I need to add an index mechanism. This is where things get a lot more complicated.

■ **Note** While we won't use the index class in the first four stages, it is good to understand this code in advance.

The Spartan_index Class

To solve the problem of indexing the data file, I implement a separate index class called Spartan_index. The index class is responsible for permitting the execution of point queries (query by index for a specific record) and range queries (a series of keys either ascending or descending), as well as the ability to cache the index for fast searching. Listing 10-5 includes the complete header file for the Spartan_index class.

Listing 10-5. Spartan_index Class Header

```
/*

  Spartan_index.h

  This header file defines a simple index class that can
  be used to store file pointer indexes (long long). The
  class keeps the entire index in memory for fast access.
  The internal-memory structure is a linked list. While
  not as efficient as a btree, it should be usable for
```

most testing environments. The constructor accepts the
max key length. This is used for all nodes in the index.

```
  File Layout:
    SOF                           max_key_len (int)
    SOF + sizeof(int)             crashed (bool)
    SOF + sizeof(int) + sizeof(bool) DATA BEGINS HERE
*/
#include "my_global.h"
#include "my_sys.h"

const long METADATA_SIZE = sizeof(int) + sizeof(bool);
/*
  This is the node that stores the key and the file
  position for the data row.
*/
struct SDE_INDEX
{
  uchar key[128];
  long long pos;
  int length;
};

/* defines (doubly) linked list for internal list */
struct SDE_NDX_NODE
{
  SDE_INDEX key_ndx;
  SDE_NDX_NODE *next;
  SDE_NDX_NODE *prev;
};

class Spartan_index
{
public:
  Spartan_index(int keylen);
  Spartan_index();
  ~Spartan_index(void);
  int open_index(char *path);
  int create_index(char *path, int keylen);
  int insert_key(SDE_INDEX *ndx, bool allow_dupes);
  int delete_key(uchar *buf, long long pos, int key_len);
  int update_key(uchar *buf, long long pos, int key_len);
  long long get_index_pos(uchar *buf, int key_len);
  long long get_first_pos();
  uchar *get_first_key();
  uchar *get_last_key();
  uchar *get_next_key();
  uchar *get_prev_key();
  int close_index();
  int load_index();
  int destroy_index();
```

```
  SDE_INDEX *seek_index(uchar *key, int key_len);
  SDE_NDX_NODE *seek_index_pos(uchar *key, int key_len);
  int save_index();
  int trunc_index();
private:
  File index_file;
  int max_key_len;
  SDE_NDX_NODE *root;
  SDE_NDX_NODE *range_ptr;
  int block_size;
  bool crashed;
  int read_header();
  int write_header();
  long long write_row(SDE_INDEX *ndx);
  SDE_INDEX *read_row(long long Position);
  long long curfpos();
};
```

Notice that the class implements the expected form of create, open, close, read, and write methods. The load_index() method reads an entire index file into memory, storing the index as a doubly linked list. All the index scanning and reference methods access the linked list in memory rather than accessing the disk. This saves a great deal of time and provides a way to keep the entire index in memory for fast insertion and deletion. A corresponding method, save_index(), permits you to write the index from memory back to disk. The way these methods should be used is to call load_index() when the table is opened and then save_index() when the table is closed.

You may be wondering if there could be size limitations with this approach. Depending on the size of the index, how many indexes are created, and how many entries there are, this implementation could have some limitations. For the purposes of this tutorial and for the foreseeable use of the Spartan storage engine, however, this isn't a problem.

Another area you may be concerned about is the use of the doubly linked list. This implementation isn't likely to be your first choice for high-speed index storage. You are more likely to use a B-tree or some variant of one to create an efficient index-access method. The linked list is easy to use, however, and it makes the implementation of a rather large set of source code a bit easier to manage. The example demonstrates how to incorporate an index class into your engine—not how to code a B-tree structure. This keeps the code simpler, because the linked list is easier to code. For the purposes of this tutorial, the linked-list structure will perform very well. In fact, you may even want to use it to form your own storage engine until you get the rest of the storage engine working, and then turn your attention to a better index class.

Listing 10-6 shows the complete source code for the Spartan_index class implementation. The code is rather lengthy, so either take some time and examine the methods or save the code reading for later and skip ahead to the description of how to start building the Spartan storage engine.

Listing 10-6. Spartan_index Class Source Code

```
/*
  Spartan_index.cc

  This class reads and writes an index file for use with the Spartan data
  class. The file format is a simple binary storage of the
  Spartan_index::SDE_INDEX structure. The size of the key can be set via
  the constructor.
*/
#include "spartan_index.h"
#include <my_dir.h>
#include <string.h>
```

```cpp
/* constuctor takes the maximum key length for the keys */
Spartan_index::Spartan_index(int keylen)
{
  root = NULL;
  crashed = false;
  max_key_len = keylen;
  index_file = -1;
  block_size = max_key_len + sizeof(long long) + sizeof(int);
}

/* constuctor (overloaded) assumes existing file */
Spartan_index::Spartan_index()
{
  root = NULL;
  crashed = false;
  max_key_len = -1;
  index_file = -1;
  block_size = -1;
}

/* destructor */
Spartan_index::~Spartan_index(void)
{
}

/* create the index file */
int Spartan_index::create_index(char *path, int keylen)
{
  DBUG_ENTER("Spartan_index::create_index");
  DBUG_PRINT("info", ("path: %s", path));
  open_index(path);
  max_key_len = keylen;
  /*
    Block size is the key length plus the size of the index
    length variable.
  */
  block_size = max_key_len + sizeof(long long);
  write_header();
  DBUG_RETURN(0);
}

/* open index specified as path (pat+filename) */
int Spartan_index::open_index(char *path)
{
  DBUG_ENTER("Spartan_index::open_index");
  /*
    Open the file with read/write mode,
    create the file if not found,
    treat file as binary, and use default flags.
  */
```

```
  index_file = my_open(path, O_RDWR | O_CREAT | O_BINARY | O_SHARE, MYF(0));
  if(index_file == -1)
    DBUG_RETURN(errno);
  read_header();
  DBUG_RETURN(0);
}

/* read header from file */
int Spartan_index::read_header()
{
  DBUG_ENTER("Spartan_index::read_header");
  if (block_size == -1)
  {
    /*
      Seek the start of the file.
      Read the maximum key length value.
    */
    my_seek(index_file, 0l, MY_SEEK_SET, MYF(0));
    i = my_read(index_file, (uchar *)&max_key_len, sizeof(int), MYF(0));
    /*
      Calculate block size as maximum key length plus
      the size of the key plus the crashed status byte.
    */
    block_size = max_key_len + sizeof(long long) + sizeof(int);
    i = my_read(index_file, (uchar *)&crashed, sizeof(bool), MYF(0));
  }
  else
  {
    i = (int)my_seek(index_file, sizeof(int) + sizeof(bool), MY_SEEK_SET, MYF(0));
  }
  DBUG_RETURN(0);
}

/* write header to file */
int Spartan_index::write_header()
{
  int i;

  DBUG_ENTER("Spartan_index::write_header");
  if (block_size != -1)
  {
    /*
      Seek the start of the file and write the maximum key length
      then write the crashed status byte.
    */
    my_seek(index_file, 0l, MY_SEEK_SET, MYF(0));
    i = my_write(index_file, (uchar *)&max_key_len, sizeof(int), MYF(0));
    i = my_write(index_file, (uchar *)&crashed, sizeof(bool), MYF(0));
  }
  DBUG_RETURN(0);
}
```

```
/* write a row (SDE_INDEX struct) to the index file */
long long Spartan_index::write_row(SDE_INDEX *ndx)
{
  long long pos;
  int i;
  int len;

  DBUG_ENTER("Spartan_index::write_row");
  /*
     Seek the end of the file (always append)
  */
  pos = my_seek(index_file, 0l, MY_SEEK_END, MYF(0));
  /*
    Write the key value.
  */
  i = my_write(index_file, ndx->key, max_key_len, MYF(0));
  memcpy(&pos, &ndx->pos, sizeof(long long));
  /*
    Write the file position for the key value.
  */
  i = i + my_write(index_file, (uchar *)&pos, sizeof(long long), MYF(0));
  memcpy(&len, &ndx->length, sizeof(int));
  /*
    Write the length of the key.
  */
  i = i + my_write(index_file, (uchar *)&len, sizeof(int), MYF(0));
  if (i == -1)
    pos = i;
  DBUG_RETURN(pos);
}

/* read a row (SDE_INDEX struct) from the index file */
SDE_INDEX *Spartan_index::read_row(long long Position)
{
  int i;
  long long pos;
  SDE_INDEX *ndx = NULL;

  DBUG_ENTER("Spartan_index::read_row");
  /*
    Seek the position in the file (Position).
  */
  pos = my_seek(index_file,(ulong) Position, MY_SEEK_SET, MYF(0));
  if (pos != -1L)
  {
    ndx = new SDE_INDEX();
    /*
      Read the key value.
    */
```

```
    i = my_read(index_file, ndx->key, max_key_len, MYF(0));
    /*
      Read the key value. If error, return NULL.
    */
    i = my_read(index_file, (uchar *)&ndx->pos, sizeof(long long), MYF(0));
    if (i == -1)
    {
        delete ndx;
        ndx = NULL;
    }
  }
  DBUG_RETURN(ndx);
}

/* insert a key into the index in memory */
int Spartan_index::insert_key(SDE_INDEX *ndx, bool allow_dupes)
{
  SDE_NDX_NODE *p = NULL;
  SDE_NDX_NODE *n = NULL;
  SDE_NDX_NODE *o = NULL;
  int i = -1;
  int icmp;
  bool dupe = false;
  bool done = false;

  DBUG_ENTER("Spartan_index::insert_key");
  /*
    If this is a new index, insert first key as the root node.
  */
  if (root == NULL)
  {
    root = new SDE_NDX_NODE();
    root->next = NULL;
    root->prev = NULL;
    memcpy(root->key_ndx.key, ndx->key, max_key_len);
    root->key_ndx.pos = ndx->pos;
    root->key_ndx.length = ndx->length;
  }
  else //set pointer to root
    p = root;
  /*
    Loop through the linked list until a value greater than the
    key to be inserted, then insert new key before that one.
  */
  while ((p != NULL) && !done)
  {
    icmp = memcmp(ndx->key, p->key_ndx.key,
                  (ndx->length > p->key_ndx.length) ?
                  ndx->length : p->key_ndx.length);
    if (icmp > 0) // key is greater than current key in list
```

```
    {
      n = p;
      p = p->next;
    }
    /*
      If dupes not allowed, stop and return NULL
    */
    else if (!allow_dupes && (icmp == 0))
    {
      p = NULL;
      dupe = true;
    }
    else
    {
      n = p->prev; //stop, insert at n->prev
      done = true;
    }
  }
  /*
    If position found (n != NULL) and dupes permitted,
    insert key. If p is NULL insert at end else insert in middle
    of list.
  */
  if ((n != NULL) && !dupe)
  {
    if (p == NULL) //insert at end
    {
      p = new SDE_NDX_NODE();
      n->next = p;
      p->prev = n;
      memcpy(p->key_ndx.key, ndx->key, max_key_len);
      p->key_ndx.pos = ndx->pos;
      p->key_ndx.length = ndx->length;
    }
    else
    {
      o = new SDE_NDX_NODE();
      memcpy(o->key_ndx.key, ndx->key, max_key_len);
      o->key_ndx.pos = ndx->pos;
      o->key_ndx.length = ndx->length;
      o->next = p;
      o->prev = n;
      n->next = o;
      p->prev = o;
    }
    i = 1;
  }
  DBUG_RETURN(i);
}
```

```
/* delete a key from the index in memory. Note:
   position is included for indexes that allow dupes */
int Spartan_index::delete_key(uchar *buf, long long pos, int key_len)
{
  SDE_NDX_NODE *p;
  int icmp;
  int buf_len;
  bool done = false;

  DBUG_ENTER("Spartan_index::delete_key");
  p = root;
  /*
    Search for the key in the list. If found, delete it!
  */
  while ((p != NULL) && !done)
  {
    buf_len = p->key_ndx.length;
    icmp = memcmp(buf, p->key_ndx.key,
                  (buf_len > key_len) ? buf_len : key_len);
    if (icmp == 0)
    {
      if (pos != -1)
      {
        if (pos == p->key_ndx.pos)
          done = true;
      }
      else
        done = true;
    }
    else
      p = p->next;
  }
  if (p != NULL)
  {
    /*
      Reset pointers for deleted node in list.
    */
    if (p->next != NULL)
      p->next->prev = p->prev;
    if (p->prev != NULL)
      p->prev->next = p->next;
    else
      root = p->next;
    delete p;
  }
  DBUG_RETURN(0);
}
```

```
/* update key in place (so if key changes!) */
int Spartan_index::update_key(uchar *buf, long long pos, int key_len)
{
  SDE_NDX_NODE *p;
  bool done = false;

  DBUG_ENTER("Spartan_index::update_key");
  p = root;
  /*
    Search for the key.
  */
  while ((p != NULL) && !done)
  {
    if (p->key_ndx.pos == pos)
      done = true;
    else
      p = p->next;
  }
  /*
    If key found, overwrite key value in node.
  */
  if (p != NULL)
  {
    memcpy(p->key_ndx.key, buf, key_len);
  }
  DBUG_RETURN(0);
}

/* get the current position of the key in the index file */
long long Spartan_index::get_index_pos(uchar *buf, int key_len)
{
  long long pos = -1;

  DBUG_ENTER("Spartan_index::get_index_pos");
  SDE_INDEX *ndx;
  ndx = seek_index(buf, key_len);
  if (ndx != NULL)
    pos = ndx->pos;
  DBUG_RETURN(pos);
}

/* get next key in list */
uchar *Spartan_index::get_next_key()
{
  uchar *key = 0;

  DBUG_ENTER("Spartan_index::get_next_key");
  if (range_ptr != NULL)
  {
    key = (uchar *)my_malloc(max_key_len, MYF(MY_ZEROFILL | MY_WME));
    memcpy(key, range_ptr->key_ndx.key, range_ptr->key_ndx.length);
    range_ptr = range_ptr->next;
```

```
  }
  DBUG_RETURN(key);
}

/* get prev key in list */
uchar *Spartan_index::get_prev_key()
{
  uchar *key = 0;

  DBUG_ENTER("Spartan_index::get_prev_key");
  if (range_ptr != NULL)
  {
    key = (uchar *)my_malloc(max_key_len, MYF(MY_ZEROFILL | MY_WME));
    memcpy(key, range_ptr->key_ndx.key, range_ptr->key_ndx.length);
    range_ptr = range_ptr->prev;
  }
  DBUG_RETURN(key);
}

/* get first key in list */
uchar *Spartan_index::get_first_key()
{
  SDE_NDX_NODE *n = root;
  uchar *key = 0;

  DBUG_ENTER("Spartan_index::get_first_key");
  if (root != NULL)
  {
    key = (uchar *)my_malloc(max_key_len, MYF(MY_ZEROFILL | MY_WME));
    memcpy(key, n->key_ndx.key, n->key_ndx.length);
  }
  DBUG_RETURN(key);
}

/* get last key in list */
uchar *Spartan_index::get_last_key()
{
  SDE_NDX_NODE *n = root;
  uchar *key = 0;

  DBUG_ENTER("Spartan_index::get_last_key");
  while (n->next != NULL)
    n = n->next;
  if (n != NULL)
  {
    key = (uchar *)my_malloc(max_key_len, MYF(MY_ZEROFILL | MY_WME));
    memcpy(key, n->key_ndx.key, n->key_ndx.length);
  }
  DBUG_RETURN(key);
}
```

```
/* just close the index */
int Spartan_index::close_index()
{
  SDE_NDX_NODE *p;

  DBUG_ENTER("Spartan_index::close_index");
  if (index_file != -1)
  {
    my_close(index_file, MYF(0));
    index_file = -1;
  }
  while (root != NULL)
  {
    p = root;
    root = root->next;
    delete p;
  }
  DBUG_RETURN(0);
}

/* find a key in the index */
SDE_INDEX *Spartan_index::seek_index(uchar *key, int key_len)
{
  SDE_INDEX *ndx = NULL;
  SDE_NDX_NODE *n = root;
  int buf_len;
  bool done = false;

  DBUG_ENTER("Spartan_index::seek_index");
  if (n != NULL)
  {
    while((n != NULL) && !done)
    {
      buf_len = n->key_ndx.length;
      if (memcmp(n->key_ndx.key, key,
          (buf_len > key_len) ? buf_len : key_len) == 0)
        done = true;
      else
        n = n->next;
    }
  }
  if (n != NULL)
  {
    ndx = &n->key_ndx;
    range_ptr = n;
  }
  DBUG_RETURN(ndx);
}
```

```
/* find a key in the index and return position too */
SDE_NDX_NODE *Spartan_index::seek_index_pos(uchar *key, int key_len)
{
  SDE_NDX_NODE *n = root;
  int buf_len;
  bool done = false;

  DBUG_ENTER("Spartan_index::seek_index_pos");
  if (n != NULL)
  {
    while((n->next != NULL) && !done)
    {
      buf_len = n->key_ndx.length;
      if (memcmp(n->key_ndx.key, key,
          (buf_len > key_len) ? buf_len : key_len) == 0)
        done = true;
      else if (n->next != NULL)
        n = n->next;
    }
  }
  DBUG_RETURN(n);
}

/* read the index file from disk and store in memory */
int Spartan_index::load_index()
{
  SDE_INDEX *ndx;
  int i = 1;

  DBUG_ENTER("Spartan_index::load_index");
  if (root != NULL)
    destroy_index();
  /*
    First, read the metadata at the front of the index.
  */
  read_header();
  while(i != 0)
  {
    ndx = new SDE_INDEX();
    i = my_read(index_file, (uchar *)&ndx->key, max_key_len, MYF(0));
    i = my_read(index_file, (uchar *)&ndx->pos, sizeof(long long), MYF(0));
    i = my_read(index_file, (uchar *)&ndx->length, sizeof(int), MYF(0));
    if (i != 0)
      insert_key(ndx, false);
  }
  DBUG_RETURN(0);
}
```

```
/* get current position of index file */
long long Spartan_index::curfpos()
{
  long long pos = 0;

  DBUG_ENTER("Spartan_index::curfpos");
  pos = my_seek(index_file, 0l, MY_SEEK_CUR, MYF(0));
  DBUG_RETURN(pos);
}

/* write the index back to disk */
int Spartan_index::save_index()
{
  SDE_NDX_NODE *n = NULL;
  int i;

  DBUG_ENTER("Spartan_index::save_index");
  i = my_chsize(index_file, 0L, '\n', MYF(MY_WME));
  write_header();
  n = root;
  while (n != NULL)
  {
    write_row(&n->key_ndx);
    n = n->next;
  }
  DBUG_RETURN(0);
}

int Spartan_index::destroy_index()
{
  SDE_NDX_NODE *n = root;

  DBUG_ENTER("Spartan_index::destroy_index");
  while (root != NULL)
  {
    n = root;
    root = n->next;
    delete n;
  }
  root = NULL;
  DBUG_RETURN(0);
}

/* Get the file position of the first key in index */
long long Spartan_index::get_first_pos()
{
  long long pos = -1;

  DBUG_ENTER("Spartan_index::get_first_pos");
  if (root != NULL)
```

```
  pos = root->key_ndx.pos;
  DBUG_RETURN(pos);
}

/* truncate the index file */
int Spartan_index::trunc_index()
{
  DBUG_ENTER("Spartan_data::trunc_table");
  if (index_file != -1)
  {
    my_chsize(index_file, 0, 0, MYF(MY_WME));
    write_header();
  }
  DBUG_RETURN(0);
}
```

Notice that, as with the Spartan_data class, I use the DBUG routines to set the trace elements for debugging. I also use the my_xxx platform-safe utility methods.

■ **Tip** These methods can be found in the mysys directory under the root of the source tree. They are normally implemented as C functions stored in a file of the same name (e.g., the my_write.c file contains the my_write() method).

The index works by storing a key using a uchar pointer to a block of memory, a position value (long long) that stores an offset location on disk used in the Spartan_data class to position the file pointer, and a length field that stores the length of the key. The length variable is used in the memory-compare method to set the comparison length. These data items are stored in a structure named SDE_INDEX. The doubly linked list node is another structure that contains an SDE_INDEX structure. The list-node structure, named SDE_NDX_NODE, also provides the next and prev pointers for the list.

When using the index to store the location of data in the Spartan_data class file, you can call the insert_index() method, passing in the key and the offset of the data item in the file. This offset is returned on the my_write() method calls. This technique allows you to store the index pointers to data on disk and reuse that information without transforming it to position the file pointer to the correct location on disk.

The index is stored on disk in consecutive blocks of data that correspond to the size of the SDE_INDEX structure. The file has a header, which is used to store a crashed status variable and a variable that stores the maximum key length. The crashed status variable is helpful to identify the rare case in which a file has become corrupted or errors have occurred during reading or writing that compromise the integrity of the file or its metadata. Rather than use a variable-length field such as the data class, I use a fixed-length memory block to simplify the read and write methods for disk access. In this case, I made a conscious decision to sacrifice space for simplicity.

Now that you've had an introduction to the dirty work of building a storage engine—the low-level I/O functions—let's see how we can build a basic storage engine. I'll return to the Spartan_data and Spartan_index classes in later sections, discussing Stages 1 and 5, respectively.

Getting Started

The following tutorial assumes that you have your development environment configured and you have compiled the server with the debug switch turned on (see Chapter 5). I examine each stage of building the Spartan storage engine. Before you get started, you need to do one very important step: create a test file to test the storage engine so that we can drive the development toward a specific goal. Chapter 4 examined the MySQL test suite and how to create and run tests. Refer to that chapter for additional details or a refresher.

░ **Tip** If you are using Windows, you may not be able to use the MySQL test suite (mysql-test-run.pl). You can use Cygwin (http://cygwin.com/) to set up a Unix-like environment and run the test suite there. If you don't want to set up a Cygwin environment, you can still create the test file, copy and paste the statements into a MySQL client program, and run the tests that way.

The first thing you should do is create a new test to test the Spartan storage engine. Even though the engine doesn't exist yet, in the spirit of test-driven development, you should create the test before writing the code. Let's do that now.

The test file should begin as a simple test to create the table and retrieve rows from it. You can create a complete test file that includes all of the operations that I'll show you, but it may be best to start out with a simple test and extend it as you progress through the stages of building the Spartan storage engine. This has the added benefit that your test will only test the current stage and not generate errors for operations not yet implemented. Listing 10-7 shows a sample basic test to test a Stage 1 Spartan storage engine.

As you go through this tutorial, you'll be adding statements to this test, effectively building the complete test for the completed Spartan storage engine as you go.

Listing 10-7. Spartan-storage-Engine Test File (Ch10s1.test)

```
#
# Simple test for the Spartan storage engine
#
--disable_warnings
drop table if exists t1;
--enable_warnings

CREATE TABLE t1 (
  col_a int,
  col_b varchar(20),
  col_c int
) ENGINE=SPARTAN;

SELECT * FROM t1;

RENAME TABLE t1 TO t2;

DROP TABLE t2;
```

You can create this file in the /mysql-test/t directory off the root of the source tree. When you execute it the first time, it's OK to have errors. In fact, you should execute the test before beginning Stage 1. That way, you know the test works (it doesn't fail). If you recall from Chapter 4, you can execute the test by using the commands from the /mysql-test directory:

```
%> touch r/Ch10s1.result
%> ./mysql-test-run.pl Ch10s1
%> cp r/cab.reject r/Ch10s1.result
%> ./mysql-test-run.pl Ch10s1
```

Did you try it? Did it produce errors? The test suite returned [failed], but if you examine the log file generated, you won't see any errors, although you will see warnings. Why didn't it fail? Well, it turns out that MySQL will use a default storage engine if the storage engine you specify on your create statement doesn't exist. In this case, my MySQL server installation issued the error that the system was using the default MyISAM storage engine because the Spartan storage engine was not found. Listing 10-8 shows an example of the /mysql-test/r/Ch10s1.log file.

Listing 10-8. Example Log File from Test Run

```
mysql> drop table if exists t1;
mysql> CREATE TABLE t1 (
    ->    col_a int,
    ->    col_b varchar(20),
    ->    col_c int
    -> ) ENGINE=SPARTAN;
ERROR 1286 (42000): Unknown storage engine 'SPARTAN'
mysql>
mysql> SELECT * FROM t1;
ERROR 1146 (42S02): Table 'test.t1' doesn't exist
mysql>
mysql> DROP TABLE t1;
ERROR 1051 (42S02): Unknown table 'test.t1'
```

Stage 1: Stubbing the Engine

The goal of this stage is to produce a stubbed storage-engine plugin. The stubbed engine will have the most basic operation of being able to choose the engine on the CREATE statement and creating the base-table meta file (.frm). I know that doesn't sound like much, and while it doesn't actually store anything,[5] creating a stage 1 engine allows you to ensure you have all of the initial code changes necessary to register the storage engine with the server. I mentioned previously that some of these changes may not be necessary in future releases of the MySQL system. It is always a good idea to check the online reference manual for the latest changes prior to working with the MySQL source code.

Creating the Spartan Plugin Source Files

First, create a directory named spartan under the /storage directory off the main source-code tree. I use the example storage engine to get us started. The MySQL reference manual suggests using the source files for the example storage engine as your basis. The example storage engine contains all the necessary methods implemented with the correct code statements. This makes it easy to create the base source files for the Spartan storage engine.

Copy the *.cc and *.h files from the /storage/example directory to the /storage/spartan directory. You should now have two files in the spartan directory: ha_example.cc and ha_example.h. The ha_ prefix indicates that the files are derived from the handler class and represent a table handler. Rename the files ha_spartan.cc and ha_spartan.h.

■ **Note** The phrase *table handler* has been replaced with the more recent phrase *storage engine*. You may encounter bits of the documentation that talk about table handlers. They are synonymous with storage engines and apply accordingly.

---

[5]The inspiration for this chapter was the lack of coverage available for those seeking to develop their own storage engines. Very few references go beyond creating a Stage 1 engine in their examples.

The next step in creating the source files is to change all occurrences of the words example and EXAMPLE to spartan and SPARTAN, respectively. You can use your favorite code editor or text processor to effect the changes. The resulting files should have all the example identifiers changed to spartan (e.g., st_example_share should become st_spartan_share). Use case sensitivity. Your storage engine won't work if you don't do this correctly.

Last, edit the ha_spartan.h file and add the include directive to include the spartan_data.h file as shown here:

```
#include "spartan_data.h"
```

Adding the CMakeLists.txt File

Since we are creating a new plugin and a new project, we need to create a CMakeLists.txt file so that the cmake tool can create the appropriate make file for the project. Open a new file in the /storage/spartan directory and name it CMakeLists.txt. Add to the file:

```
# Spartan storage engine plugin

SET(SPARTAN_PLUGIN_STATIC "spartan")
SET(SPARTAN_PLUGIN_DYNAMIC "spartan")

SET(SPARTAN_SOURCES ha_spartan.cc ha_spartan.h spartan_data.cc spartan_data.h)
MYSQL_ADD_PLUGIN(spartan ${SPARTAN_SOURCES} STORAGE_ENGINE MODULE_ONLY)
```

Notice that we use macros to define the sources for the plugin and use another macro to add the storage-engine-specific make file lines during the cmake operation.

Final Modifications

You need to make one other change. At the bottom of the ha_spartan.cc file, you should see a mysq_declare_plugin section. This is the code that the plugin interface uses to install the storage engine. See Chapter 9 for more details about this structure.

Feel free to modify this section to indicate that it is the Spartan storage engine. You can add your own name and comments to the code. This section isn't used yet, but when the storage-engine plugin architecture is complete, you'll need this section to enable the plug-in interface.

```
mysql_declare_plugin(spartan)
{
  MYSQL_STORAGE_ENGINE_PLUGIN,
  &spartan_storage_engine,
  "Spartan",
  "Chuck Bell",
  "Spartan Storage Engine Plugin",
  PLUGIN_LICENSE_GPL,
  spartan_init_func,                        /* Plugin Init */
  NULL,                              /* Plugin Deinit */
  0x0100 /* 1.0 */,
  func_status,                          /* status variables */
  spartan_system_variables,                 /* system variables */
  NULL,                             /* config options */
  0,                            /* flags */
}
mysql_declare_plugin_end;
```

If that seemed like a lot of work for a storage-engine plugin,—it is. Fortunately, this situation will improve in future releases of the MySQL system.

Compiling the Spartan Engine

Now that all of these changes have been made, it is time to compile the server and test the new Spartan storage engine. The process is the same as with other compilations. From the root of the source tree, run the commands:

```
cmake .
make
```

Compile the server in debug mode so that you can generate trace files and use an interactive debugger to explore the source code while the server is running.

Testing Stage 1 of the Spartan Engine

Once the server is compiled, you can launch it and run it. First, install the new plugin. As we saw in Chapter 9, we can copy the compiled library (ha_spartan.so) to the plugin directory (--plugin-dir) and execute the command:

```
INSTALL PLUGIN spartan SONAME 'ha_spartan.so';
```

Or, for Windows, this command:

```
INSTALL PLUGIN spartan SONAME 'ha_spartan.dll';
```

You may be tempted to test the server using the interactive MySQL client. That's OK, and I did exactly that. Listing 10-9 shows the results from the MySQL client after running a number of SQL commands. In this example, I ran the SHOW STORAGE ENGINES, CREATE TABLE, SHOW CREATE TABLE, and DROP TABLE commands. The results show that these commands work and that the test should pass when I run it.

Listing 10-9. Example Manual Test of the Stage 1 Spartan Storage Engine

```
mysql> SHOW PLUGINS \G
*************************** 1. row ***************************
   Name: binlog
 Status: ACTIVE
   Type: STORAGE ENGINE
Library: NULL
License: GPL
*************************** 2. row ***************************
   Name: mysql_native_password
 Status: ACTIVE
   Type: AUTHENTICATION
Library: NULL
License: GPL
*************************** 3. row ***************************
   Name: mysql_old_password
 Status: ACTIVE
   Type: AUTHENTICATION
Library: NULL
License: GPL
```

```
*************************** 4. row ***************************
   Name: sha256_password
 Status: ACTIVE
   Type: AUTHENTICATION
Library: NULL
License: GPL
*************************** 5. row ***************************
   Name: CSV
 Status: ACTIVE
   Type: STORAGE ENGINE
Library: NULL
License: GPL
*************************** 6. row ***************************
   Name: MRG_MYISAM
 Status: ACTIVE
   Type: STORAGE ENGINE
Library: NULL
License: GPL
*************************** 7. row ***************************
   Name: MEMORY
 Status: ACTIVE
   Type: STORAGE ENGINE
Library: NULL
License: GPL
*************************** 8. row ***************************
   Name: MyISAM
 Status: ACTIVE
   Type: STORAGE ENGINE
Library: NULL
License: GPL
*************************** 9. row ***************************
   Name: BLACKHOLE
 Status: ACTIVE
   Type: STORAGE ENGINE
Library: NULL
License: GPL
*************************** 10. row ***************************
   Name: InnoDB
 Status: ACTIVE
   Type: STORAGE ENGINE
Library: NULL
License: GPL

...

*************************** 43. row ***************************
   Name: partition
 Status: ACTIVE
   Type: STORAGE ENGINE
Library: NULL
License: GPL
43 rows in set (0.00 sec)
```

```
mysql> INSTALL PLUGIN spartan SONAME 'ha_spartan.so';
Query OK, 0 rows affected (0.00 sec)

mysql> SHOW PLUGINS \G
*************************** 1. row ***************************
   Name: binlog
 Status: ACTIVE
   Type: STORAGE ENGINE
Library: NULL
License: GPL
*************************** 2. row ***************************
   Name: mysql_native_password
 Status: ACTIVE
   Type: AUTHENTICATION
Library: NULL
License: GPL
*************************** 3. row ***************************
   Name: mysql_old_password
 Status: ACTIVE
   Type: AUTHENTICATION
Library: NULL
License: GPL
*************************** 4. row ***************************
   Name: sha256_password
 Status: ACTIVE
   Type: AUTHENTICATION
Library: NULL
License: GPL
*************************** 5. row ***************************
   Name: CSV
 Status: ACTIVE
   Type: STORAGE ENGINE
Library: NULL
License: GPL
*************************** 6. row ***************************
   Name: MRG_MYISAM
 Status: ACTIVE
   Type: STORAGE ENGINE
Library: NULL
License: GPL
*************************** 7. row ***************************
   Name: MEMORY
 Status: ACTIVE
   Type: STORAGE ENGINE
Library: NULL
License: GPL
*************************** 8. row ***************************
   Name: MyISAM
 Status: ACTIVE
   Type: STORAGE ENGINE
Library: NULL
License: GPL
```

```
*************************** 9. row ***************************
   Name: BLACKHOLE
 Status: ACTIVE
   Type: STORAGE ENGINE
Library: NULL
License: GPL
*************************** 10. row ***************************
   Name: InnoDB
 Status: ACTIVE
   Type: STORAGE ENGINE
Library: NULL
License: GPL


...


*************************** 43. row ***************************
   Name: partition
 Status: ACTIVE
   Type: STORAGE ENGINE
Library: NULL
License: GPL
*************************** 44. row ***************************
   Name: Spartan
 Status: ACTIVE
   Type: STORAGE ENGINE
Library: ha_spartan.so
License: GPL
44 rows in set (0.00 sec)

mysql> use test;
Database changed
mysql> CREATE TABLE t1 (col_a int, col_b varchar(20), col_c int) ENGINE=SPARTAN;
Query OK, 0 rows affected (0.02 sec)

mysql> SHOW CREATE TABLE t1 \G
*************************** 1. row ***************************
      Table: t1
Create Table: CREATE TABLE 't1' (
  'col_a' int(11) DEFAULT NULL,
  'col_b' varchar(20) DEFAULT NULL,
  'col_c' int(11) DEFAULT NULL
) ENGINE=SPARTAN DEFAULT CHARSET=latin1
1 row in set (0.00 sec)

mysql> DROP TABLE t1;
Query OK, 0 rows affected (0.00 sec)

mysql>
```

I know that the storage engine is working, because it is listed in the SHOW PLUGINS command and in the SHOW CREATE TABLE statement. Had the engine failed to connect, it may or may not have shown in the SHOW PLUGINS command, but the CREATE TABLE command would have specified the MyISAM storage engine instead of the Spartan storage engine.

You should also run the test you created earlier (if you're running Linux). When you run the test this time, the test passes. That's because the storage engine is now part of the server, and it can be recognized. Let's put the SELECT command in and rerun the test. It should once again pass. At this point, you could add the test results to the /r directory for automated test reporting. Listing 10-10 shows the updated test.

■ **Note**   We will make new versions of the test for each stage, naming them Ch10sX (e.g. Ch10s1, Ch10s2, etc.).

Listing 10-10. Updated Spartan Storage Engine Test File (Ch10s1.test)

```
#
# Simple test for the Spartan storage engine
#
--disable_warnings
drop table if exists t1;
--enable_warnings

CREATE TABLE t1 (
  col_a int,
  col_b varchar(20),
  col_c int
) ENGINE=SPARTAN;

SELECT * FROM t1;

DROP TABLE t1;
```

That's it for a Stage 1 engine. It is plugged in and ready for you to add the Spartan_data and spartan_index classes. In the next stage, we'll add the ability to create, open, close, and delete files. That may not sound like much, but in the spirit of incremental development, you can add that bit and then test and debug until everything works before you move on to the more challenging operations.

Stage 2: Working with Tables

The goal of this stage is to produce a stubbed storage engine that can create, open, close, and delete data files. This stage is the one in which you set up the basic file-handling routines and establish that the engine is working with the files correctly. MySQL has provided a number of file I/O routines for you that encapsulate the lower-level functions, making them platform safe. The following is a sample of some of the functions available. See the files in the /mysys directory for more details.

- my_create(...): Create files

- my_open(...): Open files

- my_read(...): Read data from files

- `my_write(...)`: Write data to files
- `my_delete(...)`: Delete file
- `fn_format(...)`: Create a platform-safe path statement

In this stage, I show you how to incorporate the Spartan_data class for the low-level I/O. I walk you through each change and include the completed method source code for each change.

Updating the Spartan Source Files

First, either download the compressed source files from the Apress Web site's catalog page for this book, and copy them into your /storage/spartan directory. Or use the spartan_data.cc and spartan_data.h files that you created earlier.

Since I'm using Spartan_data class to handle the low-level I/O, I need to create an object pointer to hold an instance of that class. I need to place it somewhere where it can be shared so that there won't be two or more instances of the class trying to read the same file. While that may be OK, it is more complicated and would require a bit more work. Instead, I place an object reference in the Spartan handler's shared structure.

■ **Tip** After you make each change, compile the spartan project to make sure there are no errors. Correct any errors before proceeding to the next change.

Updating the Header File

Open the ha_spartan.h file and add the object reference to the st_spartan_share structure. Listing 10-11 shows the completed code change (comments omitted for brevity). Once you have this change made, recompile the spartan source files to make sure there aren't any errors.

Listing 10-11. Changes to Share Structure in ha_spartan.h

```
/*
  Spartan Storage Engine Plugin
*/

#include "my_global.h"              /* ulonglong */
#include "thr_lock.h"               /* THR_LOCK, THR_LOCK_DATA */
#include "handler.h"                /* handler */
#include "spartan_data.h"

class Spartan_share : public Handler_share {
public:
  mysql_mutex_t mutex;
  THR_LOCK lock;
  Spartan_data *data_class;
  Spartan_share();
  ~Spartan_share()
  {
    thr_lock_delete(&lock);
```

```
    mysql_mutex_destroy(&mutex);
    if (data_class != NULL)
      delete data_class;
    data_class = NULL;
  }
};
```

...

Updating the Class File

The next series of modifications are done in the ha_spartan.cc file. Open that file and locate the constructor for the new Spartan_share class. Since there is an object reference now in the share structure, we need to instantiate it when the share is created. Add the instantiation of the Spartan_data class to the method. Name the object reference data_class. Listing 10-12 shows an excerpt of the method with changes.

▓ **Tip**   If you are using Windows, and IntelliSense in Visual Studio does not recognize the new Spartan_data class, you need to repair the .ncb file. Exit Visual Studio, delete the .ncb file from the source root, and then rebuild mysqld. This may take a while, but when it is done, IntelliSense will work again.

Listing 10-12. Changes to the Spartan_data class constructor in ha_spartan.cc

```
Spartan_share::Spartan_share()
{
  thr_lock_init(&lock);
  mysql_mutex_init(ex_key_mutex_Spartan_share_mutex,
                   &mutex, MY_MUTEX_INIT_FAST);
  data_class = new Spartan_data();
}
```

Naturally, you also need to destroy the object reference when the share structure is destroyed. Locate the destructor method and add the code to destroy the data-class object reference. Listing 10-13 shows an excerpt of the method with the changes.

Listing 10-13. Changes to the Spartan_data destructor in ha_spartan.h

```
class Spartan_share : public Handler_share {
public:
  mysql_mutex_t mutex;
  THR_LOCK lock;
  Spartan_data *data_class;
  Spartan_share();
  ~Spartan_share()
  {
    thr_lock_delete(&lock);
    mysql_mutex_destroy(&mutex);
    if (data_class != NULL)
```

```
      delete data_class;
    data_class = NULL;
  }
};
```

The handler instance of the Spartan storage engine also must provide the file extensions for the data files. Since there is both a data and an index file, you need to create two file extensions. Define the file extensions and add them to the ha_spartan_exts array. Use .sde for the data file and .sdi for the index file. MySQL uses these extensions for deleting files and other maintenance operations. Locate the ha_spartan_exts array, add the #defines above it, and add those definitions to the array. Listing 10-14 shows the changes to the array structure.

Listing 10-14. Changes to the ha_spartan_exts Array in ha_spartan.cc

```
#define SDE_EXT ".sde"
#define SDI_EXT ".sdi"

static const char *ha_spartan_exts[] = {
  SDE_EXT,
  SDI_EXT,
  NullS
};
```

The first operation you need to add is the create file operation. This will create the empty file to contain the data for the table. Locate the create() method and add the code to get a copy of the share structure, then call the data class create_table() method and close the table. Listing 10-15 shows the updated create method. I show you how to add the index class in a later stage.

Listing 10-15. Changes to the create() Method in ha_spartan.cc

```
int ha_spartan::create(const char *name, TABLE *table_arg,
                       HA_CREATE_INFO *create_info)
{
  DBUG_ENTER("ha_spartan::create");
  char name_buff[FN_REFLEN];

  if (!(share = get_share()))
    DBUG_RETURN(1);
  /*
    Call the data class create table method.
    Note: the fn_format() method correctly creates a file name from the
    name passed into the method.
  */
  if (share->data_class->create_table(fn_format(name_buff, name, "", SDE_EXT,
                                       MY_REPLACE_EXT|MY_UNPACK_FILENAME)))
    DBUG_RETURN(-1);
  share->data_class->close_table();
  DBUG_RETURN(0);
}
```

The next operation you need to add is the open-file operation. This will open the file that contains the data for the table. Locate the open() method and add the code to get a copy of the share structure and open the table. Listing 10-16 shows the updated open method.

Listing 10-16. Changes to the open() Method in ha_spartan.cc

```
int ha_spartan::open(const char *name, int mode, uint test_if_locked)
{
  DBUG_ENTER("ha_spartan::open");
  char name_buff[FN_REFLEN];

  if (!(share = get_share()))
    DBUG_RETURN(1);
  /*
    Call the data class open table method.
    Note: the fn_format() method correctly creates a file name from the
    name passed into the method.
  */
  share->data_class->open_table(fn_format(name_buff, name, "", SDE_EXT,
                                MY_REPLACE_EXT|MY_UNPACK_FILENAME));
  thr_lock_data_init(&share->lock,&lock,NULL);
  DBUG_RETURN(0);
}
```

The next operation you need to add is the delete-file operation. This will delete the files that contain the data for the table. Locate the delete_table() method and add the code to close the table and call the my_delete() function to delete the table. Listing 10-17 shows the updated delete method. I'll show you how to add the index class in a later stage.

Listing 10-17. Changes to the delete_table() Method in ha_spartan.cc

```
int ha_spartan::delete_table(const char *name)
{
  DBUG_ENTER("ha_spartan::delete_table");
  char name_buff[FN_REFLEN];

  /*
    Call the mysql delete file method.
    Note: the fn_format() method correctly creates a file name from the
    name passed into the method.
  */
  my_delete(fn_format(name_buff, name, "", SDE_EXT,
            MY_REPLACE_EXT|MY_UNPACK_FILENAME), MYF(0));
  DBUG_RETURN(0);
}
```

There is one last operation that many developers forget to include. The RENAME TABLE command allows users to rename tables. Your storage handler must also be able to copy the file to a new name and then delete the old one. While the MySQL server handles the rename of the .frm file, you need to perform the copy for the data file. Locate the rename_table() method and add the code to call the my_copy() function to copy the data file for the table. Listing 10-18 shows the updated rename-table method. Later, I show you how to add the index class .

Listing 10-18. *Changes to the rename_table() Method in ha_spartan.cc*

```
int ha_spartan::rename_table(const char * from, const char * to)
{
  DBUG_ENTER("ha_spartan::rename_table ");
  char data_from[FN_REFLEN];
  char data_to[FN_REFLEN];

  my_copy(fn_format(data_from, from, "", SDE_EXT,
          MY_REPLACE_EXT|MY_UNPACK_FILENAME),
          fn_format(data_to, to, "", SDE_EXT,
          MY_REPLACE_EXT|MY_UNPACK_FILENAME), MYF(0));
  /*
    Delete the file using MySQL's delete file method.
  */
  my_delete(data_from, MYF(0));
  DBUG_RETURN(0);
}
```

OK, you now have a completed Stage 2 storage engine. All that is left to do is to compile the server and run the tests.

■ **Note**   Be sure to copy the updated ha_spartan.so (or ha_spartan.dll) to your plugin directory. If you forget this step, you may spend a lot of time trying to discover why your Stage 2 engine isn't working properly.

Testing Stage 2 of the Spartan Engine

When you run the test again, you should see all of the statements complete successfully. There are, however, two things the test doesn't verify for you. First, you need to make sure the .sde file was created and deleted. Second, you need to make sure the rename command works.

Testing the commands for creating and dropping the table is easy. Launch your server and then a MySQL client. Issue the CREATE statement from the test, and then use your file browser to navigate to the /data/test folder. There you should see two files: t1.frm and t1.sde. Return to your MySQL client and issue the DROP statement. Then return to the /data/test folder and verify that the files are indeed deleted.

Testing the command that renames the table is also easy. Repeat the CREATE statement test and then issue the command:

```
RENAME TABLE t1 TO t2;
```

Once you run the RENAME command, you should be able to issue a SELECT statement and even a DROP statement that operate on the renamed table. This should produce an output like:

```
mysql> RENAME TABLE t1 to t2;
Query OK, 0 rows affected (0.00 sec)

mysql> SELECT * FROM t2;
Empty set (0.00 sec)
```

```
mysql> DROP TABLE t2;
Query OK, 0 rows affected (0.00 sec)
```

Use your file browser to navigate to the /data/test folder. There you should see two files: t2.frm and t2.sde. Return to your MySQL client and issue the DROP statement. Then return to the /data/test folder and verify that the files are indeed deleted.

Now that you have verified that the RENAME statement works, add that to the test file and rerun the test. The test should complete without errors. Listing 10-19 shows the updated Ch10s2.test file.

Listing 10-19. Updated Spartan Storage Engine Test File (Ch10s2.test)

```
#
# Simple test for the Spartan storage engine
#
--disable_warnings
drop table if exists t1;
--enable_warnings

CREATE TABLE t1 (
  col_a int,
  col_b varchar(20),
  col_c int
) ENGINE=SPARTAN;

SELECT * FROM t1;

RENAME TABLE t1 TO t2;

DROP TABLE t2;
```

Well, that's it for a Stage 2 engine. It is plugged in and creates, deletes, and renames files. In the next stage, we'll add the ability to read and write data.

Stage 3: Reading and Writing Data

The goal of this stage is to produce a working storage engine that can read and write data. In this stage, I show you how to incorporate the Spartan_data class for reading and writing data. I walk you through each change and include the completed method source code for each change.

Updating the Spartan Source Files

Making a Stage 3 engine requires updates to the basic reading process (described earlier).To implement the read operation, you'll be making changes to the rnd_init(), rnd_next(), position(), and rnd_pos() methods in the ha_spartan.cc file. The position() and rnd_pos() methods are used during large sorting operations and use an internal buffer to store the rows. The write operation requires changes to only the write_row() method.

Updating the Header File

The position methods require that you store a pointer—either a record offset position or a key value to be used in the sorting operations. Oracle provides a nifty way of doing this, as you'll see in the position methods in a moment. Open the ha_spartan.h file and add the current_position variable to the ha_spartan class. Listing 10-20 shows an excerpt with the changes.

Listing 10-20. Changes to the ha_spartan Class in ha_spartan.h

```
class ha_spartan: public handler
{
  THR_LOCK_DATA lock;        /* MySQL lock */
  Spartan_share *share;      ///< Shared lock info
  Spartan_share *get_share(); ///< Get the share
  off_t current_position;    /* Current position in the file during a file scan */

public:
  ha_spartan(handlerton *hton, TABLE_SHARE *table_ar);
  ~ha_spartan()
  {
  }
...
```

Updating the Source File

Return to the ha_spartan.cc file, as that is where the rest of the changes need to be made. The first method you need to change is rnd_init(). Here is where you need to set the initial conditions for a table scan. In this case, you set the current position to 0 (start of file) and the number of records to 0, and specify the length of the item you want to use for the sorting methods. Use a long long, since that is the data type for the current position in the file. Listing 10-21 shows the updated method with the changes.

Listing 10-21. Changes to the rnd_init() Method in ha_spartan.cc

```
int ha_spartan::rnd_init(bool scan)
{
  DBUG_ENTER("ha_spartan::rnd_init");
  current_position = 0;
  stats.records = 0;
  ref_length = sizeof(long long);
  DBUG_RETURN(0);
}
```

■ **Caution** This is the point at which we start adding functionality beyond that of the example engine. Be sure to correctly specify your return codes. The example engine tells the optimizer that a function is not supported by issuing the return statement DBUG_RETURN(HA_ERR_WRONG_COMMAND);. Be sure to change these to something other than the wrong command return code (e.g., 0).

The next method you need to change is rnd_next(), which is responsible for getting the next record from the file and detecting the end of the file. In this method, you can call the data class read_row() method, passing in the record buffer, the length of the buffer, and the current position in the file. Notice the return for the end of the file and the setting of more statistics. The method also records the current position so that the next call to the method will advance the file to the next record. Listing 10-22 shows the updated method with the changes.

Listing 10-22. Changes to the rnd_next() Method in ha_spartan.cc

```
int ha_spartan::rnd_next(uchar *buf)
{
  int rc;
  DBUG_ENTER("ha_spartan::rnd_next");
  MYSQL_READ_ROW_START(table_share->db.str, table_share->table_name.str,
                       TRUE);
  /*
    Read the row from the data file.
  */
  rc = share->data_class->read_row(buf, table->s->rec_buff_length,
                                   current_position);
  if (rc != -1)
    current_position = (off_t)share->data_class->cur_position();
  else
    DBUG_RETURN(HA_ERR_END_OF_FILE);
  stats.records++;
  MYSQL_READ_ROW_DONE(rc);
  DBUG_RETURN(rc);
}
```

The Spartan_data class is nice, because it stores the records in the same format as the MySQL internal buffer. In fact, it just writes a few uchars of a header for each record, storing a deleted flag and the record length (for use in scanning and repairing). If you were working on a storage engine that stored the data in a different format, you would need to perform the translation at this point. A sample of how that translation could be accomplished is found in the ha_tina.cc file. The process looks something like:

```
for (Field **field=table->field ; *field ; field++)
{
  /* copy field data to your own storage type */
  my_value = (*field)->val_str();
  my_store_field(my_value);
}
```

In this example, you are iterating through the field array, writing out the data in your own format. Look for the ha_tina::find_current_row() method for an example.

The next method you need to change is position(), which records the current position of the file in the MySQL pointer-storage mechanism. It is called after each call to rnd_next(). The methods for storing and retrieving these pointers are my_store_ptr() and my_get_ptr(). The store-pointer method takes a reference variable (the place you want to store something), the length of what you want to store, and the thing you want to store as parameters. The get-pointer method takes a reference variable and the length of what you are retrieving, and it returns the item stored. These methods are used in the case of an order by rows where the data will need to be sorted. Take a look at the changes for the position() method shown in Listing 10-23 to see how you can call the store-pointer method.

Listing 10-23. Changes to the position() Method in ha_spartan.cc

```
void ha_spartan::position(const uchar *record)
{
  DBUG_ENTER("ha_spartan::position");
  my_store_ptr(ref, ref_length, current_position);
  DBUG_VOID_RETURN;
}
```

The next method you need to change is rnd_pos(), which is where you'll retrieve the current position stored and then read in the row from that position. Notice that in this method we also increment the read statistic ha_read_rnd_next_count. This provides the optimizer information about how many rows there are in the table, and it can be helpful in optimizing later queries. Listing 10-24 shows the updated method with the changes.

Listing 10-24. Changes to the rnd_pos() Method in ha_spartan.cc

```
int ha_spartan::rnd_pos(uchar *buf, uchar *pos)
{
  int rc;
  DBUG_ENTER("ha_spartan::rnd_pos");
  MYSQL_READ_ROW_START(table_share->db.str, table_share->table_name.str,
                       TRUE);
  ha_statistic_increment(&SSV::ha_read_rnd_next_count);
  current_position = (off_t)my_get_ptr(pos,ref_length);
  rc = share->data_class->read_row(buf, current_position, -1);
  MYSQL_READ_ROW_DONE(rc);
  DBUG_RETURN(rc);
}
```

The next method you need to change is info(), which returns information to the optimizer to help choose an optimal execution path. This is an interesting method to implement, and when you read the comments in the source code, it'll seem humorous. What you need to do in this method is to return the number of records. Oracle states that you should always return a value of 2 or more. This disengages portions of the optimizer that are wasteful for a record set of one row. Listing 10-25 shows the updated info() method.

Listing 10-25. Changes to the info() Method in ha_spartan.cc

```
int ha_spartan::info(uint flag)
{
  DBUG_ENTER("ha_spartan::info");
  /* This is a lie, but you don't want the optimizer to see zero or 1 */
  if (stats.records < 2)
    stats.records= 2;
  DBUG_RETURN(0);
}
```

The last method you need to change is write_row(); you'll be writing the data to the data file using the Spartan_data class again. Like the read, the Spartan_data class needs only to write the record buffer to disk preceded by a delete status flag and the record length. Listing 10-26 shows the updated method with the changes.

Listing 10-26. Changes to the write_row() Method in ha_spartan.cc

```
int ha_spartan::write_row(uchar *buf)
{
  DBUG_ENTER("ha_spartan::write_row");
  long long pos;
  SDE_INDEX ndx;

  ha_statistic_increment(&SSV::ha_write_count);
  /*
    Begin critical section by locking the spartan mutex variable.
  */
```

```
mysql_mutex_lock(&share->mutex);
pos = share->data_class->write_row(buf, table->s->rec_buff_length);
/*
  End section by unlocking the spartan mutex variable.
*/
mysql_mutex_unlock(&share->mutex);
DBUG_RETURN(0);
}
```

Notice that once again I have placed a mutex (for example, critical section) around the write so that no two threads can write at the same time. Now is a good time to compile the server and debug any errors. When that is done, you'll have a completed a Stage 3 storage engine. All that is left to do is to compile the server and run the tests.

Testing Stage 3 of the Spartan Engine

When you run the test again, you should see all of the statements complete successfully. If you are wondering why I always begin with running the test from the last increment, it's because you want to make sure that none of the new code broke anything that the old code was doing. In this case, you can see that you can still create, rename, and delete tables. Now, let's move on to testing the read and write operations.

Testin these functions is easy. Launch your server and then a MySQL client. If you have deleted the test table, re-create it and then issue the command:

```
INSERT INTO t1 VALUES(1, "first test", 24);
INSERT INTO t1 VALUES(4, "second test", 43);
INSERT INTO t1 VALUES(3, "third test", -2);
```

After each statement, you should see the successful insertion of the records. If you encounter errors (which you shouldn't), launch your debugger, set breakpoints in all of the read and write methods in the ha_spartan.cc file, and then debug the problem. You should not look any further than the ha_spartan.cc file, because that is the only file that could contain the source of the error.[6]

Now you can issue a SELECT statement and see what the server sends back to you. Enter the command:

```
SELECT * FROM t1;
```

You should see all three rows returned. Listing 10-27 shows the results of running the query.

Listing 10-27. Results of Running INSERT/SELECT Statements

```
mysql> INSERT INTO t1 VALUES(1, "first test", 24);
Query OK, 1 row affected (0.00 sec)

mysql> INSERT INTO t1 VALUES(4, "second test", 43);
Query OK, 1 row affected (0.00 sec)

mysql> INSERT INTO t1 VALUES(3, "third test", -2);
Query OK, 1 row affected (0.00 sec)
```

---

[6] Well, maybe the low-level I/O source code. It's always possible that I've missed something or that something has changed in the server since I wrote that class.

```
mysql> SELECT * FROM t1;
+-------+-------------+-------+
| col_a | col_b       | col_c |
+-------+-------------+-------+
|     1 | first test  |    24 |
|     4 | second test |    43 |
|     3 | third test  |    -2 |
+-------+-------------+-------+
3 rows in set (0.00 sec)

mysql>
```

Now that you have verified that the read and writes work, add tests for those operations to the test file and rerun the test. The test should complete without errors. Listing 10-28 shows the updated Ch10s3.test file.

Listing 10-28. Updated Spartan-storage-engine Test File (Ch10s3.test)

```
#
# Simple test for the Spartan storage engine
#
--disable_warnings
drop table if exists t1;
--enable_warnings

CREATE TABLE t1 (
  col_a int,
  col_b varchar(20),
  col_c int
) ENGINE=SPARTAN;

SELECT * FROM t1;
INSERT INTO t1 VALUES(1, ìfirst testî, 24);
INSERT INTO t1 VALUES(4, ìsecond testî, 43);
INSERT INTO t1 VALUES(3, ìthird testî, -2);
SELECT * FROM t1;
RENAME TABLE t1 TO t2;
SELECT * FROM t2;
DROP TABLE t2;
```

That's it for a Stage 3 engine. It is now a basic read/write storage engine that does all of the basic necessities for reading and writing data. In the next stage, we add the ability to update and delete data.

Stage 4: Updating and Deleting Data

The goal of this stage is to produce a working storage engine that can update and delete data. In this stage, I show you how to incorporate the Spartan_data class for updating and deleting data. I walk you through each change and include the completed-method source code for each change.

The Spartan_data class performs updating in place. That is, the old data are overwritten with the new data. Deletion is performed by marking the data as deleted and skipping the deleted records on reads. The read_row() method in the Spartan_data class skips the deleted rows. This may seem as if it will waste a lot of space, and that could be true if the storage engine were used in a situation in which there are lots of deletes and inserts. To mitigate that possibility, you can always dump and then drop the table, and reload the data from the dump. This will remove the empty records. Depending on how you plan to build your own storage engine, this may be something you need to reconsider.

Updating the Spartan Source Files

This stage requires you to update the update_row(), delete_row(), and delete_all_rows() methods. The delete_all_rows() method is a time-saving method used to empty a table all at once rather than a row at a time. The optimizer may call this method for truncation operations and when it detects a mass-delete query.

Updating the Header File

There are no changes necessary to the ha_spartan.h file for a Stage 4 storage engine.

Updating the Source File

Open the ha_spartan.cc file and locate the update_row() method. This method has the old record and the new record buffers passed as parameters. This is great, because we don't have indexes and must do a table scan to locate the record! Fortunately, the Spartan_data class has the update_row() method that will do that work for you. Listing 10-29 shows the updated method with the changes.

Listing 10-29. Changes to the update_row() Method in ha_spartan.cc

```
/* update a record in place */
long long Spartan_data::update_row(uchar *old_rec, uchar *new_rec,
                                   int length, long long position)
{

  DBUG_ENTER("ha_spartan::update_row");
  /*
    Begin critical section by locking the spartan mutex variable.
  */
  mysql_mutex_lock(&share->mutex);
  share->data_class->update_row((uchar *)old_data, new_data,
                 table->s->rec_buff_length, current_position -
                 share->data_class->row_size(table->s->rec_buff_length));
  /*
    End section by unlocking the spartan mutex variable.
  */
  mysql_mutex_unlock(&share->mutex);
  DBUG_RETURN(0);
}
```

The delete_row() method is similar to the update method. In this case, we call the delete_row() method in the Spartan_data class, passing in the buffer for the row to delete, the length of the record buffer, and -1 for the current position to force the table scan. Once again, the data-class method does all the heavy lifting for you. Listing 10-30 shows the updated method with the changes.

Listing 10-30. Changes to the delete_row() Method in ha_spartan.cc

```
int ha_spartan::update_row(const uchar *old_data, uchar *new_data)
{

  DBUG_ENTER("ha_spartan::update_row");
  /*
    Begin critical section by locking the spartan mutex variable.
  */
  mysql_mutex_lock(&share->mutex);
  share->data_class->update_row((uchar *)old_data, new_data,
                table->s->rec_buff_length, current_position -
                share->data_class->row_size(table->s->rec_buff_length));
  /*
    End section by unlocking the spartan mutex variable.
  */
  mysql_mutex_unlock(&share->mutex);
  DBUG_RETURN(0);
}
```

The last method you need to update is delete_all_rows(). This deletes all data in the table. The easiest way to do that is to delete the data file and re-create it. The Spartan_data class does this a little differently. The trunc_table() method resets the file pointer to the start of the file and truncates the file using the my_chsize() method. Listing 10-31 shows the updated method with the changes.

Listing 10-31. Changes to the delete_all_rows() Method in ha_spartan.cc

```
int ha_spartan::delete_all_rows()
{
  DBUG_ENTER("ha_spartan::delete_all_rows");
  /*
    Begin critical section by locking the spartan mutex variable.
  */
  mysql_mutex_lock(&share->mutex);
  share->data_class->trunc_table();
  /*
    End section by unlocking the spartan mutex variable.
  */
  mysql_mutex_unlock(&share->mutex);
  DBUG_RETURN(0);
}
```

Now compile the server and debug any errors. When that is done, you'll have a completed Stage 4 engine. All that is left to do is to compile the server and run the tests.

Testing Stage 4 of the Spartan Engine

First, verify that everything is working in the Stage 3 engine, and then move on to testing the update and delete operations. When you run the test again, you should see all of the statements complete successfully.

The update and delete tests require you to have a table created and to have data in it. You can always add data using the normal INSERT statements as before. Feel free to add your own data and fill up the table with a few more rows.

When you have some data in the table, select one of the records and issue an update command for it using something like:

```
UPDATE t1 SET col_b = "Updated!" WHERE col_a = 1;
```

When you run that command followed by a SELECT * command, you should see the row updated. You can then delete a row by issuing a delete command such as:

```
DELETE FROM t1 WHERE col_a = 3;
```

When you run that command followed by a SELECT * command, you should see that the row has been deleted. An example of what this sequence of commands would produce is:.

```
mysql> DELETE FROM t1 WHERE col_a = 3;
Query OK, 1 row affected (0.01 sec)

mysql> SELECT * FROM t1;
+-------+-------------+-------+
| col_a | col_b       | col_c |
+-------+-------------+-------+
|     4 | second test |    43 |
|     4 | tenth test  |    11 |
|     5 | Updated!    |   100 |
+-------+-------------+-------+
3 rows in set (0.00 sec)

mysql>
```

Have we missed something? Savvy software developers may notice that this test isn't comprehensive and does not cover all possibilities that the Spartan_data class has to consider. For example, deleting a row in the middle of the data isn't the same as deleting one at the beginning or at the end of the file. Updating the data is the same.

That's OK, because you can add that functionality to the test file. You can add more INSERT statements to add some more data, and then update the first and last rows and one in the middle. You can do the same for the delete operation. Listing 10-32 shows the updated Ch10s4.test file.

Listing 10-32. Updated Spartan-storage-engine Test File (Ch10s4.test)

```
#
# Simple test for the Spartan storage engine
#
--disable_warnings
drop table if exists t1;
--enable_warnings

CREATE TABLE t1 (
  col_a int,
  col_b varchar(20),
  col_c int
) ENGINE=SPARTAN;

SELECT * FROM t1;
INSERT INTO t1 VALUES(1, ìfirst testî, 24);
INSERT INTO t1 VALUES(4, ìsecond testî, 43);
```

425

```
INSERT INTO t1 VALUES(3, ìfourth testî, -2);
INSERT INTO t1 VALUES(4, ìtenth testî, 11);
INSERT INTO t1 VALUES(1, ìseventh testî, 20);
INSERT INTO t1 VALUES(5, ìthird testî, 100);
SELECT * FROM t1;
UPDATE t1 SET col_b = ìUpdated!î WHERE col_a = 1;
SELECT * from t1;
UPDATE t1 SET col_b = ìUpdated!î WHERE col_a = 3;
SELECT * from t1;
UPDATE t1 SET col_b = ìUpdated!î WHERE col_a = 5;
SELECT * from t1;
DELETE FROM t1 WHERE col_a = 1;
SELECT * FROM t1;
DELETE FROM t1 WHERE col_a = 3;
SELECT * FROM t1;
DELETE FROM t1 WHERE col_a = 5;
SELECT * FROM t1;
RENAME TABLE t1 TO t2;
SELECT * FROM t2;

DROP TABLE t2;
```

Notice that I've added some rows that have duplicate values. You should expect the server to update and delete all matches for rows with duplicates. Run that test and see what it does. Listing 10-33 shows an example of the expected results for this test. When you run the test under the test suite, it should complete without errors.

Listing 10-33. Sample Results of Stage 4 Test

```
mysql> INSTALL PLUGIN spartan SONAME 'ha_spartan.so';
Query OK, 0 rows affected (0.01 sec)

mysql> use test;
Database changed
mysql>
mysql> CREATE TABLE t1 (
    ->    col_a int,
    ->    col_b varchar(20),
    ->    col_c int
    -> ) ENGINE=SPARTAN;
Query OK, 0 rows affected (0.01 sec)

mysql>
mysql> SELECT * FROM t1;
Empty set (0.00 sec)

mysql> INSERT INTO t1 VALUES(1, "first test", 24);
Query OK, 1 row affected (0.00 sec)

mysql> INSERT INTO t1 VALUES(4, "second test", 43);
Query OK, 1 row affected (0.00 sec)
```

```
mysql> INSERT INTO t1 VALUES(3, "fourth test", -2);
Query OK, 1 row affected (0.00 sec)

mysql> INSERT INTO t1 VALUES(4, "tenth test", 11);
Query OK, 1 row affected (0.00 sec)

mysql> INSERT INTO t1 VALUES(1, "seventh test", 20);
Query OK, 1 row affected (0.00 sec)

mysql> INSERT INTO t1 VALUES(5, "third test", 100);
Query OK, 1 row affected (0.00 sec)

mysql> SELECT * FROM t1;
+-------+--------------+-------+
| col_a | col_b        | col_c |
+-------+--------------+-------+
|     1 | first test   |    24 |
|     4 | second test  |    43 |
|     3 | fourth test  |    -2 |
|     4 | tenth test   |    11 |
|     1 | seventh test |    20 |
|     5 | third test   |   100 |
+-------+--------------+-------+
6 rows in set (0.00 sec)

mysql> UPDATE t1 SET col_b = "Updated!" WHERE col_a = 1;
Query OK, 2 rows affected (0.00 sec)
Rows matched: 2  Changed: 2  Warnings: 0

mysql> SELECT * from t1;
+-------+-------------+-------+
| col_a | col_b       | col_c |
+-------+-------------+-------+
|     1 | Updated!    |    24 |
|     4 | second test |    43 |
|     3 | fourth test |    -2 |
|     4 | tenth test  |    11 |
|     1 | Updated!    |    20 |
|     5 | third test  |   100 |
+-------+-------------+-------+
6 rows in set (0.00 sec)

mysql> UPDATE t1 SET col_b = "Updated!" WHERE col_a = 3;
Query OK, 1 row affected (0.00 sec)
Rows matched: 1  Changed: 1  Warnings: 0
```

427

```
mysql> SELECT * from t1;
+-------+-------------+-------+
| col_a | col_b       | col_c |
+-------+-------------+-------+
|     1 | Updated!    |    24 |
|     4 | second test |    43 |
|     3 | Updated!    |    -2 |
|     4 | tenth test  |    11 |
|     1 | Updated!    |    20 |
|     5 | third test  |   100 |
+-------+-------------+-------+
6 rows in set (0.01 sec)

mysql> UPDATE t1 SET col_b = "Updated!" WHERE col_a = 5;
Query OK, 1 row affected (0.00 sec)
Rows matched: 1  Changed: 1  Warnings: 0

mysql> SELECT * from t1;
+-------+-------------+-------+
| col_a | col_b       | col_c |
+-------+-------------+-------+
|     1 | Updated!    |    24 |
|     4 | second test |    43 |
|     3 | Updated!    |    -2 |
|     4 | tenth test  |    11 |
|     1 | Updated!    |    20 |
|     5 | Updated!    |   100 |
+-------+-------------+-------+
6 rows in set (0.00 sec)

mysql> DELETE FROM t1 WHERE col_a = 1;
Query OK, 2 rows affected (0.00 sec)

mysql> SELECT * FROM t1;
+-------+-------------+-------+
| col_a | col_b       | col_c |
+-------+-------------+-------+
|     4 | second test |    43 |
|     3 | Updated!    |    -2 |
|     4 | tenth test  |    11 |
|     5 | Updated!    |   100 |
+-------+-------------+-------+
4 rows in set (0.00 sec)

mysql> DELETE FROM t1 WHERE col_a = 3;
Query OK, 1 row affected (0.01 sec)
```

```
mysql> SELECT * FROM t1;
+-------+-------------+-------+
| col_a | col_b       | col_c |
+-------+-------------+-------+
|     4 | second test |    43 |
|     4 | tenth test  |    11 |
|     5 | Updated!    |   100 |
+-------+-------------+-------+
3 rows in set (0.00 sec)

mysql> DELETE FROM t1 WHERE col_a = 5;
Query OK, 1 row affected (0.00 sec)

mysql> SELECT * FROM t1;
+-------+-------------+-------+
| col_a | col_b       | col_c |
+-------+-------------+-------+
|     4 | second test |    43 |
|     4 | tenth test  |    11 |
+-------+-------------+-------+
2 rows in set (0.00 sec)

mysql> RENAME TABLE t1 TO t2;
Query OK, 0 rows affected (0.00 sec)

mysql> SELECT * FROM t2;
+-------+-------------+-------+
| col_a | col_b       | col_c |
+-------+-------------+-------+
|     4 | second test |    43 |
|     4 | tenth test  |    11 |
+-------+-------------+-------+
2 rows in set (0.00 sec)

mysql> DROP TABLE t2;
Query OK, 0 rows affected (0.00 sec)

mysql>
```

That's it for a Stage 4 engine. It is now a basic read/write/update/delete storage engine. In the next stage, we'll add the index class to make queries more efficient.

Stage 5: Indexing the Data

The goal of this stage is to produce a working storage engine that includes support for a single index (with a little work, you can make it have multiple indexes). In this stage, I show you how to incorporate the Spartan_index class for indexing the data. Many changes need to be made. I recommend reading through this section before beginning to follow along with the changes.

Begin by adding the Spartan_index class files to the CMakeLists.txt file as shown below.

```
# Spartan storage engine plugin

SET(SPARTAN_PLUGIN_STATIC "spartan")
SET(SPARTAN_PLUGIN_DYNAMIC "spartan")

SET(SPARTAN_SOURCES
   ha_spartan.cc ha_spartan.h
   spartan_data.cc spartan_data.h
   spartan_index.cc spartan_index.h
)

MYSQL_ADD_PLUGIN(spartan ${SPARTAN_SOURCES} STORAGE_ENGINE MODULE_ONLY)

TARGET_LINK_LIBRARIES(spartan mysys)
```

The Spartan_index class works by saving the record pointer to the corresponding row in the Spartan_data class. When the server searches for a record by the primary key, it can use the Spartan_index class to find the record pointer, and then access the record directly by issuing a direct read call via the Spartan_data class. This makes the process of reading a random record much faster than performing a table scan.

The source code in this section is designed to work for the most basic of indexing operations. Depending on how complex your queries become, these changes should suffice for most situations. I walk you through each change and include the completed method source code for each change.

Updating the Spartan Source Files

The Spartan_index class simply saves the current position of the file along with the key. The methods in ha_spartan.cc you'll need to update include index_read(), index_read_idx(), index_next(), index_prev(), index_first(), and index_last(). These methods read values from the index and iterate through the index, as well as go to the front and back (start, end) of the index. Fortunately, the Spartan_index class provides all of these operations.

Updating the Header File

To use the index class, first add a reference to the spartan_index.h file in the ha_spartan.h header file. Listing 10-34 shows the completed code change (I've omitted comments for brevity). Once you have this change made, recompile the spartan source files to make sure there aren't any errors.

Listing 10-34. Changes to Spartan_share class in ha_spartan.h

```
#include "my_global.h"              /* ulonglong */
#include "thr_lock.h"               /* THR_LOCK, THR_LOCK_DATA */
#include "handler.h"                /* handler */
#include "spartan_data.h"
#include "spartan_index.h"

class Spartan_share : public Handler_share {
public:
  mysql_mutex_t mutex;
```

```
  THR_LOCK lock;
  Spartan_data *data_class;
  Spartan_index *index_class;
  Spartan_share();
  ~Spartan_share()
  {
    thr_lock_delete(&lock);
    mysql_mutex_destroy(&mutex);
    if (data_class != NULL)
      delete data_class;
    data_class = NULL;
    if (index_class != NULL)
      delete index_class;
    index_class = NULL;
  }
};
...
```

Open the ha_spartan.h file and add the #include directive to include the spartan_index.h header file as shown above.

Once that is complete, open the ha_spartan.cc file and add the index-class initialization to the constructor.. Listing 10-35 shows the completed code change. Once you have this change made, recompile the spartan source files to make sure there aren't any errors.

Listing 10-35. Changes to Spartan_data constructor in ha_spartan.cc

```
Spartan_share::Spartan_share()
{
  thr_lock_init(&lock);
  mysql_mutex_init(ex_key_mutex_Spartan_share_mutex,
                   &mutex, MY_MUTEX_INIT_FAST);
  data_class = new Spartan_data();
  index_class = new Spartan_index();
}
```

You need to make a few other changes while you have the header file open. You have to add flags to tell the optimizer what index operations are supported. You also have to set the boundaries for the index parameters: the maximum number of keys supported, the maximum length of the keys, and the maximum key parts. For this stage, set the parameters as shown in Listing 10-36. I've included the entire set of changes you need to make to the file. Notice the table_flags() method. This is where you tell the optimizer what limitations the storage engine has. I have set the engine to disallow BLOBs and not permit auto-increment fields. A complete list of these flags can be found in handler.h.

Listing 10-36. Changes to the ha_spartan Class Definition in ha_spartan.h

```
  /*
    The name of the index type that will be used for display
    don't implement this method unless you really have indexes
  */
  const char *index_type(uint inx) { return "Spartan_index"; }
  /*
```

```
  The file extensions.
*/
const char **bas_ext() const;
/*
  This is a list of flags that says what the storage engine
  implements. The current table flags are documented in
  handler.h
*/
ulonglong table_flags() const
{
  return (HA_NO_BLOBS | HA_NO_AUTO_INCREMENT | HA_BINLOG_STMT_CAPABLE);
}
/*
  This is a bitmap of flags that says how the storage engine
  implements indexes. The current index flags are documented in
  handler.h. If you do not implement indexes, just return zero
  here.

  part is the key part to check. First key part is 0
  If all_parts it's set, MySQL want to know the flags for the combined
  index up to and including 'part'.
*/
ulong index_flags(uint inx, uint part, bool all_parts) const
{
  return (HA_READ_NEXT | HA_READ_PREV | HA_READ_RANGE |
          HA_READ_ORDER | HA_KEYREAD_ONLY);
}
/*
  unireg.cc will call the following to make sure that the storage engine can
  handle the data it is about to send.

  Return *real* limits of your storage engine here. MySQL will do
  min(your_limits, MySQL_limits) automatically

  There is no need to implement ..._key_... methods if you don't suport
  indexes.
*/
uint max_supported_keys()         const { return 1; }
uint max_supported_key_parts()    const { return 1; }
uint max_supported_key_length()   const { return 128; }
```

If you were to execute the SHOW INDEXES FROM command on a table created with the Spartan engine, you would see the results of the above code changes, as shown in listing 10-37. Notice the index type reported in the output.

Listing 10-37. Example of SHOW INDEXES FROM output

```
mysql> show indexes from test.t1 \G
*************************** 1. row ***************************
        Table: t1
   Non_unique: 0
     Key_name: PRIMARY
```

```
  Seq_in_index: 1
  Column_name: col_a
    Collation: A
  Cardinality: NULL
     Sub_part: NULL
       Packed: NULL
         Null:
   Index_type: Spartan_index
      Comment:
Index_comment:
1 row in set (0.00 sec)
```

One last thing needs to be added. Identifying the key in a record turns out to be easy but not very intuitive. To make things easier to work with, I've written two helper methods: get_key(), which finds the key field and returns its value or 0 if there are no keys, and get_key_len(), which returns the length of the key. Add their definitions to the class header file (ha_spartan.h):

```
uchar *get_key();
int get_key_len();
```

You will implement these methods in the ha_spartan.cc class file.

Updating the Class File

Now would be a good time to compile and check for errors. When you're done, start the modifications for the index methods.

First, go back through the open, create, close, write, update, delete, and rename methods, and add the calls to the index class to maintain the index. The code to do this involves identifying the field that is the key and then saving the key and its position to the index for retrieval later.

The open method must open both the data and the index files together. The only extra step is to load the index into memory. Locate the open() method in the class file, and add the calls to the index class for opening the index and loading the index into memory. Listing 10-38 shows the method with the changes.

Listing 10-38. Changes to the open() Method in ha_spartan.cc

```
int ha_spartan::open(const char *name, int mode, uint test_if_locked)
{
  DBUG_ENTER("ha_spartan::open");
  char name_buff[FN_REFLEN];

  if (!(share = get_share()))
    DBUG_RETURN(1);
  /*
    Call the data class open table method.
    Note: the fn_format() method correctly creates a file name from the
    name passed into the method.
  */
  share->data_class->open_table(fn_format(name_buff, name, "", SDE_EXT,
                                MY_REPLACE_EXT|MY_UNPACK_FILENAME));
  share->index_class->open_index(fn_format(name_buff, name, "", SDI_EXT,
                                 MY_REPLACE_EXT|MY_UNPACK_FILENAME));
```

```
  share->index_class->load_index();
  thr_lock_data_init(&share->lock,&lock,NULL);
  DBUG_RETURN(0);
}
```

The create method must create both the data and the index files together. Locate the create() method in the class file, and add the calls to the index class for creating the index. Listing 10-39 shows the method with the changes.

Listing 10-39. Changes to the create() Method in ha_spartan.cc

```
int ha_spartan::create(const char *name, TABLE *table_arg,
                       HA_CREATE_INFO *create_info)
{
  DBUG_ENTER("ha_spartan::create");
  char name_buff[FN_REFLEN];
  char name_buff2[FN_REFLEN];

  if (!(share = get_share()))
    DBUG_RETURN(1);
  /*
    Call the data class create table method.
    Note: the fn_format() method correctly creates a file name from the
    name passed into the method.
  */
  if (share->data_class->create_table(fn_format(name_buff, name, "", SDE_EXT,
                                      MY_REPLACE_EXT|MY_UNPACK_FILENAME)))
    DBUG_RETURN(-1);
   share->data_class->close_table();
   if (share->index_class->create_index(fn_format(name_buff2, name, "", SDI_EXT,
                                        MY_REPLACE_EXT|MY_UNPACK_FILENAME),
                                        128))
  {
    DBUG_RETURN(-1);
  }
  share->index_class->close_index();
  DBUG_RETURN(0);
}
```

The close method must close both the data and the index files together. Since the index class uses an in-memory structure to store all changes, it must be written back to disk. Locate the close() method in the class file, and add the calls to the index class for saving, destroying the in-memory structure and closing the index. Listing 10-40 shows the method with the changes.

Listing 10-40. Changes to the close() Method in ha_spartan.cc

```
int ha_spartan::close(void)
{
  DBUG_ENTER("ha_spartan::close");
  share->data_class->close_table();
  share->index_class->save_index();
  share->index_class->destroy_index();
```

```
    share->index_class->close_index();
    DBUG_RETURN(0);
}
```

Now let's make the changes to the writing and reading methods. Since it is possible that no keys will be used, the method must check that there is a key to be added. To make things easier to work with, I've written two helper methods: get_key(), which finds the key field and returns its value or 0 if there are no keys, and get_key_len(), which returns the length of the key. Listing 10-41 shows these two helper methods. Add those methods now to the ha_spartan.cc file.

Listing 10-41. Additional Helper Methods in ha_spartan.cc

```
uchar *ha_spartan::get_key()
{
  uchar *key = 0;

  DBUG_ENTER("ha_spartan::get_key");
  /*
    For each field in the table, check to see if it is the key
    by checking the key_start variable. (1 = is a key).
  */
  for (Field **field=table->field ; *field ; field++)
  {
    if ((*field)->key_start.to_ulonglong() == 1)
    {
      /*
        Copy field value to key value (save key)
      */
      key = (uchar *)my_malloc((*field)->field_length,
                               MYF(MY_ZEROFILL | MY_WME));
      memcpy(key, (*field)->ptr, (*field)->key_length());
    }
  }
  DBUG_RETURN(key);
}

int ha_spartan::get_key_len()
{
  int length = 0;

  DBUG_ENTER("ha_spartan::get_key");
  /*
    For each field in the table, check to see if it is the key
    by checking the key_start variable. (1 = is a key).
  */
  for (Field **field=table->field ; *field ; field++)
  {
    if ((*field)->key_start.to_ulonglong() == 1)
      /*
        Copy field length to key length
      */
```

```
      length = (*field)->key_length();
  }
  DBUG_RETURN(length);
}
```

The write method must both write the record to the data file and insert the key into the index file. Locate the write_row() method in the class file and add the calls to the index class to insert the key if one is found. Listing 10-42 shows the method with the changes.

Listing 10-42. Changes to the write_row() Method in ha_spartan.cc

```
int ha_spartan::write_row(uchar *buf)
{
  DBUG_ENTER("ha_spartan::write_row");
  long long pos;
  SDE_INDEX ndx;

  ha_statistic_increment(&SSV::ha_write_count);
  /*
    Begin critical section by locking the spartan mutex variable.
  */
  mysql_mutex_lock(&share->mutex);
  ndx.length = get_key_len();
  memcpy(ndx.key, get_key(), get_key_len());
  pos = share->data_class->write_row(buf, table->s->rec_buff_length);
  ndx.pos = pos;
  if ((ndx.key != 0) && (ndx.length != 0))
    share->index_class->insert_key(&ndx, false);
  /*
    End section by unlocking the spartan mutex variable.
  */
  mysql_mutex_unlock(&share->mutex);
  DBUG_RETURN(0);
}
```

The update method is also a little different. It must change both the record in the data file and the key in the index. Since the index uses an in-memory structure, the index file must be changed, saved to disk, and reloaded.

■ **Note**   Savvy programmers will note something in the code for the Spartan_index that could be made to prevent the reloading step. Do you know what it is? Here's a hint: what if the index-class update method updated the key and then repositioned it in the memory structure? I'll leave that experiment up to you. Go into the index code and improve it.

Locate the update_row() method in the class file and add the calls to the index class to update the key if one is found. Listing 10-43 shows the method with the changes.

Listing 10-43. Changes to the update_row() Method in ha_spartan.cc

```
int ha_spartan::update_row(const uchar *old_data, uchar *new_data)
{

  DBUG_ENTER("ha_spartan::update_row");
  /*
    Begin critical section by locking the spartan mutex variable.
  */
  mysql_mutex_lock(&share->mutex);
  share->data_class->update_row((uchar *)old_data, new_data,
                  table->s->rec_buff_length, current_position -
                  share->data_class->row_size(table->s->rec_buff_length));
  if (get_key() != 0)
  {
    share->index_class->update_key(get_key(), current_position -
                    share->data_class->row_size(table->s->rec_buff_length),
                    get_key_len());
    share->index_class->save_index();
    share->index_class->load_index();
  }
  /*
    End section by unlocking the spartan mutex variable.
  */
  mysql_mutex_unlock(&share->mutex);
  DBUG_RETURN(0);
}
```

The delete method isn't as complicated. In this case, the method just needs to delete the data row and remove the index from the in-memory structure, if one is found. Locate the delete_row() method in the class file and add the calls to the index class to delete the key, if one is found. Listing 10-44 shows the method with the changes.

Listing 10-44. Changes to the delete_row() Method in ha_spartan.cc

```
int ha_spartan::delete_row(const uchar *buf)
{
  DBUG_ENTER("ha_spartan::delete_row");
  long long pos;

  if (current_position > 0)
    pos = current_position -
      share->data_class->row_size(table->s->rec_buff_length);
  else
    pos = 0;
  /*
    Begin critical section by locking the spartan mutex variable.
  */
  mysql_mutex_lock(&share->mutex);
  share->data_class->delete_row((uchar *)buf,
                                table->s->rec_buff_length, pos);
  if (get_key() != 0)
    share->index_class->delete_key(get_key(), pos, get_key_len());
```

437

```
  /*
    End section by unlocking the spartan mutex variable.
  */
  mysql_mutex_unlock(&share->mutex);
  DBUG_RETURN(0);
}
```

Likewise, the method for deleting all rows is very easy. In this case, we want to delete all data from the data and index file. Locate the delete_all_rows() method in the class file and add the calls to the index class to destroy the index and truncate the index file. Listing 10-45 shows the method with the changes.

Listing 10-45. Changes to the delete_all_rows() Method in ha_spartan.cc

```
int ha_spartan::delete_all_rows()
{
  DBUG_ENTER("ha_spartan::delete_all_rows");
  /*
    Begin critical section by locking the spartan mutex variable.
  */
  mysql_mutex_lock(&share->mutex);
  share->data_class->trunc_table();
  share->index_class->destroy_index();
  share->index_class->trunc_index();
  /*
    End section by unlocking the spartan mutex variable.
  */
  mysql_mutex_unlock(&share->mutex);
  DBUG_RETURN(0);
}
```

The delete_table() method must delete both the data and index files. Locate the delete_table() method and add the code to call the my_delete() function to delete the index. Listing 10-46 shows the method with the changes.

Listing 10-46. Changes to the delete_table() Method in ha_spartan.cc

```
int ha_spartan::delete_table(const char *name)
{
  DBUG_ENTER("ha_spartan::delete_table");
  char name_buff[FN_REFLEN];

  /*
    Call the mysql delete file method.
    Note: the fn_format() method correctly creates a file name from the
    name passed into the method.
  */
  my_delete(fn_format(name_buff, name, "", SDE_EXT,
            MY_REPLACE_EXT|MY_UNPACK_FILENAME), MYF(0));
  /*
    Call the mysql delete file method.
    Note: the fn_format() method correctly creates a file name from the
    name passed into the method.
  */
```

```
my_delete(fn_format(name_buff, name, "", SDI_EXT,
        MY_REPLACE_EXT|MY_UNPACK_FILENAME), MYF(0));

DBUG_RETURN(0);
}
```

The last change to the general read and write file operations is to the rename_table() method. The rename_table() method for the index follows the same pattern as the previous changes. Locate the rename_table() method in the class file and add the code to copy the index file. Listing 10-47 shows the method with the changes.

Listing 10-47. Changes to the rename_table() Method in ha_spartan.cc

```
int ha_spartan::rename_table(const char * from, const char * to)
{
  DBUG_ENTER("ha_spartan::rename_table ");
  char data_from[FN_REFLEN];
  char data_to[FN_REFLEN];
  char index_from[FN_REFLEN];
  char index_to[FN_REFLEN];

  my_copy(fn_format(data_from, from, "", SDE_EXT,
          MY_REPLACE_EXT|MY_UNPACK_FILENAME),
          fn_format(data_to, to, "", SDE_EXT,
          MY_REPLACE_EXT|MY_UNPACK_FILENAME), MYF(0));
  my_copy(fn_format(index_from, from, "", SDI_EXT,
          MY_REPLACE_EXT|MY_UNPACK_FILENAME),
          fn_format(index_to, to, "", SDI_EXT,
          MY_REPLACE_EXT|MY_UNPACK_FILENAME), MYF(0));
  /*
    Delete the file using MySQL's delete file method.
  */
  my_delete(data_from, MYF(0));
  my_delete(index_from, MYF(0));

  DBUG_RETURN(0);
}
```

Wow! That was a lot of changes. As you can see, supporting indexes has made the code much more complicated. I hope you now have a better appreciation for just how well the existing storage engines in MySQL are built. Now, let's move on to making the changes to the indexing methods.

Several methods must be implemented to complete the indexing mechanism for a Stage 5 storage engine. Note as you go through these methods that some return a row from the data file based on the index passed in, whereas others return a key. The documentation isn't clear about this, and the name of the parameter doesn't give us much of a clue, but I show you how they are used. These methods must return either a key not found or an end-of-file return code. Take care to code these return statements correctly, or you could encounter some strange query results.

The first method is the index_read_map() method. This sets the row buffer to the row in the file that matches the key passed in. If the key passed in is null, the method should return the first key value in the file. Locate the index_read_map() method and add the code to get the file position from the index and read the corresponding row from the data file. Listing 10-48 shows the method with the changes.

Listing 10-48. Changes to the index_read_map() Method in ha_spartan.cc

```
int ha_spartan::index_read_map(uchar *buf, const uchar *key,
                               key_part_map keypart_map __attribute__((unused)),
                               enum ha_rkey_function find_flag
                               __attribute__((unused)))
{
  int rc;
  long long pos;
  DBUG_ENTER("ha_spartan::index_read");
  MYSQL_INDEX_READ_ROW_START(table_share->db.str, table_share->table_name.str);
  if (key == NULL)
    pos = share->index_class->get_first_pos();
  else
    pos = share->index_class->get_index_pos((uchar *)key, keypart_map);
  if (pos == -1)
    DBUG_RETURN(HA_ERR_KEY_NOT_FOUND);
  current_position = pos + share->data_class->row_size(table->s->rec_buff_length);
  rc = share->data_class->read_row(buf, table->s->rec_buff_length, pos);
  share->index_class->get_next_key();
  MYSQL_INDEX_READ_ROW_DONE(rc);
  DBUG_RETURN(rc);
}
```

The next index method is index_next(). This method gets the next key in the index and returns the matching row from the data file. It is called during range index scans. Locate the index_next() method and add the code to get the next key from the index and read a row from the data file. Listing 10-49 shows the method with the changes.

Listing 10-49. Changes to the index_next() Method in ha_spartan.cc

```
int ha_spartan::index_next(uchar *buf)
{
  int rc;
  uchar *key = 0;
  long long pos;

  DBUG_ENTER("ha_spartan::index_next");
  MYSQL_INDEX_READ_ROW_START(table_share->db.str, table_share->table_name.str);
  key = share->index_class->get_next_key();
  if (key == 0)
    DBUG_RETURN(HA_ERR_END_OF_FILE);
  pos = share->index_class->get_index_pos((uchar *)key, get_key_len());
  share->index_class->seek_index(key, get_key_len());
  share->index_class->get_next_key();
  if (pos == -1)
    DBUG_RETURN(HA_ERR_KEY_NOT_FOUND);
  rc = share->data_class->read_row(buf, table->s->rec_buff_length, pos);
  MYSQL_INDEX_READ_ROW_DONE(rc);
  DBUG_RETURN(rc);
}
```

The next index method is also a range query. The index_prev() method gets the previous key in the index and returns the matching row from the data file. It is called during range index scans. Locate the index_prev() method and add the code to get the previous key from the index and read a row from the data file. Listing 10-50 shows the method with the changes.

Listing 10-50. Changes to the index_prev() Method in ha_spartan.cc

```
int ha_spartan::index_prev(uchar *buf)
{
  int rc;
  uchar *key = 0;
  long long pos;

  DBUG_ENTER("ha_spartan::index_prev");
  MYSQL_INDEX_READ_ROW_START(table_share->db.str, table_share->table_name.str);
  key = share->index_class->get_prev_key();
  if (key == 0)
    DBUG_RETURN(HA_ERR_END_OF_FILE);
  pos = share->index_class->get_index_pos((uchar *)key, get_key_len());
  share->index_class->seek_index(key, get_key_len());
  share->index_class->get_prev_key();
  if (pos == -1)
    DBUG_RETURN(HA_ERR_KEY_NOT_FOUND);
  rc = share->data_class->read_row(buf, table->s->rec_buff_length, pos);
  MYSQL_INDEX_READ_ROW_DONE(rc);
  DBUG_RETURN(rc);
}
```

Notice that I had to move the index pointers around a bit to get the code for the next and previous to work. Range queries generate two calls to the index class the first time it is used: the first one gets the first key (index_read), and then the second calls the next key (index_next). Subsequent index calls are made to index_next(). Therefore, I must call the Spartan_index class method get_prev_key() to reset the keys correctly. This would be another great opportunity to rework the index class to work better with range queries in MySQL.

The next index method is also a range query. The index_first() method gets the first key in the index and returns it. Locate the index_first() method, and add the code to get the first key from the index and return the key. Listing 10-51 shows the method with the changes.

Listing 10-51. Changes to the index_first() Method in ha_spartan.cc

```
int ha_spartan::index_first(uchar *buf)
{
  int rc;
  uchar *key = 0;

  DBUG_ENTER("ha_spartan::index_first");
  MYSQL_INDEX_READ_ROW_START(table_share->db.str, table_share->table_name.str);
  key = share->index_class->get_first_key();
  if (key == 0)
    DBUG_RETURN(HA_ERR_END_OF_FILE);
  else
    rc = 0;
```

```
  memcpy(buf, key, get_key_len());
  MYSQL_INDEX_READ_ROW_DONE(rc);
  DBUG_RETURN(rc);
}
```

The last index method is one of the range queries as well. The index_last() method gets the last key in the index and returns it. Locate the index_last() method and add the code to get the last key from the index and return the key. Listing 10-52 shows the method with the changes.

Listing 10-52. Changes to the index_last() Method in ha_spartan.cc

```
int ha_spartan::index_last(uchar *buf)
{
  int rc;
  uchar *key = 0;

  DBUG_ENTER("ha_spartan::index_last");
  MYSQL_INDEX_READ_ROW_START(table_share->db.str, table_share->table_name.str);
  key = share->index_class->get_last_key();
  if (key == 0)
    DBUG_RETURN(HA_ERR_END_OF_FILE);
  else
    rc = 0;
  memcpy(buf, key, get_key_len());
  MYSQL_INDEX_READ_ROW_DONE(rc);
  DBUG_RETURN(rc);
}
```

Now compile the server and debug any errors. When that is done, you will have a completed Stage 5 engine. All that is left to do is compile the server and run the tests.

If you decide to debug the Spartan-storage-engine code, you may notice during debugging that some of the index methods may not get called. That is because the index methods are used in a variety of ways in the optimizer. The order of calls depends a lot on the choices that the optimizer makes. If you are curious (like me) and want to see each method fire, you'll need to create a much larger data set and perform more complex queries. You can also check the source code and the reference manual for more details about each of the methods supported in the handler class.

Testing Stage 5 of the Spartan Engine

When you run the test again, you should see all of the statements complete successfully. Verify that everything is working in the Stage 4 engine and then move on to testing the index operations.

The index tests will require you to have a table created and to have data in it. You can always add data using the normal INSERT statements as before. Now you need to test the index. Enter a command that has a WHERE clause on the index column (col_a), such as:

```
SELECT * FROM t1 WHERE col_a = 2;
```

When you run that command, you should see the row returned. That isn't very interesting, is it? You've done all that work, and it just returns the row anyway. The best way to know that the indexes are working is to have large data tables with a diverse range of index values. That would take a while to do, and I encourage you to do so.

There's another way. You can launch the server, attach breakpoints (using your debugger) in the source code, and issue the index-based queries. That may sound like lots of work, and you may not have time to run but a few examples.

That's fine, because you can add that functionality to the test file. You can add the key column to the CREATE and add more SELECT statements with WHERE clauses to perform point and range queries. Listing 10-53 shows the updated Ch10s5.test file.

Listing 10-53. Updated Spartan Storage Engine Test File (Ch10s5.test)

```
#
# Simple test for the Spartan storage engine
#
--disable_warnings
drop table if exists t1;
--enable_warnings

CREATE TABLE t1 (
  col_a int KEY,
  col_b varchar(20),
  col_c int
) ENGINE=SPARTAN;

INSERT INTO t1 VALUES (1, "first test", 24);
INSERT INTO t1 VALUES (2, "second test", 43);
INSERT INTO t1 VALUES (9, "fourth test", -2);
INSERT INTO t1 VALUES (3, 'eighth test', -22);
INSERT INTO t1 VALUES (4, "tenth test", 11);
INSERT INTO t1 VALUES (8, "seventh test", 20);
INSERT INTO t1 VALUES (5, "third test", 100);
SELECT * FROM t1;
UPDATE t1 SET col_b = "Updated!" WHERE col_a = 1;
SELECT * from t1;
UPDATE t1 SET col_b = "Updated!" WHERE col_a = 3;
SELECT * from t1;
UPDATE t1 SET col_b = "Updated!" WHERE col_a = 5;
SELECT * from t1;
DELETE FROM t1 WHERE col_a = 1;
SELECT * FROM t1;
DELETE FROM t1 WHERE col_a = 3;
SELECT * FROM t1;
DELETE FROM t1 WHERE col_a = 5;
SELECT * FROM t1;
SELECT * FROM t1 WHERE col_a = 4;
SELECT * FROM t1 WHERE col_a >= 2 AND col_a <= 5;
SELECT * FROM t1 WHERE col_a = 22;
DELETE FROM t1 WHERE col_a = 5;
SELECT * FROM t1;
SELECT * FROM t1 WHERE col_a = 5;
UPDATE t1 SET col_a = 99 WHERE col_a = 8;
SELECT * FROM t1 WHERE col_a = 8;
SELECT * FROM t1 WHERE col_a = 99;
RENAME TABLE t1 TO t2;
SELECT * FROM t2;
DROP TABLE t2;
```

Notice that I've changed some of the INSERT statements to make the index methods work. Run that test and see what it does. Listing 10-54 shows an example of the expected results for this test. When you run the test under the test suite, it should complete without errors.

Listing 10-54. Sample Results of Stage 5 Test

```
mysql> INSTALL PLUGIN spartan SONAME 'ha_spartan.so';
Query OK, 0 rows affected (0.01 sec)

mysql> use test;
Database changed
mysql> CREATE TABLE t1 (col_a int, col_b varchar(20), col_c int) ENGINE=SPARTAN;
Query OK, 0 rows affected (0.04 sec)

mysql> INSERT INTO t1 VALUES (1, "first test", 24);
Query OK, 1 row affected (0.00 sec)

mysql> INSERT INTO t1 VALUES (2, "second test", 43);
Query OK, 1 row affected (0.00 sec)

mysql> INSERT INTO t1 VALUES (9, "fourth test", -2);
Query OK, 1 row affected (0.00 sec)

mysql> INSERT INTO t1 VALUES (3, 'eighth test', -22);
Query OK, 1 row affected (0.00 sec)

mysql> INSERT INTO t1 VALUES (4, "tenth test", 11);
Query OK, 1 row affected (0.01 sec)

mysql> INSERT INTO t1 VALUES (8, "seventh test", 20);
Query OK, 1 row affected (0.00 sec)

mysql> INSERT INTO t1 VALUES (5, "third test", 100);
Query OK, 1 row affected (0.01 sec)

mysql> SELECT * FROM t1;
+-------+--------------+-------+
| col_a | col_b        | col_c |
+-------+--------------+-------+
|     1 | first test   |    24 |
|     2 | second test  |    43 |
|     9 | fourth test  |    -2 |
|     3 | eighth test  |   -22 |
|     4 | tenth test   |    11 |
|     8 | seventh test |    20 |
|     5 | third test   |   100 |
+-------+--------------+-------+
7 rows in set (0.00 sec)

mysql> UPDATE t1 SET col_b = "Updated!" WHERE col_a = 1;
Query OK, 1 row affected (0.00 sec)
Rows matched: 1  Changed: 1  Warnings: 0
```

```
mysql> SELECT * from t1;
+-------+--------------+-------+
| col_a | col_b        | col_c |
+-------+--------------+-------+
|     1 | Updated!     |    24 |
|     2 | second test  |    43 |
|     9 | fourth test  |    -2 |
|     3 | eighth test  |   -22 |
|     4 | tenth test   |    11 |
|     8 | seventh test |    20 |
|     5 | third test   |   100 |
+-------+--------------+-------+
7 rows in set (0.00 sec)

mysql> UPDATE t1 SET col_b = "Updated!" WHERE col_a = 3;
Query OK, 1 row affected (0.00 sec)
Rows matched: 1  Changed: 1  Warnings: 0

mysql> SELECT * from t1;
+-------+--------------+-------+
| col_a | col_b        | col_c |
+-------+--------------+-------+
|     1 | Updated!     |    24 |
|     2 | second test  |    43 |
|     9 | fourth test  |    -2 |
|     3 | Updated!     |   -22 |
|     4 | tenth test   |    11 |
|     8 | seventh test |    20 |
|     5 | third test   |   100 |
+-------+--------------+-------+
7 rows in set (0.01 sec)

mysql> UPDATE t1 SET col_b = "Updated!" WHERE col_a = 5;
Query OK, 1 row affected (0.01 sec)
Rows matched: 1  Changed: 1  Warnings: 0

mysql> SELECT * from t1;
+-------+--------------+-------+
| col_a | col_b        | col_c |
+-------+--------------+-------+
|     1 | Updated!     |    24 |
|     2 | second test  |    43 |
|     9 | fourth test  |    -2 |
|     3 | Updated!     |   -22 |
|     4 | tenth test   |    11 |
|     8 | seventh test |    20 |
|     5 | Updated!     |   100 |
+-------+--------------+-------+
7 rows in set (0.00 sec)
```

```
mysql> DELETE FROM t1 WHERE col_a = 1;
Query OK, 1 row affected (0.01 sec)

mysql> SELECT * FROM t1;
+-------+--------------+-------+
| col_a | col_b        | col_c |
+-------+--------------+-------+
|     2 | second test  |    43 |
|     9 | fourth test  |    -2 |
|     3 | Updated!     |   -22 |
|     4 | tenth test   |    11 |
|     8 | seventh test |    20 |
|     5 | Updated!     |   100 |
+-------+--------------+-------+
6 rows in set (0.00 sec)

mysql> DELETE FROM t1 WHERE col_a = 3;
Query OK, 1 row affected (0.00 sec)

mysql> SELECT * FROM t1;
+-------+--------------+-------+
| col_a | col_b        | col_c |
+-------+--------------+-------+
|     2 | second test  |    43 |
|     9 | fourth test  |    -2 |
|     4 | tenth test   |    11 |
|     8 | seventh test |    20 |
|     5 | Updated!     |   100 |
+-------+--------------+-------+
5 rows in set (0.01 sec)

mysql> DELETE FROM t1 WHERE col_a = 5;
Query OK, 1 row affected (0.00 sec)

mysql> SELECT * FROM t1;
+-------+--------------+-------+
| col_a | col_b        | col_c |
+-------+--------------+-------+
|     2 | second test  |    43 |
|     9 | fourth test  |    -2 |
|     4 | tenth test   |    11 |
|     8 | seventh test |    20 |
+-------+--------------+-------+
4 rows in set (0.00 sec)

mysql> SELECT * FROM t1 WHERE col_a = 4;
+-------+------------+-------+
| col_a | col_b      | col_c |
+-------+------------+-------+
|     4 | tenth test |    11 |
+-------+------------+-------+
1 row in set (0.01 sec)
```

```
mysql> SELECT * FROM t1 WHERE col_a >= 2 AND col_a <= 5;
+-------+-------------+-------+
| col_a | col_b       | col_c |
+-------+-------------+-------+
|     2 | second test |    43 |
|     4 | tenth test  |    11 |
+-------+-------------+-------+
2 rows in set (0.00 sec)

mysql> SELECT * FROM t1 WHERE col_a = 22;
Empty set (0.01 sec)

mysql> DELETE FROM t1 WHERE col_a = 5;
Query OK, 0 rows affected (0.00 sec)

mysql> SELECT * FROM t1;
+-------+--------------+-------+
| col_a | col_b        | col_c |
+-------+--------------+-------+
|     2 | second test  |    43 |
|     9 | fourth test  |    -2 |
|     4 | tenth test   |    11 |
|     8 | seventh test |    20 |
+-------+--------------+-------+
4 rows in set (0.00 sec)

mysql> SELECT * FROM t1 WHERE col_a = 5;
Empty set (0.00 sec)

mysql> UPDATE t1 SET col_a = 99 WHERE col_a = 8;
Query OK, 1 row affected (0.00 sec)
Rows matched: 1  Changed: 1  Warnings: 0

mysql> SELECT * FROM t1 WHERE col_a = 8;
Empty set (0.01 sec)

mysql> SELECT * FROM t1 WHERE col_a = 99;
+-------+--------------+-------+
| col_a | col_b        | col_c |
+-------+--------------+-------+
|    99 | seventh test |    20 |
+-------+--------------+-------+
1 row in set (0.00 sec)

mysql> RENAME TABLE t1 TO t2;
Query OK, 0 rows affected (0.01 sec)
```

```
mysql> SELECT * FROM t2;
+-------+--------------+-------+
| col_a | col_b        | col_c |
+-------+--------------+-------+
|     2 | second test  |    43 |
|     9 | fourth test  |    -2 |
|     4 | tenth test   |    11 |
|    99 | seventh test |    20 |
+-------+--------------+-------+
4 rows in set (0.01 sec)

mysql> DROP TABLE t2;
Query OK, 0 rows affected (0.00 sec)

mysql>
```

That's it for a Stage 5 engine. It is now a basic read/write/update/delete storage engine with indexing, which is the stage at which most of the storage engines in MySQL are implemented. Indeed, for all but transactional environments, this should be sufficient for your storage needs. In the next stage, I discuss the much more complex topic of adding transaction support.

Stage 6: Adding Transaction Support

Currently, the only storage engine in MySQL that supports transactions is InnoDB.[7] Transactions provide a mechanism that permits a set of operations to execute as a single atomic operation. For example, if a database was built for a banking institution, the macro operations of transferring money from one account to another (money removed from one account and placed in another) would preferably be executed completely without interruption. Transactions permit these operations to be encased in an atomic operation that will back out any changes should an error occur before all operations are complete, thus avoiding data being removed from one table and never making it to the next table. A sample set of operations in the form of SQL statements encased in transactional commands is shown in Listing 10-55.

Listing 10-55. Sample Transaction SQL Commands

```
START TRANSACTION;
UPDATE SavingsAccount SET Balance = Balance−100
WHERE AccountNum = 123;
UPDATE CheckingAccount SET Balance = Balance + 100
WHERE AccountNum = 345;
COMMIT;
```

In practice, most database professionals specify the MyISAM table type if they require faster access and InnoDB if they need transaction support. Fortunately, Oracle has provided the storage-engine plugin with the capability to support transactions.

The facilities for performing transactions in storage engines is supported by the start_stmt() and external_lock() methods. The start_stmt() method is called when a transaction is started. The external_lock() method is used to signal a specific lock for a table and is called when an explicit lock is issued. Your storage engine must

---

[7]The cluster storage engine (NDB) also supports transactions.

implement the new transaction in the start_stmt() method by creating a savepoint and registering the transaction with the server using the trans_register_ha() method. This method takes as parameters the current thread, whether you want to set the transaction across all threads, and the address of your handlerton. Calling this causes the transaction to start. An example implementation of the start_stmt() method is shown in Listing 10-56.

Listing 10-56. Example start_stmt() Method Implementation

```
int my_handler::start_stmt(THD *thd, thr_lock_type lock_type)
{
  DBUG_ENTER("my_handler::index_last");
  int error= 0;
  /*
    Save the transaction data
  */
  my_txn *txn= (my_txn *) thd->ha_data[my_handler_hton.slot];
  /*
    If this is a new transaction, create it and save it to the
    handler's slot in the ha_data array.
  */
  if (txn == NULL)
    thd->ha_data[my_handler_hton.slot]= txn= new my_txn;
  /*
    Start the transaction and create a savepoint then register
    the transaction.
  */
  if (txn->stmt == NULL && !(error= txn->tx_begin()))
  {
    txn->stmt= txn->new_savepoint();
    trans_register_ha(thd, FALSE, &my_handler_hton);
  }
  DBUG_RETURN(error);
}
```

Starting a transaction from external_lock() is a bit more complicated. MySQL calls the external_lock() method for every table in use at the start of a transaction. Thus, you have some more work to do to detect the transaction and process it accordingly. This can be seen in the check of the trx->active_trans flag. The start transaction operation is also implied when the external_lock() method is called for the first table. Listing 10-57 shows an example implementation of the external_lock() method (some sections are omitted for brevity). See the ha_innodb.cc file for the complete code.

Listing 10-57. Example external_lock() Method Implementation (from InnoDB)

```
int ha_innobase::external_lock(THD*  thd, int Lock_type)
{
  row_prebuilt_t* prebuilt = (row_prebuilt_t*) innobase_prebuilt;
  trx_t*    trx;

  DBUG_ENTER("ha_innobase::external_lock");
  DBUG_PRINT("enter",("lock_type: %d", lock_type));

  update_thd(thd);
```

```
  trx = prebuilt->trx;

  prebuilt->sql_stat_start = TRUE;
  prebuilt->hint_need_to_fetch_extra_cols = 0;

  prebuilt->read_just_key = 0;
  prebuilt->keep_other_fields_on_keyread = FALSE;

  if (lock_type == F_WRLCK) {

    /* If this is a SELECT, then it is in UPDATE TABLE ...
    or SELECT ... FOR UPDATE */
    prebuilt->select_lock_type = LOCK_X;
    prebuilt->stored_select_lock_type = LOCK_X;
  }

  if (lock_type != F_UNLCK)
      {
    /* MySQL is setting a new table lock */

    trx->detailed_error[0] = '\0';

    /* Set the MySQL flag to mark that there is an active
    transaction */
    if (trx->active_trans == 0) {

      innobase_register_trx_and_stmt(thd);
      trx->active_trans = 1;
    } else if (trx->n_mysql_tables_in_use == 0) {
      innobase_register_stmt(thd);
    }

    trx->n_mysql_tables_in_use++;
    prebuilt->mysql_has_locked = TRUE;

...
    DBUG_RETURN(0);
  }

  /* MySQL is releasing a table lock */

  trx->n_mysql_tables_in_use--;
  prebuilt->mysql_has_locked = FALSE;

  /* If the MySQL lock count drops to zero we know that the current SQL
  statement has ended */

  if (trx->n_mysql_tables_in_use == 0) {

...
  DBUG_RETURN(0);
}
```

Now that you've seen how to start transactions, let's see how they are stopped (also known as committed or rolled back). Committing a transaction just means writing the pending changes to disk, storing the appropriate keys, and cleaning up the transaction. Oracle provides a method in the handlerton (`int (*commit)(THD *thd, bool all)`) that can be implemented using the function description shown here. The parameters are the current thread and whether you want the entire set of commands committed.

```
int (*commit)(THD *thd, bool all);
```

Rolling back the transaction is more complicated. In this case, you have to undo everything that was done since the last start of the transaction. Oracle supports rollback using a callback in the handlerton (`int (*rollback)(THD *thd, bool all)`) that can be implemented using the function description shown here. The parameters are the current thread and whether the entire transaction should be rolled back.

```
int (*rollback)(THD *thd, bool all);
```

To implement transactions, the storage engine must provide some sort of buffer mechanism to hold the unsaved changes to the database. Some storage engines use heap-like structures; others use queues and similar internal-memory structures. If you are going to implement transactions in your storage engine, you'll need to create an internal-caching (sometimes called versioning) mechanism. When a commit is issued, the data must be taken out of the buffer and written to disk. When a rollback occurs, the operations must be canceled and their changes reversed.

Savepoints are another transaction mechanism available to you for managing data during transactions. Savepoints are areas in memory that allow you to save information. You can use them to save information during a transaction. For example, you may want to save information about an internal buffer that you implement to store the "dirty" or "uncommitted" changes. The savepoint concept was created for just such a use.

Oracle provides several savepoint operations that you can define in your handlerton. These appear in lines 13 through 15 in the handlerton structure shown in Listing 10-1. The method descriptions for the savepoint methods are:

```
uint savepoint_offset;
int (*savepoint_set)(THD *thd, void *sv);
int (*savepoint_rollback)(THD *thd, void *sv);
int (*savepoint_release)(THD *thd, void *sv);
```

The `savepoint_offset` value is the size of the memory area you want to save. The `savepoint_set()` method allows you to set a value to the parameter `sv` and save it as a savepoint. The `savepoint_rollback()` method is called when a rollback operation is triggered. In this case, the server returns the information saved in `sv` to the method. Similarly, `savepoint_release()` is called when the server responds to a release savepoint event and also returns the data via the `sv` that was set as a savepoint. For more information about savepoints, see the MySQL source code and online reference manual.

■ **Tip** For excellent examples of how the transaction facilities work, see the `ha_innodb.cc` source files. You can also find information in the online reference manual.

Simply adding transaction support using the MySQL mechanisms is not the end of the story. Storage engines that use indexes[8] must provide mechanisms to permit transactions. These operations must be capable of marking nodes that have been changed by operations in a transaction, saving the original values of the data that have changed until such time that the transaction is complete. At this point, all the changes are committed to the physical store (for both the index and the data). This will require making changes to the `Spartan_index` class.

Clearly, implementing transactions in a storage-engine plugin requires a lot of careful thought and planning. I strongly suggest that if you are going to implement transactional support in your storage engine, you study the BDB and InnoDB storage engines as well as the online reference manual. You may even want to set up your debugger and watch the transactions execute. Whichever way you go with your implementation of transactions, rest assured that if you get it working, you will have something special. There are few excellent storage engines that support transactions and none (so far) that exceed the capabilities of the native MySQL storage engines.

Summary

In this chapter, I've taken you on a tour of the storage-engine plugin source code and showed you how to create your own storage engine. Through the Spartan storage engine, you learned how to construct a storage engine that can read and write data and that supports concurrent access and indexing. Although I explain all of the stages of building this storage engine, I leave adding transactional support for you to experiment with.

I have also not implemented all possible functions of a storage handler. Rather, I implemented just the basics. Now that you've seen the basics in action and had a chance to experiment, I recommend studying the online documentation and the source code while you design your own storage engine.

If you found this chapter a challenge, it's OK. Creating a database physical-storage mechanism is not a trivial task. I hope you come away from this chapter with a better understanding of what it takes to build a storage engine and a proper respect for those MySQL storage engines that implement indexing and transaction support. Neither of these tasks are trivial endeavors.

Finally, I have seen several areas of possible improvement for the data and index classes I have provided. While the data class seems fine for most applications, the index class could be improved. If you plan to use these classes as a jumping-off point for your own storage engine, I suggest getting your storage engine working with the classes as they are now and then going back and either updating or replacing them.

I recommend updating several areas in particular in the index class. Perhaps the most important change I recommend is changing the internal buffer to a more efficient tree structure. There are many to choose from, such as the ubiquitous B-tree or hash mechanism. I also suggest that you change the way the class handles range queries. Last, changes need to be made to handle transaction support. The class needs to support whatever buffer mechanism you use to handle commits and rollbacks.

In the next chapter, I discuss some advanced topics in database-server design and implementation. The chapter will prepare you for using the MySQL server source code as an experimental platform for studying database-system internals.

---

[8]For the record, it is possible to have a Stage 6 engine that does not support indexes. Indexes are not required for transaction processing. Uniqueness should be a concern, however, and performance will suffer.

PART 3

■ ■ ■

Advanced Database Internals

Getting Started with MySQL DevelopmentPart 3 delves deeper into the MySQL system and gives you an insider's look at what makes the system work. Chapter 11 revisits the topic of query execution in the MySQL architecture and introduces how you can conduct experiments with the source code. Chapter 12 presents the MySQL internal query representation and provides an example alternative query representation. Chapter 13 introduces the MySQL internal query optimizer; it describes an example of an alternative query optimizer that uses the internal representation implementation from the previous chapter. The chapter also shows you how to alter the MySQL source code to implement the alternative query optimizer. Chapter 14 combines the techniques from the previous chapters to implement an alternative query-processing engine.

■ ■ ■

## CHAPTER 11

Database System Internals

This chapter presents some database-system internals concepts in preparation for studying database-system internals at a deeper level. I present more in-depth coverage of how queries are represented internally within the server and how queries are executed. I explore these topics from a more general viewpoint and then close the chapter with a discussion of how you can use the MySQL system to conduct your own experiments with the MySQL system internals. Last, I'll introduce the database system's internals experiment project.

Query Execution

Most database systems use either an iterative or an interpretative execution strategy. *Iterative* methods provide ways to produce a sequence of calls available for processing discrete operations (e.g., join, project, etc.), but are not designed to incorporate the features of the internal representation. Translation of queries into iterative methods uses techniques of functional programming and program transformation. Several algorithms generate iterative programs from relational algebra–based query specifications.

The implementation of the query-execution mechanism creates a set of defined compiled functional primitives, formed using a high-level language, that are then linked together via a call stack or procedural call sequence. When a query-execution plan is created and selected for execution, a compiler (usually the same one used to create the database system) is used to compile the procedural calls into a binary executable. Because of the high cost of the iterative method, compiled execution plans are typically stored for reuse for similar or identical queries.

Interpretative methods, on the other hand, perform query execution using existing compiled abstractions of basic operations. The query-execution plan chosen is reconstructed as a queue of method calls that are each taken off the queue and processed; the results are then placed in memory for use with the next or subsequent calls. Implementation of this strategy is often called *lazy evaluation,* because the available compiled methods are not optimized for best performance; rather, they are optimized for generality.

MySQL Query Execution Revisited

Query processing and execution in MySQL is interpretive. It is implemented using a threaded architecture whereby each query is given its own thread of execution. Figure 11-1 depicts a block diagram that describes the MySQL query processing methodology.

SELECT * FROM MyTable;

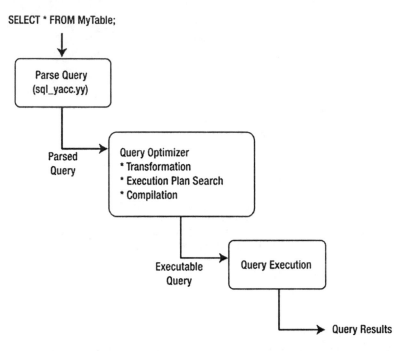

Figure 11-1. MySQL query execution

When a client issues a query, a new thread is created, and the SQL statement is forwarded to the parser for syntactic validation (or rejection due to errors). As you saw in the previous chapter, the MySQL parser is implemented using a large Lex-YACC script that is compiled with Bison. The parser constructs a data structure used to hold the query. This data structure, or query structure, can be used to execute the query. Once the query structure is created, control passes to the query processor, which performs checks such as verifying table integrity and security access. Once the required access is granted and the tables are opened (and locked if the query is an update), control is passed to individual methods that execute the basic query operations, such as select, restrict, and project. Optimization is applied to the data structure by ordering the lists of tables and operations to form a more efficient query based on common practices. This form of optimization is called a SELECT-PROJECT-JOIN query processor. The results of the query operations are returned to the client using established communication protocols and access methods.

What Is a Compiled Query?

One often confusing area understanding what "compiled" means. A compiled query is an actual compilation of an iterative query-execution plan, but some researchers (such as C. J. Date) consider a compiled query one that has been optimized and stored for future execution. As a result, you must take care when considering using a compiled query. In this work, the use of the word *compiled* is avoided, because the query optimizer and execution engine do not store the query execution plan for later reuse, nor does the query execution require any compilation or assembly to work.

▪ **Note** The concept of a stored procedure is a saved plan—it is compiled, or optimized, for execution at a later date and can be run many times on data that meet its input parameters.

Exploring MySQL Internals

How can you teach someone how an optimizer works without allowing him to get his hands dirty with a project? Furthermore, how can you be expected to know the internals of a database system without actually seeing them? I answer these questions in this section by discussing how MySQL can be used as an experimental test bed for professionals and academics alike.

Getting Started Using MySQL for Experiments

There are several ways to use MySQL to conduct experiments. For example, you could study the internal components using an interactive debugger, or you could use the MySQL system as a host for your own implementation of internal-database technologies. Another useful way to look at how the server behaves internally would be to turn on tracing and read the traces generated by using a server compiled with debug turned on. See Chapter 5 for more details on debug tracing.

If you are going to conduct experiments, use a dedicated server for the experiments. This is important if you plan to use MySQL to develop your own extensions. You don't want to risk contamination of your development server by the experiments.

Experimenting with the MySQL Source Code

The most invasive method of experimenting with MySQL is through modifications to the source code. This involves observing the system as it runs and then designing experiments to change portions by replacing an algorithm or section of code with another, and then observing the changes in behavior. Although this approach will enable you to investigate the internal workings of MySQL, making changes to the source code in this manner may result in the server becoming too unstable for use—especially if you push the envelope of the algorithms and data structures or ,worse, violate memory references. There is no better way to learn the source code than to observe it in action, however. Tests conducted in this manner can then be used to gather data for other forms of experimentation.

Using MySQL As a Host for Experimental Technologies

A less-invasive method of conducting experiments with MySQL is by using MySQL as a host for your own experimental code. This allows you to focus on the optimizer and the execution engine without worrying about the other parts of the system. There are a great many parts to a database system. To name only a few, there are subcomponents in MySQL for network communication, data input, and access control, and even utilities for using and managing files and memory. Rather than create your own subcomponents, you can use MySQL's resources in your own code.

I've implemented the experiment project described in this book using this method. I'll show you how to connect to the MySQL parser and use the MySQL parser to read, test, and accept valid commands and redirect the code to the experimental project optimizer and execution routines.

The parser and lexical analyzer identify strings of alphanumeric characters (also known as tokens) that have been defined in the parser or lexical hash. The parser tags all of the tokens with location information (the order of appearance in the stream), and identifies literals and numbers using logic that recognizes specific patterns of the nontoken strings. Once the parser is done, control returns to the lexical analyzer. The lexical analyzer in MySQL is designed to recognize specific patterns of the tokens and nontokens. Once valid commands are identified, control is then passed to the execution code for each command. The MySQL parser and lexical analyzer can be modified to include the new tokens, or keywords, for the experiment. See Chapter 7 for more details on how to modify the parser and lexical analyzer. The commands can be designed to mimic those of SQL, representing the typical data-manipulation commands, such as select, update, insert, and delete, as well as the typical data-definition commands, such as create and drop.

Once control is passed to the experimental optimization/execution engine, the experiments can be run using the MySQL internal-query-representation structures or converted to another structure. From there, experimental implementation for query optimization and execution can be run, and the results returned to the client by using the MySQL system. This allows you to use the network communication and parsing subcomponents while implementing your own internal database components.

Running Multiple Instances of MySQL

One lesser-known fact about the MySQL server is that it is possible to run multiple instances of the server on a single machine. This allows you to run your modified MySQL system on the same machine as your development installation. You may want to do this if your resources are limited or if you want to run your modified server on the same machine as another installation for comparison purposes. Running multiple instances of MySQL requires specifying certain parameters on the command line or in the configuration file.

VIRTUAL MACHINES TO THE RESCUE

You can also leverage a virtual machine to further isolate your experiments. To make the most of this option, you can configure a virtual machine with a basic MySQL server installation and then clone the machine. This permits you to run an instance of MySQL as if it were on a separate machine. Some virtual-machine environments also allow you to take snapshots of the machine while it is running, which permits you to restart the session at the moment of the snapshot. This can save you a lot of time in setting up your test environment. I often choose this method when faced with a complicated or lengthy test-environment setup.

There are many virtual environments from which to choose. The open-source Oracle VirtualBox is a great choice for academics and those looking to save money. VirtualBox runs on most platforms and offers all the features you need to set up a host of virtual MySQL servers. VMWare's software is expensive, but it offers more features. If you run Mac OS X, VMWare's Fusion and Parallel Desktop are both excellent low-cost alternatives.

At a minimum, you need to specify either a different TCP port or socket for the server to communicate on and specify different directories for the database files. An example of starting a second instance of MySQL on Windows is:

```
mysqld-debug.exe --port=3307 --datadir="c:/mysql/test_data" --console
```

In this example, I'm telling the server to use TCP port 3307 (the default is 3306) and to use a different data directory and run as a console application. To connect to the second instance of the server, I must tell the client to use the same port as the server. For example, to connect to my second instance, I'd launch the MySQL client utility with:

```
mysql.exe -uroot --port=3307
```

The --port parameter can also be used with the mysqladmin utility. For example, to shut down the second instance running on port 3307, issue the command:

```
mysqladmin.exe -uroot --port=3307 shutdown
```

There is a potential for problems with this technique. It is easy to forget which server you're connected to. One way to prevent confusion or to avoid issuing a query (such as a DELETE or DROP) to the wrong server is to change the prompt on your MySQL client utilities to indicate the server to which you are connected.

For example, issue the command prompt DBXP-> to set your prompt for the MySQL client connected to the experimental server and prompt Development-> for the MySQL client connected to the development server.

This technique allows you to see at a glance to which server you are about to issue a command. Examples of using the prompt command in the MySQL client are shown in Listing 11-1.

Listing 11-1. Example of Changing the MySQL Client Prompt for the Experimental Server

```
mysql> prompt DBXP->
PROMPT set to 'DBXP->'
DBXP->show databases;
+--------------------+
| Database           |
+--------------------+
| information_schema |
| mysql              |
| test               |
+--------------------+
3 rows in set (0.01 sec)

DBXP->
```

■ **Tip**   You can also set the current database in the prompt by using the \d option. For example, to set the prompt in the client connected to the experimental server, issue the command prompt DBXP:\d->. This sets the prompt to indicate that you are connected to the experimental server and the current database (specified by the last use command) separated by a colon (e.g., DBXP:TEST->).

You can use this technique to restrict access to your modified server. If you change the port number or socket, only those who know the correct parameters can connect to the server. This will enable you to minimize the risk of exposure of the modifications to the user population. If your development environment is diverse, with a lot of experimentation and research projects that share the same resources (which is often the case in academia), you may also want to take these steps to protect your own experiments from contamination of and by other projects. This isn't normally a problem, but it helps to take the precaution.

■ **Caution**   If you use binary, query, or slow-query logs, you must also specify an alternative location for the log files for each instance of the MySQL server. Failure to do so may result in corruption of your log files and/or data.

Limitations and Concerns

Perhaps the most challenging aspect of using MySQL for experimentation is modifying the parser to recognize the new keyword for the SQL commands (see Chapter 7). Although not precisely a complex or new implementation language, modification of the YACC files requires careful attention to the original developers' intent. The solution involves placing copies of the SQL syntax definitions for the new commands at the top of each of the parser-command definitions. This permits you to intercept the flow of the parser in order to redirect the query execution.

The most frequent and least trivial challenge of all is keeping up with the constant changes to the MySQL code base. Unfortunately, the frequency of upgrades is unpredictable. If you want to keep up to date with feature changes, the integration of the experimental technologies requires reinserting the modifications to the MySQL source files with each release of the source code. This is probably not a concern for anyone wanting to experiment with MySQL. If you find yourself wanting to keep up with the changes because of extensions you are writing, you should probably use a source-code-management tool or build a second server for experimentation and do your development on the original server.

■ **Tip** The challenge that you are most likely to encounter is examining the MySQL code base and discovering the meaning, layout, and use of the various internal data representations. The only way to overcome this is through familiarity. I encourage you to visit and read the documentation (the online MySQL reference manual) and articles on the MySQL Web site, blogs, and message forums. They are a wealth of information. While some are difficult to absorb, the concepts presented become clearer with each reading. Resist the temptation to become frustrated with the documentation. Give it a rest, then go back later and read it again. I find nuggets of useful information every time I (re)read the technical material.

The Database System Internals Experiment

I built the database experiment project (DBXP) to allow you to explore the MySQL internals and to let you explore some alternative-database-system internal implementations. You can use this experiment to learn more about how database systems are constructed and how they work under the hood.

Why an Experiment?

The DBXP is an experiment rather than a solution because it is incomplete. That is, the technologies are implemented with minimal error handling, a limited feature set, and low robustness.

This doesn't mean the DBXP technologies can't be modified for use as replacements for the MySQL system internals; rather, the DBXP is designed for exploration rather than production.

Overview of the Experiment Project

The DBXP project is a series of classes that implement alternative algorithms and mechanisms for internal-query representation, query optimization, query execution, and file access. This not only gives you an opportunity to explore an advanced implementation of query-optimization theory, but it also enables the core of the DBXP technology to execute without modification of the MySQL internal operation. This provides the additional security that the native MySQL core executable code will not be affected by the addition of the DBXP technologies. This added benefit can help mitigate some of the risks of modifying an existing system.

Implementation of the MySQL parser (see sql_parse.cc) directs control to specific instances of the execution subprocesses by making calls to functions implemented for each SQL command. For example, the SHOW command is redirected to functions implemented in the sql_show.cc file. The MySQL parser code in sql_parse.cc needs to be modified to redirect processing to the DBXP query processor.

The first step in the DBXP query processor is to convert the MySQL internal-query representation to the experimental internal representation. The internal representation chosen is called a *query tree*, in which each node contains an atomic relational operation (select, project, join, etc.) and the links represent data flow. Figure 11-2 shows a conceptual example of a query tree. In the example, I use the notation: project/select (Π), restrict (Σ), and join (Φ). The arrows represent how data would flow from the tables up to the root. A join operation is represented as a node with two children. As data are presented from each child, the join operation is able to process that data and pass the results to the next node up in the tree (its parent). Each node can have zero, one, or two children and has exactly one parent.

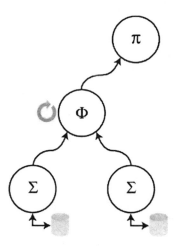

Figure 11-2. *Query tree concept*

The query tree was chosen because it permits the DBXP query optimizer to use tree-manipulation algorithms. That is, optimization uses the tree structure and tree-manipulation algorithms to arrange nodes in the tree in a more efficient execution order. Furthermore, execution of the optimized query is accomplished by traversing the tree to the leaf nodes, performing the operation as specified by the node, and passing information back up the links. This technique also made possible execution in a pipeline fashion, with data passed from the leaf nodes to the root node one data item at a time.

Traversing the tree down to a leaf for one data item and returning it back up the tree (a process known as *pulsing*) permits each node to process one data item, returning one row at a time in the result set. This pulsing, or polling, of the tree permits the execution of the pipeline. The result is a faster initial return of query results and a perceived faster transmission time of the query results to the client. Witnessing the query results returning more quickly—although not all at once—gives the user the perception of faster queries.

Using MySQL to host the DBXP implementation begins at the MySQL parser, where the DBXP code takes over the optimization and execution of the query and then returns the results to the client one row at a time using the MySQL network-communications utilities.

Components of the Experiment Project

The experiment project is designed to introduce you to alternatives to how database-systems internals could be implemented and to allow you to explore the implementations by adding your own modifications to the project. DBXP is implemented using a set of simple C++ classes that represent objects in a database system.

There are classes for tuples, relations, indexes, and the query tree. Additional classes have been added to manage multiuser access to the tables. An example high-level architecture of the DBXP is shown in Figure 11-3.

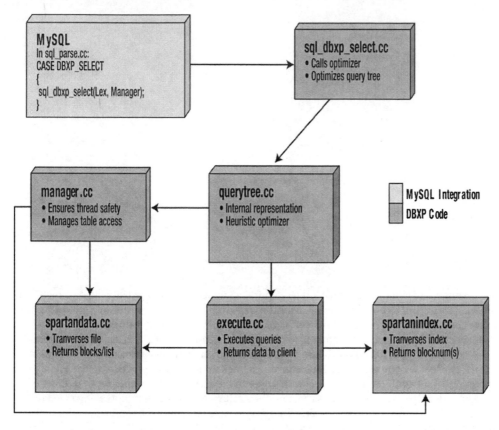

Figure 11-3. *High-level diagram of the experiment project*

A complete list of the major classes in the project is shown in Table 11-1. The classes are stored in source files by the same name as the class (e.g., the `Attribute` class is defined and implemented in the files named `attribute.h` and `attribute.cc`, respectively).

Table 11-1. *Database Internals Experiment Project Classes*

Class	Description
Query_tree	Provides internal representation of the query. Also contains thequery optimizer.
Expression	Provides an expression evaluation mechanism.
Attribute	Operations for storing and manipulating an attribute (column) for a tuple (row).

These classes represent the basic building blocks of a database system. Chapters 12 through 14 contain a complete explanation of the query tree, heuristic optimizer, and pipeline execution algorithms. The chapters also include overviews of the utility. I'll show you the implementation details of some parts (the most complex) of the DBXP implementation and leave the rest for you to implement as exercises.

■ **Note**   Suggestions on how to use the experiment project in a classroom setting are presented in the introduction section of this book.

Conducting the Experiments

Running the experiments requires modifying the cmake files for the new project and compiling them with the MySQL server. None of the project files requires any special compilation or libraries. Details of the modifications to the MySQL configuration and cmake files are discussed in the next chapter, in which I show you how to stub out the SQL commands for the experiment.

If you haven't tried the example programs from the previous chapters I've included the basic process for building and running the DBXP experiment projects below.

1. Modify the `CMakeLists.txt` file in the /sql folder.

2. Run 'cmake.' from the root of the source tree.

3. Run 'make' from the root of the source tree.

4. Stop your server and copy the executable to your binary directory.

5. Restart the server and connect via the MySQL client to run the DBXP SQL commands.

Summary

In this chapter, I have presented some of the more complex database-internal technologies. You learned about how queries are represented internally within the server and how they are executed. More important, you discovered how MySQL can be used to conduct your own database-internals experiments. The knowledge of these technologies should provide you with a greater understanding of why and how the MySQL system was built and how it executes.

In the next chapter, I show you more about internal-query representation through an example implementation of a query-tree structure. The next chapter begins a series of chapters designed as a baseline for you to implement your own query optimizer and execution engine. If you've ever wondered what it takes to build a database system, the next chapters will show you how to get started on your own query engine.

CHAPTER 12

■ ■ ■

Internal Query Representation

This chapter presents the first part of the advanced database technologies for the database-experiment project (DBXP). I begin by introducing the concept of the query tree structure, which is used for storing a query in memory. Next, I'll present the query tree structure used for the project along with the first in a series of short projects for implementing the DBXP code. The chapter concludes with a set of exercises you can use to learn more about MySQL and query trees.

The Query Tree

A query tree is a tree structure that corresponds to a query, in which leaf nodes of the tree contain nodes that access a relation and internal nodes with zero, one, or more children. The internal nodes contain the relational operators. These operators include project (depicted as π), restrict (depicted as σ), and join (depicted as either θ or $\bowtie$).[1] The edges of a tree represent data flow from bottom to top—that is, from the leaves, which correspond to reading data in the database, to the root, which is the final operator producing the query results. Figure 12-1 depicts an example of a query tree.

```
SELECT name
FROM faculty f, classes c
WHERE f.id = c.fac_id AND
f.department_id = 'CS' AND c.semester = 'F2001'
```

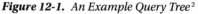

π_name$(\sigma$_department_id='CS'^semester='F2001'$ (f $\bowtie$ id=fac_id c))$

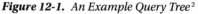

π

|

σ_department_id='CS'^semester='F2001'

|

$\bowtie$ id=fac_id

Faculty   Classes

Figure 12-1. *An Example Query Tree*[2]

---

[1]Strangely, few texts give explanations for the choice of symbol. Traditionally, θ represents a theta-join and $\bowtie$ represents a natural join, but most texts interchange these concepts, resulting in all joins represented using one or the other symbol (and sometimes both).

[2]Although similar drawings have appeared in several places in the literature, Figure 12-1 contains a subtle nuance of database theory that is often overlooked. Can you spot the often-misused trait? Hint: What is the domain of the semester attribute? Which rule has been violated by encoding data in a column?

An evaluation of the query tree consists of evaluating an internal node operation whenever its operands are available and passing the results from evaluating the operation up the tree to the parent node. The evaluation terminates when the root node is evaluated and replaced by the tuples that form the result of the query. The following sections present a variant of the query tree structure for use in storing representations of queries in memory. The advantages of using this mechanism versus a relational calculus internal representation are shown in Table 12-1.

Table 12-1. *Advantages of Using a Query Tree vs. Relational Calculus*

Operational Requirement	Query Tree	Relational Calculus
Can it be reduced?	Yes. It is possible to prune the query tree prior to evaluating query plans.	Only through application of algebraic operations.
Can it support execution?	Yes. The tree can be used to execute queries by passing dataup the tree.	No. Requires translation to another form.
Can it support relational algebra expressions?	Yes. The tree lends itself well to relational algebra.	No. Requires conversion.
Can it be implementedin database systems?	Yes. Tree structures are acommon data structure.	Only through designs that model the calculus.
Can it contain data?	Yes. The tree nodes can contain data, operations, and expressions.	No. Only the literals and variables that form the expression.

Clearly, the query-tree internal representation is superior to the more traditional mechanism employed in modern database systems. For example, the internal representation in MySQL is that of a set of classes and structures designed to contain the query and its elements for easy (fast) traversal. It organizes data for the optimization and execution.[3]

There are some disadvantages to the query-tree internal representation. Most optimizers are not designed to work within a tree structure. If you wanted to use the query tree with an optimizer, the optimizer would have to be altered. Similarly, query execution will be very different from most query-processing implementations. In this case, the query execution engine will be running from the tree rather than as a separate step. These disadvantages are addressed in later chapters as I explore an alternative optimizer and execution engine.

The DBXP query tree is a tree data structure that uses a node structure that contains all of the parameters necessary to represent these operations:

- *Restriction*: Allows you to include results that match an expression of the attributes.

- *Projection*: Provides the ability to select attributes to include in the result set.

- *Join*: Lets you combine two or more relations to form a composite set of attributes in the result set.

- *Sort (order by)*: Allows you to order the result set.

- *Distinct*: Provides the ability to reduce the result set to unique tuples.

■ **Note**   Distinct is an operation that is added to accomplish a relational operation that isn't supported by most SQL implementations and is not an inherent property of relational algebra.

---

[3]Some would say it shouldn't have to, as the MySQL internal structure is used to organize the data for the optimizer. Query trees, on the other hand, are designed to be optimized and executed in place.

Projection, restriction, and join are the basic operations. Sort and distinct are provided as additional utility operations that assist in the formulation of a complete query tree (all possible operations are represented as nodes). Join operations can have join conditions (theta-joins) or no conditions (equi-joins). The join operation is subdivided into the operations:

- *Inner*: The join of two relations returning tuples where there is a match.

- *Outer (left, right, full)*: Return all rows from at least one of the tables or views mentioned in the FROM clause, as long as those rows meet any WHERE search conditions. All rows are retrieved from the left table referenced with a left outer join, and all rows from the right table are referenced in a right outer join. All rows from both tables are returned in a full outer join. Values for attributes of nonmatching rows are returned as null values.

- *Leftouter*: The join of two relations returning tuples where there is a match, plus all tuples from the relation specified to the left, leaving nonmatching attributes specified from the other relation empty (null).

- *Rightouter*: The join of two relations returning tuples where there is a match, plus all tuples from the relation specified to the right, leaving nonmatching attributes specified from the other relation empty (null).

- *Fullouter*: The join of two relations returning all tuples from both relations, leaving nonmatching attributes specified from the other relation empty (null).

- *Crossproduct*: The join of two relations mapping each tuple from the first relation to all tuples from the other relation.

The query tree also supports some set operations. The set operations supported include:

- *Intersect*: The set operation where only matches from two relations with the same schema are returned.

- *Union*: The set operation where only the nonmatches from two relations with the same schema are returned.

What Is a Theta-Join?

You may be wondering why some joins are called equi-joins while others are called theta-joins. Equi-joins are joins in which the join condition is an equality (=). A theta-join is a join in which the join condition is an inequality (>, <, >=, <=, <>). Technically, all joins are theta-joins. Theta-joins are used less often, whereas equi-joins are common.

While the DBXP query trees provide the union and intersect operations, most database systems support unions in the form of a concatenation of result sets. Although the MySQL parser does not currently support intersect operations, however, it does support unions. Further modification of the MySQL parser is necessary to implement the intersect operation. The following sections describe the major code implementations and classes created to transform MySQL query representation to a DBXP query tree.

Query Transformation

The MySQL parser must be modified to identify and parse the SQL commands. We need, however, a way to tell the parser that we want to use the DBXP implementation and not the existing query engine. To make the changes easy, I simply added a keyword (e.g., DBXP) to the SQL commands that redirects the parsing to code that converts the MySQL internal representation into the DBXP internal representation. Although this process adds some execution time and requires a small amount of extra computational work, the implementation simplifies the modifications to the parser and provides a common mechanism to compare the DBXP data structure to that of the MySQL data structure. I refer to SQL commands with the DBXP keyword as simply DBXP SQL commands.

The process of transformation[4] begins in the MySQL parser, which identifies commands as being DBXP commands. The system then directs control to a class named `sql_dbxp_parse.cc` that manages the transformation of the parsed query from the MySQL form to the DBXP internal representation (query tree). This is accomplished by a method named `buid_query_tree`. This method is called only for SELECT and EXPLAIN SELECT statements.

DBXP Query Tree

The heart of the DBXP query optimizer is the DBXP internal representation data structure. It is used to represent the query once the SQL command has been parsed and transformed.

This structure is implemented as a tree structure (hence the name *query tree*) in which each node has zero, one, or two children. Nodes with zero children are the leaves of the tree, those with one child represent internal nodes that perform unary operations on data, and those with two children are either join or set operations. The actual node structure from the source code is shown in Listing 12-1.

Listing 12-1. DBXP Query Tree Node

```
/*
  STRUCTURE query_node

  DESCRIPTION
    This this structure contains all of the data for a query node:

    NodeId -- the internal id number for a node
    ParentNodeId -- the internal id for the parent node (used for insert)
    SubQuery -- is this the start of a subquery?
    Child -- is this a Left or Right child of the parent?
    NodeType -- synonymous with operation type
    JoinType -- if a join, this is the join operation
    join_con_type -- if this is a join, this is the "on" condition
    Expressions -- the expressions from the "where" clause for this node
    Join Expressions -- the join expressions from the "join" clause(s)
    Relations[] -- the relations for this operation (at most 4)
    PreemptPipeline -- does the pipeline need to be halted for a sort?
    Fields -- the attributes for the result set of this operation
    Left -- a pointer to the left child node
    Right -- a pointer to the right child node
*/
struct query_node
{
  query_node();
  ~query_node();
  int            nodeid;
  int            parent_nodeid;
  bool           sub_query;
  bool           child;
```

---

[4]Although many texts on the subject of query processing disagree about how each process is differentiated, they do agree that certain distinct process steps must occur.

```
query_node_type        node_type;
type_join              join_type;
join_con_type          join_cond;
Item                   *where_expr;
Item                   *join_expr;
TABLE_LIST             *relations[4];
bool                   preempt_pipeline;
List<Item>             *fields;
query_node             *left;
query_node             *right;
};
```

Some of these variables are used to manage node organization and form the tree itself. Two of the most interesting are nodeid and parent_nodeid. These are used to establish parentage of the nodes in the tree. This is necessary, because nodes can be moved up and down the tree as part of the optimization process. The use of a parent_nodeid variable avoids the need to maintain reverse pointers in the tree.[5]

The sub_query variable is used to indicate the starting node for a subquery. Thus, the data structure can support nested queries (subqueries) without additional modification of the structure. The only caveat is that the algorithms for optimization are designed to use the subquery indicator as a stop condition for tree traversal. That is, when a subquery node is detected, optimization considers the subquery a separate entity. Once detected, the query optimization routines are rerun using the subquery node as the start of the next optimization. Thus, any number of subqueries can be supported and represented as subtrees in the tree structure. This is an important feature of the query tree that overcomes the limitation found in many internal representations.

The where_expr variable is a pointer to the MySQL Item tree that manages a typical general expression tree. We will change this later to a special class that encapsulates expressions. See Chapter 13 for more details.

The relations array is used to contain pointers to relation classes that represent the abstraction of the internal record structures found in the MySQL storage engines. The relation class provides an access layer to the data stored on disk via the storage engine handler class. The array size is currently set at 4. The first two positions (0 and 1) correspond to the left and right child, respectively. The next two positions (2 and 3) represent temporary relations, such as reordering (sorting) and the application of indexes.

■ **Note** The relations array size is set at 4, which means you can process queries with up to four tables. If you need to process queries with more than four tables, you will need to change the transformation code shown later in this chapter to accept more than four tables.

The fields attribute is a pointer to the MySQL Item class that contains the list of fields for a table. It is useful in projection operations and maintaining attributes necessary for operations on relations (e.g., the propagation of attributes that satisfy expressions but that are not part of the result set).

The last variable of interest is the preempt_pipeline variable, which is used by the DBXP Execute class to implement a loop in the processing of the data from child nodes. Loops are necessary anytime an operation requires iteration through the entire set of data (rows). For example, a join that joins two relations on a common attribute in the absence of indexes that permit ordering may require iteration through one or both child nodes in order to achieve the correct mapping (join) operation.

---

[5]A practice strongly discouraged by Knuth and other algorithm gurus.

This class is also responsible for query optimization (described in Chapter 13). Since the query tree provides all of the operations for manipulating the tree and since query optimization is also a set of tree operations, optimization was accomplished using methods placed in a class that wraps the query tree structure (called the query tree class).

The optimizer methods implement a heuristic algorithm (described in Chapter 13 and in more detail in Chapter 14). Execution of these methods results in the reorganization of the tree into a more optimal tree and the separation of some nodes into two or more others that can also be relocated to form a more optimal tree. An optimal tree permits a more efficient execution of the query.

Cost optimization is also supported in this class using an algorithm that walks the tree, applying available indexes to the access methods for each leaf node (nodes that access the relation stores directly).

This structure can support a wide variety of operations, including restrict, project, join, set, and ordering (sorting). The query node structure is designed to represent each of these operations as a single node and can store all pertinent and required information to execute the operation in place. Furthermore, the EXPLAIN command was implemented as a postorder traversal of the tree, printing out the contents of each node starting at the leaves (see the show_plan method later in this chapter). The MySQL equivalent of this operation requires much more computational time and is implemented with a complex set of methods.

Thus, the query tree is an internal representation that can represent any query and provide a mechanism to optimize the query by manipulating the tree. Indeed, the tree structure itself simplifies optimization and enables the implementation of a heuristic optimizer by providing a means to associate query operations as nodes in a tree. This query tree therefore is a viable mechanism for use in any relational database system and can be generalized for use in a production system.

Implementing DBXP Query Trees in MySQL

This section presents the addition of the DBXP query tree structure to the MySQL source code. This first step in creating a relational database research tool is designed to show you how the query tree works and how to transform the MySQL query structure into a base query tree (not optimized). Later chapters will describe the optimizer and execution engine.

Rather than attempting to reuse the existing SELECT command, we will create new entries in the parser to implement a special version of the SELECT command with the string DBXP_SELECT. This will permit the modifications to be isolated and not confused with existing SELECT subcomponents in the parser. The following sections show you how to add the query tree and add stubs for executing DBXP_SELECT and EXPLAIN DBXP_SELECT commands.

▪ **Note**   The source code examples available on the Apress website for this and the following chapters contains a difference file you can use to apply to the MySQL source tree. Depending on the version of server you are using, provided it is based on version 5.6, the patch operation should apply with minimal modification. The use of difference files keeps the example code smaller and permits you to see the changes in context.

Files Added and Changed

While following the examples in this chapter, you will create several files and modify some of the MySQL source-code files. Table 12-2 lists the files that will be added and changed.

Table 12-2. *Summary of Files Added and Changed*

File	Description
mysqld.cc	Added the DBXP version number label to the MySQL version number
lex.h	Added DBXP tokens to the lexical hash
query_tree.h	DBXP query-tree header file (new file)
query_tree.cc	DBXP query-tree class file (new file)
sql_cmd.h	Add the DBXP_SELECT to the enum_sql_command list
sql_yacc.yy	Added SQL command parsing to the parser
sql_parse.cc	Added the code to handle the new commands to the "big switch"

Creating the Tests

The following section explains the process of stubbing the DBXP_SELECT command, the query tree class, and the EXPLAIN DBXP_SELECT and DBXP_SELECT commands. The goal is to permit the user to enter any valid SELECT command, process the query, and return the results.

■ **Note** Since the DBXP engine is an experimental engine, it is limited to queries that represent the basic operations for retrieving data. Keeping the length of these chapters to a manageable size and complexity requires that the DBXP engine not process queries with aggregates—those containing a HAVING, GROUP BY, or ORDER BY clause. (There is nothing prohibiting this, so you are free to implement these operations yourself.)

The following sections detail the steps necessary to create these three aspects of the DBXP code. Rather than create three small tests, I'll create a single test file and use that to test the functions. For those operations that are not implemented, you can either comment out the query statements by adding a pound sign (#) at the beginning of the command or run the test as shown and ignore the inevitable errors for commands not yet implemented (thereby keeping true to the test first development mantra). Listing 12-2 shows the Ch12.test file.

Listing 12-2. Chapter Tests (Ch12.test)

```
#
# Sample test to test the DBXP_SELECT and EXPLAIN DBXP_SELECT commands
#

# Test 1: Test stubbed DBXP_SELECT command.
DBXP_SELECT * FROM no_such_table;

# Test 2: Test stubbed Query Tree implementation.
DBXP_SELECT * FROM customer;

# Test 3: Test stubbed EXPLAIN DBXP_SELECT command.
EXPLAIN DBXP_SELECT * FROM customer;
```

Of course, you can use this test as a guide and add your own commands to explore the new code. Refer to Chapter 4 for more details on how to create and run this test using the MySQL Test Suite.

Stubbing the DBXP_SELECT Command

In this section, you'll learn how to add a custom SELECT command to the MySQL parser. You'll see how the parser can be modified to accommodate a new command that mimics the traditional SELECT command in MySQL.

Identifying the Modifications

You should first identify a MySQL server that has the DBXP technologies by adding a label to the MySQL version number to ensure that you can always tell that you're connected to the modified server.

■ **Tip** You can use the command SELECT VERSION() at any time to retrieve the version of the server. If you are using the MySQL command-line client, you can change the command prompt to indicate that the server you are connected to is the server with the DBXP code.

To append the version label, open the mysqld.cc file and locate the set_server_version method. Add a statement to append a label onto the MySQL version number string. In this case, we will use "-DBXP 2.0" to represent the printing of this book. Listing 12-3 shows the modified set_server_version method.

Listing 12-3. Changes to the mysqld.cc File

```
static void set_server_version(void)
{
  char *end= strxmov(server_version, MYSQL_SERVER_VERSION,
                     MYSQL_SERVER_SUFFIX_STR, NullS);
#ifdef EMBEDDED_LIBRARY
  end= strmov(end, "-embedded");
#endif
#ifndef DBUG_OFF
  if (!strstr(MYSQL_SERVER_SUFFIX_STR, "-debug"))
    end= strmov(end, "-debug");
#endif
  if (opt_log || opt_slow_log || opt_bin_log)
    strmov(end, "-log");                        // This may slow down system
/* BEGIN DBXP MODIFICATION */
/* Reason for Modification: */
/* This section adds the DBXP version number to the MySQL version number. */
  strmov(end, "-DBXP 2.0");
/* END DBXP MODIFICATION */
}
```

Modifying the Lexical Structures

Now, let's add the tokens you'll need to identify the DBXP_SELECT command. Open the lex.h file and add the code shown in bold in Listing 12-4 to the symbols array in context.

CHAPTER 12 ▪ INTERNAL QUERY REPRESENTATION

Listing 12-4. Changes to the lex.h File

```
static SYMBOL symbols[] = {
...
  { "DAY_MINUTE",        SYM(DAY_MINUTE_SYM)},
  { "DAY_SECOND",        SYM(DAY_SECOND_SYM)},
/* BEGIN DBXP MODIFICATION */
/* Reason for MODIFICATION */
/* This section identifies the symbols and values for the DBXP token */
  { "DBXP_SELECT",        SYM(DBXP_SELECT_SYM)},
/* END DBXP MODIFICATION */
  { "DEALLOCATE",        SYM(DEALLOCATE_SYM)},
  { "DEC",               SYM(DECIMAL_SYM)},
    ...
```

Add the Command Enumeration

This section explains how to add the new DBXP_SELECT command enumeration. The modifications begin with adding a new case statement to the parser command switch in the sql_parse.cc file. The switch uses enumerated values for the cases.

To add a new case, you must add a new enumerated value. These values are identified in the parser code and stored in the lex->sql_command member variable. To add a new enumerated value to the lexical parser, open the sql_cmd.h file and add the code shown in Listing 12-5 to the enum_sql_command enumeration.

Listing 12-5. Adding the DBXP_SELECT Command Enumeration

```
enum enum_sql_command {
...
/* BEGIN DBXP MODIFICATION */
/* Reason for Modification: */
/* This section captures the enumerations for the DBXP command tokens */
  SQLCOM_DBXP_SELECT,
  SQLCOM_DBXP_EXPLAIN_SELECT,
/* END DBXP MODIFICATION */
...
```

Adding the DBXP_SELECT Command to the MySQL Parser

Once the new enumerated value for the case statement is added, you must also add code to the parser code (sql_yacc.yy) to identify the new DBXP_SELECT statement. This is done in several parts. You'll add a new token to the parser requiring updates to three places.

The new token, once activated, will permit the parser to distinguish a normal MySQL SELECT statement from one that you want to process with the DBXP code. We program the parser so that, when the token is present, it indicates the parser should set the sql_command variable to the SQLCOM_DBXP_SELECT value instead of the normal MySQL select enumerated value (SQLCOM_SELECT). This technique allows you to issue the same basic SELECT statement to both the normal MySQL code and the DBXP code. For example, the following SELECT statements both accomplish the same task; they just will be optimized differently. The first one will be directed to the SQLCOM_SELECT case statement, whereas the second will be directed to the SQLCOM_DBXP_SELECT case statement.

```
SELECT * FROM customer;
DBXP_SELECT * FROM customer;
```

The code to add the new token is shown in Listing 12-6. Locate the list of tokens in the sql_yacc.yy file and add the code. (The list is in roughly alphabetical order).

Listing 12-6. Adding the Command Symbol to the Parser

```
%token  DAY_SECOND_SYM
%token  DAY_SYM                         /* SQL-2003-R */
/* BEGIN DBXP MODIFICATION */
/* Reason for Modification: */
/* This section defines the tokens for the DBXP commands */
%token  DBXP_SELECT_SYM
/* END DBXP MODIFICATION */
%token  DEALLOCATE_SYM                  /* SQL-2003-R */
%token  DECIMAL_NUM
```

We also need to add the new command to the type <NONE> definition. Listing 12-7 shows this modification.

Listing 12-7. Adding the Command Syntax Operations to the Parser

```
%type <NONE>
/* BEGIN DBXP MODIFICATION */
/* Reason for Modification: */
/* Add the dbxp_select statement to the NONE type definition. */
        query verb_clause create change select dbxp_select do drop insert replace insert2
/* END DBXP MODIFICATION */
```

The last area for adding the token is to add the following code to the statement section. Listing 12-8 shows the modification in context.

Listing 12-8. Adding the Command to the SELECT: section

```
statement:
...
        | select
/* BEGIN DBXP MODIFICATION */
/* Reason for Modification: */
/* Add the dbxp_select statement to the list of statements(commands). */
        | dbxp_select
/* END DBXP MODIFICATION */
        | set
...
```

We can now add the statements to enable parsing of the DBXP_SELECT command. Listing 12-9 shows the parser code needed to identify the DBXP_SELECT command and to process the normal parts of the select command. Notice that the parser identifies the select and DBXP symbols and then provides for other parsing of the select options, fields list, and FROM clause. Immediately after that line is the code that sets the sql_command. Notice that the code also places a vertical bar (|) before the original select-command parser code. This is the "or" operator that the parser syntax uses to process variations of a command. To add this change to the parser, open the sql_yacc.yy file and locate the select: label, then add the code, as shown in Listing 12-9.

Listing 12-9. Adding the Command Syntax Operations to the Parser

```
/* BEGIN DBXP MODIFICATION */
/* Reason for Modification: */
/* This section captures (parses) the SELECT DBXP statement */

dbxp_select:
        DBXP_SELECT_SYM DBXP_select_options DBXP_select_item_list
              DBXP_select_from
        {
           LEX *lex= Lex;
          lex->sql_command = SQLCOM_DBXP_SELECT;
        }
        ;

/* END DBXP MODIFICATION */

select:
        select_init
         {
           LEX *lex= Lex;
           lex->sql_command= SQLCOM_SELECT;
         }
        ;
```

Notice also that the code references several other labels. Listing 12-10 contains the code for these operations. The first is the DBXP_select_options, which identifies the valid options for the SELECT command. While this is very similar to the MySQL select options, it provides for only two options: DISTINCT and COUNT(*). The next operation is the DBXP_select_from code that identifies the tables in the FROM clause. It also calls the DBXP_where_clause operation to identify the WHERE clause. The next operation is the DBXP_select_item_list, which resembles the MySQL code. Last, the DBXP_where_clause operation identifies the parameters in the WHERE clause. Take some time to go through this code and follow the operations to their associated labels to see what each does. To add this code to the parser, locate the select_from: label and add the code above it. Although it doesn't matter where you place the code, this location seems more logical, because it is in the same area with the MySQL select operations. Listing 12-10 shows the complete source code for the DBXP_SELECT parser code.

Listing 12-10. Additional Operations for the DBXP_SELECT Command

```
/* BEGIN DBXP MODIFICATION */
/* Reason for Modification: */
/* This section captures (parses) the sub parts of the SELECT DBXP statement */

DBXP_select_options:
   /* empty */
   | DISTINCT
   {
     Select->options|= SELECT_DISTINCT;
   }
   ;

DBXP_select_from:
  FROM join_table_list DBXP_where_clause {};
```

```
DBXP_select_item_list:
  /* empty */
  | DBXP_select_item_list ',' select_item
  | select_item
  | '*'
    {
      THD *thd= YYTHD;
      Item *item= new (thd->mem_root)
                    Item_field(&thd->lex->current_select->context,
                               NULL, NULL, "*");
      if (item == NULL)
        MYSQL_YYABORT;
      if (add_item_to_list(thd, item))
        MYSQL_YYABORT;
      (thd->lex->current_select->with_wild)++;
    };

DBXP_where_clause:
  /* empty */  { Select->where= 0; }
  | WHERE expr
    {
      SELECT_LEX *select= Select;
      select->where= $2;
      if ($2)
        $2->top_level_item();
    }
    ;

/* END DBXP MODIFICATION */

...
```

■ **Note** A savvy yacc developer may spot some places in this code that can be reduced or reused from the rules for the original SELECT statement. I leave this as an exercise for those interested in optimizing this code.

Now that you've made the changes to the lexical parser, you have to generate the equivalent C source code. Fortunately, the normal cmake/make steps will take care of this. Simply execute these commands from the root of the source tree.

```
cmake .
make
```

If you want to check your code without waiting for the make file to process all of the source files, you can use Bison to generate these files. Open a command window and navigate to the /sql directory off the root of your source code tree. Run the command:

```
bison -y -d sql_yacc.yy
```

This generates two new files: y.tab.c and y.tab.h. These files replace the sql_yacc.cc and sql_yacc.h files, respectively. Before you copy them, make a backup of the original files. After you've done so, copy y.tab.c to sql_yacc.cc and y.taqb.h to sql_yacc.h.

WHAT ARE LEX AND YACC AND WHO'S BISON?

Lex stands for "lexical analyzer generator" and is used as a parser to identify tokens and literals, as well as the syntax of a language. YACC stands for "yet another compiler compiler" and is used to identify and act on the semantic definitions of the language. The use of these tools together with Bison (a YACC-compatible parser generator that generates C source code from the Lex/YACC code) provides a rich mechanism for creating subsystems that can parse and process language commands. Indeed, that is exactly how MySQL uses these technologies.

If you compile the server now, you can issue DBXP_SELECT commands, but nothing will happen. That's because you need to add the case statement to the parser switch in sql_parse.cc. Since we do not yet have a complete DBXP engine, let's make the exercise a bit more interesting by stubbing out the case statement. Listing 12-11 shows a complete set of scaffold code you can use to implement the DBXP_SELECT command. In this code, I use the MySQL utility classes to establish a record set. The first portion of the code sets up the field list for the fictional table. Following that are lines of code to write data values to the network stream and, finally, to send an end-of-file marker to the client. Writing data to the output stream requires calls to protocol->prepare_for_resend(), storing the data to be sent using protocol->store(), and then writing the buffer to the stream with protocol->write().

Listing 12-11. Modifications to the Parser Command Switch

```
/* BEGIN DBXP MODIFICATION */
/* Reason for Modification: */
/* This section adds the code to call the new DBXP_SELECT command. */
  case SQLCOM_DBXP_SELECT:
  {
    List<Item> field_list;
    /* The protocol class is used to write data to the client. */
    Protocol *protocol= thd->protocol;

    /* Build the field list and send the fields to the client */
    field_list.push_back(new Item_int("Id",(longlong) 1,21));
    field_list.push_back(new Item_empty_string("LastName",40));
    field_list.push_back(new Item_empty_string("FirstName",20));
    field_list.push_back(new Item_empty_string("Gender",2));
    if (protocol->send_ result_set_metadata (&field_list,
                        Protocol::SEND_NUM_ROWS | Protocol::SEND_EOF))
      DBUG_RETURN(TRUE);
    protocol->prepare_for_resend();

    /* Write some sample data to the buffer and send it with write() */
    protocol->store((longlong)3);
    protocol->store("Flintstone", system_charset_info);
    protocol->store("Fred", system_charset_info);
    protocol->store("M", system_charset_info);
    if (protocol->write())
      DBUG_RETURN(TRUE);

    protocol->prepare_for_resend();
    protocol->store((longlong)5);
```

```
      protocol->store("Rubble", system_charset_info);
      protocol->store("Barnie", system_charset_info);
      protocol->store("M", system_charset_info);
      if (protocol->write())
        DBUG_RETURN(TRUE);

      protocol->prepare_for_resend();
      protocol->store((longlong)7);
      protocol->store("Flintstone", system_charset_info);
      protocol->store("Wilma", system_charset_info);
      protocol->store("F", system_charset_info);
      if (protocol->write())
        DBUG_RETURN(TRUE);

      /*
        send_eof() tells the communication mechanism that we're finished
        sending data (end of file).
      */
      my_eof(thd);
      break;
  }
/* END DBXP MODIFICATION */
  case SQLCOM_PREPARE:
...
```

This stub code returns a simulated record set to the client whenever a DBXP_SELECT command is detected. Go ahead and enter this code, and then compile and run the test.

Testing the DBXP_SELECT Command

The test we want to run is issuing a DBXP_SELECT command and verifying that the statement is parsed and processed by the new stubbed case statement. You can run the test you created earlier or simply enter a SQL statement such as the following (make sure you type the DBXP part) in a MySQL command-line client:

```
DBXP_SELECT * from no_such_table;
```

It doesn't matter what you type after the DBXP as long as it is a valid SQL SELECT statement. Listing 12-12 shows an example of the output you should expect.

Listing 12-12. Results of Stub Test

```
mysql> DBXP_SELECT * from no_such_table;
+----+------------+-----------+--------+
| Id | LastName   | FirstName | Gender |
+----+------------+-----------+--------+
| 3  | Flintstone | Fred      | M      |
| 5  | Rubble     | Barnie    | M      |
| 7  | Flintstone | Wilma     | F      |
+----+------------+-----------+--------+
3 rows in set (0.23 sec)

mysql>
```

Adding the Query Tree Class

Now that you have a stubbed DBXP_SELECT command, you can begin to implement the DBXP-specific code to execute a SELECTcommand. In this section, I'll show you how to add the basic query-tree class and transform the MySQL internal structure to the query tree. I don't go all the way into the bowels of the query-tree code until the next chapter.

Adding the Query Tree Header File

Adding the query-tree class requires creating the query-tree header file and referencing it in the MySQL code. The query-tree header file is shown in Listing 12-13. Notice that I named the class Query_tree. This follows the MySQL coding guidelines by naming classes with an initial capital. Take a moment to scan through the header code. You will see there isn't a lot of code there—just the basics of the query-tree node structure and the enumerations. Notice there are enumerations for node type, join condition type, join, and aggregate types. These enumerations permit the query-tree nodes to take on unique roles in the execution of the query. I explain more about how these are used in the next chapter.

You can create the file any way you choose (or download it). Name it query_tree.h and place it in the /sql directory of your MySQL source tree. Don't worry about how to add it to the project; I show you how to do that in a later section.

Listing 12-13. The Query Tree Header File

```
/*
  query_tree.h

  DESCRIPTION
    This file contains the Query_tree class declaration. It is responsible for containing the
    internal representation of the query to be executed. It provides methods for
    optimizing and forming and inspecting the query tree. This class is the very
    heart of the DBXP query capability! It also provides the ability to store
    a binary "compiled" form of the query.

  NOTES
    The data structure is a binary tree that can have 0, 1, or 2 children. Only
    Join operations can have 2 children. All other operations have 0 or 1
    children. Each node in the tree is an operation and the links to children
    are the pipeline.

  SEE ALSO
    query_tree.cc
*/
#include "sql_priv.h"
#include "sql_class.h"
#include "table.h"
#include "records.h"

class Query_tree
{
public:
  enum query_node_type         //this enumeration lists the available
  {                             //query node (operations)
    qntUndefined = 0,
    qntRestrict = 1,
```

```
   qntProject = 2,
   qntJoin = 3,
   qntSort = 4,
   qntDistinct = 5
};

enum join_con_type          //this enumeration lists the available
{                           //join operations supported
  jcUN = 0,
  jcNA = 1,
  jcON = 2,
  jcUS = 3
};

enum type_join              //this enumeration lists the available
{                           //join types supported.
  jnUNKNOWN      = 0,       //undefined
  jnINNER        = 1,
  jnLEFTOUTER    = 2,
  jnRIGHTOUTER   = 3,
  jnFULLOUTER    = 4,
  jnCROSSPRODUCT = 5,
  jnUNION        = 6,
  jnINTERSECT    = 7
};

  enum AggregateType        //used to add aggregate functions
  {
      atNONE     = 0,
      atCOUNT    = 1
  };

/*
  STRUCTURE query_node

  DESCRIPTION
    This this structure contains all of the data for a query node:

    NodeId -- the internal id number for a node
    ParentNodeId -- the internal id for the parent node (used for insert)
    SubQuery -- is this the start of a subquery?
    Child -- is this a Left or Right child of the parent?
    NodeType -- synonymous with operation type
    JoinType -- if a join, this is the join operation
    join_con_type -- if this is a join, this is the "on" condition
    Expressions -- the expressions from the "where" clause for this node
    Join Expressions -- the join expressions from the "join" clause(s)
    Relations[] -- the relations for this operation (at most 2)
    PreemptPipeline -- does the pipeline need to be halted for a sort?
    Fields -- the attributes for the result set of this operation
```

```
        Left -- a pointer to the left child node
        Right -- a pointer to the right child node
*/
  struct query_node
  {
    query_node();
    ~query_node();
    int                nodeid;
    int                parent_nodeid;
    bool               sub_query;
    bool               child;
    query_node_type    node_type;
    type_join          join_type;
    join_con_type      join_cond;
    Item               *where_expr;
    Item               *join_expr;
    TABLE_LIST         *relations[4];
    bool               preempt_pipeline;
    List<Item>         *fields;
    query_node         *left;
    query_node         *right;
  };

  query_node *root;               //The ROOT node of the tree

  ~Query_tree(void);
  void ShowPlan(query_node *QN, bool PrintOnRight);

};
```

With the query-tree header file, you also need the query-tree source file. The source file must provide the code for the constructor and destructor methods of the query-tree class. Listing 12-14 shows the completed constructor and destructor methods. Create the query_tree.cc file and enter this code (or download it). Place this file in the /sql directory of your MySQL source tree. I show you how to add it to the project in a later section.

Listing 12-14. The Query Tree Class

```
/*
  query_tree.cc

  DESCRIPTION
    This file contains the Query_tree class. It is responsible for containing the
    internal representation of the query to be executed. It provides methods for
    optimizing and forming and inspecting the query tree. This class is the very
    heart of the DBXP query capability! It also provides the ability to store
    a binary "compiled" form of the query.

  NOTES
    The data structure is a binary tree that can have 0, 1, or 2 children. Only
    Join operations can have 2 children. All other operations have 0 or 1
    children. Each node in the tree is an operation and the links to children
    are the pipeline.
```

```
  SEE ALSO
    query_tree.h
*/
#include "query_tree.h"

Query_tree::query_node::query_node()
{
  where_expr = NULL;
  join_expr = NULL;
  child = false;
  join_cond = Query_tree::jcUN;
  join_type = Query_tree::jnUNKNOWN;
  left = NULL;
  right = NULL;
  nodeid = -1;
  node_type = Query_tree::qntUndefined;
  sub_query = false;
  parent_nodeid = -1;
}

Query_tree::query_node::~query_node()
{
  if(left)
    delete left;
  if(right)
    delete right;
}

Query_tree::~Query_tree(void)
{
  if(root)
    delete root;
}
```

Building the Query Tree from the MySQL Structure

What we need next is the code to perform the transformation from the MySQL internal structure to the query tree. Let's use a helper source file rather than add the code to the sql_parse.cc file. In fact, many of the commands represented by the case statements (in the sql_parse.cc file) are done this way. Create a new file named sql_dbxp_parse.cc. Create a new function in that file named build_query_tree as shown in Listing 12-15. The code is a basic transformation method. Take a moment to look through the code as you type it in (or download and copy and paste it into the file).

Listing 12-15. The DBXP Parser Helper File

```
/*
  sql_dbxp_parse.cc

  DESCRIPTION
    This file contains methods to execute the DBXP_SELECT query statements.
```

```
   SEE ALSO
      query_tree.cc
*/
#include "query_tree.h"

/*
  Build Query Tree

  SYNOPSIS
    build_query_tree()
    THD *thd            IN the current thread
    LEX *lex            IN the pointer to the current parsed structure
    TABLE_LIST *tables  IN the list of tables identified in the query

  DESCRIPTION
    This method returns a converted MySQL internal representation (IR) of a
    query as a query_tree.

  RETURN VALUE
    Success = Query_tree * -- the root of the new query tree.
    Failed = NULL
*/
Query_tree *build_query_tree(THD *thd, LEX *lex, TABLE_LIST *tables)
{
  DBUG_ENTER("build_query_tree");
  Query_tree *qt = new Query_tree();
  Query_tree::query_node *qn = new Query_tree::query_node();
  TABLE_LIST *table;
  int i = 0;
  int num_tables = 0;

  /* Create a new restrict node. */
  qn->parent_nodeid = -1;
  qn->child = false;
  qn->join_type = (Query_tree::type_join) 0;
  qn->nodeid = 0;
  qn->node_type = (Query_tree::query_node_type) 2;
  qn->left = 0;
  qn->right = 0;

  /* Get the tables (relations) */
  i = 0;
  for(table = tables; table; table = table->next_local)
  {
    num_tables++;
    qn->relations[i] = table;
    i++;
  }
```

```
  /* Populate attributes */
  qn->fields = &lex->select_lex.item_list;
  /* Process joins */
  if (num_tables > 0)  //indicates more than 1 table processed
    for(table = tables; table; table = table->next_local)
      if (((Item *)table->join_cond() != 0) && (qn->join_expr == 0))
        qn->join_expr = (Item *)table->join_cond();
  qn->where_expr = lex->select_lex.where;
  qt->root = qn;
  DBUG_RETURN(qt);
}
```

Notice that the build_query_tree code begins with creating a new query node, identifies the tables used in the query, populates the fields list, and captures the join and where expressions. These are all basic items needed to execute the most basic of queries.

Stubbing the Query Tree Execution

Now let's consider what it takes to create a query tree in code. Create a new function named DBXP_select_command, and copy the code from Listing 12-16. Place this function in the sql_dbxp_parse.cc file. This function will be called from the case statement in sql_parse.cc.

Listing 12-16. Handling the DBXP_SELECT Command

```
/*
  Perform Select Command

  SYNOPSIS
    DBXP_select_command()
    THD *thd              IN the current thread

  DESCRIPTION
    This method executes the SELECT command using the query tree.

  RETURN VALUE
    Success = 0
    Failed = 1
*/
int DBXP_select_command(THD *thd)
{
  DBUG_ENTER("DBXP_select_command");
  Query_tree *qt = build_query_tree(thd, thd->lex,
                                    (TABLE_LIST*) thd->lex->select_lex.table_list.first);
  List<Item> field_list;
  Protocol *protocol= thd->protocol;
  field_list.push_back(new Item_empty_string("Database Experiment Project (DBXP)",40));
  if (protocol->send_result_set_metadata(&field_list,
                        Protocol::SEND_NUM_ROWS | Protocol::SEND_EOF))
    DBUG_RETURN(TRUE);
  protocol->prepare_for_resend();
  protocol->store("Query tree was built.", system_charset_info);
```

```
  if (protocol->write())
    DBUG_RETURN(TRUE);
  my_eof(thd);
  DBUG_RETURN(0);
}
```

This code begins by calling the transformation function (build_query_tree) and then creates a stubbed result set. This time, I create a record set with only one column and one row that is used to pass a message to the client that the query tree transformation completed. Although this code isn't very interesting, it is a placeholder for you to conduct more experiments on the query tree (see exercises at the end of the chapter). Place the sql_dbxp_parse.cc file in the /sql directory of your MySQL source tree.

Stubbing the DBXP_SELECT Command Revisited

Open the sql_parse.cc file and add a function declaration for the DBXP_select_command function, placing the declaration near the phrase mysql_execute_command. Listing 12-17 shows the complete function header for the DBXP_select_command function. Enter this code above the comment block as shown.

Listing 12-17. Modifications to the Parser Command Code

```
/* BEGIN DBXP MODIFICATION */
/* Reason for Modification: */
/* This section adds the code to call the new SELECT DBXP command. */
int DBXP_select_command(THD *thd);
int DBXP_explain_select_command(THD *thd);
/* END DBXP MODIFICATION */
```

You can now change the code in the case statement (also called the parser command switch) to call the new DBXP_select_command function. Listing 12-18 shows the complete code for calling this function. Notice that the only parameter we need to pass in is the current thread (thd). The MySQL internal query structure and all other metadata for the query are referenced via the thread pointer. As you can see, this technique cleans up the case statement quite a bit. It also helps to modularize the DBXP code to make it easier to maintain and modify for your experiments.

Listing 12-18. Modifications to the Parse Command Switch (sql_parse.cc)

```
/* BEGIN DBXP MODIFICATION */
/* Reason for Modification: */
/* This section adds the code to call the new DBXP_SELECT command. */
  case SQLCOM_DBXP_SELECT:
  {
    res = DBXP_select_command(thd);
    if (res)
      goto error;
    break;
  }
/* END DBXP MODIFICATION */
  case SQLCOM_PREPARE:
  {
...
```

Before you can compile the server, you need to add the new source code files (query_tree.h, query_tree.cc, and sql_dbxp_parse.cc) to the project (make) file.

Adding the Files to the CMakeLists.txt file

Adding the project files requires modifying the CMakeLists.txt file in the /sql directory from the root of the source tree. Open the file and locate the SQL_SHARED_SOURCES_label. Add source-code files to the list of sources for compilation of the server (mysqld). Listing 12-19 shows the start of the definition and the project files added.

Listing 12-19. Modifications to the CMakeLists.txt File

```
SET(SQL_SHARED_SOURCES
  abstract_query_plan.cc
  datadict.cc
...

  sql_dbxp_parse.cc
  query_tree.cc
...
```

■ **Caution** Be sure to use spaces when formatting the lists when modifying the cmake files.

Testing the Query Tree

Once the server is compiled without errors, you can test it using a SQL statement. Unlike the last test, you should enter a valid SQL command that references objects that exist. You could either run the test (see Listing 12-20) as described in an earlier section or enter the following command in the MySQL command-line client:

```
DBXP_SELECT * from customer;
```

Listing 12-20. Results of DBXP_SELECT Test

```
mysql> DBXP_SELECT * FROM customer;

+-------------------------------------------------+
| Database Experiment Project (DBXP)              |
+-------------------------------------------------+
| Query tree was built.                           |
+-------------------------------------------------+
1 row in set (0.00 sec)

mysql>
```

You've stubbed out the DBXP_SELECT operation and built a query tree, but that isn't very interesting. What if we could see what the query looks like? We'll create a function that works like the EXPLAIN command, only instead of a list of information about the query, we'll create a graphical representation[6] of the query in tree form.

Showing Details of the Query Tree

Adding a new command requires adding a new enumeration for a new case statement in the parser switch in sql_parse.cc and adding the parser code to identify the new command. You also have to add the code to execute the new command to the sql_DBXP_parse.cc file. While creating and adding an EXPLAIN command to the parser that explains query trees sounds complicated, the EXPLAIN SELECT command is available in MySQL, so we can copy a lot of that code and reuse much of it.

Adding the EXPLAIN DBXP_SELECT Command to the MySQL Parser

To add the new enumeration to the parser, open the sql_lex.h file and add an enumeration named SQLCOM_DBXP_EXPLAIN_SELECT following the code for the SQLCOM_DBXP_SELECT enumeration. Listing 12-21 shows the completed code changes. Once the code is added, you can regenerate the lexical hash as described earlier.

Listing 12-21. Adding the EXPLAIN Enumeration

```
/* A Oracle compatible synonym for show */
describe:
/* BEGIN DBXP MODIFICATION */
/* Reason for Modification: */
/* This section captures (parses) the EXPLAIN (DESCRIBE) DBXP statements */

  describe_command DBXP_SELECT_SYM DBXP_select_options DBXP_select_item_list
              DBXP_select_from
  {
          LEX *lex= Lex;
          lex->sql_command = SQLCOM_DBXP_EXPLAIN_SELECT;
          lex->select_lex.db= 0;
          lex->verbose= 0;
  }

/* END DBXP MODIFICATION */
...
```

Notice that in this code, the parser identifies an EXPLAIN DBXP_SELECT command. In fact, it calls many of the same operations as the DBXP_SELECT parser code. The only difference is that this code sets the sql_command to the new enumeration (SQLCOM_DBXP_EXPLAIN_SELECT).

The changes to the parser switch statement in sql_parse.cc require adding the function declaration for the code in sql_DBXP_parse.cc that will execute the EXPLAIN command. Open the sql_parse.cc file and add the function declaration for the EXPLAIN function. Name the function DBXP_explain_select_command (are you starting to see a pattern?). Add this at the same location as the DBXP_select_command function declaration. Listing 12-22 shows the complete code for both DBXP commands.

---

[6]As graphical as a command-line interface will allow, anyway.

Listing 12-22. Modifications to the Parser Command Code

```
/* BEGIN DBXP MODIFICATION */
/* Reason for Modification: */
/* This section adds the code to call the new DBXP_SELECT command. */
int DBXP_select_command(THD *thd);
int DBXP_explain_select_command(THD *thd);
/* END DBXP MODIFICATION */
```

You also need to add the new case statement for the DBXP explain command. The statements are similar to the case statement for the DBXP_SELECT command. Listing 12-23 shows the new case statement added.

Listing 12-23. Modifications to the Parser Switch Statement

```
/* BEGIN DBXP MODIFICATION */
/* Reason for Modification: */
/* This section adds the code to call the new DBXP_SELECT command. */
  case SQLCOM_DBXP_SELECT:
  {
    res = DBXP_select_command(thd);
    if (res)
      goto error;
    break;
  }
  case SQLCOM_DBXP_EXPLAIN_SELECT:
  {
    res = DBXP_explain_select_command(thd);
    if (res)
      goto error;
    break;
  }
/* END DBXP MODIFICATION */
```

Creating a show_plan Function

The EXPLAIN DBXP_SELECT command shows the query path as a tree printed out within the confines of character text. The EXPLAIN code is executed in a function named show_plan in the sql_DBXP_parse.cc file. A helper function named write_printf is used to make the show_plan code easier to read. Listings 12-24 and 12-25 show the completed code for both of these methods.

Listing 12-24. Adding a Function to Capture the Protocol Store and Write Statements

```
/*
  Write to vio with printf.

  SYNOPSIS
    write_printf()
    Protocol *p     IN the Protocol class
    char *first     IN the first string to write
    char *last      IN the last string to write
```

```
DESCRIPTION
  This method writes to the vio routines printing the strings passed.

  RETURN VALUE
    Success = 0
    Failed = 1
*/
int write_printf(Protocol *p, char *first, const char *last)
{
  char *str = new char[1024];

  DBUG_ENTER("write_printf");
  strcpy(str, first);
  strcat(str, last);
  p->prepare_for_resend();
  p->store(str, system_charset_info);
  p->write();
  delete str;
  DBUG_RETURN(0);
}
```

Notice that the write_printf code calls the protocol->store and protocol->write functions to write a line of the drawing to the client. I'll let you explore the show_plan source code shown in Listing 12-25 to see how it works. I'll show you an example of the code executing in the next section. The code uses a postorder traversal to generate the query plan from the query tree, starting at the root. Add these methods to the sql_DBXP_parse.cc file.

Listing 12-25. The show_plan Source Code

```
/*
  Show Query Plan

  SYNOPSIS
    show_plan()
    Protocol *p          IN the MySQL protocol class
    query_node *Root     IN the root node of the query tree
    query_node *qn       IN the starting node to be operated on.
    bool print_on_right  IN indicates the printing should tab to the right
                            of the display.

  DESCRIPTION
    This method prints the execute plan to the client via the protocol class

  WARNING
    This is a RECURSIVE method!
    Uses postorder traversal to draw the quey plan

  RETURN VALUE
    Success = 0
    Failed = 1
```

```
*/
int show_plan(Protocol *p, Query_tree::query_node *root,
              Query_tree::query_node *qn, bool print_on_right)
{
  DBUG_ENTER("show_plan");

  /* spacer is used to fill white space in the output */
  char *spacer = (char *)my_malloc(80, MYF(MY_ZEROFILL | MY_WME));
  char *tblname = (char *)my_malloc(256, MYF(MY_ZEROFILL | MY_WME));
  int i = 0;

  if(qn != 0)
  {
    show_plan(p, root, qn->left, print_on_right);
    show_plan(p, root, qn->right, true);

    /* draw incoming arrows */
    if(print_on_right)
      strcpy(spacer, "           |               ");
    else
      strcpy(spacer, "      ");

    /* Write out the name of the database and table */
    if((qn->left == NULL) && (qn->right == NULL))
    {
      /*
         If this is a join, it has 2 children, so we need to write
         the children nodes feeding the join node. Spaces are used
         to place the tables side-by-side.
      */
      if(qn->node_type == Query_tree::qntJoin)
      {
        strcpy(tblname, spacer);
        strcat(tblname, qn->relations[0]->db);
        strcat(tblname, ".");
        strcat(tblname, qn->relations[0]->table_name);
        if(strlen(tblname) < 15)
          strcat(tblname, "                 ");
        else
          strcat(tblname, "            ");
        strcat(tblname, qn->relations[1]->db);
        strcat(tblname, ".");
        strcat(tblname, qn->relations[1]->table_name);
        write_printf(p, tblname, "");
        write_printf(p, spacer, "     |                                |");
        write_printf(p, spacer, "     |    ----------------------------");
        write_printf(p, spacer, "     |   |");
        write_printf(p, spacer, "     V   V");
      }
      else
```

```
                strcpy(tblname, spacer);
        strcat(tblname, qn->relations[0]->db);
        strcat(tblname, ".");
        strcat(tblname, qn->relations[0]->table_name);
        write_printf(p, tblname, "");
        write_printf(p, spacer, "       |");
        write_printf(p, spacer, "       |");
        write_printf(p, spacer, "       |");
        write_printf(p, spacer, "       V");
    }
}
else if((qn->left != 0) && (qn->right != 0))
{
    write_printf(p, spacer, "     |                           |");
    write_printf(p, spacer, "     |    ---------------------------");
    write_printf(p, spacer, "     |   |");
    write_printf(p, spacer, "     V   V");
}
else if((qn->left != 0) && (qn->right == 0))
{
    write_printf(p, spacer, "       |");
    write_printf(p, spacer, "       |");
    write_printf(p, spacer, "       |");
    write_printf(p, spacer, "       V");
}
else if(qn->right != 0)
{
}
write_printf(p, spacer, "-------------------");

/* Write out the node type */
switch(qn->node_type)
{
case Query_tree::qntProject:
    {
        write_printf(p, spacer, "|      PROJECT     |");
        write_printf(p, spacer, "-------------------");
        break;
    }
case Query_tree::qntRestrict:
    {
        write_printf(p, spacer, "|     RESTRICT     |");
        write_printf(p, spacer, "-------------------");
        break;
    }
case Query_tree::qntJoin:
    {
        write_printf(p, spacer, "|       JOIN       |");
        write_printf(p, spacer, "-------------------");
        break;
    }
```

491

```
      case Query_tree::qntDistinct:
        {
          write_printf(p, spacer, "|      DISTINCT      |");
          write_printf(p, spacer, "-------------------");
          break;
        }
      default:
        {        write_printf(p, spacer, "|      UNDEF      |");
          write_printf(p, spacer, "-------------------");
          break;
        }
      }
      write_printf(p, spacer, "| Access Method:  |");
      write_printf(p, spacer, "|     iterator    |");
      write_printf(p, spacer, "-------------------");
      if(qn == root)
      {
        write_printf(p, spacer, "           |");
        write_printf(p, spacer, "           |");
        write_printf(p, spacer, "           V");
        write_printf(p, spacer, "     Result Set");
      }
  }
  my_free(spacer);
  my_free(tblname);
  DBUG_RETURN(0);
}
```

The last things you need to do are to add the code to perform the DBXP EXPLAIN command, call the show_plan()
method, and return a result to the client. Listing 12-26 shows the complete code for this function. Notice that in this
function, I build the query tree and then create a field list using a single-character string column named "Execution
Path," and then call show_plan to write the plan to the client.

Listing 12-26. The DBXP EXPLAIN Command Source Code

```
/*
  Perform EXPLAIN command.

  SYNOPSIS
    DBXP_explain_select_command()
    THD *thd            IN the current thread

  DESCRIPTION
    This method executes the EXPLAIN SELECT command.

  RETURN VALUE
    Success = 0
    Failed = 1
*/
int DBXP_explain_select_command(THD *thd)
```

```
{
  DBUG_ENTER("DBXP_explain_select_command");
  Query_tree *qt = build_query_tree(thd, thd->lex,
                                    (TABLE_LIST*) thd->lex->select_lex.table_list.first);
  List<Item> field_list;
  Protocol *protocol= thd->protocol;
  field_list.push_back(new Item_empty_string("Execution Path",NAME_LEN));
  if (protocol->send_result_set_metadata(&field_list,
                          Protocol::SEND_NUM_ROWS | Protocol::SEND_EOF))
    DBUG_RETURN(TRUE);
  protocol->prepare_for_resend();
  show_plan(protocol, qt->root, qt->root, false);
  my_eof(thd);
  DBUG_RETURN(0);
}
```

Now, let's compile the server and give it a go with the test file.

Testing the DBXP EXPLAIN Command

As with the previous tests, you can either use the test described in an earlier section or enter a valid SQL command in the MySQL command-line client. Listing 12-27 shows an example of what the query-execution path would look like. It should be stated at this point that the query is not optimized and will appear as a single node. Once you add the optimizer (see Chapter 11), the query execution path will reflect the appropriate execution for the query statement entered.

Listing 12-27. Results of the DBXP EXPLAIN Test

```
mysql> EXPLAIN DBXP_SELECT * FROM customer;
```

```
15 rows in set (0.00 sec)

mysql>
```

This is much more interesting than a dull listing of facts. Adding the EXPLAIN command at this stage of the DBXP project allows you to witness and diagnose how the optimizer is forming the query tree. You'll find this very helpful when you begin your own experiments.

If you haven't been doing so thus far, you should run the complete test that tests all three portions of the code presented in this chapter.

Summary

I presented in this chapter some of the more complex database internal technologies. You learned how queries are represented internally within the MySQL server as they are parsed and processed via the "big switch." More important, you discovered how MySQL can be used to conduct your own database internal experiments with the query-tree class. Knowing these technologies should provide you with a greater understanding of why and how the MySQL internal components are built.

In the next chapter, I show you more about internal-query representation through an example implementation of a query-tree optimization strategy. If you've ever wondered what it takes to build an optimizer for a relational database system, the next chapter will show you an example of a heuristic query optimizer using the query tree class.

EXERCISES

The following lists represent the types of activities you might want to conduct as experiments (or as a class assignment) to explore relational-database technologies.

1. The query in Figure 12-1 exposes a design flaw in one of the tables. What is it? Does the flaw violate any of the normal forms? If so, which one?

2. Explore the TABLE structure and change the DBXP_SELECT stub to return information about the table and its fields.

3. Change the EXPLAIN DBXP_SELECT command to produce an output similar to the MySQL EXPLAIN SELECT command.

4. Modify the build_query_tree function to identify and process the LIMIT clause.

5. How can the query tree query_node structure be changed to accommodate HAVING, GROUP BY, and ORDER clauses?

CHAPTER 13

■ ■ ■

Query Optimization

The query-tree class shown in Chapter 12 forms the starting point for building the experimental-query optimization and execution engine for DBXP. In this chapter, I show you how to add the optimizer to the query-tree class. I begin by explaining the rationale for the heuristics (or rules) used in the optimizer and then jump into writing the code. Because the code for some of the functions is quite lengthy, the examples in this chapter are excerpts. If you are following along by coding the examples, download the source code for this chapter instead of typing in the code from scratch.

Types of Query Optimizers

The first query optimizers were designed for use in early database systems, such as System R[1] and INGRES.[2] These optimizers were developed for a particular implementation of the relational model, and they have stood the test of time as illustrations for how to implement optimizers. Many commercially available database systems are based on these works. Since then, optimizers have been created for extensions of the relational model to include object-oriented and distributed database systems.

One example is the Volcano optimizer, which uses a dynamic programming algorithm[3] to generate query plans for cost-based optimization in object-oriented database systems. Another example is concerned with how to perform optimization in heterogeneous database systems (similar to distributed systems, but there is no commonly shared concept of organization). In these environments, it is possible to use statistical methods for deriving optimization strategies.

Another area in which the requirements for query optimization generate unique needs is that of in-memory database systems. These systems are designed to contain the entire system and all of the data in the computer's secondary memory (i.e., disk). While most of these applications are implemented as embedded systems, some larger distributed systems that consist of a collection of systems use in-memory databases to expedite information-retrieval optimization in in-memory database systems require efficient algorithms, because the need for optimizing retrieval is insignificant compared to the need for processing the query itself.[4]

---

[1]P. G. Selinger, M. M. Astraham, D. D. Chamberlin, R. A. Lories, and T. G. Price. 1979. "Access Path Selection in a Relational Database Management System." *Proceedings of the ACM SIGMOD International Conference on the Management of Data*, Aberdeen, Scotland: 23–34. Considered by some to be the "Bible of Query Optimization."
[2]M. Stonebraker, E. Wong, P. Kreps. 1976. "The Design and Implementation of INGRES." *ACM Transactions* on Database Systems 1(3): 189–222.
[3]http://en.wikipedia.org/wiki/Dynamic_programming
[4]Query execution in traditional systems includes not only processing the query but also accessing the data from physical media. In-memory systems, however, do not have the long access times associated with retrieval from physical media.

All the research into traditional and nontraditional optimization is based on the firmament of the System R optimizer. The System R optimizer is a cost-based optimizer that uses information gathered about the database and the data, or statistics, in relation to forming cost estimates for how the query would perform. Additionally, the concept of arranging the internal representation of the query into different, but equivalent, internal representations (they generate the same answer) provides a mechanism to store the alternative forms. Each of these alternative forms is called a *query plan*. The plan with the least cost is chosen as the most efficient way to execute the query.

One key feature identified in the System R work was the concept of selectivity—the prediction of results based on the evaluation of an expression that contained references to attributes and their values. Selectivity is central to determining in what order the simple expressions in a conjunctive selection should be tested. The most selective expression (that is, the one with the smallest selectivity) will retrieve the smallest number of tuples (rows). Thus, that expression should be the basis for the first operation in a query. Conjunctive selections can be thought of as the "intersection" conditions. Conversely, disjunctive selections are the "union" conditions. Order has no effect among the disjunctive conditions.

Certain query optimizers, such as System R, do not process all possible join orders. Rather, they restrict the search to certain types of join orders that are known to produce more efficient execution. For example, multiway joins might be ordered so that the conditions that generate the fewest possible results are performed first. Similarly, the System R optimizer considers only those join orders in which the right operand of each join is one of the initial relations. Such join orders are called left-deep join orders. Left-deep join orders are particularly convenient for pipeline execution, because the right operand is normally a relation (versus an intermediate relation), and thus, only one input to each join is pipelined. The use of pipelining is a key element of the optimizer and execution engine for the database-experiment project.

Cost-Based Optimizers

A cost-based optimizer generates a range of query-evaluation plans from the given query by using the equivalence rules, and it chooses the one with the lowest cost based on the metrics (or statistics) gathered about the relations and operations needed to execute the query. For a complex query, many equivalent plans are possible.

The goal of cost-based optimization is to arrange the query execution and table access utilizing indexes and statistics gathered from past queries. Systems such as Microsoft SQL Server and Oracle use cost-based optimizers.

The portion of the database system responsible for acquiring and processing statistics (and many other utility functions) is called the *database catalog*. The catalog maintains statistics about the referenced relations and the access paths available on each of them. These will be used later in access-path selection to select the most efficient plan (with the lowest cost). For example, System R maintains statistics for each table on: the following:

- The cardinality of each relation

- The number of pages in the segment that hold tuples of each relation

- The fraction of data pages in the segment that hold tuples of relation (blocking factor, or fill)

- For each index:

  - The number of distinct keys in each index

  - The number of pages in each index

These statistics come from several sources within the system. The statistics are created when a relation is loaded and when an index is created. They are then updated periodically by a user command,[5] which can be run by any user. System R does not update these statistics in real time because of the extra database operations and the locking bottleneck that this would create at the system catalogs. Dynamic updating of statistics would tend to serialize accesses that modify the relation contents and thus limit the ability of the system to process simultaneous queries in a multiuser environment.

---

[5]This practice is still used today by most commercial database systems.

The use of statistics in cost-based optimization is not very complex. Most database professionals interviewed seem to think that the gathering and application of statistics is a complex and vital element of query optimization. Although cost-based query optimization and even hybrid optimization schemes use statistics for cost and/or ranking, the optimization schemes are neither complex nor critical. Take, for instance, the concept of evenly distributed values among attributes. This concept alone is proof of the imprecise nature of the application of statistics. Statistical calculations are largely categorical in nature, and they are not designed to generate a precise value. They merely assist in determining whether one query execution plan is usually more costly than another.

Frequency distribution of attribute values is a common method for predicting the size of query results. By forming a distribution of possible (or actual[6]) values of an attribute, the database system can use the distribution to calculate a cost for a given query plan by predicting the number of tuples (or rows) that the plan must process. Modern database systems, however, deal with frequency distributions of individual attributes only, because considering all possible combinations of attributes is very expensive. This essentially corresponds to what is known as the attribute value independence assumption, and although it rarely is true, it is adopted by almost all relational database systems.

Gathering the distribution data requires either constant updating of the statistics or predictive analysis of the data. Another tactic is the use of uniform distributions in which the distribution of the attribute values is assumed to be equal for all distinct values. For example, given 5,000 tuples and a possible 50 values for a given attribute, the uniform distribution assumes that each value is represented 100 times. This is rarely the case and is often incorrect. Given the absence of any statistics, however, it is still a reasonable approximation of reality in many cases.

The memory requirements and running time of dynamic programming grow exponentially with query size (i.e., number of joins) in the worst case, since all viable partial plans generated in each step must be stored to be used in the next one. In fact, many modern systems place a limit on the size of queries that can be submitted (usually around 15 joins), because for larger queries, the optimizer crashes due to very high memory requirements. Nevertheless, most queries seen in practice involve fewer than ten joins, and the algorithm has proved to be effective in such contexts. It is considered the standard in query-optimization search strategies. Some of the statistics gathered about rows (or tuples) in tables (or relations) for use in cost-based optimizers include:

- The number of tuples in the table

- The number of blocks containing rows (the block count)

- The size of the row in bytes

- The number of distinct values for each attribute (or column)

- The selection cardinality of each attribute (sometimes represented as evenly distributed)

- The fan-out of internal nodes of an index (the number of children resulting in subtrees)

- The height of the B-tree for an index

- The number of blocks at the leaf level of the index

The cost of writing the final result of an operation back to disk is ignored. Regardless of the query-evaluation plan used, this cost does not change; therefore, not including it in the calculations does not affect the choice of the plan.

Most database systems today use a form of dynamic programming to generate all possible query plans. While dynamic programming offers good performance for cost optimization, it is a complex algorithm that can require more resources for the more complex queries. While most database systems do not encounter these types of queries, researchers in the areas of distributed database systems and high-performance computing have explored alternatives and variants to dynamic programming techniques. The recent research by Kossmann and Stocker shows that we are beginning to see the limits of traditional approaches to query optimization.[7] What are needed are more efficient

---

[6]The accumulation of statistics in real time is called piggyback statistic generation.
[7]D. Kossman and K. Stocker. 2000. "Iterative Dynamic Programming: A New Class of Query Optimization Algorithms." *ACM Transactions on Database Systems* 25(1): 43–82.

optimization techniques that generate execution plans that follow good practices rather than exhaustive exploration. In other words, we need optimizers that perform well in a variety of general environments as well as optimizers that perform well in unique database environments.

Heuristic Optimizers

The goal of heuristic optimization is to apply rules that ensure good practices for query execution. Systems that use heuristic optimizers include INGRES and various academic variants. Most systems typically use heuristic optimization as a means of avoiding the really bad plans rather than as a primary means of optimization.

Heuristic optimizers use rules on how to shape the query into the most optimal form prior to choosing alternative implementations. The application of heuristics, or rules, can eliminate queries that are likely to be inefficient. Using heuristics as a basis to form the query plan ensures that the query plan is most likely (but not always) optimized prior to evaluation. Such heuristics include:

- Performing selection operations as early as possible. It is usually better to perform selections earlier than projections, because they reduce the number of tuples to be sent up the tree.

- Performing projections early.

- Determining which selection operations and join operations produce the smallest result set and using those first (left-most-deep).

- Replacing Cartesian products with join operations.

- Moving projection attributes as far down as possible in the tree.

- Identifying subtrees whose operations can be pipelined.

Heuristic optimizers are not new technologies. Researchers have created rules-based optimizers for various specialized purposes. One example is the Prairie rule-based query optimizer. This rule-based optimizer permits the creation of rules based on a given language notation. Queries are processed using the rules to govern how the optimizer performs. In this case, the Prairie optimizer is primarily a cost-based optimizer that uses rules to tune the optimizer.

Aside from examples such as Prairie and early primitives such as INGRES, no commercial database systems implement a purely heuristic optimizer. For those that do have a heuristic or rule-based optimization step, it is usually implemented as an addition to or as a preprocessor to a classic cost-based optimizer or as a preprocessing step in the optimization.

Semantic Optimizers

The goal of semantic optimization is to form query-execution plans that use the semantics, or topography, of the database and the relationships and indexes within to form queries that ensure the best practice available for executing a query in the given database. Semantic query optimization uses knowledge of the schema (e.g., integrity constraints) for transforming a query into a form that may be answered more efficiently than the original version.

Although not yet implemented in commercial database systems as the primary optimization technique, semantic optimization is currently the focus of considerable research. Semantic optimization operates on the premise that the optimizer has a basic understanding of the actual database schema. When a query is submitted, the optimizer uses its knowledge of system constraints to simplify or to ignore a particular query if it is guaranteed to return an empty result set. This technique holds great promise for providing even more improvements to query-processing efficiency in future relational database systems.

Parametric Optimizers

Ioannidis, in his work on parametric query optimization, describes a query-optimization method that combines the application of heuristic methods with cost-based optimization. The resulting query optimizer provides a means to produce a smaller set of effective query plans from which cost can be estimated, and thus, the lowest-cost plan of the set can be executed.[8] Query-plan generation is created using a random algorithm, called sipR. This permits systems that utilize parametric query optimization to choose query plans that can include the uncertainty of parameter changes (such as buffer sizes) to choose optimal plans either formed on the fly or from storage.

It is interesting to note that in his work, Ioannidis suggests that the use of dynamic programming algorithms may not be needed, and thus the overhead in using these techniques can be avoided. Furthermore, he found that database systems that use heuristics to prune or shape the query prior to applying dynamic programming algorithms for query optimization are usually an enhanced version of the original algorithm of System R. Ioannidis showed that for small queries (approximately up to 10 joins), dynamic programming is superior to randomized algorithms, whereas for large queries, the opposite holds true.

Heuristic Optimization Revisited

The heuristic-optimization process uses a set of rules that have been defined to guarantee good execution plans. Thus, the effectiveness of a heuristic optimizer to produce good plans is based solely on the effectiveness and completeness of its rules.

The following paragraphs describe the rules used to create the DBXP query optimizer. Although these rules are very basic, when they are applied to typical queries, the resulting execution is near optimal, with fast performance and accurate results.

Some basic strategies were used to construct the query tree initially. Specifically, all executions take place in the query-tree node. Restrictions and projections are processed on a branch and do not generate intermediate relations. Joins are always processed as an intersection of two paths. A multiway join would be formed using a series of two-way joins. The following rules represent the best practices for forming a set of heuristics to generate good execution plans. The DBXP optimizer is designed to apply these rules in order to transform the query tree into a form that ensures efficient execution.[9]

1. Split any nodes that contain a project and join or restrict and join. This step is necessary because some queries specify the join condition in the WHERE clause[10] and thus can "fool" the optimizer into forming join nodes that have portions of the expressions that are not part of the join condition.

2. Push all restrictions down the tree to leaves. Expressions are grouped according to their respective relations into individual query-tree nodes. Although some complex expressions cannot be reduced, most can be easily reduced to a single relation. By placing the restrictions at the leaves, the number of resulting tuples that must be passed up the tree is reduced.

3. Place all projections at the lowest point in the tree. Projections should be placed in a node above restrictions, and they will further reduce the amount of data passed through the tree by eliminating unneeded attributes from the resulting tuples. It should be noted that the projections may be modified to include attributes that are needed for operations, such as joins that reside in the parentage of the projection query tree node.

---

[8]Y. E. Ioannidis, R. T. Ng, K. Shim, and T. Sellis. 1997. "Parametric Query Optimization." *VLDB Journal* 6:132–151.
[9]In this case, efficient execution may not be the optimal solution.
[10]A common technique practiced by novice database users.

4. Place all joins at intersections of projections or restrictions of the relations contained in the join clause.[11] This ensures that the fewest amount of tuples are evaluated for the most expensive operation—joins. Intermediate query-tree nodes that order the resulting tuples from the child nodes may be necessary. These intermediate nodes, called utility operations, may sort or group the tuples depending on the type of join, and they can greatly increase the performance of the join.

■ **Note** Other heuristics can be used. The previous list contains those that generate the greatest gain in performance.

Lee, Shih, and Chen give an interesting counterargument to the practice of pushing selections and restrictions down the tree.[12] They suggest that under some conditions, some selections and projections may be more costly than joins. Their argument presents a query optimizer based on graph theory that can more accurately predict query optimization for situations in which complex selects and projections are present. Nevertheless, the general case is that "efficient" execution plans can be constructed for the majority of queries using the rules I've listed.

The DBXP Query Optimizer

Although these rules offer a complete set of operations for forming the optimal query tree, they do not address balancing multiway joins or applying indexes. These steps are considered cost-based optimizations. For this reason, most heuristic optimizers are implemented as a two-phase optimization, with the first pass generating an optimized query path and a second pass applying cost-optimization strategies.

■ **Note** DBXP optimizer is implemented as a two-pass operation. The first operation rearranges the tree for execution using a heuristic algorithm. The second pass walks the tree, changing the access method for nodes that have relations with indexes available on the attributes being operated on. I leave the implementation of the cost-optimization pass as an exercise for the reader.

Creating comprehensive tests for a heuristic optimizer would require writing SQL statements that cover all possible paths through the optimizer. In essence, you need to create a test that tests all possible queries, both valid and invalid (invalid queries are normally captured in the SQL parser code). Implementing the heuristic optimizer is only the second part of the DBXP engine, however. In the previous chapter, we created the basic query-tree internal representation and stubbed the execution methods. In this chapter, we will create the optimizer but will not be able to execute the queries. You can continue to use the stubbed execution to test the optimizer but, rather than presenting the results of the queries, you can reuse the code from the previous chapter to show the query plan instead of the query results.

With this in mind, let's design a few basic queries that exercise the optimizer to show it is processing the queries. We take care of query execution in the next chapter. Listing 13-1 shows a sample test that exercises the query optimizer.

---

[11] May disallow the use of indexes for the join operation.
[12] C. Lee, C. Shih, and Y. Chen. 2001. "A Graph-Theoretic Model for Optimizing Queries Involving Methods." V*LDB Journal* 9:327–343.

Listing 13-1. Sample DBXP Query-optimizer Test (Ch13.test)

```
#
# Sample test to test the DBXP_SELECT optimizer
#

# Test 1:
DBXP_SELECT * FROM staff;

# Test 2:
DBXP_SELECT id FROM staff WHERE staff.id = '123456789';

# Test 3:
DBXP_SELECT id, dir_name FROM staff, directorate
WHERE staff.dno = directorate.dnumber;

# Test 4:
DBXP_SELECT * FROM staff JOIN tasking ON staff.id = tasking.id
WHERE staff.id = '123456789';
```

▥ **Tip**　The database used in these examples is included in the Appendix.

You can use this test as a guide and add your own commands to explore the new code. Please refer to Chapter 4 for more details on how to create and run this test using the MySQL Test Suite.

Stubbing the DBXP_SELECT Command

Since there is no query-execution capability, the query commands can be optimized but not executed. The show plan mechanism (the EXPLAIN command) can serve as a means to demonstrate the optimizer. To add this functionality, you can open the sql_dbxp_parse.cc file and alter the DBXP_select_command() method as shown in Listing 13-2.

Listing 13-2. Stubbing the Query Optimizer for Testing

```
int DBXP_explain_select_command(THD *thd);

/*
  Perform DBXP_SELECT Command

  SYNOPSIS
    DBXP_select_command()
    THD *thd            IN the current thread

  DESCRIPTION
    This method executes the SELECT command using the query tree and optimizer.
```

```
    RETURN VALUE
      Success = 0
      Failed = 1
*/
int DBXP_select_command(THD *thd)
{
  DBUG_ENTER("DBXP_select_command");
  DBXP_explain_select_command(thd);
  DBUG_RETURN(0);
}
```

These changes alter the code to call the EXPLAIN command code rather than executing the query. This allows the tests to return a valid result set (the query plan) so that we can test the optimizer without the query execution portion.

■ **Note**   I use a function declaration above the DBXP_select_command() method. This allows the code to call forward to the DBXP_explain_select_command() method without using a header file.

There is also a change necessary to the DBXP_explain_select_command() method. You need to add the call to the new optimize methods. This includes the heuristic_optimization() and cost_optimization() methods. I discuss the heuristic optimization in more detail in the following sections. Listing 13-3 shows the modifications to the EXPLAIN code.

Listing 13-3. Modifications to the EXPLAIN Command Code

```
/*
  Perform EXPLAIN command.

  SYNOPSIS
    DBXP_explain_select_command()
    THD *thd              IN the current thread

  DESCRIPTION
    This method executes the EXPLAIN SELECT command.

  RETURN VALUE
    Success = 0
    Failed = 1
*/
int DBXP_explain_select_command(THD *thd)
{
  bool res= 0;

  DBUG_ENTER("DBXP_explain_select_command");

  /* Prepare the tables (check access, locks) */
  res = check_table_access(thd, SELECT_ACL, thd->lex->query_tables, 0, 1, 1);
  if (res)
    DBUG_RETURN(1);
```

```
res = open_and_lock_tables(thd, thd->lex->query_tables, 0,
                           MYSQL_LOCK_IGNORE_TIMEOUT);
if (res)
  DBUG_RETURN(1);

/* Create the query tree and optimize it */
Query_tree *qt = build_query_tree(thd, thd->lex,
        (TABLE_LIST*) thd->lex->select_lex.table_list.first);
qt->heuristic_optimization();
qt->cost_optimization();

/* create a field list for returning the query plan */
List<Item> field_list;

/* use the protocol class to communicate to client */
Protocol *protocol= thd->protocol;

/* write the field to the client */
field_list.push_back(new Item_empty_string("Execution Path",NAME_LEN));
if (protocol->send_result_set_metadata(&field_list,
                         Protocol::SEND_NUM_ROWS | Protocol::SEND_EOF))
  DBUG_RETURN(TRUE);
protocol->prepare_for_resend();

/* generate the query plan and send it to client */
show_plan(protocol, qt->root, qt->root, false);
my_eof(thd); /* end of file tells client no more data is coming */

/* unlock tables and cleanup memory */
mysql_unlock_read_tables(thd, thd->lock);
delete qt;
DBUG_RETURN(0);
}
```

Important MySQL Structures and Classes

There are a number of key structures and classes in the MySQL source code. You have already seen many of them in the examples thus far. Some of the more important ones are documented in the MySQL Internals manual. Unfortunately, no document lists them all. The following sections describe some of these structures and classes that you will encounter when working with the DBXP query optimizer (and later, the query execution code). These include the TABLE structure, the Field class, and a few of the common Item iterators (the Item class is discussed in Chapter 3).

TABLE Structure

The most important MySQL structure that you will work with when writing the optimizer is the TABLE structure.

This structure is important, because it contains all pertinent data for a table. It contains everything from a pointer to the appropriate storage-handler class to a list of the fields, keys, and temporary buffers for storing rows while executing the query.

While the structure is immense (like most important structures in MySQL), you will see a few key attributes over and over. Table 13-1 lists some of the more important attributes for the TABLE structure. For a detailed examination of the TABLE structure, see the handler.h file.

Table 13-1. *TABLE Structure Overview*

Attribute	Description
file	A reference to the storage-engine object.
field	An array of fields for the table.
fields	The number of fields in the field array.
next	A pointer to the next table in a list of tables.
prev	A pointer to the previous table in a list of tables.

The Field Class

The Field class contains all the attributes and methods for creating, assigning values to, and manipulating fields (or attributes) for the tables in the database. The Field class is defined in the /sql/field.h file and implemented in the /sql/field.cc file. The Field class is actually a base from which several types of fields are derived. These derived classes, named Field_XXX, can be found in several places within the MySQL source code.

Since it is only a base class,[13] many methods in the class are intended to be overwritten by the derived class (they're defined as virtual). Many of the derived classes have the same set of basic attributes and methods, however. Table 13-2 lists the attributes and methods that you will encounter in working with the DBXP source code. For a detailed examination of the Field class, see the field.h file.

Table 13-2. *The Field Class*

Attribute/Method	Description
ptr	A pointer to the field within the record buffer.
null_ptr	A pointer to a byte (or bytes) in the record buffer that indicates which attributes can contain NULL.
table_name	The table name associated with this field.
field_name	The attribute name for this field.
field_length	The length of the field. Indicates the number of bytes that can be stored.
is_null()	Checks to see if the field is NULL.
move_field()	Changes the pointer of the field in memory to point to a different location.
store()	A series of overloaded methods used to store values into the fields.
val_str()	Gets the value of the field as a string.
val_int()	Gets the value of the field as an integer.
result_type()	Gets the data type of the field.
cmp()	Returns the comparison result of the field with the value passed.

---

[13]It isn't a true abstract class, because it contains some methods that are defined in the source code. A true abstract class defines all methods as virtual and therefore they are used as interfaces rather than base classes.

Iterators

There are three types of iterators in the MySQL source code. You have already seen these iterators while working with the code in previous chapters. Iterators are special constructs that make it easy to create and navigate a list of objects, and they are typically presented as either linked lists or arrays. The iterators in MySQL are implemented as template classes, which take as a parameter the type of the data on which the list operates. The MySQL iterators are linked lists, but some behave more like queues and stacks. The following sections describe some of the available iterator classes in MySQL. These iterators are defined in the sql/sql_list.h header file.

template <> class List

The List template class is implemented as a queue or stack with methods for pushing items onto the back of the list using the push_back() method or on the front of the list using the push_front() method. Items can be retrieved using the pop() method or deleted by using the remove() method. You can loop through the list by using the next attribute of the data item, but the list is usually used to form a linked list of items (e.g., List<Item> item_list), and then one of the List_iterator classes is used to loop through the list quickly. This class is derived from the base_list class (also defined in /sql/sql_list.h).

template <> class List_iterator

The List_iterator class is implemented as a linked list with methods for moving through the list using the overloaded ++ operator. Items can be retrieved using the ref() method or deleted by using the remove() method. The list can be restarted from the front by issuing the rewind() method. This class is derived from the base_list class (also defined in /sql/sql_list.h).

template <> class List_iterator_fast

The List_iterator_fast class is essentially the same as the List_iterator class, but it is optimized for fast-forward traversal. It is implemented as a linked list with methods for moving through the list using the overloaded ++ operator. Items can be retrieved using the ref() method or deleted by using the remove() method. This class is derived from the base_list class (also defined in /sql/sql_list.h).

Examples

Using the iterators is easy. If you want to use a list to manipulate items, a simple list, such as the List<Item_field>, would be the best choice. If you want to loop through a list of fields quickly, you can create a list iterator as either a List_iterator<Item_field> or a List_iterator_fast<Item_field>. Examples of loop structures are shown in Listing 13-4.

Listing 13-4. Example Iterators

```
/* create a list and populate with some items */
List<Item> item_list;
item_list.push_back(new Item_int((int32)
        join->select_lex->select_number));
item_list.push_back(new Item_string(join->select_lex->type,
  strlen(join->select_lex->type), cs));
item_list.push_back(new Item_string(message,strlen(message),cs));
```

```
../* start a basic list iterator to iterate through the item_list */
  List_iterator<Item_field> item_list_it(*item_list);

  /* control the iteration using an offset */
  while ((curr_item= item_list_it++))
  {
    /* do something */
  }

../* start a fast list iterator to iterate through the item_list */
  List_iterator_fast<Item_field> li(item_equal->fields);

  /* control the iteration using an offset */
  while ((item= li++))
  {
    /* do something */
  }
```

The DBXP Helper Classes

I mentioned in Chapter 11 two additional classes used in the DBXP engine (Attribute and Expression). These classes are designed to make the optimizer easier to code and easier to understand. They are encapsulations of the existing MySQL classes (and structures), and they reuse many of the methods available in the MySQL code.

The first helper class is a class that encapsulates the attributes used in a query. These attributes are represented in the MySQL code as the Item class. The helper class, named Attribute, makes access to these classes easier by providing a common interface for accessing items. Listing 13-5 shows the header file for the Attribute class.

Listing 13-5. The Attribute Class Header

```
#include "sql_priv.h"
#include "sql_class.h"
#include "table.h"

class Attribute
{
public:
  Attribute(void);
  int remove_attribute(int num);
  Item *get_attribute(int num);
  int add_attribute(bool append, Item *new_item);
  int num_attributes();
  int index_of(char *table, char *value);
  int hide_attribute(Item *item, bool hide);
  char *to_string();
private:
  List<Item> attr_list;
  bool hidden[256];
};
```

The second helper class encapsulates the expressions used in a query. Like the attributes, the expressions are represented in the MySQL code as Item class instances. The helper class, named Expression, provides a common (and simplified) interface to the Item classes. Listing 13-6 shows the header file for the Expression class.

Listing 13-6. The Expression Class Header

```
#include "sql_priv.h"
#include "sql_class.h"
#include "table.h"
#include <sql_string.h>

struct expr_node
{
  Item      *left_op;
  Item      *operation;
  Item      *right_op;
  Item      *junction;
  expr_node *next;
};

class Expression
{
public:
  Expression(void);
  int remove_expression(int num, bool free);
  expr_node *get_expression(int num);
  int add_expression(bool append, expr_node *new_item);
  int num_expressions();
  int index_of(char *table, char *value);
  int reduce_expressions(TABLE *table);
  bool has_table(char *table);
  int convert(THD *thd, Item *mysql_expr);
  char *to_string();
  bool evaluate(TABLE *table 1);
  int compare_join(expr_node *expr, TABLE *t1, TABLE *t2);
  int get_join_expr(Expression *where_expr);
private:
  expr_node *root;
  Field *find_field(TABLE *tbl, char *name);
  bool compare(expr_node *expr, TABLE *t1);
  int num_expr;
};
```

I use a structure to contain the expressions in the form of left operand, operator, and right operand. This is a more simplified approach than the expression tree that the MySQL classes represents, making it easier to read the optimizer code. The simpler approach also makes it easier to evaluate the conditions in an interactive debugger.

■ **Note**　I omit some of the details of these helper classes in the text, because they are very simple abstractions of calling the MySQL methods for the TABLE structure and the Item and Field classes. The files are included in the online chapter source code, however. The source code for this book is available for download at http://www.apress.com in the Source Code section.

These helper class and header files should be placed in the /sql directory and added to your CMakeLists.txt file. I show you how to do that in the "Compiling and Testing the Code" section.

Modifications to the Existing Code

There is one other minor modification necessary to implement the optimizer: we need to add the code to use the new Attribute and Expression classes. Open the query_tree.h header file and make the changes shown in Listing 13-7. As you can see, I've changed the where_expr and join_expr attributes to use the new Expression class. Likewise, I changed the attributes attribute to use the new Attribute class.

Listing 13-7. Changes to the Query Tree Class

```
#include "attribute.h"
#include "expression.h"
#include "sql_priv.h"
#include "sql_class.h"
#include "table.h"
#include "records.h"

const int MAXNODETABLES = 4;
const int LEFTCHILD = 0;
const int RIGHTCHILD = 1;

class Query_tree
{
public:
  enum query_node_type          //this enumeration lists the available
  {                             //query node (operations)
    qntUndefined = 0,
    qntRestrict = 1,
    qntProject = 2,
    qntJoin = 3,
    qntSort = 4,
    qntDistinct = 5
  };

  enum join_con_type            //this enumeration lists the available
  {                             //join operations supported
    jcUN = 0,
    jcNA = 1,
    jcON = 2,
    jcUS = 3
  };

  enum type_join                //this enumeration lists the available
  {                             //join types supported.
    jnUNKNOWN      = 0,         //undefined
    jnINNER        = 1,
    jnLEFTOUTER    = 2,
    jnRIGHTOUTER   = 3,
```

```
    jnFULLOUTER    = 4,
    jnCROSSPRODUCT = 5,
    jnUNION        = 6,
    jnINTERSECT    = 7
};

    enum AggregateType          //used to add aggregate functions
    {
        atNONE      = 0,
        atCOUNT     = 1
    };

/*
    STRUCTURE query_node

    DESCRIPTION
      This this structure contains all of the data for a query node:

      NodeId -- the internal id number for a node
      ParentNodeId -- the internal id for the parent node (used for insert)
      SubQuery -- is this the start of a subquery?
      Child -- is this a Left or Right child of the parent?
      NodeType -- synonymous with operation type
      JoinType -- if a join, this is the join operation
      join_con_type -- if this is a join, this is the "on" condition
      Expressions -- the expressions from the "where" clause for this node
      Join Expressions -- the join expressions from the "join" clause(s)
      Relations[] -- the relations for this operation (at most 2)
      PreemptPipeline -- does the pipeline need to be halted for a sort?
      Fields -- the attributes for the result set of this operation
      Left -- a pointer to the left child node
      Right -- a pointer to the right child node
*/
  struct query_node
  {
    query_node();
    ~query_node();
    int                nodeid;
    int                parent_nodeid;
    bool               sub_query;
    int                child;
    query_node_type    node_type;
    type_join          join_type;
    join_con_type      join_cond;
    Expression         *where_expr;
    Expression         *join_expr;
    TABLE_LIST         *relations[MAXNODETABLES];
    int                eof[MAXNODETABLES];
    int                ndx[MAXNODETABLES];
    bool               preempt_pipeline;
    Attribute          *attributes;
```

```
    query_node          *left;
    query_node          *right;
};

  struct record_buff
  {
    uchar *field_ptr;
    long field_length;
    record_buff *next;
    record_buff *prev;
    READ_RECORD *record;
  };
```

A number of methods also need to be added to the query-tree class. Instead of describing the details of every method and its implementation, I have included the rest of the query-tree definition in Listing 13-8. This code is also added to the query_tree.h file.

Listing 13-8. New Methods for the Query-tree Class

```
  query_node *root;                 //The ROOT node of the tree

  Query_tree(void);
  ~Query_tree(void);
  int init_node(query_node *qn);
  int heuristic_optimization();
  int cost_optimization();
  int insert_attribute(query_node *qn, Item *c);
  bool distinct;
  int prepare(query_node *qn);
  int cleanup(query_node *qn);
  bool Eof(query_node *qn);
  READ_RECORD *get_next(query_node *qn);
  List <Item> result_fields;

private:
  bool h_opt;              //has query been optimized (rules)?
  bool c_opt;              //has query been optimized (cost)?
  READ_RECORD *lbuff;
  READ_RECORD *rbuff;
  record_buff *left_record_buff;
  record_buff *right_record_buff;
  record_buff *left_record_buffer_ptr;
  record_buff *right_record_buffer_ptr;

  int push_projections(query_node *qn, query_node *pNode);
  query_node *find_projection(query_node *qn);
  bool is_leaf(query_node *qn);
  bool has_relation(query_node *qn, char *Table);
  bool has_attribute(query_node *qn, Item *a);
  int del_attribute(query_node *qn, Item *a);
  int push_restrictions(query_node *qn, query_node *pNode);
  query_node *find_restriction(query_node *qn);
```

```
    query_node *find_join(query_node *qn);
    int push_joins(query_node *qn, query_node *pNode);
    int prune_tree(query_node *prev, query_node *cur_node);
    int balance_joins(query_node *qn);
    int split_restrict_with_project(query_node *qn);
    int split_restrict_with_join(query_node *qn);
    int split_project_with_join(query_node *qn);
    bool find_table_in_tree(query_node *qn, char *tbl);
    bool find_table_in_expr(Expression *expr, char *tbl);
    bool find_attr_in_expr(Expression *expr, char *tbl, char *value);
    int apply_indexes(query_node *qn);
    bool do_restrict(query_node *qn, READ_RECORD *t);
    READ_RECORD *do_project(query_node *qn, READ_RECORD *t);
    READ_RECORD *do_join(query_node *qn);
    int find_index_in_expr(Expression *e, char *tbl);
    TABLE *get_table(query_node *qn);
    int insertion_sort(bool left, Field *field, READ_RECORD *rcd);
    int check_rollback(record_buff *cur_left, record_buff *curr_left_prev,
        record_buff *cur_right, record_buff *cur_right_prev);
};
```

Notice that there are several public methods, including heuristic_optimization() and cost_optimization(). I have also added a public attribute, distinct, that you can use to assist in implementing the distinct operation (see the exercises at the end of the chapter). The rest of the methods are the helper methods for the optimization code. I explain some of the more interesting ones and leave the mundane for you to explore.

Now that we have some helper classes to make the optimizer easier to implement, we need to incorporate them into the translation code that translates the MySQL internal-query representation to the DBXP query tree. Open the sql_dbxp_parse.cc file and locate the build_query_tree() method. Listing 13-9 shows the changes necessary to add the new Attribute and Expression classes.

Listing 13-9. Changes to the Build-query-tree Method

```
/*
  Build Query Tree

  SYNOPSIS
    build_query_tree()
    THD *thd               IN the current thread
    LEX *lex               IN the pointer to the current parsed structure
    TABLE_LIST *tables     IN the list of tables identified in the query

  DESCRIPTION
    This method returns a converted MySQL internal representation (IR) of a
    query as a query_tree.

  RETURN VALUE
    Success = Query_tree * -- the root of the new query tree.
    Failed = NULL
*/
Query_tree *build_query_tree(THD *thd, LEX *lex, TABLE_LIST *tables)
```

```
{
  DBUG_ENTER("build_query_tree");
  Query_tree *qt = new Query_tree();
  Query_tree::query_node *qn =
    (Query_tree::query_node *)my_malloc(sizeof(Query_tree::query_node),
    MYF(MY_ZEROFILL | MY_WME));
  TABLE_LIST *table;
  int i = 0;
  Item *w;
  int num_tables = 0;

  /* create a new restrict node */
  qn->parent_nodeid = -1;
  qn->child = false;
  qn->join_type = (Query_tree::type_join) 0;
  qn->nodeid = 0;
  qn->node_type = (Query_tree::query_node_type) 2;
  qn->left = NULL;
  qn->right = NULL;
  qn->attributes = new Attribute();
  qn->where_expr = new Expression();
  qn->join_expr = new Expression();

  /* Get the tables (relations) */
  i = 0;
  for(table = tables; table; table = table->next_local)
  {
    num_tables++;
    qn->relations[i] = table;
    i++;
  }

  /* prepare the fields (find associated tables) for query */
  List <Item> all_fields;
  Name_resolution_context context;
  List_iterator <Item> it(thd->lex->select_lex.item_list);
  it++;
  if (lex->select_lex.with_wild)
  {
    bool found = FALSE;
    Field_iterator_table_ref field_iterator;
    for(table = tables; table; table = table->next_local)
    {
      field_iterator.set(table);
      for (; !field_iterator.end_of_fields(); field_iterator.next())
      {
        Item *item= field_iterator.create_item(thd);
        if (!found)
        {
          found= TRUE;
          it.replace(item); /* Replace '*' with the first found item. */
        }
```

```
        else
        {
          it.after(item);    /* Add 'item' to the SELECT list. */
        }
      }
    }
  }
if (setup_fields(thd, lex->select_lex.ref_pointer_array,
                   lex->select_lex.item_list, thd->mark_used_columns,
                   &all_fields, 1))
    DBUG_RETURN(NULL);
  qt->result_fields = lex->select_lex.item_list;

  /* get the attributes from the raw query */
  w = lex->select_lex.item_list.pop();
  while (w != 0)
  {
    uint unused_field_idx= NO_CACHED_FIELD_INDEX;
    TABLE_LIST *dummy;
    Field *f = NULL;
    for(table = tables; table; table = table->next_local)
    {
      f = find_field_in_table_ref(thd, table, ((Field *)w)->field_name,
                             strlen(((Field *)w)->field_name),
                             ((Field *)w)->field_name, NULL, NULL, NULL,
                             FALSE, FALSE, &unused_field_idx, FALSE,
                             &dummy);
      if (f)
      {
        qn->attributes->add_attribute(true, (Item *)f);
        break;
      }
    }
    w = lex->select_lex.item_list.pop();
  }

  /* get the joins from the raw query */
  if (num_tables > 0)  //indicates more than 1 table processed
    for(table = tables; table; table = table->next_local)
    {
      if (table->join_cond() != 0)
        qn->join_expr->convert(thd, (Item *)table->join_cond());
    }

  /* get the expressions for the where clause */
  qn->where_expr->convert(thd, lex->select_lex.where);

  /* get the join conditions for the joins */
  qn->join_expr->get_join_expr(qn->where_expr);
```

```
  /* if there is a where clause, set node to restrict */
  if (qn->where_expr->num_expressions() > 0)
    qn->node_type = (Query_tree::query_node_type) 1;

  qt->root = qn;
  DBUG_RETURN(qt);
}
```

At this point, the include files need adjusting to ensure that we're including everything needed to compile the code. For example, the following statements appear at the top of the query_tree.cc file:

```
#include "query_tree.h"
```

The query_tree.h header file includes the attribute and expression header files as well as the needed MySQL includes files using the following.

```
#include "query_tree.h"
#include "sql_base.h"
#include "sql_acl.h"
#include "sql_parse.h"
#include "lock.h"
```

■ **Caution** If you encounter strange errors while compiling, check that you are not including the attribute, expression, and query_tree header files in your CMakeLists.txt file. The compiler will automatically include these files by following the include directives.

Details of the Heuristic Optimizer

The heuristic optimizer is implemented using the model of the rules described earlier. The methods used in the heuristic optimizer each implement some or all the rules. These methods are listed in Table 13-3.

Table 13-3. Heuristic Methods in the Heuristic Optimizer

Method	Description
split_restrict_with_join()	Searches the tree for nodes that have a restriction (has expressions) and a join expression. It divides the node into two nodes: one for the restriction and one for the join.
split_project_with_join()	Searches the tree for nodes that have a projection (has attributes) and a join expression. It divides the node into two nodes: one for the projection and one for the join.
split_restrict_with_project()	Searches the tree for nodes that have a restriction (has expressions) and a projection (has attributes). It divides the node into two nodes: one for the restriction and one for the projection.
find_restriction()	Searches the tree for a restriction node that is not already at a leaf.

(*continued*)

Table 13-3. (*continued*)

Method	Description
push_restrictions()	Pushes the restrictions down the tree to the lowest node possible. It looks for situations in which the restriction can reside at a leaf. This method is used with find_restrictions() in a loop (the loop ends when no more restrictions that are not already at a leaf are found).
find_projection()	Searches the tree for a projection node that is not already at a leaf.
push_projections()	Pushes the projections down the tree to the lowest node possible. It looks for situations in which the projection can reside at a leaf or as a parent of a restriction. This method is used with find_projections() in a loop (the loop ends when no more projections are found that are not already at a leaf or the parent of a leaf that is a restriction).
find_join()	Searches the tree for a join node.
push_joins()	Pushes the joins down the tree to the nodes as parents to qualifying restrictions and/or projections (those that operate on the tables in the join).
prune_tree()	Identifies nodes in the tree that have been optimized away and are no longer valid (no attributes or expressions and not a join or sort), and deletes them.

The implementation of the heuristic optimizer reads very easily. Listing 13-10 shows the source-code implementation for the `heuristic_optimization()` method.

Listing 13-10. The DBXP Heuristic-optimization Method[14]

```
/*
  Perform heuristic optimization

  SYNOPSIS
    heuristic_optimization()

  DESCRIPTION
    This method performs heuristic optimization on the query tree. The
    operation is destructive in that it rearranges the original tree.

  RETURN VALUE
    Success = 0
    Failed = 1
*/
int Query_tree::heuristic_optimization()
{
  DBUG_ENTER("heuristic_optimization");
  query_node       *pNode;
  query_node       *nNode;
```

---

[14]The sentinel value in this code is derived from a classic rock album. Do you know the name of the band?

```
h_opt = true;
/*
  First, we have to correct the situation where restrict and
  project are grouped together in the same node.
*/
split_restrict_with_join(root);
split_project_with_join(root);
split_restrict_with_project(root);

/*
  Find a node with restrictions and push down the tree using
  a recursive call. continue until you get the same node twice.
  This means that the node cannot be pushed down any further.
*/
pNode = find_restriction(root);
while(pNode != 0)
{
  push_restrictions(root, pNode);
  nNode = find_restriction(root);
  /*
    If a node is found, save a reference to it unless it is
    either the same node as the last node found or
    it is a leaf node. This is done so that we can ensure we
    continue searching down the tree visiting each node once.
  */
  if(nNode != 0)
  {
    if(nNode->nodeid == pNode->nodeid)
      pNode = 0;
    else if(is_leaf(nNode))
      pNode = 0;
    else
      pNode = nNode;
  }
}

/*
  Find a node with projections and push down the tree using
  a recursive call. Continue until you get the same node twice.
  This means that the node cannot be pushed down any further.
*/
pNode = find_projection(root);
while(pNode != 0)
{
  push_projections(root, pNode);
  nNode = find_projection(root);
  /*
    If a node is found, save a reference to it unless it is
    either the same node as the last node found or
    it is a leaf node. This is done so that we can ensure we
    continue searching down the tree visiting each node once.
  */
```

```
    if(nNode != 0)
    {
      if(nNode->nodeid == pNode->nodeid)
        pNode = 0;
      else if(is_leaf(nNode))
        pNode = 0;
      else
        pNode = nNode;
    }
}


/*
  Find a join node and push it down the tree using
  a recursive call. Continue until you get the same node twice.
  This means that the node cannot be pushed down any further.
*/
pNode = find_join(root);
while(pNode != 0)
{
  push_joins(root, pNode);
  nNode = find_join(root);
  /*
    If a node is found, save a reference to it unless it is
    either the same node as the last node found or
    it is a leaf node. This is done so that we can ensure we
    continue searching down the tree visiting each node once.
  */
  if(nNode != 0)
  {
    if(nNode->nodeid == pNode->nodeid)
      pNode = 0;
    else if(is_leaf(nNode))
      pNode = 0;
    else
      pNode = nNode;
  }
  else
    pNode = nNode;
}


/*
  Prune the tree of "blank" nodes
  Blank Nodes are:
   1) projections without attributes that have at least 1 child
   2) restrictions without expressions
   BUT...Can't delete a node that has TWO children!
*/
prune_tree(0, root);
```

```
/*
  Lastly, check to see if this has the DISTINCT option.
  If so, create a new node that is a DISTINCT operation.
*/
if(distinct && (root->node_type != qntDistinct))
{
  int i;
  pNode = (query_node*)my_malloc(sizeof(query_node),
          MYF(MY_ZEROFILL | MY_WME));
  init_node(pNode);
  pNode->sub_query = 0;
  pNode->attributes = 0;
  pNode->join_cond = jcUN;  /* (join_con_type) 0; */
  pNode->join_type = jnUNKNOWN;  /* (type_join) 0; */
  pNode->left = root;
  pNode->right = 0;
  for(i = 0; i < MAXNODETABLES; i++)
    pNode->relations[i] = NULL;
  pNode->nodeid = 90125;  // sentinel value to indicate node is not set
  pNode->child = LEFTCHILD;
  root->parent_nodeid = 90125;  // sentinel value to indicate node is not set
  root->child = LEFTCHILD;
  pNode->parent_nodeid = -1;
  pNode->node_type = qntDistinct;
  pNode->attributes = new Attribute();
  pNode->where_expr = new Expression();
  pNode->join_expr = new Expression();
  root = pNode;
}
DBUG_RETURN(0);
}
```

Notice the loops for locating restrictions, projections, and joins. The code is designed to walk through the tree using a preorder traversal, applying the rules until there are no more conditions that violate the rules (i.e., no "bad" node placements).

The following listings show some of the source code for the major methods in the heuristic_optimization() method as described earlier. To save space, I omitted listing the lesser helper methods, because they are simple abstractions of the MySQL structure and class methods. You should download the source code for this chapter and examine the other helper methods to see how they work.

The split_restrict_with_join() method searches the tree for joins that have where expressions (thus are both joins and restrictions) and breaks them into two nodes: a join and a restrict node. Listing 13-11 shows the source code for this method.

Listing 13-11. Split Restrict With Join

```
/*
  Split restrictions that have joins.

  SYNOPSIS
    split_restrict_with_join()
    query_node *QN IN the node to operate on
```

DESCRIPTION
    This method looks for joins that have where expressions (thus are both
    joins and restrictions) and breaks them into two nodes.

NOTES
    This is a RECURSIVE method!

RETURN VALUE
    Success = 0
    Failed = 1
*/
```cpp
int Query_tree::split_restrict_with_join(query_node *QN)
{
  int j = 0;
  int i = 0;

  DBUG_ENTER("split_restrict_with_join");
  if(QN != 0)
  {
    if(((QN->join_expr->num_expressions() > 0) &&
      (QN->where_expr->num_expressions() > 0)) &&
       ((QN->node_type == qntJoin) || (QN->node_type == qntRestrict)))
    {
      bool isleft = true;
      /*
        Create a new node and:
          1) Move the where expressions to the new node.
          2) Set the new node's children = current node children
          3) Set the new node's relations = current node relations.
          4) Set current node's left or right child = new node;
          5) Set new node's id = current id + 200;
          6) set parent id, etc.
          7) determine which table needs to be used for the
             restrict node.
      */
      query_node *new_node = (query_node*)my_malloc(sizeof(query_node),
                        MYF(MY_ZEROFILL | MY_WME));
      init_node(new_node);
      new_node->node_type = qntRestrict;
      new_node->parent_nodeid = QN->nodeid;
      new_node->nodeid = QN->nodeid + 200;
      new_node->where_expr = QN->where_expr;
      new_node->join_expr = new Expression();
      QN->where_expr = new Expression();

      /*
        Loop through tables and move table that matches
        to the new node
      */
      for(i = 0; i < MAXNODETABLES; i++)
```

```
  {
    if (QN->relations[i] != NULL)
    {
      if (find_table_in_expr(new_node->where_expr,
            QN->relations[i]->table_name))
      {
        new_node->relations[j] = QN->relations[i];
        j++;
        if (i != 0)
          isleft = false;
        QN->relations[i] = NULL;
      }
    }
  }

  /* set children to point to balance of tree */
  new_node->right = 0;
  if (isleft)
  {
    new_node->child = LEFTCHILD;
    new_node->left = QN->left;
    QN->left = new_node;
  }
  else
  {
    new_node->child = RIGHTCHILD;
    new_node->left = QN->right;
    QN->right = new_node;
  }
  if (new_node->left)
    new_node->left->parent_nodeid = new_node->nodeid;
  j = QN->attributes->num_attributes();
  if ((QN->node_type == qntJoin) && (j > 0))
  {
    Attribute *attribs = 0;
    Item * attr;
    int ii = 0;
    int jj = 0;
    if ((QN->attributes->num_attributes() == 1) &&
        (strcasecmp("*",
        ((Field *)QN->attributes->get_attribute(0))->field_name) == 0))
    {
      new_node->attributes = new Attribute();
      new_node->attributes->add_attribute(j,
        QN->attributes->get_attribute(0));
    }
    else
    {
      attribs = new Attribute();
      for (i = 0; i < (int)new_node->relations[0]->table->s->fields; i++)
```

```
          {
            Item *f = (Item *)new_node->relations[0]->table->field[i];
            attribs->add_attribute(true, (Item *)f);
          }
          j = attribs->num_attributes();
          new_node->attributes = new Attribute();
          for (i = 0; i < j; i++)
          {
            attr = attribs->get_attribute(i);
            jj = QN->attributes->index_of(
              (char *)((Field *)attr)->table->s->table_name.str,
              (char *)((Field *)attr)->field_name);
            if (jj > -1)
            {
              new_node->attributes->add_attribute(ii, attr);
              ii++;
              QN->attributes->remove_attribute(jj);
            }
            else if (find_attr_in_expr(QN->join_expr,
              (char *)((Field *)attr)->table->s->table_name.str,
              (char *)((Field *)attr)->field_name))
            {
              new_node->attributes->add_attribute(ii, attr);
              new_node->attributes->hide_attribute(attr, true);
              ii++;
            }
          }
        }
      }
      else
      {
        QN->node_type = qntJoin;
        QN->join_type = jnINNER;
        new_node->attributes = new Attribute();
      }
    }
    split_restrict_with_join(QN->left);
    split_restrict_with_join(QN->right);
  }
  DBUG_RETURN(0);
}
```

The split_project_with_join() method searches the tree for joins that have attributes (and thus are both joins and projections) and breaks them into two nodes: a join and a project node. Listing 13-12 shows the source code for this method.

Listing 13-12. Split Project With Join

```
/*
  Split projections that have joins.

  SYNOPSIS
    split_project_with_join()
    query_node *QN IN the node to operate on

  DESCRIPTION
    This method looks for joins that have attributes (thus are both
    joins and projections) and breaks them into two nodes.

  NOTES
    This is a RECURSIVE method!

  RETURN VALUE
    Success = 0
    Failed = 1
*/
int Query_tree::split_project_with_join(query_node *QN)
{
  int j = 0;
  int i;

  DBUG_ENTER("split_project_with_join");
  if(QN != 0)
  {
    if((QN->join_expr->num_expressions() > 0) &&
       ((QN->node_type == qntJoin) || (QN->node_type == qntProject)))
    {
      /*
        Create a new node and:
          1) Move the where expressions to the new node.
          2) Set the new node's children = current node children
          3) Set the new node's relations = current node relations.
          4) Set current node's left or right child = new node;
          5) Set new node's id = current id + 300;
          6) set parent id, etc.
      */
      QN->node_type = qntJoin;
      QN->join_type = jnINNER;
      if (QN->left == 0)
      {
        query_node *new_node = (query_node*)my_malloc(sizeof(query_node),
                               MYF(MY_ZEROFILL | MY_WME));
        init_node(new_node);
        new_node->node_type = qntProject;
        new_node->parent_nodeid = QN->nodeid;
        new_node->nodeid = QN->nodeid + 300;
        for(i = 0; i < MAXNODETABLES; i++)
          new_node->relations[i] = 0;
```

```
new_node->relations[0] = QN->relations[0];
QN->relations[0] = 0;
new_node->left = QN->left;
QN->left = new_node;
new_node->right = 0;
new_node->child = LEFTCHILD;
if (new_node->left != 0)
  new_node->left->parent_nodeid = new_node->nodeid;
j = QN->attributes->num_attributes();
new_node->attributes = new Attribute();
new_node->where_expr = new Expression();
new_node->join_expr = new Expression();
if ((j == 1) &&
    (strcasecmp("*", ((Field *)QN->attributes->get_attribute(0))->field_name)==0))
{
  new_node->attributes = new Attribute();
  new_node->attributes->add_attribute(j, QN->attributes->get_attribute(0));
  if (QN->right != 0)
    QN->attributes->remove_attribute(0);
}
else if (j > 0)
{
  Attribute *attribs = 0;
  Item * attr;
  int ii = 0;
  int jj = 0;
  attribs = new Attribute();
  for (i = 0; i < (int)new_node->relations[0]->table->s->fields; i++)
  {
    Field *f = new_node->relations[0]->table->field[i];
    attribs->add_attribute(true, (Item *)f);
  }
  j = attribs->num_attributes();
  for (i = 0; i < j; i++)
  {
    attr = attribs->get_attribute(i);
    jj = QN->attributes->index_of(
      (char *)((Field *)attr)->table->s->table_name.str,
      (char *)((Field *)attr)->field_name);
    if (jj > -1)
    {
      new_node->attributes->add_attribute(ii, attr);
      ii++;
      QN->attributes->remove_attribute(jj);
    }
    else if (find_attr_in_expr(QN->join_expr,
      (char *)((Field *)attr)->table->s->table_name.str,
      (char *)((Field *)attr)->field_name))
```

```
      {
        new_node->attributes->add_attribute(ii, attr);
        new_node->attributes->hide_attribute(attr, true);
        ii++;
      }
    }
  }
}
if (QN->right == 0)
{
  query_node *new_node = (query_node*)my_malloc(sizeof(query_node),
                          MYF(MY_ZEROFILL | MY_WME));
  init_node(new_node);
  new_node->node_type = qntProject;
  new_node->parent_nodeid = QN->nodeid;
  new_node->nodeid = QN->nodeid + 400;
  for(i = 0; i < MAXNODETABLES; i++)
    new_node->relations[0] = 0;
  new_node->relations[0] = QN->relations[1];
  QN->relations[1] = 0;
  new_node->left = QN->right;
  QN->right = new_node;
  new_node->right = 0;
  new_node->child = RIGHTCHILD;
  if (new_node->left != 0)
    new_node->left->parent_nodeid = new_node->nodeid;
  j = QN->attributes->num_attributes();
  new_node->attributes = new Attribute();
  new_node->where_expr = new Expression();
  new_node->join_expr = new Expression();
  if ((j == 1) &&
      (strcasecmp("*", ((Field *)QN->attributes->get_attribute(0))->field_name)==0))
  {
    new_node->attributes = new Attribute();
    new_node->attributes->add_attribute(j, QN->attributes->get_attribute(0));
    QN->attributes->remove_attribute(0);
  }
  else
  {
    Attribute *attribs = 0;
    Item * attr;
    int ii = 0;
    int jj = 0;
    attribs = new Attribute();
    for (i = 0; i < (int)new_node->relations[0]->table->s->fields; i++)
    {
      Field *f = new_node->relations[0]->table->field[i];
      attribs->add_attribute(true, (Item *)f);
      if (j == 0)
```

```
      {
        new_node->attributes->hide_attribute((Item *)f, true);
      }
    }
    j = attribs->num_attributes();
    new_node->attributes = new Attribute();
    for (i = 0; i < j; i++)
    {
      attr = attribs->get_attribute(i);
      jj = QN->attributes->index_of(
        (char *)((Field *)attr)->table->s->table_name.str,
        (char *)((Field *)attr)->field_name);
      if (jj > -1)
      {
        new_node->attributes->add_attribute(ii, attr);
        ii++;
        QN->attributes->remove_attribute(jj);
      }
      else if (find_attr_in_expr(QN->join_expr,
        (char *)((Field *)attr)->table->s->table_name.str,
        (char *)((Field *)attr)->field_name))
      {
        new_node->attributes->add_attribute(ii, attr);
        new_node->attributes->hide_attribute(attr, true);
        ii++;
      }
    }
  }
}
split_project_with_join(QN->left);
split_project_with_join(QN->right);
}
DBUG_RETURN(0);
}
```

The split_restrict_with_project() method searches the tree for restrictions that have attributes (and thus are both projections and restrictions) and breaks them into two nodes: a restrict and a project node. Listing 13-13 shows the source code for this method.

Listing 13-13. Split Restrict With Project

```
/*
  Split restrictions that have attributes (projections).

  SYNOPSIS
    split_restrict_with_project()
    query_node *QN IN the node to operate on

  DESCRIPTION
    This method looks for restrictions that have attributes (thus are both
    projections and restrictions) and breaks them into two nodes.
```

```
  NOTES
    This is a RECURSIVE method!

  RETURN VALUE
    Success = 0
    Failed = 1
*/
int Query_tree::split_restrict_with_project(query_node *QN)
{
  DBUG_ENTER("split_restrict_with_project");
  if(QN != 0)
  {
    if(((QN->attributes->num_attributes() > 0) &&
       (QN->where_expr->num_expressions() > 0)) &&
       ((QN->node_type == qntProject) || (QN->node_type == qntRestrict)))
    {
      /*
         Create a new node and:
           1) Move the expressions to the new node.
            2) Set the new node's children = current node children
           3) Set the new node's relations = current node relations.
           4) Set current node's left child = new node;
           5) Set new node's id = current id + 1000;
           6) set parent id, etc.
      */
      query_node *new_node = (query_node*)my_malloc(sizeof(query_node),
                              MYF(MY_ZEROFILL | MY_WME));
      init_node(new_node);
      new_node->child = LEFTCHILD;
      new_node->node_type = qntRestrict;
      if(new_node->node_type == qntJoin)
      {
        new_node->join_cond = QN->join_cond;
        new_node->join_type = QN->join_type;
      }
      QN->node_type = qntProject;
      new_node->attributes = new Attribute();
      new_node->where_expr = QN->where_expr;
      new_node->join_expr = new Expression();
      QN->where_expr = new Expression();
      new_node->left = QN->left;
      new_node->right = QN->right;
      new_node->parent_nodeid = QN->nodeid;
      new_node->nodeid = QN->nodeid + 1000;
      if(new_node->left)
        new_node->left->parent_nodeid = new_node->nodeid;
      if(new_node->right)
        new_node->right->parent_nodeid = new_node->nodeid;
      for(int i = 0; i < MAXNODETABLES; i++)
```

```
      {
        new_node->relations[i] = QN->relations[i];
        QN->relations[i] = NULL;
      }
      QN->left = new_node;
      QN->right = 0;
    }
    split_restrict_with_project(QN->left);
    split_restrict_with_project(QN->right);
  }
  DBUG_RETURN(0);
}
```

The find_restriction() method searches the tree from the starting node (QN) for the next restriction in the tree. If a restriction is found, a pointer to the node is returned; otherwise, the method returns NULL. Listing 13-14 shows the source code for this method.

Listing 13-14. Find Restriction

```
/*
  Find a restriction in the subtree.

  SYNOPSIS
    find_restriction()
    query_node *QN IN the node to operate on

  DESCRIPTION
    This method looks for a node containing a restriction and returns the node
    pointer.

  NOTES
    This is a RECURSIVE method!
    This finds the first restriction and is biased to the left tree.

  RETURN VALUE
    Success = query_node * the node located
    Failed = NULL
*/
Query_tree::query_node *Query_tree::find_restriction(query_node *QN)
{
  DBUG_ENTER("find_restriction");
  query_node   *N;

  N = 0;
  if(QN != 0)
  {
    /*
      A restriction is a node marked as restrict and
      has at least one expression
    */
    if (QN->where_expr->num_expressions() > 0)
      N = QN;
    else
```

```
    {
      N = find_restriction(QN->left);
      if(N == 0)
        N = find_restriction(QN->right);
    }
  }
  DBUG_RETURN(N);
}
```

The push_restriction() method searches the tree from the starting node (QN) and pushes the restriction node (pNode) down the tree to nodes that contain the relations specified in the restriction. Listing 13-15 shows the source code for this method.

Listing 13-15. Push Restrictions

```
/*
  Push restrictions down the tree.

  SYNOPSIS
    push_restrictions()
    query_node *QN IN the node to operate on
    query_node *pNode IN the node containing the restriction attributes

  DESCRIPTION
    This method looks for restrictions and pushes them down the tree to nodes
    that contain the relations specified.

  NOTES
    This is a RECURSIVE method!
    This finds the first restriction and is biased to the left tree.

  RETURN VALUE
    Success = 0
    Failed = 1
*/
int Query_tree::push_restrictions(query_node *QN, query_node *pNode)
{
  query_node        *NewQN=0;

  DBUG_ENTER("push_restrictions");
  if((QN != 0) && (pNode != 0) && (pNode->left != 0))
  {
    /*
      Conditions:
        1) QN is a join node
        2) QN is a project node
        3) QN is a restrict node
        4) All other nodes types are ignored.
```

```
    Methods:
      1) if join or project and the children are not already restrictions
         add a new node and put where clause in new node else
         see if you can combine the child node and this one
      2) if the node has the table and it is a join,
         create a new node below it and push the restriction
         to that node.
      3) if the node is a restriction and has the table,
         just add the expression to the node's expression list
*/

/* if projection, move node down tree */
if((QN->nodeid != pNode->nodeid) && (QN->node_type == qntProject))
{
  if (QN->left != 0)
  {
    QN->left = (query_node*)my_malloc(sizeof(query_node),
               MYF(MY_ZEROFILL | MY_WME));
    init_node(QN->left);
    NewQN = QN->left;
    NewQN->left = 0;
  }
  else
  {
    NewQN = QN->left;
    QN->left = (query_node*)my_malloc(sizeof(query_node),
               MYF(MY_ZEROFILL | MY_WME));
    QN->left->left = NewQN;
    NewQN = QN->left;
  }
  NewQN->sub_query = 0;
  NewQN->join_cond = jcUN;    /* (join_con_type) 0; */
  NewQN->join_type = jnUNKNOWN;    /* (type_join) 0; */
  NewQN->right = 0;
  for(long i = 0; i < MAXNODETABLES; i++)
    NewQN->relations[i] = 0;
  NewQN->nodeid = QN->nodeid + 1;
  NewQN->parent_nodeid = QN->nodeid;
  NewQN->node_type = qntRestrict;
  NewQN->attributes = new Attribute();
  NewQN->where_expr = new Expression();
  NewQN->join_expr = new Expression();
  if (pNode->relations[0])
    NewQN->where_expr->reduce_expressions(pNode->relations[0]->table);
  if ((QN->relations[0] != NULL) && (QN->relations[0] == pNode->relations[0]))
  {
    if (QN->relations[0])
    {
      if (find_table_in_expr(pNode->where_expr, QN->relations[0]->table_name))
```

```
        {
          NewQN->relations[0] = QN->relations[0];
          QN->relations[0] = 0;
        }
      }
    }
    else
    {
      if (pNode->relations[0])
        if (find_table_in_tree(QN->left, pNode->relations[0]->table_name))
          NewQN->relations[0] = 0;
      pNode->where_expr = NULL;
      pNode->relations[0] = 0;
    }
  }
  /* if join, move restrict node down tree */
  else if((QN->nodeid != pNode->nodeid) &&
    ((QN->left == 0) || (QN->right == 0)) &&
    (QN->node_type == qntJoin))
  {
    if(QN->relations[0] != 0)
    {
      QN->left = (query_node*)my_malloc(sizeof(query_node),
                  MYF(MY_ZEROFILL | MY_WME));
      NewQN = QN->left;
      NewQN->sub_query = 0;
      NewQN->join_cond = jcUN;   /* (join_con_type) 0; */
      NewQN->join_type = jnUNKNOWN;   /* (type_join) 0; */
      NewQN->left = 0;
      NewQN->right = 0;
      for(long i = 0; i < MAXNODETABLES; i++)
        NewQN->relations[i] = 0;
      NewQN->nodeid = QN->nodeid + 1;
      NewQN->parent_nodeid = QN->nodeid;
      NewQN->node_type = qntRestrict;
      NewQN->attributes = new Attribute();
      NewQN->where_expr = new Expression();
      NewQN->join_expr = new Expression();
      NewQN->relations[0] = QN->relations[0];
      QN->relations[0] = 0;
      if (pNode->relations[0])
        NewQN->where_expr->reduce_expressions(pNode->relations[0]->table);
    }
    else if(QN->relations[1] != 0)
    {
      QN->right = (query_node*)my_malloc(sizeof(query_node),
                  MYF(MY_ZEROFILL | MY_WME));
      NewQN = QN->left;
      NewQN->sub_query = 0;
      NewQN->join_cond = jcUN;   /* (join_con_type) 0; */
      NewQN->join_type = jnUNKNOWN;   /* (type_join) 0; */
```

```
        NewQN->left = 0;
        NewQN->right = 0;
        for(long i = 0; i < MAXNODETABLES; i++)
          NewQN->relations[i] = 0;
      }
      NewQN->nodeid = QN->nodeid + 1;
      NewQN->parent_nodeid = QN->nodeid;
      NewQN->node_type = qntRestrict;
      NewQN->attributes = new Attribute();
      NewQN->where_expr = new Expression();
      NewQN->join_expr = new Expression();
      NewQN->relations[0] = QN->relations[1];
      QN->relations[1] = 0;
      NewQN->where_expr->reduce_expressions(pNode->relations[0]->table);
    }
    push_restrictions(QN->left, pNode);
    push_restrictions(QN->right, pNode);
  }
  DBUG_RETURN(0);
}
```

The find_projection() method searches the tree from the starting node (QN) for the next projection in the tree. If a projection is found, a pointer to the node is returned; otherwise, the method returns NULL. Listing 13-16 shows the source code for this method.

Listing 13-16. Find Projection

```
/*
  Find a projection in the tree

  SYNOPSIS
    find_projection()
    query_node *QN IN the node to operate on

  DESCRIPTION
    This method looks for a node containing a projection and returns the node
    pointer.

  NOTES
    This finds the first projection and is biased to the left tree.
    This is a RECURSIVE method!

  RETURN VALUE
    Success = query_node * the node located or NULL for not found
    Failed = NULL
*/
Query_tree::query_node *Query_tree::find_projection(query_node *QN)
{
  DBUG_ENTER("find_projection");
  query_node    *N;
```

```
    N = 0;
    if(QN != 0)
    {
      /*
        A projection is a node marked as project and
        has at least one attribute
      */
      if((QN->node_type == qntProject) &&
         (QN->attributes != 0))
        N = QN;
      else
      {
        N = find_projection(QN->left);
        if(N == 0)
          N = find_projection(QN->right);
      }
    }
    DBUG_RETURN(N);
}
```

The push_projection() method searches the tree from the starting node (QN) and pushes the projection node (pNode) down the tree to nodes that contain the relations specified in the projection. Listing 13-17 shows the source code for this method.

Listing 13-17. Push Projections

```
/*
  Push projections down the tree.

  SYNOPSIS
    push_projections()
    query_node *QN IN the node to operate on
    query_node *pNode IN the node containing the projection attributes

  DESCRIPTION
    This method looks for projections and pushes them down the tree to nodes
    that contain the relations specified.

  NOTES
    This is a RECURSIVE method!

  RETURN VALUE
    Success = 0
    Failed = 1
*/
int Query_tree::push_projections(query_node *QN, query_node *pNode)
{
  DBUG_ENTER("push_projections");
  Item *   a;
  int      i;
  int      j;
```

```
  if((QN != 0) && (pNode != 0))
  {
    if((QN->nodeid != pNode->nodeid) &&
       (QN->node_type == qntProject))
    {
      i = 0;
      j = QN->attributes->num_attributes();

      /* move attributes to new node */
      while(i < j)
      {
        a = QN->attributes->get_attribute(i);
        if(has_relation(QN,
          (char *)((Field *)a)->table->s->table_name.str))
        {
          if(!has_attribute(QN, a))
            insert_attribute(QN, a);
          del_attribute(pNode, a);
        }
        i++;
      }
    }
    if(pNode->attributes->num_attributes() != 0)
    {
      push_projections(QN->left, pNode);
      push_projections(QN->right, pNode);
    }
  }
  DBUG_RETURN(0);
}
```

The find_join () method searches the tree from the starting node (QN) for the next join in the tree. If a join is found, a pointer to the node is returned; otherwise, the method returns NULL. Listing 13-18 shows the source code for this method.

Listing 13-18. Find Join

```
/*
  Find a join in the subtree.

  SYNOPSIS
    find_restriction()
    query_node *QN IN the node to operate on

  DESCRIPTION
    This method looks for a node containing a join and returns the
    node pointer.

  NOTES
    This is a RECURSIVE method!
    This finds the first restriction and is biased to the left tree.
```

```
  RETURN VALUE
    Success = query_node * the node located
    Failed = NULL
*/
Query_tree::query_node *Query_tree::find_join(query_node *QN)
{
  DBUG_ENTER("find_join");
  query_node                    *N;
  N = 0;

  if(QN != 0)
  {
    /*
      if this is a restrict node or a restrict node with
      at least one expression it could be an unprocessed join
      because the default node type is restrict
    */
    if(((QN->node_type == qntRestrict) ||
      (QN->node_type == qntRestrict)) && (QN->join_expr->num_expressions() > 0))
      N = QN;
    else
    {
      N = find_join(QN->left);
      if(N == 0)
        N = find_join(QN->right);
    }
  }
  DBUG_RETURN(N);
}
```

The push_joins() method searches the tree from the starting node (QN) and pushes the join node (pNode) down the tree to a position at which the join is the parent of two nodes that contain the relations specified in the children of the join. Listing 13-19 shows the source code for this method.

Listing 13-19. Push Joins

```
/*
  Push joins down the tree.

  SYNOPSIS
    push_restrictions()
    query_node *QN IN the node to operate on
    query_node *pNode IN the node containing the join

  DESCRIPTION
    This method looks for theta joins and pushes them down the tree to the
    parent of two nodes that contain the relations specified.

  NOTES
    This is a RECURSIVE method!
```

```
    RETURN VALUE
      Success = 0
      Failed = 1
*/
int Query_tree::push_joins(query_node *QN, query_node *pNode)
{
  DBUG_ENTER("push_joins");
  Item *lField;
  Item *rField;
  expr_node *node;

  if(!pNode->join_expr)
    DBUG_RETURN(0);
  node = pNode->join_expr->get_expression(0);
  if (!node)
    DBUG_RETURN(0);
  lField = node->left_op;
  rField = node->right_op;

  /* Node must have expressions and not be null */
  if((QN != NULL) && (pNode != NULL) &&
     (pNode->join_expr->num_expressions() > 0))
  {
    /* check to see if tables in join condition exist */
    if((QN->nodeid != pNode->nodeid) &&
       (QN->node_type == qntJoin) &&
        QN->join_expr->num_expressions() == 0 &&
       ((has_relation(QN->left,
          (char *)((Field *)lField)->table->s->table_name.str) &&
        has_relation(QN->right,
          (char *)((Field *)rField)->table->s->table_name.str)) ||
       (has_relation(QN->left,
          (char *)((Field *)rField)->table->s->table_name.str) &&
        has_relation(QN->right,
          (char *)((Field *)lField)->table->s->table_name.str))))
    {
      /* move the expression */
      QN->join_expr = pNode->join_expr;
      pNode->join_expr = new Expression();
      QN->join_type = jnINNER;
      QN->join_cond = jcON;
    }
    push_joins(QN->left, pNode);
    push_joins(QN->right, pNode);
  }
  DBUG_RETURN(0);
}
```

The prune_tree() method searches the tree for blank nodes (nodes that have no longer have any operation or function) that are a result of performing heuristic optimization on the tree and deletes them. Listing 13-20 shows the source code for this method.

535

Listing 13-20. Prune Tree

```
/*
  Prune the tree of dead limbs.

  SYNOPSIS
    prune_tree()
    query_node *prev IN the previous node (parent)
    query_node *cur_node IN the current node pointer (used to delete).

  DESCRIPTION
    This method looks for nodes blank nodes that are a result of performing
    heuristic optimization on the tree and deletes them.

  NOTES
    This is a RECURSIVE method!

  RETURN VALUE
    Success = 0
    Failed = 1
*/
int Query_tree::prune_tree(query_node *prev, query_node *cur_node)
{
  DBUG_ENTER("prune_tree");
  if(cur_node != 0)
  {
    /*
      Blank Nodes are 1) projections without attributes
      that have at least 1 child, or 2) restrictions
      without expressions
    */
    if(((((cur_node->node_type == qntProject) &&
       (cur_node->attributes->num_attributes() == 0)) ||
       ((cur_node->node_type == qntRestrict) &&
       (cur_node->where_expr->num_expressions() == 0))) &&
       ((cur_node->left == 0) || (cur_node->right == 0)))
    {
      /*
        Redirect the pointers for the nodes above and
        below this node in the tree.
      */
      if(prev == 0)
      {
        if(cur_node->left == 0)
        {
          cur_node->right->parent_nodeid = -1;
          root = cur_node->right;
        }
        else
```

```
            {
              cur_node->left->parent_nodeid = -1;
              root = cur_node->left;
            }
            my_free(cur_node);
            cur_node = root;
        }
        else
        {
            if(prev->left == cur_node)
            {
              if(cur_node->left == 0)
              {
                prev->left = cur_node->right;
                if (cur_node->right != NULL)
                  cur_node->right->parent_nodeid = prev->nodeid;
              }
              else
              {
                prev->left = cur_node->left;
                if (cur_node->left != NULL)
                  cur_node->left->parent_nodeid = prev->nodeid;
              }
              my_free(cur_node);
              cur_node = prev->left;
            }
            else
            {
              if(cur_node->left == 0)
              {
                prev->right = cur_node->right;
                if (cur_node->right != NULL)
                  cur_node->right->parent_nodeid = prev->nodeid;
              }
              else
              {
                prev->right = cur_node->left;
                if (cur_node->left != NULL)
                  cur_node->left->parent_nodeid = prev->nodeid;
              }
              my_free(cur_node);
              cur_node = prev->right;
            }
        }
        prune_tree(prev, cur_node);
    }
    else
```

```
    {
      prune_tree(cur_node, cur_node->left);
      prune_tree(cur_node, cur_node->right);
    }
  }
  DBUG_RETURN(0);
}
```

Compiling and Testing the Code

If you haven't already, download the source code for this chapter and place the files in the /sql directory off the root of your source tree. In the example code, you will also find a difference file (ch13.diff) that you can use to apply the changes to the server source-code files (e.g. mysqld.cc sql_cmd.h, etc.). Or, you can use the changes from Chapter 12 as the changes to the server code is the same.

Spend a few moments looking through the source code so that you are familiar with the methods. Taking the time to look through the code now will help should you need to debug the code to work with your configuration or if you want to add other enhancements or work the exercises.

Once you have all the source-code files downloaded and have examined the code, add the files to the CMakeLists.txt file. See "Adding the Files to the CMakeLists.txt file" in Chapter 12 for the details. You will be adding the attribute and expression helper source files (attribute.cc and expression.cc). Once you have the files added to the project, navigate to the root of the source tree, run the cmake, and make commands as shown. Make sure the code compiles without compilation errors.

```
cmake .
```

```
make
```

Once you have the new code installed and compiled, run the server and perform the tests. You can run the test you created earlier or you can enter the commands in a MySQL client utility. Listing 13-21 shows the expected output of running the commands listed in the test.

Listing 13-21. Example Test Runs

```
DBXP_SELECT * FROM staff' at line 1
```

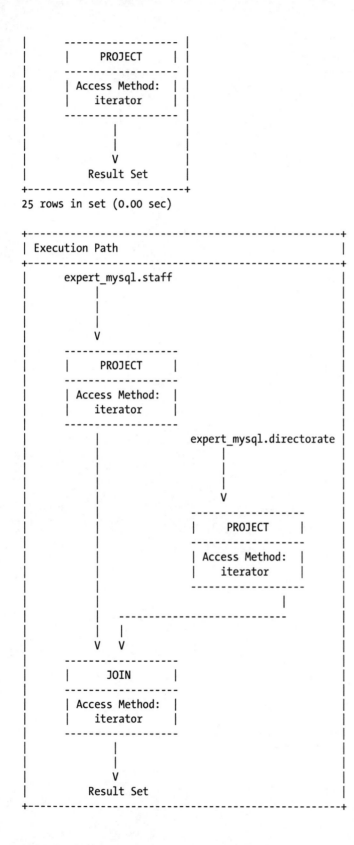

```
|      ------------------ |
|      |    PROJECT     | |
|      ------------------ |
|      | Access Method: | |
|      |    iterator    | |
|      ------------------ |
|             |           |
|             |           |
|             V           |
|         Result Set      |
+-------------------------+
```

25 rows in set (0.00 sec)

```
+-------------------------------------------------+
| Execution Path                                  |
+-------------------------------------------------+
|      expert_mysql.staff                         |
|             |                                   |
|             |                                   |
|             |                                   |
|             V                                   |
|      ------------------                         |
|      |    PROJECT     |                         |
|      ------------------                         |
|      | Access Method: |                         |
|      |    iterator    |                         |
|      ------------------                         |
|             |        expert_mysql.directorate   |
|             |               |                   |
|             |               |                   |
|             |               |                   |
|             |               V                   |
|             |        ------------------         |
|             |        |    PROJECT     |         |
|             |        ------------------         |
|             |        | Access Method: |         |
|             |        |    iterator    |         |
|             |        ------------------         |
|             |                 |                 |
|             |   ---------------------           |
|             | |                                 |
|             V V                                 |
|      ------------------                         |
|      |     JOIN       |                         |
|      ------------------                         |
|      | Access Method: |                         |
|      |    iterator    |                         |
|      ------------------                         |
|             |                                   |
|             |                                   |
|             V                                   |
|         Result Set                              |
+-------------------------------------------------+
```

```
36 rows in set (0.00 sec)

+-------------------------------------------------+
| Execution Path                                  |
+-------------------------------------------------+
|         expert_mysql.staff                      |
|               |                                 |
|               |                                 |
|               |                                 |
|               V                                 |
|        -------------------                      |
|        |    RESTRICT     |                      |
|        -------------------                      |
|        | Access Method:  |                      |
|        |    iterator     |                      |
|        -------------------                      |
|               |              expert_mysql.tasking |
|               |                     |           |
|               |                     |           |
|               |                     |           |
|               |                     V           |
|               |              -------------------  |
|               |              |     PROJECT     | |
|               |              -------------------  |
|               |              | Access Method:  | |
|               |              |    iterator     | |
|               |              -------------------  |
|               |                        |        |
|               |      -------------------         |
|               |      |  |                        |
|               V      V                           |
|        -------------------                       |
|        |      JOIN       |                       |
|        -------------------                       |
|        | Access Method:  |                       |
|        |    iterator     |                       |
|        -------------------                       |
|               |                                  |
|               |                                  |
|               V                                  |
|          Result Set                              |
+-------------------------------------------------+
36 rows in set (0.00 sec)

Query OK, 4 rows affected (0.00 sec)
mysql >
```

Notice how the query plans differ for each of the statements entered. Take some time to explore other query statements to see how the optimizer optimizes other forms of queries.

■ **Note** The output for the DBXP_SELECT commands may look a little odd at first (they are query plans) but recall from earlier that we stubbed the DBXP_select_command() method in the sql_dbxp_parser.cc file to redirect to the DBXP_explain_select_command() method. We will add the execution of the queries in the next chapter.

Summary

I presented in this chapter the most complex database internal technology—an optimizer. You learned how to expand the concept of the query tree to incorporate a query optimizer that uses the tree structure in the optimization process. More important, you discovered how to construct a heuristic query optimizer. The knowledge of heuristic optimizers should provide you with a greater understanding of the DBXP engine and how it can be used to study database technologies in more depth. It doesn't get any deeper than an optimizer!

In the next chapter, I show you more about query execution through an example implementation of a query-tree optimization strategy. The next chapter will complete the DBXP engine by linking the heuristic query optimizer, using the query-tree class, to an execution process that—surprise—also uses the query-tree structure.

EXERCISES

The following lists several areas for further exploration. They represent the types of activities you might want to conduct as experiments (or as a class assignment) to explore relational database technologies.

1. Complete the code for the balance_joins() method. Hint: You will need to create an algorithm that can move conjunctive joins around so that the join that is most restrictive is executed first (is lowest in the tree).

2. Complete the code for the cost_optimization() method. Hint: You will need to walk the tree and indicate nodes that can use indexes.

3. Examine the code for the heuristic optimizer. Does it cover all possible queries? If not, are there any other rules that can be used to complete the coverage?

4. Examine the code for the query tree and heuristic optimizer. How can you implement the distinct node type as listed in the query-tree class? Hint: See the code that follows the prune_tree() method in the heuristic_optimization() method.

5. How can you change the code to recognize invalid queries? What are the conditions that determine that a query is invalid and how would you test for them?

6. (advanced) MySQL does not currently support the intersect operation (as defined by Date). Change the MySQL parser to recognize the new keyword and process queries, such as SELECT * FROM A INTERSECT B. Are there any limitations of this operation, and are they reflected in the optimizer?

7. (advanced) How would you implement the GROUP BY, ORDER BY, and HAVING clauses? Make the changes to the optimizer to enable these clauses.

■ ■ ■

## CHAPTER 14

Query Execution

The query-tree class shown in Chapter 12 and the heuristic optimizer shown in Chapter 13 form the first two of the three components that make up the DBXP query-execution engine. In this chapter, I show you how to expand the query-tree class to process project, restrict, and join operations. This will give you a glimpse into the world of database-query execution. I begin by briefly explaining the basic principles of the query execution algorithms and then jump into writing the code. Because the code for some of the methods is quite lengthy, not all of the code examples shown in this chapter include the complete source code. If you are following along by coding the examples, consider loading the source code for this chapter and using it rather than typing in the code from scratch.

Query Execution Revisited

The query-execution process is the implementation of the various relational theory operations. These operations include project, restrict, join, cross-product, union, and intersect. Few database systems implement union and intersect.

■ **Note** Union and intersect are not the same as the UNION operator in SQL. The union and intersect relational operations are set operations, whereas the UNION operator in SQL simply combines the results of two or more SELECT statements that have compatible result columns.

Writing algorithms to implement these operations is very straightforward and often omitted from relational-theory and database-systems texts. It is unfortunate that the algorithms are omitted, because the join operation is nontrivial. The following sections describe the basic algorithms for the relational operations.

Project

The project (or projection) operation is one in which the result set contains a subset of the attributes (columns) in the original relation (table).[1] Thus, the result set can contain fewer attributes than the original relation. Users specify projections in a SQL SELECT command by listing the desired columns in the column list immediately following the SELECT keyword. For example, This command projects the first_name and last_name columns from the staff table:

```
SELECT first_name, last_name FROM staff
```

---

[1] For simplicity, I use the attribute/column, tuple/row, and relation/table terms interchangeably.

The project algorithm to implement this operation is shown in Listing 14-1.

Listing 14-1. Project Algorithm

```
begin
  do
    get next tuple from relation
    for each attribute in tuple
      if attribute.name found in column_list
        write attribute data to client
      fi
  while not end_of_relation
end
```

As you can see from the listing, the code to implement this algorithm limits sending data to the client to the data specified in the column list.

Restrict

The restrict (or restriction) operation is one in which the result set contains a subset of the tuples (rows) in the original relation (table). Thus, the result set can contain fewer tuples than the original relation. Users specify restrictions in a SQL SELECT command by listing the desired conditions in the WHERE clause immediately following the FROM clause. For example, the following command restricts the result set from the staff table to those employees who make more than $65,000.00 annually.

```
SELECT first_name, last_name FROM staff WHERE salary > 65000.00
```

The restrict algorithm to implement this operation is shown in Listing 14-2.

Listing 14-2. Restrict Algorithm

```
begin
  do
    get next tuple from relation
    if tuple attribute values match conditions
      write attribute data to client
    fi
  while not end_of_relation
end
```

As you can see from the listing, the code to implement this algorithm is where the data values in the tuple match the conditions in the WHERE clause. This algorithm is often implemented with an additional optimization step to reduce the expressions to a minimal set (e.g., omitting always true conditions).

Join

The join operation is one in which the result set contains the tuples (rows) that match a specified combination of two relations (tables). Three or more tables are joined using n-1 joins, where n is the number of tables. In the case of three tables joined (A, B, C), the join is a combination of two of the tables and the result of that join joined with the remaining table. The combinations of how the joins are linked—as a left-deep or right-deep tree or even as a bushy tree—are one of order of execution of the intermediate joins. Examples of these types of tree arrangements are shown in Figure 14-1.

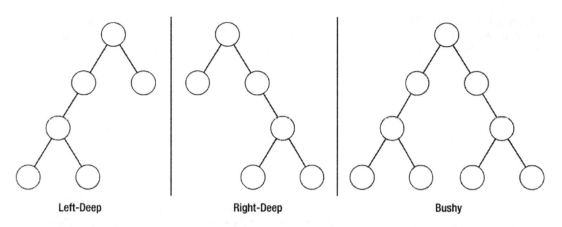

Figure 14-1. *Example tree arrangements*

Joins are most often used in a master/detail relationship in which one table (the base or master table) references one or more subtables (detail tables) in which one record in the base table matches one or more records in the detail tables. For example, you could create a customer table that contains information about customers and an orders table that contains data about the customers' orders. The customer table is the base table, and the orders table is the subtable.

```
SELECT customer.name, orders.number
FROM customer JOIN orders on customer.id = orders.customerid
```

Users specify joins in a SQL SELECT command by listing the desired tables and join conditions in the FROM clause. For example, the following command joins the records from the customer table with those records in the orders table. Note that in this case, the join condition is a simple equal relationship with a common column that the tables share.

The algorithm for a join operation is not as straightforward as those described earlier. This is because the join operation can be represented in several forms. You can choose to join using a simple column from table A = column from table B expression as in the previous example, or you can elect to control the output by including only matching rows (inner), matching and nonmatching rows (outer) from the left, right, or both tables. The join operations therefore include inner join (sometimes called natural or equi-joins[2]), left outer join, right outer join, full outer join, cross-product, union, and intersect. The following sections describe each of these operations in detail.

■ **Note** Some database texts treat the cross-product, union, and intersect as discrete operations. I consider them specialized forms of the join operation.

Inner Join

The inner-join operation is one in which the result set contains a subset of the tuples (rows) in the original relations (tables) where there is a match on the join condition. It is called an inner join because only those rows in the first relation whose join condition value matches that of a row in the second relation are included in the result set.

---

[2]Natural joins are equi-joins with the superfluous (duplicate) condition attribute values removed.

Users specify inner joins in a SQL SELECT command by listing the desired conditions in the FROM clause. For example, the following command joins the result set from the staff table to the directorate table, returning a result set of all employees who are assigned a directorate (one employee does not have a directorate assigned).

```
SELECT staff.last_name, staff.dept_name
FROM staff JOIN directorate on staff.dept_id = directorate.id
```

■ **Note** The keyword INNER is usually optional for most database systems, because the default join operation is an inner join.

The inner-join algorithm to implement this operation is shown in Listing 14-3. This algorithm is but one of several forms of join algorithms. The algorithm shown is a variant of a merge-join. Thus, it is possible to implement this algorithm using another equally capable join algorithm, such as a nested loop join algorithm.

Listing 14-3. Join Algorithm

```
begin
  sort relation a as rel_a on join column(s)
  sort relation b as rel_b on join column(s)
  do
    get next tuple from rel_a
    get next tuple from rel_b
    if join column values match join conditions
      write attribute data to client
    fi
    check rewind conditions
  while not end_of_rel_a and not end_of_rel_b
end
```

Users can also specify an inner join by including the join condition in the WHERE clause, as shown here. Some database professionals discourage this variant, because it can be mistaken for a normal SELECT command. Most agree that the variant is functionally equivalent, and most database optimizers are written to accommodate it.

```
SELECT staff.last_name, directorate.dept_name
FROM staff, directorate WHERE staff.dept_id = directorate.id
```

As you can see from the listing, the code to implement this algorithm requires the use of a sort. A sort is needed to order the rows in the tables on the join columns so that the algorithm can correctly identify all of the matches should there be any duplicate condition values among the rows. To illustrate this point, consider the tables shown in Listing 14-4.

Listing 14-4. Example Join Tables (Unordered)

staff table

id	first_name	mid_name	last_name	sex	salary	mgr_id
333445555	John	Q	Smith	M	30000	333444444
123763153	William	E	Walters	M	25000	123654321
333444444	Alicia	F	St.Cruz	F	25000	None

921312388	Goy	X	Hong	F	40000	123654321
800122337	Rajesh	G	Kardakarna	M	38000	333445555
820123637	Monty	C	Smythe	M	38000	333445555
830132335	Richard	E	Jones	M	38000	333445555
333445665	Edward	E	Engles	M	25000	333445555
123654321	Beware	D	Borg	F	55000	333444444
123456789	Wilma	N	Maxima	F	43000	333445555

directorate table

dir_code	dir_name	dir_head_id
N41	Development	333445555
N01	Human Resources	123654321
M00	Management	333444444

■ **Note** Some database systems (such as MySQL) return the rows in the original, unordered sequence. The examples shown are included in order of the internal sort for emphasis.

Notice that the tables are not ordered. If you were to run the example join shown using the algorithm without ordering the rows, you'd have to read all of the rows from one of the tables for each row, read from the other. For example, if the staff table were read in the order shown, you would read one row from the directorate table for the first join, two rows from the directorate table for the next row from staff, followed by two, one, one, one, four, two rows, with a total of 14 reads from the directorate table to complete the operation. If the tables were ordered as shown in Listing 14-5, however, you could avoid rereading the rows from the directorate table.

Listing 14-5. Example Join Tables (Ordered by Join Column)

staff table

id	first_name	mid_name	last_name	sex	salary	mgr_id
123763153	William	E	Walters	M	25000	123654321
921312388	Goy	X	Hong	F	40000	123654321
333445555	John	Q	Smith	M	30000	333444444
123654321	Beware	D	Borg	F	55000	333444444
333445665	Edward	E	Engles	M	25000	333445555
830132335	Richard	E	Jones	M	38000	333445555
820123637	Monty	C	Smythe	M	38000	333445555
800122337	Rajesh	G	Kardakarna	M	38000	333445555
123456789	Wilma	N	Maxima	F	43000	333445555
333444444	Alicia	F	St.Cruz	F	25000	None

directorate table
```
+----------+------------------+-------------+
| dir_code | dir_name         | dir_head_id |
+----------+------------------+-------------+
| NO1      | Human Resources  | 123654321   |
| MOO      | Management       | 333444444   |
| N41      | Development      | 333445555   |
+----------+------------------+-------------+
```

This creates another problem, however. How do you know not to read another row from either table? Notice the last step in the inner-join algorithm. This is where the implementation can get a bit tricky. What you need to do here is be able to reuse a row that has already been read so that you can compare one row from one table to many rows in another. This gets tricky when you consider that you may have to advance (go forward one row) or rewind (go back one row) from either table.

If you follow the algorithm by hand with the ordered example tables using staff.mgr_id = directorate.dir_head_id as the join criteria (reading from the staff table as rel_a first), you'll see that the algorithm would require the "reuse" of the directorate row with a dir_head_id of 333444444 twice and the row with and dir_head_id of 333445555 three times. The caching of the rows is sometimes called "rewinding" the table read pointers. The result set of this example is shown in Listing 14-6.

Listing 14-6. Example Inner-join Result Set

```
+------------+------------------+
| last_name  | dir_name         |
+------------+------------------+
| Smith      | Management       |
| Walters    | Human Resources  |
| Hong       | Human Resources  |
| Kardakarna | Development      |
| Smythe     | Development      |
| Jones      | Development      |
| Engles     | Development      |
| Borg       | Management       |
| Maxima     | Development      |
+------------+------------------+
```

Listing 14-6 yields only 9 rows and not 10. This is because there is one row in the directorate table that does not have a mgr_id, because she is the boss. Thus, there is no corresponding row in the directorate table to match on mgr_id = dir_head_id.

Outer Join

Outer joins are similar to inner joins, but in this case, we are interested in obtaining all of the rows from the left, right, or both tables. That is, we include the rows from the table indicated (left, right, or both—also called full) regardless of whether there is a matching row in the other table. Each of these operations can be represented by a slight variance of the general outer-join algorithm.

Users specify outer joins in a SQL SELECT command by listing the desired conditions in the FROM clause and invoking one of the options (left, right, full). Some database systems default to using left if the option is omitted. For example, the following command joins the result set from the staff table to the directorate table, returning a result set of all employees and the directorate:

```
SELECT staff.last_name, directorate.dir_name
FROM staff LEFT OUTER JOIN directorate on staff.mgr_id = directorate.dir_head_id;
```

Note that this differs from the inner join, because no rows from the left table are omitted. Listing 14-7 shows the basic outer-join algorithm. The following sections describe how the algorithm implements each of the three types of outer joins.

Listing 14-7. The Outer-join Algorithm

```
begin
  sort relation a as rel_a on join column(s)
  sort relation b as rel_b on join column(s)
  do
    get next tuple from rel_a
    get next tuple from rel_b
    if type is FULL
      if join column values match join conditions
        write attribute data from both tuples to client
      else
        if rel_a has data
          write NULLS for rel_b
        else if rel_b has data
          write NULLS for rel_a
        fi
    else if type is LEFT
      if join column values match join conditions
        write attribute data from rel_a to client
      else
        if rel_a has data
          write NULLS for rel_b
      fi
    else if type is RIGHT
      if join column values match join conditions
        write attribute data from rel_b to client
      else
        if rel_b has data
          write NULLS for rel_a
      fi
    fi
    check rewind conditions
  while not end_of_rel_a and not end_of_rel_b
end
```

Next, we discuss examples of each of the types of outer joins.

Left Outer Join

Left outer joins include all rows from the left table concatenated with rows from the right table. For those rows that do not match the join condition, null values are returned for the columns from the right table.

```
SELECT staff.last_name, directorate.dir_name
FROM staff LEFT OUTER JOIN directorate on staff.mgr_id = directorate.dir_head_id;
```

Listing 14-8 shows the result set for the left outer join of the sample tables.

Listing 14-8. Example Left Outer Join Result Set

```
+------------+-----------------+
| last_name  | dir_name        |
+------------+-----------------+
| Smith      | Management      |
| Walters    | Human Resources |
| St.Cruz    | NULL            |
| Hong       | Human Resources |
| Kardakarna | Development     |
| Smythe     | Development     |
| Jones      | Development     |
| Engles     | Development     |
| Borg       | Management      |
| Maxima     | Development     |
+------------+-----------------+
```

Notice that now we see the row containing the row from the staff table that has no matching row in the directorate table. This is because we told the optimizer to use all of the rows from the staff table (the one on the left of the join specification) and match to the right table. Thus, we see one of the many uses of outer joins—they can be used to identify any mismatches.[3]

Right Outer Join

Right outer joins include all rows from the right table concatenated with rows from the left table. For those rows that do not match the join condition, null values are returned for the columns from the left table.

```
SELECT staff.last_name, directorate.dir_name
FROM staff RIGHT OUTER JOIN directorate on staff.mgr_id = directorate.dir_head_id;
```

Listing 14-9 shows the result set for the left outer join of the sample tables.

---

[3]Forgive my generalization. They may not be mismatches exactly, because it depends on the data stored and their interpretation.

Listing 14-9. Example Right Outer Join Result Set

```
+------------+------------------+
| last_name  | dir_name         |
+------------+------------------+
| Kardakarna | Development      |
| Smythe     | Development      |
| Jones      | Development      |
| Engles     | Development      |
| Maxima     | Development      |
| Walters    | Human Resources  |
| Hong       | Human Resources  |
| Smith      | Management       |
| Borg       | Management       |
+------------+------------------+
```

Now we're back to the nine rows. That's because we instructed the optimizer to use all of the rows in the right table where there is a match in the left table and since there were no rows in the directorate table (the one on the right of the join specification) that did not match a row in the staff table, the row without a match in the left table was omitted.

Full Outer Join

Full outer joins include all rows from both tables concatenated together. For those rows that do not match the join condition, null values are returned for the columns from the nonmatching table.

```
SELECT staff.last_name, directorate.dir_name
FROM staff FULL OUTER JOIN directorate on staff.mgr_id = directorate.dir_head_id;
```

Listing 14-10 shows the result set for the full outer join of the sample tables.

Listing 14-10. Example Full Outer-join Result Set

```
+------------+------------------+
| last_name  | dir_name         |
+------------+------------------+
| Smith      | Management       |
| Walters    | Human Resources  |
| St.Cruz    | NULL             |
| Hong       | Human Resources  |
| Kardakarna | Development      |
| Smythe     | Development      |
| Jones      | Development      |
| Engles     | Development      |
| Borg       | Management       |
| Maxima     | Development      |
+------------+------------------+
```

While MySQL does not support a full outer join, the above would be representative of the output. Now consider what the output would be if the directorate table contained a row without a dir_head_id. I leave this as an exercise for you to ponder.

Cross-Product

The cross-product operation is the one in which the result set contains each row of the left table combined with every row from the right table. Thus, the result set contains n x m rows, where n represents the number of rows in the left table and m represents the number of rows in the right table. While simple in concept, not all database systems support the cross-product operation.

■ **Note**   It is possible, in most database systems, to represent a cross-product query using a query such as SELECT * FROM table1, table2. In this case, there are no join conditions, so all rows from table1 are matched with all of the rows from table2. Try it out yourself on MySQL. You'll see that MySQL supports cross-product operations using this method.

Users specify the cross-product operation by including the keyword CROSS in place of JOIN in the FROM clause. You may be thinking that this operation has limited applicability, but you'd be surprised at its usefulness. Suppose you were modeling possible outcomes for an artificial-intelligence algorithm. You may have tables that store possible next moves (outcomes) and other tables that store stimuli. If you wanted to find all possible combinations, given a list of stimuli selected from one table and the possible effects on the moves selected from another, you can produce a result set that shows all of the combinations. Listing 14-11 presents an example of such a scenario.

Listing 14-11. Sample Cross-product Scenario

```
CREATE TABLE next_stim
SELECT source, stimuli_id FROM stimuli WHERE likelihood >= 0.75
+------------+------------+
| source     | stimuli_id |
+------------+------------+
| obstacle   | 13         |
| other_bot  | 14         |
| projectile | 15         |
| chasm      | 23         |
+------------+------------+

CREATE TABLE next_moves
SELECT move_name, next_move_id, likelihood FROM moves WHERE likelihood >= 0.90
+------------+--------------+------------+
| move_name  | next_move_id | likelihood |
+------------+--------------+------------+
| turn left  | 21           | 0.25       |
| reverse    | 18           | 0.40       |
| turn right | 22           | 0.45       |
+------------+--------------+------------+

SELECT * FROM next_stim CROSS next_moves
+------------+------------+------------+--------------+------------+
| source     | stimuli_id | move_name  | next_move_id | likelihood |
+------------+------------+------------+--------------+------------+
| obstacle   | 13         | turn left  | 21           | 0.25       |
| obstacle   | 13         | reverse    | 18           | 0.40       |
| obstacle   | 13         | turn right | 22           | 0.45       |
```

other_bot	14	turn left	21	0.25
other_bot	14	reverse	18	0.40
other_bot	14	turn right	22	0.45
projectile	15	turn left	21	0.25
projectile	15	reverse	18	0.40
projectile	15	turn right	22	0.45
chasm	23	turn left	21	0.25
chasm	23	reverse	18	0.40
chasm	23	turn right	22	0.45

Listing 14-12 shows the cross-product algorithm. Notice that this sample is written using two steps: one to combine the rows and one to remove the duplicates.

Listing 14-12. The Cross-product Algorithm

```
begin
  do
    get next tuple from rel_a
    do
      get next tuple from rel_b
      write tuple from rel_a concat tuple from rel_b to client
    while not end_of_rel_b
  while not end_of_rel_a
  remove duplicates from temp_table
  return data from temp_table to client
end
```

As you can see from the listing, the code to implement this algorithm is really one of two loops where the rows from the left table are concatenated with the rows from the right table (i.e., a nested loop algorithm).

Union

The union operation is the same as the set operation of the same name. In this case, the join is the union of all of the rows in both tables with duplicate rows removed. Naturally, the tables must be of the same design for this operation to work. This differs from the SQL union in that the SQL union includes rows from all SELECT commands (with compatible column lists) regardless of duplicates. Unlike the other joins, the implementation of the union operation is sometimes implemented in two steps: one to combine the tables and another to remove the duplicates.

Users specify the union command by including the keyword UNION in place of JOIN in the FROM clause. Let's say you wanted to combine two employee tables (one that includes all employees who work in the United States and another that includes employees who work in Canada) and ensure you get a result set that has all of the employees listed once. You could unite the two using a command like the following:

```
SELECT * from us_employees UNION ca_employees
```

Let's look at this one a little closer. Listing 14-13 shows examples of the tables mentioned. A quick glance will show that there are two employees who work both in the United States and Canada. If you used the SQL UNION command, you'd get the contents of both tables, with those two employees counted twice. Listing 14-14 shows the results of the union operation using the sample tables.

Listing 14-13. Sample Employee Tables

US employees table

```
+------------+-----------+-----------+---------+
| first_name | last_name | id        | dept_id |
+------------+-----------+-----------+---------+
| Chad       | Borg      | 990441234 | 1       |
| Alicia     | Wallace   | 330506781 | 4       |
| Howard     | Bell      | 333445555 | 5       |
| Tamra      | English   | 453453453 | 5       |
| Bill       | Smith     | 123456789 | 5       |
+------------+-----------+-----------+---------+
```

Canada employees table

```
+------------+-----------+-----------+---------+
| first_name | last_name | id        | dept_id |
+------------+-----------+-----------+---------+
| William    | Wallace   | 220059009 | <null>  |
| Aaron      | Hill      | 987987987 | 4       |
| Lillian    | Wallace   | 987654321 | 4       |
| Howard     | Bell      | 333445555 | 5       |
| Bill       | Smith     | 123456789 | 5       |
+------------+-----------+-----------+---------+
```

Listing 14-14. Example Union Result Set

```
+------------+-----------+-----------+---------+
| first_name | last_name | id        | dept_id |
+------------+-----------+-----------+---------+
| Chad       | Borg      | 990441234 | 1       |
| Alicia     | Wallace   | 330506781 | 4       |
| Howard     | Bell      | 333445555 | 5       |
| Tamra      | English   | 453453453 | 5       |
| Bill       | Smith     | 123456789 | 5       |
| William    | Wallace   | 220059009 | <null>  |
| Aaron      | Hill      | 987987987 | 4       |
| Lillian    | Wallace   | 987654321 | 4       |
+------------+-----------+-----------+---------+
```

Listing 14-15 shows the union algorithm. Notice that this sample is written using two steps to combine and then remove duplicates.

■ **Note** In MySQL, you can use the ALL option for the UNION clause to skip removal of duplicates.

Listing 14-15. The Union Algorithm

```
begin
  do
    get next tuple from rel_a
    write tuple from rel_a to temp_table
    get next tuple from rel_b
    write tuple from rel_b to temp_table
  while not (end_of_rel_a or end_of_rel_b)
  remove duplicates from temp_table
  return data from temp_table to client
end
```

Intersect

The intersect operation is the same as the set operation of the same name. In this case, the join is the intersection of the rows that are in both tables, with duplicate rows removed. Naturally, the tables must be of the same design for this operation to work.

Users specify the intersect operation by including the keyword INTERSECT in place of JOIN in the FROM clause. Let's say you wanted to combine two employee tables (one that includes all employees who work in the United States and another that includes employees who work in Canada) and ensure you get a result set that has all of the employees who work in both the United States and Canada. You could intersect the two using a command like:

```
SELECT * from us_employees INTERSECT ca_employees
```

Let's look at this one a little more closely. Using the example tables from Listing 14-13, you will see that there are two employees who work both in the United States and Canada. Listing 14-16 shows the results of the intersect operation using the sample tables. Listing 14-17 shows the intersect algorithm.

Listing 14-16. Example Intersect Result Set

```
+------------+-----------+-----------+---------+
| first_name | last_name | id        | dept_id |
+------------+-----------+-----------+---------+
| Howard     | Bell      | 333445555 | 5       |
| Bill       | Smith     | 123456789 | 5       |
+------------+-----------+-----------+---------+
```

Listing 14-17. The Intersect Algorithm

```
begin
  do
    get next tuple from rel_a
    get next tuple from rel_b
    if join column values match intersection conditions
      write tuple from rel_a to client
  while not (end_of_rel_a or end_of_rel_b)
end
```

DBXP Query Execution

Query execution in DBXP is accomplished using the optimized query tree. The tree structure itself is used as a pipeline for processing the query. When a query is executed, a get_next() method is issued on each of the children of the root node. Another get_next() method call is made to each of their children. This process continues as the tree is traversed to the lowest level of the tree containing a reference to a single table. Consider the query:

```
SELECT col1, col2 FROM table_a JOIN
(SELECT col2, col8 FROM table_b WHERE col6 = 7)
ON col8 WHERE table_a.col7 > 14
```

The query is retrieving data from table_a that matches a subset of the data in table_b. Notice that I wrote the subset as a subquery. The query-tree execution easily accommodates a subquery mechanism in which a subquery would be represented as a subtree. Figure 14-2 shows a high-level view of the concept.

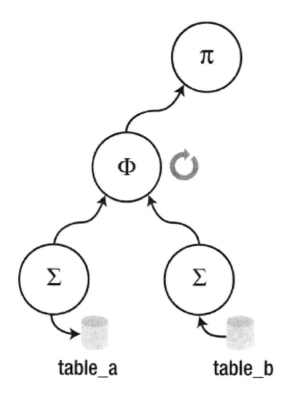

Figure 14-2. Query-tree execution

The operation for each node is executed for one row in the relation. Upon completion, the result of that operation passes the result up to the next operation in the tree. If no result is produced, control remains in the current node until a result is produced or there are no more results to process. As the tree is being climbed back to the root, the results are passed to each parent in turn until the root node is reached. Once the operation in the root node is complete, the resulting tuple is passed to the client. In this way, execution of the query appears to produce results faster because data (results) are shown to the client much earlier than if the query were to be executed for the entire set of operations before any results are given to the client.

The Query_tree class is designed to include the operations necessary to execute the query. Operations are included for project, restrict, and join. A prepare() method is called at the start of query execution. The prepare() method walks the query tree, initializing all the nodes for execution. Execution is accomplished by using a while loop that iterates through the result set, issuing a pulse to the tree starting at the root node. A pulse is a call to the get_next() method that is propagated down the tree. Each node that is pulsed issues a pulse to each of its children, starting with the left child. A separate parameterized method is provided for each of the following operations: do_restrict(), do_project(), and do_join().[4] These methods operate using one or two tuples as input and return either a null or a tuple. A null return indicates that the tuple or tuples do not satisfy the current operation. For example, a do_restrict() operation accepting a tuple operates using the expression class to evaluate the values in the tuple. If the expression evaluates to false, a null result is returned. If the expression evaluates to true, the same tuple is returned.[5]

This process is repeated throughout the tree, passing a single tuple up the tree to the root. The resulting tuple from the root is then processed by the external while loop and presented to the client via the existing MySQL client-communication protocols. This form of execution is called a pipeline because of the way nodes are traversed, passing a single node through the tree and thus through all of the operations in the query.

Designing the Tests

Creating comprehensive tests for a query execution would require writing SQL statements that cover all possible paths through the optimizer. In essence, you would need to create a test that tests all possible queries, both valid and invalid. The DBXP execution is incomplete, however. Although the project and restrict operations are fully implemented, only the inner join is implemented in the do_join() method. This permits you to create your own implementations for the remaining join operations in the stable DBXP environment.

With this in mind, let's design a few basic queries that exercise the execution engine to see how the DBXP engine processes queries. Listing 14-18 shows a sample test to exercise the query optimizer. Feel free to add your own queries to test the limits of the DBXP engine.

Listing 14-18. Sample DBXP Query-execution Test (Ch14.test)

```
#
# Sample test to test the DBXP_SELECT execution
#

# Test 1:
DBXP_SELECT first_name, last_name, sex, id FROM staff;

# Test 2:
DBXP_SELECT id FROM staff;

# Test 3:
DBXP_SELECT dir_name FROM directorate;

# Test 4a:
DBXP_SELECT id, dir_name FROM staff
JOIN directorate ON staff.mgr_id = directorate.dir_head_id;
```

---

[4]Set operations (intersect, union) and sorting are implemented as specialized forms of join operations.
[5]Actually, all tuples are passed by reference so the item returned is the same pointer.

```
# Test 4b:
DBXP_SELECT id, dir_name FROM staff, directorate
WHERE staff.mgr_id = directorate.dir_head_id;

# Test 5:
DBXP_SELECT * FROM staff WHERE staff.id = '123456789';

# Test 6:
DBXP_SELECT first_name, last_name FROM staff join directorate ON staff.mgr_id =
directorate.dir_head_id
WHERE directorate.dir_code = 'N41';

# Test 7:
DBXP_SELECT * FROM directorate JOIN building ON directorate.dir_code = building.dir_code;

# Test 8:
DBXP_SELECT directorate.dir_code, dir_name, building, dir_head_id
FROM directorate JOIN building ON directorate.dir_code = building.dir_code;
```

Notice that there are two queries for test case 4. What do you expect to be displayed by these two different queries? Why would I include them? I include them because they are really the same query (they generate the same result set). Due to the flexibility of the SQL command structure[6], it is possible to write a single query using several forms of the syntax. In this case, they should result in the same join and thus produce the same output. It also makes for a good test for an optimizer and an execution engine.

■ **Tip** The database used in these examples is included in the Appendix.

Please refer to Chapter 4 for more details on how to create and run the test in Listing 14-18 using the MySQL Test Suite.

Updating the DBXP SELECT Command

Since we now have a means to execute queries, we can replace the code in the DBXP_select_command() method with code that runs the SELECT commands. This method will check table access, open and lock the tables, execute the query, send results to the client, and unlock the tables. Listing 14-19 shows the completed DBXP_select_command().

Listing 14-19. Completed DBXP SELECT Command

```
/*
  Perform Select Command

  SYNOPSIS
    DBXP_select_command()
    THD *thd            IN the current thread
```

---

[6]Some would argue that this is an inherent weakness, and I am inclined to agree.

```
    DESCRIPTION
        This method executes the SELECT command using the query tree and optimizer.

    RETURN VALUE
        Success = 0
        Failed = 1
*/
int DBXP_select_command(THD *thd)
{
    bool res;
    READ_RECORD *record;
    select_result *result = thd->lex->result;

    DBUG_ENTER("DBXP_select_command");

    /* Prepare the tables (check access, locks) */
    res = check_table_access(thd, SELECT_ACL, thd->lex->query_tables, 0, 1, 1);
    if (res)
        DBUG_RETURN(1);
    res = open_and_lock_tables(thd, thd->lex->query_tables, 0,
                                MYSQL_LOCK_IGNORE_TIMEOUT);
    if (res)
        DBUG_RETURN(1);

    /* Create the query tree and optimize it */
    Query_tree *qt = build_query_tree(thd, thd->lex,
                        (TABLE_LIST*) thd->lex->select_lex.table_list.first);
    qt->heuristic_optimization();
    qt->cost_optimization();
    qt->prepare(qt->root);
    if (!(result= new select_send()))
        DBUG_RETURN(1);

    /* use the protocol class to communicate to client */
    Protocol *protocol= thd->protocol;

    /* write the field list for returning the query results */
    if (protocol->send_result_set_metadata(&qt->result_fields,
                            Protocol::SEND_NUM_ROWS | Protocol::SEND_EOF))
        DBUG_RETURN(1);

    /* pulse the execution engine to get a row from the result set */
    while (!qt->Eof(qt->root))
    {
        record = qt->get_next(qt->root);
        if (record != NULL)
        {
            /* send the data to the client */
            send_data(protocol, qt->result_fields, thd);
        }
    }
    my_eof(thd);
```

559

```
/* unlock tables and cleanup memory */
qt->cleanup(qt->root);
mysql_unlock_read_tables(thd, thd->lock);
delete qt;
DBUG_RETURN(0);
}
```

This implementation now has all the elements necessary to execute queries. It begins with checking table access and opening the tables. Assuming these steps complete successfully, the DBXP query-engine calls are next, beginning with building the query tree and then optimizing, and, finally, executing the query in a loop.

Notice that the loop is a simple while not end of file loop that calls the get_next() method on the root node. If a tuple (record) is returned, the code writes the row to the client; otherwise, it calls the get_next() method until the end of the file is detected. When all tuples have been processed, the code frees all used memory and unlocks the tables.

Since I placed the code that sends data to the client in one place outside the query-tree methods, the implementation for all of the relational operations is simplified a bit. As you will see in the following section, the query-tree methods resemble those of the theoretical algorithms.

The DBXP Algorithms

Now that the code to operate the DBXP query engine is complete, let's turn our attention to how the DBXP Query_tree class implements the relational operations.

Project

The DBXP project operation is implemented in a method called do_project() of the Query_tree class. This method is easy to implement, because the MySQL base classes provide a fast way to do the projection. Instead of looping through the attributes in the row, we can use the MySQL base classes to send the data to the client.

The do_project() method can be simplified to just store the current row in the buffer and return the row to the next node in the tree. When control returns to the DBXP_select_command() method, a helper method named send_data() is used to send the data to the client. Listing 14-20 shows the code for the do_project() method.

Listing 14-20. DBXP Project Method

```
/*
  Perform project operation.

  SYNOPSIS
    do_project()
    query_node *qn IN the operational node in the query tree.
    READ_RECORD *t -- the tuple to apply the operation to.

  DESCRIPTION
    This method performs the relational model operation entitled "project".
    This operation is a narrowing of the result set vertically by
    restricting the set of attributes in the output tuple.

  NOTES
    Returns 0 (null) if no tuple satisfies child operation (does NOT indicate
    the end of the file or end of query operation. Use Eof() to verify.
```

```
RETURN VALUE
    Success = new tuple with correct attributes
    Failed = NULL
*/
READ_RECORD *Query_tree::do_project(query_node *qn, READ_RECORD *t)
{
  DBUG_ENTER("do_project");
  if (t != NULL)
  {
    if (qn == root)

      /*
          If the left table isn't NULL, copy the record buffer from
          the table into the record buffer of the relations class.
          This completes the read from the storage engine and now
          provides the data for the projection (which is accomplished
          in send_data().
      */
      if (qn->relations[0] != NULL)
        memcpy((uchar *)qn->relations[0]->table->record[0],
          (uchar *)t->rec_buf,
          qn->relations[0]->table->s->rec_buff_length);
  }
  DBUG_RETURN(t);
}
```

Notice that in this code, all that must be done is copying the data read from the storage engine into the record buffer of the table object. I accomplish this by copying the memory from the READ_RECORD read from the storage engine into the table's first READ_RECORD buffer, copying in the number of bytes specified in the rec_buff_length attribute of the table.

Restrict

The DBXP restrict operation is implemented in a method called do_restrict() of the Query_tree class. The code uses the where_expr member variable of the Query_tree class that contains an instantiation of the Expression helper class. The implementation of the restrict operation is therefore simplified to calling the evaluate() method of the Expression class. Listing 14-21 shows the code for the do_restrict() method.

Listing 14-21. DBXP Restrict Method

```
/*
  Perform restrict operation.

  SYNOPSIS
    do_restrict()
    query_node *qn IN the operational node in the query tree.
    READ_RECORD *t -- the tuple to apply the operation to.
```

```
DESCRIPTION
    This method performs the relational model operation entitled "restrict".
    This operation is a narrowing of the result set horizontally by
    satisfying the expressions listed in the where clause of the SQL
    statement being executed.

RETURN VALUE
    Success = true
    Failed = false
*/
bool Query_tree::do_restrict(query_node *qn, READ_RECORD *t)
{
  bool found = false;

  DBUG_ENTER("do_restrict");
  if (qn != NULL)
  {
    /*
        If the left table isn't NULL, copy the record buffer from
        the table into the record buffer of the relations class.
        This completes the read from the storage engine and now
        provides the data for the projection (which is accomplished
        in send_data().

        Lastly, evaluate the where clause. If the where clause
        evaluates to true, we keep the record else we discard it.
    */
    if (qn->relations[0] != NULL)
      memcpy((uchar *)qn->relations[0]->table->record[0], (uchar *)t->rec_buf,
        qn->relations[0]->table->s->rec_buff_length);
    if (qn->where_expr != NULL)
      found = qn->where_expr->evaluate(qn->relations[0]->table);
  }
  DBUG_RETURN(found);
}
```

When a match is found, the data are copied to the record buffer of the table. This associates the data in the current record buffer with the table. It also allows the use of the many MySQL methods to manipulate fields and send data to the client.

Join

The DBXP join operation is implemented in a method called do_join() of the Query_tree class. The code uses the join_expr member variable of the Query_tree class that contains an instantiation of the Expression helper class. The implementation of the evaluation of the join conditions is therefore simplified to calling the evaluate() method of the Expression class.

This method is the most complex of all of the DBXP code. The reason for the complexity is due in part to the many conditions under which a join must be evaluated. The theoretical join algorithm described previously and the examples shown illustrate the complexity. I will expand on that a bit here in preparation for your examination of the do_join() source code. Listing 14-22 presents the simplified pseudocode for the do_join() method.

Listing 14-22. The DBXP Join Algorithm

```
begin
  if preempt_pipeline
    do
      if no left child
        get next tuple from left relation
      else
        get next tuple from left child
      fi
      insert tuple in left buffer in order by join column for left relation
    until eof
    do
      if no right child
        get next tuple from right relation
      else
        get next tuple from right child
      fi
      insert tuple in right buffer in order by join column for right relation
    until eof
  fi
  if left record pointer is NULL
    get next tuple from left buffer
  fi
  if right record pointer is NULL
    get next tuple from right buffer
  fi
  if there are tuples to process
    write attribute data of both tuples to table record buffers
    if join column values match join conditions
      check rewind conditions
      clear record pointers
      check for end of file
      set return record to left record pointer (indicates a match)
  else if left join value < right tuple join value
        set return record to NULL (no match)
        set left record pointer to NULL
      else if left join value > right tuple join value
        set return record to NULL (no match)
        set right record pointer to NULL
    fi
  else
    set return record to NULL (no match)
  fi
end
```

Since the join method is called repeatedly from the get_next() method, the algorithm has been altered to use the preempt_pipeline member variable from the query_node. This variable is set to TRUE during the prepare() method prior to executing the query tree. This allows the join method to detect when the first call is made so that the temporary buffers can be created. In this way, the traversal of the tree is pre-empted until the join operation completes for the first match (or the end of the file if no matches).

Notice that the algorithm uses two buffers to store the ordered rows from the incoming tables. These buffers are used to read records for the join operation, and they are represented using a record pointer for each buffer. If a match is found, both record pointers are set to NULL, which forces the code to read the next record. If the evaluation of the join condition indicates that the join value from the left table is less than the right, the left record pointer is set to NULL so that on the next call to the do_join() method, the next record is read from the left record buffer. Similarly, if the left join value is greater than the right, the right record pointer is set to NULL and on the next call a new record is read from the right record buffer.

Now that the basics of the do_join() method have been explained, take a look at the source code. Listing 14-23 shows the code for the do_join() method.

■ **Note**   I chose to not use a helper function to create the temporary buffers for the first step of the join operation so that I could keep the code together for easier debugging. Thus, the decision was purely for convenience. You can save a bit of code if you want by making this part of the code a helper function.

Listing 14-23. DBXP Join Method

```
/*
  Perform join operation.

  SYNOPSIS
    do_join()
    query_node *qn IN the operational node in the query tree.
    READ_RECORD *t -- the tuple to apply the operation to.

  DESCRIPTION
    This method performs the relational model operation entitled
    "join". This operation is the combination of two relations to
    form a composite view. This algorithm implements ALL variants
    of the join operation.

  NOTES
    Returns 0 (null) if no tuple satisfies child operation (does
    NOT indicate the end of the file or end of query operation.
    Use Eof() to verify.

  RETURN VALUE
    Success = new tuple with correct attributes
    Failed = NULL
*/
READ_RECORD *Query_tree::do_join(query_node *qn)
{
  READ_RECORD *next_tup=0;
  int i;
  TABLE *ltable = NULL;
  TABLE *rtable = NULL;
  Field *fright = NULL;
  Field *fleft = NULL;
```

```
record_buff *lprev=0;
record_buff *rprev=0;
expr_node *expr;

DBUG_ENTER("do_join");
if (qn == NULL)
  DBUG_RETURN(NULL);

/* check join type because some joins require other processing */
switch (qn->join_type)
{
  case (jnUNKNOWN) :
    break;
  case (jnINNER) :
  case (jnLEFTOUTER) :
  case (jnRIGHTOUTER) :
  case (jnFULLOUTER) :
  {

    /*
      preempt_pipeline == true means we need to stop the pipeline
      and sort the incoming rows. We do that by making an in-memory
      copy of the record buffers stored in left_record_buff and
      right_record_buff
    */
    if (qn->preempt_pipeline)
    {
      left_record_buff = NULL;
      right_record_buff = NULL;
      next_tup = NULL;

      /* Build buffer for tuples from left child. */
      do
      {
        /* if left child exists, get row from it */
        if (qn->left != NULL)
          lbuff = get_next(qn->left);

        /* else, read the row from the table (the storage handler) */
        else
        {
          /*
            Create space for the record buffer and
            store pointer in lbuff
          */
          lbuff = (READ_RECORD *) my_malloc(sizeof(READ_RECORD),
                              MYF(MY_ZEROFILL | MY_WME));
          lbuff->rec_buf =
            (uchar *) my_malloc(qn->relations[0]->table->s->rec_buff_length,
                              MYF(MY_ZEROFILL | MY_WME));
```

```
      /* check for end of file. Store result in eof array */
      qn->eof[0] =
        qn->relations[0]->table->file->ha_rnd_next(lbuff->rec_buf);
      if (qn->eof[0] != HA_ERR_END_OF_FILE)
        qn->eof[0] = false;
      else
      {
        lbuff = NULL;
        qn->eof[0] = true;
      }
    }
    /* if the left buffer is not null, get a new row from table */
    if (lbuff != NULL)
    {
      /* we need the table information for processing fields */
      if (qn->left == NULL)
        ltable = qn->relations[0]->table;
      else
        ltable = get_table(qn->left);
      if (ltable != NULL)
        memcpy((uchar *)ltable->record[0], (uchar *)lbuff->rec_buf,
          ltable->s->rec_buff_length);

      /* get the join expression */
      expr = qn->join_expr->get_expression(0);
      for (Field **field = ltable->field; *field; field++)
        if (strcasecmp((*field)->field_name, ((Field *)expr->left_op)->field_name)==0)
          fleft = (*field);

      /*
         If field was found, add the row to the in-memory buffer
         ordered by the join column.
      */
      if ((fleft != NULL) && (!fleft->is_null()))
        insertion_sort(true, fleft, lbuff);
    }
  } while (lbuff != NULL);
  /* Build buffer for tuples from right child. */
  do
  {
    /* if right child exists, get row from it */
    if (qn->right != NULL)
      rbuff = get_next(qn->right);

    /* else, read the row from the table (the storage handler) */
    else
    {
      /*
         Create space for the record buffer and
         store pointer in rbuff
      */
```

```
        rbuff = (READ_RECORD *) my_malloc(sizeof(READ_RECORD),
                            MYF(MY_ZEROFILL | MY_WME));
        rbuff->rec_buf =
          (uchar *) my_malloc(qn->relations[0]->table->s->rec_buff_length,
                            MYF(MY_ZEROFILL | MY_WME));

        /* check for end of file. Store result in eof array */
        qn->eof[1] =
          qn->relations[1]->table->file->ha_rnd_next(rbuff->rec_buf);
        if (qn->eof[1] != HA_ERR_END_OF_FILE)
          qn->eof[1] = false;
        else
        {
          rbuff = NULL;
          qn->eof[1] = true;
        }
      }
      /* if the right buffer is not null, get a new row from table */
      if (rbuff != NULL)
      {
        /* we need the table information for processing fields */
        if (qn->right == NULL)
          rtable = qn->relations[1]->table;
        else
          rtable = get_table(qn->right);
        if (rtable != NULL)
          memcpy((uchar *)rtable->record[0], (uchar *)rbuff->rec_buf,
            rtable->s->rec_buff_length);

        /* get the join expression */
        expr = qn->join_expr->get_expression(0);
        for (Field **field = rtable->field; *field; field++)
          if (strcasecmp((*field)->field_name, ((Field *)expr->right_op)->field_name)==0)
            fright = (*field);

        /*
            If field was found, add the row to the in-memory buffer
            ordered by the join column.
        */
        if ((fright != NULL) && (!fright->is_null()))
          insertion_sort(false, fright, rbuff);
      }
  } while (rbuff != NULL);
  left_record_buffer_ptr = left_record_buff;
  right_record_buffer_ptr = right_record_buff;
  qn->preempt_pipeline = false;
}
/*
  This is where the actual join code begins.
  We get a tuple from each table and start the compare.
*/
```

```
/*
   if lbuff is null and the left record buffer has data
   get the row from the buffer
*/
if ((lbuff == NULL) && (left_record_buffer_ptr != NULL))
{
  lbuff = left_record_buffer_ptr->record;
  lprev = left_record_buffer_ptr;
  left_record_buffer_ptr = left_record_buffer_ptr->next;
}

/*
   if rbuff is null and the right record buffer has data
   get the row from the buffer
*/
if ((rbuff == NULL) && (right_record_buffer_ptr != NULL))
{
  rbuff = right_record_buffer_ptr->record;
  rprev = right_record_buffer_ptr;
  right_record_buffer_ptr = right_record_buffer_ptr->next;
}

/*
   if the left buffer was null, check to see if a row is
   available from left child.
*/
if (ltable == NULL)
{
  if (qn->left == NULL)
    ltable = qn->relations[0]->table;
  else
    ltable = get_table(qn->left);
}
/*
   if the right buffer was null, check to see if a row is
   available from right child.
*/
if (rtable == NULL)
{
  if (qn->right == NULL)
    rtable = qn->relations[1]->table;
  else
    rtable = get_table(qn->right);
}
/*
   If there are two rows to compare, copy the record buffers
   to the table record buffers. This transfers the data
   from the internal buffer to the record buffer. It enables
   us to reuse the MySQL code for manipulating fields.
*/
```

```
if ((lbuff != NULL) && (rbuff != NULL))
{
  memcpy((uchar *)ltable->record[0], (uchar *)lbuff->rec_buf,
    ltable->s->rec_buff_length);
  memcpy((uchar *)rtable->record[0], (uchar *)rbuff->rec_buf,
    rtable->s->rec_buff_length);

  /* evaluate the join condition */
  i = qn->join_expr->compare_join(qn->join_expr->get_expression(0),
    ltable, rtable);

  /* if there is a match...*/
  if (i == 0)
  {
    /* return the row in the next_tup pointer */
    next_tup = lbuff;

    /* store next rows from buffer (already advanced 1 row) */
    record_buff *left = left_record_buffer_ptr;
    record_buff *right = right_record_buffer_ptr;

    /*
       Check to see if either buffer needs to be rewound to
       allow us to process many rows on one side to one row
       on the other
    */
    check_rewind(left_record_buffer_ptr, lprev,
      right_record_buffer_ptr, rprev);

    /* set poointer to null to force read on next loop */
    lbuff = NULL;
    rbuff = NULL;

    /*
      If the left buffer has been changed and if the
      buffer is not at the end, set the buffer to the next row.
    */
    if (left != left_record_buffer_ptr)
    {
      if (left_record_buffer_ptr != NULL)
      {
        lbuff = left_record_buffer_ptr->record;
      }
    }

    /*
      If the right buffer has been changed and if the
      buffer is not at the end, set the buffer to the next row.
    */
    if (right != right_record_buffer_ptr)
```

```
    {
      if (right_record_buffer_ptr != NULL)
      {
        rbuff = right_record_buffer_ptr->record;
      }
    }

    /* Now check for end of file and save results in eof array */
    if (left_record_buffer_ptr == NULL)
      qn->eof[2] = true;
    else
      qn->eof[2] = false;
    if (right_record_buffer_ptr == NULL)
      qn->eof[3] = true;
    else
      qn->eof[3] = false;
  }

  /* if the rows didn't match...*/
  else
  {
    /* get next rows from buffers (already advanced) */
    record_buff *left = left_record_buffer_ptr;
    record_buff *right = right_record_buffer_ptr;

    /*
       Check to see if either buffer needs to be rewound to
       allow us to process many rows on one side to one row
       on the other. The results of this rewind must be
       saved because there was no match and we may have to
       reuse one or more of the rows.
    */
    check_rewind(left_record_buffer_ptr, lprev,
      right_record_buffer_ptr, rprev);

    /*
       If the left buffer has been changed and if the
       buffer is not at the end, set the buffer to the next row
       and copy the data into the record buffer/
    */
    if (left != left_record_buffer_ptr)
    {
      if (left_record_buffer_ptr != NULL)
      {
        memcpy((uchar *)ltable->record[0],
          (uchar *)left_record_buffer_ptr->record->rec_buf,
          ltable->s->rec_buff_length);
        lbuff = left_record_buffer_ptr->record;
      }
    }
```

```
      /*
        If the right buffer has been changed and if the
        buffer is not at the end, set the buffer to the next row
        and copy the data into the record buffer/
      */
      if (right_record_buffer_ptr != NULL)
        if ((right_record_buffer_ptr->next == NULL) &&
            (right_record_buffer_ptr->prev == NULL))
          lbuff = NULL;
      if (right != right_record_buffer_ptr)
      {
        if (right_record_buffer_ptr != NULL)
        {
          memcpy((uchar *)rtable->record[0],
            (uchar *)right_record_buffer_ptr->record->rec_buf,
            rtable->s->rec_buff_length);
          rbuff = right_record_buffer_ptr->record;
        }
      }

      /* Now check for end of file and save results in eof array */
      if (left_record_buffer_ptr == NULL)
        qn->eof[2] = true;
      else
        qn->eof[2] = false;
      if (right_record_buffer_ptr == NULL)
        qn->eof[3] = true;
      else
        qn->eof[3] = false;

      next_tup = NULL;
    }
  }
  else
  {
    next_tup = NULL; /* at end, return null */
  }
  break;
}

/* placeholder for exercise... */
case (jnCROSSPRODUCT) :
{
  break;
}
/*
  placeholder for exercises...
  Union and intersect are mirrors of each other -- same code will
  work for both except the dupe elimination/inclusion part (see below)
*/
case (jnUNION) :
case (jnINTERSECT) :
```

```
    {
      break;
    }
  }
  DBUG_RETURN(next_tup);
}
```

Notice in the code that under any condition other than a match, the record returned from the code is set to NULL. This allows the loop in the get_next() method to repeatedly call the do_join() method until a match is returned. This is similar to the way the do_restrict() method call is made.

I have not implemented the code for any of the other join operations. The main reason is that it allows you to experiment with the code (see the exercises at end of this chapter). Fortunately, you should find that the code can be modified with a few simple alterations to allow the processing of the outer joins. Adding code for the cross-product, union, and intersect operations can be accomplished by implementing the theoretical algorithm described in the first part of this chapter.

After you have studied the pseudocode for the method, you should find reading the code easier. The most complex part of this code is the check_rewind() method. This is implemented as a function in the class in order to make the code less complex and easier to read. Several other helper methods are described in more detail in the following section.

Other Methods

Several helper methods make up the DBXP execution engine. Table 14-1 lists the new methods and their uses. The more complex methods are described in more detail in the text that follows.

Table 14-1. *The DBXP Execution Engine Helper Methods*

Class::Method	Description
Query_tree::get_next()	Retrieves next tuple from child node.
Query_tree::insertion_sort()	Creates an ordered buffer of READ_RECORD pointers. Used in the join operations for ordering the incoming tuples.
Query_tree::eof()	Checks for the end-of-file condition for the storage engine or temporary buffers.
Query_tree::check_rewind()	Checks to see if the record buffers need to be adjusted to reread tuples for multiple matches.
send_data()	Sends data to the client. See sql_dbxp_parse.cc.
Expression::evaluate()	Evaluates the WHERE clause for a restrict operation.
Expression::compare_join()	Evaluates the join condition for a join operation.
Handler::rnd_init()	Initializes read from storage engine (see Chapter 10).
Handler::rnd_next()	Reads the next tuple from storage engine (see Chapter 10).

The get_next() Method

The get_next() method is the heart of the query-execution flow in DBXP. It is responsible for calling the do_... methods that implement the query operations. It is called once from the while loop in the DBXP_select_command() method. Once this method is initiated the first time, it performs the operation for the current node, calling the children nodes to get their result. The process is repeated in a recursive fashion until all the children in the current node have returned a single tuple. Listing 14-24 shows the code for the get_next() method.

Listing 14-24. The get_next() Method

```
/*
  Get the next tuple (row) in the result set.

  SYNOPSIS
    Eof()
    query_node *qn IN the operational node in the query tree.

  DESCRIPTION
    This method is used to get the next READ_RECORD from the pipeline.
    The idea is to call prepare() after you've validated the query then call
    get_next to get the first tuple in the pipeline.

  RETURN VALUE
    Success = next tuple in the result set
    Failed = NULL
*/
READ_RECORD *Query_tree::get_next(query_node *qn)
{
  READ_RECORD *next_tup = NULL;
  DBUG_ENTER("get_next");

  /*
    For each of the possible node types, perform the query operation
    by calling the method for the operation. These implement a very
    high-level abstraction of the operation. The real work is left
    to the methods.
  */
  switch (qn->node_type)
  {
    /* placeholder for exercises... */
    case Query_tree::qntDistinct :
      break;

    /* placeholder for exercises... */
    case Query_tree::qntUndefined :
      break;

    /* placeholder for exercises... */
    case Query_tree::qntSort :
      if (qn->preempt_pipeline)
        qn->preempt_pipeline = false;
      break;

    /*
      For restrict, get a row (tuple) from the table and
      call the do_restrict method looping until a row is returned
```

```
     (data matches conditions), then return result to main loop
     in DBXP_select_command.
  */
  case Query_tree::qntRestrict :
    do
    {
      /* if there is a child, get row from child */
      if (qn->left != NULL)
        next_tup = get_next(qn->left);

      /* else get the row from the table stored in this node */
      else
      {
        /* create space for the record buffer */
        if (next_tup == NULL)
          next_tup = (READ_RECORD *) my_malloc(sizeof(READ_RECORD),
                                        MYF(MY_ZEROFILL | MY_WME));
        next_tup->rec_buf = (uchar *) my_malloc(qn->relations[0]->table->s->rec_buff_length,
                                        MYF(MY_ZEROFILL | MY_WME));

        /* read row from table (storage handler */
        qn->eof[0] = qn->relations[0]->table->file->ha_rnd_next(next_tup->rec_buf);

        /* check for end of file */
        if (qn->eof[0] != HA_ERR_END_OF_FILE)
          qn->eof[0] = false;
        else
        {
          qn->eof[0] = true;
          next_tup = NULL;
        }
      }

      /* if there is a row, call the do_restrict method */
      if (next_tup)
        if(!do_restrict(qn, next_tup))
        {
          /* if no row to return, free memory used */
          my_free(next_tup->rec_buf);
          my_free(next_tup);
          next_tup = NULL;
        }
    } while ((next_tup == NULL) && !Eof(qn));
    break;

  /*
    For project, get a row (tuple) from the table and
    call the do_project method. If successful,
    return result to main loop in DBXP_select_command.
  */
  case Query_tree::qntProject :
```

```
/* if there is a child, get row from child */
if (qn->left != NULL)
{
  next_tup = get_next(qn->left);
  if (next_tup)
    if (!do_project(qn, next_tup))
    {
      /* if no row to return, free memory used */
      my_free(next_tup->rec_buf);
      my_free(next_tup);
      next_tup = NULL;
    }
}

/* else get the row from the table stored in this node */
else
{
  /* create space for the record buffer */
  if (next_tup == NULL)
    next_tup = (READ_RECORD *) my_malloc(sizeof(READ_RECORD),
                            MYF(MY_ZEROFILL | MY_WME));
  next_tup->rec_buf = (uchar *) my_malloc(qn->relations[0]->table->s->rec_buff_length + 20,
                            MYF(MY_ZEROFILL | MY_WME));

  /* read row from table (storage handler) */
  qn->eof[0] = qn->relations[0]->table->file->ha_rnd_next(next_tup->rec_buf);

  /* check for end of file */
  if (qn->eof[0] != HA_ERR_END_OF_FILE)
  {
    qn->eof[0] = false;
  }
  else
  {
    qn->eof[0] = true;
    next_tup = NULL;
  }

  /* if there is a row, call the do_project method */
  if (next_tup)
  {
    if (!do_project(qn, next_tup))
    {
      /* no row to return, free memory used */
      my_free(next_tup->rec_buf);
      my_free(next_tup);
      next_tup = NULL;
    }
  }
}
break;
```

```
  /*
    For join, loop until either a row is returned from the
    do_join method or we are at end of file for both tables.
    If successful (data matches conditions),
    return result to main loop in DBXP_select_command.
  */
  case Query_tree::qntJoin :
    do
    {
      if (next_tup)
      {
        /* if no row to return, free memory used */
        my_free(next_tup->rec_buf);
        my_free(next_tup);
        next_tup = NULL;
      }
      next_tup = do_join(qn);
    }
    while ((next_tup == NULL) && !Eof(qn));
    break;
  }
  DBUG_RETURN(next_tup);
}
```

The send_data() Method

The send_data() method is a helper router that writes data to the client using the MySQL Protocol class to handle the communication chores. This method was borrowed from the MySQL source code and rewritten slightly to accommodate the (relative) simplistic execution of the DBXP execution engine. In this case, the Item superclass is used to send the field values to the client using the item->send() method. Listing 14-25 shows the code for the send_data() method.

Listing 14-25. The send_data() Method

```
/*
  Send data

  SYNOPSIS
    send_data()
    Protocol *p         IN the Protocol class
    THD *thd            IN the current thread
    List<Item> *items   IN the list of fields identified in the row

  DESCRIPTION
    This method sends the data to the clien using the protocol class.

  RETURN VALUE
    Success = 0
    Failed = 1
```

```
*/
bool send_data(Protocol *protocol, List<Item> &items, THD *thd)
{

  /* use a list iterator to loop through items */
  List_iterator_fast<Item> li(items);

  char buff[MAX_FIELD_WIDTH];
  String buffer(buff, sizeof(buff), &my_charset_bin);
  DBUG_ENTER("send_data");

  /* this call resets the transmission buffers */
  protocol->prepare_for_resend();

  /* for each item in the list (a field), send data to the client */
  Item *item;
  while ((item=li++))
  {
    /*
      Use the MySQL send method for the item class to write to network.
      If unsuccessful, free memory and send error message to client.
    */
    if (item->send(protocol, &buffer))
    {
      protocol->free();          /* Free used buffer */
      my_message(ER_OUT_OF_RESOURCES, ER(ER_OUT_OF_RESOURCES), MYF(0));
      break;
    }
  }
  /* increment row count */
  thd->inc_sent_row_count(1);

  /* if network write was ok, return */
  if (thd->vio_ok())
    DBUG_RETURN(protocol->write());

  DBUG_RETURN(0);
}
```

The method uses the item class, calling the send() method and passing in a pointer to an instance of the protocol class. This is how data for a field item is written to the client. The send_data() method is one in which the projection and join column lists are processed to complete the operations. This is one of the nicest touches in the MySQL source code. But, how do the MySQL classes know what columns to send? Take a look back at the build_query_tree() method. Recall that there is a list identified in the select_lex class. The DBXP code captures these fields in the line of code shown here. This list is directly from the columns list in the SELECT command and populated by the parser code.

```
qt->result_fields = lex->select_lex.item_list;
```

These fields are captured in the thread extended structure. The MySQL code simply writes out any data that are present in this list of fields.

The check_rewind() Method

This method is the part of the join algorithms that is most often omitted in database texts. The method adjusts the buffers for rows coming from the tables to allow the algorithm to reuse processed rows. This is necessary because one row from one table may match more than one row from another. While the concept of the method is relatively straightforward, it can be a challenge to write the code yourself. Fortunately, I've saved you the trouble.

The code works by examining the rows in the record buffers. It takes as input pointers to the record buffers along with the previous record pointer in the buffer. The record buffer is implemented as a doubly linked list to allow movement forward and back through the buffers.

This code must process several conditions in order to keep the flow of data to the do_join() method. These conditions are the result of the evaluation of the join condition(s) after a match has been detected. The result of a failed match is handled in the do_join() method.

- If the next record in the left buffer is a match to the right buffer, rewind the right buffer until the join condition of the right buffer is less than the left.

- If the next record in the left buffer is not a match to the right buffer, set the right buffer to the previous right record pointer.

- If the left record buffer is at the end and there are still records in the right buffer, and if the join value of the previous left record pointer is a match to the right record pointer, set the left record pointer to the previous left record pointer.

The method is implemented with a bias to the left record buffer. In other words, the code keeps the right buffer synchronized with the left buffer (also called a left-deep join execution). Listing 14-26 shows the code for the check_rewind() method.

Listing 14-26. The check_rewind() Method

```
/*
  Adjusts pointers to record buffers for join.

  SYNOPSIS
    check_rewind()
    record_buff *cur_left IN the left record buffer
    record_buff *cur_left_prev IN the left record buffer previous
    record_buff *cur_right IN the left record buffer
    record_buff *cur_right_prev IN the left record buffer previous

  DESCRIPTION
    This method is used to push a tuple back into the buffer
    during a join operation that preempts the pipeline.

  NOTES
    Now, here's where we have to check the next tuple in each
    relation to see if they are the same. If one of them is the
    same and the other isn't, push one of them back.

    We need to rewind if one of the following is true:
    1. The next record in R2 has the same join value as R1
    2. The next record in R1 has the same join value as R2
    3. The next record in R1 has the same join value and R2 is
       different (or EOF)
    4. The next record in R2 has the same join value and R1 is
       different (or EOF)
```

```
  RETURN VALUE
    Success = int index number
    Failed = -1
*/
int Query_tree::check_rewind(record_buff *cur_left,
                             record_buff *curr_left_prev,
                             record_buff *cur_right,
                             record_buff *curr_right_prev)
{
  record_buff *left_rcd_ptr = cur_left;
  record_buff *right_rcd_ptr = cur_right;
  int i;
  DBUG_ENTER("check_rewind");

  /*
    If the next tuple in right record is the same as the present tuple
      AND the next tuple in right record is different, rewind until
      it is the same
    else
      Push left record back.
  */

  /* if both buffers are at EOF, return -- nothing to do */
  if ((left_rcd_ptr == NULL) && (right_rcd_ptr == NULL))
    DBUG_RETURN(0);

  /* if the currently processed record is null, get the one before it */
  if (cur_right == NULL)
    right_rcd_ptr = curr_right_prev;

  /*
    if left buffer is not at end, check to see
    if we need to rewind right buffer
  */
  if (left_rcd_ptr != NULL)
  {
    /* compare the join conditions to check order */
    i = memcmp(left_rcd_ptr->field_ptr, right_rcd_ptr->field_ptr,
      left_rcd_ptr->field_length < right_rcd_ptr->field_length ?
      left_rcd_ptr->field_length : right_rcd_ptr->field_length);

    /*
      i == 0 means the rows are the same. In this case, we need to
      check to see if we need to advance or rewind the right buffer.
    */
    if (i == 0)
```

```
{
  /*
    If there is a next row in the right buffer, check to see
    if it matches the left row. If the right row is greater
    than the left row, rewind the right buffer to one previous
    to the current row or until we hit the start.
  */
  if (right_rcd_ptr->next != NULL)
  {
    right_rcd_ptr = right_rcd_ptr->next;
    i = memcmp(left_rcd_ptr->field_ptr, right_rcd_ptr->field_ptr,
      left_rcd_ptr->field_length < right_rcd_ptr->field_length ?
      left_rcd_ptr->field_length : right_rcd_ptr->field_length);
    if (i > 0)
    {
      do
      {
        if (right_rcd_ptr->prev != NULL)
        {
          right_rcd_ptr = right_rcd_ptr->prev;
          i = memcmp(left_rcd_ptr->field_ptr, right_rcd_ptr->field_ptr,
            left_rcd_ptr->field_length < right_rcd_ptr->field_length ?
            left_rcd_ptr->field_length : right_rcd_ptr->field_length);
        }
      }
      while ((i == 0) && (right_rcd_ptr->prev != NULL));

      /* now advance one more to set pointer to correct location */
      if (right_rcd_ptr->next != NULL)
        right_rcd_ptr = right_rcd_ptr->next;
    }
    /* if no next right row, rewind to previous row */
    else
      right_rcd_ptr = right_rcd_ptr->prev;
  }
  /*
    If there is a next row in the left buffer, check to see
    if it matches the right row. If there is a match and the right
    buffer is not at start, rewind the right buffer to one previous
    to the current row.
  */
  else if (left_rcd_ptr->next != NULL)
  {
    if (right_rcd_ptr->prev != NULL)
    {
      i = memcmp(left_rcd_ptr->field_ptr, right_rcd_ptr->prev->field_ptr,
        left_rcd_ptr->field_length < right_rcd_ptr->prev->field_length ?
        left_rcd_ptr->field_length : right_rcd_ptr->prev->field_length);
    }
```

```
        if ((i == 0) && (right_rcd_ptr->prev != NULL))
          right_rcd_ptr = right_rcd_ptr->prev;
      }
    }
    /* if the left row is less than right row, rewind right buffer */
    else if (i < 0)
    {
      if (right_rcd_ptr->prev != NULL)
        right_rcd_ptr = right_rcd_ptr->prev;
    }
    /* if the right row is less than the left row, advance right row */
    else
    {
      if (right_rcd_ptr->next != NULL)
        right_rcd_ptr = right_rcd_ptr->next;
    }
  }
  /*
    Rows don't match, so advance the right buffer and check match again.
    if they still match, rewind left buffer.
  */
  else
  {
    if (right_rcd_ptr->next != NULL)
    {
      i = memcmp(curr_left_prev->field_ptr, right_rcd_ptr->field_ptr,
        curr_left_prev->field_length < right_rcd_ptr->field_length ?
        curr_left_prev->field_length : right_rcd_ptr->field_length);
      if (i == 0)
        left_rcd_ptr = curr_left_prev;
    }
  }
  /* set buffer pointers to adjusted rows from buffers */
  left_record_buffer_ptr = left_rcd_ptr;
  right_record_buffer_ptr = right_rcd_ptr;
  DBUG_RETURN(0);
}
```

Now that you've had a close look at the source code for the DBXP query execution, it's time to compile the code and take it for a test ride.

Compiling and Testing the Code

If you haven't already, download the source code for this chapter and place the files in the /sql directory off the root of your source tree. In the example code, you will also find a difference file you can use to apply the changes to the server source code files (e.g. mysqld.cc sql_cmd.h, etc.). Or you can use the changes from Chapter 13 as the changes to the server code is the same.

Spend a few moments looking through the source code so that you are familiar with the methods. Taking the time to look through the code now will help should you need to debug the code to work with your configuration or if you want to add other enhancements or work the exercises.

■ **Tip** See Chapter 11 for details on how to add the source files to the project and compile them.

Once you have the new code installed and compiled, you can run the server and perform the tests. You can run the test you created earlier, or you can enter the commands in a MySQL client utility. Listing 14-27 shows the expected output of running the commands listed in the test.

Listing 14-27. Example Test Runs

```
mysql> SELECT DBXP first_name, last_name, sex, id FROM staff;

+------------+------------+------+-----------+
| first_name | last_name  | sex  | id        |
+------------+------------+------+-----------+
| John       | Smith      | M    | 333445555 |
| William    | Walters    | M    | 123763153 |
| Alicia     | St.Cruz    | F    | 333444444 |
| Goy        | Hong       | F    | 921312388 |
| Rajesh     | Kardakarna | M    | 800122337 |
| Monty      | Smythe     | M    | 820123637 |
| Richard    | Jones      | M    | 830132335 |
| Edward     | Engles     | M    | 333445665 |
| Beware     | Borg       | F    | 123654321 |
| Wilma      | Maxima     | F    | 123456789 |
+------------+------------+------+-----------+
10 rows in set (0.01 sec)

mysql> DBXP_SELECT id FROM staff;
+-----------+
| id        |
+-----------+
| 333445555 |
| 123763153 |
| 333444444 |
| 921312388 |
| 800122337 |
| 820123637 |
| 830132335 |
| 333445665 |
| 123654321 |
| 123456789 |
+-----------+
10 rows in set (0.00 sec)
```

```
mysql> DBXP_SELECT dir_name FROM directorate;
+-----------------+
| dir_name        |
+-----------------+
| Development     |
| Human Resources |
| Management      |
+-----------------+
3 rows in set (0.00 sec)

mysql> DBXP_SELECT id, dir_name FROM staff
JOIN directorate ON staff.mgr_id = directorate.dir_head_id;
+-----------+-----------------+
| id        | dir_name        |
+-----------+-----------------+
| 123763153 | Human Resources |
| 921312388 | Human Resources |
| 333445555 | Management      |
| 123654321 | Management      |
| 800122337 | Development     |
| 820123637 | Development     |
| 830132335 | Development     |
| 333445665 | Development     |
| 123456789 | Development     |
+-----------+-----------------+
9 rows in set (0.00 sec)

mysql> DBXP_SELECT id, dir_name FROM staff, directorate
WHERE staff.mgr_id = directorate.dir_head_id;
+-----------+-----------------+
| id        | dir_name        |
+-----------+-----------------+
| 123763153 | Human Resources |
| 921312388 | Human Resources |
| 333445555 | Management      |
| 123654321 | Management      |
| 800122337 | Development     |
| 820123637 | Development     |
| 830132335 | Development     |
| 333445665 | Development     |
| 123456789 | Development     |
+-----------+-----------------+
9 rows in set (0.00 sec)

mysql> DBXP_SELECT * FROM staff WHERE staff.id = '123456789';
+-----------+------------+----------+-----------+------+--------+-----------+
| id        | first_name | mid_name | last_name | sex  | salary | mgr_id    |
+-----------+------------+----------+-----------+------+--------+-----------+
| 123456789 | Wilma      | N        | Maxima    | F    |  43000 | 333445555 |
+-----------+------------+----------+-----------+------+--------+-----------+
1 row in set (0.00 sec)
```

583

```
mysql> DBXP_SELECT first_name, last_name FROM staff join directorate ON staff.mgr_id = directorate.
dir_head_id WHERE directorate.dir_code = 'N41';
+------------+------------+
| first_name | last_name  |
+------------+------------+
| Rajesh     | Kardakarna |
| Monty      | Smythe     |
| Richard    | Jones      |
| Edward     | Engles     |
| Wilma      | Maxima     |
+------------+------------+
5 rows in set (0.00 sec)

mysql> DBXP_SELECT * FROM directorate JOIN building ON directorate.dir_code = building.dir_code;
+----------+-----------------+-------------+----------+----------+
| dir_code | dir_name        | dir_head_id | dir_code | building |
+----------+-----------------+-------------+----------+----------+
| M00      | Management      | 333444444   | M00      | 1000     |
| N01      | Human Resources | 123654321   | N01      | 1453     |
| N41      | Development     | 333445555   | N41      | 1300     |
| N41      | Development     | 333445555   | N41      | 1301     |
| N41      | Development     | 333445555   | N41      | 1305     |
+----------+-----------------+-------------+----------+----------+
5 rows in set (0.00 sec)

mysql> DBXP_SELECT directorate.dir_code, dir_name, building, dir_head_id
FROM directorate JOIN building ON directorate.dir_code = building.dir_code;
+----------+-----------------+----------+-------------+
| dir_code | dir_name        | building | dir_head_id |
+----------+-----------------+----------+-------------+
| M00      | Management      | 1000     | 333444444   |
| N01      | Human Resources | 1453     | 123654321   |
| N41      | Development     | 1300     | 333445555   |
| N41      | Development     | 1301     | 333445555   |
| N41      | Development     | 1305     | 333445555   |
+----------+-----------------+----------+-------------+
5 rows in set (0.00 sec)

mysql>
```

Summary

I presented in this chapter the internal-database query-execution operations. You learned how to expand the concept of the query tree to incorporate a query-execution engine that uses the tree structure in the execution process. The knowledge of these technologies should provide you with a greater understanding of the DBXP engine and how it can be used to study database technologies in more depth.

You've reached the end of the book and may be wondering what else there is to do. This part of the book has provided you with an experimental engine based in MySQL that will allow you to explore your own implementation of the internal-database technologies. Best of all, you can tweak the DBXP code any way you wish. Perhaps you just want to experiment, but you may also want to implement the union and intersect operations, or just expand the DBXP engine to implement the full set of query features in MySQL. Whatever you choose to do with what you have learned from this section of the book, you can always amaze your friends and coworkers by implementing an alternative query engine for MySQL!

EXERCISES

The following lists several areas for further exploration. They represent the types of activities you might want to conduct as experiments (or as a class assignment) to explore relational-database technologies.

1. Complete the code for the `do_join()` method to support all of the join types supported in MySQL. Hint: You must be able to identify the type of join before you begin optimization. Look to the parser for details.

2. Examine the code for the `check_rewind()` method in the `Query_tree` class. Change the implementation to use temporary tables to avoid high memory usage when joining large tables.

3. Evaluate the performance of the DBXP query engine. Run multiple test runs and record execution times. Compare these results to the same queries using the native MySQL query engine. How does the DBXP engine compare to MySQL?

4. Why is the remove duplicates operation not necessary for the intersect operation? Are there any conditions where this is false? If so, what are they?

5. (advanced) MySQL does not currently support a cross-product or intersect operation (as defined by Date). Change the MySQL parser to recognize these new keywords and process queries, such `SELECT * FROM A CROSS B` and `SELECT * FROM A INTERSECT B`, and add these functions to the execution engine. Hint: See the `do_join()` method.

6. (advanced) Form a more complete list of test queries and examine the limitations of the DBXP engine. What modifications are necessary to broaden the capabilities of the DBXP engine?

APPENDIX

This appendix contains a consolidated list of the references used in this book along with the description of the sample database used in the examples.

Bibliography

The following bibliography contains additional sources of interesting articles and papers. The bibliography is arranged by topic.

Database Theory

- A. Belussi, E. Bertino, and B. Catania. *An Extended Algebra for Constraint Databases* (IEEE Transactions on Knowledge and Data Engineering 10.5 (1998): 686–705).

- C. J. Date and H. Darwen. *Foundation for Future Database Systems: The Third Manifesto*. (Reading: Addison-Wesley, 2000).

- C. J. Date. *The Database Relational Model: A Retrospective Review and Analysis*. (Reading: Addison-Wesley, 2001).

- R. Elmasri and S. B. Navathe. *Fundamentals of Database Systems*. 4th ed. (Boston: Addison-Wesley, 2003).

- M. J. Franklin, B. T. Jonsson, and D. Kossmann. *Performance Tradeoffs for Client-server Query Processing* (Proceedings of the 1996 ACM SIGMOD International Conference on Management of Data Montreal, Canada 1996. 149–160).

- P. Gassner, G. M. Lohman, K. B. Schiefer, and Y. Wang. *Query Optimization in the IBM DB2 Family* (Bulletin of the Technical Committee on Data Engineering 16.4 (1993): 4–17).

- Y. E. Ioannidis, R. T. Ng, K. Shim, and T. Sellis. *Parametric query optimization* (VLDB Journal 6 (1997):132–151).

- D. Kossman, and K. Stocker. *Iterative Dynamic Programming: A New Class of Query Optimization Algorithms* (ACM Transactions on Database Systems 25.1 (2000): 43–82).

- C. Lee, C. Shih, and Y. Chen. *A graph-theoretic model for optimizing queries involving methods*. (VLDB Journal 9 (2001):327–343).

- P. G. Selinger, M. M. Astraham, D. D. Chamberlin, R. A. Lories, and T. G. Price. *Access Path Selection in a Relational Database Management System* (Proceedings of the ACM SIGMOD International Conference on the Management of Data. Aberdeen, Scotland: 1979. 23–34).

- M. Stonebraker, E. Wong, P. Kreps. *The Design and Implementation of INGRES* (ACM Transactions on Database Systems 1.3 (1976): 189–222).

- M. Stonebraker and J. L. Hellerstein. *Readings in Database Systems 3rd edition*, Michael Stonebraker ed., (Morgan Kaufmann Publishers, 1998).

- A. B. Tucker. *Computer Science Handbook*. 2nd ed. (Boca Raton, Florida: CRC Press LLCC, 2004).

- Brian Werne. Inside the SQL Query Optimizer (Progress Worldwide Exchange 2001, Washington D.C. 2001) http://www.peg.com/techpapers/2001Conf/

General

- D. Rosenberg, M. Stephens, M. Collins-Cope. *Agile Development with ICONIX Process*, (Berkeley, CA: Apress, 2005).

MySQL

- Robert A. Burgelman, Andrew S. Grove, Philip E. Meza, *Strategic Dynamics*. (New York: McGraw-Hill, 2006).

- M. Kruckenberg and J. Pipes. *Pro MySQL*, (Berkeley, CA: Apress, 2005).

Open Source

- Paulson, James W. "An Empirical Study of Open-Source and Closed-Source Software Products" IEEE Transactions on Software Engineering, Vol.30, No.5 April 2004.

Websites

- www.opensource.org -- The open source consortium.

- http://dev.mysql.com -- MySQL's developer's site.

- http://www.mysql.com/ -- All things MySQL.

- www.gnu.org/licenses/gpl.html -- The GNU Public License.

- http://www.activestate.org -- ActivePerl for Windows.

- http://www.gnu.org/software/diffutils/diffutils.html -- Diff for Linux.

- http://www.gnu.org/software/patch/ -- GNU Patch.

- http://www.gnu.org/software/gdb/documentation -- GDB Documentation.

- ftp://www.gnu.org/gnu/ddd -- GNU Data Display Debugger.

- http://undo-software.com -- Undo Software.

- http://gnuwin32.sourceforge.net/packages/bison.htm -- Bison.

- http://www.gnu.org -- Yacc.

- http://www.postgresql.org/ -- Postgresql.

Sample Database

The following sample database is used in the later chapters of this text. The following listing shows the SQL dump of the database.

Listing A-1. Sample Database Create Statements

```
-- MySQL dump 10.10
--
-- Host: localhost    Database: expert_mysql
-- --------------------------------------------------------
-- Server version        5.1.9-beta-debug-DBXP 1.0

/*!40101 SET @OLD_CHARACTER_SET_CLIENT=@@CHARACTER_SET_CLIENT */;
/*!40101 SET @OLD_CHARACTER_SET_RESULTS=@@CHARACTER_SET_RESULTS */;
/*!40101 SET @OLD_COLLATION_CONNECTION=@@COLLATION_CONNECTION */;
/*!40101 SET NAMES utf8 */;
/*!40103 SET @OLD_TIME_ZONE=@@TIME_ZONE */;
/*!40103 SET TIME_ZONE='+00:00' */;
/*!40014 SET @OLD_UNIQUE_CHECKS=@@UNIQUE_CHECKS, UNIQUE_CHECKS=0 */;
/*!40014 SET @OLD_FOREIGN_KEY_CHECKS=@@FOREIGN_KEY_CHECKS, FOREIGN_KEY_CHECKS=0
*/;
/*!40101 SET @OLD_SQL_MODE=@@SQL_MODE, SQL_MODE='NO_AUTO_VALUE_ON_ZERO' */;
/*!40111 SET @OLD_SQL_NOTES=@@SQL_NOTES, SQL_NOTES=0 */;

CREATE DATABASE IF NOT EXISTS expert_mysql;


--
-- Table structure for table 'expert_mysql'.'building'
--

DROP TABLE IF EXISTS 'expert_mysql'.'building';
CREATE TABLE 'expert_mysql'.'building' (
  'dir_code' char(4) NOT NULL,
  'building' char(6) NOT NULL
) ENGINE=MyISAM DEFAULT CHARSET=latin1;


--
-- Dumping data for table 'expert_mysql'.'building'
--


/*!40000 ALTER TABLE 'expert_mysql'.'building' DISABLE KEYS */;
LOCK TABLES 'expert_mysql'.'building' WRITE;
INSERT INTO 'expert_mysql'.'building' VALUES
('N41','1300'),
('N01','1453'),
('M00','1000'),
('N41','1301'),
('N41','1305');
UNLOCK TABLES;
/*!40000 ALTER TABLE 'expert_mysql'.'building' ENABLE KEYS */;
```

```
--
-- Table structure for table 'expert_mysql'.'directorate'
--

DROP TABLE IF EXISTS 'expert_mysql'.'directorate';
CREATE TABLE 'expert_mysql'.'directorate' (
  'dir_code' char(4) NOT NULL,
  'dir_name' char(30) DEFAULT NULL,
  'dir_head_id' char(9) DEFAULT NULL,
  PRIMARY KEY ('dir_code')
) ENGINE=MyISAM DEFAULT CHARSET=latin1;


--
-- Dumping data for table 'expert_mysql'.'directorate'
--


/*!40000 ALTER TABLE 'expert_mysql'.'directorate' DISABLE KEYS */;
LOCK TABLES 'expert_mysql'.'directorate' WRITE;
INSERT INTO 'expert_mysql'.'directorate' VALUES
('N41','Development','333445555'),
('N01','Human Resources','123654321'),
('M00','Management','333444444');
UNLOCK TABLES;
/*!40000 ALTER TABLE 'directorate' ENABLE KEYS */;


--
-- Table structure for table 'expert_mysql'.'staff'
--

DROP TABLE IF EXISTS 'expert_mysql'.'staff';
CREATE TABLE 'expert_mysql'.'staff' (
  'id' char(9) NOT NULL,
  'first_name' char(20) DEFAULT NULL,
  'mid_name' char(20) DEFAULT NULL,
  'last_name' char(30) DEFAULT NULL,
  'sex' char(1) DEFAULT NULL,
  'salary' int(11) DEFAULT NULL,
  'mgr_id' char(9) DEFAULT NULL,
  PRIMARY KEY ('id')
) ENGINE=MyISAM DEFAULT CHARSET=latin1;


--
-- Dumping data for table 'expert_mysql'.'staff'
--


/*!40000 ALTER TABLE 'expert_mysql'.'staff' DISABLE KEYS */;
LOCK TABLES 'expert_mysql'.'staff' WRITE;
INSERT INTO 'expert_mysql'.'staff' VALUES
('333445555','John','Q','Smith','M',30000,'333444444'),
```

```
('123763153','William','E','Walters','M',25000,'123654321'),
('333444444','Alicia','F','St.Cruz','F',25000,NULL),
('921312388','Goy','X','Hong','F',40000,'123654321'),
('800122337','Rajesh','G','Kardakarna','M',38000,'333445555'),
('820123637','Monty','C','Smythe','M',38000,'333445555'),
('830132335','Richard','E','Jones','M',38000,'333445555'),
('333445665','Edward','E','Engles','M',25000,'333445555'),
('123654321','Beware','D','Borg','F',55000,'333444444'),
('123456789','Wilma','N','Maxima','F',43000,'333445555');
UNLOCK TABLES;
/*!40000 ALTER TABLE 'expert_mysql'.'staff' ENABLE KEYS */;


--
-- Table structure for table 'tasking'
--

DROP TABLE IF EXISTS 'expert_mysql'.'tasking';
CREATE TABLE 'expert_mysql'.'tasking' (
  'id' char(9) NOT NULL,
  'project_number' char(9) NOT NULL,
  'hours_worked' double DEFAULT NULL
) ENGINE=MyISAM DEFAULT CHARSET=latin1;


--
-- Dumping data for table 'tasking'
--


/*!40000 ALTER TABLE 'tasking' DISABLE KEYS */;
LOCK TABLES 'expert_mysql'.'tasking' WRITE;
INSERT INTO 'expert_mysql'.'tasking' VALUES
('333445555','405',23),
('123763153','405',33.5),
('921312388','601',44),
('800122337','300',13),
('820123637','300',9.5),
('830132335','401',8.5),
('333445555','300',11),
('921312388','500',13),
('800122337','300',44),
('820123637','401',500.5),
('830132335','400',12),
('333445665','600',300.25),
('123654321','607',444.75),
('123456789','300',1000);
UNLOCK TABLES;
/*!40000 ALTER TABLE 'expert_mysql'.'tasking' ENABLE KEYS */;
/*!40103 SET TIME_ZONE=@OLD_TIME_ZONE */;

/*!40101 SET SQL_MODE=@OLD_SQL_MODE */;
/*!40014 SET FOREIGN_KEY_CHECKS=@OLD_FOREIGN_KEY_CHECKS */;
```

```sql
/*!40014 SET UNIQUE_CHECKS=@OLD_UNIQUE_CHECKS */;
/*!40101 SET CHARACTER_SET_CLIENT=@OLD_CHARACTER_SET_CLIENT */;
/*!40101 SET CHARACTER_SET_RESULTS=@OLD_CHARACTER_SET_RESULTS */;
/*!40101 SET COLLATION_CONNECTION=@OLD_COLLATION_CONNECTION */;
/*!40111 SET SQL_NOTES=@OLD_SQL_NOTES */;

# Source on localhost: ... connected.

# Exporting metadata from bvm

DROP DATABASE IF EXISTS bvm;

CREATE DATABASE bvm;

USE bvm;

# TABLE: bvm.books

CREATE TABLE 'books' (

  'ISBN' varchar(15) DEFAULT NULL,

  'Title' varchar(125) DEFAULT NULL,

  'Authors' varchar(100) DEFAULT NULL,

  'Quantity' int(11) DEFAULT NULL,

  'Slot' int(11) DEFAULT NULL,

  'Thumbnail' varchar(100) DEFAULT NULL,

  'Description' text,

  'Pages' int(11) DEFAULT NULL,

  'Price' double DEFAULT NULL,

  'PubDate' date DEFAULT NULL

) ENGINE=MyISAM DEFAULT CHARSET=latin1;

# TABLE: bvm.settings

CREATE TABLE 'settings' (

  'FieldName' char(30) DEFAULT NULL,

  'Value' char(250) DEFAULT NULL

) ENGINE=MyISAM DEFAULT CHARSET=latin1;
```

```
#...done.

USE bvm;

# Exporting data from bvm

# Data for table bvm.books:

INSERT INTO bvm.books VALUES (978-1590595053, 'Pro MySQL', 'Michael Kruckenberg, Jay Pipes and Brian
Aker', 5, 1, 'bcs01.gif', NULL, 798, 49.99, '2005-07-15');

INSERT INTO bvm.books VALUES (978-1590593325, 'Beginning MySQL Database Design and Optimization',
'Chad Russell and Jon Stephens', 6, 2, 'bcs02.gif', NULL, 520, 44.99, '2004-10-28');

INSERT INTO bvm.books VALUES (978-1893115514, 'PHP and MySQL 5', 'W. Jason Gilmore', 4, 3, 'bcs03.gif',
NULL, 800, 39.99, '2004-06-21');

INSERT INTO bvm.books VALUES (978-1590593929, 'Beginning PHP 5 and MySQL E-Commerce', 'Cristian
Darie and Mihai Bucica', 5, 4, 'bcs04.gif', NULL, 707, 46.99, '2008-02-21');

INSERT INTO bvm.books VALUES (978-1590595091, 'PHP 5 Recipes', 'Frank M. Kromann, Jon Stephens,
Nathan A. Good and Lee Babin', 8, 5, 'bcs05.gif', NULL, 672, 44.99, '2005-10-04');

INSERT INTO bvm.books VALUES (978-1430227939, 'Beginning Perl', 'James Lee', 3, 6, 'bcs06.gif',
NULL, 464, 39.99, '2010-04-14');

INSERT INTO bvm.books VALUES (978-1590595350, 'The Definitive Guide to MySQL 5', 'Michael Kofler',
2, 7, 'bcs07.gif', NULL, 784, 49.99, '2005-10-04');

INSERT INTO bvm.books VALUES (978-1590595626, 'Building Online Communities with Drupal, phpBB, and
WordPress', 'Robert T. Douglass, Mike Little and Jared W. Smith', 1, 8, 'bcs08.gif', NULL, 560, 49.99,
'2005-12-16');

INSERT INTO bvm.books VALUES (978-1590595084, 'Pro PHP Security', 'Chris Snyder and Michael
Southwell', 7, 9, 'bcs09.gif', NULL, 528, 44.99, '2005-09-08');

INSERT INTO bvm.books VALUES (978-1590595312, 'Beginning Perl Web Development', 'Steve Suehring',
8, 10, 'bcs10.gif', NULL, 376, 39.99, '2005-11-07');

# Blob data for table books:

UPDATE bvm.books SET 'Description' = "Pro MySQL is the first book that exclusively covers
intermediate and advanced features of MySQL, the world's most popular open source database server.
Whether you are a seasoned MySQL user looking to take your skills to the next level, or youre a
database expert searching for a fast-paced introduction to MySQL's advanced features, this book is
for you." WHERE 'ISBN' = 978-1590595053;

UPDATE bvm.books SET 'Description' = "Beginning MySQL Database Design and Optimization shows you
how to identify, overcome, and avoid gross inefficiencies. It demonstrates how to maximize the many
data manipulation features that MySQL includes. This book explains how to include tests and branches
in your queries, how to normalize your database, and how to issue concurrent queries to boost
```

performance, among many other design and optimization topics. You'll also learn about some features new to MySQL 4.1 and 5.0 like subqueries, stored procedures, and views, all of which will help you build even more efficient applications." WHERE 'ISBN' = 978-1590593325;

UPDATE bvm.books SET 'Description' = "Beginning PHP 5 and MySQL: From Novice to Professional offers a comprehensive introduction to two of the most popular open-source technologies on the planet: the PHP scripting language and the MySQL database server. You are not only exposed to the core features of both technologies, but will also gain valuable insight into how they are used in unison to create dynamic data-driven web applications, not to mention learn about many of the undocumented features of the most recent versions." WHERE 'ISBN' = 978-1893115514;

UPDATE bvm.books SET 'Description' = "Beginning PHP 5 E-Commerce: From Novice to Professional is an ideal reference for intermediate PHP 5 and MySQL developers, and programmers familiar with web development technologies. This book covers every step of the design and build process, and provides rich examples that will enable you to build high-quality, extendable e-commerce websites." WHERE 'ISBN' = 978-1590593929;

UPDATE bvm.books SET 'Description' = "We are confident PHP 5 Recipes will be a useful and welcome companion throughout your PHP journey, keeping you on the cutting edge of PHP development, ahead of the competition, and giving you all the answers you need, when you need them." WHERE 'ISBN' = 978-1590595091;

UPDATE bvm.books SET 'Description' = "This is a book for those of us who believed that we didn't need to learn Perl, and now we know it is more ubiquitous than ever. Perl is extremely flexible and powerful, and it isn't afraid of Web 2.0 or the cloud. Originally touted as the duct tape of the Internet, Perl has since evolved into a multipurpose, multiplatform language present absolutely everywhere: heavy-duty web applications, the cloud, systems administration, natural language processing, and financial engineering. Beginning Perl, Third Edition provides valuable insight into Perl's role regarding all of these tasks and more." WHERE 'ISBN' = 978-1430227939;

UPDATE bvm.books SET 'Description' = "This is the first book to offer in-depth instruction about the new features of the world's most popular open source database server. Updated to reflect changes in MySQL version 5, this book will expose you to MySQL's impressive array of new features: views, stored procedures, triggers, and spatial data types." WHERE 'ISBN' = 978-1590595350;

UPDATE bvm.books SET 'Description' = "Building Online Communities with Drupal, phpBB, and Wordpress is authored by a team of experts. Robert T. Douglass created the Drupal-powered blog site NowPublic.com. Mike Little is a founder and contributing developer of the WordPress project. And Jared W. Smith has been a longtime support team member of phpBBHacks.com and has been building sites with phpBB since the first beta releases." WHERE 'ISBN' = 978-1590595626;

UPDATE bvm.books SET 'Description' = "Pro PHP Security is one of the first books devoted solely to PHP security. It will serve as your complete guide for taking defensive and proactive security measures within your PHP applications. The methods discussed are compatible with PHP versions 3, 4, and 5." WHERE 'ISBN' = 978-1590595084;

UPDATE bvm.books SET 'Description' = "Beginning Perl Web Development: From Novice to Professional introduces you to the world of Perl Internet application development. This book tackles all areas crucial to developing your first web applications and includes a powerful combination of real-world examples coupled with advice. Topics range from serving and consuming RSS feeds, to monitoring Internet servers, to interfacing with e-mail. You'll learn how to use Perl with ancillary packages like Mason and Nagios." WHERE 'ISBN' = 978-1590595312;

```
# Data for table bvm.settings:

INSERT INTO bvm.settings VALUES ('ImagePath', 'c://mysql_embedded//images//');

#...done.
```

Chapter Exercise Notes

This section contains some hints and helpful direction for the exercises included in Chapters 12, 13, and 14. Some of the exercises are practical exercises whereby the solutions would be too long to include in an appendix. For those exercises that require programming to solve I include some hints as to how to write the code for the solution. In other cases, I include additional information that should assist you in completing the exercise.

Chapter 12

The following questions are from Chapter 12, "Internal Query Representation."

Question 1. The query in figure 12-1 exposes a design flaw in one of the tables. What is it? Does the flaw violate any of the normal forms? If so, which one?

Look at the semester attribute. How many values does the data represent? Packing data like this makes for some really poor performing queries if you need to access part of the attribute (field). For example, to query for all of the semesters in 2001, you would have to use a WHERE clause and use the LIKE operator: WHERE semester LIKE '%2001'. This practice of packing fields (also called multi-valued fields) violates First Normal Form.

Question 2. Explore the TABLE structure and change the SELECT DBXP stub to return information about the table and its fields

Change the code to return information like we did in Chapter 8 when we explored the show_disk_usage_command() method. Only this time, include the metadata about the table. Hint: see the table class.

Question 3. Change the EXPLAIN SELECT DBXP command to produce an output similar to the MySQL EXPLAIN SELECT command

Change the code to produce the information in a table like that of the MySQL EXPLAIN command. Note that you will need additional methods in the Query_tree class to gather information about the optimized query.

Question 4. Modify the build_query_tree function to identify and process the LIMIT clause

The changes to the code require you to identify when a query has the LIMIT clause and to abbreviate the results accordingly. By way of a hint, here is the code to capture the value of the LIMIT clause. You will need to modify the code in the DBXP_select_command() method to handle the rest of the operation.

```
SELECT_LEX_UNIT *unit= &lex->unit;
unit->set_limit(unit->global_parameters);
```

Question 5. How can the query tree query_node structure be changed to accommodate HAVING, GROUP BY, and ORDER clauses?

The best design is one that stays true to the query tree concept. That is, consider a design where each of these clauses is a separate node in the tree. Consider also if there are any heuristics that may apply to these operations. Hint: would it not be more efficient to process the HAVING clause nearest the leaf nodes? Lastly, consider rules that govern how many of each of these nodes can exist in the tree.

Chapter 13

The following questions are from Chapter 13, "Query Optimization."

Question 1. Complete the code for the balance_joins() method. Hints: you will need to create an algorithm that can move conjunctive joins around so that the join that is most restrictive is executed first (is lowest in the tree)

This exercise is all about how to move joins around in the tree to push the most restrictive joins down. The tricky part is using the statistics of the tables to determine which joins will produce the fewest results. Look to the handler and table classes for information about accessing this data. Beyond that, you will need helper methods to traverse the tree and get information about the tables. This is necessary because it is possible (and likely) that the joins will be higher in the tree and may not contain direct reference to the table.

Question 2. Complete the code for the cost_optimization() method. Hints: you will need to walk the tree and indicate nodes that can use indexes

This exercise requires you to interrogate the handler and table classes to determine which tables have indexes and what those columns are.

Question 3. Examine the code for the heuristic optimizer. Does it cover all possible queries? If not, are there any other rules (heuristics) that can be used to complete the coverage?

You should discover that there are many such heuristics and that this optimizer covers only the most effective of the heuristics. For example, you could implement heuristics that take into account the GROUP BY and HAVING operations treating them in a similar fashion as project or restrict pushing the nodes down the tree for greater optimization.

Question 4. Examine the code for the query tree and heuristic optimizer. How can you implement the distinct node type as listed in the query tree class? Hint: see the code that follows the prune_tree() method in the heuristic_optimization() method

Most of the hints for this exercise are in the sample code. The following excerpt shows how you can identify when a DISTINCT option is specified on the query.

Question 5. How can you change the code to recognize invalid queries? What are the conditions that determine a query is invalid and how would you test for them?

Part of the solution for this exercise is done for you. For example, a query statement that is syntactically incorrect will be detected by the parser and an appropriate error displayed. However, for those queries that are syntactically correct by semantically meaningless, you will need to add additional error handling code to detect. Try a query that is syntactically correct but references the wrong fields for a query. Create tests of this nature and trace (debug) the code as you do. You should see places in the code where additional error handling can be placed. Lastly, you could also create a method in the Query_tree class that validates the query tree itself. This could be particularly handy if you attempt to create additional node types or implement other heuristic methods.

Question 6. (advanced) MySQL does not currently support the INTERSECT operation (as defined by Date). Change the MySQL parser to recognize the new keyword and process queries like SELECT * FROM A INTERSECT B. Are there any limitations of this operation and are they reflected in the optimizer?

What sounds like a very difficult problem has a very straight-forward solution. Consider adding a new node type named "intersect" that has two children. The operation merely returns those rows that are in both tables. Hint: use one of the many merge sort variants to accomplish this.

Question 7. (advanced) How would you implement the GROUP BY, ORDER BY, and HAVING clauses? Make the changes to the optimizer to enable these clauses.

There are many ways to accomplish this. In keeping with the design of the Query_tree class, each of these operations can be represented as another node type. You can build a method to handle each of these just as we did with restrict, project, and join. Note however that the HAVING clause is used with the GROUP BY clause and the ORDER BY clause is usually processed last.

Chapter 14

The following questions are from Chapter 14, "Query Execution."

Question 1. Complete the code for the do_join() method to support all of the join types supported in MySQL. Hint: you need to be able to identify the type of join before you begin optimization. Look to the parser for details

To complete this exercise, you may want to restructure the code in the do_join() method. The example I used keeps all of the code together, but a more elegant solution would be one where the select-case statement in the do_join() method called helper methods for each type of join and possibly other helper methods for common operations (i.e., see the preempt_pipeline code). The code for the other forms of joins is going to be very similar to the join implemented in the example code.

Question 2. Examine the code for the check_rewind() method in the Query_tree class. Change the implementation to use temporary tables to avoid high memory usage when joining large tables

This exercise also has a straight-forward solution. See the MySQL code in the `sql_select.cc` file for details on how to create a temporary table. Hint: it's very much the same as create table and insert. You could also use the base `Spartan` classes and create a temporary table that stores the record buffers.

Question 3. Evaluate the performance of the DBXP query engine. Run multiple test runs and record execution times. Compare these results to the same queries using the native MySQL query engine. How does the DBXP engine compare to MySQL?

There are many ways to record execution time. You could use a simple stopwatch and record the time based on observation or you could add code that captures the system time. This later method is perhaps the quickest and most reliable way to determine relative speed. I say relative because there are many factors concerning the environment and what is running at the time of the execution that could affect performance. When you conduct your test runs, be sure to use multiple test runs and perform statistical analysis on the results. This will give you a normalized set of data to compare.

Question 4. Why is the remove duplicates operation not necessary for the intersect operation? Are there any conditions where this is false? If so, what are they?

Let us consider what an intersect operation is. It is simply the rows that appear in each of the tables involved (you can intersect on more than two tables). Duplicates in this case are not possible if the tables themselves do not have duplicates. However, if the tables are the result of operations performed in the tree below and have not had the duplicates removed and the `DISTINCT` operation is included in the query, you will need to remove duplicates. Basically, this is an "it depends" answer.

Question 5. (advanced) MySQL does not currently support a CROSS PRODUCT or INTERSECT operation (as defined by Date). Change the MySQL parser to recognize these new keywords and process queries like SELECT * FROM A CROSS B and SELECT * FROM A INTERSECT B and add these functions to the execution engine. Hint: see the do_join() method

The files you need to change are the same files we changed when adding the DBXP keyword. These include `lex.h` and `sql_yacc.yy`. You may need to extend the `sql_lex` structure to include provisions for recording the operation type.

Question 6. (advanced) Form a more complete list of test queries and examine the limitations of the DBXP engine. What modifications are necessary to broaden the capabilities of the DBXP engine?

First, the query tree should be expanded to include the HAVING, GROUP BY, and ORDER BY clauses. You should also consider adding the capabilities for processing aggregate functions. These aggregate functions (e.g., max(), min(), etc.) could be fit into the Expression class whereby new methods are created to parse and evaluate the aggregate functions.

Index

■ R

Radio frequency identification card (RFID)
    authentication mechanism, 348
    authentication plugins
        architecture, 355–356
        client-side plugin, 358–363
        CMakeLists.txt file, 357
        compilation, 365
        include files and definitions, 357–358
        INFORMATION_SCHEMA.plugins view, 365
        logging, 366–367
        mysqladmin client application, 367
        --plugin-dir option, 365
        rfid_auth.ini file, 364–365
        server-side plugin, 363–364
        verification, 366
    module
        board, 349–350
        card identification numbers, 353
        driver installation, 351–353
        keycard, 349, 351
        securing, 354–355
        SparkFun's RFID starter kit, 349–350
    more-secure user-login mechanism, 367
    mysql.plugin table, 367
    operations, 349
    tag, 348
    validate_password plugin, 367
RAID device, 122
Rand_log_event, 306
READ_RECORD, 561
read_row() method, 422
Record command, 135
Refactoring, 119
ref() method, 505
register_slave() method, 330–331
Regression testing, 127
Relational database system (RDBMS)
    client applications, 27
    file-access mechanism
        cache mechanism, 37
        file organization, 37
        index mechanisms, 38
        (I/O) system, 36–37
        performance trade-offs, 37
    internal query representation, 34
    vs. MYSQL, 27
    query execution
        compiled query, 35
        data access, 36
        interpretative methods, 35
        iterative methods, 35
        join operation, 36
        query operations, 35

    query interface, 29
    query optimization
        cost-based optimizer, 33
        heuristic optimizers, 33
        hybrid optimizer, 34
        parametric query optimization, 34
        plan-based query-processing, 32
        semantic optimization, 34
        unbound parameters, 34
    query processing
        data independence, 30
        logical query, 30–31
        query optimization, 31
        query shipping, 30
        query tree, 31
        steps, 31
    query results, 38
    SQL, 26
    storage repository database, 26
Relay slave, 281
remove() method, 505
rename_table() method, 416, 439
Replication
    architecture, 296–297
    binary log (*see* Binary log)
    definition, 281
    extension, 322
        slave connect logging (*see* Slave
            connect logging)
        STOP SLAVE command (*see* STOP
            SLAVE command)
        subsystem, 311
    failover, 283
    GTIDs, 283–284
    master configuration
        GRANT statement, 287
        log_bin variable, 286
        mysql_bin, 286
        REPLICATION SLAVE privilege, 287
        server_id, 286
        SHOW MASTER STATUS command, 287
        variable setting, 286
    master-slave connection, 288–290
    mysqlfailover, 283
    requirements, 284–286
    role switching, 283
    server roles, 281
    slave configuration, 288
    source code, 297–299
        files, 297–299
    log events (*see* Log events)
    switchover, 283
    usage, 282–283
RESET MASTER command, 288
Restrict algorithm, 544

CPSIA information can be obtained at www.ICGtesting.com
Printed in the USA
LVOW122140231212

312989LV00016B/695/P